OSF™ DCE
Application Development Reference

Revision 1.0

Open Software Foundation

P T R Prentice Hall, Englewood Cliffs, New Jersey 07632

Cover design: **BETH FAGAN**
Cover illistration: **STEVE LEWONTIN**

This book was formatted with troff

Published by Prentice-Hall, Inc.
A Simon & Schuster Company
Englewood Cliffs, New Jersey 07632

Printed in the United States of America
10 9 8 7 6 5 4 3 2 1

ISBN 0-13-643834-2

Prentice-Hall International (UK) Limited, *London*
Prentice-Hall of Australia Pty. Limited, *Sydney*
Prentice-Hall Canada Inc., *Toronto*
Prentice-Hall Hispanoamericana, S.A., *Mexico*
Prentice-Hall of India Private Limited, *New Delhi*
Prentice-Hall of Japan, Inc., *Tokyo*
Simon & Schuster Asia Pte. Ltd., *Singapore*
Editora Prentice-Hall do Brasil, Ltda., *Rio de Janeiro*

Contents

Preface

The *OSF DCE Application Development Reference* provides complete and detailed reference information to help application programmers use the correct syntax for Distributed Computing Environment (DCE) calls when writing UNIX applications for a distributed computing environment.

Audience

This document is written for application programmers who want to write Distributed Computing Environment applications for a UNIX environment.

Applicability

This is Revision 1.0 of this document. It applies to the OSF™ DCE Version 1.0 offering and related updates. See your software license for details.

Purpose

The purpose of this document is to assist application programmers when writing UNIX applications for a distributed computing environment. After reading this manual, application programmers should be able to use the correct syntax for DCE calls.

Document Usage

This document is organized into seven chapters.

- For DCE Threads, see Chapter 1.
- For DCE Remote Procedure Call, see Chapter 2.
- For DCE Directory Service, see Chapter 3.
- For DCE Distributed Time Service, see Chapter 4.
- For DCE Security Service, see Chapter 5.
- For DCE Distributed File Service, see Chapter 6.
- For DCE Routines, see Chapter 7.

Related Documents

For additional information about the Distributed Computing Environment, refer to the following documents:

- *Introduction to OSF DCE*
- *OSF DCE User's Guide and Reference*
- *OSF DCE Application Development Guide*
- *OSF DCE Administration Guide*
- *OSF DCE Administration Reference*
- *OSF DCE Porting and Testing Guide*
- *OSF DCE Technical Supplement*
- *OSF DCE Release Notes*
- *Application Environment Specification (AES)/Distributed Computing*

Typographic and Keying Conventions

This document uses the following typographic conventions:

Bold	**Bold** words or characters represent system elements that you must use literally, such as commands, flags, and pathnames.
Italic	*Italic* words or characters represent variable values that you must supply.
`Constant width`	Examples and information that the system displays appear in `constant width` typeface.
[ ]	Brackets enclose optional items in format and syntax descriptions.
{ }	Braces enclose a list from which you must choose an item in format and syntax descriptions.
|	A vertical bar separates items in a list of choices.

< >	Angle brackets enclose the name of a key on the keyboard.
...	Horizontal ellipsis points indicate that you can repeat the preceding item one or more times.

This document uses the following keying conventions:

<Ctrl-*x*> or ^*x*	The notation **<Ctrl-*x*>** or ^*x* followed by the name of a key indicates a control character sequence. For example, **<Ctrl-c>** means that you hold down the control key while pressing **<c>**.
<Return>	The notation **<Return>** refers to the key on your terminal or workstation that is labeled with the word Return or Enter, or with a left arrow.

Problem Reporting

If you have any problems with the software or documentation, please contact your software vendor's customer service department.

Pathnames of Directories and Files in DCE Documentation

For a list of the pathnames for directories and files referred to in this document, see the *OSF DCE Administration Guide* and the *OSF DCE Release Notes*.

Permuted Index

Chapter 1

DCE Threads

intro

Purpose Introduction to DCE Threads

Description

DCE Threads is a set of routines that you can call to create a multithreaded program. Multithreading is used to improve the performance of a program. Routines implemented by DCE Threads that are not specified by Draft 4 of the POSIX 1003.4a standard are indicated by an **_np** suffix on the name. These routines are not portable.

The Threads routines sort alphabetically in the reference pages; however, this introduction lists the routines in the following functional groups:

- Threads Routines
- Attributes Object Routines
- Mutex Routines
- Condition Variable Routines
- Thread-Specific Data Routines
- Threads Cancellation Routines
- Threads Priority and Scheduling Routines
- Cleanup Routines
- The **atfork( )** Routine
- The **exceptions( )** Routine

Threads Routines	
Routine	**Description**
pthread_create()	Creates a thread
pthread_delay_np()	Causes a thread to wait for a period of time
pthread_detach()	Marks a thread for deletion
pthread_exit()	Terminates the calling thread
pthread_join()	Causes the calling thread to wait for the termination of a specified thread
pthread_once()	Calls an initialization routine to be executed only once
pthread_self()	Obtains the identifier of the current thread
pthread_yield()	Notifies the scheduler that the current thread will release its processor to other threads of the same or higher priority

Attributes Object Routines	
Routine	**Description**
pthread_attr_create()	Creates a thread attributes object
pthread_attr_delete()	Deletes a thread attributes object
pthread_attr_getinheritsched()	Obtains the inherit scheduling attribute
pthread_attr_getprio()	Obtains the scheduling priority attribute
pthread_attr_getsched()	Obtains the scheduling policy attribute
pthread_attr_getstacksize()	Obtains the stacksize attribute
pthread_attr_setinheritsched()	Changes the inherit scheduling attribute
pthread_attr_setprio()	Changes the scheduling priority attribute
pthread_attr_setsched()	Changes the scheduling policy attribute
pthread_attr_setstacksize()	Changes the stacksize attribute
pthread_condattr_create()	Creates a condition variable attributes object
pthread_condattr_delete()	Deletes a condition variable attributes object
pthread_mutexattr_create()	Creates a mutex attributes object
pthread_mutexattr_delete()	Deletes a mutex attributes object
pthread_mutexattr_getkind_np()	Obtains the mutex type attribute
pthread_mutexattr_setkind_np()	Changes the mutex type attribute

Mutex Routines	
Routine	**Description**
pthread_lock_global_np( )	Locks a global mutex
pthread_mutex_destroy( )	Deletes a mutex
pthread_mutex_init( )	Creates a mutex
pthread_mutex_lock( )	Locks a mutex and waits if the mutex is already locked
pthread_mutex_trylock( )	Locks a mutex and returns if the mutex is already locked
pthread_mutex_unlock( )	Unlocks a mutex
pthread_unlock_global_np( )	Unlocks a global mutex

Condition Variable Routines	
Routine	**Description**
pthread_cond_broadcast( )	Wakes all threads waiting on a condition variable
pthread_cond_destroy( )	Deletes a condition variable
pthread_cond_init( )	Creates a condition variable
pthread_cond_signal( )	Wakes one thread waiting on a condition variable
pthread_cond_timedwait( )	Causes a thread to wait for a specified period of time for a condition variable to be signaled or broadcast
pthread_cond_wait( )	Causes a thread to wait for a condition variable to be signaled or broadcast
pthread_get_expiration_np( )	Obtains a value representing a desired expiration time

Thread-Specific Data	
Routine	**Description**
pthread_getspecific( )	Obtains the thread-specific data associated with the specified key
pthread_keycreate( )	Generates a unique thread-specific data key value
pthread_setspecific( )	Sets the thread-specific data associated with the specified key

Threads Cancellation Routines	
Routine	**Description**
pthread_cancel( )	Allows a thread to request termination
pthread_setasynccancel( )	Enables or disables the current thread's asynchronous cancelability
pthread_setcancel( )	Enables or disables the current thread's general cancelability
pthread_signal_to_cancel_np( )	Cancels a thread if a signal is received by the process
pthread_testcancel( )	Requests delivery of a pending cancel

Threads Priority and Scheduling Routines	
Routine	**Description**
pthread_getprio( )	Obtains the current priority of a thread
pthread_getscheduler( )	Obtains the current scheduling policy of a thread
pthread_setprio( )	Changes the current priority of a thread
pthread_setscheduler( )	Changes the current scheduling policy and priority of a thread

Cleanup Routines	
Routine	**Description**
pthread_cleanup_pop( )	Removes a cleanup handler from the stack
pthread_cleanup_push( )	Establishes a cleanup handler

The atfork( ) Routine	
Routine	**Description**
atfork( )	Arranges for fork cleanup handling

Exceptions in DCE Threads	
Routine	**Description**
exceptions( )	Describes exception handling in DCE Threads

atfork

Purpose Arranges for fork cleanup handling

Synopsis **#include <pthread.h>**

void atfork
    void (**user_state*,
    void (**pre_fork)( )*,
    void (**parent_fork)( )*,
    void (**child_fork)( )*);

Parameters

user_state	Pointer to the user state that is passed to each routine.
pre_fork	Routine to be called before performing the fork.
parent_fork	Routine to be called in the parent after the fork.
child_fork	Routine to be called in the child after the fork.

Description

The **atfork**( ) routine allows you to register three routines to be executed at different times relative to a fork. The different times and/or places are as follows:

Just prior to the fork in the parent process.
Just after the fork in the parent process.
Just after the fork in the created (child) process.

Use these routines to clean up just prior to **fork**( ), to set up after **fork**( ), and to perform locking relative to **fork**( ). You are allowed to provide one parameter to be used in conjunction with all the routines. This parameter must be *user_state*.

Return Values

The **atfork**( ) routine does not return a value. Instead, an exception is raised if there is insufficient table space to record the handler addresses.

Related Information

Functions: **fork(2)**.

exceptions

Purpose Exception handling in DCE Threads

Description

DCE Threads provides the following two ways to obtain information about the status of a threads routine:

- The routine returns a status value to the thread.
- The routine raises an exception.

Before you write a multithreaded program, you must choose only one of the preceding two methods of receiving status. These two methods cannot be used together in the same code module.

The POSIX P1003.4a (pthreads) draft standard specifies that errors be reported to the thread by setting the external variable **errno** to an error code and returning a function value of 1. The threads reference pages document this status value-returning interface. However, an alternative to status values is provided by DCE Threads in the exception-returning interface.

Access to exceptions from the C language is defined by the macros in the **exc_handling.h** file. The **exc_handling.h** header file is included automatically when you include **pthread_exc.h.**

To use the exception-returning interface, replace

```
#include <pthread.h>
```

with the following include statement:

```
#include <pthread_exc.h>
```

The following example shows the syntax for handling exceptions:

```
TRY
    try_block
[CATCH (exception_name)
    handler_block]...
[CATCH_ALL
    handler_block]
ENDTRY
```

pthread_attr_create

Purpose Creates a thread attributes object

Synopsis

```
#include <pthread.h>

int pthread_attr_create
        pthread_attr_t *attr);
```

Parameters

attr Thread attributes object created.

Description

The **pthread_attr_create( )** routine creates a thread attributes object that is used to specify the attributes of threads when they are created. The attributes object created by this routine is only used in calls to **pthread_create( )**.

The individual attributes (internal fields) of the attributes object are set to default values. (The default values of each attribute are discussed in the descriptions of the following services.) Use the following routines to change the individual attributes:

- **pthread_attr_setinheritsched( )**
- **pthread_attr_setprio( )**
- **pthread_attr_setsched( )**
- **pthread_attr_setstacksize( )**

When an attributes object is used to create a thread, the values of the individual attributes determine the characteristics of the new object. Attributes objects perform in a manner similar to additional parameters. Changing individual attributes does not affect any objects that were previously created using the attributes object.

Return Values

If an error condition occurs, this routine returns -1 and sets **errno** to the corresponding error value. Possible return values are as follows:

Return	Error	Description
0		Successful completion.
-1	[**ENOMEM**]	Insufficient memory exists to create the thread attributes object.
-1	[**EINVAL**]	The value specified by *attr* is invalid.

Related Information

Functions: **pthread_attr_delete(3thr)**, **pthread_attr_setinheritsched(3thr)**, **pthread_attr_setprio(3thr)**, **pthread_attr_setsched(3thr)**, **pthread_attr_setstacksize(3thr)**, **pthread_create(3thr)**.

pthread_attr_delete

Purpose Deletes a thread attributes object

Synopsis

```
#include <pthread.h>

int pthread_attr_delete(
        pthread_attr_t *attr);
```

Parameters

attr Thread attributes object deleted.

Description

The **pthread_attr_delete()** routine deletes a thread attributes object and gives permission to reclaim storage for the thread attributes object. Threads that were created using this thread attributes object are not affected by the deletion of the thread attributes object.

The results of calling this routine are unpredictable if the value specified by the *attr* parameter refers to a thread attributes object that does not exist.

Return Values

If an error condition occurs, this routine returns -1 and sets **errno** to the corresponding error value. Possible return values are as follows:

Return	Error	Description
0		Successful completion.
-1	[**EINVAL**]	The value specified by *attr* is invalid.

Related Information

Functions: **pthread_attr_create(3thr)**.

pthread_attr_getinheritsched

Purpose

Obtains the inherit scheduling attribute

Synopsis

#include <pthread.h>

int pthread_attr_getinheritsched(
    pthread_attr_t *attr***);**

Parameters

attr Thread attributes object whose inherit scheduling attribute is obtained.

Description

The **pthread_attr_getinheritsched( )** routine obtains the value of the inherit scheduling attribute in the specified thread attributes object. The inherit scheduling attribute specifies whether threads created using the attributes object inherit the scheduling attributes of the creating thread, or use the scheduling attributes stored in the attributes object that is passed to **pthread_create( )**.

The default value of the inherit scheduling attribute is **PTHREAD_INHERIT_SCHED**.

Return Values

On successful completion, this routine returns the inherit scheduling attribute value.

If an error condition occurs, this routine returns -1 and sets **errno** to the corresponding error value. Possible return values are as follows:

Return	Error	Description
Inherit scheduling attribute		Successful completion.
-1	[**EINVAL**]	The value specified by *attr* is invalid.

Related Information

Functions: **pthread_attr_create(3thr)**, **pthread_attr_setinheritsched(3thr)**, **pthread_create(3thr)**.

pthread_attr_getprio

Purpose Obtains the scheduling priority attribute

Synopsis **#include <pthread.h>**

int pthread_attr_getprio(
    pthread_attr_t *attr***);**

Parameters

attr Thread attributes object whose priority attribute is obtained.

Description

The **pthread_attr_getprio( )** routine obtains the value of the scheduling priority of threads created using the thread attributes object specified by the *attr* parameter.

Return Values

On successful completion, this routine returns the scheduling priority attribute value.

If an error condition occurs, this routine returns -1 and sets **errno** to the corresponding error value. Possible return values are as follows:

Return	Error	Description
Scheduling priority attribute		Successful completion.
-1	[**EINVAL**]	The value specified by *attr* is invalid.

Related Information

Functions: **pthread_attr_create(3thr)**, **pthread_attr_setprio(3thr)**, **pthread_create(3thr)**.

pthread_attr_getsched

Purpose Obtains the value of the scheduling policy attribute

Synopsis **#include <pthread.h>**

int pthread_attr_getsched(
    pthread_attr_t *attr*)**;**

Parameters

attr Thread attributes object whose scheduling policy attribute is obtained.

Description

The **pthread_attr_getsched( )** routine obtains the scheduling policy of threads created using the thread attributes object specified by the *attr* parameter. The default value of the scheduling attribute is **SCHED_OTHER**.

Return Values

On successful completion, this routine returns the value of the scheduling policy attribute.

If an error condition occurs, this routine returns -1 and sets **errno** to the corresponding error value. Possible return values are as follows:

Return	Error	Description
Scheduling policy attribute		Successful completion.
-1	[**EINVAL**]	The value specified by *attr* is invalid.

Related Information

Functions: **pthread_attr_create(3thr)**, **pthread_attr_setsched(3thr)**, **pthread_create(3thr)**.

pthread_attr_getstacksize

Purpose Obtains the value of the stacksize attribute

Synopsis **#include <pthread.h>**

long pthread_attr_getstacksize(
pthread_attr_t *attr***);**

Parameters

attr Thread attributes object whose stacksize attribute is obtained.

Description

The **pthread_attr_getstacksize( )** routine obtains the minimum size (in bytes) of the stack for a thread created using the thread attributes object specified by the *attr* parameter.

Return Values

On successful completion, this routine returns the stacksize attribute value.

If an error condition occurs, this routine returns -1 and sets **errno** to the corresponding error value. Possible return values are as follows:

Return	Error	Description
Stacksize attribute		Successful completion.
-1	[EINVAL]	The value specified by *attr* is invalid.

Related Information

Functions: **pthread_attr_create(3thr)**, **pthread_attr_setstacksize(3thr)**, **pthread_create(3thr)**.

pthread_attr_setinheritsched

Purpose Changes the inherit scheduling attribute

Synopsis

```
#include <pthread.h>

int pthread_attr_setinheritsched(
        pthread_attr_t *attr,
        int inherit);
```

Parameters

attr Thread attributes object to be modified.

inherit New value for the inherit scheduling attribute. Valid values are as follows:

PTHREAD_INHERIT_SCHED
This is the default value. The created thread inherits the current priority and scheduling policy of the thread calling **pthread_create( )**.

PTHREAD_DEFAULT_SCHED
The created thread starts execution with the priority and scheduling policy stored in the thread attributes object.

Description

The **pthread_attr_setinheritsched( )** routine changes the inherit scheduling attribute of thread creation. The inherit scheduling attribute specifies whether threads created using the specified thread attributes object inherit the scheduling attributes of the creating thread, or use the scheduling attributes stored in the thread attributes object that is passed to **pthread_create( )**.

The first thread in an application that is not created by an explicit call to **pthread_create( )** has a scheduling policy of **SCHED_OTHER**. (See the **pthread_attr_setprio( )** and **pthread_attr_setsched( )** routines for more information on valid priority values and valid scheduling policy values, respectively.)

Inheriting scheduling attributes (instead of using the scheduling attributes stored in the attributes object) is useful when a thread is creating several helper threads—threads that are intended to work closely with the creating thread to cooperatively solve the same problem. For example, inherited scheduling attributes ensure that helper threads created in a sort routine execute with the same priority as the calling thread.

Return Values

If an error condition occurs, this routine returns -1 and sets **errno** to the corresponding error value. Possible return values are as follows:

Return	Error	Description
0		Successful completion.
-1	[**EINVAL**]	The value specified by *attr* is invalid.

Related Information

Functions: **pthread_attr_create(3thr)**, **pthread_attr_getinheritsched(3thr)**, **pthread_attr_setprio(3thr)**, **pthread_attr_setsched(3thr)**, **pthread_create(3thr)**.

pthread_attr_setprio

Purpose Changes the scheduling priority attribute of thread creation

Synopsis **#include <pthread.h>**

int pthread_attr_setprio(
    pthread_attr_t **attr*,
    int *priority*);

Parameters

attr Thread attributes object modified.

priority New value for the priority attribute. The priority attribute depends on scheduling policy. Valid values fall within one of the following ranges:

- **PRI_OTHER_MIN** <= *priority* <= **PRI_OTHER_MAX** (use with the **SCHED_OTHER** policy)
- **PRI_FIFO_MIN** <= *priority* <= **PRI_FIFO_MAX** (use with the **SCHED_FIFO** policy)
- **PRI_RR_MIN** <= *priority* <= **PRI_RR_MAX** (use with the **SCHED_RR** policy)
- **PRI_FG_MIN_NP** <= *priority* <= **PRI_FG_MAX_NP** (use with the **SCHED_FG_NP** policy)
- **PRI_BG_MIN_NP** <= *priority* <= **PRI_BG_MAX_NP** (use with the **SCHED_BG_NP** policy)

The default priority is the midpoint between **PRI_OTHER_MIN** and **PRI_OTHER_MAX**. To specify a minimum or maximum priority, use the appropriate symbol; for example, **PRI_FIFO_MIN** or **PRI_FIFO_MAX**. To specify a value between the minimum and maximum, use an appropriate arithmetic expression. For example, to specify a priority midway between the minimum and maximum for the Round Robin scheduling policy, specify the following concept using your programming language's syntax:

```
pri_rr_mid = (PRI_RR_MIN + PRI_RR_MAX)/2
```

If your expression results in a value outside the range of minimum to maximum, an error results when you attempt to use it.

Description

The **pthread_attr_setprio( )** routine sets the execution priority of threads that are created using the attributes object specified by the *attr* parameter.

By default, a created thread inherits the priority of the thread calling **pthread_create( )**. To specify a priority using this routine, scheduling inheritance must be disabled at the time the thread is created. Before calling this routine and **pthread_create( )**, call **pthread_attr_setinheritsched( )** and specify the value **PTHREAD_DEFAULT_SCHED** for the *inherit* parameter.

An application specifies priority only to express the urgency of executing the thread relative to other threads. Priority is not used to control mutual exclusion when accessing shared data. With a sufficient number of processors executing, all ready threads, regardless of priority, execute simultaneously.

Return Values

If an error condition occurs, this routine returns -1 and sets **errno** to the corresponding error value. Possible return values are as follows:

Return	Error	Description
0		Successful completion.
-1	[**EINVAL**]	The value specified by *attr* is invalid.
-1	[**ERANGE**]	One or more parameters supplied have an invalid value.

Related Information

Functions: **pthread_attr_create(3thr)**, **pthread_attr_getprio(3thr)**, **pthread_attr_setinheritsched(3thr)**, **pthread_create(3thr)**.

pthread_attr_setsched

Purpose Changes the scheduling policy attribute of thread creation

Synopsis **#include <pthread.h>**

int pthread_attr_setsched(
    pthread_attr_t **attr*
    int **scheduler*);

Parameters

attr Thread attributes object modified.

scheduler New value for the scheduling policy attribute. Valid values are as follows:

SCHED_FIFO (First In, First Out) The highest-priority thread runs until it blocks. If there is more than one thread with the same priority, and that priority is the highest among other threads, the first thread to begin running continues until it blocks.

SCHED_RR (Round Robin) The highest-priority thread runs until it blocks; however, threads of equal priority, if that priority is the highest among other threads, are timesliced. Timeslicing is a process in which threads alternate using available processors.

SCHED_OTHER (Default) All threads are timesliced. **SCHED_OTHER** ensures that all threads, regardless of priority, receive some scheduling so that no thread is completely denied execution time. (However, **SCHED_OTHER** threads can be denied execution time by **SCHED_FIFO** or **SCHED_RR** threads.)

SCHED_FG_NP (Foreground) Same as **SCHED_OTHER**. Threads are timesliced and priorities can be modified dynamically by the scheduler to ensure fairness.

SCHED_BG_NP (Background) Ensures that all threads, regardless of priority, receive some scheduling. However, **SCHED_BG_NP** can be denied execution by **SCHED_FIFO** or **SCHED_RR** threads.

Description

The **pthread_attr_setsched( )** routine sets the scheduling policy of a thread that is created using the attributes object specified by the *attr* parameter. The default value of the scheduling attribute is **SCHED_OTHER**.

Return Values

If an error condition occurs, this routine returns -1 and sets **errno** to the corresponding error value. Possible return values are as follows:

Return	Error	Description
0		Successful completion.
-1	[**EINVAL**]	The value specified by *attr* is invalid.
-1	[**EPERM**]	The caller does not have the appropriate privileges to set the priority of the specified thread.

Related Information

Functions: **pthread_attr_create(3thr)**, **pthread_attr_getsched(3thr)**, **pthread_attr_setinheritsched(3thr)**, **pthread_create(3thr)**.

pthread_attr_setstacksize

Purpose Changes the stacksize attribute of thread creation

Synopsis **#include <pthread.h>**

int pthread_attr_setstacksize(
    pthread_attr_t ***attr*,**
    long *stacksize***);**

Parameters

attr Thread attributes object modified.

stacksize New value for the stacksize attribute. The *stacksize* parameter specifies the minimum size (in bytes) of the stack needed for a thread.

Description

The **pthread_attr_setstacksize( )** routine sets the minimum size (in bytes) of the stack needed for a thread created using the attributes object specified by the *attr* parameter. Use this routine to adjust the size of the writable area of the stack. The default value of the stacksize attribute is machine specific.

A thread's stack is fixed at the time of thread creation. Only the main or initial thread can dynamically extend its stack.

Most compilers do not check for stack overflow. Ensure that your thread stack is large enough for anything that you call from the thread.

Return Values

If an error condition occurs, this routine returns -1 and sets **errno** to the corresponding error value. Possible return values are as follows:

Return	Error	Description
0		Successful completion.
-1	[EINVAL]	The value specified by *attr* is invalid.

Related Information

Functions: **pthread_attr_create(3thr)**, **pthread_attr_getstacksize(3thr)**, **pthread_create(3thr)**.

pthread_cancel

Purpose Allows a thread to request that it or another thread terminate execution

Synopsis

```
#include <pthread.h>

int pthread_cancel(
        pthread_t thread);
```

Parameters

thread Thread that receives a cancel request.

Description

The **pthread_cancel()** routine sends a cancel to the specified thread. A cancel is a mechanism by which a calling thread informs either itself or the called thread to terminate as quickly as possible. Issuing a cancel does not guarantee that the canceled thread receives or handles the cancel. The canceled thread can delay processing the cancel after receiving it. For instance, if a cancel arrives during an important operation, the canceled thread can continue if what it is doing cannot be interrupted at the point where the cancel is requested.

Because of communications delays, the calling thread can only rely on the fact that a cancel eventually becomes pending in the designated thread (provided that the thread does not terminate beforehand). Furthermore, the calling thread has no guarantee that a pending cancel is to be delivered because delivery is controlled by the designated thread.

Termination processing when a cancel is delivered to a thread is similar to **pthread_exit()**. Outstanding cleanup routines are executed in the context of the target thread, and a status of -1 is made available to any threads joining with the target thread.

This routine is preferred in implementing Ada's **abort** statement and any other language (or software-defined construct) for requesting thread cancellation.

The results of this routine are unpredictable if the value specified in *thread* refers to a thread that does not currently exist.

Return Values

If an error condition occurs, this routine returns -1 and sets **errno** to the corresponding error value. Possible return values are as follows:

Return	Error	Description
0		Successful completion.
-1	[**EINVAL**]	The specified thread is invalid.
-1	[**ERSCH**]	The specified thread does not refer to a currently existing thread.

Related Information

Functions: **pthread_exit(3thr)**, **pthread_join(3thr)**, **pthread_setasynccancel(3thr)**, **pthread_setcancel(3thr)**, **pthread_testcancel(3thr)**.

pthread_cleanup_pop

Purpose Removes the cleanup handler at the top of the cleanup stack and optionally executes it

Synopsis **#include <pthread.h>**

void pthread_cleanup_pop(
  int *execute* **);**

Parameters

execute Integer that specifies whether the cleanup routine that is popped should be executed or just discarded. If the value is nonzero, the cleanup routine is executed.

Description

The **pthread_cleanup_pop( )** routine removes the routine specified in **pthread_cleanup_push( )** from the top of the calling thread's cleanup stack and executes it if the value specified in *execute* is nonzero.

This routine and **pthread_cleanup_push( )** are implemented as macros and must be displayed as statements and in pairs within the same lexical scope. You can think of the **pthread_cleanup_push( )** macro as expanding to a string whose first character is a { (left brace) and **pthread_cleanup_pop** as expanding to a string containing the corresponding } (right brace).

Return Values

This routine must be used as a statement.

Related Information

Functions: **pthread_cleanup_push(3thr)**.

pthread_cleanup_push

Purpose Establishes a cleanup handler

Synopsis **#include <pthread.h>**

void pthread_cleanup_push(
    void *routine*,
    pthread_addr_t *arg*);

Parameters

routine Routine executed as the cleanup handler.

arg Parameter executed with the cleanup routine.

Description

The **pthread_cleanup_push( )** routine pushes the specified routine onto the calling thread's cleanup stack. The cleanup routine is popped from the stack and executed with the *arg* parameter when any of the following actions occur:

- The thread calls **pthread_exit( )**.
- The thread is canceled.
- The thread calls **pthread_cleanup_pop( )** and specifies a nonzero value for the *execute* parameter.

This routine and **pthread_cleanup_pop( )** are implemented as macros and must be displayed as statements and in pairs within the same lexical scope. You can think of the **pthread_cleanup_push( )** macro as expanding to a string whose first character is a **{** (left brace) and **pthread_cleanup_pop( )** as expanding to a string containing the corresponding **}** (right brace).

Return Values

This routine must be used as a statement.

Related Information

Functions: **pthread_cancel(3thr)**, **pthread_cleanup_pop(3thr)**, **pthread_exit(3thr)**, **pthread_testcancel(3thr)**.

pthread_cond_broadcast

Purpose Wakes all threads that are waiting on a condition variable

Synopsis **#include <pthread.h>**

int pthread_cond_broadcast(
pthread_cond_t **cond***);**

Parameters

cond Condition variable broadcast.

Description

The **pthread_cond_broadcast( )** routine wakes all threads waiting on a condition variable. Calling this routine implies that data guarded by the associated mutex has changed so that it might be possible for one or more waiting threads to proceed. If any one waiting thread might be able to proceed, call **pthread_cond_signal( )**.

Call this routine when the associated mutex is either locked or unlocked.

Return Values

If an error condition occurs, this routine returns -1 and sets **errno** to the corresponding error value. Possible return values are as follows:

Return	Error	Description
0		Successful completion.
-1	[**EINVAL**]	The value specified by *cond* is invalid.

Related Information

Functions: **pthread_cond_destroy(3thr)**, **pthread_cond_init(3thr)**, **pthread_cond_signal(3thr)**, **pthread_cond_timedwait(3thr)**, **pthread_cond_wait(3thr)**.

pthread_cond_destroy

Purpose Deletes a condition variable

Synopsis **#include <pthread.h>**

int pthread_cond_destroy(
pthread_cond_t ***cond*);**

Parameters

cond Condition variable deleted.

Description

The **pthread_cond_destroy( )** routine deletes a condition variable. Call this routine when a condition variable is no longer referenced. The effect of calling this routine is to give permission to reclaim storage for the condition variable.

The results of this routine are unpredictable if the condition variable specified in *cond* does not exist.

The results of this routine are also unpredictable if there are threads waiting for the specified condition variable to be signaled or broadcast when it is deleted.

Return Values

If an error condition occurs, this routine returns -1 and sets **errno** to the corresponding error value. Possible return values are as follows:

Return	Error	Description
0		Successful completion.
-1	[**EINVAL**]	The value specified by *cond* is invalid.
-1	[**EBUSY**]	A thread is currently executing a **pthread_cond_timedwait( )** routine or **pthread_cond_wait( )** on the condition variable specified in *cond*.

Related Information

Functions: **pthread_cond_broadcast(3thr)**, **pthread_cond_init(3thr)**, **pthread_cond_signal(3thr)**, **pthread_cond_timedwait(3thr)**, **pthread_cond_wait(3thr)**.

pthread_cond_init

Purpose Creates a condition variable

Synopsis **#include <pthread.h>**

int pthread_cond_init(
    pthread_cond_t **cond*,
    pthread_condattr_t *attr***);**

Parameters

cond Condition variable that is created.

attr Condition variable attributes object that defines the characteristics of the condition variable created. If you specify **pthread_condattr_default**, default attributes are used.

Description

The **pthread_cond_init()** routine creates and initializes a condition variable. A condition variable is a synchronization object used in conjunction with a mutex. A mutex controls access to shared data; a condition variable allows threads to wait for that data to enter a defined state. The state is defined by a Boolean expression called a predicate.

A condition variable is signaled or broadcast to indicate that a predicate might have become true. The broadcast operation indicates that all waiting threads need to resume and reevaluate the predicate. The signal operation is used when any one waiting thread can continue.

If a thread that holds a mutex determines that the shared data is not in the correct state for it to proceed (the associated predicate is not true), it waits on a condition variable associated with the desired state. Waiting on the condition variable automatically releases the mutex so that other threads can modify or examine the shared data. When a thread modifies the state of the shared data so that a predicate might be true, it signals or broadcasts on the appropriate condition variable so that threads waiting for that predicate can continue.

It is important that all threads waiting on a particular condition variable at any time hold the *same* mutex. If they do not, the behavior of the wait operation is unpredictable (an implementation can use the mutex to control internal access to the condition variable object). However, it is legal for a client to store condition variables and mutexes and later reuse them in different combinations. The client must ensure that no threads use the condition variable with the old mutex. At any time, an arbitrary number of condition variables can be associated with a single mutex, each representing a different predicate of the shared data protected by that mutex.

Condition variables are not owned by a particular thread. Any associated storage is not automatically deallocated when the creating thread terminates.

Return Values

If an error condition occurs, this routine returns -1, the condition variable is not initialized, and the contents of *cond* are undefined. This routine sets **errno** to the corresponding error value. Possible return values are as follows:

Return	Error	Description
0		Successful completion.
-1	[**EAGAIN**]	The system lacks the necessary resources to initialize another condition variable.
-1	[**ENOMEM**]	Insufficient memory exists to initialize the condition variable.

Related Information

Functions: **pthread_cond_broadcast(3thr)**, **pthread_cond_destroy(3thr)**, **pthread_cond_signal(3thr)**, **pthread_cond_timedwait(3thr)**, **pthread_cond_wait(3thr)**.

pthread_cond_signal

Purpose Wakes one thread that is waiting on a condition variable

Synopsis **#include <pthread.h>**

int pthread_cond_signal(
pthread_cond_t **cond*);

Parameters

cond Condition variable signaled.

Description

The **pthread_cond_signal()** routine wakes one thread waiting on a condition variable. Calling this routine implies that data guarded by the associated mutex has changed so that it is possible for a single waiting thread to proceed. Call this routine when any thread waiting on the specified condition variable might find its predicate true, but only one thread needs to proceed.

The scheduling policy determines which thread is awakened. For policies **SCHED_FIFO** and **SCHED_RR** a blocked thread is chosen in priority order.

Call this routine when the associated mutex is either locked or unlocked.

Return Values

If an error condition occurs, this routine returns -1 and sets **errno** to the corresponding error value. Possible return values are as follows:

Return	Error	Description
0		Successful completion.
-1	[EINVAL]	The value specified by *cond* is invalid.

Related Information

Functions: **pthread_cond_broadcast(3thr)**, **pthread_cond_destroy(3thr)**, **pthread_cond_init(3thr)**, **pthread_cond_timedwait(3thr)**, **pthread_cond_wait(3thr)**.

pthread_cond_timedwait

Purpose Causes a thread to wait for a condition variable to be signaled or broadcast

Synopsis **#include <pthread.h>**

int pthread_cond_timedwait(
pthread_cond_t **cond*,
pthread_mutex_t **mutex*,
struct timespec **abstime*);

Parameters

cond Condition variable waited on.

mutex Mutex associated with the condition variable specified in *cond*.

abstime Absolute time at which the wait expires, if the condition has not been signaled or broadcast. (See the **pthread_get_expiration_np( )** routine, which you can use to obtain a value for this parameter.)

Description

The **pthread_cond_timedwait( )** routine causes a thread to wait until one of the following occurs:

- The specified condition variable is signaled or broadcast.
- The current system clock time is greater than or equal to the time specified by the *abstime* parameter.

This routine is identical to **pthread_cond_wait( )** except that this routine can return before a condition variable is signaled or broadcast—specifically, when a specified time expires.

If the current time equals or exceeds the expiration time, this routine returns immediately, without causing the current thread to wait.

Call this routine after you lock the mutex specified in *mutex*. The results of this routine are unpredictable if this routine is called without first locking the mutex.

Return Values

If an error condition occurs, this routine returns -1 and **errno** is set to the corresponding error value. Possible return values are as follows:

Return	Error	Description
0		Successful completion.
-1	[**EINVAL**]	The value specified by *cond*, *mutex*, or *abstime* is invalid.
-1	[**EAGAIN**]	The time specified by *abstime* expired.
-1	[**EDEADLK**]	A deadlock condition is detected.

Related Information

Functions: **pthread_cond_broadcast(3thr)**, **pthread_cond_destroy(3thr)**, **pthread_cond_init(3thr)**, **pthread_cond_signal(3thr)**, **pthread_cond_wait(3thr)**, **pthread_get_expiration_np(3thr)**.

pthread_cond_wait

Purpose Causes a thread to wait for a condition variable to be signaled or broadcast

Synopsis **#include <pthread.h>**

```
int pthread_cond_wait(
        pthread_cond_t *cond,
        pthread_mutex_t *mutex);
```

Parameters

cond Condition variable waited on.

mutex Mutex associated with the condition variable specified in *cond*.

Description

The **pthread_cond_wait( )** routine causes a thread to wait for a condition variable to be signaled or broadcast. Each condition corresponds to one or more predicates based on shared data. The calling thread waits for the data to reach a particular state (for the predicate to become true).

Call this routine after you have locked the mutex specified in *mutex*. The results of this routine are unpredictable if this routine is called without first locking the mutex.

This routine automatically releases the mutex and causes the calling thread to wait on the condition. If the wait is satisfied as a result of some thread calling **pthread_cond_signal( )** or **pthread_cond_broadcast( )**, the mutex is reacquired and the routine returns.

A thread that changes the state of storage protected by the mutex in such a way that a predicate associated with a condition variable might now be true must call either **pthread_cond_signal( )** or **pthread_cond_broadcast( )** for that condition variable. If neither call is made, any thread waiting on the condition variable continues to wait.

This routine might (with low probability) return when the condition variable has not been signaled or broadcast. When a spurious wakeup occurs, the mutex is reacquired before the routine returns. (To handle this type of situation, enclose this routine in a loop that checks the predicate.)

Return Values

If an error condition occurs, this routine returns -1 and **errno** is set to the corresponding error value. Possible return values are as follows:

Return	Error	Description
0		Successful completion.
-1	[**EINVAL**]	The value specified by *cond* or *mutex* is invalid.
-1	[**EDEADLK**]	A deadlock condition is detected.

Related Information

Functions: **pthread_cond_broadcast(3thr)**, **pthread_cond_destroy(3thr)**, **pthread_cond_init(3thr)**, **pthread_cond_signal(3thr)**, **pthread_cond_timedwait(3thr)**.

pthread_condattr_create

Purpose Creates a condition variable attributes object

Synopsis **#include <pthread.h>**

```
int pthread_condattr_create(
        pthread_condattr_t *attr);
```

Parameters

attr Condition variable attributes object that is created.

Description

The **pthread_condattr_create()** routine creates a condition variable attributes object that is used to specify the attributes of condition variables when they are created. The condition variable attributes object is initialized with the default value for all of the attributes defined by a given implementation.

When a condition variable attributes object is used to create a condition variable, the values of the individual attributes determine the characteristics of the new object. Attributes objects act like additional parameters to object creation. Changing individual attributes does not affect objects that were previously created using the attributes object.

Return Values

The created condition variable attributes object is returned to the *attr* parameter. If an error condition occurs, this routine returns -1 and sets **errno** to the corresponding error value. Possible return values are as follows:

Return	Error	Description
0		Successful completion.
-1	[**EINVAL**]	The value specified by *attr* is invalid.
-1	[**ENOMEM**]	Insufficient memory exists to create the condition variable attributes object.

Related Information

Functions: **pthread_condattr_delete(3thr)**, **pthread_cond_init(3thr)**.

pthread_condattr_delete

Purpose

Deletes a condition variable attributes object

Synopsis

#include <pthread.h>

int pthread_condattr_delete(
pthread_condattr_t **attr***);**

Parameters

attr Condition variable attributes object deleted.

Description

The **pthread_condattr_delete( )** routine deletes a condition variable attributes object. Call this routine when a condition variable attributes object created by **pthread_condattr_create( )** is no longer referenced.

This routine gives permission to reclaim storage for the condition variable attributes object. Condition variables that are created using this attributes object are not affected by the deletion of the condition variable attributes object.

The results of calling this routine are unpredictable if the handle specified by the *attr* parameter refers to an attributes object that does not exist.

Return Values

Possible return values are as follows:

Return	Error	Description
0		Successful completion.
-1	[**EINVAL**]	The value specified by *attr* is invalid.

Related Information

Functions: **pthread_condattr_create(3thr)**.

pthread_create

Purpose

Creates a thread object and thread

Synopsis

#include <pthread.h>

int pthread_create(
  pthread_t **thread*,
  pthread_attr_t *attr*,
  pthread_startroutine_t *start_routine*,
  pthread_addr_t *arg*);

Parameters

thread — Handle to the thread object created.

attr — Thread attributes object that defines the characteristics of the thread being created. If you specify **pthread_attr_default**, default attributes are used.

start_routine — Function executed as the new thread's start routine.

arg — Address value copied and passed to the thread's start routine.

Description

The **pthread_create( )** routine creates a thread object and a thread. A thread is a single, sequential flow of control within a program. It is the active execution of a designated routine, including any nested routine invocations. A thread object defines and controls the executing thread.

Creating a Thread

Calling this routine sets into motion the following actions:

- An internal thread object is created to describe the thread.
- The associated executable thread is created with attributes specified by the *attr* parameter (or with default attributes if **pthread_attr_default** is specified).
- The *thread* parameter receives the new thread.
- The *start_routine* function is called when this routine completes successfully.

Thread Execution

The thread is created in the ready state and therefore might immediately begin executing the function specified by the *start_routine* parameter. The newly created thread begins running before **pthread_create( )** completes if the new thread follows the **SCHED_RR** or **SCHED_FIFO** scheduling policy or has a priority higher than the creating thread, or both. Otherwise, the new thread begins running at its turn, which with sufficient processors might also be before **pthread_create( )** returns.

The *start_routine* parameter is passed a copy of the *arg* parameter. The value of the *arg* parameter is unspecified.

The thread object exists until the **pthread_detach( )** routine is called or the thread terminates, whichever occurs last.

The synchronization between the caller of **pthread_create( )** and the newly created thread is through the use of the **pthread_join( )** routine (or any other mutexes or condition variables they agree to use).

Terminating a Thread

A thread terminates when one of the following events occurs:

- The thread returns from its start routine.
- The thread exits (within a routine) as the result of calling the **pthread_exit( )** routine.
- The thread is canceled.

When a Thread Terminates

The following actions are performed when a thread terminates:

- If the thread terminates by returning from its start routine or calling **pthread_exit( )**, the return value is copied into the thread object. If the start routine returns normally and the start routine is a procedure that does not return a value, then the result obtained by **pthread_join( )** is unpredictable. If the thread has been canceled, a return value of -1 is copied into the thread object. The return value can be retrieved by other threads by calling the **pthread_join( )** routine.
- A destructor for each thread-specific data point is removed from the list of destructors for this thread and then is called. This step destroys all the thread-specific data associated with the current thread.

- Each cleanup handler that has been declared by **pthread_cleanup_push( )** and not yet removed by **pthread_cleanup_pop( )** is called. The most recently pushed handler is called first.
- A flag is set in the thread object indicating that the thread has terminated. This flag must be set in order for callers of **pthread_join( )** to return from the call.
- A broadcast is made so that all threads currently waiting in a call to **pthread_join( )** can return from the call.
- The thread object is marked to indicate that it is no longer needed by the thread itself. A check is made to determine if the thread object is no longer needed by other threads; that is, if **pthread_detach( )** has been called. If that routine is called, then the thread object is deallocated.

Return Values

If an error condition occurs, no thread is created, the contents of *thread* are undefined, and this routine returns -1 and sets **errno** to the corresponding error value. Possible return values are as follows:

Return	Error	Description
0		Successful completion.
-1	[**EAGAIN**]	The system lacks the necessary resources to create another thread.
-1	[**ENOMEM**]	Insufficient memory exists to create the thread object. This is not a temporary condition.

Related Information

Functions: **pthread_attr_create(3thr)**, **pthread_cancel(3thr)**, **pthread_detach(3thr)**, **pthread_exit(3thr)**, **pthread_join(3thr)**.

pthread_delay_np

Purpose Causes a thread to wait for a specified period

Synopsis

```
#include <pthread.h>

int pthread_delay_np(
        struct timespec *interval);
```

Parameters

interval Number of seconds and nanoseconds that the calling thread waits before continuing execution. The value specified must be greater than or equal to 0 (zero).

Description

The **pthread_delay_np( )** routine causes a thread to delay execution for a specified period of elapsed wall clock time. The period of time the thread waits is at least as long as the number of seconds and nanoseconds specified in the *interval* parameter.

Specifying an interval of 0 seconds and 0 nanoseconds is allowed and can result in the thread giving up the processor or delivering a pending cancel.

The **struct timespec** structure contains two fields, as follows:

- The **tv_sec** field is an integer number of seconds.
- The **tv_nsec** field is an integer number of nanoseconds.

This routine is not portable.

Return Values

If an error condition occurs, this routine returns -1 and sets **errno** to the corresponding error value. Possible return values are as follows:

Return	Error	Description
0		Successful completion.
-1	[**EINVAL**]	The value specified by *interval* is invalid.

Related Information

Functions: **pthread_yield(3thr)**.

pthread_detach

Purpose

Marks a thread object for deletion

Synopsis

#include <pthread.h>

int pthread_detach(
pthread_t **thread***);**

Parameters

thread Thread object marked for deletion.

Description

The **pthread_detach**( ) routine indicates that storage for the specified thread is reclaimed when the thread terminates. This includes storage for the *thread* parameter's return value. If *thread* has not terminated when this routine is called, this routine does not cause it to terminate.

Call this routine when a thread object is no longer referenced. Additionally, call this routine for every thread that is created to ensure that storage for thread objects does not accumulate.

You cannot join with a thread after the thread has been detached.

The results of this routine are unpredictable if the value of *thread* refers to a thread object that does not exist.

Return Values

If an error condition occurs, this routine returns -1 and sets **errno** to the corresponding error value. Possible return values are as follows:

Return	Error	Description
0		Successful completion.
-1	[**EINVAL**]	The value specified by *thread* is invalid.
-1	[**ESRCH**]	The value specified by *thread* does not refer to an existing thread.

Related Information

Functions: **pthread_cancel(3thr)**, **pthread_create(3thr)**, **pthread_exit(3thr)**, **pthread_join(3thr)**.

pthread_exit

Purpose Terminates the calling thread

Synopsis **#include <pthread.h>**

void pthread_exit(
pthread_addr_t *status*);

Parameters

status Address value copied and returned to the caller of **pthread_join( )**.

Description

The **pthread_exit( )** routine terminates the calling thread and makes a status value available to any thread that calls **pthread_join( )** and specifies the terminating thread.

An implicit call to **pthread_exit( )** is issued when a thread returns from the start routine that was used to create it. The function's return value serves as the thread's exit status. If the return value is -1, an error exit is forced for the thread instead of a normal exit. The process exits when the last running thread calls **pthread_exit( )**, with an undefined exit status.

Restrictions

The **pthread_exit( )** routine does not work in the main (initial) thread because DCE Threads relies on information at the base of thread stacks; this information does not exist in the main thread.

Return Values

No value is returned.

Related Information

Functions: **pthread_create(3thr)**, **pthread_detach(3thr)**, **pthread_join(3thr)**.

pthread_get_expiration_np

Purpose

Obtains a value representing a desired expiration time

Synopsis

#include <pthread.h>

int pthread_get_expiration_np(
  struct timespec ***delta*,**
  struct timespec ***abstime*);**

Parameters

delta — Number of seconds and nanoseconds to add to the current system time. The result is the time when a timed wait expires.

abstime — Value representing the expiration time.

Description

The **pthread_get_expiration_np( )** routine adds a specified interval to the current absolute system time and returns a new absolute time. This new absolute time is used as the expiration time in a call to **pthread_cond_timedwait( )**.

This routine is not portable.

The **struct timespec** structure contains two fields, as follows:

- The **tv_sec** field is an integer number of seconds.
- The **tv_nsec** field is an integer number of nanoseconds.

Return Values

If an error condition occurs, this routine returns -1 and sets **errno** to the corresponding error value. Possible return values are as follows:

Return	Error	Description
0		Successful completion.
-1	[EINVAL]	The value specified by *delta* is invalid.

Related Information

Functions: **pthread_cond_timedwait(3thr)**.

pthread_getprio

Purpose Obtains the current priority of a thread

Synopsis **#include <pthread.h>**

```
int pthread_getprio(
        pthread_t thread);
```

Parameters

thread Thread whose priority is obtained.

Description

The **pthread_getprio( )** routine obtains the current priority of a thread. The current priority is different from the initial priority of the thread if the **pthread_setprio( )** routine is called.

The exact effect of different priority values depends upon the scheduling policy assigned to the thread.

Return Values

The current priority value of the thread specified in *thread* is returned. (See the **pthread_setprio( )** reference page for valid values.)

If an error condition occurs, this routine returns -1 and sets **errno** to the corresponding error value. Possible return values are as follows:

Return	Error	Description
Priority value		Successful completion.
-1	[**EINVAL**]	The value specified by *thread* is invalid.
-1	[**ESRCH**]	The value specified by *thread* does not refer to an existing thread.

Related Information

Functions: **pthread_attr_setprio(3thr)**, **pthread_setprio(3thr)**, **pthread_setscheduler(3thr)**.

pthread_getscheduler

Purpose Obtains the current scheduling policy of a thread

Synopsis **#include <pthread.h>**

int pthread_getscheduler(
pthread_t *thread*);

Parameters

thread Thread whose scheduling policy is obtained.

Description

The **pthread_getscheduler( )** routine obtains the current scheduling policy of a thread. The current scheduling policy of a thread is different from the initial scheduling policy if the **pthread_setscheduler( )** routine is called.

Return Values

The current scheduling policy value of the thread specified in *thread* is returned. (See the **pthread_setscheduler( )** reference page for valid values.)

If an error condition occurs, this routine returns -1 and sets **errno** to the corresponding error value. Possible return values are as follows:

Return	Error	Description
Current scheduling policy		Successful completion.
-1	[**EINVAL**]	The value specified by *thread* is invalid.
-1	[**ESRCH**]	The value specified by *thread* does not refer to an existing thread.

Related Information

Functions: **pthread_attr_setscheduler(3thr)**, **pthread_setscheduler(3thr)**.

pthread_getspecific

Purpose Obtains the thread-specific data associated with the specified key

Synopsis **#include <pthread.h>**

int pthread_getspecific(
  pthread_key_t *key***,**
  pthread_addr_t **value***);**

Parameters

key Context key value that identifies the data value obtained. This key value must be obtained from **pthread_keycreate( )**.

value Address of the current thread-specific data value associated with the specified key.

Description

The **pthread_getspecific( )** routine obtains the thread-specific data associated with the specified key for the current thread.

Return Values

If an error condition occurs, this routine returns -1 and sets **errno** to the corresponding error value. Possible return values are as follows:

Return	Error	Description
0		Successful completion.
-1	[**EINVAL**]	The key value is invalid.

Related Information

Functions: **pthread_keycreate(3thr)**, **pthread_setspecific(3thr)**.

pthread_join

Purpose Causes the calling thread to wait for the termination of a specified thread

Synopsis **#include <pthread.h>**

int pthread_join(
    pthread_t *thread***,**
    pthread_addr_t **status***);**

Parameters

thread Thread whose termination is awaited by the caller of this routine.

status Status value of the terminating thread when that thread calls **pthread_exit**( ).

Description

The **pthread_join**( ) routine causes the calling thread to wait for the termination of a specified thread. A call to this routine returns after the specified thread has terminated.

Any number of threads can call this routine. All threads are awakened when the specified thread terminates.

If the current thread calls this routine, a deadlock results.

The results of this routine are unpredictable if the value for *thread* refers to a thread object that no longer exists.

Return Values

If the thread terminates normally, the exit status is the value that is optionally returned from the thread's start routine.

If an error condition occurs, this routine returns -1 and sets **errno** to the corresponding error value. The following return values are possible:

Return	Error	Description
0		Successful completion.
-1	[**EINVAL**]	The value specified by *thread* is invalid.
-1	[**ESRCH**]	The value specified by *thread* does not refer to a currently existing thread.
-1	[**EDEADLK**]	A deadlock is detected.

Related Information

Functions: **pthread_create(3thr)**, **pthread_detach(3thr)**, **pthread_exit(3thr)**.

pthread_keycreate

Purpose Generates a unique thread-specific data key value

Synopsis **#include <pthread.h>**

int pthread_keycreate(
    pthread_key_t ******key*,
    pthread_destructor_t *destructor*);

Parameters

key Value of the new thread-specific data key.

destructor Procedure to be called to destroy a data value associated with the created key when the thread terminates.

Description

The **pthread_keycreate()** routine generates a unique thread-specific data key value. This key value identifies a thread-specific data value, which is an address of memory generated by the client containing arbitrary data of any size.

Thread-specific data allows client software to associate information with the current thread.

For example, thread-specific data can be used by a language runtime library that needs to associate a language-specific thread-private data structure with an individual thread. The thread-specific data routines also provide a portable means of implementing the class of storage called thread-private static, which is needed to support parallel decomposition in the FORTRAN language.

This routine generates and returns a new key value. Each call to this routine within a process returns a key value that is unique within an application invocation. Calls to **pthread_keycreate()** must occur in initialization code guaranteed to execute only once in each process. The **pthread_once()** routine provides a way of specifying such code.

When multiple facilities share access to thread-specific data, the facilities must agree on the key value that is associated with the context. The key value must be created only once and needs to be stored in a location known to each facility. (It may be desirable to encapsulate the creation of a key, and the setting and getting of context values for that key, within a special facility created for that purpose.)

When a thread terminates, thread-specific data is automatically destroyed. For each thread-specific data currently associated with the thread, the **destructor** routine associated with the key value of that context is called. The order in which per-thread context destructors are called at thread termination is undefined.

Return Values

If an error condition occurs, this routine returns -1 and sets **errno** to the corresponding error value. Possible return values are as follows:

Return	Error	Description
0		Successful completion.
-1	[**EINVAL**]	The value specified by *key* is invalid.
-1	[**ENOMEM**]	An attempt was made to allocate a key when the key namespace is exhausted. This is not a temporary condition.
-1	[**EAGAIN**]	Insufficient memory exists to create the key.

Related Information

Functions: **pthread_getspecific(3thr)**, **pthread_setspecific(3thr)**.

pthread_lock_global_np

Purpose Locks the global mutex

Synopsis **#include <pthread.h>**

void pthread_lock_global_np( );

Description

The **pthread_lock_global_np( )** routine locks the global mutex. If the global mutex is currently held by another thread when a thread calls this routine, the thread waits for the global mutex to become available.

The thread that has locked the global mutex becomes its current owner and remains the owner until the same thread has unlocked it. This routine returns with the global mutex in the locked state and with the current thread as the global mutex's current owner.

Use the global mutex when calling a library package that is not designed to run in a multithreaded environment. (Unless the documentation for a library function specifically states that it is compatible with multithreading, assume that it is not compatible; in other words, assume it is nonreentrant.)

The global mutex is one lock. Any code that calls any function that is not known to be reentrant uses the same lock. This prevents dependencies among threads calling library functions and those functions calling other functions, and so on.

The global mutex is a recursive mutex. A thread that has locked the global mutex can relock it without deadlocking. (The locking thread must call **pthread_unlock_global_np( )** as many times as it called this routine to allow another thread to lock the global mutex.)

This routine is not portable.

Return Values

No value is returned.

Related Information

Functions: **pthread_mutexattr_setkind_np(3thr)**, **pthread_mutex_lock(3thr)**, **pthread_mutex_unlock(3thr)**, **pthread_unlock_global_np(3thr)**.

pthread_mutex_destroy

Purpose Deletes a mutex

Synopsis **#include <pthread.h>**

int pthread_mutex_destroy(
pthread_mutex_t ***mutex*);**

Parameters

mutex Mutex to be deleted.

Description

The **pthread_mutex_destroy**( ) routine deletes a mutex and must be called when a mutex object is no longer referenced. The effect of calling this routine is to reclaim storage for the mutex object.

It is illegal to delete a mutex that has a current owner (in other words, is locked).

The results of this routine are unpredictable if the mutex object specified in the *mutex* parameter does not currently exist.

Return Values

If an error condition occurs, this routine returns -1 and sets **errno** to the corresponding error value. Possible return values are as follows:

Return	Error	Description
0		Successful completion.
-1	[**EBUSY**]	An attempt was made to destroy a mutex that is locked.
-1	[**EINVAL**]	The value specified by *mutex* is invalid.

Related Information

Functions: **pthread_mutex_init(3thr)**, **pthread_mutex_lock(3thr)**, **pthread_mutex_trylock(3thr)**, **pthread_mutex_unlock(3thr)**.

pthread_mutex_init

Purpose Creates a mutex

Synopsis **#include <pthread.h>**

int pthread_mutex_init(
    pthread_mutex_t ***mutex*,**
    pthread_mutexattr_t *attr***);**

Parameters

mutex Mutex that is created.

attr Attributes object that defines the characteristics of the created mutex. If you specify **pthread_mutexattr_default**, default attributes are used.

Description

The **pthread_mutex_init( )** routine creates a mutex and initializes it to the unlocked state. If the thread that called this routine terminates, the created mutex is not automatically deallocated, because it is considered shared among multiple threads.

Return Values

If an error condition occurs, this routine returns -1, the mutex is not initialized, and the contents of *mutex* are undefined. This routine sets **errno** to the corresponding error value. Possible return values are as follows:

Return	Error	Description
0		Successful completion.
-1	[**EAGAIN**]	The system lacks the necessary resources to initialize another mutex.
-1	[**ENOMEM**]	Insufficient memory exists to initialize the mutex.

Related Information

Functions: **pthread_mutexattr_create(3thr)**, **pthread_mutexattr_getkind_np(3thr)**, **pthread_mutexattr_setkind_np(3thr)**, **pthread_mutex_lock(3thr)**, **pthread_mutex_trylock(3thr)**, **pthread_mutex_unlock(3thr)**.

pthread_mutex_lock

Purpose Locks an unlocked mutex

Synopsis

```
#include <pthread.h>

int pthread_mutex_lock(
        pthread_mutex_t *mutex);
```

Parameters

mutex Mutex that is locked.

Description

The **pthread_mutex_lock()** routine locks a mutex. If the mutex is locked when a thread calls this routine, the thread waits for the mutex to become available.

The thread that has locked a mutex becomes its current owner and remains the owner until the same thread has unlocked it. This routine returns with the mutex in the locked state and with the current thread as the mutex's current owner.

If you specified a fast mutex in a call to **pthread_mutexattr_setkind_np()**, a deadlock can result if the current owner of a mutex calls this routine in an attempt to lock the mutex a second time. If you specified a recursive mutex in a call to **pthread_mutexattr_setkind_np()**, the current owner of a mutex can relock the same mutex without blocking. If you specify a nonrecursive mutex in a call to **pthread_mutexattr_setkind_np()**, an error is returned and the thread does not block if the current owner of a mutex calls this routine in an attempt to lock the mutex a second time.

The preemption of a lower-priority thread that locks a mutex possibly results in the indefinite blocking of higher-priority threads waiting for the same mutex. The execution of the waiting higher-priority threads is blocked for as long as there is a sufficient number of runable threads of any priority between the lower-priority and higher-priority values. Priority inversion occurs when any resource is shared between threads with different priorities.

Return Values

If an error condition occurs, this routine returns -1 and sets **errno** to the corresponding error value. Possible return values are as follows:

Return	Error	Description
0		Successful completion.
-1	[**EINVAL**]	The value specified by *mutex* is invalid.
-1	[**EDEADLK**]	A deadlock condition is detected.

Related Information

Functions: **pthread_mutexattr_setkind_np(3thr)**, **pthread_mutex_destroy(3thr)**, **pthread_mutex_init(3thr)**, **pthread_mutex_trylock(3thr)**, **pthread_mutex_unlock(3thr)**.

pthread_mutex_trylock

Purpose Locks a mutex

Synopsis

```
#include <pthread.h>
int pthread_mutex_trylock(
        pthread_mutex_t *mutex);
```

Parameters

mutex Mutex that is locked.

Description

The **pthread_mutex_trylock**( ) routine locks a mutex. If the specified mutex is locked when a thread calls this routine, the calling thread does not wait for the mutex to become available.

When a thread calls this routine, an attempt is made to lock the mutex immediately. If the mutex is successfully locked, 1 is returned and the current thread is then the mutex's current owner.

If the mutex is locked by another thread when this routine is called, 0 (zero) is returned and the thread does not wait to acquire the lock. If a fast mutex is owned by the current thread, 0 is returned. If a recursive mutex is owned by the current thread, 1 is returned and the mutex is relocked. (To unlock a recursive mutex, each call to **pthread_mutex_trylock**( ) must be matched by a call to the **pthread_mutex_unlock**( ) routine.)

Return Values

If an error condition occurs, this routine returns -1 and sets **errno** to the corresponding error value. Possible return values are as follows:

Return	Error	Description
1		Successful completion.
0		The mutex is locked; therefore, it was not acquired.
-1	[**EINVAL**]	The value specified by *mutex* is invalid.

Related Information

Functions: **pthread_mutexattr_setkind_np(3thr)**, **pthread_mutex_destroy(3thr)**, **pthread_mutex_init(3thr)**, **pthread_mutex_lock(3thr)**, **pthread_mutex_unlock(3thr)**.

pthread_mutex_unlock

Purpose Unlocks a mutex

Synopsis

```
#include <pthread.h>

int pthread_mutex_unlock(
        pthread_mutex_t *mutex);
```

Parameters

mutex Mutex that is unlocked.

Description

The **pthread_mutex_unlock( )** routine unlocks a mutex. If no threads are waiting for the mutex, the mutex unlocks with no current owner. If one or more threads are waiting to lock the specified mutex, this routine causes one thread to return from its call to **pthread_mutex_lock( )**. The scheduling policy is used to determine which thread acquires the mutex. For the **SCHED_FIFO** and **SCHED_RR** policies, a blocked thread is chosen in priority order.

The results of calling this routine are unpredictable if the mutex specified in *mutex* is unlocked. The results of calling this routine are also unpredictable if the mutex specified in *mutex* is currently owned by a thread other than the calling thread.

Return Values

If an error condition occurs, this routine returns -1 and sets **errno** to the corresponding error value. Possible return values are as follows:

Return	Error	Description
0		Successful completion.
-1	[EINVAL]	The value specified by *mutex* is invalid.

Related Information

Functions: **pthread_mutexattr_setkind_np(3thr)**, **pthread_mutex_destroy(3thr)**, **pthread_mutex_init(3thr)**, **pthread_mutex_lock(3thr)**, **pthread_mutex_trylock(3thr)**, **pthread_unlock_global_np(3thr)**.

pthread_mutexattr_create

Purpose Creates a mutex attributes object

Synopsis **#include <pthread.h>**

int pthread_mutexattr_create(
pthread_mutexattr_t **attr*);

Parameters

attr Mutex attributes object created.

Description

The **pthread_mutexattr_create**( ) routine creates a mutex attributes object used to specify the attributes of mutexes when they are created. The mutex attributes object is initialized with the default value for all of the attributes defined by a given implementation.

When a mutex attributes object is used to create a mutex, the values of the individual attributes determine the characteristics of the new object. Attributes objects act like additional parameters to object creation. Changing individual attributes does not affect any objects that were previously created using the attributes object.

Return Values

The created mutex attributes object is returned to the *attr* parameter.

If an error condition occurs, this routine returns -1 and sets **errno** to the corresponding error value. Possible return values are as follows:

Return	Error	Description
0		Successful completion.
-1	[**EINVAL**]	The value specified by *attr* is invalid.
-1	[**ENOMEM**]	Insufficient memory exists to create the mutex attributes object.

Related Information

Functions: **pthread_create(3thr)**, **pthread_mutexattr_delete(3thr)**, **pthread_mutexattr_getkind_np(3thr)**, **pthread_mutexattr_setkind_np(3thr)**, **pthread_mutex_init(3thr)**.

pthread_mutexattr_delete

Purpose Deletes a mutex attributes object

Synopsis **#include <pthread.h>**

int pthread_mutexattr_delete(
pthread_mutexattr_t ***attr*);**

Parameters

attr Mutex attributes object deleted.

Description

The **pthread_mutexattr_delete( )** routine deletes a mutex attributes object. Call this routine when a mutex attributes object is no longer referenced by the **pthread_mutexattr_create( )** routine.

This routine gives permission to reclaim storage for the mutex attributes object. Mutexes that were created using this attributes object are not affected by the deletion of the mutex attributes object.

The results of calling this routine are unpredictable if the attributes object specified in the *attr* parameter does not exist.

Return Values

Possible return values are as follows:

Return	Error	Description
0		Successful completion.
-1	[**EINVAL**]	The value specified by *attr* is invalid.

Related Information

Functions: **pthread_mutexattr_create(3thr)**.

pthread_mutexattr_getkind_np

Purpose Obtains the mutex type attribute used when a mutex is created

Synopsis **#include <pthread.h>**

int pthread_mutexattr_getkind_np(
pthread_mutexattr_t ***attr*);**

Parameters

attr Mutex attributes object whose mutex type is obtained.

Description

The **pthread_mutexattr_getkind_np( )** routine obtains the mutex type attribute that is used when a mutex is created. See the **pthread_mutexattr_setkind_np( )** reference page for information about mutex type attributes.

This routine is not portable.

Return Values

If an error condition occurs, this routine returns -1 and sets **errno** to the corresponding error value. Possible return values are as follows:

Return	Error	Description
Mutex type attribute		Successful completion.
-1	[EINVAL]	The value specified by *attr* is invalid.

Related Information

Functions: **pthread_mutexattr_create(3thr)**, **pthread_mutexattr_setkind_np(3thr)**, **pthread_mutex_init(3thr)**.

pthread_mutexattr_setkind_np

Purpose Specifies the mutex type attribute

Synopsis **#include <pthread.h>**

int pthread_mutexattr_setkind_np(
pthread_mutexattr_t **attr*,
int *kind***);**

Parameters

attr Mutex attributes object modified.

kind New value for the mutex type attribute. The *kind* parameter specifies the type of mutex that is created. Valid values are **MUTEX_FAST_NP** (default), **MUTEX_RECURSIVE_NP**, and **MUTEX_NONRECURSIVE_NP**.

Description

The **pthread_mutexattr_setkind_np( )** routine sets the mutex type attribute that is used when a mutex is created.

A fast mutex is locked and unlocked in the fastest manner possible. A fast mutex can only be locked (obtained) once. All subsequent calls to **pthread_mutex_lock( )** cause the calling thread to block until the mutex is freed by the thread that owns it. If the thread that owns the mutex attempts to lock it again, the thread waits for itself to release the mutex (causing a deadlock).

A recursive mutex can be locked more than once by the same thread without causing that thread to deadlock. In other words, a single thread can make consecutive calls to **pthread_mutex_lock( )** without blocking. The thread must then call **pthread_mutex_unlock( )** the same number of times as it called **pthread_mutex_lock( )** before another thread can lock the mutex.

A nonrecursive mutex is locked only once by a thread, like a fast mutex. If the thread tries to lock the mutex again without first unlocking it, the thread receives an error. Thus, nonrecursive mutexes are more informative than fast mutexes because fast mutexes block in such a case, leaving it up to you to determine why the thread no longer executes. Also, if someone other than the owner tries to unlock a nonrecursive mutex, an error is returned.

Never use a recursive mutex with condition variables because the implicit unlock performed for a **pthread_cond_wait( )** or **pthread_cond_timedwait( )** might not actually release the mutex. In that case, no other thread can satisfy the condition of the predicate.

This routine is not portable.

Return Values

If an error condition occurs, this routine returns -1 and sets **errno** to the corresponding error value. Possible return values are as follows:

Return	Error	Description
0		Successful completion.
-1	[**EINVAL**]	The value specified by *attr* or *kind* is invalid.
-1	[**EPERM**]	The caller does not have the appropriate privileges.
-1	[**ERANGE**]	One or more parameters supplied have an invalid value.

Related Information

Functions: **pthread_mutexattr_create(3thr)**, **pthread_mutexattr_getkind_np(3thr)**, **pthread_mutex_init(3thr)**.

pthread_once

Purpose Calls an initialization routine executed by one thread, a single time

Synopsis **#include <pthread.h>**

int pthread_once(
pthread_once_t ***once_block*,**
pthread_initroutine_t *init_routine***);**

Parameters

once_block Address of a record that defines the one-time initialization code. Each one-time initialization routine must have its own unique **pthread_once_t** data structure.

init_routine Address of a procedure that performs the initialization. This routine is called only once, regardless of the number of times it and its associated *once_block* are passed to **pthread_once( )**.

Description

The **pthread_once( )** routine calls an initialization routine executed by one thread, a single time. This routine allows you to create your own initialization code that is guaranteed to be run only once, even if called simultaneously by multiple threads or multiple times in the same thread.

For example, a mutex or a thread-specfic data key must be created exactly once. Calling **pthread_once( )** prevents the code that creates a mutex or thread-specific data from being called by multiple threads. Without this routine, the execution must be serialized so that only one thread performs the initialization. Other threads that reach the same point in the code are delayed until the first thread is finished.

This routine initializes the control record if it has not been initialized and then determines if the client one-time initialization routine has executed once. If it has not executed, this routine calls the initialization routine specified in *init_routine*. If the client one-time initialization code has executed once, this routine returns.

The **pthread_once_t** data structure is a record that allows client initialization operations to guarantee mutual exclusion of access to the initialization routine, and that each initialization routine is executed exactly once.

The client code must declare a variable of type **pthread_once_t** to use the client initialization operations. This variable must be initialized using the **pthread_once_init** macro, as follows:

```
static pthread_once_t myOnceBlock = pthread_once_init;
```

Return Values

If an error occurs, this routine returns -1. No error values have been specified. Possible return values are as follows:

Return	Error	Description
0		Successful completion.
-1		Invalid parameter.

pthread_self

Purpose Obtains the identifier of the current thread

Synopsis **#include <pthread.h>**

pthread_t pthread_self( );

Description

The **pthread_self( )** routine allows a thread to obtain its own identifier. For example, this identifier allows a thread to set its own priority.

This value becomes meaningless when the thread object is deleted; that is, when the thread terminates its execution and **pthread_detach( )** is called.

Return Values

Returns the identifier of the calling thread to **pthread_t**.

Related Information

Functions: **pthread_create(3thr)**, **pthread_setprio(3thr)**, **pthread_setscheduler(3thr)**.

pthread_setasynccancel

Purpose Enables or disables the current thread's asynchronous cancelability

Synopsis **#include <pthread.h>**

int pthread_setasynccancel(
    int *state***);**

Parameters

state State of asynchronous cancelability set for the calling thread. On return, receives the prior state of asynchronous cancelability. Valid values are as follows:

CANCEL_ON Asynchronous cancelability is enabled.

CANCEL_OFF Asynchronous cancelability is disabled.

Description

The **pthread_setasynccancel( )** routine enables or disables the current thread's asynchronous cancelability and returns the previous cancelability state to the *state* parameter.

When general cancelability is set to **CANCEL_OFF**, a cancel cannot be delivered to the thread, even if a cancelable routine is called or asynchronous cancelability is enabled. When general cancelability is set to **CANCEL_ON**, cancelability depends on the state of the thread's asynchronous cancelability.

When general cancelability is set to **CANCEL_ON** and asynchronous cancelability is set to **CANCEL_OFF**, the thread can only receive a cancel at specific cancellation points (for example, condition waits, thread joins, and calls to the **pthread_testcancel( )** routine). If both general cancelability and asynchronous cancelability are set to **CANCEL_ON**, the thread can be canceled at any point in its execution.

When a thread is created, the default asynchronous cancelability state is **CANCEL_OFF**.

If you call this routine to enable asynchronous cancels, call it in a region of code where asynchronous delivery of cancels is disabled by a previous call to this routine. Do not call threads routines in regions of code where asynchronous delivery of cancels is enabled. The previous state of asynchronous delivery can be restored later by another call to this routine.

Return Values

If an error condition occurs, this routine returns -1 and sets **errno** to the corresponding error value. Possible return values are as follows:

Return	Error	Description
CANCEL_ON		Asynchronous cancelability was on.
CANCEL_OFF		Asynchronous cancelability was off.
-1	[**EINVAL**]	The specified state is not **CANCEL_ON** or **CANCEL_OFF**.

Related Information

Functions: **pthread_cancel(3thr)**, **pthread_setcancel(3thr)**, **pthread_testcancel(3thr)**.

pthread_setcancel

Purpose Enables or disables the current thread's general cancelability

Synopsis

```
#include <pthread.h>
int pthread_setcancel(
        int state);
```

Parameters

state State of general cancelability set for the calling thread. On return, receives the prior state of general cancelability. Valid values are as follows:

CANCEL_ON General cancelability is enabled.

CANCEL_OFF General cancelability is disabled.

Description

The **pthread_setcancel( )** routine enables or disables the current thread's general cancelability and returns the previous cancelability state to the *state* parameter.

When general cancelability is set to **CANCEL_OFF**, a cancel cannot be delivered to the thread, even if a cancelable routine is called or asynchronous cancelability is enabled.

When a thread is created, the default general cancelability state is **CANCEL_ON**.

Possible Dangers of Disabling Cancelability

The most important use of cancels is to ensure that indefinite wait operations are terminated. For example, a thread waiting on some network connection, which may take days to respond (or may never respond), is normally made cancelable.

However, when cancelability is disabled, no routine is cancelable. Waits must be completed normally before a cancel can be delivered. As a result, the program stops working and the user is unable to cancel the operation.

When disabling cancelability, be sure that no long waits can occur or that it is necessary for other reasons to defer cancels around that particular region of code.

Return Values

If an error condition occurs, this routine returns -1 and sets **errno** to the corresponding error value. Possible return values are as follows:

Return	Error	Description
CANCEL_ON		Asynchronous cancelability was on.
CANCEL_OFF		Asynchronous cancelability was off.
-1	[**EINVAL**]	The specified state is not **CANCEL_ON** or **CANCEL_OFF**.

Related Information

Functions: **pthread_cancel(3thr)**, **pthread_setasynccancel(3thr)**, **pthread_testcancel(3thr)**.

pthread_setprio

Purpose Changes the current priority of a thread

Synopsis **#include <pthread.h>**

int pthread_setprio(
pthread_t *thread*,
int *priority*);

Parameters

thread Thread whose priority is changed.

priority New priority value of the thread specified in *thread*. The priority value depends on scheduling policy. Valid values fall within one of the following ranges:

- **PRI_OTHER_MIN <=** *priority* <= **PRI_OTHER_MAX**
- **PRI_FIFO_MIN <=** *priority* <= **PRI_FIFO_MAX**
- **PRI_RR_MIN <=** *priority* <= **PRI_RR_MAX**
- **PRI_FG_MIN_NP <=** *priority* <= **PRI_FG_MAX_NP**
- **PRI_BG_MIN_NP <=** *priority* <= **PRI_BG_MAX_NP**

If you create a new thread without specifying a threads attributes object that contains a changed priority attribute, the default priority of the newly created thread is the midpoint between **PRI_OTHER_MIN** and **PRI_OTHER_MAX** (the midpoint between the minimum and the maximum for the **SCHED_OTHER** policy).

When you call this routine to specify a minimum or maximum priority, use the appropriate symbol; for example, **PRI_FIFO_MIN** or **PRI_FIFO_MAX**. To specify a value between the minimum and maximum, use an appropriate arithmetic expression. For example, to specify a priority midway between the minimum and maximum for the Round Robin scheduling policy, specify the following concept using your programming language's syntax:

```
pri_rr_mid = (PRI_RR_MIN + PRI_RR_MAX)/2
```

If your expression results in a value outside the range of minimum to maximum, an error results when you use it.

Description

The **pthread_setprio( )** routine changes the current priority of a thread. A thread can change its own priority using the identifier returned by **pthread_self( )**.

Changing the priority of a thread can cause it to start executing or be preempted by another thread. The effect of setting different priority values depends on the scheduling priority assigned to the thread. The initial scheduling priority is set by calling the **pthread_attr_setprio( )** routine.

Note that **pthread_attr_setprio( )** sets the priority attribute that is used to establish the priority of a new thread when it is created. However, **pthread_setprio( )** changes the priority of an existing thread.

Return Values

If successful, this routine returns the previous priority. If an error condition occurs, this routine returns -1 and sets **errno** to the corresponding error value. Possible return values are as follows:

Return	Error	Description
Previous priority		Successful completion.
-1	[**EINVAL**]	The value specified by *thread* is invalid.
-1	[**ENOTSUP**]	An attempt is made to set the policy to an unsupported value.
-1	[**ESRCH**]	The value specified by *thread* does not refer to an existing thread.
-1	[**EPERM**]	The caller does not have the appropriate privileges to set the priority of the specified thread.

Related Information

Functions: **pthread_attr_setprio(3thr)**, **pthread_attr_setsched(3thr)**, **pthread_create(3thr)**, **pthread_self(3thr)**, **pthread_setscheduler(3thr)**.

pthread_setscheduler

Purpose Changes the current scheduling policy and priority of a thread

Synopsis **#include <pthread.h>**

int pthread_setscheduler(
pthread_t *thread*,
int *scheduler*,
int *priority*)**;**

Parameters

thread Thread whose scheduling policy is to be changed.

scheduler New scheduling policy value for the thread specified in *thread*. Valid values are as follows:

SCHED_FIFO (First In, First Out) The highest-priority thread runs until it blocks. If there is more than one thread with the same priority, and that priority is the highest among other threads, the first thread to begin running continues until it blocks.

SCHED_RR (Round Robin) The highest-priority thread runs until it blocks; however, threads of equal priority, if that priority is the highest among other threads, are timesliced. Timeslicing is a process in which threads alternate using available processors.

SCHED_OTHER (Default) All threads are timesliced. **SCHED_OTHER** ensures that all threads, regardless of priority, receive some scheduling, and thus no thread is completely denied execution time. (However, **SCHED_OTHER** threads can be denied execution time by **SCHED_FIFO** or **SCHED_RR** threads.)

SCHED_FG_NP (Foreground) Same as **SCHED_OTHER**. Threads are timesliced and priorities can be modified dynamically by the scheduler to ensure fairness.

SCHED_BG_NP (Background) Like **SCHED_OTHER**, ensures that all threads, regardless of priority, receive some scheduling. However, **SCHED_BG_NP** can be denied execution by any of the other scheduling policies.

priority New priority value of the thread specified in *thread*. The priority attribute depends on scheduling policy. Valid values fall within one of the following ranges:

- **PRI_OTHER_MIN** <= *priority* <= **PRI_OTHER_MAX**
- **PRI_FIFO_MIN** <= *priority* <= **PRI_FIFO_MAX**
- **PRI_RR_MIN** <= *priority* <= **PRI_RR_MAX**
- **PRI_FG_MIN_NP** <= *priority* <= **PRI_FG_MAX_NP**
- **PRI_BG_MIN_NP** <= *priority* <= **PRI_BG_MAX_NP**

If you create a new thread without specifying a threads attributes object that contains a changed priority attribute, the default priority of the newly created thread is the midpoint between **PRI_OTHER_MIN** and **PRI_OTHER_MAX** (the midpoint between the minimum and the maximum for the **SCHED_OTHER** policy).

When you call this routine to specify a minimum or maximum priority, use the appropriate symbol; for example, **PRI_FIFO_MIN** or **PRI_FIFO_MAX**. To specify a value between the minimum and maximum, use an appropriate arithmetic expression. For example, to specify a priority midway between the minimum and maximum for the Round Robin scheduling policy, specify the following concept using your programming language's syntax:

```
pri_rr_mid = (PRI_RR_MIN + PRI_RR_MAX)/2
```

If your expression results in a value outside the range of minimum to maximum, an error results when you use it.

Description

The **pthread_setscheduler( )** routine changes the current scheduling policy and priority of a thread. Call this routine to change both the priority and scheduling policy of a thread at the same time. To change only the priority, call the **pthread_setprio( )** routine.

A thread changes its own scheduling policy and priority by using the identifier returned by **pthread_self( )**. Changing the scheduling policy or priority, or both, of a thread can cause it to start executing or to be preempted by another thread.

This routine differs from **pthread_attr_setprio( )** and **pthread_attr_setsched( )** because those routines set the priority and scheduling policy attributes that are used to establish the priority and scheduling policy of a new thread when it is created. This routine, however, changes the priority and scheduling policy of an existing thread.

Return Values

If an error condition occurs, this routine returns -1 and sets **errno** to the corresponding error value. Possible return values are as follows:

Return	Error	Description
0		Successful completion.
-1	[**EINVAL**]	The value specified by *thread* is invalid.
-1	[**ENOTSUP**]	An attempt is made to set the policy to an unsupported value.
-1	[**ESRCH**]	The value specified by *thread* does not refer to an existing thread.
-1	[**EPERM**]	The caller does not have the appropriate privileges to set the priority of the specified thread.

Related Information

Functions: **pthread_attr_setprio(3thr)**, **pthread_attr_setsched(3thr)**, **pthread_create(3thr)**, **pthread_self(3thr)**, **pthread_setprio(3thr)**.

pthread_setspecific

Purpose Sets the thread-specific data associated with the specified key for the current thread

Synopsis **#include <pthread.h>**

int pthread_setspecific(
pthread_key_t *key*,
pthread_addr_t *value*);

Parameters

key Context key value that uniquely identifies the context value specified in *value*. This key value must have been obtained from **pthread_keycreate( )**.

value Address containing data to be associated with the specified key for the current thread; this is the thread-specific data.

Description

The **pthread_setspecific( )** routine sets the thread-specific data associated with the specified key for the current thread. If a value has already been defined for the key in this thread, the new value is substituted for it.

Different threads can bind different values to the same key. These values are typically pointers to blocks of dynamically allocated memory that are reserved for use by the calling thread.

Return Values

If an error condition occurs, this routine returns -1 and sets **errno** to the corresponding error value. Possible return values are as follows:

Return	Error	Description
0		Successful completion.
-1	[**EINVAL**]	The key value is invalid.

Related Information

Functions: **pthread_getspecific(3thr)**, **pthread_keycreate(3thr)**.

pthread_signal_to_cancel_np

Purpose Cancels the specified thread

Synopsis **#include <pthread.h>**

int pthread_signal_to_cancel_np(
sigset_t **sigset*,
pthread_t **thread*);

Parameters

sigset Signal mask containing a list of signals that, when received by the process, cancels the specified thread.

thread Thread canceled if a valid signal is received by the process.

Description

The **pthread_signal_to_cancel_np( )** routine requests that the specified thread be canceled if one of the signals specified in the signal mask is received by the process. The set of legal signals is the same as that for the **sigwait( )** service. The *sigset* parameter is not validated. If it is invalid, this routine will return successfully but neither the specified thread nor the previously specified thread will be canceled if a signal occurs.

Note that the address of the specified thread is saved in a per-process global variable. Therefore, any subsequent call to this routine by your application or any library function will supercede the thread specified in the previous call, and that thread will not be canceled if one of the signals specified for it is delivered to the process. In other words, take care when you call this routine; if another thread calls it after you do, the expected result of this routine will not occur.

Return Values

If an error condition occurs, this routine returns -1 and sets **errno** to the corresponding error value. Possible return values are as follows:

Return	Error	Description
0		Successful completion.
-1	[**EINVAL**]	The value specified by *thread* is invalid.

Related Information

Functions: **pthread_cancel(3thr)**.

pthread_testcancel

Purpose Requests delivery of a pending cancel to the current thread

Synopsis **#include <pthread.h>**

void pthread_testcancel( );

Description

The **pthread_testcancel( )** routine requests delivery of a pending cancel to the current thread. The cancel is delivered only if a cancel is pending for the current thread and general cancel delivery is not currently disabled. (A thread disables delivery of cancels to itself by calling the **pthread_setcancel( )** routine.)

This routine, when called within very long loops, ensures that a pending cancel is noticed within a reasonable amount of time.

Return Values

No value is returned.

Related Information

Functions: **pthread_cancel(3thr)**, **pthread_setasynccancel(3thr)**, **pthread_setcancel(3thr)**.

pthread_unlock_global_np

Purpose Unlocks a global mutex

Synopsis **#include <pthread.h>**

void pthread_unlock_global_np( );

Description

The **pthread_unlock_global_np( )** routine unlocks the global mutex when each call to **pthread_lock_global_np( )** is matched by a call to this routine. For example, if you called **pthread_lock_global_np( )** three times, **pthread_unlock_global_np( )** unlocks the global mutex when you call it the third time. If no threads are waiting for the global mutex, it becomes unlocked with no current owner. If one or more threads are waiting to lock the global mutex, one thread returns from its call to **pthread_lock_global_np( )**. The scheduling policy is used to determine which thread acquires the global mutex. For the policies **SCHED_FIFO** and **SCHED_RR**, a blocked thread is chosen in priority order.

The results of calling this routine are unpredictable if the global mutex is already unlocked. The results of calling this routine are also unpredictable if the global mutex is owned by a thread other than the calling thread.

This routine is not portable.

Return Values

No value is returned.

Related Information

Functions: **pthread_lock_global_np(3thr)**, **pthread_mutexattr_setkind_np(3thr)**, **pthread_mutex_lock(3thr)**, **pthread_mutex_unlock(3thr)**.

pthread_yield

Purpose Notifies the scheduler that the current thread is willing to release its processor

Synopsis **#include <pthread.h>**

void pthread_yield( );

Description

The **pthread_yield( )** routine notifies the scheduler that the current thread is willing to release its processor to other threads of the same priority. (A thread releases its processor to a thread of a higher priority without calling this routine.)

If the current thread's scheduling policy (as specified in a call to the **pthread_attr_setsched( )** or **pthread_setscheduler( )** routine) is **SCHED_FIFO** or **SCHED_RR**, this routine yields the processor to other threads of the same or a higher priority. If no threads of the same priority are ready to execute, the thread continues.

This routine allows knowledge of the details of an application to be used to increase fairness. It increases fairness of access to the processor by removing the current thread from the processor. It also increases fairness of access to shared resources by removing the current thread from the processor as soon as it is finished with the resource.

Call this routine when a thread is executing code that denies access to other threads on a uniprocessor if the scheduling policy is **SCHED_FIFO**.

Use **pthread_yield( )** carefully because misuse causes unnecessary context switching, which increases overhead without increasing fairness. For example, it is counterproductive for a thread to yield while it has a needed resource locked.

Return Values

No value is returned.

Related Information

Functions: **pthread_attr_setsched(3thr)**, **pthread_setscheduler(3thr)**.

Chapter 2

DCE Remote Procedure Call

intro

Purpose Introduction to the DCE RPC programmer commands

Description

DCE RPC provides the following programmer commands:

- The **idl** command invokes the Interface Definition Language (IDL) compiler to convert an interface definition, written in IDL, to output files.
- The **nidl_to_idl** command translates an interface definition written in Network Interface Definition Language (NIDL) to a DCE IDL interface definition.
- The **uuidgen** command creates a UUID string that you assign to an object to uniquely distinguish it from other objects.

See each command's reference page for further information.

IDL Base Data Types and IDL-to-C

The following table lists the IDL base data type specifiers. Where applicable, the table shows the size of the corresponding transmittable type and the type macro emitted by the IDL compiler for resulting declarations.

Base Data Type Specifiers — intro(1rpc)				
	Specifier			Type Macro
(sign)	(size)	(type)	Size	Emitted by idl
	small	int	8 bits	idl_small_int
	short	int	16 bits	idl_short_int
	long	int	32 bits	idl_long_int
	hyper	int	64 bits	idl_hyper_int
unsigned	small	int	8 bits	idl_usmall_int
unsigned	short	int	16 bits	idl_ushort_int
unsigned	long	int	32 bits	idl_ulong_int
unsigned	hyper	int	64 bits	idl_uhyper_int
		float	32 bits	idl_short_float
		double	64 bits	idl_long_float
		char	8 bits	idl_char
		boolean	8 bits	idl_boolean
		byte	8 bits	idl_byte
		void	—	idl_void_p_t
		handle_t	—	—

Note that you can use the **idl_** macros in the code you write for an application to ensure that your type declarations are consistent with those in the stubs, even when the application is ported to another platform. The **idl_** macros are especially useful when passing constant values to RPC calls. For maximum portability, all constants passed to RPC calls declared in your network interfaces should be cast to the appropriate type because the size of integer constants (like the size of the **int** data type) is unspecified in the C language.

The **idl_** macros are defined in **dce/idlbase.h**, which is included by header files that the IDL compiler generates.

Related Information

Commands: **idl(1rpc)**, **nidl_to_idl(1rpc)**, **uuidgen(1rpc)**.

Messages: **idl_messages(7rpc)**, **nidl_to_idl_messages(7rpc)**, **uuidgen_messages(7rpc)**.

Books: *OSF DCE Application Development Guide*.

idl

Purpose Invokes the Interface Definition Language (IDL) compiler

Synopsis **idl** *filename* [*argument*] ...

Arguments

-client *file_type* Determines which client files to generate. If you do not specify this argument, the compiler generates all client files. The file types are as follows:

none Does not generate client files.

stub Generates only a client stub file.

aux Generates only a client auxiliary file. A client auxiliary file is generated only if the interface contains any out-of-line or self-pointing types.

all Generates client stub and client auxiliary files. This is the default and is the same as not specifying the **-client** argument.

-server *file_type* Determines which server files to generate. If you do not specify this argument, the compiler generates all server files. The file types are as follows:

none Does not generate server files.

stub Generates only a server stub file.

aux Generates only a server auxiliary file. A server auxiliary file is generated only if the interface contains any out-of-line, self-pointing, or pipe types.

all Generates server stub and server auxiliary files. This is the default and is the same as not specifying the **-server** argument.

-cstub *filename* Specifies a pathname for the client stub file. When you give a filename, do not give a file extension; the **idl** compiler appends **.c** to the C source file and **.o** to the object file. If you do not use the **-cstub** argument, the **idl** compiler appends **_cstub.c** to the C source file and **_cstub.o** to the object file.

-sstub *filename* Specifies a pathname for the server stub file. When you give a filename, do not give a file extension; the **idl** compiler appends **.c** to the C source file and **.o** to the object file. If you do not use the **-sstub** argument, the **idl** compiler appends **_sstub.c** to the C source file and **_sstub.o** to the object file.

-caux *filename* Specifies a pathname for the client auxiliary file. When you give a filename, do not give a file extension; the **idl** compiler appends **.c** to the C source file and **.o** to the object file. If you do not use the **-caux** argument, the **idl** compiler appends **_caux.c** to the C source file and **_caux.o** to the object file.

-saux *filename* Specifies a pathname for the server auxiliary file. When you give a filename, do not give a file extension; the **idl** compiler appends **.c** to the C source file and **.o** to the object file. If you do not use the **-caux** argument, the **idl** compiler appends **_saux.c** to the C source file and **_saux.o** to the object file.

-header *header_file*
Allows you to specify a name for the generated header file. By default the compiler takes the basename of the IDL file and appends the **.h** extension to it.

-out *directory* Places the output files in the directory you specify. By default the compiler places the output files in the current working directory.

-I*directory* Specifies a directory name that contains imported interface definition files. You can specify more than one directory by specifying additional **-I***directory* arguments on the command line. The compiler searches the directories in the order you list them. If a file is present in more than one directory, the compiler takes the first occurrence of the file. The default behavior of the compiler is to first search the current directory, then all directories you specify, then the system IDL directory. The directory you specify is also passed to the C preprocessor and the C compiler.

-no_def_idir Specifies that the compiler search only the current directory for imported files. When you use this with **-I***directory*, the compiler searches only the directories you list, not the current directory, and not the system IDL directory.

-no_mepv Causes the compiler to not generate a manager Entry Point Vector (EPV) in the server stub. Use this argument if the manager code and IDL file do not use the same operation names. If you specify this argument you must provide an EPV within the manager code that can be used when the interface is registered with the RPC server runtime. The name of the type that you construct an EPV with is *if_name*_**v***major-version*_*minor-version*_**epv_t** where *if_name* is the interface name. It is not necessary to use this argument if the operation names in the manager code and IDL file are the same. In this case, the compiler generates a manager EPV in the server stub using the names of the operations in the IDL file. (For information on registering the server, see the **intro(3rpc)** and **rpc_server_register_if(3rpc)** reference pages later in this chapter. See also the *OSF DCE Application Development Guide*.)

-cepv Generates local routines in the client stub file (*filename*_**cstub.c**) and defines a Client Entry Point Vector (CEPV) of the name *if_name*_**v***major-version*_*minor-version*_**c_epv** where *if_name* is the interface name. The CEPV contains the addresses of the local routines. The client code must call the routines indirectly by using the addresses in the CEPV; otherwise, the stub routines in the client stub file must have the same names as the operations in the IDL file. (For information on registering the server, see the **intro(3rpc)** and **rpc_server_register_if(3rpc)** reference pages later in this chapter. See also the *OSF DCE Application Development Guide*.)

-cpp_cmd *'c_preprocessor_command_line'*
Allows you to specify a C preprocessor other than the default. The compiler invokes the C preprocessor found in that command line. The output of the C preprocessor is an expanded version of the input file(s) containing replacement text for any preprocessor directives (for example, the **#include** preprocessor directive).

-cpp_opt *'command_options'*
Specifies additional options to be passed to the C preprocessor. You can add options to the command line used to invoke the C preprocessor independent of the **-cpp_cmd** argument. The IDL compiler concatenates the **-cpp_cmd, -cpp_opt, -D, -U, -I** arguments and the source filename into a command used to invoke the C preprocessor.

The compiler repeats this process for each Attribute Configuration File (ACF) and IDL file.

-no_cpp Does not invoke the C preprocessor. Note that the C preprocessor must be run on files that contain preprocessor directives (such as **#include**) in the interface definition.

-cc_cmd *'command_line'*
Invokes the C compiler and compiler options you specify in the *'command_line'* argument rather than the default C compiler and compiler options.

-cc_opt *'command_options'*
Specifies additional options to be passed to the C compiler. You can add options to the command line used to invoke the C compiler independent of the **-cc_cmd** argument. The IDL compiler concatenates the **-cc_cmd**, **-cc_opt**, **-I** arguments and the source filename into a command that invokes the C compiler. This procedure is done for each generated stub or auxiliary file.

-D*name*[=*definition*]
Defines a symbol name and an optional value to be passed to the C preprocessor. You can use this method of defining a symbol instead of using **#define** in the source code. You can use more than one **-D***name* argument on the command line. This argument has no effect if you use the **-no_cpp** argument.

-U*name* Removes (undefines) any initial definition of a symbol name as defined by **-D***name*. You can use this method to remove a symbol name instead of using **#undef** in the source code. You can use more than one **-U***name* argument on the command line. This argument has no effect if you use the **-no_cpp** argument. If you define and undefine a name on the same command line, undefining takes precedence.

-space_opt Generates code for the marshalling and unmarshalling of data that is optimized for space, rather than speed.

-syntax_only Checks only the syntax of the IDL file, but does not generate any output files.

-keep *file_types* Specifies which files to retain. To produce the object modules, the IDL compiler first creates C source modules, then invokes the target C compiler to produce object modules, and finally, deletes the C source modules. If you do not use **-keep**, only the object modules are saved.

The file types are as follows:

none Does not save the C source or the object modules. Does not invoke the C compiler.

c_source Saves only the C source modules. Does not invoke the C compiler.

object Saves only the object modules.

all Saves both the C source and the object modules.

-bug *n*, **-no_bug** *n* Retains (**-bug**) or does not retain (**-no_bug**) a specified bug from earlier IDL compiler versions. This is desirable if a bug fix introduces incompatibilities between the old incorrect behavior (**-bug**) and the new correct behavior (**-no_bug**). The *n* specifies the number of the bug in the NCS Version 1 Network Interface Definition Language (NIDL) compiler that may be incompatible with the new DCE IDL compiler. You can specify more than one bug or no bug argument on the command line. By default, no bugs are preserved. Bug numbers are as follows:

-bug 1 If a varying **[v1_array]** with no elements is marshalled, required pad bytes preceding subsequent parameters are sometimes missing.

-bug 2 If a varying **[v1_array]** with no elements is marshalled, extra pad bytes preceding subsequent parameters are sometimes included.

-bug 3 Defines the value of **ndr_true** to be 0xFF, instead of 0x01. For new development in DCE RPC, the symbol **idl_true** and the obsolete symbol **ndr_true** are defined as 0x01. However, if you specify the **-bug 3** argument, both symbols are defined with the value 0xFF.

-stdin Takes the standard output of a previous utility as the input to the **idl** command. For example:

```
$ cat my_filename.idl | idl -stdin
```

-version Displays the current version of the IDL compiler.

-v Prints informational messages (verbose mode) on the screen while the compiler is running.

-no_warn Suppresses compiler warning messages.

-confirm Displays all the **idl** command arguments you chose, but does not compile the source IDL file. If you use this with the **-v** argument, informational messages about how the compiler behaves if you do not use **-confirm** are displayed but no corresponding actions are performed.

Description

The **idl** command invokes the IDL compiler to convert an interface definition, written in IDL, into output files. The output files include a header file, server stub file, client stub file, and auxiliary files. The compiler constructs the names of the output files by keeping the basename of the interface definition source file but replacing the filename extension with the new extension (or suffix and extension) appropriate to the newly generated type of output file. For example, **math.idl** could produce **math_sstub.c** or **math_sstub.o** for the server stub.

The **idl** command accepts the following input:

- An interface definition filename.
- Arguments to indicate either special actions to be performed by the compiler, or special properties of the input or output files.

The IDL compiler searches through directories for any related ACF. For example, if you compile a file named **source.idl**, the compiler automatically searches for a file named **source.acf**. The compiler also searches for any imported IDL file (and its related ACF). The compiler searches for these files using the following order:

1. The current working directory. The compiler always searches this directory unless you specify the **-no_def_idir** and **-I***directory* arguments together.
2. Any imported directory. The compiler searches each directory you are specifying in the **-I***directory* argument.
3. The system IDL directory. The compiler automatically imports **nbase.idl**, which resides in the system IDL directory. The compiler always searches this directory unless you specify the **-no_def_idir** argument.
4. The directory specified in the source filename. If you explicitly specify a directory in the source IDL pathname, then that directory is searched for the corresponding ACF. For example,

   $ **idl /path/pathname/my_source.idl**

   causes the IDL compiler to look for **/path/pathname/my_source.acf** if **my_source.acf** is not found in the directories in 1 through 3 above.

Note that this directory is not searched for any imported IDL file or its corresponding ACF.

Restrictions

The following filenames are reserved by the IDL compiler. Naming an IDL file with one of these names may result in unexpected behavior.

iovector.idl	**lbase.idl**	**nbase.idl**	**ncastat.idl**
ndrold.idl	**rpc.idl**	**rpcbase.idl**	**rpcpvt.idl**
rpcsts.idl	**rpctypes.idl**	**twr.idl**	**uuid.idl**

Cautions

The IDL compiler generates ANSI C code. It also supports C compilers that are not fully ANSI compliant although a warning message may occur during compilation of the stubs by the C compiler. A C compiler that is not fully ANSI compliant may generate the following warning messages:

- `warning: & before array or function: ignored`
- `warning: enumeration type clash, operator =`

Files

/lib/cpp	C preprocessor
dceshared/**bin/idl**	Compiler
dceshared/**include**	System IDL directory for imported files
dceshared/**include/nbase.idl**	Predefined IDL types
dceshared/**include/nbase.acf**	Predefined ACF types
dceshared/**nls/msg/***LANG*/**idl.cat**	Compiler error messages
dceshared/**share/include/***file.ext*	All **.idl** or **.h** files that are part of DCE RPC

Examples

1. Invoke the IDL compiler to compile the interface definition file **test.idl** and keep the generated C source modules. Only server files are generated. The server stub default filename is overridden by creating a file named **test_ss.c** for the server stub module. The server auxiliary default filename is overridden by creating a file named **test_sa.c** for the server auxiliary module.

   $ **idl test.idl -keep c_source -client none -sstub test_ss.c -saux test_sa.c**

2. Invoke the IDL compiler to compile the interface definition file **test.idl**, but do not run the C preprocessor. The manager entry point vector is not defined in the generated server stub module. The IDL compiler searches the parent directory of the current directory for any IDL files that **test.idl** could

import. The generated output files are located in the **output** subdirectory under the current directory.

$ **idl test.idl -no_cpp -no_mepv -I.. -out ./output**

Related Information

Books: *OSF DCE Application Development Guide*.

nidl_to_idl

Purpose Translates files written in NIDL to files written in IDL

Synopsis **nidl_to_idl** *filename* [*argument*] ...

Arguments

-confirm Displays all the **nidl_to_idl** command arguments you choose, but does not translate the source IDL file.

-cpp_cmd *'c_preprocessor_command_line'*
Allows you to specify a C preprocessor other than the default. The compiler invokes the C preprocessor found in that command line. The output of the C preprocessor is an expanded version of the input file(s) containing replacement text for any preprocessor directives (for example, the **#include** preprocessor directive).

-def*name*[=*definition*]
Defines a symbol name, and an optional value to be passed to the C preprocessor. You can use this method of defining a symbol on the command line instead of using **#define** in the source code. You can use more than one **-def***name* argument on the command line.

-exts *extension_name*
Specifies a filename extension other than the default filename extension for the output interface definition file. The default filename extension is **_v2.idl**.

-acf_exts *acf_extension_name*
Specifies a filename extension for the output ACF (if an ACF is needed) other than the default filename extension. The default ACF filename extension is **_v2.acf**.

-idir *directory_name*
Specifies a directory name that contains imported interface definition files. You can specify more than one directory by using additional **-idir** arguments. The translator searches the directories in the order you list them on the command line. If a file is present in more than one directory, the translator takes the first occurrence of the file. The default behavior of the translator is to first search the current directory, then all directories you specify with **-idir**, then the system IDL directory.

-no_def_idir Searches through only the current directory for imported interface definition files. When you use this argument with **-idir**, the translator searches through only the directories you list, not the current directory, and not the system IDL directory.

-no_warn Suppresses translator warning messages.

-out *directory* Places the output files in the directory you specify. If you do not use the **-out** argument, the translator places the output files in the current working directory.

-version Displays the current version of the translator.

Description

The **nidl_to_idl** command translates interface definitions written in the Network Interface Definition Language (NIDL) to DCE IDL interface definitions. The command also generates an Attribute Configuration File (ACF), if one is needed. Use the DCE IDL compiler to compile the translated files. These files are compatible with the DCE RPC runtime library.

The **nidl_to_idl** command accepts the following input:

- An interface definition file that compiled successfully under the NCS Version 1 NIDL compiler
- Arguments to indicate either special actions to be performed by the translator, or special properties of the input or output files

The translator cannot handle some NIDL features because no direct translation exists. When a feature cannot be translated, the translator issues a warning and you must manually correct the DCE IDL output file.

If the code translates without error, the automated translation is complete. Use the DCE IDL compiler to compile the translated output file. Errors issued by DCE IDL are related to NIDL. You must correct these errors manually and make some changes in the application code.

Notes

NCS Version 1 compatibility is provided only for transitional purposes and is available for only a limited number of DCE update releases. For new applications, use DCE RPC.

Files

The **nidl_to_idl** command constructs the output filenames by keeping the name of the interface definition source file but adding a suffix to the newly generated output file. For example, the input file named **test.idl** is translated to **test_v2.idl** (and **test_v2.acf**, if an ACF is needed).

Examples

Translate **my_old.idl** file to **my_old_v2.idl** file. Search first through the sales directory, then through the credit directory for imported interface definition files, but do not search through the current directory or the system IDL directory.

```
$ nidl_to_idl my_old.idl -idir sales -idir credit -no_def_idir
```

uuidgen

Purpose Generates a Universal Unique Identifier (UUID)

Synopsis **uuidgen** [*argument*] ...

Arguments

-i Produces an Interface Definition Language (IDL) file template and includes the generated UUID string in the template.

-o *filename*
Redirects the generated UUID string to the file you specify.

-s Generates a UUID string as an initialized C structure.

-t *old_style_uuid_string*
Translates the old-style (NCS Version 1) UUID string format to the new-style string format.

-v Displays the version number of the UUID generator, but does not generate a UUID.

-h Displays information about the **uuidgen** command arguments. The arguments **-h** and **-?** can be used interchangeably.

-? Displays information about the **uuidgen** command arguments. The arguments **-?** and **-h** can be used interchangeably.

-n *number_of_uuid_strings*
Generates a specified number of UUID strings.

Description

The **uuidgen** command creates a UUID string that you assign to an object to uniquely identify it. One such use is in the UUID interface attribute of an IDL interface definition. The format for representing a UUID string consists of eight hexadecimal digits followed by a dash, followed by three groups of four hexadecimal digits separated by dashes, followed by a dash and twelve hexadecimal digits:

01234567-89AB-CDEF-0123-456789ABCDEF

Files

The locations of files have the following pathnames:

dceshared/**bin/uuidgen**	Generator
dceshared/**nls/msg/***LANG*/**uuidgen.cat**	Generator error messages

Examples

1. Generate a UUID string:

   $ **uuidgen**

   ```
   23C67E00-71B6-11C9-9DFC-08002B0ECEF1
   ```

2. Generate a partial template, containing a generated UUID string, to be used to develop an interface definition:

   $ **uuidgen -i**

   ```
   [
   uuid(828BF780-71B6-11C9-B5A8-08002B0ECEF1),
   version (1.0)
   ]
   interface INTERFACENAME
   {

   }
   ```

3. Convert a UUID string from the old-style format to the new format:

   $ **uuidgen -t 34DC23469EAF.AB.A2.01.7C.5F.2C.ED.A3**

   ```
   34DC2346-9EAF-0000-ABA2-017C5F2CEDA3
   ```

4. Generate four UUID strings:

   $ **uuidgen -n 4**

   ```
   612C0B00-71B8-11C9-973A-08002B0ECEF1
   612C0B01-71B8-11C9-973A-08002B0ECEF1
   612C0B02-71B8-11C9-973A-08002B0ECEF1
   612C0B03-71B8-11C9-973A-08002B0ECEF1
   ```

intro

Purpose Introduction to the DCE RPC API runtime

Description

This introduction gives general information about the DCE RPC Application Programming Interface (API) and an overview of the following parts of the DCE RPC API runtime:

- Runtime services
- Environment variables
- Data types and structures
- Permissions required
- Frequently used routine arguments

General Information

The following subsections contain topics, beyond those directly related to the RPC API, that application programmers need to know.

IDL-to-C Mappings

The Interface Definition Language (IDL) compiler converts an interface definition into output files. The **intro(1rpc)** reference page at the beginning of this chapter contains a summary of the **idl** command, which invokes the IDL compiler.

Additional information about the IDL compiler appears in the following table, which shows the IDL base types and the IDL-to-C mappings.

The following table lists the IDL base data type specifiers. Where applicable, the table shows the size of the corresponding transmittable type and the type macro emitted by the IDL compiler for resulting declarations.

Base Data Type Specifiers — intro(3rpc)				
	Specifier			Type Macro
(sign)	(size)	(type)	Size	Emitted by idl
	small	**int**	8 bits	**idl_small_int**
	short	**int**	16 bits	**idl_short_int**
	long	**int**	32 bits	**idl_long_int**
	hyper	**int**	64 bits	**idl_hyper_int**
unsigned	**small**	**int**	8 bits	**idl_usmall_int**
unsigned	**short**	**int**	16 bits	**idl_ushort_int**
unsigned	**long**	**int**	32 bits	**idl_ulong_int**
unsigned	**hyper**	**int**	64 bits	**idl_uhyper_int**
		float	32 bits	**idl_short_float**
		double	64 bits	**idl_long_float**
		char	8 bits	**idl_char**
		boolean	8 bits	**idl_boolean**
		byte	8 bits	**idl_byte**
		void	—	**idl_void_p_t**
		handle_t	—	—

Note that you can use the **idl_** macros in the code you write for an application to ensure that your type declarations are consistent with those in the stubs, even when the application is ported to another platform. The **idl_** macros are especially useful when passing constant values to RPC calls. For maximum portability, all constants passed to RPC calls declared in your network interfaces should be cast to the appropriate type because the size of integer constants (like the size of the **int** data type) is unspecified in the C language.

The **idl_** macros are defined in **dce/idlbase.h**, which is included by header files that the IDL compiler generates.

Management Commands for Programmers

In addition to the **idl** command for programmers, DCE RPC provides two management commands for the RPC control program and the RPC daemon, as follows:

- The **rpccp** control program accesses RPCCP, the RPC control program. This program provides a set of commands for accessing the operations of the RPC Name Service Interface (NSI operations). RPCCP also supports showing the elements of the local endpoint map and removing elements from it.

  You can manage the name service with RPCCP commands or with DCE RPC runtime routines. For example, suppose you want to obtain the members of a group. You can give the **show group** command to RPCCP or you can write an application program that calls the following DCE RPC runtime routines:

— **rpc_ns_group_mbr_inq_begin( )**

— **rpc_ns_group_mbr_inq_next( )**

— **rpc_ns_group_mbr_inq_done( )**

- The **rpcd** command starts the RPC daemon. The daemon maintains the local endpoint map for RPC servers and looks up endpoints for RPC clients.

See the *OSF DCE Administration Reference* for more information about these two management commands.

Overview of DCE RPC Runtime Services

The RPC runtime services consist of RPC routines that perform a variety of operations.

Note that the RPC API is thread safe and synchronous cancel safe (in the context of POSIX threads). However, the RPC API is not asynchronous cancel safe. For more information about threads and their cancellation, see the *OSF DCE Application Development Guide*.

The rest of this overview consists of the following items:

- A list of stub support routines
- An explanation of abbreviations in the names of the nonstub support routines
- A list of nonstub support routines

An alphabetical list of the RPC stub support routines follows. With each routine name is its description and the type of application program that most likely calls the routine.

Note that **rpc_if_register_auth_info( )** is unavailable in DCE RPC Version 1.0.1.

rpc_if_register_auth_info( )
Registers authentication and authorization information for an interface. (Client).

rpc_ss_allocate( )
Allocates memory within the RPC stub memory management scheme. (Usually server, possibly client).

rpc_ss_client_free( )
Frees memory returned from a client stub. (Usually server, possibly client).

rpc_ss_destroy_client_context( )
Reclaims the client memory resources for the context handle, and sets the context handle to **NULL**. (Client).

rpc_ss_disable_allocate( )
Releases resources and allocated memory. (Client).

rpc_ss_enable_allocate( )
Enables the allocation of memory by the **rpc_ss_allocate( )** routine when not in manager code. (Client).

rpc_ss_free( )
Frees memory allocated by the **rpc_ss_allocate( )** routine. (Usually server, possibly client).

rpc_ss_get_thread_handle( )
Gets a thread handle for the manager code before it spawns additional threads, or for the client code when it becomes a server. (Usually server, possibly client).

rpc_ss_set_client_alloc_free( )
Sets the memory allocation and freeing mechanism used by the client stubs, thereby overriding the default routines the client stub uses to manage memory for pointed-to nodes. (Client).

rpc_ss_set_thread_handle( )
Sets the thread handle for either a newly created spawned thread or for a server that was formerly a client and is ready to be a client again. (Usually server, possibly client).

rpc_ss_swap_client_alloc_free( )
Exchanges the current memory allocation and freeing mechanism used by the client stubs with one supplied by the client. (Client).

An alphabetical list of abbreviations in the names of the nonstub support routines follows. The list can help you remember the names more easily. For example, consider the routine name **rpc_mgmt_ep_elt_inq_begin( )**. Use the next list to expand the name to ‘‘RPC management endpoint element inquiry begin,’’ which summarizes the description ‘‘Creates an inquiry context for viewing the elements in a local or remote endpoint map. (Management).’’

auth authentication, authorization

com	communications
dce	distributed computing environment
dflt	default
elt	element
ep	endpoint
exp	expiration
fn	function
id	identifier
if	interface
inq	inquiry
mbr	member
mgmt	management
ns	name service
protseq	protocol sequence
rpc	remote procedure call
stats	statistics

An alphabetical list of the RPC nonstub support routines follows. With each routine name is its description and the type of application program that most likely calls the routine.

Note that DCE RPC Version 1.0 supports authenticated RPC for the connectionless (datagram) protocol only. The related routines in the following list are **rpc_mgmt_inq_dflt_protect_level( )** and the five routines whose names contain **auth**.

dce_error_inq_text( )
Returns the message text for a DCE component status code. (Client, server, or management).

rpc_binding_copy( )
Returns a copy of a binding handle. (Client or server).

rpc_binding_free( )
Releases binding handle resources. (Client or server).

rpc_binding_from_string_binding( )
Returns a binding handle from a string representation of a binding handle. (Client or management).

rpc_binding_inq_auth_client( )
Returns authentication and authorization information from the binding handle for an authenticated client. (Server).

rpc_binding_inq_auth_info( )
Returns authentication and authorization information from a server binding handle. (Client).

rpc_binding_inq_object( )
Returns the object UUID from a binding handle. (Client or server).

rpc_binding_reset( )
Resets a server binding handle so the host remains specified, but the server instance on that host is unspecified. (Client or management).

rpc_binding_server_from_client( )
Converts a client binding handle to a server binding handle. (Server).

rpc_binding_set_auth_info( )
Sets authentication and authorization information into a server binding handle. (Client).

rpc_binding_set_object( )
Sets the object UUID value into a server binding handle. (Client).

rpc_binding_to_string_binding( )
Returns a string representation of a binding handle. (Client, server, or management).

rpc_binding_vector_free( )
Frees the memory used to store a vector and binding handles. (Client or server).

rpc_ep_register( )
Adds to, or replaces, server address information in the local endpoint map. (Server).

rpc_ep_register_no_replace( )
Adds to server address information in the local endpoint map. (Server).

rpc_ep_resolve_binding( )
Resolves a partially bound server binding handle into a fully bound server binding handle. (Client or management).

rpc_ep_unregister( )
Removes server address information from the local endpoint map. (Server).

rpc_if_id_vector_free( )
Frees a vector and the interface identifier structures it contains. (Client, server, or management).

rpc_if_inq_id( )
Returns the interface identifier for an interface specification. (Client or server).

rpc_mgmt_ep_elt_inq_begin( )
Creates an inquiry context for viewing the elements in a local or remote endpoint map. (Management).

rpc_mgmt_ep_elt_inq_done( )
Deletes the inquiry context for viewing the elements in a local or remote endpoint map. (Management).

rpc_mgmt_ep_elt_inq_next( )
Returns one element at a time from a local or remote endpoint map. (Management).

rpc_mgmt_ep_unregister( )
Removes server address information from a local or remote endpoint map. (Management).

rpc_mgmt_inq_com_timeout( )
Returns the communications time-out value in a binding handle. (Client).

rpc_mgmt_inq_dflt_protect_level( )
Returns the default protection level for an authentication service. (Client or server).

rpc_mgmt_inq_if_ids( )
Returns a vector of interface identifiers of interfaces a server offers. (Client, server, or management).

rpc_mgmt_inq_server_princ_name( )
Returns a server's principal name. (Client, server, or management).

rpc_mgmt_inq_stats( )
Returns RPC runtime statistics. (Client, server, or management).

rpc_mgmt_is_server_listening( )
Tells whether a server is listening for remote procedure calls. (Client, server, or management).

rpc_mgmt_set_authorization_fn( )
Establishes an authorization function for processing remote calls to a server's management routines. (Server).

rpc_mgmt_set_cancel_timeout( )
Sets the lower bound on the time to wait before timing out after forwarding a cancel. (Client).

rpc_mgmt_set_com_timeout( )
Sets the communications time-out value in a binding handle. (Client).

rpc_mgmt_set_server_stack_size( )
Specifies the stack size for each server thread. (Server).

rpc_mgmt_stats_vector_free( )
Frees a statistics vector. (Client, server, or management).

rpc_mgmt_stop_server_listening( )
Tells a server to stop listening for remote procedure calls. (Client, server, or management).

rpc_network_inq_protseqs( )
Returns all protocol sequences supported by both the RPC runtime and the operating system. (Client or server).

rpc_network_is_protseq_valid( )
Tells whether the specified protocol sequence is supported by both the RPC runtime and the operating system. (Client or server).

rpc_ns_binding_export( )
Establishes a name service database entry with binding handles or object UUIDs for a server. (Server).

rpc_ns_binding_import_begin( )
Creates an import context for an interface and an object in the name service database. (Client).

rpc_ns_binding_import_done( )
Deletes the import context for searching the name service database. (Client).

rpc_ns_binding_import_next( )
Returns a binding handle of a compatible server (if found) from the name service database. (Client).

rpc_ns_binding_inq_entry_name( )
Returns the name of an entry in the name service database from which the server binding handle came. (Client).

rpc_ns_binding_lookup_begin( )
Creates a lookup context for an interface and an object in the name service database. (Client).

rpc_ns_binding_lookup_done( )
Deletes the lookup context for searching the name service database. (Client).

rpc_ns_binding_lookup_next( )
Returns a list of binding handles of one or more compatible servers (if found) from the name service database. (Client).

rpc_ns_binding_select( )
Returns a binding handle from a list of compatible server binding handles. (Client).

rpc_ns_binding_unexport( )
Removes the binding handles for an interface, or object UUIDs, from an entry in the name service database. (Server).

rpc_ns_entry_expand_name( )
Expands the name of a name service entry. (Client, server, or management).

rpc_ns_entry_object_inq_begin( )
Creates an inquiry context for viewing the objects of an entry in the name service database. (Client, server, or management).

rpc_ns_entry_object_inq_done( )
Deletes the inquiry context for viewing the objects of an entry in the name service database. (Client, server, or management).

rpc_ns_entry_object_inq_next( )
Returns one object at a time from an entry in the name service database. (Client, server, or management).

rpc_ns_group_delete( )
Deletes a group attribute. (Client, server, or management).

rpc_ns_group_mbr_add( )
Adds an entry name to a group; if necessary, creates the entry. (Client, server, or management).

rpc_ns_group_mbr_inq_begin( )
Creates an inquiry context for viewing group members. (Client, server, or management).

rpc_ns_group_mbr_inq_done( )
Deletes the inquiry context for a group. (Client, server, or management).

rpc_ns_group_mbr_inq_next( )
Returns one member name at a time from a group. (Client, server, or management).

rpc_ns_group_mbr_remove( )
Removes an entry name from a group. (Client, server, or management).

rpc_ns_mgmt_binding_unexport( )
Removes multiple binding handles, or object UUIDs, from an entry in the name service database. (Management).

rpc_ns_mgmt_entry_create( )
Creates an entry in the name service database. (Management).

rpc_ns_mgmt_entry_delete( )
Deletes an entry from the name service database. (Management).

rpc_ns_mgmt_entry_inq_if_ids( )
Returns the list of interfaces exported to an entry in the name service database. (Client, server, or management).

rpc_ns_mgmt_handle_set_exp_age( )
Sets a handle's expiration age for local copies of name service data. (Client, server, or management).

rpc_ns_mgmt_inq_exp_age( )
Returns the application's global expiration age for local copies of name service data. (Client, server, or management).

rpc_ns_mgmt_set_exp_age( )
Modifies the application's global expiration age for local copies of name service data. (Client, server, or management).

rpc_ns_profile_delete( )
Deletes a profile attribute. (Client, server, or management).

rpc_ns_profile_elt_add( )
Adds an element to a profile. If necessary, creates the entry. (Client, server, or management).

rpc_ns_profile_elt_inq_begin( )
Creates an inquiry context for viewing the elements in a profile. (Client, server, or management).

rpc_ns_profile_elt_inq_done( )
Deletes the inquiry context for a profile. (Client, server, or management).

rpc_ns_profile_elt_inq_next( )
Returns one element at a time from a profile. (Client, server, or management).

rpc_ns_profile_elt_remove( )
Removes an element from a profile. (Client, server, or management).

rpc_ns_set_authn( )
Turns authentication on and off for RPC name service routines. (Client, server, or management)

rpc_object_inq_type( )
Returns the type of an object. (Server).

rpc_object_set_inq_fn( )
Registers an object inquiry function. (Server).

rpc_object_set_type( )
Assigns the type of an object. (Server).

rpc_protseq_vector_free( )
Frees the memory used by a vector and its protocol sequences. (Client or server).

rpc_server_inq_bindings( )
Returns binding handles for communication with a server. (Server).

rpc_server_inq_if( )
Returns the manager entry point vector registered for an interface. (Server).

rpc_server_listen( )
Tells the RPC runtime to listen for remote procedure calls. (Server).

rpc_server_register_auth_info( )
Registers authentication information with the RPC runtime. (Server).

rpc_server_register_if( )
Registers an interface with the RPC runtime. (Server).

rpc_server_unregister_if( )
Unregisters an interface from the RPC runtime. (Server).

rpc_server_use_all_protseqs( )
Tells the RPC runtime to use all supported protocol sequences for receiving remote procedure calls. (Server).

rpc_server_use_all_protseqs_if( )
Tells the RPC runtime to use all the protocol sequences and endpoints specified in the interface specification for receiving remote procedure calls. (Server).

rpc_server_use_protseq( )
Tells the RPC runtime to use the specified protocol sequence for receiving remote procedure calls. (Server).

rpc_server_use_protseq_ep( )
Tells the RPC runtime to use the specified protocol sequence combined with the specified endpoint for receiving remote procedure calls. (Server).

rpc_server_use_protseq_if( )
Tells the RPC runtime to use the specified protocol sequence combined with the endpoints in the interface specification for receiving remote procedure calls. (Server).

rpc_string_binding_compose( )
Combines the components of a string binding into a string binding. (Client or server).

rpc_string_binding_parse( )
Returns, as separate strings, the components of a string binding. (Client or server).

rpc_string_free( )
Frees a character string allocated by the runtime. (Client, server, or management).

uuid_compare( )
Compares two UUIDs and determines their order. (Client, server, or management).

uuid_create( )
Creates a new UUID. (Client, server, or management).

uuid_create_nil( )
Creates a nil UUID. (Client, server, or management).

uuid_equal( )
Determines if two UUIDs are equal. (Client, server, or management).

uuid_from_string( )
Converts a string UUID to its binary representation. (Client, server, or management).

uuid_hash( )
Creates a hash value for a UUID. (Client, server, or management).

uuid_is_nil( )
Determines if a UUID is nil. (Client, server, or management).

uuid_to_string( )
Converts a UUID from a binary representation to a string representation. (Client, server, or management).

Environment Variables

The RPC Name Service Interface (NSI) routines use the following environment variables:

- **RPC_DEFAULT_ENTRY**

  Designates the default entry in the name service database that the import and lookup routines use as the starting point to search for binding information for a compatible server. Normally, the starting entry is a profile.

  An application that uses a default entry name must define this environment variable. The RPC runtime does not provide a default.

  For example, suppose that a client application needs to search the name service database for a server binding handle. The application can use the **rpc_ns_binding_import_begin( )** routine as part of the search. If so, the application must specify, to the routine's *entry_name* parameter, the name of the entry in the name service database at which to begin the search. If the search is to begin at the entry that the **RPC_DEFAULT_ENTRY** environment variable specifies, then the application must specify the value **NULL** to parameter *entry_name* in **rpc_ns_binding_import_begin()**.

- **RPC_DEFAULT_ENTRY_SYNTAX**

  Specifies the syntax of the name provided in the **RPC_DEFAULT_ENTRY** environment variable. In addition, provides the syntax for those RPC NSI routines that allow a default value for the name syntax argument.

If the **RPC_DEFAULT_ENTRY_SYNTAX** environment variable is not defined, the RPC runtime uses the **rpc_c_ns_syntax_dce** name syntax.

(For the valid name syntaxes in this reference page and for the valid syntax values, see the table in the description of the frequently used routine argument *name_syntax*, which appears later in this reference page.)

- **RPC_DEBUG**

  Appears for the sole purpose of telling you not to set it and not to use it.

Optionally, each application defines either or both of the first two environment variables. The application can change the value of either one, or both, at any time during runtime.

RPC Data Types and Structures

The following subsections contain the data types and structures used by client, server, and management application programs.

Much of the information in this section is derived from the *OSF DCE Application Development Guide*. You may want to refer to the Guide as you read this section. For example, this section contains a brief description of a binding handle. The RPC section of the *OSF DCE Application Development Guide* explains binding handles in detail. It also explains concepts related to binding handles, such as binding information and string bindings.

Binding Handle

A binding handle is a pointer-size opaque variable containing information the RPC runtime uses to manage binding information. The RPC runtime uses binding information to establish a client/server relationship that allows the execution of remote procedure calls.

Based on the context where it is created, a binding handle is considered a server binding handle or a client binding handle.

A server binding handle is a reference to the binding information necessary for a client to establish a relationship with a specific server. Many RPC API runtime routines return a server binding handle that you can use to make a remote procedure call.

A server binding handle refers to several components of binding information. One is the network address of a server's host system. Each server instance has one or more transport addresses (endpoints). A well-known endpoint is a stable address on the host, while a dynamic endpoint is an address that the RPC runtime requests for the server. Some transport protocols provide fewer well-known endpoints than dynamic endpoints.

If binding information contains an endpoint, the corresponding binding handle is a fully bound binding handle. If the information lacks an endpoint, the binding handle is a partially bound binding handle.

The RPC runtime creates and provides a client binding handle to a called remote procedure as the **handle_t** parameter. The client binding handle contains information about the calling client. A client binding handle cannot be used to make a remote procedure call. A server uses the client binding handle. The **rpc_binding_server_from_client( )** routine converts a client binding handle to a server binding handle. You can use the resulting server binding handle to make a remote procedure call.

For an explanation of making a remote procedure call with a partially bound binding handle, see the *OSF DCE Application Development Guide*. For an explanation of failures associated with such a call, see the explanation of status code **rpc_s_wrong_boot_time** in the **rpc_status_codes(7rpc)** reference page later in this chapter.

Binding information can contain an object UUID. The default object UUID associated with a binding handle is a nil UUID. Clients can obtain a non-nil UUID in various ways, such as from a string representation of binding information (a string binding), or by importing it.

The following table contains the RPC runtime routines that operate on binding handles. The table also specifies the type of binding handle, client or server, allowed.

Client and Server Binding Handles		
Routine	**Input Argument**	**Output Argument**
rpc_binding_copy( )	Server	Server
rpc_binding_free( )	Server	None
rpc_binding_from_string_binding( )	None	Server
rpc_binding_inq_auth_client( )	Client	None
rpc_binding_inq_auth_info( )	Server	None
rpc_binding_inq_object( )	Server or client	None
rpc_binding_reset( )	Server	None
rpc_binding_server_from_client( )	Client	Server
rpc_binding_set_auth_info( )	Server	None
rpc_binding_set_object( )	Server	None
rpc_binding_to_string_binding( )	Server or client	None
rpc_binding_vector_free( )	Server	None
rpc_ns_binding_export( )	Server	None
rpc_ns_binding_import_next( )	None	Server
rpc_ns_binding_inq_entry_name( )	Server	None
rpc_ns_binding_lookup_next( )	None	Server
rpc_ns_binding_select( )	Server	Server
rpc_server_inq_bindings( )	None	Server

If the input argument type is only a client or only a server, the routines return the status code **rpc_s_wrong_kind_of_binding** when an application provides the incorrect binding handle type.

An application can share a single binding handle across multiple threads of execution. The RPC runtime, instead of the application, manages binding handle concurrency control across concurrent remote procedure calls that use a single binding handle. However, the client application has responsibility for binding handle concurrency control for operations that read or modify a binding handle. The related routines are as follows:

- **rpc_binding_free( )**
- **rpc_binding_reset( )**
- **rpc_binding_set_auth_info( )**

- **rpc_binding_set_object( )**
- **rpc_ep_resolve_binding( )**
- **rpc_mgmt_set_com_timeout( )**

For example, suppose an application shares a binding handle across two threads of execution and it resets the binding handle endpoint in one of the threads (by calling **rpc_binding_reset( )**). The binding handle in the other thread is then also reset. Similarly, freeing the binding handle in one thread (by calling **rpc_binding_free( )**) frees the binding handle in the other thread.

If you do not want this effect, your application can create a copy of a binding handle by calling **rpc_binding_copy( )**. An operation on one binding handle then has no effect on the second binding handle.

Clients and servers can access and set object UUIDs using the **rpc_binding_inq_object( )** and **rpc_binding_set_object( )** routines.

Routines requiring a binding handle as an argument show a data type of **rpc_binding_handle_t**. Binding handle arguments are passed by value.

Binding Vector

The binding vector data structure contains a list of binding handles over which a server application can receive remote procedure calls.

The binding vector contains a count member (*count*), followed by an array of binding handle (*binding_h*) elements.

The C language representation of a binding vector is as follows:

```
typedef struct {
        unsigned32   count;
        rpc_binding_handle_t binding_h[1];
        } rpc_binding_vector_t;
```

The RPC runtime creates binding handles when a server application registers protocol sequences. To obtain a binding vector, a server application calls the **rpc_server_inq_bindings( )** routine.

A client application obtains a binding vector of compatible servers from the name service database by calling **rpc_ns_binding_lookup_next( )**.

In both routines, the RPC runtime allocates memory for the binding vector. An application calls the **rpc_binding_vector_free( )** routine to free the binding vector.

An application, when it is finished with an individual binding handle in a binding vector, frees the binding handle by calling **rpc_binding_free( )**. This routine also sets the corresponding pointer in the binding vector to **NULL**.

Note that you should not decrement the *count* field in a binding vector structure when you call the **rpc_binding_free( )** routine to free an individual binding handle.

The following routines require a binding vector and show an argument data type of **rpc_binding_vector_t**:

- **rpc_binding_vector_free( )**
- **rpc_ep_register( )**
- **rpc_ep_register_no_replace( )**
- **rpc_ep_unregister( )**
- **rpc_ns_binding_export( )**
- **rpc_ns_binding_lookup_next( )**
- **rpc_ns_binding_select( )**
- **rpc_server_inq_bindings( )**

Boolean

Routines that require a Boolean-valued argument or return a Boolean value show a data type of **boolean32**. DCE RPC provides the integer constants TRUE (1) and FALSE (0) for use as Boolean values.

Endpoint Map Inquiry Handle

An endpoint map inquiry handle is a pointer-size opaque variable containing information the RPC runtime uses to access the elements in a local or remote endpoint map. The description of the **rpc_ep_register( )** routine lists the contents of an element.

The following routines require an endpoint map inquiry handle and show an argument data type of **rpc_ep_inq_handle_t**:

- **rpc_mgmt_ep_elt_inq_begin( )**
- **rpc_mgmt_ep_elt_inq_done( )**
- **rpc_mgmt_ep_elt_inq_next( )**

Global Name

The Name Service Interface (NSI) uses global names for the names of name service entries. A global name includes both a cell name and a cell-relative name composed of a directory pathname and a leaf name. For a description of global names, see the *OSF DCE Application Development Guide*. The cell name is assigned to a cell root at its creation. When you specify only a cell-relative name to an NSI operation, the NSI automatically expands the name into a global name by inserting the local cell name. Thus, the name of a member in a group or in a profile element is always stored as a global name. When returning the name of a name service entry or a member, NSI operations return global names.

For example, even when you specify a cell-relative name as the *member_name* parameter to routine **rpc_ns_group_mbr_add( )**, when you read that group member (by calling **rpc_ns_group_mbr_inq_next( )**), you will receive the corresponding global name.

Interface Handle and Specification

An interface handle is a pointer-size opaque variable containing information the RPC runtime uses to access the interface specification data structure.

The DCE IDL compiler automatically creates an interface specification data structure from each IDL file and creates a global variable of type **rpc_if_handle_t** for the interface specification.

The DCE IDL compiler places an interface handle declaration in the generated *interface-name***.h** file. The compiler generates this include file for each interface.

Routines requiring the interface handle as an argument show a data type of **rpc_if_handle_t**.

The form of each interface handle name is as follows:

- For the client:

  *if-name*_**v***major-version*_*minor-version*_**c_ifspec**

- For the server:

  *if-name*_**v***major-version*_*minor-version*_**s_ifspec**

where

- The *if-name* variable is the interface identifier specified in the IDL file.
- The *major-version* variable is the interface's major-version number specified in the IDL file.
- The *minor-version* variable is the interface's minor-version number specified in the IDL file.

An example is **notes_v1_2_c_ifspec**

The maximum combined length of the interface identifier and interface version number is 19 characters.

Since the major-version and minor-version numbers must each be at least 1 character, the interface name can be no more than 17 characters. This limits the interface handle name to 31 or fewer characters. No concurrency control is required for interface handles.

The following routines require an interface handle and show an argument data type of **rpc_if_handle_t**:

- **rpc_ep_register( )**
- **rpc_ep_register_no_replace( )**
- **rpc_ep_resolve_binding( )**
- **rpc_ep_unregister( )**
- **rpc_if_inq_id( )**
- **rpc_if_register_auth_info( )**
- **rpc_ns_binding_export( )**
- **rpc_ns_binding_import_begin( )**
- **rpc_ns_binding_lookup_begin( )**
- **rpc_ns_binding_unexport( )**
- **rpc_server_inq_if( )**
- **rpc_server_register_if( )**
- **rpc_server_unregister_if( )**
- **rpc_server_use_all_protseqs_if( )**
- **rpc_server_use_protseq_if( )**

Interface Identifier

The interface identifier (id) data structure contains the interface UUID and major-version and minor-version numbers of an interface. The interface identifier is a subset of the data contained in the interface specification structure.

The C language representation of an interface identifier structure is as follows:

```
typedef struct {
        uuid_t     uuid;
        unsigned16 vers_major;
        unsigned16 vers_minor;
        } rpc_if_id_t;
```

Routines that require an interface identifier structure show a data type of **rpc_if_id_t**. In those routines, the application is responsible for providing memory for the structure.

The **rpc_if_inq_id( )** routine returns the interface identifier from an interface specification. The following routines require an interface identifier:

- **rpc_mgmt_ep_elt_inq_begin( )**
- **rpc_mgmt_ep_elt_inq_next( )**
- **rpc_mgmt_ep_unregister( )**
- **rpc_ns_mgmt_binding_unexport( )**
- **rpc_ns_profile_elt_add( )**
- **rpc_ns_profile_elt_inq_begin( )**
- **rpc_ns_profile_elt_inq_next( )**
- **rpc_ns_profile_elt_remove( )**

Interface Identifier Vector

The interface identifier (id) vector data structure contains a list of interfaces offered by a server. The interface identifier vector contains a count member (*count*), followed by an array of pointers to interface identifiers (*rpc_if_id_t*).

The C language representation of an interface identifier vector is as follows:

```
typedef struct {
        unsigned32   count;
        rpc_if_id_t  *if_id[1];
        } rpc_if_id_vector_t;
```

The interface identifier vector is a read-only vector. To obtain a vector of the interface identifiers registered by a server with the RPC runtime, an application calls the **rpc_mgmt_inq_if_ids( )** routine. To obtain a vector of the interface identifiers exported by a server to a name service database, an application calls the **rpc_ns_mgmt_entry_inq_if_ids( )** routine.

The RPC runtime allocates memory for the interface identifier vector. The application calls the **rpc_if_id_vector_free( )** routine to free the interface identifier vector.

Manager Entry Point Vector

The manager Entry Point Vector (EPV) is an array of pointers to remote procedures.

The DCE IDL compiler automatically generates a manager EPV data type, into the header file generated by the IDL compiler, for use in constructing manager EPVs. The data type is named as follows:

*if-name*_**v***major-version*_*minor-version*_**epv_t**

where

- The *if-name* variable is the interface identifier specified in the IDL file.
- The *major-version* variable is the interface's major-version number specified in the IDL file.
- The *minor-version* variable is the interface's minor-version number specified in the IDL file.

By default, the DCE IDL compiler automatically creates and initializes a manager EPV. DCE IDL creates this EPV assuming that a manager routine of the same name exists for each procedure in the interface (as specified in the IDL file).

The DCE IDL compiler can define a client Entry Point Vector with addresses of local routines. Client applications can call these routines. For more information about client entry point vectors, see the explanation of the **-cepv** argument in the **idl(1rpc)** reference page.

If the server offers multiple implementations of the same interface, the server must create additional manager EPVs, one for each implementation. Each EPV must contain exactly one entry point (address of a function) for each procedure defined in the IDL file. The server application declares and initializes one manager EPV variable of type *if-name*_**v***major-version*_*minor-version*_**epv_t** for each implementation of the interface.

The **rpc_server_register_if( )** and **rpc_server_inq_if( )** routines use the manager EPV data type and show the manager EPV argument as having an **rpc_mgr_epv_t** data type.

Name Service Handle

A name service handle is a pointer-size opaque variable containing information the RPC runtime uses to return the following RPC data from the name service database:

- Server binding handles
- UUIDs of resources offered by a server
- Profile members
- Group members

The following routines require a name service handle and show an argument data type of **rpc_ns_handle_t**:

- **rpc_ns_binding_import_begin( )**
- **rpc_ns_binding_import_next( )**
- **rpc_ns_binding_import_done( )**
- **rpc_ns_binding_lookup_begin( )**
- **rpc_ns_binding_lookup_next( )**
- **rpc_ns_binding_lookup_done( )**
- **rpc_ns_entry_object_inq_begin( )**
- **rpc_ns_entry_object_inq_next( )**
- **rpc_ns_entry_object_inq_done( )**
- **rpc_ns_group_mbr_inq_begin( )**
- **rpc_ns_group_mbr_inq_next( )**
- **rpc_ns_group_mbr_inq_done( )**
- **rpc_ns_profile_elt_inq_begin( )**
- **rpc_ns_profile_elt_inq_next( )**
- **rpc_ns_profile_elt_inq_done( )**
- **rpc_ns_mgmt_handle_set_exp_age( )**

The scope of a name service handle is from a ***_begin( )** routine through the corresponding ***_done( )** routine.

Applications have responsibility for concurrency control of name service handles across threads.

Protocol Sequence

A protocol sequence is a character string identifying the network protocols used to establish a relationship between a client and server. The protocol sequence contains a set of options that the RPC runtime must know about. The following options are in this set:

- The RPC protocol used for communications (choices are **ncacn** and **ncadg**).
- The format used in the network address supplied in the binding (choice is **ip**).
- The transport protocol used for communications (choices are **tcp** and **udp**).

Because only certain combinations of these options are valid (are useful for interoperation), RPC provides predefined strings that represent the valid combinations. RPC applications use only these strings.

The following table contains predefined strings representing valid protocol sequences. In the descriptions NCA is an abbreviation of Network Computing Architecture.

Valid Protocol Sequences	
Protocol Sequence	**Description**
ncacn_ip_tcp	NCA Connection over Internet Protocol: Transmission Control Protocol
ip or **ncadg_ip_udp**	NCA Datagram over Internet Protocol: User Datagram Protocol

A server application can use a particular protocol sequence only if the operating system software supports that protocol. A server chooses to accept remote procedure calls over some or all of the supported protocol sequences.

Client and server applications can determine if a protocol sequence is supported by both the RPC runtime and the operating system. The applications make this determination by calling the following routines:

- **rpc_network_inq_protseqs( )**
- **rpc_network_is_protseq_valid( )**

The following routines allow server applications to register protocol sequences with the runtime:

- **rpc_server_use_all_protseqs( )**
- **rpc_server_use_all_protseqs_if( )**
- **rpc_server_use_protseq( )**
- **rpc_server_use_protseq_ep( )**
- **rpc_server_use_protseq_if( )**

Those routines requiring a protocol sequence argument show a data type of **unsigned_char_t** *.

A client can use the protocol sequence strings to construct a string binding using the **rpc_string_binding_compose( )** routine.

Protocol Sequence Vector

The protocol sequence vector data structure contains a list of protocol sequences over which the RPC runtime can send or receive remote procedure calls. The protocol sequence vector contains a count member (*count*), followed by an array of pointers to protocol sequence strings (*protseq*).

The C language representation of a protocol sequence vector is as follows:

```
typedef struct {
        unsigned32      count;
        unsigned_char_t *protseq[1];
        } rpc_protseq_vector_t;
```

The protocol sequence vector is a read-only vector. To obtain a protocol sequence vector, a server application calls the **rpc_network_inq_protseqs( )** routine. The RPC runtime allocates memory for the protocol sequence vector. The server application calls the **rpc_protseq_vector_free( )** routine to free the protocol sequence vector.

Statistics Vector

The statistics vector data structure contains statistics from the RPC runtime on a per address space basis. The statistics vector contains a count member (*count*), followed by an array of statistics. Each array element contains an **unsigned32** value. The following list describes the statistics indexed by the specified constant:

rpc_c_stats_calls_in The number of remote procedure calls received by the runtime.

rpc_c_stats_calls_out The number of remote procedure calls initiated by the runtime.

rpc_c_stats_pkts_in The number of network packets received by the runtime.

rpc_c_stats_pkts_out The number of network packets sent by the runtime.

The C language representation of a statistics vector is as follows:

```
typedef struct {
        unsigned32     count;
        unsigned32     stats[1];
        } rpc_stats_vector_t;
```

To obtain runtime statistics, an application calls the **rpc_mgmt_inq_stats( )** routine. The RPC runtime allocates memory for the statistics vector. The application calls the **rpc_mgmt_stats_vector_free( )** routine to free the statistics vector.

String Binding

A string binding contains the character representation of a binding handle.

String bindings are a convenient way of representing portions of a binding handle. However, you cannot use string bindings directly to make remote procedure calls. You must first call the routine **rpc_binding_from_string_binding( )**, which converts a string binding to a binding handle.

A string binding does not contain all the information from a binding handle. For example, a call to the routine **rpc_binding_to_string_binding( )** does not translate the authentication information sometimes associated with a binding handle into the resulting string binding.

You can begin the development of a distributed application by having its servers communicate their binding information to clients by using string bindings. This communication allows a server to establish a client/server relationship without using the local endpoint map or the name service database.

In this case, the server calls none of the **rpc_ep_register( )**, **rpc_ep_register_no_replace( )**, and **rpc_ns_binding_export( )** routines. Instead, the server calls only routine **rpc_server_inq_bindings( )** to obtain a vector of binding handles. The server obtains binding handles one at a time from the vector and calls routine **rpc_binding_to_string_binding( )** to convert each binding handle into a string binding. The resulting string binding is always fully bound and may contain a non-nil object UUID. The server then makes some or all of its string bindings available to clients. One way is placing the string bindings in a file to be read by clients or users or both. Another way is delivering the string bindings to clients or users by means of a file, mail, or paper.

You can continue the distributed application's development by changing the application so that servers use the local endpoint map and the name service database to communicate their binding information.

To find the server, a client obtains a string binding containing a protocol sequence that the client runtime supports and, optionally, an object UUID that the client requires. The client then calls routine **rpc_binding_from_string_binding( )** to convert the string binding into a server binding handle.

Other useful routines for working with string bindings are **rpc_string_binding_compose( )**, which creates a string binding from its component parts, and **rpc_string_binding_parse( )**, which separates a string binding into its component parts.

The two formats of a string binding follow. The four fields represent the object UUID, RPC protocol sequence, network address, and endpoint and network options of the binding. A delimiter character such as @ (at sign) or **:** (colon) separates each field. A string binding does not contain any white space.

object-uuid @ *rpc-protocol-sequence* **:** *nw-addr* [*endpoint***,** *option* ...]

or

object-uuid

This field specifies the UUID of the object operated on by the remote procedure that is called with this string binding. The RPC runtime, at the server, maps the object's type to a manager Entry Point Vector (EPV) to invoke the correct manager routine. The explanation of the routine **rpc_server_register_if( )** discusses mapping object UUIDs to manager EPVs.

This field is optional. If you do not provide it the RPC runtime assumes a nil UUID.

@ This symbol is the delimiter character for the object UUID field. If you specify an object UUID you must follow it with this symbol.

rpc-protocol-sequence
This field specifies the protocol sequence used for making remote procedure calls. The valid protocol sequences are as follows:

ncacn_ip_tcp

ncadg_ip_udp

More information about these valid protocol sequences appears in the previous table.

This field is required.

: This symbol is the delimiter character for the RPC protocol sequence field.

nw-addr
This field specifies the address (*addr*) of a host on a network (*nw*) that receives remote procedure calls made with this string binding. The format and content of the network address depends on the value of *rpc-protocol-sequence* as follows:

ncacn_ip_tcp and **ncadg_ip_udp**

Specify an Internet address using the common Internet address notation or hostname.

Two examples with common Internet address notation are `128.10.2.30` and `#126.15.1.28`. The second example shows the use of the optional **#** (number sign) character.

An example with a host name is `ko`.

If the specified hostname is multihomed, the binding handle returned from routine **rpc_binding_from_string_binding( )** contains a host address. It is the first host address returned from the system library call that translates a hostname to a host address for the network address format in the protocol sequence. To control the host address used, specify the network address using the common Internet address notation instead of a hostname.

The network address field is optional. If you do not supply this field, the string binding refers to your local host.

[This symbol is the delimiter character specifying that one endpoint and zero or more options follow. If the string binding contains at least one endpoint, this symbol is required.

endpoint

This field specifies the endpoint, or address of a specific server instance on a host, to receive remote procedure calls made with this string binding. Optionally the keyword **endpoint=** can precede the endpoint specifier.

The format and content of the endpoint depends on the specified protocol sequence as follows:

ncacn_ip_tcp and **ncadg_ip_udp**

Specify an Internet port number.

An example of an Internet port number is `1025`.

The endpoint field is optional. For more information about endpoints, see the information on binding handles in this reference page.

, This symbol is the delimiter character specifying that option data follows. If an option follows, this delimiter is required.

option

This field specifies any options. Each option is specified as *option name=option value*.

The format and content of the option depends on the specified protocol sequence as follows:

ncacn_ip_tcp and **ncadg_ip_udp**

There are no Internet options.

The *option* field is optional.

] This symbol is the delimiter character specifying that one endpoint and zero or more options precede. If the string binding contains at least one endpoint, this symbol is required.

The \ (backslash) character is treated as an escape character for all string binding fields.

Examples of valid string bindings follow. In each example *obj-uuid* represents a UUID in string form. In other words, the symbol *obj-uuid* can represent the UUID `308FB580-1EB2-11CA-923B-08002B1075A7`.

obj-uuid`@ncacn_ip_tcp:16.20.16.27[2001]`
obj-uuid`@ncacn_ip_tcp:16.20.16.27[endpoint=2001]`

String UUID

A string UUID contains the character representation of a UUID.
A string UUID consists of multiple fields of hexadecimal characters.
Each field has a fixed length, and dashes separate the fields.

An example of a string UUID follows:

```
989C6E5C-2CC1-11CA-A044-08002B1BB4F5
```

When you supply a string UUID as an input argument to an RPC runtime routine, you can enter the alphabetic hexadecimal characters in either uppercase or lowercase letters. The RPC runtime routines that return a string UUID always return the hexadecimal characters in uppercase letters. The following routines require a string UUID:

- **rpc_string_binding_parse( )**
- **uuid_from_string( )**

The following routines return a string UUID:

- **rpc_string_binding_compose( )**
- **uuid_to_string( )**

Unsigned Character String

DCE RPC treats all characters in strings as unsigned characters. Those routines with character string arguments show a data type of **unsigned_char_t** *.

UUID Vector

The UUID vector data structure contains a list of UUIDs. The UUID vector contains a count member (*count*), followed by an array of pointers to UUIDs.

The C language representation of a UUID vector is as follows:

```
typedef struct
{
  unsigned32   count;
  uuid_t       *uuid[1];
} uuid_vector_t;
```

An application constructs a UUID vector to contain object UUIDs to be exported or unexported from the name service database. The following routines require a UUID vector and show an argument data type of **uuid_vector_t**:

- **rpc_ep_register( )**
- **rpc_ep_register_no_replace( )**
- **rpc_ep_unregister( )**

- **rpc_ns_binding_export( )**
- **rpc_ns_binding_unexport( )**
- **rpc_ns_mgmt_binding_unexport( )**

Permissions Required

To use the Name Service Interface (NSI) routines to access entries in a Cell Directory Service (CDS) database, you need Access Control List (ACL) permissions. Depending on the NSI operation, you need ACL permissions to the parent directory or the CDS object entry (the name service entry) or both.

The ACL permissions are as follows:

- To create an entry, you need insert permission to the parent directory.
- To read an entry, you need read permission to the CDS object entry.
- To write to an entry, you need write permission to the CDS object entry.
- To delete an entry, you need delete permission either to the CDS object entry or to the parent directory.
- To test an entry, you need either test permission or read permission to the CDS object entry.

Note that write permission does not imply read permission.

To find the ACL permissions for the NSI routines whose names begin with **rpc_ns**, see these routines' reference pages.

The non-NSI routines whose names do not begin with **rpc_ns** do not need ACL permissions, so their reference pages do not specify any.

Frequently Used Routine Parameters

A few parameters are common to many of the DCE RPC routines. These parameters are described fully here and again briefly on the specific routine reference pages.

binding Used as an input or output parameter.

Returns a binding handle for making remote procedure calls to a server.

A client obtains a binding handle by calling one of the following routines:

- **rpc_binding_copy( )**

- **rpc_binding_from_string_binding( )**
- **rpc_ns_binding_import_next( )**
- **rpc_ns_binding_select( )**

Creating a binding handle establishes a relationship between a client and a server. However, the relationship does not involve any communications between the client and server. The communications occur when a client makes a remote procedure call.

As an input parameter to a remote procedure call, *binding* specifies a binding handle that refers to binding information. The client's RPC runtime uses this binding information to make a remote procedure call to a server.

Server manager routines can extract client information from a client binding handle by using the following routines:

- **rpc_binding_inq_auth_client( )**
- **rpc_binding_inq_object( )**
- **rpc_binding_to_string_binding( )**
- **rpc_string_binding_parse( )**

name Used as an input/output parameter.

When used as an input parameter, the value of this parameter depends on the syntax selected in the *name_syntax* parameter. If it is allowed by the called routine, the value **NULL** specifies that the routine uses the name specified in the **RPC_DEFAULT_ENTRY** environment variable. Specifying **NULL** also has the called routine use the name syntax that the environment variable **RPC_DEFAULT_ENTRY_SYNTAX** specifies.

For a *name_syntax* value of **rpc_c_ns_syntax_dce**, use the DCE naming rules to specify parameter *name*.

As an output parameter, returns an entry in the name service database in the form of a character string that includes a terminating **NULL** character. The value of this parameter depends on the syntax selected in *name_syntax*.

For a *name_syntax* value of **rpc_c_ns_syntax_dce**, *name* is returned using the DCE naming syntax.

The DCE RPC runtime allocates memory for the returned string. The application is responsible for calling the **rpc_string_free( )** routine to deallocate the string.

If an application does not want a returned name string, the application usually specifies **NULL** for this parameter. The one exception is routine **rpc_ns_entry_expand_name**( ); it always returns a name string.

name_syntax

Used as an input parameter, an integer value that specifies the syntax of an entry name. When allowed by the called routine, a value of **rpc_c_ns_syntax_default** specifies that the routine uses the syntax specified in the **RPC_DEFAULT_ENTRY_SYNTAX** environment variable. The following table lists the valid syntaxes that applications can use in DCE RPC for entries in the name service database.

Valid Name Syntaxes		
Constant	**Value**	**Description**
rpc_c_ns_syntax_default	0	Default syntax
rpc_c_ns_syntax_dce	3	DCE

The *name_syntax* parameter tells routines how to parse the entry name specified in an input *name* parameter or specifies the syntax to use when returning an entry name as an output *name* parameter.

If the **RPC_DEFAULT_ENTRY_SYNTAX** environment variable is not defined, the RPC runtime uses the **rpc_c_ns_syntax_dce** name syntax.

string

Used as an input or output parameter.

Returns a character string, which always includes the terminating null character **\0**. The DCE RPC runtime allocates memory for the returned string. The application calls the **rpc_string_free**( ) routine to deallocate the memory occupied by the string.

If there is no data for the requested string, the routine returns the string **\0**. For example, if the string binding passed to routine **rpc_string_binding_parse**( ) does not contain an object UUID, the routine returns **\0** as the value of the object UUID string. The application must call the **rpc_string_free**( ) routine to deallocate the memory occupied by this string.

If an application does not require a returned output string, the application specifies **NULL** for this parameter.

status

Each routine in the RPC API returns a DCE status code indicating whether the routine completed successfully or, if not, why not. A return value of **rpc_s_ok** indicates success. All other return values signify routine failure. The status codes listed for each RPC runtime routine are the most likely, but not necessarily all, the status codes that the routine can return. The status code argument has a data type of **unsigned32**.

To translate a DCE status code to a text message, call the routine **dce_error_inq_text( )**.

Note that RPC exceptions are equivalent to RPC status codes. To identify the status code that corresponds to a given exception, replace the **_x_** string of the exception with the string **_s_**; for example, the exception **rpc_x_already_listening** is equivalent to the status code **rpc_s_already_listening**.

The **rpc_status_codes(7rpc)** reference page later in this chapter documents the RPC status codes in alphabetical order. The documentation for each status code includes the message text, the explanation, and the suggested user action.

uuid Used as an input or output parameter.

When you need to specify a nil UUID to a *uuid* input parameter in any of the DCE RPC routines, you can supply the value **NULL**.

Related Information

Books: *OSF DCE Administration Reference*, *OSF DCE Application Development Guide*.

dce_error_inq_text

Purpose Returns the message text for a DCE component status code

Used by client, server, or management applications.

Any DCE component, not only RPC, can call this routine.

Synopsis

```
#include <dce/rpc.h>
#include <dce/dce_error.h>

void dce_error_inq_text(
        unsigned long status_to_convert,
        unsigned char *error_text,
        int *status);
```

Parameters

Input

status_to_convert Specifies the DCE status code to convert to a text string.

Output

error_text Returns a **NULL**-terminated character string message corresponding to the *status_to_convert* parameter.

status Returns the status code from this routine, indicating whether the routine completed successfully or, if not, why not. The possible status codes and their meanings are as follows:

0 Success.

-1 Failure.

Description

The **dce_error_inq_text()** routine returns a **NULL**-terminated, character-string message for the DCE status code specified.

The application must provide memory for the returned message. The largest returned message is **dce_c_error_string_len()** characters long, including the terminating **NULL** character.

If the call fails, this routine returns a message as well as a failure code in the *status* parameter.

Before calling this routine, the environment variable **NLSPATH** must be set to point to DCE message catalog files. A general C-shell command to set this environment variable follows:

% **setenv NLSPATH** *dceshared***/nls/msg/***LANG***/%N**

Note that *LANG* is a variable instead of a literal. A specific example of this general command follows:

% **setenv NLSPATH /usr/lib/nls/msg/en_US.88591/%N**

The explanations of status codes from the RPC runtime routines and associated user actions are listed alphabetically by the status codes in the **rpc_status_codes( )** reference page later in this chapter.

Return Values

No value is returned.

rpc_binding_copy

Purpose Returns a copy of a binding handle

Used by client or server applications.

Synopsis **#include <dce/rpc.h>**

void rpc_binding_copy(
rpc_binding_handle_t *source_binding*,
rpc_binding_handle_t **destination_binding*,
unsigned32 **status*);

Parameters

Input

source_binding
Specifies the server binding handle whose referenced binding information is copied.

Output

destination_binding
Returns the server binding handle that refers to the copied binding information.

status Returns the status code from this routine. This status code indicates whether the routine completed successfully or, if not, why not.

The possible status codes and their meanings are as follows:

rpc_s_ok	Success.
rpc_s_invalid_binding	Invalid binding handle.
rpc_s_wrong_kind_of_binding	Wrong kind of binding for operation.

Description

The **rpc_binding_copy( )** routine copies the server binding information referenced by the binding handle specified in the *source_binding* parameter. This routine returns a new server binding handle for the copied binding information. The new server binding handle is returned in the *destination_binding* parameter.

Use the **rpc_binding_copy( )** routine if you want a change (made to binding information by one thread) *not* to affect the binding information used by other threads. The explanation of binding handles in the **intro(3rpc)** reference page has more detail about this use of routine **rpc_binding_copy( )**.

After calling this routine, operations performed on the *source_binding* binding handle do not affect the binding information referenced by the *destination_binding* binding handle. Similarly, operations performed on the *destination_binding* binding handle do not affect the binding information referenced by the *source_binding* binding handle.

If you want the changes made to binding information by one thread to affect the binding information used by other threads, your program must share a single binding handle across the threads. In this case the application controls binding handle concurrency.

When an application is finished using the binding handle specified by the *destination_binding* parameter, the application calls the **rpc_binding_free( )** routine to release the memory used by the *destination_binding* binding handle and its referenced binding information.

Return Values

No value is returned.

Related Information

Functions: **rpc_binding_free(3rpc)**.

rpc_binding_free

Purpose Releases binding handle resources

Used by client or server applications.

Synopsis **#include <dce/rpc.h>**

```
void rpc_binding_free
        rpc_binding_handle_t *binding,
        unsigned32 *status);
```

Parameters

Input/Output

binding Specifies the server binding handle to free.

Output

status Returns the status code from this routine. This status code indicates whether the routine completed successfully or, if not, why not.

The possible status codes and their meanings are as follows:

rpc_s_ok	Success.
rpc_s_invalid_binding	Invalid binding handle.
rpc_s_wrong_kind_of_binding	Wrong kind of binding for operation.

Description

The **rpc_binding_free( )** routine frees the memory used by a server binding handle and its referenced binding information. Use this routine when your application is finished using a server binding handle that was dynamically created during program execution.

If the free-binding operation succeeds, the *binding* parameter returns the value **NULL**.

An application can dynamically create binding handles by calling any of the following routines:

- **rpc_binding_copy( )**
- **rpc_binding_from_string_binding( )**
- **rpc_ns_binding_import_next( )**
- **rpc_ns_binding_select( )**
- **rpc_server_inq_bindings( )**

Return Values

No value is returned.

Related Information

Functions: **rpc_binding_copy(3rpc)**, **rpc_binding_from_string_binding(3rpc)**, **rpc_binding_vector_free(3rpc)**, **rpc_ns_binding_import_next(3rpc)**, **rpc_ns_binding_lookup_next(3rpc)**, **rpc_ns_binding_select(3rpc)**, **rpc_server_inq_bindings(3rpc)**.

rpc_binding_from_string_binding

Purpose Returns a binding handle from a string representation

Used by client or management applications.

Synopsis **#include <dce/rpc.h>**

void rpc_binding_from_string_binding(
unsigned_char_t **string_binding*,
rpc_binding_handle_t **binding*,
unsigned32 **status***);**

Parameters

Input

string_binding
Specifies a string representation of a binding handle.

Output

binding Returns the server binding handle.

status Returns the status code from this routine. This status code indicates whether the routine completed successfully or, if not, why not.

The possible status codes and their meanings are as follows:

rpc_s_ok	Success.
rpc_s_invalid_arg	Invalid argument.
rpc_s_invalid_endpoint_format	Invalid endpoint format.
rpc_s_invalid_rpc_protseq	Invalid protocol sequence.
rpc_s_invalid_string_binding	Invalid string binding.
rpc_s_protseq_not_supported	Protocol sequence not supported on this host.
uuid_s_bad_version	Bad UUID version.
uuid_s_invalid_string_uuid	Invalid format for a string UUID.

Description

The **rpc_binding_from_string_binding( )** routine creates a server binding handle from a string representation of a binding handle.

The *string_binding* parameter does not need to contain an object UUID. In this case, the returned *binding* contains a nil UUID.

If the provided *string_binding* parameter does not contain an endpoint field, the returned *binding* parameter is a partially bound server binding handle.

If the provided *string_binding* parameter does contain an endpoint field, the returned *binding* parameter is a fully bound server binding handle with a well-known endpoint.

If the provided *string_binding* parameter does not contain a host address field, the returned *binding* parameter refers to the local host.

To create a string binding, call the **rpc_string_binding_compose( )** routine or call the **rpc_binding_to_string_binding( )** routine or provide a character string constant.

When an application finishes using the *binding* parameter, the application calls the **rpc_binding_free( )** routine to release the memory used by the binding handle.

The **intro(3rpc)** reference page contains an explanation of partially and fully bound binding handles.

Return Values

No value is returned.

Related Information

Functions: **rpc_binding_copy(3rpc)**, **rpc_binding_free(3rpc)**, **rpc_binding_to_string_binding(3rpc)**, **rpc_string_binding_compose(3rpc)**.

rpc_binding_inq_auth_client

Purpose Returns authentication and authorization information from the binding handle for an authenticated client

Used by server applications.

Synopsis

```
#include <dce/rpc.h>
#include <dce/id_base.h>

void rpc_binding_inq_auth_client(
        rpc_binding_handle_t binding,
        rpc_authz_handle_t *privs,
        unsigned_char_t **server_princ_name,
        unsigned32 *protect_level,
        unsigned32 *authn_svc,
        unsigned32 *authz_svc,
        unsigned32 *status);
```

Parameters

Input

binding Specifies the client binding handle from which to return the authentication and authorization information.

Output

privs Returns a handle to the authorization information for the client that made the remote procedure call on *binding*.

The server must cast this handle to the data type specified by *authz_svc*. The following table shows how to cast the return value.

Casts for Authorization Information		
For *authz_svc value*:	*privs* **contains this data:**	**Use this cast:**
rpc_c_authz_none	A **NULL** value.	None
rpc_c_authz_name	The calling client's principal name.	**(unsigned_char_t *)**
rpc_c_authz_dce	The calling client's privilege attribute certificate.	**(sec_id_pac_t *)**

The data referenced by this parameter is read-only and should not be modified by the server. If the server wants to preserve any of the returned data, it must copy the data into server-allocated memory.

server_princ_name

Returns a pointer to the server principal name specified by the client that made the remote procedure call on *binding*. The content of the returned name and its syntax is defined by the authentication service in use.

Specifying **NULL** prevents the routine from returning this parameter. In this case, the caller does not have to call the **rpc_string_free( )** routine.

protect_level

Returns the protection level requested by the client that made the remote procedure call on *binding*. The protection level determines the degree to which authenticated communications between the client and the server are protected.

Specifying **NULL** prevents the routine from returning this parameter.

The possible protection levels are as follows:

rpc_c_protect_level_default Uses the default protection level for the specified authentication service.

rpc_c_protect_level_none Performs no protection.

rpc_c_protect_level_connect Performs protection only when the client establishes a relationship with the server.

rpc_c_protect_level_call Performs protection only at the beginning of each remote procedure call when the server receives the request.

rpc_c_protect_level_pkt Ensures that all data received is from the expected client.

rpc_c_protect_level_pkt_integ Ensures and verifies that none of the data transferred between client and server has been modified.

rpc_c_protect_level_pkt_privacy
Performs protection as specified by all of the previous levels and also encrypt each remote procedure call argument value.

authn_svc
Returns the authentication service requested by the client that made the remote procedure call on *binding*.

Specifying **NULL** prevents the routine from returning this parameter.

The possible authentication services are as follows:

rpc_c_authn_none	No authentication.
rpc_c_authn_dce_secret	DCE shared-secret key authentication.
rpc_c_authn_dce_public	DCE public key authentication (reserved for future use).
rpc_c_authn_default	DCE default authentication service.

authz_svc
Returns the authorization service requested by the client that made the remote procedure call on *binding*.

Specifying **NULL** prevents the routine from returning this parameter.

The possible authorization services are as follows:

rpc_c_authz_name	Server performs authorization based on the client principal name.
rpc_c_authz_dce	Server performs authorization using the client's DCE Privilege Attribute Certificate (PAC) sent to the server with each remote procedure call made with *binding*. Generally, access is checked against DCE Access Control Lists (ACLs).

status Returns the status code from this routine. This status code indicates whether the routine completed successfully or, if not, why not.

The possible status codes and their meanings are as follows:

rpc_s_ok	Success.
rpc_s_invalid_binding	Invalid binding handle.
rpc_s_wrong_kind_of_binding	Wrong kind of binding for operation.
rpc_s_binding_has_no_auth	Binding has no authentication information.

Description

The **rpc_binding_inq_auth_client( )** routine returns authentication and authorization information associated with the client identified by *binding*. The calling server manager routine can use the returned data for authorization purposes.

The RPC runtime allocates memory for the returned *server_princ_name* parameter. The server is responsible for calling the **rpc_string_free( )** routine for the returned parameter string.

For applications in which the client side uses the IDL **auto_handle** or **implicit_handle** attribute, the server side needs to be built with the IDL **explicit_handle** attribute specified in the Attribute Configuration File (ACF). Using **explicit_handle** provides *binding* as the first parameter to each server manager routine.

Return Values

No value is returned.

Related Information

Functions: **rpc_binding_inq_auth_info(3rpc)**, **rpc_binding_set_auth_info(3rpc)**, **rpc_string_free(3rpc)**.

rpc_binding_inq_auth_info

Purpose Returns authentication and authorization information from a server binding handle

Used by client applications.

Synopsis **#include <dce/rpc.h>**
#include <dce/sec_login.h>

```
void rpc_binding_inq_auth_info(
        rpc_binding_handle_t binding,
        unsigned_char_t **server_princ_name,
        unsigned32 *protect_level,
        unsigned32 *authn_svc,
        rpc_auth_identity_handle_t *auth_identity,
        unsigned32 *authz_svc,
        unsigned32 *status);
```

Parameters

Input

binding Specifies the server binding handle from which to return the authentication and authorization information.

Output

server_princ_name
Returns a pointer to the expected principal name of the server referenced by *binding*. The content of the returned name and its syntax is defined by the authentication service in use.

Specifying **NULL** prevents the routine from returning this parameter. In this case, the caller does not have to call the **rpc_string_free( )** routine.

protect_level
Returns the protection level used for remote procedure calls made with *binding*. The protection level determines the degree to which authenticated communications between the client and the server are protected.

Note that the returned level may be different from the level specified for *protect_level* on the call to **rpc_binding_set_auth_info( )**. If the RPC runtime or the RPC protocol in the bound protocol sequence does not support a specified level, the level is automatically upgraded to the next higher supported level.

Specifying **NULL** prevents the routine from returning this parameter.

The possible protection levels are as follows:

rpc_c_protect_level_default Uses the default protection level for the specified authentication service.

rpc_c_protect_level_none Performs no protection.

rpc_c_protect_level_connect Performs protection only when the client establishes a relationship with the server.

rpc_c_protect_level_call Performs protection only at the beginning of each remote procedure call when the server receives the request.

rpc_c_protect_level_pkt Ensures that all data received is from the expected client.

rpc_c_protect_level_pkt_integ Ensures and verifies that none of the data transferred between client and server has been modified.

rpc_c_protect_level_pkt_privacy
Performs protection as specified by all of the previous levels and also encrypt each remote procedure call parameter value.

authn_svc

Returns the authentication service used for remote procedure calls made with *binding*.

Specifying **NULL** prevents the routine from returning this argument.

The possible authentication services are as follows:

rpc_c_authn_none No authentication.

rpc_c_authn_dce_secret DCE shared-secret key authentication.

rpc_c_authn_dce_public	DCE public key authentication (reserved for future use).
rpc_c_authn_default	DCE default authentication service.

auth_identity

Returns a handle for the data structure that contains the client's authentication and authorization credentials. This parameter must be cast as appropriate for the authentication and authorization services established via **rpc_binding_set_auth_info( )** or **rpc_if_register_auth_info( )**.

When using the **rpc_c_authn_dce_secret** authentication service and any authorization service, this value must be a **sec_login_handle_t** obtained from one of the following routines:

- **sec_login_setup_identity( )**
- **sec_login_get_current_context( )**
- **sec_login_newgroups( )**

These routines are described in Chapter 5 of this manual.

Specifying **NULL** prevents the routine from returning this parameter.

authz_svc

Returns the authorization service used for remote procedure calls made with *binding*.

Specifying **NULL** prevents the routine from returning this parameter.

The possible authorization services are as follows:

rpc_c_authz_none	Server performs no authorization.
rpc_c_authz_name	Server performs authorization based on the client principal name.
rpc_c_authz_dce	Server performs authorization using the client's DCE Privilege Attribute Certificate (PAC) sent to the server with each remote procedure call made with *binding*. Generally, access is checked against DCE Access Control Lists (ACLs).

status Returns the status code from this routine. This status code indicates whether the routine completed successfully or, if not, why not.

The possible status codes and their meanings are as follows:

rpc_s_ok	Success.
rpc_s_invalid_binding	Invalid binding handle.
rpc_s_wrong_kind_of_binding	Wrong kind of binding for operation.
rpc_s_binding_has_no_auth	Binding has no authentication information.

Description

The **rpc_binding_inq_auth_info( )** routine returns authentication and authorization information associated with the specified server binding handle. The calling client associates the authentication and authorization data with the server binding handle by a prior call to the **rpc_binding_set_auth_info( )** routine.

The RPC runtime allocates memory for the returned *server_princ_name* parameter. The caller is responsible for calling the **rpc_string_free( )** routine for the returned parameter string.

Return Values

No value is returned.

Related Information

Functions: **rpc_binding_set_auth_info(3rpc)**, **rpc_if_register_auth_info(3rpc)**, **rpc_string_free(3rpc)**.

rpc_binding_inq_object

Purpose Returns the object UUID from a binding handle

Used by client or server applications.

Synopsis **#include <dce/rpc.h>**

void rpc_binding_inq_object(
  rpc_binding_handle_t *binding*,
  uuid_t **object_uuid*,
  unsigned32 **status*);

Parameters

Input

binding Specifies a client or server binding handle.

Output

object_uuid
Returns the object UUID found in the *binding* parameter. The object UUID is a unique identifier for an object for which a remote procedure call can be made.

status Returns the status code from this routine. This status code indicates whether the routine completed successfully or, if not, why not.

The possible status codes and their meanings are as follows:

rpc_s_ok	Success.
rpc_s_invalid_binding	Invalid binding handle.

Description

The **rpc_binding_inq_object()** routine obtains the object UUID associated with a client or server binding handle. If no object UUID has been associated with the binding handle, this routine returns a nil UUID.

Return Values

No value is returned.

Related Information

Functions: **rpc_binding_set_object(3rpc)**.

rpc_binding_reset

Purpose Resets a server binding handle

Used by client or management applications.

Synopsis **#include <dce/rpc.h>**

void rpc_binding_reset(
rpc_binding_handle_t *binding*,
unsigned32 **status*);

Parameters

Input

binding Specifies the server binding handle to reset.

Output

status Returns the status code from this routine. This status code indicates whether the routine completed successfully or, if not, why not.

The possible status codes and their meanings are as follows:

rpc_s_ok	Success.
rpc_s_invalid_binding	Invalid binding handle.
rpc_s_wrong_kind_of_binding	Wrong kind of binding for operation.

Description

The **rpc_binding_reset()** routine disassociates a server instance from the server binding handle specified in the *binding* parameter. This routine removes the endpoint portion of the server address in the binding handle as well as any other server instance information in the binding handle. The host portion of the server address remains unchanged. The result is a partially bound server binding handle. This binding handle can rebind to another server instance on the previous host when it is later used to make a remote procedure call. The **intro(3rpc)** reference page contains an explanation of partially and fully bound binding handles.

This routine does not affect any authentication information for the *binding* parameter.

Suppose that a client can be serviced by any compatible server instance on the host specified in the binding handle. Then, the client can call the **rpc_binding_reset( )** routine before making a remote procedure call using the binding handle specified in *binding*.

When the client makes the next remote procedure call using the reset server binding handle in *binding*, the client's RPC runtime uses a well-known endpoint from the client's interface specification, if any. Otherwise, the client's RPC runtime automatically communicates with the RPC Daemon (RPCD) on the specified remote host, to obtain the endpoint of a compatible server from the local endpoint map. If a compatible server is located, the RPC runtime updates *binding* with a new endpoint.

However, if a compatible server is not located, the client's remote procedure call fails. If the failed call uses a connection protocol (**ncacn**), it receives the **rpc_s_endpoint_not_found** status code. If the failed call uses a datagram protocol (**ncadg**), it receives the **rpc_s_comm_failure** status code.

If a server application wants to be available to clients making a remote procedure call on a reset binding handle, it registers all binding handles by calling **rpc_ep_register( )** or **rpc_ep_register_no_replace( )**. If, however, the IDL-generated file contains endpoint address information, then the application does not have to call either of these two routines.

Return Values

No value is returned.

Related Information

Functions: **rpc_ep_register(3rpc)**, **rpc_ep_register_no_replace(3rpc)**.

rpc_binding_server_from_client

Purpose

Converts a client binding handle to a server binding handle

Used by server applications.

Synopsis

#include <dce/rpc.h>

void rpc_binding_server_from_client(
  rpc_binding_handle_t *client_binding***,**
  rpc_binding_handle_t **server_binding***,**
  unsigned32 **status***);**

Parameters

Input

client_binding
Specifies the client binding handle to convert to a server binding handle.

Output

server_binding
Returns a server binding handle.

status Returns the status code from this routine. This status code indicates whether the routine completed successfully or, if not, why not.

The possible status codes and their meanings are as follows:

rpc_s_ok	Success.
rpc_s_invalid_binding	Invalid binding handle.
rpc_s_wrong_kind_of_binding	Wrong kind of binding.

Description

When a remote procedure call arrives at a server, the RPC runtime creates a client binding handle to refer to information about the calling client (client binding information). The RPC runtime passes the client binding handle to the called remote procedure as the first input argument (which uses the **handle_t** type).

The **rpc_binding_server_from_client()** routine converts client binding information into server binding information corresponding to the client's system.

When calling this routine, the called remote procedure specifies the client binding handle, and the routine returns a partially bound server binding handle (that is, the newly constructed server binding information contains a network address for the client's system, but lacks an endpoint). The server binding information also lacks authentication information, but the called procedure can add it by calling **rpc_binding_set_auth_info**( ). The object UUID from the client binding information remains.

The **rpc_binding_server_from_client( )** routine is relevant when a called remote procedure (the first remote procedure) needs to make its own remote procedure call (a nested procedure call) to a second remote procedure offered by a server on the system of the client that called the first remote procedure (that is, the original client). The partially bound server binding handle returned by the **rpc_binding_server_from_client( )** routine ensures that a nested call requests the second remote procedure on the original client's system.

In a multithreaded RPC application, the second remote procedure can belong to a server that shares the original client's address space (that is, the server and client can operate jointly as a server/client instance). If the original client belongs to a server/client instance and the application requires the nested call to execute in that instance, the application must guarantee that the nested remote procedure call uses one of the instances' endpoints.

An application can provide this guarantee by meeting any of the following conditions:

- The interface possesses its own well-known endpoints, and the server elects to use these interface-specific endpoints (by calling **rpc_server_use_protseq_if**( ) or **rpc_server_use_all_protseqs_if**( )).

- The server uses server-specific endpoints, and the interface is offered by only one server/client instance per system.

  To use server-specific endpoints, a server either requests dynamic endpoints (by calling **rpc_server_use_protseq**( ) or **rpc_server_use_all_protseqs**( )) or specifies its own well-known endpoints (by calling **rpc_server_use_protseq_ep**( )). The server must also register its server-specific endpoints in the local endpoint map (by calling **rpc_ep_register**( )).

- The original client sets an object UUID into the server binding information of the first call (by calling **rpc_binding_set_object**( )); the object UUID identifies the server/client instance.

  The client can obtain the object UUID from the list of object UUIDs used to register the endpoints of the server/client instance. The client must select an object UUID that belongs exclusively to its instance.

Server binding information containing an object UUID impacts the selection of a manager for a remote procedure call; see the *OSF DCE Application Development Guide* for a description of manager selection. The object UUID can either identify a particular resource offered by the companion server or, used as an instance UUID, the object UUID can identify the original client's server/client instance.

The object UUID is passed in the first remote procedure call as part of the client binding information and is retained in the server binding information. This server binding information is newly constructed by the **rpc_binding_server_from_client( )** routine. When the second remote procedure call arrives at the original client's system, the RPC daemon uses the object UUID to look for associated endpoints in the local endpoint map. To ensure that the object UUID is associated with the endpoints of the original server/client instance, the server must complete the following steps:

1. Obtain the UUID (for example, by calling **uuid_create( )**).
2. Specify the UUID as part of registering endpoints for the interface of the second remote procedure (by calling **rpc_ep_register( )** or **rpc_ep_register_no_replace( )**).

If the second remote procedure call will be routed to a manager of a non-nil type, then the server must also do the following:

1. Specify the type for the manager that implements that interface (by calling **rpc_server_register_if( )**).
2. Set the object UUID to the same type as the manager (by calling **rpc_object_set_type( )**).

- The first remote procedure call contains a distinct call argument used by the original client to pass server information that identifies its server/client instance.

  The first remote procedure call uses this information to route the second remote procedure call to the original server/client instance. For example, server information can be as follows:

  — A fully bound string binding that identifies the client's server/client instance.

If the first remote procedure receives this string binding, calling the **rpc_binding_server_from_client** routine is unnecessary. Instead, the first remote procedure requests a server binding handle for the string binding (by calling **rpc_binding_from_string_binding( )**).

— An object UUID that is associated in the endpoint map with one or more endpoints of the original server/client instance.

The client can obtain the object UUID from the list of object UUIDs used to register the endpoints of the server/client instance. The client must select an object UUID that belongs exclusively to its instance, and pass that UUID as a call argument.

After calling the **rpc_binding_server_from_client( )** routine, add the object UUID from the call argument to the newly constructed server binding information (by calling **rpc_binding_set_object( )**).

Return Values

No value is returned.

Related Information

Functions: **rpc_binding_free(3rpc)**, **rpc_binding_set_object(3rpc)**, **rpc_ep_register(3rpc)**, **rpc_ep_register_no_replace(3rpc)**.

Books: *DCE OSF Application Development Guide*.

rpc_binding_set_auth_info

Purpose Sets authentication and authorization information for a server binding handle

Used by client applications.

Synopsis

```
#include <dce/rpc.h>
#include <dce/sec_login.h>
void rpc_binding_set_auth_info(
        rpc_binding_handle_t binding,
        unsigned_char_t **server_princ_name,
        unsigned32 protect_level,
        unsigned32 authn_svc,
        rpc_auth_identity_handle_t auth_identity,
        unsigned32 authz_svc,
        unsigned32 *status);
```

Parameters

Input

binding Specifies the server binding handle for which to set the authentication and authorization information.

server_princ_name
Specifies the principal name of the server referenced by *binding*. The content of the name and its syntax is defined by the authentication service in use.

A client that does not know the server principal name can call the **rpc_mgmt_inq_server_princ_name( )** routine to obtain the principal name of a server that is registered for the required authentication service. Using a principal name obtained in this way means that the client is interested in one-way authentication. In other words, it means that the client does not care which server principal received the remote procedure call request. The server, though, still verifies that the client is who the client claims to be.

protect_level
Specifies the protection level for remote procedure calls made using *binding*. The protection level determines the degree to which authenticated communications between the client and the server are protected.

If the RPC runtime or the RPC protocol in the bound protocol sequence does not support a specified level, the level is automatically upgraded to the next higher supported level. The possible protection levels are as follows:

rpc_c_protect_level_default Uses the default protection level for the specified authentication service.

rpc_c_protect_level_none Performs no protection.

rpc_c_protect_level_connect Performs protection only when the client establishes a relationship with the server.

rpc_c_protect_level_call Performs protection only at the beginning of each remote procedure call when the server receives the request.

This level does not apply to remote procedure calls made over a connection-based protocol sequence (that is, **ncacn_ip_tcp**). If this level is specified and the binding handle uses a connection-based protocol sequence, the routine uses the **rpc_c_protect_level_pkt** level instead.

rpc_c_protect_level_pkt Ensures that all data received is from the expected client.

rpc_c_protect_level_pkt_integ

Ensures and verifies that none of the data transferred between client and server has been modified.

This is the highest protection level that is guaranteed to be present in the RPC runtime.

rpc_c_protect_level_pkt_privacy

Performs protection as specified by all of the previous levels and also encrypt each remote procedure call argument value.

This is the highest protection level, but it may not be available in the RPC runtime.

authn_svc

Specifies the authentication service to use. The supported authentication services are as follows:

rpc_c_authn_none	No authentication.
rpc_c_authn_dce_secret	DCE shared-secret key authentication.
rpc_c_authn_dce_public	DCE public key authentication (reserved for future use).
rpc_c_authn_default	DCE default authentication service.

Specify **rpc_c_authn_none** to turn authentication off for remote procedure calls made using *binding*.

If **rpc_c_authn_default** is specified, the RPC runtime uses the **rpc_c_authn_dce_secret** authentication service for remote procedure calls made using *binding*.

auth_identity

Specifies a handle for the data structure that contains the client's authentication and authorization credentials appropriate for the selected authentication and authorization services.

When using the **rpc_c_authn_dce_secret** authentication service and any authorization service, this value must be a **sec_login_handle_t** obtained from one of the following routines:

- **sec_login_setup_identity**( )
- **sec_login_get_current_context**( )
- **sec_login_newgroups**( )

These routines are described in Chapter 5 of this manual.

Specify **NULL** to use the default security login context for the current address space.

authz_svc

Specifies the authorization service implemented by the server for the interface of interest. The validity and trustworthiness of authorization data, like any application data, is dependent on the authentication service and protection level specified. The supported authorization services are as follows:

rpc_c_authz_none	Server performs no authorization. This is valid only if the *authn_svc* parameter is **rpc_c_authn_none**.
rpc_c_authz_name	Server performs authorization based on the client principal name.
rpc_c_authz_dce	Server performs authorization using the client's DCE Privilege Attribute Certificate (PAC) sent to the server with each remote procedure call made with *binding*. Generally, access is checked against DCE Access Control Lists (ACLs).

Output

status Returns the status code from this routine. This status code indicates whether the routine completed successfully or, if not, why not.

The possible status codes and their meanings are as follows:

rpc_s_ok	Success.
rpc_s_invalid_binding	Invalid binding handle.
rpc_s_wrong_kind_of_binding	Wrong kind of binding for operation.
rpc_s_unknown_authn_service	Unknown authentication service.
rpc_s_authn_authz_mismatch	Requested authorization service is not supported by the requested authentication service.
rpc_s_unsupported_protect_level	Requested protection level is not supported.

Description

The **rpc_binding_set_auth_info( )** routine sets up the specified server binding handle so that it can be used to make authenticated remote procedure calls, including authorization information.

Unless a client calls this routine, all remote procedure calls made on the *binding* binding handle are unauthenticated. A client is not required to call this routine.

If a client is using the IDL **auto_handle** attribute and wants to perform authenticated RPC, it needs to call the stub support library routine **rpc_if_register_auth_info( )**. Some authentication services (*authn_svc*) may need to communicate with the Security service to perform this operation. Otherwise, they may receive the **rpc_s_comm_failure** status.

Return Values

No value is returned.

Related Information

Functions: **rpc_binding_inq_auth_info(3rpc)**, **rpc_if_register_auth_info(3rpc)**, **rpc_mgmt_inq_dflt_protect_level(3rpc)**, **rpc_mgmt_inq_server_princ_name(3rpc)**, **sec_login_get_current_context(3sec)**, **sec_login_newgroups(3sec)**, **sec_login_setup_identity(3sec)**.

rpc_binding_set_object

Purpose

Sets the object UUID value into a server binding handle

Used by client applications.

Synopsis

#include <dce/rpc.h>

void rpc_binding_set_object(
    rpc_binding_handle_t *binding*,
    uuid_t **object_uuid*,
    unsigned32 **status*);

Parameters

Input

binding Specifies the server binding into which parameter *object_uuid* is set. Supply **NULL** to specify a nil UUID for this parameter.

object_uuid
Specifies the UUID of the object serviced by the server specified in the *binding* parameter. The object UUID is a unique identifier for an object for which a remote procedure call can be made.

Output

status Returns the status code from this routine. This status code indicates whether the routine completed successfully or, if not, why not.

The possible status codes and their meanings are as follows:

rpc_s_ok	Success.
rpc_s_invalid_binding	Invalid binding handle.
rpc_s_wrong_kind_of_binding	Wrong kind of binding for operation.

Description

The **rpc_binding_set_object()** routine associates an object UUID with a server binding handle. This operation replaces the previously associated object UUID with the UUID in the *object_uuid* parameter.

To set the object UUID to the nil UUID, specify **NULL** or the nil UUID for the *object_uuid* parameter.

Return Values

No value is returned.

Related Information

Functions: **rpc_binding_from_string_binding(3rpc)**,
rpc_binding_inq_object(3rpc).

rpc_binding_to_string_binding

Purpose

Returns a string representation of a binding handle

Used by client, server, or management applications.

Synopsis

#include <dce/rpc.h>

void rpc_binding_to_string_binding(
    rpc_binding_handle_t *binding*,
    unsigned_char_t ***string_binding*,
    unsigned32 **status*);

Parameters

Input

binding Specifies a client or server binding handle to convert to a string representation of a binding handle.

Output

string_binding
Returns a pointer to the string representation of the binding handle specified in the *binding* parameter.

status Returns the status code from this routine. This status code indicates whether the routine completed successfully or, if not, why not.

The possible status codes and their meanings are as follows:

rpc_s_ok	Success.
rpc_s_invalid_binding	Invalid binding handle.

Description

The **rpc_binding_to_string_binding()** routine converts a client or server binding handle to its string representation.

The RPC runtime allocates memory for the string returned in the *string_binding* parameter. The application calls the **rpc_string_free()** routine to deallocate that memory.

If the binding handle in the *binding* parameter contains a nil object UUID, the object UUID field is not included in the returned string.

To parse the returned *string_binding* parameter, call **rpc_string_binding_parse( )**.

Return Values

No value is returned.

Related Information

Functions: **rpc_binding_from_string_binding(3rpc)**, **rpc_string_binding_parse(3rpc)**, **rpc_string_free(3rpc)**.

rpc_binding_vector_free

Purpose

Frees the memory used to store a vector and binding handles

Used by client or server applications.

Synopsis

#include <dce/rpc.h>

void rpc_binding_vector_free(
    rpc_binding_vector_t *******binding_vector***,**
    unsigned32 *******status***);**

Parameters

Input/Output

binding_vector
Specifies the address of a pointer to a vector of server binding handles. On return the pointer is set to **NULL**.

Output

status Returns the status code from this routine. This status code indicates whether the routine completed successfully or, if not, why not.

The possible status codes and their meanings are as follows:

rpc_s_ok	Success.
rpc_s_invalid_arg	Invalid argument.
rpc_s_invalid_binding	Invalid binding handle.
rpc_s_wrong_kind_of_binding	Wrong kind of binding for operation.

Description

The **rpc_binding_vector_free( )** routine frees the memory used to store a vector of server binding handles. The freed memory includes both the binding handles and the vector itself.

A server obtains a vector of binding handles by calling **rpc_server_inq_bindings( )**. A client obtains a vector of binding handles by calling **rpc_ns_binding_lookup_next( )**. Call **rpc_binding_vector_free( )** if you have used either of these routines.

The **rpc_binding_free( )** routine frees individual elements of the vector. If an element is freed with this routine, the **NULL** element entry replaces it; **rpc_binding_vector_free( )** ignores such an entry.

Return Values

No value is returned.

Related Information

Functions: **rpc_binding_free(3rpc)**, **rpc_ns_binding_lookup_next(3rpc)**, **rpc_server_inq_bindings(3rpc)**.

rpc_ep_register

Purpose Adds to, or replaces, server address information in the local endpoint map

Used by server applications.

Synopsis **#include <dce/rpc.h>**

void rpc_ep_register(
  rpc_if_handle_t *if_handle*,
  rpc_binding_vector_t **binding_vec*,
  uuid_vector_t **object_uuid_vec*,
  unsigned_char_t **annotation*,
  unsigned32 **status*);

Parameters

Input

if_handle
Specifies an interface specification to register with the local endpoint map.

binding_vec
Specifies a vector of binding handles over which the server can receive remote procedure calls.

object_uuid_vec
Specifies a vector of object UUIDs that the server offers. The server application constructs this vector.

Supply the value **NULL** to indicate there are no object UUIDs to register.

annotation
Defines a character string comment applied to each cross product element added to the local endpoint map. The string can be up to 64 characters long, including the **NULL** terminating character. Specify **NULL** or the string **\0** if there is no annotation string.

The string is used by applications for informational purposes only. The RPC runtime does not use this string to determine which server instance a client communicates with, or for enumerating endpoint map elements.

Output

status Returns the status code from this routine. This status code indicates whether the routine completed successfully or, if not, why not.

The possible status codes and their meanings are as follows:

rpc_s_ok	Success.
ept_s_cant_access	Error reading endpoint database.
ept_s_cant_create	Error creating endpoint database.
ept_s_cant_perform_op	Cannot perform requested operation.
ept_s_database_invalid	Endpoint map database invalid.
ept_s_invalid_entry	Invalid database entry.
ept_s_update_failed	Update failed.
rpc_s_comm_failure	Communications failure.
rpc_s_invalid_binding	Invalid binding handle.
rpc_s_no_bindings	No bindings.
rpc_s_wrong_kind_of_binding	Wrong kind of binding for operation.

Description

The **rpc_ep_register**( ) routine adds elements to, or replaces elements in, the local host's endpoint map.

Each element in the local endpoint map logically contains the following:

- Interface ID, consisting of an interface UUID and versions (major and minor)
- Binding information
- Object UUID (optional)
- Annotation (optional)

A server uses this routine, instead of **rpc_ep_register_no_replace**( ), when only a single instance of the server runs on the server's host. Use this routine if, at any time, no more than one server instance offers the same interface UUID, object UUID, and protocol sequence.

When local endpoint map elements are not replaced, obsolete elements accumulate each time a server instance stops running without calling **rpc_ep_unregister( )**. Periodically the RPC Daemon (RPCD) identifies these obsolete elements and removes them. However, during the time between these removals the obsolete elements increase the chance that a client will receive endpoints to nonexistent servers. The client then wastes time trying to communicate with these servers before obtaining another endpoint.

Using this routine to replace any existing local endpoint map elements reduces the chance that a client will receive the endpoint of a nonexistent server instance.

Suppose an existing element in the local endpoint map matches the interface UUID, binding information exclusive of the endpoint, and object UUID of an element this routine provides. The routine changes the endpoint map according to the elements' interface major and minor version numbers, as shown in the following table:

Existing Element	Relationship	Provided Element	Routine's Action
Major version number	Not equal to	Major version number	Ignores minor version number relationship and adds a new endpoint map element. The existing element remains unchanged.
Major version number	Equal to	Major version number	Acts according to the minor version number relationship.
Minor version number	Equal to	Minor version number	Replaces the endpoint of the existing element based on the provided information.
Minor version number	Less than	Minor version number	Replaces the existing element based on the provided information.
Minor version number	Greater than	Minor version number	Ignores the provided information. The existing element remains unchanged.

For example, suppose under these circumstances that the existing interface version number is 1.3 (major.minor) and the provided version number is 2.0. The routine adds a new endpoint map element with interface version number 2.0 and does not change the element with version number 1.3. However, if the existing interface version number is 1.5 and the provided version number is 1.4, the routine does not change the endpoint map.

A server program calls this routine to register endpoints that have been specified by calling any of the following routines:

- **rpc_server_use_all_protseqs( )**
- **rpc_server_use_protseq( )**
- **rpc_server_use_protseq_ep( )**

A server that calls only the **rpc_server_use_all_protseqs_if( )** or **rpc_server_use_protseq_if( )** routines does not need to call this routine. In such cases, the client's runtime uses an endpoint from the client's interface specification to fill in a partially bound binding handle. However, it is recommended that you also register well-known endpoints that the server specifies (registering endpoints from interface definitions is unnecessary).

If the server also exports to the name service database, the server calls this routine with the same *if_handle*, *binding_vec* and *object_uuid_vec* parameters as the server uses when calling the **rpc_ns_binding_export( )** routine.

The **rpc_ep_register( )** routine communicates with the RPC Daemon (RPCD), which in turn communicates with the local endpoint map. The routine communicates using one of the protocol sequences specified in one of the binding handles in *binding_vec*. Attempting to register a binding that specifies a protocol sequence that the RPC daemon is not listening on results in the failure of **rpc_ep_register( )**. The routine indicates this failure by placing the value **rpc_s_comm_failure** into *status*.

For information about how the endpoint map service (the RPC daemon) selects an element for an interface ID and an object UUID, see the RPC information in the *OSF DCE Application Development Guide*. This guide explains how the endpoint map service searches for the endpoint of a server that is compatible with a client. If the client supplies a non-nil object UUID that is not in the endpoint map, or the client supplies a nil object UUID, the search can succeed, but only if the server has registered a nil object UUID using the **rpc_ep_register( )** or **rpc_ep_register_no_replace( )** routines. The *object_uuid_vec* parameter can contain both nil and non-nil object UUIDs for the routine to place into endpoint map elements.

For an explanation of how a server can establish a client/server relationship without using the local endpoint map, see the explanation of a string binding in the **intro(3rpc)** reference page.

This routine creates a cross product from the *if_handle*, *binding_vec* and *object_uuid_vec* parameters, and adds each element in the cross product as a separate registration in the local endpoint map. If you supply **NULL** to *object_uuid_vec*, the corresponding elements in the cross product contain a nil object UUID.

For example, suppose that *if_handle* has the value **ifhand**, *binding_vec* has the values **b1**, **b2**, **b3**, and *object_uuid_vec* has the values **u1**, **u2**, **u3**, **u4**. The resulting 12 elements in the cross product are as follows:

(ifhand,b1,u1) (ifhand,b1,u2) (ifhand,b1,u3) (ifhand,b1,u4)
(ifhand,b2,u1) (ifhand,b2,u2) (ifhand,b2,u3) (ifhand,b2,u4)
(ifhand,b3,u1) (ifhand,b3,u2) (ifhand,b3,u3) (ifhand,b3,u4)

(An annotation string is part of each of these 12 elements.)

Return Values

No value is returned.

Related Information

Functions: **rpc_ep_register_no_replace(3rpc)**, **rpc_ep_resolve_binding(3rpc)**, **rpc_ep_unregister(3rpc)**, **rpc_mgmt_ep_unregister(3rpc)**, **rpc_ns_binding_export(3rpc)**, **rpc_server_inq_bindings(3rpc)**, **rpc_server_use_all_protseqs(3rpc)**, **rpc_server_use_all_protseqs_if(3rpc)**, **rpc_server_use_protseq(3rpc)**, **rpc_server_use_protseq_ep(3rpc)**, **rpc_server_use_protseq_if(3rpc)**.

Books: *OSF DCE Application Development Guide*.

rpc_ep_register_no_replace

Purpose Adds to server address information in the local endpoint map

Used by server applications.

Synopsis **#include <dce/rpc.h>**

void rpc_ep_register_no_replace(
  rpc_if_handle_t *if_handle*,
  rpc_binding_vector_t **binding_vec*,
  uuid_vector_t **object_uuid_vec*,
  unsigned_char_t **annotation*,
  unsigned32 **status*);

Parameters

Input

if_handle
Specifies an interface specification to register with the local endpoint map.

binding_vec
Specifies a vector of binding handles over which the server can receive remote procedure calls.

object_uuid_vec
Specifies a vector of object UUIDs that the server offers. The server application constructs this vector.

Supply the value **NULL** to indicate there are no object UUIDs to register.

annotation
Defines a character string comment applied to each cross-product element added to the local endpoint map. The string can be up to 64 characters long, including the **NULL** terminating character. Specify **NULL** or the string **\0** if there is no annotation string.

The string is used by applications for informational purposes only. The RPC runtime does not use this string to determine which server instance a client communicates with, or for enumerating endpoint map elements.

Output

status Returns the status code from this routine. This status code indicates whether the routine completed successfully or, if not, why not.

The possible status codes and their meanings are as follows:

rpc_s_ok	Success.
ept_s_cant_access	Error reading endpoint database.
ept_s_cant_create	Error creating endpoint database.
ept_s_cant_perform_op	Cannot perform requested operation.
ept_s_database_invalid	Endpoint map database invalid.
ept_s_invalid_entry	Invalid database entry.
ept_s_update_failed	Update failed.
rpc_s_comm_failure	Communications failure.
rpc_s_invalid_binding	Invalid binding handle.
rpc_s_no_bindings	No bindings.
rpc_s_wrong_kind_of_binding	Wrong kind of binding for operation.

Description

The **rpc_ep_register_no_replace()** routine adds elements to the local host's endpoint map. The routine does not replace existing elements. Otherwise, this routine is identical to **rpc_ep_register()**.

Each element in the local endpoint map logically contains the following:

- Interface ID, consisting of an interface UUID and versions (major and minor)
- Binding information
- Object UUID (optional)
- Annotation (optional)

A server uses this routine, instead of **rpc_ep_register()**, when multiple instances of the server run on the same host. Use this routine if, at any time, more than one server instance offers the same interface UUID, object UUID, and protocol sequence.

Since this routine does not replace elements, calling servers must unregister (that is, remove) themselves before they stop running. Otherwise, when local endpoint map elements are not replaced, obsolete elements accumulate each time a server instance stops running without calling **rpc_ep_unregister( )**. Periodically the RPC Daemon (RPCD) identifies obsolete elements and removes them from the local endpoint map. However, during the time between these removals, the obsolete elements increase the chance that a client will receive endpoints to nonexistent servers. The client then wastes time trying to communicate with these servers before obtaining another endpoint.

A server program calls this routine to register endpoints that were specified by calling any of the following routines:

- **rpc_server_use_all_protseqs( )**
- **rpc_server_use_protseq( )**
- **rpc_server_use_protseq_ep( )**

A server that calls only the **rpc_server_use_all_protseqs_if( )** or **rpc_server_use_protseq_if( )** routine does not need to call this routine. In such cases, the client's runtime uses an endpoint from the client's interface specification to fill in a partially bound binding handle. However, it is recommended that you also register well-known endpoints that the server specifies (registering endpoints from interface definitions is unnecessary).

If the server also exports to the name service database, the server calls this routine with the same *if_handle*, *binding_vec* and *object_uuid_vec* parameters as the server uses when calling the **rpc_ns_binding_export( )** routine.

The **rpc_ep_register_no_replace( )** routine communicates with the RPC Daemon (RPCD), which in turn communicates with the local endpoint map. The routine communicates using one of the protocol sequences specified in one of the binding handles in *binding_vec*. Attempting to register a binding that specifies a protocol sequence that the RPC daemon is not listening on results in the failure of **rpc_ep_register_no_replace( )**. The routine indicates this failure by placing the value **rpc_s_comm_failure** into *status*.

For information about how the endpoint map service selects an element for an interface ID and an object UUID, see the RPC information in the *OSF DCE Application Development Guide*. This guide explains how the endpoint map service searches for the endpoint of a server that is compatible with a client. If the client supplies a non-nil object UUID that is not in the endpoint map, or the client supplies a nil object UUID, the search can succeed, but only if the server has registered a nil object UUID using the **rpc_ep_register_no_replace( )** or **rpc_ep_register( )** routine. The *object_uuid_vec* parameter can contain both nil and non-nil object UUIDs for the routine to place into endpoint map elements.

For an explanation of how a server can establish a client/server relationship without using the local endpoint map, see the explanation of a string binding in the **intro(3rpc)** reference page.

This routine creates a cross-product from the *if_handle*, *binding_vec* and *object_uuid_vec* parameters, and adds each element in the cross-product as a separate registration in the local endpoint map. If you supply **NULL** to *object_uuid_vec*, the corresponding elements in the cross-product contain a nil object UUID. The **rpc_ep_register( )** routine's reference page summarizes the contents of an element in the local endpoint map.

Return Values

No value is returned.

Related Information

Functions: **rpc_ep_register(3rpc)**, **rpc_ep_resolve_binding(3rpc)**, **rpc_ep_unregister(3rpc)**, **rpc_mgmt_ep_unregister(3rpc)**, **rpc_ns_binding_export(3rpc)**, **rpc_server_inq_bindings(3rpc)**, **rpc_server_use_all_protseqs(3rpc)**, **rpc_server_use_all_protseqs_if(3rpc)**, **rpc_server_use_protseq(3rpc)**, **rpc_server_use_protseq_ep(3rpc)**, **rpc_server_use_protseq_if(3rpc)**.

Books: *OSF DCE Application Development Guide*.

rpc_ep_resolve_binding

Purpose Resolves a partially bound server binding handle into a fully bound server binding handle

Used by client and management applications.

Synopsis **#include <dce/rpc.h>**

void rpc_ep_resolve_binding(
rpc_binding_handle_t *binding*,
rpc_if_handle_t *if_handle*,
unsigned32 **status*);

Parameters

Input/Output

binding Specifies a partially bound server binding handle to resolve into a fully bound server binding handle.

if_handle
Contains a stub-generated data structure that specifies the interface of interest.

Output

status Returns the status code from this routine. This status code indicates whether the routine completed successfully or, if not, why not.

The possible status codes and their meanings are as follows:

rpc_s_ok	Success.
ept_s_not_registered	No entries found.
rpc_s_invalid_binding	Invalid binding handle.
rpc_s_wrong_kind_of_binding	Wrong kind of binding for operation.

Description

An application calls the **rpc_ep_resolve_binding( )** routine to resolve a partially bound server binding handle into a fully bound server binding handle.

Resolving binding handles requires an interface UUID and an object UUID. The object UUID can be a nil UUID. The RPC runtime requests the RPC Daemon (RPCD), on the host that the *binding* parameter specifies, to look up an endpoint for a compatible server instance. The RPC daemon finds the endpoint by looking in the local endpoint map for the interface UUID from the *if_handle* parameter and for the object UUID in the *binding* parameter.

The **rpc_ep_resolve_binding( )** routine depends on whether the specified binding handle is partially bound or fully bound. When the application specifies a partially bound handle, the routine produces the following results:

- If no compatible server instances are registered in the local endpoint map, the routine returns the **ept_s_not_registered** status code.
- If one compatible server instance is registered in the local endpoint map, the routine returns a fully bound binding handle in *binding* and the **rpc_s_ok** status code.
- If more than one compatible server instance is registered in the local endpoint map, the routine randomly selects one. It then returns the corresponding fully bound binding handle in *binding* and the **rpc_s_ok** status code.

When the application specifies a fully bound binding handle, the routine returns the specified binding handle in *binding* and the **rpc_s_ok** status code. The routine makes no request of the RPC daemon.

In neither the partially bound case nor the fully bound case does the routine contact a compatible server instance.

Using This Routine

For each server instance, the RPC runtime automatically provides routines (the **rpc_mgmt_*** routines) that form an RPC management interface. If a server instance registers any application-provided interfaces, the RPC runtime automatically registers the RPC-provided management interface with the local endpoint map for that server instance.

An application can call **rpc_ep_resolve_binding( )** at any time with either a partially bound or a fully bound handle. However, applications typically call this routine to avoid calling a routine in the management interface with a partially bound handle.

An application can have a partially bound binding handle at the following times:

- After importing a binding handle.
- After resetting a binding handle.
- After converting a string binding without an endpoint to a binding handle.

If an application calls an application-provided remote procedure using a partially bound handle, the RPC runtime automatically asks the RPC daemon to resolve the binding handle into a fully bound handle. This fully bound binding handle corresponds to the RPC interface of the called remote procedure and the requested object, if any. The application can then use this fully bound handle to make remote management calls, so calling the **rpc_ep_resolve_binding( )** routine is unnecessary.

When a high proportion of all servers in an environment offers the same interface, the interface is known as a pervasive one. The RPC management interface is a pervasive interface in all environments that use DCE RPC.

Using this routine to unambiguously locate compatible server instances applies to application-pervasive interfaces as well as to the RPC management interface.

Partially Bound Handles with a Non-nil Object UUID

If the application has a partially bound handle with a non-nil object UUID, the application can decide not to call the **rpc_ep_resolve_binding( )** routine before calling a procedure in the management interface. In this case the remote management call is sent to a server instance, registered on the remote host, that offers that object UUID.

After completing the remote management call, the application has a fully bound handle to that server instance. The server instance that the handle specifies probably offers the non-management interfaces of interest to the calling application. However, if you want to be certain of obtaining a fully bound handle to a server instance that offers the interfaces needed for later remote procedure calls, call the **rpc_ep_resolve_binding( )** routine.

Partially Bound Handles with a Nil Object UUID

When an application makes a remote procedure or management call using a partially bound handle with a nil object UUID, the RPC daemon searches for a compatible server instance. The search is based on the nil object UUID and the UUID of the interface to which the call belongs.

All server instances that register any RPC interface automatically offer the RPC management interface. When an application makes a remote management call using a partially bound handle with a nil object UUID, the RPC daemon on the remote host cannot distinguish among server instances registered in the local endpoint map.

When the RPC daemon cannot distinguish among these instances it selects *any* server instance. After completing the remote management call, the calling application has a fully bound handle. However, the server instance that the handle represents probably does not offer the non-management interfaces that interest the application.

The remote RPC management routines avoid this ambiguity. They do this by returning the status **rpc_s_binding_incomplete** if the provided binding handle is a partially bound one with a nil object UUID.

An application wanting to contact servers that have exported and registered interfaces with a nil object UUID calls routine **rpc_ep_resolve_binding( )**. The application obtains a fully bound binding handle for calling remote management procedures in a server instance that also offers the remote procedures in the application-specific interface.

Note that an application that wants to manage all the server instances on a host does not call **rpc_ep_resolve_binding( )**. Instead, the application obtains fully bound binding handles for each server instance by calling **rpc_mgmt_ep_elt_inq_begin( )**, **rpc_mgmt_ep_elt_inq_next( )**, and **rpc_mgmt_ep_elt_inq_done( )**.

Return Values

No value is returned.

Related Information

Functions: **rpc_ep_register(3rpc)**, **rpc_ep_register_no_replace(3rpc)**, **rpc_mgmt_ep_elt_inq_begin(3rpc)**, **rpc_mgmt_ep_elt_inq_done(3rpc)**, **rpc_mgmt_ep_elt_inq_next(3rpc)**, **rpc_binding_from_string_binding(3rpc)**, **rpc_binding_reset(3rpc)**.

rpc_ep_unregister

Purpose Removes server address information from the local endpoint map

Used by server applications.

Synopsis **#include <dce/rpc.h>**

void rpc_ep_unregister(
  rpc_if_handle_t *if_handle*,
  rpc_binding_vector_t **binding_vec*,
  uuid_vector_t **object_uuid_vec*,
  unsigned32 **status*);

Parameters

Input

if_handle
Specifies an interface specification to remove (that is, unregister) from the local endpoint map.

binding_vec
Specifies a vector of binding handles to remove.

object_uuid_vec
Specifies a vector of object UUIDs to remove. The server application constructs this vector. This routine removes all local endpoint map elements that match the specified *if_handle* parameter, *binding_vec* parameter, and object UUIDs.

This is an optional parameter. The value **NULL** indicates there are no object UUIDs to remove.

Output

status Returns the status code from this routine. This status code indicates whether the routine completed successfully or, if not, why not.

The possible status codes and their meanings are as follows:

rpc_s_ok	Success.
ept_s_cant_access	Error reading endpoint database.
ept_s_cant_create	Error creating endpoint database.
ept_s_cant_perform_op	Cannot perform requested operation.
ept_s_database_invalid	Endpoint map database invalid.
ept_s_invalid_entry	Invalid database entry.
ept_s_update_failed	Update failed.
rpc_s_invalid_binding	Invalid binding handle.
rpc_s_no_bindings	No bindings.
rpc_s_wrong_kind_of_binding	Wrong kind of binding for operation.

Description

The **rpc_ep_unregister()** routine removes elements from the local host's endpoint map. A server application calls this routine only if the server has registered endpoints previously and the server wishes to remove that address information from the local endpoint map.

A server program is able to remove its own local endpoint map elements (server address information) based on either of the following:

- The interface specification.
- The interface specification and the object UUIDs of resources offered.

The server calls the **rpc_server_inq_bindings()** routine to obtain the required *binding_vec* parameter. To remove selected endpoints, the server can remove individual elements from *binding_vec* before calling this routine. (See the explanation of a binding vector in the **intro(3rpc)** reference page for more information about removing a single element from a vector of binding handles.)

This routine creates a cross product from the *if_handle*, *binding_vec* and *object_uuid_vec* parameters and removes each element in the cross product from the local endpoint map. The **rpc_ep_register()** routine's reference page summarizes the contents of a cross product in the local endpoint map.

Servers must always call the **rpc_ep_unregister()** routine to remove their endpoints from the local endpoint map before they exit. Otherwise, stale information will be in the local endpoint map. However, if a server prematurely removes endpoints (the server is not in the process of exiting), clients that do not already have fully bound binding handles to the server will not be able to send remote procedure calls to the server.

Return Values

No value is returned.

Related Information

Functions: **rpc_ep_register(3rpc)**, **rpc_ep_register_no_replace(3rpc)**, **rpc_mgmt_ep_unregister(3rpc)**, **rpc_ns_binding_unexport(3rpc)**, **rpc_server_inq_bindings(3rpc)**.

rpc_if_id_vector_free

Purpose Frees a vector and the interface identifier structures it contains

Used by client, server, or management applications.

Synopsis **#include <dce/rpc.h>**

void rpc_if_id_vector_free(
  rpc_if_id_vector_t *******if_id_vector***,**
  unsigned32 *******status***);**

Parameters

Input/Output

if_id_vector Specifies the address of a pointer to a vector of interface information. On return the pointer is set to **NULL**.

Output

status Returns the status code from this routine. This status code indicates whether the routine completed successfully or, if not, why not.

The possible status codes and their explanations are as follows:

rpc_s_ok	Success.
rpc_s_invalid_arg	Invalid argument.

Description

The **rpc_if_id_vector_free( )** routine frees the memory used to store a vector of interface identifiers. This includes memory used by the interface identifiers and the vector itself. On return this routine sets the *if_id_vector* parameter to **NULL**.

To obtain a vector of interface identifiers, call **rpc_ns_mgmt_entry_inq_if_ids( )** or **rpc_mgmt_inq_if_ids( )**. Call **rpc_if_id_vector_free( )** if you have used either of these routines.

Return Values

No value is returned.

Related Information

Functions: **rpc_if_inq_id(3rpc)**, **rpc_mgmt_inq_if_ids(3rpc)**, **rpc_ns_mgmt_entry_inq_if_ids(3rpc)**.

rpc_if_inq_id

Purpose

Returns the interface identifier for an interface specification

Used by client or server applications.

Synopsis

#include <dce/rpc.h>

void rpc_if_inq_id(
  rpc_if_handle_t *if_handle*,
  rpc_if_id_t **if_id*,
  unsigned32 **status*);

Parameters

Input

if_handle Represents a stub-generated data structure that specifies the interface specification to inquire about.

Output

if_id Returns the interface identifier. The application provides memory for the returned data.

status Returns the status code from this routine. This status code indicates whether the routine completed successfully or, if not, why not.

The possible status code and its meaning is as follows:

rpc_s_ok Success.

Description

An application calls the **rpc_if_inq_id**( ) routine to obtain a copy of the interface identifier from the provided interface specification.

The returned interface identifier consists of the interface UUID and interface version numbers (major and minor) specified in the DCE IDL file's interface specification.

Return Values

No value is returned.

Related Information

Functions: **rpc_if_id_vector_free(3rpc)**, **rpc_mgmt_inq_if_ids(3rpc)**, **rpc_ns_mgmt_entry_inq_if_ids(3rpc)**.

rpc_if_register_auth_info

Purpose

Registers authentication and authorization information for an interface

Used by client applications.

Synopsis

#include <dce/rpc.h>
#include <dce/sec_login.h>

void rpc_if_register_auth_info(
  rpc_if_handle_t *if_handle*,
  unsigned_char_t **server_princ_name*,
  unsigned32 *protect_level*,
  unsigned32 *authn_svc*,
  rpc_auth_identity_handle_t *auth_identity*,
  unsigned32 *authz_svc*,
  unsigned32 **status*);

Parameters

Input

if_handle
: Specifies the interface specification for which to register the authentication and authorization information. The specified information applies to all remote procedure calls in the interface, where bindings are obtained via **auto_handle**.

server_princ_name
: Specifies the principal name of the server responsible for processing remote procedure calls for the specified interface. The content of the name and its syntax is defined by the authentication service in use.

  A client that does not know the server principal name can call **rpc_mgmt_inq_server_princ_name( )** to obtain the name of a server that is registered for the required authentication service. Using a principal name obtained in this way means that the client is interested in one-way authentication. In other words, it means that the client does not care which server principal received the remote procedure call request. The server, though, still verifies that the client is who the client claims to be.

protect_level

Specifies the protection level for remote procedure calls belonging to *if_handle*. The protection level determines the degree to which authenticated communications between the client and the server are protected.

If the RPC runtime does not support a specified level, it automatically upgrades the level to the next higher supported level.

The possible protection levels are as follows:

rpc_c_protect_level_default
Uses the default protection level for the specified authentication service.

rpc_c_protect_level_none
Performs no protection.

rpc_c_protect_level_connect
Performs protection only when the client establishes a relationship with the server.

rpc_c_protect_level_call
Performs protection only at the beginning of each remote procedure call when the server receives the request.

This level does not apply to remote procedure calls made over a connection-based protocol sequence (that is, **ncacn_ip_tcp**). If this level is specified and the binding handle uses a connection-based protocol sequence, the routine uses the **rpc_c_protect_level_pkt** level instead.

rpc_c_protect_level_pkt
Ensures that all data received is from the expected client.

rpc_c_protect_level_pkt_integ
Ensures and verifies that none of the data transferred between client and server has been modified.

This is the highest authentication level that is guaranteed to be present in the RPC runtime.

rpc_c_protect_level_pkt_privacy
Performs protection as specified by all of the previous levels and also encrypts each remote procedure call argument value.

This is the highest authentication level, but it may not be available in the RPC runtime.

authn_svc
Specifies the authentication service to use. The supported authentication services are as follows:

rpc_c_authn_none No authentication. This service turns authentication off for all remote procedure calls belonging to *if_handle*.

rpc_c_authn_dce_secret
DCE shared-secret key authentication.

rpc_c_authn_dce_public
DCE public key authentication (reserved for future use).

rpc_c_authn_default
DCE default authentication service.

auth_identity
Specifies a handle for the data structure that contains the client's authentication and authorization credentials appropriate for the selected authentication and authorization services.

When using the **rpc_c_authn_dce_secret** authentication service and any authorization service, this value must be a **sec_login_handle_t** obtained from one of the following routines:

- **sec_login_setup_identity( )**
- **sec_login_get_current_context( )**
- **sec_login_newgroups( )**

These routines are described in Chapter 5 of this manual.

Specify **NULL** to use the security login context for the current address space.

authz_svc

Specifies the authorization service implemented by the server for the specified interface. The validity and trustworthiness of authorization data, like any application data, depends on the authentication service and protection level specified. The supported authorization services are as follows:

rpc_c_authz_none	Supplies no authorization.
rpc_c_authz_name	Supplies authorization based on the client principal name.
rpc_c_authz_dce	Supplies authorization using the client's DCE Privilege Attribute Certificate (PAC) sent to the server with each remote procedure call request. Generally, access is checked against DCE Access Control Lists (ACLs).

Output

status Returns the status code from this routine. This status code indicates whether the routine completed successfully or, if not, why not.

The possible status codes and their meanings are as follows:

rpc_s_ok	Success.
rpc_s_unknown_authn_service	Unknown authentication service.

Description

The **rpc_if_register_auth_info( )** routine registers authentication and authorization information for the interface specification identified by *if_handle*.

After a client calls this routine, the RPC runtime automatically applies the authentication and authorization information to all remote procedure calls that the client makes using implicit binding handles. An example is when the client uses an implicit handle with the IDL **auto_handle** attribute or a customized handle with the **handle** attribute.

Unless a client calls this routine, all **auto_handle** remote procedure calls that the client makes on the *if_handle* interface are unauthenticated. A client is not required to call this routine.

Return Values

No value is returned.

Related Information

Functions: **rpc_binding_inq_auth_info(3rpc)**, **rpc_binding_set_auth_info(3rpc)**, **rpc_mgmt_inq_dflt_protect_level(3rpc)**, **rpc_mgmt_inq_server_princ_name(3rpc)**, **sec_login_get_current_context(3sec)**, **sec_login_newgroups(3sec)**, **sec_login_setup_identity(3sec)**.

rpc_mgmt_ep_elt_inq_begin

Purpose Creates an inquiry context for viewing the elements in an endpoint map

Used by management applications.

Synopsis **#include <dce/rpc.h>**

void rpc_mgmt_ep_elt_inq_begin(
    rpc_binding_handle_t *ep_binding*,
    unsigned32 *inquiry_type*,
    rpc_if_id_t **if_id*,
    unsigned32 *vers_option*,
    uuid_t **object_uuid*,
    rpc_ep_inq_handle_t **inquiry_context*,
    unsigned32 **status*);

Parameters

Input

ep_binding

Specifies the host whose local endpoint map elements you receive. To receive elements from the same host as the calling application, specify **NULL**.

To receive local endpoint map elements from another host, specify a server binding handle for that host. You can specify the same binding handle you are using to make other remote procedure calls. The object UUID associated with this parameter must be a nil UUID. If you specify a non-nil UUID, the routine fails with the status code **ept_s_cant_perform_op**. Other than the host information and object UUID, all information in this parameter is ignored.

inquiry_type

Specifies an integer value that indicates the type of inquiry to perform on the local endpoint map. The following table shows the valid inquiry types:

Valid Inquiries on Local Endpoint Maps	
Value	**Description**
rpc_c_ep_all_elts	Returns every element from the local endpoint map. The *if_id*, *vers_option*, and *object_uuid* parameters are ignored.
rpc_c_ep_match_by_if	Searches the local endpoint map for those elements that contain the interface identifier specified by the *if_id* and *vers_option* values. The *object_uuid* parameter is ignored.
rpc_c_ep_match_by_obj	Searches the local endpoint map for those elements that contain the object UUID specified by the *object_uuid* parameter. The *if_id* and *vers_option* parameters are ignored.
rpc_c_ep_match_by_both	Searches the local endpoint map for those elements that contain the interface identifier and object UUID specified by the *if_id*, *vers_option*, and *object_uuid* parameters.

if_id Specifies the interface identifier of the local endpoint map elements to be returned by the **rpc_mgmt_ep_elt_inq_next**( ) routine.

Use this parameter only when specifying a value of **rpc_c_ep_match_by_if** or **rpc_c_ep_match_by_both** for the *inquiry_type* parameter. Otherwise, this parameter is ignored and the value **NULL** can be specified.

vers_option

Specifies how the **rpc_mgmt_ep_elt_inq_next**( ) routine uses the *if_id* parameter. Use this parameter only when specifying a value of **rpc_c_ep_match_by_if** or **rpc_c_ep_match_by_both** for the *inquiry_type* parameter. Otherwise, this parameter is ignored and a 0 (zero) value can be specified. The following table presents the valid values for this parameter.

Valid values of vers_option	
Value	**Description**
rpc_c_vers_all	Returns local endpoint map elements that offer the specified interface UUID, regardless of the version numbers. For this value, specify 0 (zero) for both the major and minor versions in *if_id*.
rpc_c_vers_compatible	Returns local endpoint map elements that offer the same major version of the specified interface UUID and a minor version greater than or equal to the minor version of the specified interface UUID.
rpc_c_vers_exact	Returns local endpoint map elements that offer the specified version of the specified interface UUID.
rpc_c_vers_major_only	Returns local endpoint map elements that offer the same major version of the specified interface UUID (ignores the minor version). For this value, specify 0 (zero) for the minor version in *if_id*.
rpc_c_vers_upto	Returns local endpoint map elements that offer a version of the specified interface UUID less than or equal to the specified major and minor version. (For example, suppose *if_id* contains V2.0 and the local endpoint map contained elements with the following versions: V1.3, V2.0, and V2.1. The **rpc_mgmt_ep_elt_inq_next** routine returns the elements with V1.3 and V2.0.)

object_uuid

Specifies the object UUID that **rpc_mgmt_ep_elt_inq_next( )** looks for in local endpoint map elements.

This parameter is used only when you specify a value of **rpc_c_ep_match_by_obj** or **rpc_c_ep_match_by_both** for the *inquiry_type* parameter. Otherwise, this parameter is ignored and you can supply **NULL** to specify a nil UUID.

Output

inquiry_context

Returns an inquiry context for use with the **rpc_mgmt_ep_elt_inq_next( )** and **rpc_mgmt_ep_elt_inq_done( )** routines.

status Returns the status code from this routine. This status code indicates whether the routine completed successfully or, if not, why not.

The possible status codes and their meanings are as follows:

rpc_s_ok	Success.
rpc_s_invalid_inquiry_context	Invalid inquiry context.
rpc_s_invalid_inquiry_type	Invalid inquiry type.
rpc_s_invalid_vers_option	Invalid version option.
rpc_s_wrong_kind_of_binding	Wrong kind of binding for operation.

Description

The **rpc_mgmt_ep_elt_inq_begin( )** routine creates an inquiry context for viewing server address information stored in the local endpoint map.

Using the *inquiry_type* and *vers_option* parameters, an application specifies which of the following local endpoint map elements are returned from calls to the **rpc_mgmt_ep_elt_inq_next( )** routine:

- All elements.
- Those elements with the specified interface identifier.
- Those elements with the specified object UUID.
- Those elements with both the specified interface identifier and object UUID.

Before calling the **rpc_mgmt_ep_elt_inq_next( )** routine, the application must first call this routine to create an inquiry context.

After viewing the local endpoint map elements, the application calls the **rpc_mgmt_ep_elt_inq_done( )** routine to delete the inquiry context.

Return Values

No value is returned.

Related Information

Functions: **rpc_ep_register(3rpc)**, **rpc_ep_register_no_replace(3rpc)**, **rpc_ep_unregister(3rpc)**, **rpc_mgmt_ep_elt_inq_done(3rpc)**, **rpc_mgmt_ep_elt_inq_next(3rpc)**, **rpc_mgmt_ep_unregister(3rpc)**.

rpc_mgmt_ep_elt_inq_done

Purpose Deletes the inquiry context for viewing the elements in an endpoint map

Used by management applications.

Synopsis **#include <dce/rpc.h>**

void rpc_mgmt_ep_elt_inq_done(
rpc_ep_inq_handle_t ***inquiry_context*,**
unsigned32 ***status*);**

Parameters

Input/Output

inquiry_context

Specifies the inquiry context to delete. (An inquiry context is created by calling **rpc_mgmt_ep_elt_inq_begin()**.)

Returns the value **NULL**.

Output

status Returns the status code from this routine. This status code indicates whether the routine completed successfully or, if not, why not.

The possible status codes and their meanings are as follows:

rpc_s_ok	Success.
rpc_s_invalid_inquiry_context	Invalid inquiry context.

Description

The **rpc_mgmt_ep_elt_inq_done()** routine deletes an inquiry context. The **rpc_mgmt_ep_elt_inq_begin()** routine created the inquiry context.

An application calls this routine after viewing local endpoint map elements using the **rpc_mgmt_ep_elt_inq_next()** routine.

Return Values

No value is returned.

Related Information

Functions: **rpc_mgmt_ep_elt_inq_begin(3rpc)**, **rpc_mgmt_ep_elt_inq_next(3rpc)**.

rpc_mgmt_ep_elt_inq_next

Purpose Returns one element from an endpoint map

Used by management applications.

Synopsis **#include <dce/rpc.h>**

void rpc_mgmt_ep_elt_inq_next(
rpc_ep_inq_handle_t *inquiry_context*,
rpc_if_id_t **if_id*,
rpc_binding_handle_t **binding*,
uuid_t **object_uuid*,
unsigned_char_t ***annotation*,
unsigned32 **status*);

Parameters

Input

inquiry_context
Specifies an inquiry context. This inquiry context is returned from the **rpc_mgmt_ep_elt_inq_begin( )** routine.

Output

if_id Returns the interface identifier of the local endpoint map element.

binding Returns the binding handle from the local endpoint map element.

Specify **NULL** to prevent the routine from returning this parameter. In this case the application does not call the **rpc_binding_free( )** routine.

object_uuid
Returns the object UUID from the local endpoint map element.

Specify **NULL** to prevent the routine from returning this parameter.

annotation
Returns the annotation string for the local endpoint map element. If there is no annotation string in the local endpoint map element, the string **\0** is returned.

Specify **NULL** to prevent the routine from returning this argument. In this case the application does not call the **rpc_string_free( )** routine.

status Returns the status code from this routine. This status code indicates whether the routine completed successfully or, if not, why not.

The possible status codes and their meanings are as follows:

rpc_s_ok	Success.
ept_s_cant_perform_op	Cannot perform the requested operation.
rpc_s_comm_failure	Communications failure.
ept_s_database_invalid	Endpoint map database invalid.
rpc_s_fault_context_mismatch	Fault context mismatch.
ept_s_invalid_context	Invalid inquiry type for this context.
ept_s_invalid_entry	Invalid database entry.
rpc_s_invalid_arg	Invalid argument.
rpc_s_invalid_inquiry_context	Invalid inquiry context.
rpc_s_invalid_inquiry_type	Invalid inquiry type.
rpc_s_no_more_elements	No more elements.

Description

The **rpc_mgmt_ep_elt_inq_next**( ) routine returns one element from the local endpoint map. Regardless of the selector value specified for the *inquiry_type* parameter in **rpc_mgmt_ep_elt_inq_begin**( ), this routine returns all the components of a selected local endpoint map element. The **rpc_ep_register**( ) routine's reference page summarizes the contents of an element in the local endpoint map.

An application can view all the selected local endpoint map elements by repeatedly calling the **rpc_mgmt_ep_elt_inq_next**( ) routine. When all the elements have been viewed, this routine returns an **rpc_s_no_more_elements** status. The returned elements are unordered.

If a remote endpoint map contains elements that include a protocol sequence that your system does not support, this routine does not return the elements. (A protocol sequence is part of the binding information component of an endpoint map element.) To receive all possible elements from a remote endpoint map, your application must run on a system that supports the protocol sequences included in the elements.

For example, if your system does not support protocol sequence **ncacn_ip_tcp** and a remote endpoint map contains elements that include this protocol sequence, this routine does not return these elements to your application. If your application ran on a system that supported protocol sequence **ncacn_ip_tcp**, this routine would return the elements.

The RPC runtime allocates memory for the returned *binding* and the *annotation* string on each call to this routine. The application calls the **rpc_binding_free( )** routine for each returned *binding* and the **rpc_string_free( )** routine for each returned *annotation* string.

After viewing the local endpoint map's elements, the application must call the **rpc_mgmt_ep_elt_inq_done( )** routine to delete the inquiry context.

Return Values

No value is returned.

Related Information

Functions: **rpc_binding_free(3rpc)**, **rpc_ep_register(3rpc)**, **rpc_ep_register_no_replace(3rpc)**, **rpc_mgmt_ep_elt_begin(3rpc)**, **rpc_mgmt_ep_elt_done(3rpc)**, **rpc_string_free(3rpc)**.

rpc_mgmt_ep_unregister

Purpose Removes server address information from an endpoint map

Used by management applications.

Synopsis **#include <dce/rpc.h>**

```
void rpc_mgmt_ep_unregister(
        rpc_binding_handle_t ep_binding,
        rpc_if_id_t *if_id,
        rpc_binding_handle_t binding,
        uuid_t *object_uuid,
        unsigned32 *status);
```

Parameters

Input

ep_binding
Specifies the host whose local endpoint map elements you unregister (that is, remove). To remove elements from the same host as the calling application, specify **NULL**.

To remove local endpoint map elements from another host, specify a server binding handle for that host. You can specify the same binding handle you are using to make other remote procedure calls. The object UUID associated with this parameter must be a nil UUID. If you specify a non-nil UUID, the routine fails with the status code **ept_s_cant_perform_op**. Other than the host information and object UUID, all information in this parameter is ignored.

if_id Specifies the interface identifier to remove from the local endpoint map.

binding Specifies the binding handle to remove.

object_uuid
Specifies an optional object UUID to remove.

The value **NULL** indicates there is no object UUID to consider in the removal.

Output

status Returns the status code from this routine. This status code indicates whether the routine completed successfully or, if not, why not.

The possible status codes and their meanings are as follows:

rpc_s_ok	Success.
ept_s_cant_access	Error reading the endpoint database.
ept_s_cant_perform_op	Cannot perform the requested operation.
rpc_s_comm_failure	Communications failure.
ept_s_database_invalid	Endpoint map database is invalid.
ept_s_invalid_entry	Invalid database entry.
ept_s_not_registered	No entries found.
ept_s_update_failed	Update failed.
rpc_s_invalid_binding	Invalid binding handle.
rpc_s_no_interfaces	No interfaces registered.
rpc_s_wrong_kind_of_binding	Wrong kind of binding for operation.

Description

The **rpc_mgmt_ep_unregister**( ) routine unregisters (that is, removes) an element from a local endpoint map. A management program calls this routine to remove addresses of servers that are no longer available, or to remove addresses of servers that support objects that are no longer offered.

Use this routine cautiously; removing elements from the local endpoint map may make servers unavailable to client applications that do not already have a fully bound binding handle to the server.

A management application calls the **rpc_mgmt_ep_inq_next**( ) routine to view local endpoint map elements. The application can then remove the elements using the **rpc_mgmt_ep_unregister**( ) routine.

Return Values

No value is returned.

Related Information

Functions: **rpc_ep_register(3rpc)**, **rpc_ep_register_no_replace(3rpc)**, **rpc_ns_binding_unexport(3rpc)**, **rpc_mgmt_ep_elt_inq_begin(3rpc)**, **rpc_mgmt_ep_elt_inq_done(3rpc)**, **rpc_mgmt_ep_elt_inq_next(3rpc)**.

rpc_mgmt_inq_com_timeout

Purpose Returns the communications time-out value in a binding handle

Used by client applications.

Synopsis **#include <dce/rpc.h>**

void rpc_mgmt_inq_com_timeout(
rpc_binding_handle_t *binding*,
unsigned32 **timeout*,
unsigned32 **status*);

Parameters

Input

binding Specifies a server binding handle.

Output

timeout Returns the communications time-out value from the *binding* parameter.

status Returns the status code from this routine. This status code indicates whether the routine completed successfully or, if not, why not.

The possible status codes and their meanings are as follows:

rpc_s_ok	Success.
rpc_s_invalid_binding	Invalid binding handle.
rpc_s_wrong_kind_of_binding	Wrong kind of binding for operation.

Description

The **rpc_mgmt_inq_com_timeout**( ) routine returns the communications time-out value in a server binding handle. The time-out value specifies the relative amount of time to spend trying to communicate with the server. Depending on the protocol sequence for the specified binding handle, the value in *timeout* acts only as advice to the RPC runtime.

The **rpc_mgmt_set_com_timeout(3rpc)** reference page explains the time-out values returned in *timeout*. To change the timeout value, a client calls **rpc_mgmt_set_com_timeout( )**.

Return Values

No value is returned.

Related Information

Functions: **rpc_mgmt_set_com_timeout(3rpc)**.

rpc_mgmt_inq_dflt_protect_level

Purpose Returns the default protection level for an authentication service

Used by client and server applications.

Synopsis **#include <dce/rpc.h>**

```
void rpc_mgmt_inq_dflt_protect_level(
        unsigned32 authn_svc,
        unsigned32 *protect_level,
        unsigned32 *status);
```

Parameters

Input

authn_svc

Specifies the authentication service for which to return the default protection level.

The supported authentication services are as follows:

rpc_c_authn_none	No authentication.
rpc_c_authn_dce_secret	DCE shared-secret key authentication.
rpc_c_authn_dce_public	DCE public key authentication (reserved for future use).
rpc_c_authn_default	DCE default authentication service.

Output

protect_level

Returns the default protection level for the specified authentication service. The protection level determines the degree to which authenticated communications between the client and the server are protected.

The possible protection levels are as follows:

rpc_c_protect_level_default	Uses the default protection level for the specified authentication service.

rpc_c_protect_level_none Performs no protection.

rpc_c_protect_level_connect Performs protection only when the client establishes a relationship with the server.

rpc_c_protect_level_call Performs protection only at the beginning of each remote procedure call when the server receives the request.

rpc_c_protect_level_pkt Ensures that all data received is from the expected client.

rpc_c_protect_level_pkt_integ
Ensures and verifies that none of the data transferred between client and server has been modified.

rpc_c_protect_level_pkt_privacy
Performs protection as specified by all of the previous levels and also encrypts each remote procedure call argument value.

status Returns the status code from this routine. This status code indicates whether the routine completed successfully or, if not, why not.

The possible status codes and their meanings are as follows:

rpc_s_ok Success.

rpc_s_unknown_auth_service Unknown authentication service.

Description

The **rpc_mgmt_inq_dflt_protect_level()** routine returns the default protection level for the specified authentication service.

A client can call this routine to learn the default protection level before specifying **rpc_c_protect_level_default** for the *protect_level* parameter in the **rpc_binding_set_auth_info()** or **rpc_if_register_auth_info()** routine. If the default level is inappropriate, the client can specify a different, explicit level.

A called remote procedure within a server application can call this routine to obtain the default protection level for a given authentication service. By calling routine **rpc_binding_inq_auth_client()** in the remote procedure, the server can obtain the protection level set up by the calling client. The server can then compare the client-specified protection level with the default level to determine whether to allow the remote procedure to execute.

Alternatively, a remote procedure can compare the client's protection level against a level other than the default level. In this case there is no need for the server's remote procedure to call this routine.

Return Values

No value is returned.

Related Information

Functions: **rpc_binding_inq_auth_client(3rpc)**, **rpc_binding_set_auth_info(3rpc)**, **rpc_if_register_auth_info(3rpc)**.

rpc_mgmt_inq_if_ids

Purpose Returns a vector of interface identifiers of interfaces a server offers

Used by client, server, or management applications.

Synopsis **#include <dce/rpc.h>**

void rpc_mgmt_inq_if_ids(
rpc_binding_handle_t *binding*,
rpc_if_id_vector_t ***if_id_vector*,
unsigned32 **status*);

Parameters

Input

binding Specifies a binding handle. To receive interface identifiers from a remote application, specify a server binding handle for that application. To receive interface information about your own (local) application, specify **NULL**.

If the binding handle you supply refers to partially bound binding information and the binding information contains a nil object UUID, this routine returns the **rpc_s_binding_incomplete** status code. In this case, the RPC Daemon (RPCD) does not know which server instance to select from the local endpoint map because the RPC management interface is automatically registered (by the RPC runtime) for all RPC servers.

To avoid this situation, you can obtain a fully bound server binding handle by calling the **rpc_ep_resolve_binding( )** routine.

Output

if_id_vector
Returns the address of an interface identifier vector.

status Returns the status code from this routine, which indicates whether the routine completed successfully or, if not, why not. The possible status codes and their meanings are as follows:

rpc_s_ok	Success.
rpc_s_binding_incomplete	Binding incomplete (no object ID and no endpoint).
rpc_s_comm_failure	Communications failure.
rpc_s_invalid_arg	Invalid argument.
rpc_s_invalid_binding	Invalid binding handle.
rpc_s_mgmt_op_disallowed	Management operation disallowed.
rpc_s_no_interfaces	No interfaces registered.
rpc_s_wrong_kind_of_binding	Wrong kind of binding for operation.

In addition to the values above, *status* can return the value of parameter *status* from the application-defined authorization function (**rpc_mgmt_authorization_fn_t**). The prototype for such a function is defined in the *authorization_fn* parameter listed in the reference page for the **rpc_mgmt_set_authorization_fn(3rpc)** routine.

Description

An application calls the **rpc_mgmt_inq_if_ids**( ) routine to obtain a vector of interface identifiers listing the interfaces registered by a server with the RPC runtime.

If a server has not registered any interfaces with the runtime, this routine returns a **rpc_s_no_interfaces** status code and an *if_id_vector* parameter value of **NULL**.

The application calls the **rpc_if_id_vector_free**( ) routine to release the memory used by the vector.

By default, the RPC runtime allows all clients to remotely call this routine. To restrict remote calls of this routine, a server application supplies an authorization function using the **rpc_mgmt_set_authorization_fn**( ) routine.

Return Values

No value is returned.

Related Information

Functions: **rpc_ep_resolve_binding(3rpc)**, **rpc_if_id_vector_free(3rpc)**, **rpc_mgmt_set_authorization_fn(3rpc)**, **rpc_server_register_if(3rpc)**.

rpc_mgmt_inq_server_princ_name

Purpose Returns a server's principal name

Used by client, server, or management applications.

Synopsis **#include <dce/rpc.h>**

void rpc_mgmt_inq_server_princ_name(
  rpc_binding_handle_t *binding*,
  unsigned32 *authn_svc*,
  unsigned_char_t ***server_princ_name*,
  unsigned32 **status*);

Parameters

Input

binding Specifies a binding handle. If a client application receives the principal name from a server application, supply a server binding handle for that server. For a server application to receive a principal name of itself, supply the value **NULL**.

If the binding handle you supply refers to partially bound binding information and the binding information contains a nil object UUID, this routine returns the **rpc_s_binding_incomplete** status code. In this case the RPC Daemon (RPCD) does not know which server instance to select from the local endpoint map because the RPC runtime automatically registers the RPC management interface for all RPC servers.

You can avoid this situation by calling **rpc_ep_resolve_binding( )** to obtain a fully bound server binding handle.

authn_svc

Specifies the authentication service for which a principal name is returned. The **rpc_binding_set_auth_info(3rpc)** reference page, in its explanation of the *authn_svc* parameter, contains a list of supported authentication services.

Output

server_princ_name
Returns a principal name. This name is registered for the authentication service in parameter *authn_svc* by the server referenced in parameter *binding*. If the server registered multiple principal names, only one of them is returned.

status Returns the status code from this routine. This status code indicates whether the routine completed successfully or, if not, why not.

The possible status codes and their meanings are as follows:

rpc_s_ok	Success.
rpc_s_binding_incomplete	Binding incomplete (no object ID and no endpoint).
rpc_s_comm_failure	Communications failure.
rpc_s_mgmt_op_disallowed	Management operation disallowed.
rpc_s_unknown_authn_service	Unknown authentication service.
rpc_s_wrong_kind_of_binding	Wrong kind of binding for operation.

In addition to the above values, *status* can return the value of parameter *status* from the application-defined authorization function (**rpc_mgmt_authorization_fn_t**). The prototype for such a function is defined in the *authorization_fn* parameter in the reference page for **rpc_mgmt_set_authorization_fn(3rpc)**.

Description

An application calls the **rpc_mgmt_inq_server_princ_name( )** routine to obtain the principal name a server registered for a specified authentication service.

A client (or management) application uses this routine when it wants to allow one-way authentication with the server specified by *binding*. This means that the client does not care which server principal receives the remote procedure call request. However, the server verifies that the client is who the client claims to be. For one-way authentication, a client calls this routine before calling **rpc_binding_set_auth_info( )**.

A server application uses this routine to obtain the principal name it registered by calling **rpc_server_register_auth_info( )**.

The RPC runtime allocates memory for the string returned in *server_princ_name*. The application calls **rpc_string_free( )** to deallocate that memory.

By default, the RPC runtime allows all clients to call this routine remotely. To restrict these calls, a server application supplies an authorization function by calling **rpc_mgmt_set_authorization_fn( )**.

Return Values

No value is returned.

Related Information

Functions: **rpc_binding_inq_object(3rpc)**, **rpc_binding_set_auth_info(3rpc)**, **rpc_ep_resolve_binding(3rpc)**, **rpc_mgmt_set_authorization_fn(3rpc)**, **rpc_server_register_auth_info(3rpc)**, **rpc_string_free(3rpc)**, **uuid_is_nil(3rpc)**.

rpc_mgmt_inq_stats

Purpose Returns RPC runtime statistics

Used by client, server, or management applications.

Synopsis **#include <dce/rpc.h>**

void rpc_mgmt_inq_stats(
rpc_binding_handle_t *binding***,**
rpc_stats_vector_t ***statistics***,**
unsigned32 **status***);**

Parameters

Input

binding Specifies a binding handle. To receive statistics about a remote application, specify a server binding handle for that application. To receive statistics about your own (local) application, specify **NULL**.

If the binding handle you supply refers to partially bound binding information and the binding information contains a nil object UUID, this routine returns the **rpc_s_binding_incomplete** status code. In this case, the RPC Daemon (RPCD) does not know which server instance to select from the local endpoint map because the RPC management interface is automatically registered (by the RPC runtime) for all RPC servers.

To avoid this situation, you can obtain a fully bound server binding handle by calling the **rpc_ep_resolve_binding( )** routine.

Output

statistics Returns the statistics vector for the server specified by the *binding* parameter. Each statistic is a value of the type **unsigned32**.

status Returns the status code from this routine. This status code indicates whether the routine completed successfully or, if not, why not.

The possible status codes and their meanings are as follows:

rpc_s_ok	Success.
rpc_s_binding_incomplete	Binding incomplete (no object ID and no endpoint).

rpc_s_comm_failure	Communications failure.
rpc_s_invalid_binding	Invalid binding handle.
rpc_s_mgmt_op_disallowed	Management operation disallowed.
rpc_s_wrong_kind_of_binding	Wrong kind of binding for operation.

In addition to the above values, *status* can return the value of parameter *status* from the application-defined authorization function **rpc_mgmt_authorization_fn_t( )**. The prototype for such a function is defined in the *authorization_fn* parameter in the reference page for **rpc_mgmt_set_authorization_fn(3rpc)**.

Description

The **rpc_mgmt_inq_stats( )** routine returns statistics from the RPC runtime about a specified server.

The explanation of a statistics vector in the **intro(3rpc)** reference page lists the elements of the vector.

The RPC runtime allocates memory for the statistics vector. The application calls the **rpc_mgmt_stats_vector_free( )** routine to release the memory that the statistics vector used.

By default, the RPC runtime allows all clients to remotely call this routine. To restrict remote calls of this routine, a server application supplies an authorization function using the **rpc_mgmt_set_authorization_fn( )** routine.

Return Values

No value is returned.

Related Information

Functions: **rpc_ep_resolve_binding(3rpc)**, **rpc_mgmt_set_authorization_fn(3rpc)**, **rpc_mgmt_stats_vector_free(3rpc)**.

rpc_mgmt_is_server_listening

Purpose Tells whether a server is listening for remote procedure calls

Used by client, server, or management applications.

Synopsis **#include <dce/rpc.h>**

boolean32 rpc_mgmt_is_server_listening(
rpc_binding_handle_t *binding*,
unsigned32 **status*);

Parameters

Input

binding Specifies a server binding handle. To determine if a remote application is listening for remote procedure calls, specify a server binding handle for that application. To determine if your own (local) application is listening for remote procedure calls, specify **NULL**.

If the binding handle you supply refers to partially bound binding information and the binding information contains a nil object UUID, this routine returns the **rpc_s_binding_incomplete** status code. In this case, the RPC Daemon (RPCD) does not know which server instance to select from the local endpoint map because the RPC management interface is automatically registered (by the RPC runtime) for all RPC servers.

To avoid this situation, you can obtain a fully bound server binding handle by calling the **rpc_ep_resolve_binding( )** routine.

Output

status Returns the status code from this routine. This status code indicates whether the routine completed successfully or, if not, why not.

The possible status codes and their meanings are as follows:

rpc_s_ok	Success.
rpc_s_binding_incomplete	Binding incomplete (no object ID and no endpoint).
rpc_s_comm_failure	Communications failure.

rpc_s_invalid_binding Invalid binding handle.

rpc_s_mgmt_op_disallowed Management operation disallowed.

rpc_s_wrong_kind_of_binding Wrong kind of binding for operation.

In addition to the above values, *status* can return the value of parameter *status* from the application-defined authorization function (**rpc_mgmt_authorization_fn_t**). The prototype for such a function is defined in the *authorization_fn* parameter in the reference page for **rpc_mgmt_set_authorization_fn(3rpc)**.

Description

The **rpc_mgmt_is_server_listening( )** routine determines whether the server specified in the *binding* parameter is listening for remote procedure calls.

This routine returns a value of TRUE if the server is blocked in the **rpc_server_listen( )** routine.

By default, the RPC runtime allows all clients to remotely call this routine. To restrict remote calls of this routine, a server application supplies an authorization function using the **rpc_mgmt_set_authorization_fn( )** routine.

Return Values

Your program must examine the return value of the *status* parameter and the return value of the routine to understand the meaning of the routine value. The following table summarizes the values that this routine can return.

Values Returned by rpc_mgmt_is_server_listening( )		
Value Returned	**Status Code**	**Explanation**
TRUE	**rpc_s_ok**	The specified server is listening for remote procedure calls.
FALSE	One of the status codes listed for the *status* parameter	The specified server is not listening for remote procedure calls, or the server cannot be reached.

Related Information

Functions: **rpc_ep_resolve_binding(3rpc)**, **rpc_mgmt_set_authorization_fn(3rpc)**, **rpc_server_listen(3rpc)**.

rpc_mgmt_set_authorization_fn

Purpose

Establishes an authorization function for processing remote calls to a server's management routines

Used by server applications.

Synopsis

#include <dce/rpc.h>

void rpc_mgmt_set_authorization_fn(
rpc_mgmt_authorization_fn_t *authorization_fn***,**
unsigned32 ****status*);**

Parameters

Input

authorization_fn

Specifies a pointer to an authorization function. The RPC server runtime automatically calls this function whenever the server runtime receives a client request to execute one of the RPC management routines.

Specify **NULL** to unregister a previously registered authorization function. In this case, the default authorizations (as described later) are used.

The following C definition for **rpc_mgmt_authorization_fn_t** illustrates the prototype for the authorization function:

```
typedef boolean32 (*rpc_mgmt_authorization_fn_t)
 (
  rpc_binding_handle_t client_binding,        /* in */
  unsigned32          requested_mgmt_operation, /* in */
  unsigned32          *status                 /* out */
 );
```

The following table shows the *requested_mgmt_operation* **Values** passed by the RPC runtime to the authorization function.

Operation Values Passed to Authorization Function	
Called Remote Routine	*requested_mgmt_operation* **Value**
rpc_mgmt_inq_if_ids( )	**rpc_c_mgmt_inq_if_ids**
rpc_mgmt_inq_server_princ_name( )	**rpc_c_mgmt_inq_princ_name**
rpc_mgmt_inq_stats( )	**rpc_c_mgmt_inq_stats**
rpc_mgmt_is_server_listening( )	**rpc_c_mgmt_is_server_listen**
rpc_mgmt_stop_server_listening( )	**rpc_c_mgmt_stop_server_listen**

Output

status Returns the status code from this routine. This status code indicates whether the routine completed successfully or, if not, why not.

The possible status code and its meaning is as follows:

rpc_s_ok Success.

Description

The **rpc_mgmt_set_authorization_fn**( ) routine sets up an authorization function to control remote access to the calling server's remote management routines.

If a server does not provide an authorization function, the RPC runtime controls client application access to the server's remote management routines as shown in the next table. In the table, an Enabled authorization allows all clients to execute the remote routine and a Disabled authorization prevents all clients from executing the remote routine.

Default Controls for Remote Management Routines	
Remote Routine	**Default Authorization**
rpc_mgmt_inq_if_ids( )	Enabled
rpc_mgmt_inq_server_princ_name( )	Enabled
rpc_mgmt_inq_stats( )	Enabled
rpc_mgmt_is_server_listening( )	Enabled
rpc_mgmt_stop_server_listening( )	Disabled

A server can modify the default authorizations by calling **rpc_mgmt_set_authorization_fn( )** to specify an authorization function. When an authorization function is provided, the RPC runtime automatically calls that function to control the execution of all remote management routines called by clients.

The specified function must provide access control for all of the remote management routines.

If the authorization function returns TRUE, the management routine is allowed to execute. If the authorization function returns FALSE, the management routine does not execute, and the called routine returns to the client the status code returned from the **rpc_mgmt_authorization_fn_t** function. However, if the status code that the **rpc_mgmt_authorization_fn_t** function returns is 0 (zero) or **rpc_s_ok**, then the status code **rpc_s_mgmt_op_disallowed** is returned to the client.

The RPC runtime calls the server-provided authorization function with the following two input arguments:

- The binding handle of the calling client.
- An integer value denoting which management routine the client has called.

Using these arguments, the authorization function determines whether the calling client is allowed to execute the requested management routine. For example, the authorization function can call **rpc_binding_inq_auth_client( )** to obtain authentication and authorization information about the calling client and determine if that client is authorized to execute the requested management routine.

Return Values

No value is returned.

Related Information

Functions: **rpc_mgmt_ep_unregister(3rpc)**, **rpc_mgmt_inq_if_ids(3rpc)**, **rpc_mgmt_inq_server_princ_name(3rpc)**, **rpc_mgmt_inq_stats(3rpc)**, **rpc_mgmt_is_server_listening(3rpc)**, **rpc_mgmt_stop_server_listening(3rpc)**.

rpc_mgmt_set_cancel_timeout

Purpose

Sets the lower bound on the time to wait before timing out after forwarding a cancel

Used by client applications.

Synopsis

#include <dce/rpc.h>

void rpc_mgmt_set_cancel_timeout(
signed32 *seconds*,
unsigned32 **status*);

Parameters

Input

seconds An integer specifying the number of seconds to wait for a server to acknowledge a cancel. To specify that a client waits an infinite amount of time, supply the value **rpc_c_cancel_infinite_timeout**.

Output

status Returns the status code from this routine. This status code indicates whether the routine completed successfully or, if not, why not.

The possible status code and its meaning is as follows:

rpc_s_ok	Success.

Description

The **rpc_mgmt_set_cancel_timeout**( ) routine resets the amount of time the RPC runtime waits for a server to acknowledge a cancel before orphaning the call.

The application specifies either to wait forever or to wait a length of time specified in seconds. If the value of *seconds* is 0 (zero), the remote procedure call is immediately orphaned when the RPC runtime detects and forwards a pending cancel; control returns immediately to the client application. The default value, **rpc_c_cancel_infinite_timeout**, specifies waiting forever for the call to complete.

The value for the cancel time-out applies to all remote procedure calls made in the current thread. A multithreaded client that wishes to change the time-out value must call this routine in each thread of execution.

For more information about canceled threads and orphaned remote procedure calls, see the *OSF DCE Application Development Guide*.

Return Values

No value is returned.

Related Information

Functions: **pthread_cancel(3thr)**, **pthread_setcancel(3thr)**.

Books: *OSF DCE Application Development Guide*.

rpc_mgmt_set_com_timeout

Purpose Sets the communications time-out value in a binding handle

Used by client applications.

Synopsis **#include <dce/rpc.h>**

void rpc_mgmt_set_com_timeout(
    rpc_binding_handle_t *binding*,
    unsigned32 *timeout*,
    unsigned32 **status*);

Parameters

Input

binding Specifies the server binding handle whose time-out value is set.

timeout Specifies a communications time-out value.

Output

status Returns the status code from this routine. This status code indicates whether the routine completed successfully or, if not, why not.

The possible status codes and their meanings are as follows:

rpc_s_ok	Success.
rpc_s_invalid_binding	Invalid binding handle.
rpc_s_invalid_timeout	Invalid time-out value.
rpc_s_wrong_kind_of_binding	Wrong kind of binding for operation.

Description

The **rpc_mgmt_set_com_timeout()** routine resets the communications time-out value in a server binding handle. The time-out value specifies the relative amount of time to spend trying to communicate with the server. Depending on the protocol sequence for the specified binding handle, the *timeout* value acts only as advice to the RPC runtime.

After the initial relationship is established, subsequent communications for the binding handle can revert to not less than the default time-outs for the protocol service. This means that after setting a short initial time-out, establishing a connection, calls in progress are not timed out any sooner than the default.

The time-out value can be any integer value from 0 (zero) to 10. Note that these values do *not* represent seconds. They represent a relative amount of time to spend to establish a client/server relationship (a binding).

Constants are provided for certain values in the time-out range. The following table lists the binding time-out values, describing the DCE RPC predefined values that an application can use for the *timeout* parameter.

Predefined Time-Out Values

Name	Value	Description
rpc_c_binding_min_timeout	0	Attempts to communicate for the minimum amount of time for the network protocol being used. This value favors response time over correctness in determining whether the server is running.
rpc_c_binding_default_timeout	5	Attempts to communicate for an average amount of time for the network protocol being used. This value gives equal consideration to response time and correctness in determining whether a server is running. This is the default value.
rpc_c_binding_max_timeout	9	Attempts to communicate for the longest finite amount of time for the network protocol being used. This value favors correctness in determining whether a server is running over response time.
rpc_c_binding_infinite_timeout	10	Attempts to communicate forever.

Return Values

No value is returned.

Related Information

Functions: **rpc_mgmt_inq_com_timeout(3rpc)**.

rpc_mgmt_set_server_stack_size

Purpose Specifies the stack size for each server thread

Used by server applications.

Synopsis **#include <dce/rpc.h>**

void rpc_mgmt_set_server_stack_size(
    unsigned32 *thread_stack_size*,
    unsigned32 **status*);

Parameters

Input

thread_stack_size
Specifies, in bytes, the stack size allocated for each thread created by **rpc_server_listen**( ). This value is applied to all threads created for the server. Select this value based on the stack requirements of the remote procedures offered by the server.

Output

status Returns the status code from this routine. This status code indicates whether the routine completed successfully or, if not, why not.

The possible status codes and their meanings are as follows:

rpc_s_ok	Success.
rpc_s_invalid_arg	Invalid argument.
rpc_s_not_supported	Not supported.

Description

The **rpc_mgmt_set_server_stack_size**( ) routine specifies the thread stack size to use when the RPC runtime creates call threads for executing remote procedure calls. The *max_calls_exec* parameter in **rpc_server_listen**( ) specifies the number of call execution threads created.

A server, provided it knows the stack requirements of all the manager routines in the interfaces it offers, can call **rpc_mgmt_set_server_stack_size( )** to ensure that each call thread has the necessary stack size.

This routine is optional. When it is used, it must be called before the server calls **rpc_server_listen( )**. If a server does not call this routine, the default per thread stack size from the underlying threads package is used.

Some thread packages do not support the specification or modification of thread stack sizes. The packages cannot perform such operations or the concept of a thread stack size is meaningless to them.

Return Values

No value is returned.

Related Information

Functions: **rpc_server_listen(3rpc)**.

rpc_mgmt_stats_vector_free

Purpose Frees a statistics vector

Used by client, server, or management applications.

Synopsis **#include <dce/rpc.h>**

void rpc_mgmt_stats_vector_free(
**rpc_stats_vector_t *****stats_vector*,
**unsigned32 ****status*);

Parameters

Input/Output

stats_vector Specifies the address of a pointer to a statistics vector. On return, *stats_vector* contains the value **NULL**.

Output

status Returns the status code from this routine. This status code indicates whether the routine completed successfully or, if not, why not.

The possible status code and its meaning is as follows:

rpc_s_ok Success.

Description

An application calls **rpc_mgmt_stats_vector_free( )** to release the memory used to store a vector of statistics.

An application calls **rpc_mgmt_inq_stats( )** to obtain a vector of statistics. Follow a call to **rpc_mgmt_inq_stats( )** with a call to **rpc_mgmt_stats_vector_free( )**.

Return Values

No value is returned.

Related Information

Functions: **rpc_mgmt_inq_stats(3rpc)**.

rpc_mgmt_stop_server_listening

Purpose Tells a server to stop listening for remote procedure calls

Used by client, server, or management applications.

Synopsis **#include <dce/rpc.h>**

void rpc_mgmt_stop_server_listening(
  rpc_binding_handle_t *binding*,
  unsigned32 **status*);

Parameters

Input

binding Specifies a server binding handle. To direct a remote server to stop listening for remote procedure calls, specify a server binding handle to that server. To direct your own (local) server to stop listening for remote procedure calls, specify **NULL**.

If the binding handle you supply refers to partially bound binding information and the binding information contains a nil object UUID, this routine returns the **rpc_s_binding_incomplete** status code. In this case, the RPC Daemon (RPCD) does not know which server instance to select from the local endpoint map because the RPC management interface is automatically registered (by the RPC runtime) for all RPC servers.

To avoid this situation, you can obtain a fully bound server binding handle by calling **rpc_ep_resolve_binding( )**.

Output

status Returns the status code from this routine. This status code indicates whether the routine completed successfully or, if not, why not.

The possible status codes and their meanings are as follows:

rpc_s_ok	Success.
rpc_s_binding_incomplete	Binding incomplete (no object ID and no endpoint).
rpc_s_comm_failure	Communications failure.

rpc_s_invalid_binding	Invalid binding handle.
rpc_s_mgmt_op_disallowed	Management operation disallowed.
rpc_s_unknown_if	Unknown interface.
rpc_s_wrong_kind_of_binding	Wrong kind of binding for operation.

In addition to the above values, *status* can return the value of parameter *status* from the application-defined authorization function **rpc_mgmt_authorization_fn_t( )**. The prototype for such a function is defined in the *authorization_fn* parameter in the reference page for **rpc_mgmt_set_authorization_fn(3rpc)**.

Description

The **rpc_mgmt_stop_server_listening( )** routine directs a server to stop listening for remote procedure calls.

On receiving such a request, the DCE RPC runtime stops accepting new remote procedure calls. Executing calls are allowed to complete.

After all calls complete, **rpc_server_listen( )** returns to the caller.

By default, the RPC runtime does not allow any client to remotely call this routine. To allow clients to execute this routine, a server application supplies an authorization function using **rpc_mgmt_set_authorization_fn( )**.

Return Values

No value is returned.

Related Information

Functions: **rpc_ep_resolve_binding(3rpc)**,
rpc_mgmt_set_authorization_fn(3rpc), **rpc_server_listen(3rpc)**.

rpc_network_inq_protseqs

Purpose Returns all protocol sequences supported by both the RPC runtime and the operating system

Used by client and server applications.

Synopsis **#include <dce/rpc.h>**

```
void rpc_network_inq_protseqs(
        rpc_protseq_vector_t **protseq_vector,
        unsigned32 *status);
```

Parameters

Input

None.

Output

protseq_vector	Returns the address of a protocol sequence vector.
status	Returns the status code from this routine. This status code indicates whether the routine completed successfully or, if not, why not.

The possible status codes and their meanings are as follows:

rpc_s_ok	Success.
rpc_s_no_protseqs	No supported protocol sequences.

Description

The **rpc_network_inq_protseqs**( ) routine obtains a vector containing the protocol sequences supported by the RPC runtime and the operating system. A server chooses to accept remote procedure calls over some or all of the supported protocol sequences. If there are no supported protocol sequences, this routine returns the **rpc_s_no_protseqs** status code and the value **NULL** in the *protseq_vector* parameter.

The application calls **rpc_protseq_vector_free**( ) to release the memory used by the vector.

Return Values

No value is returned.

Related Information

Functions: **rpc_network_is_protseq_valid(3rpc)**, **rpc_protseq_vector_free(3rpc)**.

rpc_network_is_protseq_valid

Purpose Tells whether the specified protocol sequence is supported by both the RPC runtime and the operating system

Used by client and server applications.

Synopsis **#include <dce/rpc.h>**

boolean32 rpc_network_is_protseq_valid(
unsigned_char_t ***protseq*,**
unsigned32 ***status*);**

Parameters

Input

protseq Specifies a string identifier for a protocol sequence. (See the table of valid protocol sequences in the **intro(3rpc)** reference page for a list of acceptable values.)

The **rpc_network_is_protseq_valid( )** routine determines whether this parameter contains a valid protocol sequence. If not, the routine returns FALSE and the *status* parameter contains the **rpc_s_invalid_rpc_protseq** status code.

Output

status Returns the status code from this routine. This status code indicates whether the routine completed successfully or, if not, why not.

The possible status codes and their meanings are as follows:

rpc_s_ok	Success.
rpc_s_invalid_rpc_protseq	Invalid protocol sequence.
rpc_s_protseq_not_supported	Protocol sequence not supported on this host.

Description

The **rpc_network_is_protseq_valid( )** routine determines whether a specified protocol sequence is available for making remote procedure calls. A server chooses to accept remote procedure calls over some or all of the supported protocol sequences.

A protocol sequence is valid if the RPC runtime and the operating system support the protocol sequence. DCE RPC supports the protocol sequences pointed to by the explanation of the *protseq* parameter.

An application calls **rpc_network_inq_protseqs( )** to obtain all the supported protocol sequences.

Return Values

This routine can return the following values:

TRUE — The RPC runtime supports the protocol sequence specified in the *protseq* parameter. The routine returns the status code **rpc_s_ok** in the *status* parameter.

FALSE — The RPC runtime does not support the protocol sequence specified in the *protseq* parameter.

Related Information

Functions: **rpc_network_inq_protseqs(3rpc)**, **rpc_string_binding_parse(3rpc)**.

rpc_ns_binding_export

Purpose

Establishes a name service database entry with binding handles or object UUIDs for a server

Used by server applications.

Synopsis

#include <dce/rpc.h>

void rpc_ns_binding_export(
    unsigned32 *entry_name_syntax*,
    unsigned_char_t **entry_name*,
    rpc_if_handle_t *if_handle*,
    rpc_binding_vector_t **binding_vec*,
    uuid_vector_t **object_uuid_vec*,
    unsigned32 **status*);

Parameters

Input

entry_name_syntax
An integer value that specifies the syntax of the *entry_name* parameter. To use the syntax specified in the **RPC_DEFAULT_ENTRY_SYNTAX** environment variable, provide the value **rpc_c_ns_syntax_default**.

entry_name
Specifies the entry name to which binding handles and object UUIDs are exported. This can be either the global or cell-relative name.

if_handle
Specifies a stub-generated data structure that identifies the interface to export. Specifying the value **NULL** indicates there are no binding handles to export (only object UUIDs are exported) and the *binding_vec* parameter is ignored.

binding_vec
Specifies a vector of server bindings to export. Specify the value **NULL** for this parameter in cases where there are no binding handles to export (only object UUIDs are exported).

object_uuid_vec
Identifies a vector of object UUIDs offered by the server. The server application constructs this vector. **NULL** indicates there are no object UUIDs to export (only binding handles are exported).

Output

status Returns the status code from this routine. This status code indicates whether the routine completed successfully or, if not, why not.

The possible status codes and their meanings are as follows:

rpc_s_ok	Success.
rpc_s_incomplete_name	Incomplete name.
rpc_s_invalid_binding	Invalid binding handle.
rpc_s_invalid_name_syntax	Invalid name syntax.
rpc_s_name_service_unavailable	Name service unavailable.
rpc_s_no_ns_permission	No permission for name service operation.
rpc_s_nothing_to_export	Nothing to export.
rpc_s_unsupported_name_syntax	Unsupported name syntax.
rpc_s_wrong_kind_of_binding	Wrong kind of binding for operation.

Description

The **rpc_ns_binding_export()** routine allows a server application to publicly offer, in the name service database, an interface that any client application can use. A server application can also use this routine to publicly offer the object UUIDs of the application's resources.

To export an interface, the server application calls the routine with an interface and the server binding handles that a client can use to access the server.

A server can export interfaces and objects in a single call to this routine, or it can export them separately.

If the entry in the name service database specified by the *entry_name* parameter does not exist, **rpc_ns_binding_export()** tries to create it. In this case a server must have the correct permissions to create the entry. Otherwise, a management application with the necessary permissions creates the entry by calling **rpc_ns_mgmt_entry_create( )** before the server runs.

A server is not required to export its interfaces to the name service database. When a server does not export any interfaces, only clients that privately know of that server's binding information can access its interfaces. For example, a client that has the information needed to construct a string binding can call **rpc_binding_from_string_binding( )** to create a binding handle for making remote procedure calls to a server.

Before calling **rpc_ns_binding_export( )** to export interfaces (but not to export object UUIDs), a server must do the following:

- Register one or more protocol sequences with the local RPC runtime by calling one of the following routines:

  rpc_server_use_protseq( )
  rpc_server_use_protseq_ep( )
  rpc_server_use_protseq_if( )
  rpc_server_use_all_protseqs( )
  rpc_server_use_all_protseqs_if( )

- Obtain a list of server bindings by calling **rpc_server_inq_bindings( )**.

  The vector returned from **rpc_server_inq_bindings( )** becomes the *binding_vec* parameter for this routine. To prevent a binding from being exported, set the selected vector element to the value **NULL**. (See the section on RPC data types and structures in the **intro(3rpc)** reference page.)

If a server exports an interface to the same entry in the name service database more than once, the second and subsequent calls to this routine add the binding information and object UUIDs only if they differ from the ones in the server entry. Existing data is not removed from the entry.

To remove binding handles and object UUIDs from the name service database, a server application calls **rpc_ns_binding_unexport( )** and a management application calls **rpc_ns_mgmt_binding_unexport( )**.

For an explanation of how a server can establish a client/server relationship without using the name service database, see the explanation of a string binding in the **intro(3rpc)** reference page.

In addition to calling this routine, a server that called either **rpc_server_use_all_protseqs( )** or **rpc_server_use_protseq( )** must also register with the local endpoint map by calling **rpc_ep_register( )** or **rpc_ep_register_no_replace( )**.

Permissions Required

You need both read permission and write permission to the CDS object entry (the target name service entry). If the entry does not exist, you also need insert permission to the parent directory.

Return Values

No value is returned.

Related Information

Functions: **rpc_ep_register(3rpc)**, **rpc_ep_register_no_replace(3rpc)**, **rpc_ns_binding_unexport(3rpc)**, **rpc_ns_mgmt_binding_unexport(3rpc)**, **rpc_ns_mgmt_entry_create(3rpc)**, **rpc_server_inq_bindings(3rpc)**, **rpc_server_use_all_protseqs(3rpc)**, **rpc_server_use_all_protseqs_if(3rpc)**, **rpc_server_use_protseq(3rpc)**, **rpc_server_use_protseq_ep(3rpc)**, **rpc_server_use_protseq_if(3rpc)**.

rpc_ns_binding_import_begin

Purpose Creates an import context for an interface and an object in the name service database

Used by client applications.

Synopsis **#include <dce/rpc.h>**

void rpc_ns_binding_import_begin(
unsigned32 *entry_name_syntax*,
unsigned_char_t **entry_name*,
rpc_if_handle_t *if_handle*,
uuid_t **obj_uuid*,
rpc_ns_handle_t **import_context*,
unsigned32 **status*);

Parameters

Input

entry_name_syntax
An integer value that specifies the syntax of parameter *entry_name*.

To use the syntax specified in the **RPC_DEFAULT_ENTRY_SYNTAX** environment variable, provide the value **rpc_c_ns_syntax_default**.

entry_name
Specifies the entry name where the search for compatible binding handles begins. This can be either the global or cell-relative name.

To use the entry name found in the **RPC_DEFAULT_ENTRY** environment variable, supply **NULL** or a null string (**\0**) for this parameter. When this entry name is used, the RPC runtime automatically uses the default name syntax specified in the **RPC_DEFAULT_ENTRY_SYNTAX** environment variable.

if_handle
A stub-generated data structure specifying the interface to import. If the interface specification has not been exported or is of no concern to the caller, specify **NULL** for this parameter. In this case the bindings returned are only guaranteed to be of a compatible and supported protocol sequence and, depending on the value of parameter *obj_uuid*, contain the specified object UUID. The desired interface may not be supported by the contacted server.

obj_uuid Specifies an optional object UUID.

If you specify **NULL** or a nil UUID for this parameter, the returned binding handles contain one of the object UUIDs that the compatible server exported. If the server did not export any object UUIDs, the returned compatible binding handles contain a nil object UUID.

If you specify a non-nil UUID, compatible binding handles are returned from an entry only if the server has exported the specified object UUID. Each returned binding handle contains the specified non-nil object UUID.

Output

import_context
Returns the name service handle for use with the **rpc_ns_binding_import_next()** and **rpc_ns_binding_import_done()** routines.

status Returns the status code from this routine. This status code indicates whether the routine completed successfully or, if not, why not.

The possible status codes and their meanings are as follows:

rpc_s_ok	Success.
rpc_s_incomplete_name	Incomplete name.
rpc_s_invalid_name_syntax	Invalid name syntax.
rpc_s_invalid_object	Invalid object.
rpc_s_no_env_setup	Environment variable not set up.
rpc_s_unsupported_name_syntax	Unsupported name syntax.

Description

The **rpc_ns_binding_import_begin( )** routine creates an import context for importing compatible server binding handles for servers. These servers offer the specified interface and object UUID in the respective *if_handle* and *obj_uuid* parameters.

Before calling **rpc_ns_binding_import_next( )**, the client must first call this routine to create an import context. The arguments to this routine control the operation of **rpc_ns_binding_import_next( )**.

After importing binding handles, the client calls **rpc_ns_binding_import_done( )** to delete the import context.

Permissions Required

No permissions are required.

Return Values

No value is returned.

Related Information

Functions: **rpc_ns_binding_import_done(3rpc)**,
rpc_ns_binding_import_next(3rpc),
rpc_ns_mgmt_handle_set_exp_age(3rpc).

rpc_ns_binding_import_done

Purpose Deletes the import context for searching the name service database

Used by client applications.

Synopsis **#include <dce/rpc.h>**

void rpc_ns_binding_import_done(
rpc_ns_handle_t **import_context*,
unsigned32 **status***);**

Parameters

Input/Output

import_context
Specifies the name service handle to delete. (A name service handle is created by calling **rpc_ns_binding_import_begin( )**.)

Returns the value **NULL**.

Output

status Returns the status code from this routine. This status code indicates whether the routine completed successfully or, if not, why not.

The possible status codes and their meanings are as follows:

rpc_s_ok	Success.
rpc_s_invalid_ns_handle	Invalid name service handle.

Description

The **rpc_ns_binding_import_done( )** routine deletes an import context created by calling **rpc_ns_binding_import_begin( )**. This deletion does not affect any previously imported bindings.

Typically, a client calls this routine after completing remote procedure calls to a server using a binding handle returned from **rpc_ns_binding_import_next( )**. A client program calls this routine for each created import context, regardless of the status returned from **rpc_ns_binding_import_next( )**, or the success in making remote procedure calls.

Permissions Required

No permissions are required.

Return Values

No value is returned.

Related Information

Functions: **rpc_ns_binding_import_begin(3rpc)**, **rpc_ns_binding_import_next(3rpc)**.

rpc_ns_binding_import_next

Purpose Returns a binding handle of a compatible server (if found) from the name service database

Used by client applications.

Synopsis **#include <dce/rpc.h>**

void rpc_ns_binding_import_next(
rpc_ns_handle_t *import_context*,
rpc_binding_handle_t **binding*,
unsigned32 **status*);

Parameters

Input

import_context
Specifies a name service handle. This handle is returned from the **rpc_ns_binding_import_begin( )** routine.

Output

binding Returns a compatible server binding handle.

status Returns the status code from this routine. This status code indicates whether the routine completed successfully or, if not, why not.

The possible status codes and their meanings are as follows:

rpc_s_ok	Success.
rpc_s_class_version_mismatch	RPC class version mismatch.
rpc_s_entry_not_found	Name service entry not found.
rpc_s_invalid_ns_handle	Invalid name service handle.
rpc_s_name_service_unavailable	Name service unavailable.
rpc_s_no_more_bindings	No more bindings.

rpc_s_no_ns_permission	No permission for name service operation.
rpc_s_not_rpc_entry	Not an RPC entry.

Description

The **rpc_ns_binding_import_next( )** routine returns one compatible (to the client) server binding handle selected at random from the name service database. The server offers the interface and object UUID specified by the respective *if_handle* and *obj_uuid* parameters in **rpc_ns_binding_import_begin( )**.

A similar routine is **rpc_ns_binding_lookup_next( )**, which returns a vector of compatible server binding handles for one or more servers.

The **rpc_ns_binding_import_next( )** routine communicates only with the name service database, not directly with servers.

The returned compatible binding handle always contains an object UUID. Its value depends on the value specified in the *obj_uuid* parameter of the **rpc_ns_binding_import_begin( )** routine, as follows:

- If *obj_uuid* contains a non-nil object UUID, the returned binding handle contains that object UUID.
- If *obj_uuid* contains a nil object UUID or **NULL**, the object UUID returned in the binding handle depends on how the server exported object UUIDs:
  - If the server did not export any object UUIDs, the returned binding handle contains a nil object UUID.
  - If the server exported one object UUID, the returned binding handle contains that object UUID.
  - If the server exported multiple object UUIDs, the returned binding handle contains one of the object UUIDs. The import-next operation selects the returned object UUID in a nondeterministic way. So, a different object UUID can be returned for each compatible binding handle from a single server entry.

The client application can use the returned binding handle to make a remote procedure call to the server. If the client fails to communicate with the server, it can call the **rpc_ns_binding_import_next( )** routine again.

Each time the client calls **rpc_ns_binding_import_next( )**, the routine returns another server binding handle. The binding handles returned are unordered. Multiple binding handles can refer to different protocol sequences from the same server.

When the search finishes, the routine returns a status code of **rpc_s_no_more_bindings** and returns the value **NULL** in *binding*.

A client application calls **rpc_ns_binding_inq_entry_name**( ) to obtain the name of the entry in the name service database where the binding handle came from.

The **rpc_ns_binding_import_next**( ) routine allocates memory for the returned *binding* parameter. When a client application finishes with the binding handle, it must call **rpc_binding_free**( ) to deallocate the memory. Each call to **rpc_ns_binding_import_next**( ) requires a corresponding call to **rpc_binding_free**( ).

The client calls the **rpc_ns_binding_import_done**( ) routine after it has satisfactorily used one or more returned server binding handles. The **rpc_ns_binding_import_done**( ) routine deletes the import context. The client also calls **rpc_ns_binding_import_done**( ) if the application wants to start a new search for compatible servers (by calling **rpc_ns_binding_import_begin**( )). The order of binding handles returned can be different for each new search. This means that the order in which binding handles are returned to an application can be different each time the application is run.

Permissions Required

You need read permission to the specified CDS object entry (the starting name service entry) and to any CDS object entry in the resulting search path.

Return Values

No value is returned.

Related Information

Functions: **rpc_ns_binding_import_begin(3rpc)**, **rpc_ns_binding_import_done(3rpc)**, **rpc_ns_binding_inq_entry_name(3rpc)**, **rpc_ns_binding_lookup_begin(3rpc)**, **rpc_ns_binding_lookup_done(3rpc)**, **rpc_ns_binding_lookup_next(3rpc)**, **rpc_ns_binding_select(3rpc)**.

rpc_ns_binding_inq_entry_name

Purpose Returns the name of an entry in the name service database from which the server binding handle came

Used by client applications.

Synopsis **#include <dce/rpc.h>**

void rpc_ns_binding_inq_entry_name(
rpc_binding_handle_t *binding*,
unsigned32 *entry_name_syntax*,
unsigned_char_t ***entry_name*,
unsigned32 **status*);

Parameters

Input

binding Specifies a server binding handle whose entry name in the name service database is returned.

entry_name_syntax
An integer value that specifies the syntax of returned parameter *entry_name*.

To use the syntax specified in the **RPC_DEFAULT_ENTRY_SYNTAX** environment variable, provide the value **rpc_c_ns_syntax_default**.

Output

entry_name
Returns the name of the entry in the name service database in which *binding* was found. The returned name is a global name.

Specify **NULL** to prevent the routine from returning this parameter. When you specify this value, the client does not need to call **rpc_string_free( )**.

status Returns the status code from this routine, which indicates whether the routine completed successfully or, if not, why not.

The possible status codes and their meanings are as follows:

rpc_s_ok	Success.
rpc_s_incomplete_name	Incomplete name.
rpc_s_invalid_binding	Invalid binding handle.
rpc_s_invalid_name_syntax	Invalid name syntax.
rpc_s_no_entry_name	No entry name for binding.
rpc_s_unsupported_name_syntax	Unsupported name syntax.
rpc_s_wrong_kind_of_binding	Wrong kind of binding for operation.

Description

The **rpc_ns_binding_inq_entry_name()** routine returns the global name of the entry in the name service database from which a binding handle for a compatible server came.

The RPC runtime allocates memory for the string returned in the *entry_name* parameter. Your application calls **rpc_string_free()** to deallocate that memory.

An entry name is associated only with binding handles returned from the **rpc_ns_binding_import_next()**, **rpc_ns_binding_lookup_next()**, and **rpc_ns_binding_select()** routines.

If the binding handle specified in the *binding* parameter is not returned from an entry in the name service database (for example, the binding handle is created by calling **rpc_binding_from_string_binding()**), this routine returns the **rpc_s_no_entry_name** status code.

Permissions Required

No permissions are required.

Return Values

No value is returned.

Related Information

Functions: **rpc_binding_from_string_binding(3rpc)**, **rpc_ns_binding_import_next(3rpc)**, **rpc_ns_binding_lookup_next(3rpc)**, **rpc_ns_binding_select(3rpc)**, **rpc_string_free(3rpc)**.

rpc_ns_binding_lookup_begin

Purpose

Creates a lookup context for an interface and an object in the name service database

Used by client applications.

Synopsis

#include <dce/rpc.h>

void rpc_ns_binding_lookup_begin(
    unsigned32 *entry_name_syntax*,
    unsigned_char_t **entry_name*,
    rpc_if_handle_t *if_handle*,
    uuid_t **object_uuid*,
    unsigned32 *binding_max_count*,
    rpc_ns_handle_t **lookup_context*,
    unsigned32 **status***);**

Parameters

Input

entry_name_syntax

An integer value that specifies the syntax of the *entry_name* parameter.

To use the syntax specified in the **RPC_DEFAULT_ENTRY_SYNTAX** environment variable, provide the value **rpc_c_ns_syntax_default**.

entry_name

Specifies the entry name at which the search for compatible binding handles begins. This can be either the global or cell-relative name.

To use the entry name found in the **RPC_DEFAULT_ENTRY** environment variable, supply **NULL** or a null string (**\0**) for this parameter. When this entry name is used, the RPC runtime automatically uses the default name syntax specified in the **RPC_DEFAULT_ENTRY_SYNTAX** environment variable.

if_handle
A stub-generated data structure specifying the interface to look up. If the interface specification has not been exported or is of no concern to the caller, specify **NULL** for this parameter. In this case the bindings returned are only guaranteed to be of a compatible and supported protocol sequence and contain the specified object UUID. The desired interface might not be supported by the contacted server.

object_uuid
Specifies an optional object UUID.

If you specify **NULL** or a nil UUID for this parameter, the returned binding handles contain one of the object UUIDs exported by the compatible server. If the server did not export any object UUIDs, the returned compatible binding handles contain a nil object UUID.

For a non-nil UUID, compatible binding handles are returned from an entry only if the server has exported the specified object UUID. Each returned binding handle contains the specified non-nil object UUID.

binding_max_count
Sets the maximum number of bindings to return in the *binding_vector* parameter of **rpc_ns_binding_lookup_next( )**. Specify **rpc_c_binding_max_count_default** to use the default count.

Output

lookup_context
Returns the name service handle for use with the **rpc_ns_binding_lookup_next( )** and **rpc_ns_binding_lookup_done( )** routines.

status Returns the status code from this routine. This status code indicates whether the routine completed successfully or, if not, why not.

The possible status codes and their meanings are as follows:

rpc_s_ok	Success.
rpc_s_incomplete_name	Incomplete name.
rpc_s_invalid_name_syntax	Invalid name syntax.
rpc_s_invalid_object	Invalid object.
rpc_s_no_env_setup	Environment variable not set up.
rpc_s_unsupported_name_syntax	Unsupported name syntax.

Description

The **rpc_ns_binding_lookup_begin( )** routine creates a lookup context for locating compatible server binding handles for servers. These servers offer the specified interface and object UUID in the respective *if_handle* and *object_uuid* parameters.

Before calling **rpc_ns_binding_lookup_next( )**, the client application must first create a lookup context by calling **rpc_ns_binding_lookup_begin( )**. The parameters to this routine control the operation of **rpc_ns_binding_lookup_next( )**.

When finished locating binding handles, the client application calls the **rpc_ns_binding_lookup_done( )** routine to delete the lookup context.

Permissions Required

No permissions are required.

Return Values

No value is returned.

Related Information

Functions: **rpc_ns_binding_lookup_done(3rpc)**, **rpc_ns_binding_lookup_next(3rpc)**, **rpc_ns_mgmt_handle_set_exp_age(3rpc)**.

rpc_ns_binding_lookup_done

Purpose Deletes the lookup context for searching the name service database

Used by client applications.

Synopsis **#include <dce/rpc.h>**

void rpc_ns_binding_lookup_done(
rpc_ns_handle_t ******lookup_context*,
unsigned32 ******status*);

Parameters

Input/Output

lookup_context

Specifies the name service handle to delete. (A name service handle is created by calling **rpc_ns_binding_lookup_begin( )**.)

Returns the value **NULL**.

Output

status Returns the status code from this routine. This status code indicates whether the routine completed successfully or, if not, why not.

The possible status codes and their meanings are as follows:

rpc_s_ok	Success.
rpc_s_invalid_ns_handle	Invalid name service handle.

Description

The **rpc_ns_binding_lookup_done( )** routine deletes a lookup context created by calling **rpc_ns_binding_lookup_begin( )**.

Typically, a client calls this routine after completing remote procedure calls to a server using a binding handle returned from **rpc_ns_binding_lookup_next( )**. A client program calls this routine for each created lookup context, regardless of the status returned from **rpc_ns_binding_lookup_next( )**, or success in making remote procedure calls.

Permissions Required

No permissions are required.

Return Values

No value is returned.

Related Information

Functions: **rpc_ns_binding_lookup_begin(3rpc)**, **rpc_ns_binding_lookup_next(3rpc)**.

rpc_ns_binding_lookup_next

Purpose Returns a list of binding handles of one or more compatible servers (if found) from the name service database

Used by client applications.

Synopsis **#include <dce/rpc.h>**

void rpc_ns_binding_lookup_next(
rpc_ns_handle_t *lookup_context*,
rpc_binding_vector_t ***binding_vec*,
unsigned32 **status*);

Parameters

Input

lookup_context
Specifies a name service handle. This handle is returned from the **rpc_ns_binding_lookup_begin( )** routine.

Output

binding_vec Returns a vector of compatible server binding handles.

status Returns the status code from this routine, which indicates whether the routine completed successfully or, if not, why not.

The possible status codes and their meanings are as follows:

rpc_s_ok	Success.
rpc_s_class_version_mismatch	RPC class version mismatch.
rpc_s_entry_not_found	Name service entry not found.
rpc_s_invalid_ns_handle	Invalid name service handle.
rpc_s_name_service_unavailable	Name service unavailable.

rpc_s_no_more_bindings	No more bindings.
rpc_s_no_ns_permission	No permission for name service operation.
rpc_s_not_rpc_entry	Not an RPC entry.

Description

The **rpc_ns_binding_lookup_next( )** routine returns a vector of compatible (to the client) server binding handles. The servers offer the interface and object UUID specified by the respective *if_handle* and *object_uuid* parameters in **rpc_ns_binding_lookup_begin( )**. The number of binding handles that **rpc_ns_binding_lookup_next( )** attempts to return is the value of *binding_max_count* in the **rpc_ns_binding_lookup_begin( )** routine.

A similar routine is **rpc_ns_binding_import_next( )**, which returns *one* compatible server binding handle.

The **rpc_ns_binding_lookup_next( )** routine communicates only with the name service database, not directly with servers.

This routine traverses entries in the name service database, returning compatible server binding handles from each entry. The routine can return multiple binding handles from each entry. The search operation obeys the following rules for traversing the entries:

- At each entry visited, the search operation randomly processes binding information, then group members, then profile members. Profile members with different priorities are returned according to their priorities, highest priority first.
- The search operation returns members of a group in random order.
- The search operation returns members of a profile with the same priority in random order.

If the entry where the search begins (see the *entry_name* parameter in **rpc_ns_binding_lookup_begin( )**) contains binding handles as well as an RPC group and/or a profile, **rpc_ns_binding_lookup_next( )** returns the binding handles from *entry_name* before searching the group or profile. This means that **rpc_ns_binding_lookup_next( )** can return a partially full vector before processing the members of the group or profile.

Each binding handle in the returned vector always contains an object UUID. Its value depends on the value specified in the *object_uuid* parameter of **rpc_ns_binding_lookup_begin( )** as follows:

- If *object_uuid* contains a non-nil object UUID, each returned binding handle contains that object UUID.
- If *object_uuid* contains a nil object UUID or **NULL**, the object UUID returned in each binding handle depends on how the server exported object UUIDS:
  - — If the server did not export any object UUIDs, each returned binding handle contains a nil object UUID.
  - — If the server exported one object UUID, each returned binding handle contains that object UUID.
  - — If the server exported multiple object UUIDs, each returned binding handle contains one of the object UUIDs. The lookup-next operation selects the returned object UUID in a nondeterministic way. So, a different object UUID can be returned for each compatible binding handle from a single server entry.

From the returned vector of server binding handles, the client application can employ its own criteria for selecting individual binding handles, or the application can call **rpc_ns_binding_select( )** to select a binding handle. The **rpc_binding_to_string_binding( )** and **rpc_string_binding_parse( )** routines are useful for a client creating its own selection criteria.

The client application can use the selected binding handle to attempt a remote procedure call to the server. If the client fails to communicate with the server, it can select another binding handle from the vector. When all the binding handles in the vector are used, the client application calls **rpc_ns_binding_lookup_next( )** again.

Each time the client calls **rpc_ns_binding_lookup_next( )**, the routine returns another vector of binding handles. The binding handles returned in each vector are unordered, as is the order in which the vectors are returned from multiple calls to this routine.

When looking up compatible binding handles from a profile, the binding handles from entries of equal profile priority are unordered in the returned vector. In addition, the vector returned from a call to **rpc_ns_binding_lookup_next( )** contains only compatible binding handles from entries of equal profile priority. This means the returned vector may be partially full.

For example, if the *binding_max_count* parameter value in **rpc_ns_binding_lookup_begin( )** was **5** and **rpc_ns_binding_lookup_next( )**

finds only three compatible binding handles from profile entries of priority 0 (zero), **rpc_ns_binding_lookup_next( )** returns a partially full binding vector (with three binding handles). The next call to **rpc_ns_binding_lookup_next( )** creates a new binding vector and begins looking for compatible binding handles from profile entries of priority 1.

When the search finishes, the routine returns a status code of **rpc_s_no_more_bindings** and returns the value **NULL** in *binding_vec*.

A client application calls **rpc_ns_binding_inq_entry_name( )** to obtain the name of the entry in the name service database where the binding handle came from.

The **rpc_ns_binding_lookup_next( )** routine allocates memory for the returned *binding_vec*. When a client application finishes with the vector, it must call **rpc_binding_vector_free( )** to deallocate the memory. Each call to **rpc_ns_binding_lookup_next( )** requires a corresponding call to **rpc_binding_vector_free( )**.

The client calls **rpc_ns_binding_lookup_done( )**, which deletes the lookup context. The client also calls **rpc_ns_binding_lookup_done( )** if the application wants to start a new search for compatible servers (by calling **rpc_ns_binding_lookup_begin( )**). The order of binding handles returned can be different for each new search. This means that the order in which binding handles are returned to an application can be different each time the application is run.

Permissions Required

You need read permission to the specified CDS object entry (the starting name service entry) and to any CDS object entry in the resulting search path.

Return Values

No value is returned.

Related Information

Functions: **rpc_binding_to_string_binding(3rpc)**, **rpc_binding_vector_free(3rpc)**, **rpc_ns_binding_import_next(3rpc)**, **rpc_ns_binding_inq_entry_name(3rpc)**, **rpc_ns_binding_lookup_begin(3rpc)**, **rpc_ns_binding_lookup_done(3rpc)**, **rpc_ns_binding_select(3rpc)**, **rpc_string_binding_parse(3rpc)**.

rpc_ns_binding_select

Purpose

Returns a binding handle from a list of compatible server binding handles

Used by client applications.

Synopsis

#include <dce/rpc.h>

void rpc_ns_binding_select(
    rpc_binding_vector_t ***binding_vec*,**
    rpc_binding_handle_t ***binding*,**
    unsigned32 ***status*);**

Parameters

Input/Output

binding_vec
Specifies the vector of compatible server binding handles from which a binding handle is selected. The returned binding vector no longer references the selected binding handle (returned separately in the *binding* parameter).

Output

binding Returns a selected server binding handle.

status Returns the status code from this routine, which indicates whether the routine completed successfully or, if not, why not.

The possible status codes and their meanings are as follows:

rpc_s_ok	Success.
rpc_s_no_more_bindings	No more bindings.

Description

The **rpc_ns_binding_select( )** routine randomly chooses and returns a server binding handle from a vector of server binding handles.

Each time the client calls **rpc_ns_binding_select( )**, the routine returns another binding handle from the vector.

When all of the binding handles are returned from the vector, the routine returns a status code of **rpc_s_no_more_bindings** and returns the value **NULL** in *binding*.

The select operation allocates storage for the data referenced by the returned *binding* parameter. When a client finishes with the binding handle, it calls **rpc_binding_free( )** to deallocate the storage. Each call to the **rpc_ns_binding_select( )** routine requires a corresponding call to **rpc_binding_free( )**.

Instead of using this routine, client applications can select a binding handle according to their specific needs. In this case the **rpc_binding_to_string_binding( )** and **rpc_string_binding_parse( )** routines are useful to the applications since the routines work together to extract the individual fields of a binding handle for examination.

Permissions Required

No permissions are required.

Return Values

No value is returned.

Related Information

Functions: **rpc_binding_free(3rpc)**, **rpc_binding_to_string_binding(3rpc)**, **rpc_ns_binding_lookup_next(3rpc)**, **rpc_string_binding_parse(3rpc)**.

rpc_ns_binding_unexport

Purpose Removes the binding handles for an interface, or object UUIDs, from an entry in the name service database

Used by server applications.

Synopsis **#include <dce/rpc.h>**

void rpc_ns_binding_unexport(
unsigned32 *entry_name_syntax*,
unsigned_char_t **entry_name*,
rpc_if_handle_t *if_handle*,
uuid_vector_t **object_uuid_vec*,
unsigned32 **status*);

Parameters

Input

entry_name_syntax
An integer value that specifies the syntax of the *entry_name* parameter.

To use the syntax specified in the **RPC_DEFAULT_ENTRY_SYNTAX** environment variable, provide the value **rpc_c_ns_syntax_default**.

entry_name
Specifies an entry name whose binding handles or object UUIDs are removed. This can be either the global or cell-relative name.

if_handle
Specifies an interface specification for the binding handles to be removed from the name service database. The value **NULL** indicates that no binding handles are removed (only object UUIDs are removed).

object_uuid_vec
Specifies a vector of object UUIDs to be removed from the name service database. The application constructs this vector. The value **NULL** indicates that no object UUIDs are removed (only binding handles are removed).

Output

status Returns the status code from this routine. This status code indicates whether the routine completed successfully or, if not, why not.

The possible status codes and their meanings are as follows:

rpc_s_ok	Success.
rpc_s_class_version_mismatch	RPC class version mismatch.
rpc_s_entry_not_found	Name service entry not found.
rpc_s_incomplete_name	Incomplete name.
rpc_s_interface_not_found	Interface not found.
rpc_s_invalid_name_syntax	Invalid name syntax.
rpc_s_invalid_vers_option	Invalid version option.
rpc_s_name_service_unavailable	Name service unavailable.
rpc_s_no_ns_permission	No permission for name service operation.
rpc_s_not_all_objs_unexported	Not all objects unexported.
rpc_s_nothing_to_unexport	Nothing to unexport.
rpc_s_not_rpc_entry	Not an RPC entry.
rpc_s_unsupported_name_syntax	Unsupported name syntax.

Description

The **rpc_ns_binding_unexport( )** routine allows a server application to unexport (that is, remove) one of the following from an entry in the name service database:

- All the binding handles for an interface.
- One or more object UUIDs for a resource or resources.
- Both binding handles and object UUIDs.

The **rpc_ns_binding_unexport( )** routine removes only those binding handles that match the interface UUID and the major and minor interface version numbers found in the *if_handle* parameter. To remove multiple versions of an interface, use **rpc_ns_mgmt_binding_unexport( )**.

A server application can remove an interface and objects in a single call to this routine, or it can remove them separately.

If **rpc_ns_binding_unexport( )** does not find any binding handles for the specified interface, it returns an **rpc_s_interface_not_found** status code and does not remove the object UUIDs, if any are specified.

If one or more binding handles for the specified interface are found and removed without error, **rpc_ns_binding_unexport( )** removes the specified object UUIDs, if any.

If any of the specified object UUIDs are not found, **rpc_ns_binding_unexport( )** returns the status code **rpc_s_not_all_objs_unexported**.

A server application, in addition to calling this routine, also calls **rpc_ep_unregister( )** to unregister any endpoints that the server previously registered with the local endpoint map.

Use this routine with caution, only when you expect a server to be unavailable for an extended time; for example, when it is permanently removed from service.

Additionally, keep in mind that name service databases are designed to be relatively stable. In replicated name service databases, frequent use of **rpc_ns_binding_export( )** and **rpc_ns_binding_unexport( )** causes the name service to remove and replace the same entry repeatedly, and can cause performance problems.

Permissions Required

You need both read permission and write permission to the CDS object entry (the target name service entry).

Return Values

No value is returned.

Related Information

Functions: **rpc_ep_unregister(3rpc)**, **rpc_ns_binding_export(3rpc)**, **rpc_ns_mgmt_binding_unexport(3rpc)**.

rpc_ns_entry_expand_name

Purpose

Expands the name of a name service entry

Used by client, server, or management applications.

Synopsis

#include <dce/rpc.h>

void rpc_ns_entry_expand_name(
    unsigned32 *entry_name_syntax*,
    unsigned_char_t **entry_name*,
    unsigned_char_t ***expanded_name*,
    unsigned32 **status*);

Parameters

Input

entry_name_syntax
An integer value that specifies the syntax of the *entry_name* parameter.

To use the syntax specified in the **RPC_DEFAULT_ENTRY_SYNTAX** environment variable, provide a value of **rpc_c_ns_syntax_default**.

entry_name
Specifies the entry name to expand. This can be either the global or cell-relative name.

Output

expanded_name
Returns a pointer to the expanded version of *entry_name*. Do *not* specify **NULL** since the routine always returns a name string.

status
Returns the status code from this routine. This status code indicates whether the routine completed successfully or, if not, why not.

The possible status codes and their meanings are as follows:

rpc_s_ok	Success.
rpc_s_incomplete_name	Incomplete name.

Description

An application calls **rpc_ns_entry_expand_name**( ) to obtain a fully expanded entry name.

The RPC runtime allocates memory for the returned *expanded_name* parameter. The application is responsible for calling **rpc_string_free**( ) for that returned parameter string.

The returned and expanded entry name accounts for local name translations and differences in locally defined naming schemas. For example, suppose the entry in the name service is

```
/.:/subsys/PrintQ/server1
```

Upon return from **rpc_ns_entry_expand_name**( ), the expanded name could be

```
/.../abc.com/subsys/PrintQ/server1
```

For more information about local names and their expansions, see the information on the DCE Directory Service in the *OSF DCE Administration Guide*.

Permissions Required

No permissions are required.

Return Values

No value is returned.

Related Information

Functions: **rpc_string_free(3rpc)**.

Books: *OSF DCE Administration Guide*.

rpc_ns_entry_object_inq_begin

Purpose Creates an inquiry context for viewing the objects of an entry in the name service database

Used by client, server, or management applications.

Synopsis **#include <dce/rpc.h>**

void rpc_ns_entry_object_inq_begin(
unsigned32 *entry_name_syntax*,
unsigned_char_t **entry_name*,
rpc_ns_handle_t **inquiry_context*,
unsigned32 **status*);

Parameters

Input

entry_name_syntax
An integer value that specifies the syntax of the *entry_name* parameter.

To use the syntax specified in the **RPC_DEFAULT_ENTRY_SYNTAX** environment variable, provide a value of **rpc_c_ns_syntax_default**.

entry_name
Specifies the entry in the name service database for which object UUIDs are viewed. This can be either the global or cell-relative name.

Output

inquiry_context
Returns a name service handle for use with the **rpc_ns_entry_object_inq_next()** routine, and with the **rpc_ns_entry_object_inq_done()** routine.

status Returns the status code from this routine, indicating whether the routine completed successfully or, if not, why not.

The possible status codes and their meanings are as follows:

rpc_s_ok	Success.
rpc_s_incomplete_name	Incomplete name.

rpc_s_invalid_name_syntax	Invalid name syntax.
rpc_s_unsupported_name_syntax	Unsupported name syntax.

Description

The **rpc_ns_entry_object_inq_begin( )** routine creates an inquiry context for viewing the object UUIDs exported to *entry_name*.

Before calling **rpc_ns_entry_object_inq_next( )**, the application must first call this routine to create an inquiry context.

When finished viewing the object UUIDs, the application calls the **rpc_ns_entry_object_inq_done( )** routine to delete the inquiry context.

Permissions Required

No permissions are required.

Return Values

No value is returned.

Related Information

Functions: **rpc_ns_binding_export(3rpc)**, **rpc_ns_entry_object_inq_done(3rpc)**, **rpc_ns_entry_object_inq_next(3rpc)**, **rpc_ns_mgmt_handle_set_exp_age(3rpc)**.

rpc_ns_entry_object_inq_done

Purpose Deletes the inquiry context for viewing the objects of an entry in the name service database

Used by client, server, or management applications.

Synopsis **#include <dce/rpc.h>**

void rpc_ns_entry_object_inq_done(
  rpc_ns_handle_t ***inquiry_context*,**
  unsigned32 ***status*);**

Parameters

Input/Output

inquiry_context
Specifies the name service handle to delete. (A name service handle is created by calling **rpc_ns_entry_object_inq_begin( )**.)

Returns the value **NULL**.

Output

status Returns the status code from this routine. This status code indicates whether the routine completed successfully or, if not, why not.

The possible status codes and their meanings are as follows:

rpc_s_ok	Success.
rpc_s_invalid_ns_handle	Invalid name service handle.

Description

The **rpc_ns_entry_object_inq_done( )** routine deletes an inquiry context created by calling **rpc_ns_entry_object_inq_begin( )**.

An application calls this routine after viewing exported object UUIDs using the **rpc_ns_entry_object_inq_next**( ) routine.

Permissions Required

No permissions are required.

Return Values

No value is returned.

Related Information

Functions: **rpc_ns_entry_object_inq_begin(3rpc)**, **rpc_ns_entry_object_inq_next(3rpc)**.

rpc_ns_entry_object_inq_next

Purpose Returns one object at a time from an entry in the name service database

Used by client, server, or management applications.

Synopsis **#include <dce/rpc.h>**

void rpc_ns_entry_object_inq_next(
rpc_ns_handle_t *inquiry_context*,
uuid_t **obj_uuid*,
unsigned32 **status*);

Parameters

Input

inquiry_context
Specifies a name service handle. This handle is returned from the **rpc_ns_entry_object_inq_begin( )** routine.

Output

obj_uuid Returns an exported object UUID.

status Returns the status code from this routine. This status code indicates whether the routine completed successfully or, if not, why not.

The possible status codes and their meanings are as follows:

rpc_s_ok	Success.
rpc_s_class_version_mismatch	RPC class version mismatch.
rpc_s_entry_not_found	Name service entry not found.
rpc_s_incomplete_name	Incomplete name.
rpc_s_invalid_ns_handle	Invalid name service handle.
rpc_s_name_service_unavailable	Name service unavailable.

rpc_s_no_more_members	No more members.
rpc_s_no_ns_permission	No permission for name service operation.
rpc_s_not_rpc_entry	Not an RPC entry.

Description

The **rpc_ns_entry_object_inq_next( )** routine returns one of the object UUIDs exported to an entry in the name service database. The *entry_name* parameter in the **rpc_ns_entry_object_inq_begin( )** routine specified the entry.

An application can view all of the exported object UUIDs by repeatedly calling the **rpc_ns_entry_object_inq_next( )** routine. When all the object UUIDs are viewed, this routine returns an **rpc_s_no_more_members** status. The returned object UUIDs are unordered.

The application supplies the memory for the object UUID returned in the *obj_uuid* parameter.

After viewing the object UUIDs, the application must call the **rpc_ns_entry_object_inq_done( )** routine to delete the inquiry context.

The order in which **rpc_ns_entry_object_inq_next( )** returns object UUIDs can be different for each viewing of an entry. Therefore, the order in which an application receives object UUIDs can be different each time the application is run.

Permissions Required

You need read permission to the CDS object entry (the target name service entry).

Return Values

No value is returned.

Related Information

Functions: **rpc_ns_binding_export(3rpc)**, **rpc_ns_entry_object_inq_begin(3rpc)**, **rpc_ns_entry_object_inq_done(3rpc)**.

rpc_ns_group_delete

Purpose Deletes a group attribute

Used by client, server, or management applications.

Synopsis

```
#include <dce/rpc.h>

void rpc_ns_group_delete(
        unsigned32 group_name_syntax,
        unsigned_char_t *group_name,
        unsigned32 *status);
```

Parameters

Input

group_name_syntax
An integer value that specifies the syntax of the *group_name* parameter.

To use the syntax specified in the **RPC_DEFAULT_ENTRY_SYNTAX** environment variable, provide the integer value **rpc_c_ns_syntax_default**.

group_name
Specifies the RPC group to delete. This can be either the global or cell-relative name.

Output

status Returns the status code from this routine. This status code indicates whether the routine completed successfully or, if not, why not.

The possible status codes and their meanings are as follows:

rpc_s_ok	Success.
rpc_s_entry_not_found	Name service entry not found.
rpc_s_incomplete_name	Incomplete name.
rpc_s_invalid_name_syntax	Invalid name syntax.
rpc_s_name_service_unavailable	Name service unavailable.

rpc_s_no_ns_permission	No permission for name service operation.
rpc_s_unsupported_name_syntax	Unsupported name syntax.

Description

The **rpc_ns_group_delete( )** routine deletes the group attribute from the specified entry in the name service database.

Neither the specified entry nor the entries represented by the group members are deleted.

Permissions Required

You need write permission to the CDS object entry (the target group entry).

Return Values

No value is returned.

Related Information

Functions: **rpc_ns_group_member_add(3rpc)**, **rpc_ns_group_member_delete(3rpc)**.

rpc_ns_group_mbr_add

Purpose Adds an entry name to a group; if necessary, creates the entry

Used by client, server, or management applications.

Synopsis **#include <dce/rpc.h>**

void rpc_ns_group_mbr_add(
unsigned32 *group_name_syntax*,
unsigned_char_t **group_name*,
unsigned32 *member_name_syntax*,
unsigned_char_t **member_name*,
unsigned32 **status*);

Parameters

Input

group_name_syntax
An integer value that specifies the syntax of the *group_name* parameter.

To use the syntax specified in the **RPC_DEFAULT_ENTRY_SYNTAX** environment variable, provide **rpc_c_ns_syntax_default**.

group_name
Specifies the RPC group that receives a new member. This can be either the global or cell-relative name.

member_name_syntax
An integer value that specifies the syntax of *member_name*.

To use the syntax specified in the **RPC_DEFAULT_ENTRY_SYNTAX** environment variable, provide **rpc_c_ns_syntax_default**.

member_name
Name of the new RPC group member. This can be either the global or cell-relative name.

Output

status Returns the status code from this routine, indicating whether the routine completed successfully or, if not, why not.

The possible status codes and their meanings are as follows:

rpc_s_ok	Success.
rpc_s_class_version_mismatch	RPC class version mismatch.
rpc_s_incomplete_name	Incomplete name.
rpc_s_invalid_name_syntax	Invalid name syntax.
rpc_s_name_service_unavailable	Name service unavailable.
rpc_s_no_ns_permission	No permission for name service operation.
rpc_s_unsupported_name_syntax	Unsupported name syntax.

Description

The **rpc_ns_group_mbr_add( )** routine adds, to the name service database, an entry name as a member to the Name Service Interface (NSI) group attribute of an entry. The *group_name* parameter specifies the entry.

If the specified *group_name* entry does not exist, this routine creates the entry with a group attribute and adds the group member specified by the *member_name* parameter. In this case, the application must have permission to create the entry. Otherwise, a management application with the necessary permissions creates the entry by calling **rpc_ns_mgmt_entry_create( )** before the application is run.

An application can add the entry in *member_name* to a group before it creates the entry itself.

Permissions Required

You need both read permission and write permission to the CDS object entry (the target group entry). If the entry does not exist, you also need insert permission to the parent directory.

Return Values

No value is returned.

Related Information

Functions: **rpc_ns_group_mbr_remove(3rpc)**,
rpc_ns_mgmt_entry_create(3rpc).

rpc_ns_group_mbr_inq_begin

Purpose Creates an inquiry context for viewing group members

Used by client, server, or management applications.

Synopsis **#include <dce/rpc.h>**

void rpc_ns_group_mbr_inq_begin(
unsigned32 *group_name_syntax*,
unsigned_char_t **group_name*,
unsigned32 *member_name_syntax*,
rpc_ns_handle_t **inquiry_context*,
unsigned32 **status*);

Parameters

Input

group_name_syntax
An integer value that specifies the syntax of the *group_name* parameter.

To use the syntax specified in the **RPC_DEFAULT_ENTRY_SYNTAX** environment variable, provide **rpc_c_ns_syntax_default**.

group_name
Specifies the name of the RPC group to view.

member_name_syntax
An integer value that specifies the syntax of *member_name* in the **rpc_ns_group_mbr_inq_next( )** routine.

To use the syntax specified in the **RPC_DEFAULT_ENTRY_SYNTAX** environment variable, provide **rpc_c_ns_syntax_default**.

Output

inquiry_context
Returns a name service handle for use with the **rpc_ns_group_mbr_inq_next( )** and **rpc_ns_group_mbr_inq_done( )** routines.

status Returns the status code from this routine. This status code indicates whether the routine completed successfully or, if not, why not.

The possible status codes and their meanings are as follows:

rpc_s_ok	Success.
rpc_s_incomplete_name	Incomplete name.
rpc_s_invalid_name_syntax	Invalid name syntax.
rpc_s_unsupported_name_syntax	Unsupported name syntax.

Description

The **rpc_ns_group_mbr_inq_begin( )** routine creates an inquiry context for viewing the members of an RPC group.

Before calling **rpc_ns_group_mbr_inq_next( )**, the application must first call this routine to create an inquiry context.

When finished viewing the RPC group members, the application calls the **rpc_ns_group_mbr_inq_done( )** routine to delete the inquiry context.

Permissions Required

No permissions are required.

Return Values

No value is returned.

Related Information

Functions: **rpc_ns_group_mbr_add(3rpc)**, **rpc_ns_group_mbr_inq_done(3rpc)**, **rpc_ns_group_mbr_inq_next(3rpc)**, **rpc_ns_mgmt_handle_set_exp_age(3rpc)**.

rpc_ns_group_mbr_inq_done

Purpose Deletes the inquiry context for a group

Used by client, server, or management applications.

Synopsis **#include <dce/rpc.h>**

void rpc_ns_group_mbr_inq_done(
    rpc_ns_handle_t ***inquiry_context*,**
    unsigned32 ***status*);**

Parameters

Input/Output

inquiry_context
Specifies the name service handle to delete. (A name service handle is created by calling **rpc_ns_group_mbr_inq_begin( )**.)

Returns the value **NULL**.

Output

status Returns the status code from this routine. This status code indicates whether the routine completed successfully or, if not, why not.

The possible status codes and their meanings are as follows:

rpc_s_ok	Success.
rpc_s_invalid_ns_handle	Invalid name service handle.

Description

The **rpc_ns_group_mbr_inq_done( )** routine deletes an inquiry context created by calling **rpc_ns_group_mbr_inq_begin( )**.

An application calls this routine after viewing RPC group members using the **rpc_ns_group_mbr_inq_next( )** routine.

Permissions Required

No permissions are required.

Return Values

No value is returned.

Related Information

Functions: **rpc_ns_group_mbr_inq_begin(3rpc)**, **rpc_ns_group_mbr_inq_next(3rpc)**.

rpc_ns_group_mbr_inq_next

Purpose Returns one member name at a time from a group

Used by client, server, or management applications.

Synopsis **#include <dce/rpc.h>**

void rpc_ns_group_mbr_inq_next(
rpc_ns_handle_t *inquiry_context*,
unsigned_char_t ***member_name*,
unsigned32 **status*);

Parameters

Input

inquiry_context
Specifies a name service handle. This handle is returned from the **rpc_ns_group_mbr_inq_begin( )** routine.

Output

member_name
Returns a pointer to a (global) RPC group member name.

The syntax of the returned name is specified by the *member_name_syntax* parameter in **rpc_ns_group_mbr_inq_begin( )**.

Specify **NULL** to prevent the routine from returning this parameter. In this case, the application does not call **rpc_string_free( )**.

status Returns the status code from this routine. This status code indicates whether the routine completed successfully or, if not, why not.

The possible status codes and their meanings are as follows:

rpc_s_ok	Success.
rpc_s_class_version_mismatch	RPC class version mismatch.
rpc_s_entry_not_found	Name service entry not found.
rpc_s_invalid_ns_handle	Invalid name service handle.

rpc_s_name_service_unavailable	Name service unavailable.
rpc_s_no_more_members	No more members.
rpc_s_no_ns_permission	No permission for name service operation.
rpc_s_not_rpc_entry	Not an RPC entry.

Description

The **rpc_ns_group_mbr_inq_next( )** routine returns one member of the RPC group specified by the *group_name* parameter in the **rpc_ns_group_mbr_inq_begin( )** routine.

An application can view all the members of an RPC group by calling the **rpc_ns_group_mbr_inq_next( )** routine repeatedly. When all the group members have been viewed, this routine returns an **rpc_s_no_more_members** status. The returned group members are unordered.

On each call to this routine that returns a member name (as a global name), the RPC runtime allocates memory for the returned *member_name*. The application calls **rpc_string_free( )** for each returned *member_name* string.

After viewing the RPC group's members, the application must call the **rpc_ns_group_mbr_inq_done( )** routine to delete the inquiry context.

Permissions Required

You need read permission to the CDS object entry (the target group entry).

Return Values

No value is returned.

Related Information

Functions: **rpc_ns_group_mbr_inq_begin(3rpc)**, **rpc_ns_group_mbr_inq_done(3rpc)**, **rpc_string_free(3rpc)**.

rpc_ns_group_mbr_remove

Purpose Removes an entry name from a group

Used by client, server, or management applications.

Synopsis **#include <dce/rpc.h>**

void rpc_ns_group_mbr_remove(
  unsigned32 *group_name_syntax*,
  unsigned_char_t **group_name*,
  unsigned32 *member_name_syntax*,
  unsigned_char_t **member_name*,
  unsigned32 **status*);

Parameters

Input

group_name_syntax
: An integer value that specifies the syntax of the *group_name* parameter.

  To use the syntax specified in the **RPC_DEFAULT_ENTRY_SYNTAX** environment variable, provide **rpc_c_ns_syntax_default**.

group_name
: Specifies the RPC group from which to remove *member_name*. This can be either the global or cell-relative name.

member_name_syntax
: An integer value that specifies the syntax of *member_name*.

  To use the syntax specified in the **RPC_DEFAULT_ENTRY_SYNTAX** environment variable, provide **rpc_c_ns_syntax_default**.

member_name
: Specifies the member to remove from the Name Service Interface (NSI) group attribute in the *group_name* entry. This member can be either the global or cell-relative name.

Output

status Returns the status code from this routine. This status code indicates whether the routine completed successfully or, if not, why not.

The possible status codes and their meanings are as follows:

rpc_s_ok	Success.
rpc_s_entry_not_found	Name service entry not found.
rpc_s_group_member_not_found	Group member not found.
rpc_s_incomplete_name	Incomplete name.
rpc_s_invalid_name_syntax	Invalid name syntax.
rpc_s_name_service_unavailable	Name service unavailable.
rpc_s_no_ns_permission	No permission for name service operation.
rpc_s_unsupported_name_syntax	Unsupported name syntax.

Description

The **rpc_ns_group_mbr_remove( )** routine removes a member from the NSI group attribute in the *group_name* entry.

Permissions Required

You need both read permission and write permission to the CDS object entry (the target group entry).

Return Values

No value is returned.

Related Information

Functions: **rpc_ns_group_mbr_add(3rpc)**.

rpc_ns_mgmt_binding_unexport

Purpose Removes multiple binding handles, or object UUIDs, from an entry in the name service database

Used by management applications.

Synopsis **#include <dce/rpc.h>**

void rpc_ns_mgmt_binding_unexport(
unsigned32 *entry_name_syntax*,
unsigned_char_t **entry_name*,
rpc_if_id_t **if_id*,
unsigned32 *vers_option*,
uuid_vector_t **object_uuid_vec*,
unsigned32 **status*);

Parameters

Input

entry_name_syntax
An integer value that specifies the syntax of the *entry_name* parameter.

To use the syntax specified in the **RPC_DEFAULT_ENTRY_SYNTAX** environment variable, provide **rpc_c_ns_syntax_default**.

entry_name
Specifies an entry name whose binding handles or object UUIDs are removed. This can be either the global or cell-relative name.

if_id Specifies an interface identifier for the binding handles to be removed from the name service database. The value **NULL** indicates that no binding handles are removed (only object UUIDs are removed).

vers_option
Specifies how the **rpc_ns_mgmt_binding_unexport( )** routine uses the *vers_major* and the *vers_minor* fields of the *if_id* parameter. The following table presents the accepted values for this parameter.

Uses of vers_major and vers_minor fields of if_id	
Value	**Description**
rpc_c_vers_all	Unexports (removes) all bindings for the interface UUID in *if_id*, regardless of the version numbers. For this value, specify 0 (zero) for both the major and minor versions in *if_id*.
rpc_c_vers_compatible	Removes those bindings for the interface UUID in *if_id* with the same major version as in *if_id*, and with a minor version greater than or equal to the minor version in *if_id*.
rpc_c_vers_exact	Removes those bindings for the interface UUID in *if_id* with the same major and minor versions as in *if_id*.
rpc_c_vers_major_only	Removes those bindings for the interface UUID in *if_id* with the same major version as in *if_id* (ignores the minor version). For this value, specify 0 (zero) for the minor version in *if_id*.
rpc_c_vers_upto	Removes those bindings that offer a version of the specified interface UUID less than or equal to the specified major and minor version. (For example, if *if_id* contains V2.0 and the name service entry contains binding handles with the versions V1.3, V2.0, and V2.1, the **rpc_ns-_mgmt_binding_unexport()** routine removes the binding handles with V1.3 and V2.0.)

object_uuid_vec

Specifies a vector of object UUIDs to be removed from the name service database. The application constructs this vector. The value **NULL** indicates that no object UUIDs are removed (only binding handles are removed).

Output

status Returns the status code from this routine. This status code indicates whether the routine completed successfully or, if not, why not.

The possible status codes and their meanings are as follows:

rpc_s_ok Success.

rpc_s_entry_not_found Name service entry not found.

rpc_s_incomplete_name	Incomplete name.
rpc_s_interface_not_found	Interface not found.
rpc_s_invalid_name_syntax	Invalid name syntax.
rpc_s_invalid_vers_option	Invalid version option.
rpc_s_name_service_unavailable	Name service unavailable.
rpc_s_no_ns_permission	No permission for name service operation.
rpc_s_not_all_objs_unexported	Not all objects unexported.
rpc_s_nothing_to_unexport	Nothing to unexport.
rpc_s_not_rpc_entry	Not an RPC entry.
rpc_s_unsupported_name_syntax	Unsupported name syntax.

Description

The **rpc_ns_mgmt_binding_unexport( )** routine allows a management application to unexport (that is, remove) one of the following from an entry in the name service database:

- All the binding handles for a specified interface UUID, qualified by the interface version numbers (major and minor).
- One or more object UUIDs of resources.
- Both binding handles and object UUIDs of resources.

A management application can remove an interface and objects in a single call to this routine, or it can remove them separately.

If the **rpc_ns_mgmt_binding_unexport( )** routine does not find any binding handles for the specified interface, the routine returns an **rpc_s_interface_not_found** status and does not remove the object UUIDs, if any are specified.

If one or more binding handles for the specified interface are found and removed without error, **rpc_ns_mgmt_binding_unexport( )** removes the specified object UUIDs, if any.

If any of the specified object UUIDs are not found, **rpc_ns_mgmt_binding_unexport( )** returns the **rpc_not_all_objs_unexported** status code.

A management application, in addition to calling this routine, also calls the **rpc_mgmt_ep_unregister( )** routine to remove any servers that have registered with the local endpoint map.

Use this routine with caution, only when you expect a server to be unavailable for an extended time; for example, when it is permanently removed from service.

Additionally, keep in mind that name service databases are designed to be relatively stable. In replicated name service databases, frequent use of the **rpc_ns_binding_export( )** and **rpc_ns_mgmt_binding_unexport( )** routines causes the name service to remove and replace the same entry repeatedly, and can cause performance problems.

Permissions Required

You need both read permission and write permission to the CDS object entry (the target name service entry).

Return Values

No value is returned.

Related Information

Functions: **rpc_mgmt_ep_unregister(3rpc)**, **rpc_ns_binding_export(3rpc)**, **rpc_ns_binding_unexport(3rpc)**.

rpc_ns_mgmt_entry_create

Purpose Creates an entry in the name service database

Used by management applications.

Synopsis **#include <dce/rpc.h>**

void rpc_ns_mgmt_entry_create(
unsigned32 *entry_name_syntax*,
unsigned_char_t **entry_name*,
unsigned32 **status*);

Parameters

Input

entry_name_syntax
An integer value that specifies the syntax of the *entry_name* parameter.

To use the syntax specified in the **RPC_DEFAULT_ENTRY_SYNTAX** environment variable, provide **rpc_c_ns_syntax_default**.

entry_name
Specifies the name of the entry to create. This can be either the global or cell-relative name.

Output

status Returns the status code from this routine. This status code indicates whether the routine completed successfully or, if not, why not.

The possible status codes and their meanings are as follows:

rpc_s_ok	Success.
rpc_s_entry_already_exists	Name service entry already exists.
rpc_s_incomplete_name	Incomplete name.
rpc_s_invalid_name_syntax	Invalid name syntax.
rpc_s_name_service_unavailable	Name service unavailable.

rpc_s_no_ns_permission	No permission for name service operation.
rpc_s_unsupported_name_syntax	Unsupported name syntax.

Description

The **rpc_ns_mgmt_entry_create( )** routine creates an entry in the name service database.

A management application can call **rpc_ns_mgmt_entry_create( )** to create an entry in the name service database for use by another application that does not itself have the necessary name service permissions to create an entry.

Permissions Required

You need both read permission and write permission to the CDS object entry (the target name service entry). You also need insert permission to the parent directory.

Return Values

No value is returned.

Related Information

Functions: **rpc_ns_mgmt_entry_delete(3rpc)**.

rpc_ns_mgmt_entry_delete

Purpose Deletes an entry from the name service database

Used by management applications.

Synopsis **#include <dce/rpc.h>**

void rpc_ns_mgmt_entry_delete(
unsigned32 *entry_name_syntax*,
unsigned_char_t **entry_name*,
unsigned32 **status*);

Parameters

Input

entry_name_syntax
An integer value that specifies the syntax of the *entry_name* parameter.

To use the syntax specified in the **RPC_DEFAULT_ENTRY_SYNTAX** environment variable, provide **rpc_c_ns_syntax_default**.

entry_name
Specifies the name of the entry to delete. This can be either the global or cell-relative name.

Output

status Returns the status code from this routine. This status code indicates whether the routine completed successfully or, if not, why not.

The possible status codes and their meanings are as follows:

rpc_s_ok	Success.
rpc_s_entry_not_found	Name service entry not found.
rpc_s_incomplete_name	Incomplete name.
rpc_s_invalid_name_syntax	Invalid name syntax.
rpc_s_name_service_unavailable	Name service unavailable.
rpc_s_no_ns_permission	No permission for name service operation.

rpc_s_not_rpc_entry	Not an RPC entry.
rpc_s_unsupported_name_syntax	Unsupported name syntax.

Description

The **rpc_ns_mgmt_entry_delete( )** routine removes an RPC entry from the name service database.

Management applications use this routine only when an entry is no longer needed, such as when a server is permanently removed from service. If the entry is a member of a group or profile, it must also be deleted from the group or profile.

Use this routine cautiously. Since name service databases are designed to be relatively stable, the frequent use of **rpc_ns_mgmt_entry_delete( )** can result in the following difficulties:

- Performance problems

  Creating and deleting entries in client or server applications causes the name service to remove and replace the same entry repeatedly in the name service database, which can lead to performance problems.

- Lost entry updates

  When multiple applications access a single entry through different replicas of a name service database, updates to the entry can be lost.

  In this situation, if one application deletes the entry and another application updates the entry before the replicas are synchronized, the delete operation takes precedence over the update operation. When the replicas are synchronized, the update is lost because the entry is deleted from all replicas.

Permissions Required

You need read permission to the CDS object entry (the target name service entry). You also need delete permission to the CDS object entry or to the parent directory.

Return Values

No value is returned.

Related Information

Functions: **rpc_ns_mgmt_entry_create(3rpc)**.

rpc_ns_mgmt_entry_inq_if_ids

Purpose Returns the list of interfaces exported to an entry in the name service database

Used by client, server, or management applications.

Synopsis **#include <dce/rpc.h>**

void rpc_ns_mgmt_entry_inq_if_ids(
unsigned32 *entry_name_syntax*,
unsigned_char_t **entry_name*,
rpc_if_id_vector_t ***if_id_vec*,
unsigned32 **status*);

Parameters

Input

entry_name_syntax
An integer value that specifies the syntax of argument *entry_name*.

To use the syntax specified in the **RPC_DEFAULT_ENTRY_SYNTAX** environment variable, provide **rpc_c_ns_syntax_default**.

entry_name
Specifies the entry in the name service database for which an interface identifier vector is returned. This can be either the global or cell-relative name.

Output

if_id_vec Returns the address of the interface identifier vector.

status Returns the status code from this routine, indicating whether the routine completed successfully or, if not, why not.

The possible status codes and their meanings are as follows:

rpc_s_ok	Success.
rpc_s_entry_not_found	Name service entry not found.
rpc_s_incomplete_name	Incomplete name.

rpc_s_invalid_name_syntax	Invalid name syntax.
rpc_s_name_service_unavailable	Name service unavailable.
rpc_s_no_interfaces_exported	No interfaces were exported to entry.
rpc_s_no_ns_permission	No permission for name service operation.
rpc_s_unsupported_name_syntax	Unsupported name syntax.

Description

The **rpc_ns_mgmt_entry_inq_if_ids( )** routine returns an interface identifier vector containing the interfaces of binding handles exported to argument *entry_name*.

This routine uses an expiration age of 0 (zero) to cause an immediate update of the local copy of name service data. The **rpc_ns_mgmt_inq_exp_age( )** routine's reference page contains an explanation of the expiration age.

The application calls **rpc_if_id_vector_free( )** to release memory used by the returned vector.

Permissions Required

You need read permission to the CDS object entry (the target name service entry).

Return Values

No value is returned.

Related Information

Functions: **rpc_if_id_vector_free(3rpc)**, **rpc_if_inq_id(3rpc)**, **rpc_ns_binding_export(3rpc)**.

rpc_ns_mgmt_handle_set_exp_age

Purpose Sets a handle's expiration age for local copies of name service data

Used by client, server, or management applications.

Synopsis **#include <dce/rpc.h>**

void rpc_ns_mgmt_handle_set_exp_age(
rpc_ns_handle_t *ns_handle*,
unsigned32 *expiration_age*,
unsigned32 **status*);

Parameters

Input

ns_handle

Specifies the name service handle for which you supply an expiration age. An RPC Name Service Interface (NSI) inquiry begin operation returns a name service handle. An example is the operation that **rpc_ns_entry_object_inq_begin()** performs; it returns a name service handle in its *inquiry_context* parameter.

expiration_age

This integer value specifies the expiration age, in seconds, of local name service data. This data is read by all RPC NSI next routines that use the specified *ns_handle* parameter. An example is the **rpc_ns_entry_object_inq_next()** routine; it accepts a name service handle in its *inquiry_context* parameter.

An expiration age of 0 (zero) causes an immediate update of the local name service data.

Output

status Returns the status code from this routine. This status code indicates whether the routine completed successfully or, if not, why not.

The possible status codes and their meanings are as follows:

rpc_s_ok Success.

rpc_s_invalid_ns_handle Invalid name service handle.

Description

The **rpc_ns_mgmt_handle_set_exp_age( )** routine sets an expiration age for a specified name service handle (in *ns_handle*). The expiration age is the amount of time, in seconds, that a local copy of data from a name service attribute can exist, before a request from the application for the attribute requires updating the local copy. When an application begins running, the RPC runtime specifies a random value of between 8 and 12 hours as the default expiration age. The default is global to the application. An expiration age applies only to a specific name service handle and temporarily overrides the current global expiration age.

Normally, avoid using this routine; instead, rely on the application's global expiration age.

A handle's expiration age is used exclusively by RPC NSI next operations (which read data from name service attributes). A next operation normally starts by looking for a local copy of the attribute data being requested by an application. In the absence of a local copy, the next operation creates one with fresh attribute data from the name service database. If a local copy already exists, the operation compares its actual age to the expiration age being used by the application (which in this case is the expiration age set for the name service handle). If the actual age exceeds the handle's expiration age, the operation automatically tries to update the local copy with fresh attribute data. If updating is impossible, the old local data remains in place and the next operation fails, returning the **rpc_s_name_service_unavailable** status code.

The scope of a handle's expiration age is a single series of RPC NSI next operations. The **rpc_ns_mgmt_handle_set_exp_age( )** routine operates as follows:

1. An RPC NSI begin operation, such as the one performed by **rpc_ns_group_mbr_inq_begin( )** creates a name service handle.

2. A call to **rpc_ns_mgmt_handle_set_exp_age( )** creates an expiration age for the handle.

3. A series of corresponding RPC NSI next operations for the name service handle uses the handle's expiration age.

4. A corresponding RPC NSI done operation for the name service handle deletes both the handle and its expiration age.

Permissions Required

No permissions are required.

Cautions

Use this routine with extreme caution.

Setting the handle's expiration age to a small value causes the RPC NSI next operations to frequently update local data for any name service attribute requested by your application. For example, setting the expiration age to 0 (zero) forces the next operation to update local data for the name service attribute requested by your application. Therefore, setting a small expiration age for a name service handle can create performance problems for your application. Also, if your application is using a remote server with the name service database, a small expiration age can adversely affect network performance for all applications.

Limit the use of this routine to the following types of situations:

- When you *must* always get accurate name service data.

  For example, during management operations to update a profile, you may need to always see the profile's current contents. In this case, before beginning to inquire about a profile, your application must call **rpc_ns_mgmt_handle_set_exp_age**( ) and specify 0 (zero) for the *expiration_age* parameter.

- When a request using the default expiration age fails, and your application needs to retry the operation.

  For example, a client application using import must first try to obtain bindings using the application's default expiration age. However, sometimes the import-next operation returns either no binding handles or an insufficient number of them. In this case, the client can retry the import operation and, after **rpc_ns_binding_import_begin**( ) terminates, include a **rpc_ns_mgmt_handle_set_exp_age**( ) routine that specifies 0 (zero) for the *expiration_age* parameter. When the client calls the import-next routine again, the small expiration age for the name service handle causes the import-next operation to update the local attribute data.

Return Values

No value is returned.

Related Information

Functions: **rpc_ns_binding_import_begin(3rpc)**, **rpc_ns_binding_lookup_begin(3rpc)**, **rpc_ns_entry_object_inq_begin(3rpc)**, **rpc_ns_group_mbr_inq_begin(3rpc)**, **rpc_ns_mgmt_inq_exp_age(3rpc)**, **rpc_ns_mgmt_set_exp_age(3rpc)**, **rpc_ns_profile_elt_inq_begin(3rpc)**.

rpc_ns_mgmt_inq_exp_age

Purpose Returns the application's global expiration age for local copies of name service data

Used by client, server, or management applications.

Synopsis **#include <dce/rpc.h>**

void rpc_ns_mgmt_inq_exp_age(
**unsigned32 ****expiration_age*,
**unsigned32 ****status*);

Parameters

Input

None.

Output

expiration_age
Returns the default expiration age (in seconds). All the RPC Name Service Interface (NSI) read operations (all the next operations) use this value.

status Returns the status code from this routine. This status code indicates whether the routine completed successfully or, if not, why not.

The possible status code and its meaning is as follows:

rpc_s_ok Success.

Description

The **rpc_ns_mgmt_inq_exp_age( )** routine returns the global expiration age that the application is using. The *expiration_age* parameter represents the amount of time, in seconds, that a local copy of data from a name service attribute can exist before a request from the application for the attribute requires updating the local copy. When an application begins running, the RPC runtime specifies a random value of between 8 and 12 hours as the default expiration age. The default is global to the application.

The RPC NSI next operations, which read data from name service attributes, use an expiration age. A next operation normally starts by looking for a local copy of the attribute data that an application requests. In the absence of a local copy, the next operation creates one with fresh attribute data from the name service database. If a local copy already exists, the operation compares its actual age to the expiration age being used by the application. If the actual age exceeds the expiration age, the operation automatically tries to update the local copy with fresh attribute data from the name service database. If updating is impossible, the old local data remains in place and the next operation fails, returning the **rpc_s_name_service_unavailable** status code.

Applications normally use only the default expiration age. For special cases, an application can substitute a user-supplied global expiration age for the default by calling **rpc_ns_mgmt_set_exp_age( )**. The **rpc_ns_mgmt_inq_exp_age( )** routine returns the current global expiration age, whether it is a default or a user-supplied value.

An application can also override the global expiration age temporarily by calling **rpc_ns_mgmt_handle_set_exp_age( )**.

Permissions Required

No permissions are required.

Return Values

No value is returned.

Related Information

Functions: **rpc_ns_mgmt_handle_set_exp_age(3rpc)**, **rpc_ns_mgmt_set_exp_age(3rpc)**.

rpc_ns_mgmt_set_exp_age

Purpose Modifies the application's global expiration age for local copies of name service data

Used by client, server, or management applications.

Synopsis **#include <dce/rpc.h>**

void rpc_ns_mgmt_set_exp_age(
    unsigned32 *expiration_age*,
    unsigned32 **status*);

Parameters

Input

expiration_age
An integer value that specifies the default expiration age, in seconds, for local name service data. This expiration age applies to all RPC name service interface (NSI) read operations (all the next operations).

An expiration age of 0 (zero) causes an immediate update of the local name service data.

To reset the expiration age to an RPC-assigned random value between 8 and 12 hours, specify a value of **rpc_c_ns_default_exp_age**.

Output

status Returns the status code from this routine. This status code indicates whether the routine completed successfully or, if not, why not.

The possible status code and its meaning is as follows:

rpc_s_ok Success.

Description

The **rpc_ns_mgmt_set_exp_age()** routine modifies the global expiration age that the application is using. The *expiration_age* parameter represents the amount of time, in seconds, that a local copy of data from a name service attribute can exist before a request from the application for the attribute requires updating the local copy. When an application begins running, the RPC runtime specifies a random value of between 8 and 12 hours as the default expiration age. The default is global to the application.

Normally, you should avoid using this routine; instead, rely on the default expiration age.

The RPC NSI next operations, which read data from name service attributes, use an expiration age. A next operation normally starts by looking for a local copy of the attribute data that an application requests. In the absence of a local copy, the next operation creates one with fresh attribute data from the name service database. If a local copy already exists, the operation compares its actual age to the expiration age being used by the application. If the actual age exceeds the expiration age, the operation automatically tries to update the local copy with fresh attribute data from the name service database. If updating is impossible, the old local data remains in place and the next operation fails, returning the **rpc_s_name_service_unavailable** status code.

Permissions Required

No permissions are required.

Cautions

Use this routine with extreme caution.

Setting the expiration age to a small value causes the RPC NSI next operations to frequently update local data for any name service attribute that your application requests. For example, setting the expiration age to 0 (zero) forces all next operations to update local data for the name service attribute that your application has requested. Therefore, setting small expiration ages can create performance problems for your application. Also, if your application is using a remote server with the name service database, a small expiration age can adversely affect network performance for all applications.

Return Values

No value is returned.

Related Information

Functions: **rpc_ns_mgmt_handle_set_exp_age(3rpc)**, **rpc_ns_mgmt_set_exp_age(3rpc)**.

rpc_ns_profile_delete

Purpose

Deletes a profile attribute

Used by client, server, or management applications.

Synopsis

#include <dce/rpc.h>

void rpc_ns_profile_delete(
  unsigned32 *profile_name_syntax*,
  unsigned_char_t **profile_name*,
  unsigned32 **status*);

Parameters

Input

profile_name_syntax
An integer value that specifies the syntax of the *profile_name* parameter.

To use the syntax specified in the **RPC_DEFAULT_ENTRY_SYNTAX** environment variable, provide **rpc_c_ns_syntax_default**.

profile_name
Specifies the name of the profile to delete. This can be either the global or cell-relative name.

Output

status Returns the status code from this routine. This status code indicates whether the routine completed successfully or, if not, why not.

The possible status codes and their meanings are as follows:

rpc_s_ok	Success.
rpc_s_entry_not_found	Name service entry not found.
rpc_s_incomplete_name	Incomplete name.
rpc_s_invalid_name_syntax	Invalid name syntax.
rpc_s_name_service_unavailable	Name service unavailable.

rpc_s_no_ns_permission	No permission for name service operation.
rpc_s_unsupported_name_syntax	Unsupported name syntax.

Description

The **rpc_ns_profile_delete( )** routine deletes the profile attribute from the specified entry in the name service database (the *profile_name* parameter).

Neither the specified entry nor the entry names included as members in each profile element are deleted.

Use this routine cautiously; deleting a profile may break a hierarchy of profiles.

Permissions Required

You need write permission to the CDS object entry (the target profile entry).

Return Values

No value is returned.

Related Information

Functions: **rpc_ns_profile_elt_add(3rpc)**, **rpc_ns_profile_elt_remove(3rpc)**.

rpc_ns_profile_elt_add

Purpose Adds an element to a profile; if necessary, creates the entry

Used by client, server, or management applications.

Synopsis **#include <dce/rpc.h>**

void rpc_ns_profile_elt_add(
unsigned32 *profile_name_syntax*,
unsigned_char_t **profile_name*,
rpc_if_id_t **if_id*,
unsigned32 *member_name_syntax*,
unsigned_char_t **member_name*,
unsigned32 *priority*,
unsigned_char_t **annotation*,
unsigned32 **status***);**

Parameters

Input

profile_name_syntax
An integer value that specifies the syntax of the *profile_name* parameter.

To use the syntax specified in the **RPC_DEFAULT_ENTRY_SYNTAX** environment variable, provide **rpc_c_ns_syntax_default**.

profile_name
Specifies the RPC profile that receives a new element. This can be either the global or cell-relative name.

if_id Specifies the interface identifier of the new profile element. To add or replace the default profile element, specify **NULL**.

member_name_syntax
An integer value that specifies the syntax of *member_name*.

To use the syntax specified in the **RPC_DEFAULT_ENTRY_SYNTAX** environment variable, provide **rpc_c_ns_syntax_default**.

member_name
Specifies the entry in the name service database to include in the new profile element. This can be either the global or cell-relative name.

priority An integer value (0 to 7) that specifies the relative priority for using the new profile element during the import and lookup operations. A value of 0 (zero) is the highest priority. A value of 7 is the lowest priority. Two or more elements can have the same priority.

When adding the default profile member, use a value of 0 (zero).

annotation

Specifies an annotation string that is stored as part of the new profile element. The string can be up to 17 characters long. Specify **NULL** or the string **\0** if there is no annotation string.

The string is used by applications for informational purposes only. For example, an application can use this string to store the interface name string (specified in the IDL file).

DCE RPC does not use this string during lookup or import operations, or for enumerating profile elements.

Output

status Returns the status code from this routine. This status code indicates whether the routine completed successfully or, if not, why not.

The possible status codes and their meanings are as follows:

rpc_s_ok	Success.
rpc_s_class_version_mismatch	RPC class version mismatch.
rpc_s_incomplete_name	Incomplete name.
rpc_s_invalid_name_syntax	Invalid name syntax.
rpc_s_invalid_priority	Invalid profile element priority.
rpc_s_name_service_unavailable	Name service unavailable.
rpc_s_no_ns_permission	No permission for name service operation.
rpc_s_unsupported_name_syntax	Unsupported name syntax.

Description

The **rpc_ns_profile_elt_add( )** routine adds an element to the profile attribute of the entry in the name service database specified by the *profile_name* parameter.

If the *profile_name* entry does not exist, this routine creates the entry with a profile attribute and adds the profile element specified by the *if_id*, *member_name*, *priority*, and *annotation* parameters. In this case, the application must have permission to create the entry. Otherwise, a management application with the necessary permissions creates the entry by calling **rpc_ns_mgmt_entry_create( )** before the application is run.

If an element with the specified member name and interface identifier are already in the profile, this routine updates the element's priority and annotation string using the values provided in the *priority* and *annotation* parameters.

An application can add the entry in the *member_name* parameter to a profile before it creates the entry itself.

Permissions Required

You need both read permission and write permission to the CDS object entry (the target profile entry). If the entry does not exist, you also need insert permission to the parent directory.

Return Values

No value is returned.

Related Information

Functions: **rpc_if_inq_id(3rpc)**, **rpc_ns_mgmt_entry_create(3rpc)**, **rpc_ns_profile_elt_remove(3rpc)**.

rpc_ns_profile_elt_inq_begin

Purpose Creates an inquiry context for viewing the elements in a profile

Used by client, server, or management applications.

Synopsis **#include <dce/rpc.h>**

void rpc_ns_profile_elt_inq_begin(
unsigned32 *profile_name_syntax*,
unsigned_char_t **profile_name*,
unsigned32 *inquiry_type*,
rpc_if_id_t **if_id*,
unsigned32 *vers_option*,
unsigned32 *member_name_syntax*,
unsigned_char_t **member_name*,
rpc_ns_handle_t **inquiry_context*,
unsigned32 **status*);

Parameters

Input

profile_name_syntax
An integer value that specifies the syntax of the *profile_name* parameter.

To use the syntax specified in the **RPC_DEFAULT_ENTRY_SYNTAX** environment variable, provide **rpc_c_ns_syntax_default**.

profile_name
Specifies the name of the profile to view. This can be either the global or cell-relative name.

inquiry_type
An integer value that specifies the type of inquiry to perform on the profile. The following table describes the valid inquiry types.

Valid Values of *inquiry_ type*	
Value	**Description**
rpc_c_profile_default_elt	Searches the profile for the default profile element, if any. The *if_id*, *vers_option*, and *member_name* parameters are ignored.
rpc_c_profile_all_elts	Returns every element from the profile. The *if_id*, *vers_option*, and *member_name* parameters are ignored.
rpc_c_profile_match_by_if	Searches the profile for those elements that contain the interface identifier specified by the *if_id* and *vers_option* values. The *member_name* parameter is ignored.
rpc_c_profile_match_by_mbr	Searches the profile for those elements that contain the member name specified by the *member_name* parameter. The *if_id* and *vers_option* parameters are ignored.
rpc_c_profile_match_by_both	Searches the profile for those elements that contain the interface identifier and member name specified by the *if_id*, *vers_option*, and *member_name* parameters.

if_id Specifies the interface identifier of the profile elements to be returned by **rpc_ns_profile_elt_inq_next( )**.

This parameter is used only when specifying a value of either **rpc_c_profile_match_by_if** or **rpc_c_profile_match_by_both** for the *inquiry_type* parameter. Otherwise, this parameter is ignored and you can specify the value **NULL**.

vers_option

Specifies how **rpc_ns_profile_elt_inq_next( )** uses the *if_id* parameter.

This parameter is used only when specifying a value of either **rpc_c_profile_match_by_if** or **rpc_c_profile_match_by_both** for the *inquiry_type* parameter. Otherwise, this parameter is ignored and you can specify the value 0 (zero). The following table describes the valid values for this parameter.

Valid Values of *vers_option*	
Value	**Description**
rpc_c_vers_all	Returns profile elements that offer the specified interface UUID, regardless of the version numbers. For this value, specify 0 (zero) for both the major and minor versions in *if_id*.
rpc_c_vers_compatible	Returns profile elements that offer the same major version of the specified interface UUID and a minor version greater than or equal to the minor version of the specified interface UUID.
rpc_c_vers_exact	Returns profile elements that offer the specified version of the specified interface UUID.
rpc_c_vers_major_only	Returns profile elements that offer the same major version of the specified interface UUID (ignores the minor version). For this value, specify 0 (zero) for the minor version in *if_id*.
rpc_c_vers_upto	Returns profile elements that offer a version of the specified interface UUID less than or equal to the specified major and minor version. (For example, if *if_id* contains V2.0 and the profile contains elements with the versions V1.3, V2.0, and V2.1, **rpc_ns_profile_elt_inq_next()** returns the elements with V1.3 and V2.0.)

member_name_syntax

An integer value that specifies the syntax of the *member_name* parameter in this routine and the syntax of the *member_name* parameter in **rpc_ns_profile_elt_inq_next( )**.

To use the syntax specified in the **RPC_DEFAULT_ENTRY_SYNTAX** environment variable, provide **rpc_c_ns_syntax_default**.

member_name

Specifies the member name that **rpc_ns_profile_elt_inq_next( )** looks for in profile elements. This can be either the global or cell-relative name.

This parameter is used only when specifying a value of either **rpc_c_profile_match_by_mbr** or **rpc_c_profile_match_by_both** for the *inquiry_type* parameter. Otherwise, this parameter is ignored and you specify the value **NULL**.

Output

inquiry_context
Returns a name service handle for use with the **rpc_ns_profile_elt_inq_next( )** and **rpc_ns_profile_elt_inq_done( )** routines.

status Returns the status code from this routine. This status code indicates whether the routine completed successfully or, if not, why not.

The possible status codes and their meanings are as follows:

rpc_s_ok	Success.
rpc_s_incomplete_name	Incomplete name.
rpc_s_invalid_inquiry_type	Invalid inquiry type.
rpc_s_invalid_name_syntax	Invalid name syntax.
rpc_s_invalid_vers_option	Invalid version option.
rpc_s_unsupported_name_syntax	Unsupported name syntax.

Description

The **rpc_ns_profile_elt_inq_begin( )** routine creates an inquiry context for viewing the elements in a profile.

Using the *inquiry_type* and *vers_option* parameters, an application specifies which of the following profile elements will be returned from calls to **rpc_ns_profile_elt_inq_next( )**:

- The default element.
- All elements.
- Those elements with the specified interface identifier.
- Those elements with the specified member name.
- Those elements with both the specified interface identifier and member name.

Before calling **rpc_ns_profile_elt_inq_next( )**, the application must first call this routine to create an inquiry context.

When finished viewing the profile elements, the application calls the **rpc_ns_profile_elt_inq_done**( ) routine to delete the inquiry context.

Permissions Required

No permissions are required.

Return Values

No value is returned.

Related Information

Functions: **rpc_if_inq_id(3rpc)**, **rpc_ns_mgmt_handle_set_exp_age(3rpc)**, **rpc_ns_profile_elt_inq_done(3rpc)**, **rpc_ns_profile_elt_inq_next(3rpc)**.

rpc_ns_profile_elt_inq_done

Purpose Deletes the inquiry context for a profile

Used by client, server, or management applications.

Synopsis **#include <dce/rpc.h>**

void rpc_ns_profile_elt_inq_done(
rpc_ns_handle_t ******inquiry_context*,
unsigned32 ******status*);

Parameters

Input/Output

inquiry_context
Specifies the name service handle to delete. (A name service handle is created by calling **rpc_ns_profile_elt_inq_begin( )**.)

Returns the value **NULL**.

Output

status Returns the status code from this routine. This status code indicates whether the routine completed successfully or, if not, why not.

The possible status codes and their meanings are as follows:

rpc_s_ok	Success.
rpc_s_invalid_ns_handle	Invalid name service handle.

Description

The **rpc_ns_profile_elt_inq_done( )** routine deletes an inquiry context created by calling **rpc_ns_profile_elt_inq_begin( )**.

An application calls this routine after viewing profile elements using the **rpc_ns_profile_elt_inq_next( )** routine.

Permissions Required

No permissions are required.

Return Values

No value is returned.

Related Information

Functions: **rpc_ns_profile_elt_inq_begin(3rpc)**, **rpc_ns_profile_elt_inq_next(3rpc)**.

rpc_ns_profile_elt_inq_next

Purpose Returns one element at a time from a profile

Used by client, server, or management applications.

Synopsis **#include <dce/rpc.h>**

void rpc_ns_profile_elt_inq_next(
rpc_ns_handle_t *inquiry_context*,
rpc_if_id_t **if_id*,
unsigned_char_t ***member_name*,
unsigned32 **priority*,
unsigned_char_t ***annotation*,
unsigned32 **status*);

Parameters

Input

inquiry_context
Specifies a name service handle. This handle is returned from the **rpc_ns_profile_elt_inq_begin( )** routine.

Output

if_id Returns the interface identifier of the profile element.

member_name
Returns a pointer to the profile element's member name. The name is a global name.

The syntax of the returned name is specified by the *member_name_syntax* parameter in **rpc_ns_profile_elt_inq_begin( )**.

Specify **NULL** to prevent the routine from returning this parameter. In this case the application does not call **rpc_string_free( )**.

priority Returns the profile element priority.

annotation
Returns the annotation string for the profile element. If there is no annotation string in the profile element, the string **\0** is returned.

Specify **NULL** to prevent the routine from returning this parameter. In this case the application does not need to call **rpc_string_free( )**.

status Returns the status code from this routine. This status code indicates whether the routine completed successfully or, if not, why not.

The possible status codes and their meanings are as follows:

rpc_s_ok	Success.
rpc_s_class_version_mismatch	RPC class version mismatch.
rpc_s_entry_not_found	Name service entry not found.
rpc_s_incomplete_name	Incomplete name.
rpc_s_invalid_ns_handle	Invalid name service handle.
rpc_s_name_service_unavailable	Name service unavailable.
rpc_s_no_more_elements	No more elements.
rpc_s_no_ns_permission	No permission for name service operation.
rpc_s_not_rpc_entry	Not an RPC entry.

Description

The **rpc_ns_profile_elt_inq_next( )** routine returns one element from the profile specified by the *profile_name* parameter in the **rpc_ns_profile_elt_inq_begin( )** routine.

The selection criteria for the element returned are based on the *inquiry_type* parameter in the **rpc_ns_profile_elt_inq_begin( )** routine. The **rpc_ns_profile_elt_inq_next( )** routine returns all the components (interface identifier, member name, priority, annotation string) of a profile element.

An application can view all the selected profile entries by repeatedly calling the **rpc_ns_profile_elt_inq_next( )** routine. When all the elements have been viewed, this routine returns an **rpc_s_no_more_elements** status code. The returned elements are unordered.

On each call to this routine that returns a profile element, the DCE RPC runtime allocates memory for the returned *member_name* (which points to a global name) and *annotation* strings. The application is responsible for calling the **rpc_string_free( )** routine for each returned *member_name* and *annotation* string.

After viewing the profile's elements, the application must call the **rpc_ns_profile_elt_inq_done( )** routine to delete the inquiry context.

Permissions Required

You need read permission to the CDS object entry (the target profile entry).

Return Values

No value is returned.

Related Information

Functions: **rpc_ns_profile_elt_begin(3rpc)**, **rpc_ns_profile_elt_done(3rpc)**, **rpc_string_free(3rpc)**.

rpc_ns_profile_elt_remove

Purpose Removes an element from a profile

Used by client, server, or management applications.

Synopsis **#include <dce/rpc.h>**

void rpc_ns_profile_elt_remove(
unsigned32 *profile_name_syntax*,
unsigned_char_t **profile_name*,
rpc_if_id_t **if_id***L*,
unsigned32 *member_name_syntax*,
unsigned_char_t **member_name*,
unsigned32 **status*);

Parameters

Input

profile_name_syntax
An integer value that specifies the syntax of the *profile_name* parameter. To use the syntax specified in the **RPC_DEFAULT_ENTRY_SYNTAX** environment variable, provide **rpc_c_ns_syntax_default**.

profile_name
Specifies the profile from which to remove an element. This can be either the global or cell-relative name.

if_id Specifies the interface identifier of the profile element to be removed. Specify **NULL** to remove the default profile member.

member_name_syntax
An integer value that specifies the syntax of *member_name*. To use the syntax specified in the **RPC_DEFAULT_ENTRY_SYNTAX** environment variable, provide **rpc_c_ns_syntax_default**.

member_name
Specifies the name service entry name in the profile element to remove. This can be either the global or cell-relative name.

Output

status Returns the status code from this routine. This status code indicates whether the routine completed successfully or, if not, why not.

The possible status codes and their meanings are as follows:

rpc_s_ok	Success.
rpc_s_entry_not_found	Name service entry not found.
rpc_s_incomplete_name	Incomplete name.
rpc_s_invalid_name_syntax	Invalid name syntax.
rpc_s_name_service_unavailable	Name service unavailable.
rpc_s_no_ns_permission	No permission for name service operation.
rpc_s_profile_element_not_found	Profile element not found.
rpc_s_unsupported_name_syntax	Unsupported name syntax.

Description

The **rpc_ns_profile_elt_remove( )** routine removes a profile element from the profile attribute in the *profile_name* entry. Note that the *member_name* parameter and the *if_id* parameter must match exactly for an element to be removed.

The entry (*member_name*) referred to as a member in the profile element is not deleted.

Use this routine cautiously; removing elements from a profile may break a hierarchy of profiles.

Permissions Required

You need both read permission and write permission to the CDS object entry (the target profile entry).

Return Values

No value is returned.

Related Information

Functions: **rpc_ns_profile_delete(3rpc)**, **rpc_ns_profile_elt_add(3rpc)**.

rpc_ns_set_authn

Purpose Turns authentication on and off for RPC name service routines

Used by client, server, or management applications.

Synopsis **#include <dce/rpc.h>**

void rpc_ns_set_authn
  boolean32 *authn*,
  boolean32 * *previous_authn*,
  **unsigned32 ***status*);

Parameters

Input

authn Specifies whether authentication should be on or off during subsequent calls of name service routines from the calling thread. The value TRUE means to turn on authentication. The value FALSE means to turn off authentication.

Output

previous_authn
A Boolean value that returns the previous value of the *authn* parameter for the calling thread. The value TRUE means that authentication was on. The value FALSE means that authentication was off.

status Returns the status code from this routine. This status code indicates whether the routine completed successfully or, if not, why not.

The possible status code and its meaning is as follows:

rpc_s_ok Success.

Description

By default, authentication is turned on for all RPC name service routines. The names of these routines begin with **rpc_ns_**.

An application calls **rpc_ns_set_authn( )** to turn authentication on or off for subsequent calls to RPC name service routines. The authentication behavior that **rpc_ns_set_authn( )** sets applies only to the thread that called the routine.

An application can use the **rpc_ns_set_authn( )** routine so that subsequent calls to **rpc_ns_*( )** routines might succeed. However, success will occur only if both of the following conditions are true:

- Security services are not available.
- The name service is not using the security services.

Permissions Required

No permissions are required.

Return Values

No value is returned.

Related Information

Functions: **rpc_ns_*(3rpc)**.

rpc_object_inq_type

Purpose Returns the type of an object

Used by server applications.

Synopsis **#include <dce/rpc.h>**

void rpc_object_inq_type(
uuid_t **obj_uuid*,
uuid_t **type_uuid*,
unsigned32 **status*);

Parameters

Input

obj_uuid Specifies the object UUID whose associated type UUID is returned. Supply **NULL** to specify a nil UUID for this parameter.

Output

type_uuid Returns the type UUID corresponding to the object UUID supplied in the *obj_uuid* parameter.

Specifying **NULL** here prevents the return of a type UUID. An application, by specifying **NULL** here, can determine from the value returned in *status* whether *obj_uuid* is registered. This determination occurs without the application specifying an output type UUID variable.

status Returns the status code from this routine. This status code indicates whether the routine completed successfully or, if not, why not.

The possible status codes and their meanings are as follows:

rpc_s_ok	Success.
rpc_s_object_not_found	Object not found.
uuid_s_bad_version	Bad UUID version.

Description

A server application calls the **rpc_object_inq_type( )** routine to obtain the type UUID of an object.

If the object is registered with the RPC runtime using the **rpc_object_set_type( )** routine, the registered type is returned.

Optionally, an application can maintain an object/type registration privately. In this case, if the application provides an object inquiry function (see the **rpc_object_set_inq_fn(3rpc)** reference page), the RPC runtime uses that function to determine an object's type.

The table below shows how **rpc_object_inq_type( )** obtains the returned type UUID.

Rules for Returning an Object's Type		
Was object UUID registered (using rpc_object_set_type)?	**Was an object inquiry function registered(using rpc_object_set_inq_fn)?**	**Return Value**
Yes	Ignored	Returns the object's registered type UUID.
No	Yes	Returns the type UUID returned from calling the inquiry function.
No	No	Returns the nil UUID.

Return Values

No value is returned.

Related Information

Functions: **rpc_object_set_inq_fn(3rpc)**, **rpc_object_set_type(3rpc)**.

rpc_object_set_inq_fn

Purpose Registers an object inquiry function

Used by server applications.

Synopsis **#include <dce/rpc.h>**

void rpc_object_set_inq_fn(
rpc_object_inq_fn_t *inquiry_fn*,
unsigned32 ***status*);**

Parameters

Input

inquiry_fn Specifies a pointer to an object type inquiry function. When an application calls the **rpc_object_inq_type( )** routine and the RPC runtime finds that the specified object is not registered, the runtime automatically calls the **rpc_object_inq_type( )** routine to determine the object's type. Specify **NULL** to remove a previously set inquiry function.

The following C language definition for **rpc_object_inq_fn_t** illustrates the prototype for this function:

```
typedef void (*rpc_object_inq_fn_t)
        (
          uuid_t      *object_uuid, /* in */
          uuid_t      *type_uuid,   /* out */
          unsigned32  *status       /* out */
        );
```

The returned **type_uuid** and **status** values are returned as the output arguments from the **rpc_object_inq_type( )** routine.

If you specify **NULL**, the **rpc_object_set_inq_fn( )** routine unregisters (that is, removes) a previously registered object type inquiry function.

Output

status Returns the status code from this routine. This status code indicates whether the routine completed successfully or, if not, why not.

The possible status code and its meaning is as follows:

rpc_s_ok Success.

Description

A server application calls **rpc_object_set_inq_fn( )** to specify a function to determine an object's type. If an application privately maintains object/type registrations, the specified inquiry function returns the type UUID of an object from that registration.

The RPC runtime automatically calls the inquiry function when the application calls **rpc_object_inq_type( )** and the object was not previously registered by **rpc_object_set_type( )**. The RPC runtime also automatically calls the inquiry function for every remote procedure call it receives if the object was not previously registered.

Cautions

Use this routine with caution. When the RPC runtime automatically calls this routine in response to a received remote procedure call, the inquiry function can be called from the context of runtime internal threads with runtime internal locks held. The inquiry function should not block or at least not block for long (for example, the inquiry function should not perform a remote procedure call). Also, the inquiry function must not unwind because of an exception. In general, the inquiry function should not call back into the RPC runtime. It is legal to call **rpc_object_set_type( )** or any of the **uuid_*** routines. Failure to comply with these restrictions will result in undefined behavior.

Return Values

No value is returned.

Related Information

Functions: **rpc_object_inq_type(3rpc)**, **rpc_object_set_type(3rpc)**.

rpc_object_set_type

Purpose Registers the type of an object with the RPC runtime

Used by server applications.

Synopsis **#include <dce/rpc.h>**

void rpc_object_set_type(
uuid_t **obj_uuid*,
uuid_t **type_uuid*,
unsigned32 **status*);

Parameters

Input

obj_uuid Specifies an object UUID to associate with the type UUID in the *type_uuid* parameter. Do not specify **NULL** or a nil UUID.

type_uuid
Specifies the type UUID of the *obj_uuid* parameter.

Specify an argument value of **NULL** or a nil UUID to reset the object type to the default association of object UUID/nil type UUID.

Output

status Returns the status code from this routine. This status code indicates whether the routine completed successfully or, if not, why not.

The possible status codes and their meanings are as follows:

rpc_s_ok	Success.
rpc_s_already_registered	Object already registered.
rpc_s_invalid_object	Invalid object.
uuid_s_bad_version	Bad UUID version.

Description

The **rpc_object_set_type( )** routine assigns a type UUID to an object UUID.

By default, the RPC runtime assumes that the type of all objects is nil. A server program that contains one implementation of an interface (one manager entry point vector) does not need to call this routine, provided that the server registered the interface with the nil type UUID (see the **rpc_server_register_if(3rpc)** reference page).

A server program that contains multiple implementations of an interface (multiple manager entry point vectors; that is, multiple type UUIDs) calls this routine once for each object UUID the server offers. Associating each object with a type UUID tells the RPC runtime which manager entry point vector (interface implementation) to use when the server receives a remote procedure call for a non-nil object UUID.

The RPC runtime allows an application to set the type for an unlimited number of objects.

To remove the association between an object UUID and its type UUID (established by calling this routine), a server calls this routine again and specifies the value **NULL** or a nil UUID for the *type_uuid* parameter. This resets the association between an object UUID and type UUID to the default.

A server cannot register a nil object UUID. The RPC runtime automatically registers the nil object UUID with a nil type UUID. Attempting to set the type of a nil object UUID will result in the routine's returning the status code **rpc_s_invalid_object**.

Servers that want to maintain their own object UUID to type UUID mapping can use **rpc_object_set_inq_fn( )** in place of, or in addition to, **rpc_object_set_type( )**.

Return Values

No value is returned.

Related Information

Functions: **rpc_object_set_inq_fn(3rpc)**, **rpc_server_register_if(3rpc)**.

rpc_protseq_vector_free

Purpose Frees the memory used by a vector and its protocol sequences

Used by client or server applications.

Synopsis **#include <dce/rpc.h>**

void rpc_protseq_vector_free(
rpc_protseq_vector_t ***protseq_vector*,**
unsigned32 **status*);**

Parameters

Input/Output

protseq_vector
Specifies the address of a pointer to a vector of protocol sequences. On return the pointer is set to **NULL**.

Output

status Returns the status code from this routine. This status code indicates whether the routine completed successfully or, if not, why not.

The possible status code and its meaning is as follows:

rpc_s_ok Success.

Description

The **rpc_protseq_vector_free( )** routine frees the memory used to store a vector of protocol sequences. The freed memory includes both the protocol sequences and the vector itself.

Call **rpc_network_inq_protseqs( )** to obtain a vector of protocol sequences. Follow a call to **rpc_network_inq_protseqs( )** with a call to **rpc_protseq_vector_free( )**.

Return Values

No value is returned.

Related Information

Functions: **rpc_network_inq_protseqs(3rpc)**.

rpc_server_inq_bindings

Purpose Returns binding handles for communications with a server

Used by server applications.

Synopsis **#include <dce/rpc.h>**

void rpc_server_inq_bindings(
rpc_binding_vector_t ***binding_vector*,
unsigned32 **status*);

Parameters

Input

None.

Output

binding_vector Returns the address of a vector of server binding handles.

status Returns the status code from this routine. This status code indicates whether the routine completed successfully or, if not, why not.

The possible status codes and their meanings are as follows:

rpc_s_ok	Success.
rpc_s_no_bindings	No bindings.

Description

The **rpc_server_inq_bindings( )** routine obtains a vector of server binding handles. Binding handles are created by the RPC runtime when a server application calls any of the following routines to register protocol sequences:

- **rpc_server_use_all_protseqs( )**
- **rpc_server_use_all_protseqs_if( )**
- **rpc_server_use_protseq( )**

- **rpc_server_use_protseq_ep( )**
- **rpc_server_use_protseq_if( )**

The returned binding vector can contain binding handles with dynamic endpoints and binding handles with well-known endpoints, depending on which of the preceding routines the server application called. The **intro(3rpc)** reference page contains an explanation of dynamic and well-known endpoints.

A server uses the vector of binding handles for exporting to the name service, for registering with the local endpoint map, or for conversion to string bindings.

If there are no binding handles (no registered protocol sequences), this routine returns the **rpc_s_no_bindings** status code and returns the value **NULL** to the *binding_vector* parameter.

The server is responsible for calling the **rpc_binding_vector_free( )** routine to deallocate the memory used by the vector.

Return Values

No value is returned.

Related Information

Functions: **rpc_binding_vector_free(3rpc)**, **rpc_ep_register(3rpc)**, **rpc_ep_register_no_replace(3rpc)**, **rpc_ns_binding_export(3rpc)**, **rpc_server_use_all_protseqs(3rpc)**, **rpc_server_use_all_protseqs_if(3rpc)**, **rpc_server_use_protseq(3rpc)**, **rpc_server_use_protseq_ep(3rpc)**, **rpc_server_use_protseq_if(3rpc)**.

rpc_server_inq_if

Purpose

Returns the manager entry point vector registered for an interface

Used by server applications.

Synopsis

#include <dce/rpc.h>

void rpc_server_inq_if(
rpc_if_handle_t *if_handle***,**
uuid_t ****mgr_type_uuid*,**
rpc_mgr_epv_t ****mgr_epv*,**
unsigned32 ****status*);**

Parameters

Input

if_handle Specifies the interface specification whose manager Entry Point Vector (EPV) pointer is returned in the *mgr_epv* parameter.

mgr_type_uuid
Specifies a type UUID for the manager whose EPV pointer is returned in the *mgr_epv* parameter.

Specifying the value **NULL** (or a nil UUID) has this routine return a pointer to the manager EPV that is registered with *if_handle* and the nil type UUID of the manager.

Output

mgr_epv Returns a pointer to the manager EPV corresponding to *if_handle* and *mgr_type_uuid.*

status Returns the status code from this routine. This status code indicates whether the routine completed successfully or, if not, why not.

The possible status codes and their meanings are as follows:

rpc_s_ok	Success.
rpc_s_unknown_if	Unknown interface.
rpc_s_unknown_mgr_type	Unknown manager type.

Description

A server application calls the **rpc_server_inq_if( )** routine to determine the manager EPV for a registered interface and type UUID of the manager.

Return Values

No value is returned.

Related Information

Functions: **rpc_server_register_if(3rpc)**.

rpc_server_listen

Purpose Tells the RPC runtime to listen for remote procedure calls

Used by server applications.

Synopsis **#include <dce/rpc.h>**

void rpc_server_listen(
    unsigned32 *max_calls_exec*,
    unsigned32 **status*);

Parameters

Input

max_calls_exec

Specifies the maximum number of concurrent executing remote procedure calls.

Use the value **rpc_c_listen_max_calls_default** to specify the default value.

Also, the five **rpc_server_use_*protseq*** routines limit (according to their *max_call_requests* parameter) the number of concurrent remote procedure call requests that a server can accept.

Output

status Returns the status code from this routine. This status code indicates whether the routine completed successfully or, if not, why not.

The possible status codes and their meanings are as follows:

rpc_s_ok	Success.
rpc_s_already_listening	Server already listening.
rpc_s_max_calls_too_small	Maximum calls value too small.
rpc_s_no_protseqs_registered	No protocol sequences registered.

Description

The **rpc_server_listen( )** routine makes a server listen for remote procedure calls. DCE RPC allows a server to simultaneously process multiple calls. The *max_calls_exec* parameter specifies the maximum number of concurrent remote procedure calls the server executes. Each remote procedure call executes in a call execution thread. The implementation of the RPC architecture determines whether it reuses call execution threads for the execution of subsequent remote procedure calls or, instead, it creates a new thread for each execution of a subsequent remote procedure call.

The following conditions affect the number of concurrent remote procedure calls that a server can process:

- Sufficient network resources must be available to accept simultaneous call requests arriving over a particular protocol sequence. The value of *max_call_requests* in the five **rpc_server_use_*protseq*** routines advises the RPC runtime about the runtime's request of network resources.
- Enough call threads must be available to execute the simultaneous call requests once they have been accepted. The value of *max_calls_exec* in **rpc_server_listen( )** specifies the number of call threads.

These conditions are independent of each other.

A server application that specifies a value for *max_calls_exec* greater than 1 is responsible for concurrency control among the remote procedures since each executes in a separate thread.

If the server receives more remote procedure calls than it can execute (more calls than the value of *max_calls_exec*), the RPC runtime accepts and queues additional remote procedure calls until a call execution thread is available. From the client's perspective, a queued remote procedure call appears the same as one that the server is actively executing. A client call remains blocked and in the queue until any one of the following events occurs:

- The remote procedure call is assigned to an available call execution thread and the call runs to completion.
- The client no longer can communicate with the server.
- The client thread is canceled and the remote procedure call does not complete within the cancel time-out limits.

The implementation of the RPC architecture determines the amount of queuing it provides.

The RPC runtime continues listening for remote procedure calls (that is, the routine does not return to the server) until one of the following events occurs:

- One of the server application's manager routines calls **rpc_mgmt_stop_server_listening( )**.
- A client is allowed to, and makes, a remote **rpc_mgmt_stop_server_listening( )** call to the server.

On receiving a request to stop listening, the RPC runtime stops accepting new remote procedure calls for all registered interfaces. Executing calls and existing queued calls are allowed to complete.

After all calls complete, **rpc_server_listen( )** returns to the caller, which is a server application.

For more information about a server's listening for and handling incoming remote procedure calls, refer to the *OSF DCE Application Development Guide*. It also contains information about canceled threads.

Return Values

No value is returned.

Related Information

Functions: **rpc_mgmt_server_stop_listening(3rpc)**, **rpc_server_register_if(3rpc)**, **rpc_server_use_all_protseqs(3rpc)**, **rpc_server_use_all_protseqs_if(3rpc)**, **rpc_server_use_protseq(3rpc)**, **rpc_server_use_protseq_ep(3rpc)**, **rpc_server_use_protseq_if(3rpc)**.

Books: *OSF DCE Application Development Guide.*

rpc_server_register_auth_info

Purpose Registers authentication information with the RPC runtime

Used by server applications.

Synopsis **#include <dce/rpc.h>**

void rpc_server_register_auth_info(
unsigned_char_t **server_princ_name*,
unsigned32 *authn_svc*,
rpc_auth_key_retrieval_fn_t *get_key_fn*,
void **arg*,
unsigned32 **status*);

Parameters

Input

server_princ_name
Specifies the principal name to use for the server when authenticating remote procedure calls using the service specified by *authn_svc*. The content of the name and its syntax is defined by the authentication service in use.

authn_svc Specifies the authentication service to use when the server receives a remote procedure call request. The following authentication services are supported:

rpc_c_authn_none	No authentication.
rpc_c_authn_dce_secret	DCE shared-secret key authentication.
rpc_c_authn_dce_public	DCE public key authentication (reserved for future use).
rpc_c_authn_default	DCE default authentication service.

get_key_fn Specifies the address of a server-provided routine that returns encryption keys.

Specifying **NULL** uses the default method of acquiring encryption keys. In this case, *authn_svc* must specify **rpc_c_authn_default**.

The following table shows the RPC runtime behavior for acquiring encryption keys for each supported authentication service.

RPC Key Acquisition for Authentication Services			
authn_svc	*get_key_fn*	*arg*	**Runtime Behavior**
rpc_c_authn_default	Ignored	**NULL**	Uses the default method of encryption key acquisition from the default key table.
rpc_c_authn_default	Ignored	non-**NULL**	Uses the default method of encryption key acquisition from the default key table. The specified argument is passed to the default acquisition function.
rpc_c_authn_none	Ignored	Ignored	No authentication performed.
rpc_c_authn_dce_secret	**NULL**	**NULL**	Uses the default method of encryption key acquisition from the default key table.
rpc_c_authn_dce_secret	**NULL**	non-**NULL**	Uses the default method of encryption key acquisition from the specified key Table. The specified argument is passed to the default acquisition function.
rpc_c_authn_dce_secret	non-**NULL**	**NULL**	Uses the specified encryption key acquisition routine to obtain keys from the default key table.
rpc_c_authn_dce_secret	non-**NULL**	non-**NULL**	Uses the specified encryption key acquisition routine to obtain keys from the specified key table. The specified argument is passed to the acquisition function.
rpc_c_authn_dce_public	Ignored	Ignored	(Reserved for future use.)

The following C definition for **rpc_auth_key_retrieval_fn_t** illustrates the prototype for the encryption key acquisition routine:

```
typedef void (*rpc_auth_key_retrieval_fn_t)
(
 void          *arg,              /* in */
 unsigned_char_t *server_princ_name, /* in */
 unsigned32     key_ver,          /* in */
 void          **key,             /* out */
 unsigned32     *status           /* out */
);
```

The RPC runtime passes the *server_princ_name* parameter value specified on the call to **rpc_server_register_auth_info( )**, as the *server_princ_name* parameter value, to the *get_key_fn* key acquisition routine. The RPC runtime automatically provides a value for the key version (*key_ver*) parameter. For a *key_ver* value of 0 (zero), the key acquisition routine must return the most recent key available. The routine returns the key in the *key* parameter.

If the key acquisition routine, when called from the **rpc_server_register_auth_info( )** routine, returns a status other than **rpc_s_ok**, the **rpc_server_register_auth_info( )** routine fails and returns the error status to the calling server.

If the key acquisition routine, when called by the RPC runtime while authenticating a client remote procedure call request, returns a status other than **rpc_s_ok**, the request fails and the RPC runtime returns the error status to the client.

arg Specifies an argument to pass to the *get_key_fn* key acquisition routine, if specified. (See the description of the *get_key_fn* parameter for details.)

Output

status Returns the status code from this routine. This status code indicates whether the routine completed successfully or, if not, why not.

The possible status codes and their meanings are as follows:

rpc_s_ok	Success.
rpc_s_unknown_authn_service	Unknown authentication service.

Description

The **rpc_server_register_auth_info( )** routine registers an authentication service to use for authenticating remote procedure calls to a particular server principal. A server calls this routine once for each authentication service and principal name combination that it wants to register.

The authentication service specified by a client (using the **rpc_binding_set_auth_info( )** or **rpc_if_register_auth_info( )** routine) must be one of the authentication services registered by the server. If it is not, the client's remote procedure call request fails with an **rpc_s_unknown_authn_service** status code.

Return Values

No value is returned.

Related Information

Functions: **rpc_binding_set_auth_info(3rpc)**, **rpc_if_register_auth_info(3rpc)**.

rpc_server_register_if

Purpose Registers an interface with the RPC runtime

Used by server applications.

Synopsis **#include <dce/rpc.h>**

void rpc_server_register_if(
rpc_if_handle_t *if_handle***,**
uuid_t **mgr_type_uuid***,**
rpc_mgr_epv_t *mgr_epv***,**
unsigned32 **status***);**

Parameters

Input

if_handle
An IDL-generated data structure specifying the interface to register.

mgr_type_uuid
Specifies a type UUID to associate with the *mgr_epv* parameter. Specifying the value **NULL** (or a nil UUID) registers the *if_handle* with a nil type UUID.

mgr_epv Specifies the manager routines' entry point vector. To use the IDL-generated default entry point vector, specify **NULL**.

Output

status Returns the status code from this routine. This status code indicates whether the routine completed successfully or, if not, why not.

The possible status codes and their meanings are as follows:

rpc_s_ok	Success.
rpc_s_type_already_registered	An interface with the given type of UUID is already registered.

Description

The **rpc_server_register_if()** routine registers a server interface with the RPC runtime. A server can register an unlimited number of interfaces. Once registered, an interface is available to clients through any binding handle of the server, provided that the binding handle is compatible for the client.

A server must provide the following information to register an interface:

- An interface specification, which is a data structure generated by the IDL compiler. The server specifies the interface specification of the interface using the *if_handle* parameter.
- A type UUID and manager Entry Point Vector (EPV), a data pair that determines which manager routine executes when a server receives a remote procedure call request from a client.

  The server specifies the type UUID and EPV using the *mgr_type_uuid* and *mgr_epv* parameters, respectively. Note that when a non-nil type UUID is specified, the server must also call the **rpc_object_set_type()** routine to register objects of this non-nil type.

A server that only offers a single manager for an interface calls **rpc_server_register_if()** once for that interface. In the simple case where the single manager's entry point names are the same as the operation names in the IDL interface definition, the IDL-generated default manager EPV for the interface may be used. The value **NULL** in *mgr_epv* specifies the default manager EPV.

Note that if a server offers multiple implementations of an interface, the server code must register a separate manager entry point vector for each interface implementation.

Rules for Invoking Manager Routines

The RPC runtime dispatches an incoming remote procedure call to a manager that offers the requested RPC interface. When multiple managers are registered for an interface, the RPC runtime must select one of them. To select a manager, the RPC runtime uses the object UUID specified by the call's binding handle.

The following table summarizes the rules applied for invoking manager routines.

Rules for Invoking Manager Routines			
Object UUID of Call[1]	**Has Server Set Type of Object UUID?**[2]	**Has Server Registered Type for Manager EPV?**[3]	**Dispatching Action**
Nil	Not applicable[4]	Yes	Uses the manager with the nil type UUID.
Nil	Not applicable[4]	No	Error (**rpc_s_unknown_mgr_type**). Rejects the remote procedure call.
Non-nil	Yes	Yes	Uses the manager with the same type UUID.
Non-nil	No	Ignored	Uses the manager with the nil type UUID. If no manager with the nil type UUID, error (**rpc_s_unknown_mgr_type**). Rejects the remote procedure call.
Non-nil	Yes	No	Error (**rpc_s_unknown_mgr_type**). Rejects the remote procedure call.

1 This is the object UUID found in a binding handle for a remote procedure.

2 By calling **rpc_object_set_type()** to specify the type UUID for an object.

3 By calling **rpc_server_register_if()** using the same type UUID.

4 The nil object UUID is always automatically assigned the nil type UUID. It is illegal to specify a nil object UUID in **rpc_object_set_type()**.

For more information about registering server interfaces and invoking manager routines, refer to the *OSF DCE Application Development Guide*.

Return Values

No value is returned.

Related Information

Functions: **rpc_binding_set_object(3rpc)**, **rpc_ep_register(3rpc)**, **rpc_ep_register_no_replace(3rpc)**, **rpc_ns_binding_export(3rpc)**, **rpc_object_set_type(3rpc)**, **rpc_server_unregister_if(3rpc)**.

Books: *OSF DCE Application Development Guide*.

rpc_server_unregister_if

Purpose Removes an interface from the RPC runtime

Used by server applications.

Synopsis **#include <dce/rpc.h>**

void rpc_server_unregister_if(
    rpc_if_handle_t *if_handle*,
    uuid_t **mgr_type_uuid*,
    unsigned32 **status*);

Parameters

Input

if_handle Specifies an interface specification to unregister (remove).

Specify **NULL** to remove all interfaces previously registered with the type UUID value given in the *mgr_type_uuid* parameter.

mgr_type_uuid
Specifies the type UUID for the manager Entry Point Vector (EPV) to remove. This needs to be the same value as provided in a call to the **rpc_server_register_if(**) routine.

Specify **NULL** to remove the interface given in the *if_handle* parameter for all previously registered type UUIDs.

Specify a nil UUID to remove the IDL-generated default manager EPV. In this case all manager EPVs registered with a non-nil type UUID remain registered.

Output

status Returns the status code from this routine. This status code indicates whether the routine completed successfully or, if not, why not.

The possible status codes and their meanings are as follows:

rpc_s_ok	Success.
rpc_s_unknown_if	Unknown interface.
rpc_s_unknown_mgr_type	Unknown manager type.

Description

The **rpc_server_unregister_if()** routine removes the association between an interface and a manager Entry Point Vector (EPV).

Specify the manager EPV to remove by providing, in the *mgr_type_uuid* parameter, the type UUID value specified in a call to the **rpc_server_register_if()** routine. Once removed, an interface is no longer available to client applications.

When an interface is removed, the RPC runtime stops accepting new calls for that interface. Executing calls (on that interface) are allowed to complete.

The table below summarizes the actions of this routine.

Rules for Removing an Interface		
if_handle	*mgr_type_uuid*	**Action**
non-**NULL**	non-**NULL**	Removes the manager EPV associated with the specified parameters.
non-**NULL**	**NULL**	Removes all manager EPVs associated with parameter *if_handle*.
NULL	non-**NULL**	Removes all manager EPVs associated with parameter *mgr_type_uuid*.
NULL	**NULL**	Removes all manager EPVs.

Note that when both of the parameters *if_handle* and *mgr_type_uuid* are given the value **NULL**, this call has the effect of preventing the server from receiving any new remote procedure calls since all the manager EPVs for all interfaces have been removed.

Return Values

No value is returned.

Related Information

Functions: **rpc_server_register_if(3rpc)**.

rpc_server_use_all_protseqs

Purpose Tells the RPC runtime to use all supported protocol sequences for receiving remote procedure calls

Used by server applications.

Synopsis **#include <dce/rpc.h>**

void rpc_server_use_all_protseqs(
    unsigned32 *max_call_requests*,
    unsigned32 **status*);

Parameters

Input

max_call_requests
Specifies the maximum number of concurrent remote procedure call requests that the server can accept.

The RPC runtime guarantees that the server can accept at least this number of concurrent call requests. The actual number of these requests can be greater than the value of *max_call_requests* and can vary for each protocol sequence.

Use the value **rpc_c_protseq_max_reqs_default** to specify the default parameter value.

Note that in this version of DCE RPC, any number you specify is replaced by the default value.

Also, the **rpc_server_listen( )** routine limits (according to its *max_calls_exec* parameter) the amount of concurrent remote procedure call execution. See the **rpc_server_listen(3rpc)** reference page for more information.

Output

status Returns the status code from this routine. This status code indicates whether the routine completed successfully or, if not, why not.

The possible status codes and their meanings are as follows:

rpc_s_ok	Success.
rpc_s_cant_create_socket	Cannot create socket.
rpc_s_max_descs_exceeded	Exceeded maximum number of network descriptors.
rpc_s_no_protseqs	No supported protocol sequences.

Description

The **rpc_server_use_all_protseqs( )** routine registers all supported protocol sequences with the RPC runtime. A server must register at least one protocol sequence with the RPC runtime to receive remote procedure call requests.

For each protocol sequence registered by a server, the RPC runtime creates one or more binding handles. Each binding handle contains a dynamic endpoint that the RPC runtime and operating system generated.

The *max_call_requests* parameter allows you to specify the maximum number of concurrent remote procedure call requests the server handles.

After registering protocol sequences, a server typically calls the following routines:

rpc_server_inq_bindings( )	Obtains a vector containing all of the server's binding handles.
rpc_ep_register( )	Registers the binding handles with the local endpoint map.
rpc_ep_register_no_replace( )	Registers the binding handles with the local endpoint map.
rpc_ns_binding_export( )	Places the binding handles in the name service database for access by any client.
rpc_binding_vector_free( )	Frees the vector of server binding handles.
rpc_server_register_if( )	Registers with the RPC runtime those interfaces that the server offers.
rpc_server_listen( )	Enables the reception of remote procedure calls.

To register protocol sequences selectively, a server calls one of the following routines:

rpc_server_use_protseq( )
rpc_server_use_protseq_if( )
rpc_server_use_all_protseqs_if( )
rpc_server_use_protseq_ep( )

For an explanation of how a server can establish a client/server relationship without using the local endpoint map or the name service database, see the information on string bindings in the **intro(3rpc)** reference page.

Return Values

No value is returned.

Related Information

Functions: **rpc_binding_from_string_binding(3rpc)**, **rpc_binding_to_string_binding(3rpc)**, **rpc_binding_vector_free(3rpc)**, **rpc_ep_register(3rpc)**, **rpc_ep_register_no_replace(3rpc)**, **rpc_ns_binding_export(3rpc)**, **rpc_server_inq_bindings(3rpc)**, **rpc_server_listen(3rpc)**, **rpc_server_register_if(3rpc)**, **rpc_server_use_all_protseqs_if(3rpc)**, **rpc_server_use_protseq(3rpc)**, **rpc_server_use_protseq_ep(3rpc)**, **rpc_server_use_protseq_if(3rpc)**.

rpc_server_use_all_protseqs_if

Purpose Tells the RPC runtime to use all the protocol sequences and endpoints specified in the interface specification for receiving remote procedure calls

Used by server applications.

Synopsis **#include <dce/rpc.h>**

void rpc_server_use_all_protseqs_if(
unsigned32 *max_call_requests***,**
rpc_if_handle_t *if_handle***,**
unsigned32 ****status*);**

Parameters

Input

max_call_requests
Specifies the maximum number of concurrent remote procedure call requests that the server can accept.

The RPC runtime guarantees that the server can accept at least this number of concurrent call requests. The actual number of these requests can be greater that the value of *max_call_requests* and can vary for each protocol sequence.

Use the value **rpc_c_protseq_max_reqs_default** to specify the default parameter value.

Note that in this version of DCE RPC, any number you specify is replaced by the default value.

Also, the **rpc_server_listen()** routine limits (according to its *max_calls_exec* parameter) the amount of concurrent remote procedure call execution. See the **rpc_server_listen(3rpc)** reference page for more information.

if_handle
Specifies an interface specification containing the protocol sequences and their corresponding endpoint information to use in creating binding handles. Each created binding handle contains a well-known (nondynamic) endpoint contained in the interface specification.

Output

status Returns the status code from this routine. This status code indicates whether the routine completed successfully or, if not, why not.

The possible status codes and their meanings are as follows:

rpc_s_ok	Success.
rpc_s_calls_too_large_for_wk_ep	Maximum concurrent calls too large.
rpc_s_cant_bind_socket	Cannot bind to socket.
rpc_s_cant_create_socket	Cannot create socket.
rpc_s_cant_inq_socket	Cannot inquire endpoint from socket.
rpc_s_invalid_endpoint_format	Invalid interface handle.
rpc_s_max_descs_exceeded	Exceeded maximum number of network descriptors.
rpc_s_no_protseqs	No supported protocol sequences.

Description

The **rpc_server_use_all_protseqs_if**( ) routine registers all protocol sequences and associated endpoint address information provided in the IDL file with the RPC runtime. A server must register at least one protocol sequence with the RPC runtime to receive remote procedure call requests.

For each protocol sequence registered by a server, the RPC runtime creates one or more binding handles. Each binding handle contains the well-known endpoint specified in the IDL file.

The *max_call_requests* parameter allows you to specify the maximum number of concurrent remote procedure call requests the server handles.

If you want to register selected protocol sequences specified in the IDL, your server uses **rpc_server_use_protseq_if**( ).

The explanation of **rpc_server_use_all_protseqs**( ) contains a list of the routines a server typically calls after calling this routine. (However, a server that uses only **rpc_server_use_all_protseqs_if**( ) does not subsequently call **rpc_ep_register**( ) or **rpc_ep_register_no_replace**( ).) For an explanation of how a server can establish a client/server relationship without using the local endpoint map or the name service database, see the information on string bindings in the **intro(3rpc)** reference page.

Return Values

No value is returned.

Related Information

Functions: **rpc_binding_vector_free(3rpc)**, **rpc_ep_register(3rpc)**, **rpc_ep_register_no_replace(3rpc)**, **rpc_ns_binding_export(3rpc)**, **rpc_server_inq_bindings(3rpc)**, **rpc_server_listen(3rpc)**, **rpc_server_register_if(3rpc)**, **rpc_server_use_all_protseqs(3rpc)**, **rpc_server_use_protseq(3rpc)**, **rpc_server_use_protseq_ep(3rpc)**, **rpc_server_use_protseq_if(3rpc)**.

rpc_server_use_protseq

Purpose

Tells the RPC runtime to use the specified protocol sequence for receiving remote procedure calls

Used by server applications.

Synopsis

#include <dce/rpc.h>

void rpc_server_use_protseq(
    unsigned_char_t **protseq*,
    unsigned32 *max_call_requests*,
    unsigned32 **status*);

Parameters

Input

protseq Specifies a string identifier for the protocol sequence to register with the RPC runtime. (For a list of string identifiers, see the table of valid protocol sequences in the **intro(3rpc)** reference page.)

max_call_requests

Specifies the maximum number of concurrent remote procedure call requests that the server can accept.

The RPC runtime guarantees that the server can accept at least this number of concurrent call requests. The actual number of these requests can be greater than the value of *max_call_requests* and can vary for each protocol sequence.

Use the value **rpc_c_protseq_max_reqs_default** to specify the default parameter value.

Note that in this version of DCE RPC, any number you specify is replaced by the default value.

Also, **rpc_server_listen( )** limits (according to its *max_calls_exec* parameter) the amount of concurrent remote procedure call execution. See the **rpc_server_listen(3rpc)** reference page for more information.

Output

status Returns the status code from this routine. This status code indicates whether the routine completed successfully or, if not, why not.

The possible status codes and their meanings are as follows:

rpc_s_ok	Success.
rpc_s_cant_create_socket	Cannot create socket.
rpc_s_invalid_rpc_protseq	Invalid protocol sequence.
rpc_s_max_descs_exceeded	Exceeded maximum number of network descriptors.
rpc_s_protseq_not_supported	Protocol sequence not supported on this host.

Description

The **rpc_server_use_protseq()** routine registers a single protocol sequence with the RPC runtime. A server must register at least one protocol sequence with the RPC runtime to receive remote procedure call requests. A server can call this routine multiple times to register additional protocol sequences.

For each protocol sequence registered by a server, the RPC runtime creates one or more binding handles. Each binding handle contains a dynamic endpoint that the RPC runtime and operating system generated.

The *max_call_requests* parameter allows you to specify the maximum number of concurrent remote procedure call requests the server handles.

A server calls **rpc_server_use_all_protseqs()** to register all protocol sequences.

The explanation of the **rpc_server_use_all_protseqs()** routine contains a list of the routines a server typically calls after calling this routine. For an explanation of how a server can establish a client/server relationship without using the local endpoint map or the name service database, see the information on string bindings in the **intro(3rpc)** reference page.

Return Values

No value is returned.

Related Information

Functions: **rpc_binding_vector_free(3rpc)**, **rpc_ep_register(3rpc)**, **rpc_ep_register_no_replace(3rpc)**, **rpc_network_is_protseq_valid(3rpc)**, **rpc_ns_binding_export(3rpc)**, **rpc_server_inq_bindings(3rpc)**, **rpc_server_listen(3rpc)**, **rpc_server_register_if(3rpc)**, **rpc_server_use_all_protseqs(3rpc)**, **rpc_server_use_all_protseqs_if(3rpc)**, **rpc_server_use_protseq_ep(3rpc)**, **rpc_server_use_protseq_if(3rpc)**.

rpc_server_use_protseq_ep

Purpose Tells the RPC runtime to use the specified protocol sequence combined with the specified endpoint for receiving remote procedure calls

Used by server applications.

Synopsis **#include <dce/rpc.h>**

void rpc_server_use_protseq_ep(
  unsigned_char_t **protseq*,
  unsigned32 *max_call_requests*,
  unsigned_char_t **endpoint*,
  unsigned32 **status*);

Parameters

Input

protseq Specifies a string identifier for the protocol sequence to register with the RPC runtime. (For a list of string identifiers, see the table of valid protocol sequences in the **intro(3rpc)** reference page.

max_call_requests
Specifies the maximum number of concurrent remote procedure call requests that the server can accept.

The RPC runtime guarantees that the server can accept at least this number of concurrent call requests. The actual number of these requests can be greater than the value of *max_call_requests* and can vary for each protocol sequence.

Use the value **rpc_c_protseq_max_reqs_default** to specify the default parameter value.

Note that in this version of DCE RPC, any number you specify is replaced by the default value.

Also, **rpc_server_listen( )** limits (according to its *max_calls_exec* parameter) the amount of concurrent remote procedure call execution. See the **rpc_server_listen(3rpc)** reference page for more information.

endpoint Specifies address information for an endpoint. This information is used in creating a binding handle for the protocol sequence specified in the *protseq* parameter.

Output

status Returns the status code from this routine. This status code indicates whether the routine completed successfully or, if not, why not.

The possible status codes and their meanings are as follows:

rpc_s_ok	Success.
rpc_s_calls_too_large_for_wk_ep	Maximum concurrent calls too large.
rpc_s_cant_bind_socket	Cannot bind to socket.
rpc_s_cant_create_socket	Cannot create socket.
rpc_s_invalid_endpoint_format	Invalid endpoint format.
rpc_s_invalid_rpc_protseq	Invalid protocol sequence.
rpc_s_max_descs_exceeded	Exceeded maximum number of network descriptors.
rpc_s_protseq_not_supported	Protocol sequence not supported on this host.

Description

The **rpc_server_use_protseq_ep()** routine registers a protocol sequence and its specified endpoint address information with the RPC runtime. A server must register at least one protocol sequence with the RPC runtime to receive remote procedure call requests. A server can call this routine multiple times to register additional protocol sequences and endpoints.

For each protocol sequence registered by a server, the RPC runtime creates one or more binding handles. Each binding handle contains the well-known endpoint specified in the *endpoint* parameter.

The *max_call_requests* parameter allows you to specify the maximum number of concurrent remote procedure call requests the server handles.

The explanation of **rpc_server_use_all_protseqs()** contains a list of the routines a server typically calls after calling this routine. For an explanation of how a server can establish a client/server relationship without using the local endpoint map or the name service database, see the information on string bindings in the **intro(3rpc)** reference page.

Return Values

No value is returned.

Related Information

Functions: **rpc_binding_vector_free(3rpc)**, **rpc_ep_register(3rpc)**, **rpc_ep_register_no_replace(3rpc)**, **rpc_ns_binding_export(3rpc)**, **rpc_server_inq_bindings(3rpc)**, **rpc_server_listen(3rpc)**, **rpc_server_register_if(3rpc)**, **rpc_server_use_all_protseqs(3rpc)**, **rpc_server_use_all_protseqs_if(3rpc)**, **rpc_server_use_protseq(3rpc)**, **rpc_server_use_protseq_ep(3rpc)**.

rpc_server_use_protseq_if

Purpose Tells the RPC runtime to use the specified protocol sequence combined with the endpoints in the interface specification for receiving remote procedure calls

Used by server applications.

Synopsis **#include <dce/rpc.h>**

void rpc_server_use_protseq_if(
unsigned_char_t **protseq*,
unsigned32 *max_call_requests*,
rpc_if_handle_t *if_handle*,
unsigned32 **status*);

Parameters

Input

protseq Specifies a string identifier for the protocol sequence to register with the RPC runtime. For a list of string identifiers, see the table of valid protocol sequences in the **intro(3rpc)** reference page.

max_call_requests
Specifies the maximum number of concurrent remote procedure call requests that the server can accept.

The RPC runtime guarantees that the server can accept at least this number of concurrent call requests. The actual number of these requests can be greater than the value of *max_call_requests* and can vary for each protocol sequence.

Use the value **rpc_c_protseq_max_reqs_default** to specify the default parameter value.

Note that in this version of DCE RPC, any number you specify is replaced by the default value.

Also, the **rpc_server_listen( )** routine limits (according to its *max_calls_exec* parameter) the amount of concurrent remote procedure call execution. See the **rpc_server_listen(3rpc)** reference page for more information.

if_handle Specifies an interface specification whose endpoint information is used in creating a binding for the protocol sequence specified in *protseq*.

Each created binding handle contains a well-known (nondynamic) endpoint contained in the interface specification.

Output

status Returns the status code from this routine. This status code indicates whether the routine completed successfully or, if not, why not.

The possible status codes and their meanings are as follows:

rpc_s_ok	Success.
rpc_s_calls_too_large_for_wk_ep	Maximum concurrent calls too large.
rpc_s_cant_bind_socket	Cannot bind to socket.
rpc_s_invalid_endpoint_format	Invalid endpoint format.
rpc_s_invalid_rpc_protseq	Invalid protocol sequence.
rpc_s_max_descs_exceeded	Exceeded maximum number of network descriptors.
rpc_s_protseq_not_supported	Protocol sequence not supported on this host.

Description

The **rpc_server_use_protseq_if**( ) routine registers one protocol sequence with the RPC runtime, including its endpoint address information as provided in the specified IDL file.

A server must register at least one protocol sequence with the RPC runtime to receive remote procedure call requests. A server can call this routine multiple times to register additional protocol sequences.

For each protocol sequence registered by a server, the RPC runtime creates one or more binding handles. Each binding handle contains the well-known endpoint specified in the IDL file.

The *max_call_requests* parameter allows you to specify the maximum number of concurrent remote procedure call requests the server handles.

To register all protocol sequences from the IDL, a server calls the **rpc_server_use_all_protseqs_if**( ) routine.

The explanation of **rpc_server_use_all_protseqs**( ) contains a list of the routines a server typically calls after calling this routine. However, a server that uses only **rpc_server_use_protseq_if**( ) does not subsequently call **rpc_ep_register**( ) or

rpc_ep_register_no_replace( ). For an explanation of how a server can establish a client/server relationship without using the local endpoint map or the name service database, see the information on string bindings in the **intro(3rpc)** reference page.

Return Values

No value is returned.

Related Information

Functions: **rpc_binding_vector_free(3rpc)**, **rpc_ep_register(3rpc)**, **rpc_ep_register_no_replace(3rpc)**, **rpc_ns_binding_export(3rpc)**, **rpc_server_inq_bindings(3rpc)**, **rpc_server_listen(3rpc)**, **rpc_server_register_if(3rpc)**, **rpc_server_use_all_protseqs(3rpc)**, **rpc_server_use_all_protseqs_if(3rpc)**, **rpc_server_use_protseq(3rpc)**, **rpc_server_use_protseq_ep(3rpc)**.

rpc_ss_allocate

Purpose Allocates memory within the RPC stub memory management scheme

Used by server or possibly by client applications.

Synopsis **#include <dce/rpc.h>**

idl_void_p_t rpc_ss_allocate (idl_size_t *size*);

Parameters

Input

size Specifies, in bytes, the size of memory to be allocated.

Note that in ANSI standard C environments, **idl_void_p_t** is defined as **void** * and in other environments is defined as **char** *.

Description

Usually, the **rpc_ss_allocate**( ) routine is used in the manager code that is called from a server stub. Memory allocated by **rpc_ss_allocate** is released by the server stub after marshalling any output parameters at the end of the remote call in which the memory was allocated. If you want to release memory allocated by **rpc_ss_allocate**( ) before returning from the manager code use **rpc_ss_free**( ).

You can also use **rpc_ss_free**( ) in manager code to release memory pointed to by a full pointer (**ptr**) in an input parameter.

When the server uses **rpc_ss_allocate**( ), the server stub creates the environment the routine needs. If the parameters of the operation include any pointers other than those used for passing parameters by reference, the environment is set up automatically.

If you need to use **rpc_ss_allocate**( ) in a manager code routine that does not have a pointer in any of its parameters, use an ACF and apply the **enable_allocate** attribute to the relevant operation. This causes the generated server stub to set up the necessary environment.

Note that memory allocated by allocators other than **rpc_ss_allocate**( ) is not released when the operation on the server side completes execution.

If you want to use **rpc_ss_allocate( )** outside the code called from a server stub, you must first create an environment for it by calling **rpc_ss_enable_allocate( )**. See the *OSF DCE Application Development Guide* for more information.

Return Values

A pointer to the allocated memory.

An exception, **rpc_x_no_memory**, when no memory is available for allocation.

Related Information

Functions: **rpc_ss_free(3rpc)**, **rpc_ss_enable_allocate(3rpc)**, **rpc_ss_disable_allocate(3rpc)**, **rpc_ss_get_thread_handle(3rpc)**, **rpc_ss_set_thread_handle(3rpc)**.

Books: *OSF DCE Application Development Guide*.

rpc_ss_client_free

Purpose Frees memory returned from a client stub

Used by server or possibly by client applications.

Synopsis **#include <dce/rpc.h>**

void rpc_ss_client_free (idl_void_p_t *node_to_free***);**

Parameters

Input

node_to_free Specifies a pointer to memory returned from a client stub.

Description

The **rpc_ss_client_free( )** routine releases memory allocated and returned from a client stub. The thread calling **rpc_ss_client_free( )** must have the same thread handle as the thread that made the RPC call.

This routine enables a routine to deallocate dynamically allocated memory returned by an RPC call without knowledge of the memory management environment from which it was called.

Return Values

No value is returned.

Related Information

Functions: **rpc_ss_free(3rpc)**, **rpc_ss_get_thread_handle(3rpc)**, **rpc_ss_set_client_alloc_free(3rpc)**, **rpc_ss_set_thread_handle(3rpc)**, **rpc_ss_swap_client_alloc_free(3rpc)**.

rpc_ss_destroy_client_context

Purpose Reclaims the client memory resources for the context handle, and sets the context handle to **NULL**

Used by client applications.

Synopsis **#include <dce/rpc.h>**

void rpc_ss_destroy_client_context(
void *****p_unusable_context_handle***);**

Parameters

Input

p_unusable_context_handle Specifies the context handle that can no longer be accessed.

Description

The **rpc_ss_destroy_client_context( )** routine is used by the client application to reclaim the client resources used in maintaining an active context handle. Only call this after a communications error makes the context handle unusable. When **rpc_ss_destroy_client_context( )** reclaims the memory resources, it also sets the context handle to **NULL**.

Return Values

No value is returned.

The **rpc_ss_destroy_client_context( )** routine raises no exceptions.

rpc_ss_disable_allocate

Purpose Releases resources and allocated memory

Used by client applications.

Synopsis **#include <dce/rpc.h>**

void rpc_ss_disable_allocate (void);

Description

The **rpc_ss_disable_allocate( )** routine releases (disables) all resources acquired by a call to **rpc_ss_enable_allocate( )**, and any memory allocated by calls to **rpc_ss_allocate( )** after the call to **rpc_ss_enable_allocate( )** was made.

The **rpc_ss_enable_allocate( )** and **rpc_ss_disable_allocate( )** routines must be used in matching pairs.

For information about rules for using memory management routines, see the *OSF DCE Application Development Guide*.

Related Information

Functions: **rpc_ss_allocate(3rpc)**, **rpc_ss_enable_allocate(3rpc)**.

Books: *OSF DCE Application Development Guide*.

rpc_ss_enable_allocate

Purpose Enables the allocation of memory by the **rpc_ss_allocate()** routine when not in manager code

Used by client applications.

Synopsis **#include <dce/rpc.h>**

void rpc_ss_enable_allocate(void);

Description

In sophisticated servers, it may be necessary to call manager code routines from different environments. This occurs, for example, when the application is both a client and a server of the same interface. Therefore, a manager code routine may need to be called both by the application code and by the stub code. If code, other than manager code, calls the **rpc_ss_allocate()** routine, it must first call **rpc_ss_enable_allocate()** to initialize the memory management environment that **rpc_ss_allocate()** uses.

For information about rules for using memory management routines, see the *OSF DCE Application Development Guide*.

Return Values

An exception, **rpc_x_no_memory**, when there is insufficient memory available to set up necessary data structures.

Related Information

Functions: **rpc_ss_allocate(3rpc)**, **rpc_ss_disable_allocate(3rpc)**.

Books: *OSF DCE Application Development Guide*.

rpc_ss_free

Purpose Frees memory allocated by the **rpc_ss_allocate( )** routine

Used by server or possibly by client applications.

Synopsis **#include <dce/rpc.h>**

void rpc_ss_free (idl_void_p_t *node_to_free***);**

Parameters

Input

node_to_free Specifies a pointer to memory allocated by **rpc_ss_allocate( )**.

Note that in ANSI standard C environments, **idl_void_p_t** is defined as **void *** and in other environments is defined as **char ***.

Description

The **rpc_ss_free( )** routine releases memory allocated by **rpc_ss_allocate( )**. The thread calling **rpc_ss_free( )** must have the same thread handle as the thread that allocated the memory with **rpc_ss_allocate( )**. Use it only in an environment where **rpc_ss_allocate( )** is used.

If the manager code allocates memory with **rpc_ss_allocate( )** and the memory is not released by **rpc_ss_free( )** during manager code execution, then the server stub automatically releases the memory when the manager code completes execution and returns control to the stub.

Manager code can also use **rpc_ss_free( )** to release memory that is pointed to by a full pointer in an input parameter.

For information about rules for using memory management routines, see the *OSF DCE Application Development Guide*.

Related Information

Functions: **rpc_ss_allocate(3rpc)**, **rpc_ss_get_thread_handle(3rpc)**, **rpc_ss_set_thread_handle(3rpc)**.

Books: *OSF DCE Application Development Guide*.

rpc_ss_get_thread_handle

Purpose Gets a thread handle for the manager code before it spawns additional threads, or for the client code when it becomes a server

Used by server or possibly by client applications.

Synopsis **#include <dce/rpc.h>**

rpc_ss_thread_handle_t rpc_ss_get_thread_handle(void);

Description

The **rpc_ss_get_thread_handle( )** routine is used by a server manager thread when it spawns additional threads. To spawn additional threads that are able to perform memory management, the server manager code calls **rpc_ss_get_thread_handle( )** and passes the thread handle to each spawned thread. Each spawned thread that uses **rpc_ss_allocate( )** and **rpc_ss_free( )** for memory management must first call **rpc_ss_set_thread_handle( )**, using the handle obtained by the original manager thread.

The **rpc_ss_get_thread_handle( )** routine can also be used when a program changes from being a client to being a server. The program gets a handle on its environment as a client by calling **rpc_ss_get_thread_handle( )**. When the program reverts to being a client it reestablishes the client environment by calling **rpc_ss_set_thread_handle( )**, supplying the previously obtained handle as a parameter.

Return Values

A thread handle.

Examples

This function determines the thread handle, creates a thread, and passes the thread handle to the thread so it can share the memory management environment of the calling thread.

```
#include <pthread.h>
#include <idlbase.h>

pthread_t Launch_thread(
    int (*routine_to_launch)(
       pthread_addr_t th
       )
    )
{
    rpc_ss_thread_handle_t th = rpc_ss_get_thread_handle();
    pthread_t t;

    /*
     * Create the thread and pass to it the thread handle
     * so it can use rpc_ss_set_thread_handle.
     */
    pthread_create (&t, pthread_attr_default,
        (pthread_startroutine_t)routine_to_launch,
        (pthread_addr_t)th);

    return t;
}
```

Related Information

Functions: **rpc_ss_allocate(3rpc)**, **rpc_ss_free(3rpc)**, **rpc_ss_set_thread_handle(3rpc)**.

rpc_ss_set_client_alloc_free

Purpose Sets the memory allocation and freeing mechanism used by the client stubs, thereby overriding the default routines the client stub uses to manage memory for pointed-to nodes

Used by client applications.

Synopsis

```
#include <dce/rpc.h>

void rpc_ss_set_client_alloc_free(
        idl_void_p_t (*p_allocate)(
        idl_size_t size),
        void (*p_free)(
        idl_void_p_t *ptr)
        );
```

Parameters

Input

p_allocate Specifies a pointer to a routine that has the same procedure declaration as the **malloc( )** routine and that is used by the client stub to allocate memory.

p_free Specifies a pointer to a routine that has the same procedure declaration as the **free( )** routine and that is used to free memory that was allocated using the routine pointed at by *p_allocate*.

Note that in ANSI standard C environments, **idl_void_p_t** is defined as **void *** and in other environments is defined as **char ***.

Description

The **rpc_ss_set_client_alloc_free( )** routine overrides the default routines that the client stub uses to manage memory for pointed-to nodes. The default memory management routines are **malloc( )** and **free( )**, except when the remote call occurs within manager code, in which case the default memory management routines are **rpc_ss_allocate( )** and **rpc_ss_free( )**.

For information about rules for using memory management routines, see the *OSF DCE Application Development Guide*.

Return Values

An exception, **rpc_x_no_memory**, when there is insufficient memory available to set up necessary data structures.

Related Information

Functions: **rpc_ss_allocate(3rpc)**, **rpc_ss_free(3rpc)**.

Books: *OSF DCE Application Development Guide*.

rpc_ss_set_thread_handle

Purpose

Sets the thread handle for either a newly created spawned thread or for a server that was formerly a client and is ready to be a client again

Used by server or possibly by client applications.

Synopsis

#include <dce/rpc.h>

void rpc_ss_set_thread_handle(
    rpc_ss_thread_handle_t *id*
    );

Parameters

Input

id A thread handle returned by a call to **rpc_ss_get_thread_handle( )**.

Description

The **rpc_ss_set_thread_handle( )** routine is used by a thread spawned in the manager code to associate itself with the main RPC manager thread. Each spawned thread that uses **rpc_ss_allocate( )** and **rpc_ss_free( )** for memory management must call **rpc_ss_set_thread_handle( )**, using the handle that the main RPC manager thread obtained through **rpc_ss_get_thread_handle( )**.

The **rpc_ss_set_thread_handle( )** routine can also be used by a program that originally was a client, then became a server, and is now reverting to a client. The program must reestablish the client environment by calling the **rpc_ss_set_thread_handle( )** routine, supplying the handle it received (through **rpc_ss_get_thread_handle( )**) prior to becoming a server, as a parameter.

Return Values

An exception, **rpc_x_no_memory**, when there is insufficient memory available to set up necessary data structures.

Examples

When this function is invoked within a spawned thread, its argument is the thread handle of the calling thread. This example assumes the data passed to the thread consists of only the middle thread.

```
#include <pthread.h>
#include <dce/idlbase.h>

 int helper_thread (
     pthread_addr_t th
     )
 {
     /*
      * Set the memory management environment to match
      * the parent environment.
      */
      rpc_ss_set_thread_handle(rpc_ss_thread_handle_t)th;
     /*
      * Real work of this thread follows here ...
      */
  }
```

Related Information

Functions: **rpc_ss_get_thread_handle(3rpc)**, **rpc_ss_allocate(3rpc)**, **rpc_ss_free(3rpc)**.

Books: *OSF DCE Application Development Guide*.

rpc_ss_swap_client_alloc_free

Purpose Exchanges the current memory allocation and freeing mechanism used by the client stubs with one supplied by the client

Used by client applications.

Synopsis **#include <dce/rpc.h>**

```
void rpc_ss_swap_client_alloc_free(
        idl_void_p_t (*p_allocate)(
        idl_size_t size),
        void (*p_free)(
        idl_void_p_t ptr),
        idl_void_p_t (**p_p_old_allocate)(
        idl_size_t size),
        void (**p_p_old_free)(
        idl_void_p_t ptr)
        );
```

Parameters

Input

p_allocate Specifies a pointer to a routine that has the same procedure declaration as the **malloc( )** routine and that is used for allocating client stub memory.

p_free Specifies a pointer to a routine that has the same procedure declaration as the **free( )** routine and that is used for freeing client stub memory.

Output

p_p_old_allocate
Specifies a pointer to a pointer to a routine that has the same procedure declaration as the **malloc( )** routine. A pointer to the routine that was previously used to allocate client stub memory is returned in this parameter.

p_p_old_free Specifies a pointer to a pointer to a routine that has the same procedure declaration as the **free( )** routine. A pointer to the routine that was previously used to free client stub memory is returned in this parameter.

Note that in ANSI standard C environments, **idl_void_p_t** is defined as **void** * and in other environments is defined as **char** *.

Description

The **rpc_ss_swap_client_alloc_free( )** routine exchanges the current client allocate and free mechanism used by the client stubs for one supplied by the caller. If it is appropriate for the client code called by an application to use a certain memory allocation and freeing mechanism, regardless of its caller's state, the client code can swap its own mechanism into place on entry, replacing its caller's mechanism. It can then swap the caller's mechanism back into place prior to returning.

For information about rules for using memory management routines, see the *OSF DCE Application Development Guide*.

Return Values

An exception, **rpc_x_no_memory**, is returned when there is insufficient memory available to set up necessary data structures.

Related Information

Functions: **rpc_ss_allocate(3rpc)**, **rpc_ss_free(3rpc)**, **rpc_ss_set_client_alloc_free(3rpc)**.

Books: *OSF DCE Application Development Guide*.

rpc_string_binding_compose

Purpose

Combines the components of a string binding into a string binding

Used by client or server applications.

Synopsis

#include <dce/rpc.h>

void rpc_string_binding_compose(
  unsigned_char_t **obj_uuid*,
  unsigned_char_t **protseq*,
  unsigned_char_t **network_addr*,
  unsigned_char_t **endpoint*,
  unsigned_char_t **options*,
  unsigned_char_t ***string_binding*,
  unsigned32 **status*);

Parameters

Input

obj_uuid Specifies a **NULL**-terminated string representation of an object UUID.

protseq Specifies a **NULL**-terminated string representation of a protocol sequence.

network_addr
Specifies a **NULL**-terminated string representation of a network address.

endpoint Specifies a **NULL**-terminated string representation of an endpoint.

options Specifies a **NULL**-terminated string representation of network options.

Output

string_binding
Returns a pointer to a **NULL**-terminated string representation of a binding handle.

Specify **NULL** to prevent the routine from returning this parameter. In this case the application does not call **rpc_string_free( )**.

status Returns the status code from this routine. This status code indicates whether the routine completed successfully or, if not, why not.

The possible status code and its meaning is as follows:

rpc_s_ok Success.

Description

The **rpc_string_binding_compose()** routine combines string binding handle components into a string binding handle.

The RPC runtime allocates memory for the string returned in the *string_binding* parameter. The application calls **rpc_string_free()** to deallocate that memory.

Specify **NULL** or provide a null string (**\0**) for each input string that has no data.

Return Values

No value is returned.

Related Information

Functions: **rpc_binding_from_string_binding(3rpc)**, **rpc_binding_to_string_binding(3rpc)**, **rpc_string_binding_parse(3rpc)**, **rpc_string_free(3rpc)**, **uuid_to_string(3rpc)**.

rpc_string_binding_parse

Purpose Returns, as separate strings, the components of a string binding

Used by client or server applications.

Synopsis **#include <dce/rpc.h>**

void rpc_string_binding_parse(
unsigned_char_t **string_binding*,
unsigned_char_t ***obj_uuid*,
unsigned_char_t ***protseq*,
unsigned_char_t ***network_addr*,
unsigned_char_t ***endpoint*,
unsigned_char_t ***network_options*,
unsigned32 **status*);

Parameters

Input

string_binding
Specifies a **NULL**-terminated string representation of a binding.

Output

obj_uuid Returns a pointer to a **NULL**-terminated string representation of an object UUID.

Specify **NULL** to prevent the routine from returning this parameter. In this case the application does not call **rpc_string_free()**.

protseq Returns a pointer to a **NULL**-terminated string representation of a protocol sequence.

Specify **NULL** to prevent the routine from returning this parameter. In this case the application does not call **rpc_string_free()**.

network_addr
Returns a pointer to a **NULL**-terminated string representation of a network address.

Specify **NULL** to prevent the routine from returning this parameter. In this case the application does not call **rpc_string_free()**.

endpoint Returns a pointer to a **NULL**-terminated string representation of an endpoint.

Specify **NULL** to prevent the routine from returning this parameter. In this case the application does not call **rpc_string_free( )**.

network_options
Returns a pointer to a **NULL**-terminated string representation of network options.

Specify **NULL** to prevent the routine from returning this parameter. In this case the application does not call **rpc_string_free( )**.

status Returns the status code from this routine. This status code indicates whether the routine completed successfully or, if not, why not.

The possible status codes and their meanings are as follows:

rpc_s_ok	Success.
rpc_s_invalid_string_binding	Invalid string binding.

Description

The **rpc_string_binding_parse( )** routine parses a string representation of a binding handle into its component fields.

The RPC runtime allocates memory for each component string the routine returns. The application calls **rpc_string_free( )** once for each returned string to deallocate the memory for that string.

If any field of the *string_binding* field is empty, **rpc_string_binding_parse( )** returns the empty string in the corresponding output parameter.

Return Values

No value is returned.

Related Information

Functions: **rpc_binding_from_string_binding(3rpc)**, **rpc_binding_to_string_binding(3rpc)**, **rpc_string_binding_compose(3rpc)**, **rpc_string_free(3rpc)**, **uuid_from_string(3rpc)**.

rpc_string_free

Purpose Frees a character string allocated by the runtime

Used by client, server, or management applications.

Synopsis **#include <dce/rpc.h>**

void rpc_string_free(
    unsigned_char_t ***string*,**
    unsigned32 **status*);**

Parameters

Input/Output

string Specifies the address of the pointer to the character string to free.

The value **NULL** is returned.

Output

status Returns the status code from this routine. This status code indicates whether the routine completed successfully or, if not, why not.

The possible status code and its meaning is as follows:

rpc_s_ok Success.

Description

The **rpc_string_free()** routine deallocates the memory occupied by a character string returned by the RPC runtime.

An application must call this routine once for each character string allocated and returned by calls to other RPC runtime routines. The names of these routines appear at the end of this reference page.

Return Values

No value is returned.

Related Information

Functions: **dce_error_inq_text(3rpc)**, **rpc_binding_inq_auth_client(3rpc)**, **rpc_binding_inq_auth_info(3rpc)**, **rpc_binding_to_string_binding(3rpc)**, **rpc_mgmt_ep_elt_inq_next(3rpc)**, **rpc_mgmt_inq_server_princ_name(3rpc)**, **rpc_ns_binding_inq_entry_name(3rpc)**, **rpc_ns_entry_expand_name(3rpc)**, **rpc_ns_group_mbr_inq_next(3rpc)**, **rpc_ns_profile_elt_inq_next(3rpc)**, **rpc_string_binding_compose(3rpc)**, **rpc_string_binding_parse(3rpc)**, **uuid_to_string(3rpc)**.

uuid_compare

Purpose

Compares two UUIDs and determines their order

Used by client, server, or management applications.

Synopsis

#include <dce/uuid.h>

signed32 uuid_compare(
uuid_t ***uuid1*,**
uuid_t ***uuid2*,**
unsigned32 ***status*);**

Parameters

Input

uuid1 Specifies a pointer to a UUID. This UUID is compared with the UUID specified in *uuid2*.

Use the value **NULL** to specify a nil UUID for this parameter.

uuid2 Specifies a pointer to a UUID. This UUID is compared with the UUID specified in *uuid1*.

Use the value **NULL** to specify a nil UUID for this parameter.

Output

status Returns the status code from this routine. This status code indicates whether the routine completed successfully or, if not, why not.

The possible status codes and their meanings are as follows:

uuid_s_ok	Success.
uuid_s_bad_version	Bad UUID version.

Description

The **uuid_compare**( ) routine compares two UUIDs and determines their order. A nil UUID is considered the first element in order. The order of UUIDs is defined by the RPC architecture and is not a temporal (related to time) ordering. Comparing two specific UUIDs always returns the same result regardless of the implementation or system architecture.

You can use this routine to sort data with UUIDs as a key.

Return Values

Returns one of the following constants:

-1 The *uuid1* parameter precedes the *uuid2* parameter in order.

0 The *uuid1* parameter is equal to the *uuid2* parameter in order.

1 The *uuid1* parameter follows the *uuid2* parameter in order.

Note that a value of 0 (zero) has the same meaning as if **uuid_equal**(*&uuid1*, *&uuid2*) returned a value of TRUE.

A nil UUID is the first UUID in order. This means the following:

- If *uuid1* is **NULL** and *uuid2* is non-nil, the routine returns -1.
- If *uuid1* is **NULL** and *uuid2* is **NULL**, the routine returns 0.
- If *uuid1* is non-nil and *uuid2* is **NULL**, the routine returns 1.

Related Information

Functions: **uuid_equal(3rpc)**, **uuid_is_nil(3rpc)**.

uuid_create

Purpose Creates a new UUID

Used by client, server, or management applications.

Synopsis

```
#include <dce/uuid.h>

void uuid_create(
        uuid_t *uuid,
        unsigned32 *status);
```

Parameters

Input

None.

Output

uuid Returns the new UUID.

status Returns the status code from this routine. This status code indicates whether the routine completed successfully or, if not, why not.

The possible status codes and their meanings are as follows:

uuid_s_ok	Success.
uuid_s_getconf_failure	Cannot get network interface device configuration.
uuid_s_no_address	Cannot get Ethernet hardware address.
uuid_s_socket_failure	Cannot create socket.

Description

The **uuid_create**( ) routine creates a new UUID.

Return Values

No value is returned.

Related Information

Functions: **uuid_create_nil(3rpc)**, **uuid_from_string(3rpc)**, **uuid_to_string(3rpc)**.

uuid_create_nil

Purpose Creates a nil UUID

Used by client, server, or management applications.

Synopsis **#include <dce/uuid.h>**

void uuid_create_nil(
uuid_t ***nil_uuid*,**
unsigned32 ***status*);**

Parameters

Input

None.

Output

nil_uuid Returns a nil UUID.

status Returns the status code from this routine. This status code indicates whether the routine completed successfully or, if not, why not.

The possible status code and its meaning is as follows:

uuid_s_ok Success.

Description

The **uuid_create_nil( )** routine creates a nil UUID.

Return Values

No value is returned.

Related Information

Functions: **uuid_create(3rpc)**.

uuid_equal

Purpose Determines if two UUIDs are equal

Used by client, server, or management applications.

Synopsis

```
#include <dce/uuid.h>

boolean32 uuid_equal(
        uuid_t *uuid1,
        uuid_t *uuid2,
        unsigned32 *status);
```

Parameters

Input

uuid1 Specifies a pointer to a UUID. This UUID is compared with the UUID specified in *uuid2*. Supply the value **NULL** to specify a nil UUID for this parameter.

uuid2 Specifies a pointer to a UUID. This UUID is compared with the UUID specified in *uuid1*. Supply the value **NULL** to specify a nil UUID for this parameter.

Output

status Returns the status code from this routine. This status code indicates whether the routine completed successfully or, if not, why not.

The possible status codes and their meanings are as follows:

uuid_s_ok	Success.
uuid_s_bad_version	Bad UUID version.

Description

The **uuid_equal**( ) routine compares two UUIDs and determines if they are equal.

Return Values

The possible return values and their meanings are as follows:

TRUE — The *uuid1* parameter is equal to the *uuid2* parameter. Parameter *status* contains the status code **uuid_s_ok**.

FALSE — The *uuid1* parameter is not equal to the *uuid2* parameter.

Related Information

Functions: **uuid_compare(3rpc)**.

uuid_from_string

Purpose Converts a string UUID to its binary representation

Used by client, server, or management applications.

Synopsis **#include <dce/uuid.h>**

void uuid_from_string(
  **unsigned_char_t ****string_uuid*,
  **uuid_t ****uuid*,
  **unsigned32 ****status*);

Parameters

Input

string_uuid Specifies a string representation of a UUID. Supply the value **NULL** or the null string (**\0**) to specify a nil UUID.

Output

uuid Returns the binary form of the UUID specified by the *string_uuid* parameter into the address specified by this parameter.

status Returns the status code from this routine. This status code indicates whether the routine completed successfully or, if not, why not.

The possible status codes and their meanings are as follows:

uuid_s_ok	Success.
uuid_s_bad_version	Bad UUID version.
uuid_s_invalid_string_uuid	Invalid format for a string UUID.

Description

An application calls the **uuid_from_string()** routine to convert a string UUID to its binary representation.

Return Values

No value is returned.

Related Information

Functions: **uuid_to_string(3rpc)**.

uuid_hash

Purpose

Creates a hash value for a UUID

Used by client, server, or management applications.

Synopsis

#include <dce/uuid.h>

```
unsigned16 uuid_hash(
        uuid_t *uuid,
        unsigned32 *status);
```

Parameters

Input

uuid Specifies the UUID for which a hash value is created. Supply **NULL** to specify a nil UUID for this parameter.

Output

status Returns the status code from this routine. This status code indicates whether the routine completed successfully or, if not, why not.

The possible status codes and their meanings are as follows:

uuid_s_ok	Success.
uuid_s_bad_version	Bad UUID version.

Description

The **uuid_hash( )** routine generates a hash value for a specified UUID.

Note that the return value for a single *uuid* value may differ across platforms.

Return Values

Returns a hash value for the specified UUID.

uuid_is_nil

Purpose

Determines if a UUID is nil

Used by client, server, or management applications.

Synopsis

#include <dce/uuid.h>

boolean32 uuid_is_nil(
uuid_t ***uuid*,**
unsigned32 ***status*);**

Parameters

Input

uuid Specifies a UUID to test as a nil UUID. Supply **NULL** to specify a nil UUID for this parameter.

Output

status Returns the status code from this routine. This status code indicates whether the routine completed successfully or, if not, why not.

The possible status codes and their meanings are as follows:

uuid_s_ok	Success.
uuid_s_bad_version	Bad UUID version.

Description

The **uuid_is_nil()** routine determines whether the specified UUID is a nil UUID. This routine yields the same result as if an application did the following:

- Called the **uuid_create_nil()** routine.
- Called the **uuid_equal()** routine to compare the returned nil UUID to the UUID specified in the *uuid* parameter.

Return Values

The possible return values and their meanings are as follows:

TRUE The *uuid* parameter is a nil UUID. Parameter *status* contains the status code **uuid_s_ok**.

FALSE The *uuid* parameter is not a nil UUID.

Related Information

Functions: **uuid_compare(3rpc)**, **uuid_create_nil(3rpc)**, **uuid_equal(3rpc)**.

uuid_to_string

Purpose Converts a UUID from a binary representation to a string representation

Used by client, server, or management applications.

Synopsis **#include <dce/uuid.h>**

void uuid_to_string(
uuid_t ******uuid*,
unsigned_char_t *******string_uuid*,
unsigned32 ******status*);

Parameters

Input

uuid Specifies a UUID in its binary format. Supply **NULL** to specify a nil UUID for this parameter.

Output

string_uuid Returns a pointer to the string representation of the UUID specified in the *uuid* parameter. Specify **NULL** for this parameter to prevent the routine from returning this information.

status Returns the status code from this routine. This status code indicates whether the routine completed successfully or, if not, why not.

The possible status codes and their meanings are as follows:

uuid_s_ok	Success.
uuid_s_bad_version	Bad UUID version.

Description

The **uuid_to_string()** routine converts a UUID from its binary representation to its string representation.

The RPC runtime allocates memory for the string returned in the *string_uuid* parameter. The application calls **rpc_string_free()** to deallocate that memory. It is not necessary to call **rpc_string_free()** when you supply **NULL** for the *string_uuid* parameter.

Return Values

No value is returned.

Related Information

Functions: **rpc_string_free(3rpc)**, **uuid_from_string(3rpc)**.

idl_messages

Purpose IDL compiler error messages

Description

This reference page documents the IDL compiler error messages in alphabetical order. The documentation for each error message includes the message text, the explanation, and the suggested user action.

A conformant field must be the last field in the structure

Explanation: The IDL compiler restricts arrays with bounds that are not fixed and that occur in structures to only the last field in the structure.

User Action: If the structure contains more than one conformant array, remove all but one of them. Move the conformant array so it is the last field in the structure definition.

A conformant **[v1_array]** must also be varying

Explanation: An array with the **[v1_array]** attribute that has a conformant upper bound that is not fixed must also be varying (it must have a **[last_is]** or **[length_is]** attribute in addition to the **[max_is]** or **[size_is]** attribute).

User Action: If compatibility with NCS Version 1 NIDL is not necessary, remove the **[v1_array]** attribute. Otherwise, add a **[last_is]** or **[length_is]** attribute to the declaration.

A **[first_is]** variable must be a **small**, **short**, or **long** integer

Explanation: The **[first_is]** attribute specifies a field or parameter that contains the lower data limit of a varying array. Array data limits must be nonhyper integers.

User Action: Change the data limit field or parameter referenced by the **[first_is]** clause to integer data type.

A **[handle]** binding parameter must be **[in]** or **[in,out]**

Explanation: A parameter of a data type with the **[handle]** attribute as the first parameter in an operation is used to establish a binding to a server of the interface. It must be an **[in]** or **[in,out]** parameter.

User Action: Place the **[in]** attribute on the **[handle]** parameter.

A **handle_t** as other than the first parameter requires a **[transmit_as]**

Explanation: Data type **handle_t** is only meaningful when used as the data type of the first parameter in an operation. A bound handle is used to deliver the call to the correct server of the interface. A bound **handle_t** parameter itself is not transmittable. When the **handle_t** type is used in other than the first parameter, it must have a **[transmit_as]** clause to convert it to a transmittable type.

User Action: Use data type **handle_t** only as the data type of the first parameter in an operation, unless the defined data type has a **[transmit_as]** clause.

A **handle_t** binding parameter must be an **[in]** parameter

Explanation: A parameter of type **handle_t** as the first parameter in an operation establishes a binding to a server of the interface. It must be an **[in]** parameter only.

User Action: Remove the **[out]** attribute from the **handle_t** parameter.

A **handle_t** first parameter must not have **[transmit_as]** type

Explanation: A parameter of type **handle_t**, when used as the data type of the first parameter in an operation, is used to establish a binding to a server of the interface. It is not sent over the wire; therefore, it is incorrect for it to have a **[transmit_as]** data type.

User Action: Remove the **[transmit_as]** clause from the type's declaration.

A **hyper** constant type is not allowed

Explanation: A **hyper** constant is not allowed.

User Action: Modify the **constant** type to one of the supported types: **long, char, boolean, void *,** or **char ***.

A **[last_is]** variable must be a **small**, **short**, or **long** integer

Explanation: The **[last_is]** attribute specifies a field or parameter that contains the upper data limit of a varying array. Array data limits must be nonhyper integers.

User Action: Change the upper data limit field or parameter referenced by the **[last_is]** clause to be of integer data type.

A **[length_is]** variable must be a **small**, **short**, or **long** integer

Explanation: The **[length_is]** attribute specifies a field or parameter that contains the data length of a varying array. The field or parameter must be a nonhyper integer.

User Action: Change the field or parameter referenced by the **[length_is]** clause to be of integer data type.

A **[max_is]** parameter must have the **[in]** attribute

Explanation: The **[max_is]** attribute specifies a parameter that contains the upper bound of a conformant array. This must be an **[in]** attribute so the server stub code knows how much space to allocate for the array.

User Action: Change the upper bound parameter referenced by the **[max_is]** clause to have the **[in]** attribute.

A **[max_is]** variable must be a **small**, **short**, or **long** integer

Explanation: The **[max_is]** attribute specifies a field or parameter that contains the upper bound of a conformant array. Array bounds must be nonhyper integers.

User Action: Change the upper bound field or parameter referenced by the **[max_is]** clause to be of integer data type.

A **[maybe]** operation cannot have **[out]** parameters or a function result

Explanation: The **[maybe]** attribute specifies that the operation's caller does not require and does not receive a response or fault indication. Do not use an **[out]** parameter or a function result in a **[maybe]** operation.

User Action: Remove the **[maybe]** attribute from the operation, or remove all **[out]** parameters from the function and declare its result type as **void**.

A nonlocal interface cannot import a local interface

Explanation: The **[local]** interface attribute implies that the interface is not part of an RPC application, but used only to generate header files. This causes IDL to suppress any errors specific to RPC that the interface uses as part of an RPC application.

User Action: Remove the **[local]** attribute from the imported interface definition. The imported interface does not need a UUID unless the interface defines an operation and you compile it independently.

A parameter must have either or both the **[in]** and **[out]** attributes

Explanation: The direction of a parameter must be declared. The **[in]** attribute tells IDL that the parameter is passed from client to server. The **[out]** attribute tells IDL that the parameter is passed from server to client.

User Action: Add the **[in]**, **[out]**, or **[in,out]** attribute to the parameter.

A parameter with [*attribute-name*] cannot be passed by value

Explanation: The [*attribute-name*] attribute can only be applied to a parameter if that parameter has an explicit * (asterisk).

User Action: Modify the parameter signature to have a top-level *.

A parameter with [*attribute-name*] must be an **[out]** parameter

Explanation: A **[comm_status]** or **[fault_status]** parameter is used to return an error code if a certain type of error occurs during execution of an operation. Thus, it must be an **[out]** parameter.

User Action: Place the **[out]** attribute on the parameter.

A parameter with [*attribute-name*] must be of type **error_status_t**

Explanation: A **[comm_status]** or **[fault_status]** parameter or function result is used to return an error code if a certain type of error occurs during execution of an operation. The data type of the variable must be **error_status_t**.

User Action: Declare the variable to be of data type **error_status_t**.

A **pipe** cannot have a **[transmit_as]** type

Explanation: A pipe is a specialized object handled by RPC that, by itself, is not a transmittable object. Thus, a **[transmit_as]** clause is invalid on a **pipe** definition.

User Action: Remove the **[transmit_as]** attribute.

A **[ref]** function result is not valid

Explanation: Unlike **[out]** parameters, there is never any preexisting storage in the caller for pointer valued function results. The pointer always indicates new storage. This is the capability provided by full pointers only, not **[ref]** pointers.

User Action: Remove the **[ref]** attribute from the type definition of the data type of the function result.

A size attribute variable must not have a **[represent_as]** type

Explanation: The parameter or field referenced in a **[max_is]**, **[size_is]**, **[first_is]**, **[last_is]**, or **[length_is]** clause must not be of a data type that is declared to have a **[represent_as]** type.

User Action: Change the referenced parameter or field data type, or the data type definition itself.

A size attribute variable must not have a **[transmit_as]** type

Explanation: The parameter or field referenced in a **[max_is]**, **[size_is]**, **[first_is]**, **[last_is]**, or **[length_is]** clause must not be of a data type that is declared to have a **[transmit_as]** type.

User Action: Change the referenced parameter or field data type, or the data type definition itself.

A size specifier is required; **long** assumed

Explanation: A size specifier is required when specifying the **int** data type.

User Action: Place a size specifier (**short, small, long,** or **hyper**) before the **int** keyword.

A **[size_is]** parameter must have the **[in]** attribute

Explanation: The **[size_is]** attribute specifies a parameter that contains size information of a conformant array. This must be an **[in]** attribute so the server stub code knows how much space to allocate for the array.

User Action: Change the size parameter referenced by the **[size_is]** clause to have the **[in]** attribute.

A **[size_is]** variable must be a **small**, **short**, or **long** integer

Explanation: The **[size_is]** attribute specifies a field or parameter that contains size information of a conformant array. Array bounds, and thus array size, must be nonhyper integers.

User Action: Change the size information field or parameter referenced by the **[size_is]** clause to be of integer data type.

A source IDL filename is required

Explanation: The command line does not contain a source IDL file to compile.

User Action: You must specify a source IDL file. You may have erroneously specified the source IDL file when actually you gave a value to a command option.

A **[string]** array cannot have varying array attributes

Explanation: The **[string]** attribute says that the length of a string is an intrinsic property of the string itself; for example, C strings are 0 (zero) terminated.

User Action: Remove any **[first_is]**, **[last_is]**, or **[length_is]** clauses from the string declaration.

A translated transmittable type cannot contain [*attribute-name*] pointers

Explanation: A transmittable type that is derived by calling a translation routine, for example, a **from_local** translation of a **[represent_as]** type or a **to_xmit** translation of a **[transmit_as]** type, cannot contain pointers of the indicated type.

User Action: Define a transmittable type that does not contain invalid pointers. If using **[represent_as]**, reconsider using it.

A **[transmit_as]** or **[represent_as]** type cannot be a conformant array

Explanation: A type specified in a **[transmit_as]** clause or a type with the **[transmit_as]** or **[represent_as]** attribute cannot be a conformant array, since there is nowhere to attach the size information attribute that is needed to transmit the data.

User Action: Define a structure that contains a conformant array and a size information field instead of using a conformant array directly.

A type used in a **[transmit_as]** clause cannot have a **[represent_as]** type

Explanation: The type used in a **[transmit_as]** clause specifies an alternative type that a base IDL type is translated to or from and before or after transmission over the network. The type used in a **[represent_as]** clause is an alternative type that a base IDL type is translated from or to at the application code-to-stub code interface. Going from base IDL type to transmittable type and then to a **[represent_as]** type (that may not be transmittable) is invalid.

User Action: You may have meant to put a **[represent_as]** clause on the base IDL type, not its transmittable type.

A type with **[transmit_as]** cannot have other type attributes

Explanation: A data type with the **[transmit_as]** attribute (the presented type) has an associated transmittable type, and you must write routines to convert the presented type to or from the transmittable type. Only the transmittable type is relevant to the RPC mechanism; thus, it is incorrect for the presented type to have additional RPC-specific attributes.

User Action: Remove any type attributes other than **[transmit_as]**.

A **union** discriminator type must be **small, short, long, char, boolean,** or **enum**

Explanation: The discriminator of a **union**, that determines which case of the **union** is used, is restricted to integer, character, enumeration, and Boolean data types. Also, **hyper int** discriminators are not allowed.

User Action: Change the discriminator to one of the valid data types. Make sure the data type of the **constant** values in the **case** clauses within the **union** agree with the discriminator data type.

A **[v1_array]** can be conformant or varying in first dimension only

Explanation: An array with the **[v1_array]** attribute is limited to a conformant or varying upper data limit in the first dimension only.

User Action: Remove the **[v1_array]** attribute from the array declaration.

A **[v1_string]** must be an array of **char** with fixed bounds

Explanation: A **[v1_string]** is compatible with the NCS Version 1 NIDL **string0** data type. It must be a single dimensioned array of **char** with a 0 (zero) lower bound and a fixed upper bound.

User Action: If compatibility with NCS Version 1 NIDL is required, change the declaration accordingly. Otherwise, see the documentation regarding the **[string]** attribute.

ACF **include** statement advised for definition of type *name*

Explanation: An Attribute Configuration File (ACF) declares a type that is not defined in an IDL file. The type is referenced in the generated stub code; thus, its definition needs to be included into the stub code as well.

User Action: Place an **include** statement in the ACF to cause your module that defines the type to be included into the generated header file.

ACF interface name *name* differs from IDL interface name *name*

Explanation: The interface name in an interface's Attribute Configuration File must be identical to the interface name in the IDL source.

User Action: Change the ACF to use the correct interface name.

An arm of a **union** cannot be or contain a **[ref]** pointer

Explanation: IDL-generated server stub code must allocate storage for objects pointed to by **[ref]** pointers. IDL does not allow a **[ref]** pointer within a **union** because the valid arm of the **union**, and therefore the object for which storage is allocated, is not known at compile time.

User Action: Change the pointer within the **union** declaration to a full pointer.

An array with a pointer attribute is valid only as a parameter

Explanation: An array that is a parameter in an operation can have a pointer attribute because arrays are implicitly passed by reference pointer. Otherwise, an array cannot have a pointer attribute.

User Action: Remove the pointer attribute from the parameter or type definition, or define a new type without a pointer attribute.

An attribute is defined multiple times

Explanation: An attribute is repeated multiple times in an attribute list.

User Action: Remove all but one occurrence of the offending attribute.

An attribute variable cannot be an indirect field reference

Explanation: An indirect field reference is used in a field attribute; indirection is not allowed in this context.

User Action: Remove the indirection. For example, if the referenced field was **long *sp;** and the attribute expression was **[size_is(*sp**]), then change the field to **long s;** and the attribute expression to **[size_is(s**]).

An **[implicit_handle]** variable must either be of type **handle_t** or have the **[handle]** attribute

Explanation: The **[implicit_handle]** variable declared in the ACF must be a handle, either a primitive handle of data type **handle_t**; or a customized handle, a data type with the **[handle]** attribute.

User Action: Specify a valid handle data type for the **[implicit_handle]**.

An operation result cannot be a **pipe**

Explanation: Pipes are not allowed as operation results.

User Action: Change the operation so the **pipe** is an extra **[out]** parameter instead of the operation result.

An operation with [*attribute-name*] must return a value of type **error_status_t**

Explanation: The **[comm_status]** or **[fault_status]** attribute on an operation signifies that the return value of the operation is used to return an error code if a certain type of error occurs during execution of an operation. Thus, the operation must be declared to deliver a result of data type **error_status_t**.

User Action: Declare the operation result to be of data type **error_status_t**.

An **[out]** conformant array must be a top-level parameter or under a full pointer

Explanation: An array with unspecified lower and/or upper bounds requires size information. If the array is a top-level parameter, the size information must be in additional **[in]** parameters. If the array is contained within a structure, the size information must be in additional fields of the structure, and the parameter containing the structure must be **[in]** or **[in,out]**. In both cases, the size information must be **[in]** so the server stub knows how much storage to allocate for the array. The exception to this latter case is any **[out]** conformant array that is pointed to by a full **[ptr]** pointer or that indirectly lies under a full **[ptr]** pointer. In this case the semantics are that the user-written manager code either allocates and/or manages the storage for the array and any other data below the full **[ptr]** pointer or returning a **NULL** value for the full **[ptr]** pointer.

User Action: Change the parameter to be **[in,out]**, pass the array as a separate **[out]** parameter with **[in]** size information parameters, or change the data structure and the code that manipulates it so the conformant array is under a full **[ptr]** pointer.

An **[out,ptr]** parameter is not valid

Explanation: The **[ptr]** parameter attribute implies that the value of the pointer may be **NULL**. It is invalid on an **[out]** only parameter, since the possible nullity is not shipped to the server (for example, in the **[in]** direction).

User Action: If the pointer cannot be **NULL** remove the **[ptr]** attribute. Otherwise, make the parameter an **[in,out,ptr]** parameter.

Array elements cannot be conformant arrays or structures

Explanation: Array elements must be of fixed size.

User Action: If the element type is an array, make sure that the array has fixed bounds. If the element type is a structure, make sure that any arrays in the structure have fixed bounds.

Array elements cannot be context handles

Explanation: Arrays of context handles are not allowed.

User Action: Change the definition of the array so its elements are not context handles. If you want to declare an array of context handles, you must use alternative means.

Array elements cannot be of type **handle_t**

Explanation: Data type **handle_t** is only meaningful when used as the data type of the first parameter in an operation. It is used to establish a binding to a server of the interface.

User Action: Do not declare arrays of type **handle_t**.

Array size information required for *identifier*

Explanation: The IDL code uses an array with bounds that are not fixed without specifying the appropriate size attributes.

User Action: Modify the array declaration to include the appropriate **[max_is]** or **[size_is]** attribute. If the array is a parameter, an additional parameter is used to specify size information. If the array is a field in a structure, an additional field is used to specify size information.

Arrays can be conformant in the first dimension only

Explanation: IDL only allows an array to be conformant in its first dimension.

User Action: Modify the array declaration so dimensions other than the first have fixed bounds.

Arrays can be varying in the first dimension only

Explanation: IDL only allows an array to be varying in its first dimension.

User Action: Remove the **[first_is]**, **[last_is]**, or **[length_is]** attributes that refer to dimensions other than the first.

Array elements cannot be pipes

Explanation: Array elements cannot be pipes.

User Action: Change the definition of the array so its elements are not of a **pipe** data type. If you want to declare an array of pipes, you must use alternative means.

Arrays with **[transmit_as]** cannot be conformant or varying

Explanation: IDL does not allow a conformant or varying array with the **[transmit_as]** attribute.

User Action: Change the declaration so the array is of fixed size and has no data limit attributes, or remove the **[transmit_as]** attribute.

At least one operation must have the **[code]** attribute

Explanation: All of the operations in the interface are marked so no code is generated for them in the stub modules.

User Action: If you used the ACF **[nocode]** attribute on the interface, be sure to specify **[code]** on at least one operation. To disable stub generation entirely, use a command line option.

Attribute **[context_handle]** only applies to **void** * types

Explanation: The attribute **[context_handle]** indicates that the data is a pointer-sized object that serves as the handle, or method of accessing, some object. To the called operation, the data is often an address of a structure in memory, although it need not be. A context handle is opaque to, and must never be written by, the caller code. To emphasize this, IDL requires that context handles are defined as type **void** *.

User Action: Change the declaration with the **[context_handle]** attribute to data type **void** *.

Case label must be a **constant** from the enumeration of the discriminant

Explanation: The value of a **case** expression in a discriminated **union** is from a different enumeration data type than the enumeration data type of the discriminator variable in the **switch** clause.

User Action: Change the discriminator declaration or the **case** expression so the enumeration data types match.

Case label type does not agree with discriminator type

Explanation: The value of a **case** expression in a discriminated **union** is not the same data type as the discriminator variable in the **switch** clause.

User Action: Change the discriminator declaration or the **case** expression so the data types match.

Character constant cannot be portable across character sets

Explanation: You used an integer value to specify a character. This cannot be portable across different character sets (ASCII and EBCDIC).

User Action: Consider your portability requirements.

Command option **-bug** *number* conflicts with **-no_bug** *number*

Explanation: The command line options conflict with each other.

User Action: Remove one of the conflicting options.

Command option **-bug** *number* is not known

Explanation: The documentation defines all the valid integers that can accompany the **-bug** and **-no_bug** options. You have chosen an invalid value.

User Action: Refer to the documentation for the correct number.

Command option **-no_bug** *number* is not known

Explanation: The documentation defines all the valid integers that can accompany the **-bug** and **-no_bug** options. You have chosen an invalid value.

User Action: Refer to the documentation for the correct number.

Command option *-option-name option-value* is not valid

Explanation: The *option-value* specified is not valid for the option with which it is used.

User Action: Refer to the documentation for the correct command line syntax.

Command option *option* does not take a value

Explanation: You specified a value with a command line option that does not take a value.

User Action: If the value is meant to be the source file, it must be separated from the command option with a space.

Compilation aborted

Explanation: Previous errors caused the compilation to abort.

User Action: Correct the errors and recompile.

Conformant array or structure is invalid within a **union**

Explanation: The IDL compiler does not allow an array with bounds that are not fixed in a discriminated **union**. Each member of a **union** must be of fixed size.

User Action: It is possible to have a **union** case that is a full **[ptr]** pointer to a conformant array or conformant structure. Change the declaration and associated code accordingly.

Constant name: *name* not found

Explanation: The named **constant** is not defined.

User Action: Modify the interface and specify a known constant.

Constant type does not agree with constant expression

Explanation: You used a constant expression that is inappropriate for the constant type.

User Action: Modify the constant definition so the expression matches the type.

Context handle is not valid as a member of a **union**

Explanation: A context handle cannot be a member of a **union**.

User Action: Pass a context handle as a separate parameter to an operation, rather than embedding it as a member of a **union**.

Context handles are not valid as structure fields

Explanation: A context handle is not allowed as a field of a structure.

User Action: Pass a context handle as a separate parameter to an operation, rather than embedding it as a field of a structure.

Could not invoke the C preprocessor

Explanation: The IDL compiler is unable to invoke the C preprocessor to preprocess the IDL file before compiling it.

User Action: If you do not need the C preprocessor, you can use a command line option to prevent the IDL compiler from calling it. If you specified the C preprocessor to invoke with a command line option, check to make sure you gave the correct file specification. If you do not specify a C preprocessor, the IDL compiler looks in a default directory for it. The C preprocessor may not be installed in the expected directory.

Data type **error_status_t** must be defined in **nbase.idl**

Explanation: You specified an additional **[comm_status]** or **[fault_status]** parameter for an operation in the Attribute Configuration File (ACF). This requires that data type **error_status_t** be defined.

User Action: Usually, **error_status_t** is a predefined type in the RPC-supplied imported interface **nbase.idl**. Make sure you are accessing the RPC-supplied **nbase.idl**.

DCE IDL compiler version *version*

Explanation: Identifies the current version of the IDL compiler.

User Action: Use this version number when submitting bug reports.

Declaration of *name* cannot contain an anonymous type

Explanation: The type specification for the parameter, field or **union** arm *name* contains a data type that is an anonymous **struct** or **union**. Since such a type is unique and not compatible with any other type, the generated stubs cannot generate code to access the type.

User Action: Move the **struct** or **union** declaration into a **typedef** and modify the declaration of *name* to use the newly created type name.

Definition of tag *name* is not yet complete

Explanation: The tag *name* is forward referenced in a context that requires it to be completely defined. References to **struct** or **union** types by means of the tag name before the **struct** or **union** is completely defined is only allowed in contexts in which the size is not needed (a pointer to the type or in a **typedef**). Although IDL can process such references, the resulting stub cannot be compiled by most C compilers.

User Action: Move the declaration of the **struct** or **union** prior to this reference.

Duplicate **case** label value

Explanation: A discriminated **union** contains more than one **case** label with the same value. Each **case** label value in a discriminated **union** can be used at most once.

User Action: Remove one of the conflicting **case** labels.

Duplicate protocol specification in endpoint list; "*endpoint*" ignored

Explanation: Each protocol can be listed at most once in the endpoint list. The specified endpoint specification duplicates another endpoint specification and is ignored.

User Action: Use each protocol at most once in the endpoint list.

Extraneous punctuation character *character* ignored

Explanation: A punctuation character was found in a location where it is not allowed in the IDL language syntax.

User Action: If it is only an extra punctuation character, remove it. If the character appears correct, then the error may be caused by another nearby syntax error. Correct the other syntax errors and recompile the interface.

File *filename* is a system-defined IDL filename

Explanation: The file *filename* has the same name as an RPC-supplied system IDL file. This can cause unexpected compilation errors, such as missing declarations of IDL predefined types.

User Action: Rename *filename* so it does not conflict with any of the system-defined IDL filenames.

File *filename* not found

Explanation: A file, specified by the user either in the IDL source or ACF file, does not exist.

User Action: Check the filenames you specified. Determine the location of any imported or included files that are needed to compile the IDL source file specified. If any are not in the directories that the IDL compiler searches by default, you must use a command line option to specify additional directories to search.

File *filename*, line *number*

Explanation: Identifies the filename and source line number associated with an error.

User Action: None. This is an informational message.

File *filename*, line *number*: *source text*

Explanation: Identifies the filename, source line number, and source text associated with an error.

User Action: None. This is an informational message.

File is not a directory: *filename*

Explanation: A file that is not a directory is specified in a context where a directory is required; for example, as the command line option that specifies an output directory.

User Action: Specify a filename that is a directory.

Floating point constants not supported

Explanation: Floating-point constants cannot be specified in IDL.

User Action: Remove the **float** constant specification.

Full pointers to context handles are not allowed

Explanation: IDL does not allow full pointers to context handles.

User Action: If the declaration has the **[ptr]** attribute, either explicitly or by default, change it to a **[ref]** pointer. If the declaration is an operation result, it cannot be a **[ref]** pointer; thus, an operation result of type pointer to context handle is not possible.

Generated name too long at line *number*

Explanation: The compiler generated an identifier that is too long for some standard C compiler implementations.

User Action: Shorten the name at the specified line.

Identifier: *name* too long; maximum is *number* chars

Explanation: The length identifier exceeds the maximum number of characters allowed by IDL for portability.

User Action: Shorten the identifier name to within the allowed limit. Make sure the shortened identifier name is unique.

include filename must not contain a file extension

Explanation: The filename specified in an **include** statement in the Attribute Configuration File (ACF) must not contain a file extension. In a future IDL version, you will be able to specify a programming language, and the IDL compiler will automatically append the appropriate extension.

User Action: Remove the file extension. The current IDL compiler always assumes an **.h** extension.

Integer constant *integer* is invalid

Explanation: The integer contains incorrect characters.

User Action: Correct the specification of the integer.

Integer division by zero

Explanation: The evaluation of an integer constant expression resulted in an integer divided by zero.

User Action: Correct the expression so a division by zero does not occur.

Integer value overflows *size*

Explanation: The integer value specified is too large to be contained in the destination of size *size*.

User Action: Either reduce the size of the integer value, or increase the size of the destination declaration.

Interface attributes **[auto_handle]** and **[implicit_handle]** cannot occur together

Explanation: The **[auto_handle]** and **[implicit_handle]** attributes are two distinct mechanisms for managing the binding between client and server at runtime. You cannot specify both of these attributes.

User Action: Refer to the documentation to determine which binding mechanism to use. Then remove one of the conflicting attributes from the interface attribute list in the Attribute Configuration File (ACF).

Interface attributes **[code]** and **[nocode]** cannot occur together

Explanation: The **[code]** or **[nocode]** attribute on an interface establishes the default for operations in the interface. You can specify only one of these attributes.

User Action: Remove one of the conflicting attributes.

Interface attributes **[in_line]** and **[out_of_line]** cannot occur together

Explanation: The **[in_line]** or **[out_of_line]** attribute on an interface establishes the default for types in the interface. You can specify only one of these attributes.

User Action: Remove one of the conflicting attributes.

Interface UUID must be specified

Explanation: The interface does not have the **[uuid]** attribute required for the complete definition of the interface.

User Action: Either add the **[local]** attribute to the interface, or generate a UUID with the **uuidgen** utility supplied with IDL and specify the UUID value in the interface **[uuid]** attribute.

Internal IDL compiler error: Module *module*, Line *line*

Explanation: An internal IDL compiler error was found.

User Action: Submit a Software Performance Report and notify your software support representative so the appropriate action can be taken.

Invalid array bound type

Explanation: Array indices must be integers.

User Action: Change the array declaration so the fixed bounds are integer constants.

Invalid **case** label type

Explanation: The values in **case** clauses in discriminated **union**s must be integer, enumeration, Boolean, or character values that match the data type of the **union** discriminator.

User Action: Modify the invalid clause to use a value of the correct data type.

Invalid character literal

Explanation: The specification of the character literal is invalid.

User Action: Character literals can be specified as a single printing character or one of the following escape sequences: **\n**, **\t**, **\v**, **\b**, **\r**, **\f**, **\a**, ****, **\?**, **\'**, **\"**, ****\ *ooo*, **\x***hh* (where *ooo* are octal digits, and *hh* are hexadecimal digits).

Invalid octal digit in *integer*

Explanation: An octal integer contains a digit that is not valid. Integer constants with a leading 0 (zero) are interpreted as octal values. Only the digits 0 through 7 are valid in octal value.

User Action: If the integer is not intended to be specified in octal, remove the leading 0s (zeros). Otherwise, correct the value to contain only octal digits.

Invalid parameters on command line:

Explanation: There are extra parameters on the command line.

User Action: You may have attempted to use a value on a option that does not take a value, or attempted to compile more than one interface at once. Refer to the documentation for the proper command line syntax.

Invalid use of tag *name*

Explanation: You used a previously defined tag name in a declaration of a different type. Tag names can be used for a **struct** or **union** declaration, but not both.

User Action: Either make sure that each use of the tag name specifies the same type, or use different tag names with each type.

Legal values are:

Explanation: Identifies a list of legal values for a command option.

User Action: Reenter the option using one of the legal values.

Maximum identifier length for interface name is *number* characters

Explanation: The IDL compiler constructs new identifier names that are referenced by generated stub code from the interface name. Therefore, the number of characters allowed in an interface name is less than for other identifiers.

User Action: Shorten the interface name.

Maximum identifier length for type with **[transmit_as]** is *number* characters

Explanation: The IDL compiler constructs new identifier names that are referenced by generated stub code from the names of any **[transmit_as]** data types. Therefore, the number of characters allowed in such a data type is less than for other identifiers.

User Action: Shorten the data type name.

Maximum identifier length for **[handle]** type is *number* characters

Explanation: The IDL compiler constructs new identifier names that are referenced by generated stub code from the names of any **[handle]** data types. Therefore, the number of characters allowed in such a data type is less than for other identifiers.

User Action: Shorten the data type name.

Maximum identifier length for **[context_handle]** type is *number* characters

Explanation: The IDL compiler constructs new identifier names that are referenced by generated stub code from the names of any **[context_handle]** data types. Therefore, the number of characters allowed in such a data type is less than for other identifiers.

User Action: Shorten the data type name.

Maximum identifier length for pointed-to type is *number* characters

Explanation: The IDL compiler constructs new identifier names that are referenced by generated stub code from the names of any pointed-to data types. Therefore, the number of characters allowed in such a data type is less than for other identifiers.

User Action: Shorten the data type name.

Maximum identifier length for **pipe** type is *number* characters

Explanation: The IDL compiler constructs new identifier names that are referenced by generated stub code from the names of any **pipe** data types. Therefore, the number of characters allowed in such a data type is less than for other identifiers.

User Action: Shorten the data type name.

Maximum identifier length for **[represent_as]** type is *number* characters

Explanation: The IDL compiler constructs new identifier names that are referenced by generated stub code from the names of any **[represent_as]** data types. Therefore, the number of characters allowed in such a data type is less than for other identifiers.

User Action: Shorten the data type name.

Maximum identifier length for **[out_of_line]** type is *number* characters

Explanation: The IDL compiler constructs new identifier names that are referenced by generated stub code from the names of any **[out_of_line]** data types. Therefore, the number of characters allowed in such a data type is less than for other identifiers.

User Action: Shorten the data type name.

Members of **union**s cannot be of type **handle_t**

Explanation: Data type **handle_t** is only meaningful when used as the data type of the first parameter in an operation. It is used to establish a binding to a server of the interface.

User Action: Do not declare **union** members of data type **handle_t**.

Missing] on array bound

Explanation: The right bracket on an array bound specification was not found. It may have been omitted, or some other syntax error may cause IDL to overlook the bracket.

User Action: Add the right bracket if it is missing; otherwise, make sure there are no other syntax errors.

Missing] on attribute list

Explanation: The right bracket on an attribute list was not found. It may have been omitted, or some other syntax error may cause IDL to overlook the bracket.

User Action: Add the right bracket if it is missing; otherwise, make sure there are no other syntax errors.

Missing pointer class for *name*; **[ptr]** or **[ref]** required

Explanation: A pointer declaration does not have a pointer class attribute and no **[pointer_default]** attribute was specified on the interface.

User Action: All pointers must have one of the pointer class attributes: **[ptr]** or **[ref]**. Either add one of these attributes at the location of the pointer declaration, or add the **[pointer_default]** attribute to the interface to specify the class to be used as the default for the module.

Missing result type on operation declaration

Explanation: No data type was found for the result of an operation while processing what appeared to be an operation declaration. All operations must have an explicit result type.

User Action: If the result type of an operation is omitted, explicitly specify it. If no result is returned from the operation, specify **void** as the result type. This error can also occur due to a previous syntax error.

Missing type on parameter declaration

Explanation: No data type is found for the parameter.

User Action: If the parameter type is omitted, explicitly specify it. This error can also occur due to a previous syntax error.

Missing } on interface declaration

Explanation: The right brace on the interface declaration was not found. It may have been omitted, the nesting of other braces may be incorrect, or some other syntax error may cause IDL to overlook a brace.

User Action: Add the right brace if missing; otherwise, make sure all other braces are specified in pairs, and there are no other syntax errors.

Must compile stubs with ANSI C compiler to avoid promotion of float to double

Explanation: The operation contains a **float** parameter passed by value. Non-ANSI C compilers that do not support function prototypes, automatically promote **float** to **double**. Function prototypes within generated C stubs are conditional on the IDL_PROTOTYPES preprocessor symbol. When you compile a stub with a non-ANSI C compiler, IDL_PROTOTYPES must not be defined (causing the nonprototyped definitions to compile) and thus causing **float** to **double** promotion. This breaks the marshalling logic in the stub that expects a **float**, not a **double**.

User Action: Problems do not occur as long as you compile stubs with an ANSI C compiler. However, to maximize portability, it is highly recommended that you modify any **float** parameter passed by value to either a **double** passed by value or a **float** passed by reference. This message is informational.

Name already declared: *name*

Explanation: The name referenced is already declared.

User Action: Modify the interface and select a unique name for the given item.

Name *identifier* is declared in file *filename*, line *number*

Explanation: Gives the source file and line number of source text to help you diagnose the previous error.

User Action: None. This is an informational message.

Name is not a constant: *name*

Explanation: The name used to define a new constant is not the name of a **constant**.

User Action: Modify the **constant** definition to use a predefined **constant** name.

Name is not a field: *name*

Explanation: The name referenced in an array attribute is not declared as a field in the structure being defined.

User Action: Declare a field in the structure that can be used in the array attribute.

Name is not a parameter: *name*

Explanation: The name referenced in an array attribute is not declared as a parameter in the operation being defined.

User Action: Declare a parameter in the operation that can be used in the array attribute.

Name is not a type: *name*

Explanation: The name referenced is not a type definition.

User Action: Modify the interface to specify a unique type specification instead of the name referenced.

Name is referenced in file *filename*, line *number*

Explanation: Gives the source file and line number of source text to help you diagnose the previous error.

User Action: None. This is an informational message.

Name *name* previously declared in file *filename*, line *line*

Explanation: The name referenced was previously declared at the specified location.

User Action: Remove this declaration, if it is redundant, or change the spelling so it does not conflict with the existing name.

Name not found: *name*

Explanation: The referenced name is not defined.

User Action: Modify the interface to define an appropriate type for the specified name.

NLS message catalog version mismatch in *filename*, Expected: *version*, Actual: *version*

Explanation: The error messages reported by the IDL compiler are stored in an NLS message catalog. The catalog *filename* is not the same version as the IDL compiler being invoked. The error messages reported may therefore be incorrect or cause the compiler to terminate abnormally.

User Action: Check the definition of the NLS environment variable **NLSPATH** and verify that it searches the appropriate directories. The default location for the IDL compiler message catalog is *dceshared***/nls/msg/***LANG***/***%***N**.

No endpoint can be found in the endpoint specification *endpoint specification*

Explanation: The syntax specified in the **endpoint** specification string does not contain an **endpoint** specification. The entire string is assumed to be the protocol name and the **endpoint** remains unspecified in the generated stubs.

User Action: Correct the syntax of the **endpoint** specification.

Noninteger values are not allowed in expressions

Explanation: One of the values in the expression is not an integer (or one that can be promoted to integer).

User Action: Correct the expression to contain only integer values.

Object file for *source file* placed in current working directory

Explanation: A command option specifies a directory other than the current working directory in which to place a generated C source and object file. The IDL compiler does not place the file in the requested directory if you use the **-cc_cmd** argument on the command line. Also, the IDL compiler does not place the file in the requested directory on systems on which the mechanism it usually uses for the placement does not work.

User Action: IDL provides a command option that allows you to pass command options to the C compiler. Use the appropriate C compiler option to ensure that the object files are placed in the correct directory.

Obsolete feature encountered; Use translator

Explanation: A feature of NCS Version 1 NIDL was encountered that is not supported in the IDL compiler. You may be compiling an NCS Version 1 NIDL source file.

User Action: If the input is an NCS Version 1 NIDL source file, process it with the translator utility (the **nidl_to_idl** command) that converts an NCS Version 1 NIDL source file into the format expected by the IDL compiler. Then compile the translated source file. Otherwise, remove the reference to the obsolete feature.

Old UUID format must be replaced with new format

Explanation: The UUID specified in the interface attribute list is in an old format.

User Action: Although the old format is compatible with the new format, we recommend that you switch to the new format. If the input is an NCS Version 1 NIDL source file, process it with the translator utility (the **nidl_to_idl** command) that converts an NCS Version 1 NIDL source file into the format expected by the IDL compiler. You can also use the **uuidgen** command to convert the old format UUID to the new format. When you have the new format for the UUID, compile the translated source file.

Operation attributes **[code]** and **[nocode]** cannot occur together

Explanation: The **[code]** and **[nocode]** attributes have directly opposite meanings. Do not use both.

User Action: Remove one of the conflicting attributes.

Operation *name* has no binding handle parameter; **[auto_handle]** assumed

Explanation: When an operation uses parametric binding, its first parameter is a handle parameter that determines the location of a server of the interface. Operations whose first parameter is not of type **handle_t** and does not have the **[handle]** attribute are assumed to use nonparametric binding known as **auto_handle**, whereby a binding is automatically established by the RPC runtime library.

User Action: Refer to the documentation on the various binding techniques to determine the best method for your application.

Operation name *name* referenced in ACF is not defined

Explanation: Any operation referenced in an Attribute Configuration File (ACF) must be defined in the corresponding IDL file.

User Action: Check for typographical errors in either file.

Options table:

Explanation: Caption for options table printed in usage message.

User Action: None. This is an informational message.

Out of memory

Explanation: The system-defined limit of memory available to the compiler was exceeded.

User Action: Either have the system-defined limit of memory raised, or simplify the source file being compiled by breaking it into multiple modules or eliminating unnecessary imports.

Output parameters must be passed by reference

Explanation: Parameters with the **[out]** or **[in,out]** attributes must be passed by reference, so the changed value of the parameter can be reflected back to the caller.

User Action: Add an * (asterisk) to the parameter declaration to indicate pass-by-reference calling mechanism.

Output parameters require an explicit top-level *

Explanation: Parameters with the **[out]** or **[in,out]** attributes must be passed by reference, so the changed value of the parameter can be reflected back to the caller. IDL does not allow an * (asterisk) in a type definition to serve as a passing mechanism *.

User Action: Change the declaration of the parameter so it contains an explicit *.

Parameter name *name* referenced in ACF operation *name* is not defined

Explanation: Any parameter referenced within an operation declaration in an Attribute Configuration File (ACF) must be defined in the corresponding operation definition in the IDL file.

User Action: Check for typographical errors in either file.

Pipes are not valid as members of **union**s

Explanation: Pipes are not allowed as members of **union**s.

User Action: Pass a **pipe** as a separate parameter to an operation, rather than embedding it as a member of a **union**.

Pipes are not valid as structure fields

Explanation: Pipes are not allowed as fields of structures.

User Action: Pass a **pipe** as a separate parameter to an operation, rather than embedding it as a field of a structure.

Pipes must be defined with a **typedef**

Explanation: The IDL compiler constructs routine names that are referenced by generated stub code from the name of any **pipe** data type. Therefore, the type cannot be anonymous.

User Action: Declare the **pipe** data type with a **typedef** so the **pipe** has a name associated with it.

Pointers to conformant arrays are not allowed

Explanation: An IDL declaration attempts to use mixed pointer * (an asterisk) and array [ ] (brackets) syntax to declare a pointer to an array that has bounds that are not fixed. It is ambiguous whether size attributes apply to the pointer or the array; thus, IDL does not allow mixing pointer and array syntax when size attributes are present.

User Action: If the declaration is a parameter declaration and the top-level * is a pointer to an array, that * is unnecessary. This is because arrays are implicitly passed by reference, as in C. Remove the top-level *. If the declaration is more complex, investigate alternative ways to achieve your desired result, such as using a pointer to a structure that has the required information.

Pointers to context handles are valid only in parameter declarations

Explanation: IDL does not allow pointers to context handles, except in parameter declarations.

User Action: Do not declare a pointer to a **[context_handle]**, except as a parameter.

Pointers to pipes are valid only in parameter declarations

Explanation: IDL does not allow a pointer to a **pipe**, except in a parameter declaration.

User Action: Do not declare a pointer to a **pipe**, except as a parameter.

Pointers to type **handle_t** are valid only in parameter declarations

Explanation: Data type **handle_t** is only meaningful when used as the data type of the first parameter in an operation. It is used to establish a binding to a server of the interface.

User Action: Do not declare a pointer to data type **handle_t**, except as a parameter.

Pointers to **[v1_enum]** types are not allowed

Explanation: An enumeration type with the **[v1_enum]** attribute follows NCS Version 1 NIDL semantics, and does not allow pointers to enumerations except as a reference passing mechanism on a parameter.

User Action: If compatibility with NCS Version 1 NIDL is not necessary, remove the **[v1_enum]** attribute.

Pointers to varying arrays are not allowed

Explanation: An IDL declaration attempts to use mixed pointer * (an asterisk) and array [ ] (brackets) syntax to declare a pointer to an array that has varying bounds. Usually, it is ambiguous whether size attributes apply to the pointer or the array; thus, IDL does not allow mixing pointer and array syntax when size attributes are present.

User Action: If the declaration is a parameter declaration and the top-level * is a pointer to an array, that * is unnecessary. This is because arrays are implicitly passed by reference, as in C. Remove the top-level *. If the declaration is more complex, investigate alternative ways to achieve results, such as using a pointer to a structure that has the required information.

Reached maximum of *number* warnings; exiting

Explanation: The IDL compiler has a predefined maximum number of warnings it produces before aborting the compilation. This feature suppresses what may be the same warning over and over.

User Action: Fix the warnings that you get, or recompile the IDL file or specify the **-no_warn** option.

Rename of *filename1* to *filename2* failed

Explanation: The call to rename *filename1* to *filename2* returned a failing status.

User Action: Make sure the filenames and paths are valid, that you have privilege to perform the rename operation, and there is enough free space on the destination device.

Semantic checking prevented by other reported errors

Explanation: One or more of the reported errors prevented the compiler from completing the semantic checking of the interface. This can cause some semantic errors in the interface to go unreported.

User Action: Correct the reported errors and compile the interface again.

Size attributes can only be applied to array types

Explanation: Array bound attributes are only valid when used on array types or pointers used as an array.

User Action: Remove the array bound attribute or correct the type to be an array.

Structure fields cannot be of type **handle_t**

Explanation: Data type **handle_t** is only meaningful when used as the data type of the first parameter in an operation. It is used to establish a binding to a server of the interface.

User Action: Do not declare structure fields of data type **handle_t**.

Structures containing conformant arrays must be passed by reference

Explanation: The size of a structure that contains a conformant array is not a compile-time constant. It is not possible to pass such a structure by value.

User Action: Change the parameter declaration to pass the structure by reference by adding an * (asterisk) to the left of the parameter name.

Structures with **[transmit_as]** or **[represent_as]** cannot be conformant

Explanation: IDL does not allow a conformant structure with the **[transmit_as]** or **[represent_as]** attribute.

User Action: Change the declaration so the structure fields are of fixed size and have none of the conformant array attributes **[max_is]** or **[size_is]**, or remove the **[transmit_as]** or **[represent_as]** attribute.

Syntax error

Explanation: The source input is incorrect and no interpretation can be made.

User Action: Examine the source input on and near the source listed and correct any errors.

Syntax error in attribute list

Explanation: The syntax of the attribute list is not correct. It must contain a list of attributes separated by **,** (commas).

User Action: Make sure the attribute list contains only valid attribute names and values, that their spellings are correct, and that they form a valid list.

Syntax error in endpoint specification *endpoint*

Explanation: The syntax of the string describing the endpoint must be of the form *protocol*:[*endpoint*]. Although not in the expected format, the string *endpoint* is assumed to be the desired endpoint specification and is put into the generated stubs.

User Action: Correct the syntax of the **endpoint** specification.

Syntax error in UUID format

Explanation: The UUID specified in the **[uuid]** attribute of an interface is not in a valid format.

User Action: Make sure the UUID is transcribed correctly and contains the required punctuation.

Syntax error near *source-text*

Explanation: The source input is incorrect and no interpretation can be made for *source-text*.

User Action: Examine the source input on and near the source listed and correct any errors.

System error message: *message-text*

Explanation: Identifies the cause of the previous error.

User Action: Refer to the system documentation for an explanation of the error message.

The array size attribute variable *name* cannot have the **[ptr]** attribute

Explanation: An array size attribute clause in the source IDL specifies its value by dereferencing a pointer parameter. This is invalid if the pointer variable has the **[ptr]** attribute, since it allows the pointer to be **NULL**. If the pointer is **NULL**, there is no way to determine the size of the array.

User Action: Either redeclare the size variable as a scalar rather than a pointer, or change the size variable to a **[ref]** pointer.

The attribute [*attribute-name*] can occur at most once per operation

Explanation: A **[comm_status]** or **[fault_status]** parameter or operation result is used to return an error code if a certain type of error occurs during execution of an operation. Do not use either attribute more than once per operation.

User Action: Remove the redundant usages of the attribute from the interface's Attribute Configuration File (ACF).

The attribute [*attribute-name*] on a field is not allowed

Explanation: The specified attribute is not valid on a field.

User Action: Remove the attribute.

The attribute [*attribute-name*] on a parameter is not allowed

Explanation: The specified attribute is not valid on a parameter declaration.

User Action: Remove the attribute.

The attribute [*attribute-name*] on a type is not allowed

Explanation: The specified attribute is not valid on a type declaration.

User Action: Remove the attribute.

The attribute [*attribute-name*] on a **union** member is not allowed

Explanation: The specified attribute is not valid on a **union** member declaration.

User Action: Remove the attribute.

The attribute [*attribute-name*] on an interface is not allowed

Explanation: The specified attribute is not valid on a interface declaration.

User Action: Remove the attribute.

The attribute [*attribute-name*] on an operation is not allowed

Explanation: The specified attribute is not valid on an operation.

User Action: Remove the attribute.

The attribute **[broadcast]** is not valid on an operation with pipes

Explanation: IDL does not allow pipes to be used in **[broadcast]** operations.

User Action: Remove the **[broadcast]** attribute from the operation, or remove the **pipe** parameter from the operation.

The attribute **[idempotent]** is not valid on an operation with pipes

Explanation: An operation that uses pipes cannot be **idempotent** because the **pipe** data stream can break at unpredictable times.

User Action: Remove the **[idempotent]** attribute from the operation, or remove the **pipe** parameter from the operation.

The attribute **[ignore]** is valid only for pointers

Explanation: The **[ignore]** attribute is valid only for pointers.

User Action: Remove the **[ignore]** attribute from the declaration.

The attribute **[ignore]** on array elements is not allowed

Explanation: The **[ignore]** attribute is not allowed on array elements.

User Action: Remove the **[ignore]** attribute from the relevant declaration.

The attribute is no longer allowed in this context; use translator

Explanation: An attribute list is encountered in an invalid context. In NCS Version 1 NIDL, attributes are allowed in this position. You may be compiling an NCS Version 1 NIDL source file.

User Action: If the input is an NCS Version 1 NIDL source file, process it with the **nidl_to_idl** translator utility that converts an NCS Version 1 NIDL source file into the format expected by the IDL compiler. Then compile the translated source file. Otherwise, move the attributes to a valid location.

The attribute **[max_is]** cannot be applied to dimension *n*; upper bound is not dynamic

Explanation: A **[max_is]** variable is only valid for array dimensions that have an upper bound that is not fixed.

User Action: If the array is multidimensional, you may have specified the **[max_is]** variable for the wrong dimension. Refer to the documentation for the proper syntax. If the array has only one dimension, the **[max_is]** clause is invalid, since the array's upper bound is fixed. You may have meant to use a **[last_is]** clause. Refer to the documentation for the distinctions between conformant and varying arrays and their attributes.

The attribute **[max_is]** or **[size_is]** is required

Explanation: An array with an upper bound that is not fixed is used as a field of a structure or as a parameter of an operation. You must specify a field or parameter that determines the allocation of the array at runtime.

User Action: Use a **[max_is]** or **[size_is]** attribute to specify the field or parameter that contains the size information.

The attribute **[nocode]** does not apply to server stub

Explanation: A server for an interface must support all of the routines in that interface; therefore, the **[nocode]** ACF attribute is not valid when you use IDL to generate only server stub code.

User Action: This is a warning, so no action is required. If you want to remove the warning message, create a new ACF for the interface that does not use the **[nocode]** attribute. Or change the command line used so stub generation is not limited to the server stub.

The attribute **[out_of_line]** is not allowed on parameters

Explanation: IDL does not allow the **[out_of_line]** attribute on parameters.

User Action: Apply the **[out_of_line]** attribute to the type definition rather than the parameter. If you do not want all instances of the type **[out_of_line]**, define two separate types, one of which has the **[out_of_line]** attribute.

The attribute **[ptr]** is invalid on a binding **handle** parameter

Explanation: The first parameter in an operation is a **handle** parameter, either of type **handle_t** or a type with the **[handle]** attribute. It cannot have the **[ptr]** attribute, since it cannot be **NULL**.

User Action: Remove the **[ptr]** attribute from the parameter.

The attribute **[ptr]** is not valid on **pipe** parameters

Explanation: IDL does not allow the **[ptr]** attribute on **pipe** parameters.

User Action: Remove the **[ptr]** attribute from the parameter.

The attribute **[ptr]** is valid only for pointer or array types

Explanation: The **[ptr]** attribute modifies the default behavior of a pointer or array data type. It is not valid on other data types.

User Action: You may have missed an * (asterisk) in your declaration. If not, remove the **[ptr]** attribute.

The attribute **[ref]** is valid only for pointer or array types

Explanation: The **[ref]** attribute modifies the default behavior of a pointer or array data type. It is not valid on other data types.

User Action: You may have missed an * (asterisk) in your declaration. If not, remove the **[ref]** attribute.

The attribute **[size_is]** cannot be applied to dimension *n*; upper bound is not dynamic

Explanation: A **[size_is]** variable is only valid for array dimensions that have an upper bound that is not fixed.

User Action: If the array is multidimensional, you may have specified the **[size_is]** variable for the wrong dimension. Refer to the documentation for the proper syntax. If the array has only one dimension, the **[size_is]** clause is invalid, since the array's upper data limit is fixed. You may have meant to use a **[length_is]** clause. Refer to the documentation for the distinctions between conformant and varying arrays and their attributes.

The attribute **[string]** cannot be applied to a **[v1_array]**

Explanation: A string that is compatible with the NCS Version 1 NIDL **string0** data type must have the **[v1_array]** and **[v1_string]** attributes. The **[string]** attribute only applies without the **[v1_array]** attribute. A **[v1_array]** is for compatibility with NCS Version 1 NIDL.

User Action: If compatibility with NCS Version 1 NIDL is required, place the **[v1_string]** attribute on the declaration. Otherwise, remove the **[v1_array]** attribute from the array declaration.

The attribute **[string]** is valid only for one-dimensional array of **char, byte** type, or **byte** structure

Explanation: The **[string]** attribute flags that an array is a string. Strings must be arrays whose base type is **char**, **byte**, or a structure whose fields are all scalar byte fields.

User Action: Remove the **[string]** attribute, or change the data type so it is a valid string.

The attribute **[uuid]** is invalid when the **[local]** attribute is specified

Explanation: The **[local]** interface attribute flags that an interface is not for RPC use, but is only a local header generation mechanism. The **[uuid]** attribute is only used for RPC interfaces.

User Action: Remove one of the conflicting attributes.

The attribute **[v1_array]** cannot occur with the **[first_is]** attribute

Explanation: With the **[v1_array]** attribute, the only valid array attributes are **[max_is]**, **[last_is]**, and **[length_is]**.

User Action: If compatibility with NCS Version 1 NIDL is necessary, the lower bound of the array must be fixed; remove the **[first_is]** attribute and change the array declaration. Otherwise, remove the **[v1_array]** attribute.

The attribute **[v1_array]** cannot occur with the **[first_is]** or **[min_is]** attributes

Explanation: A **[v1_array]** specifies that the array be handled in a manner compatible with NCS Version 1 NIDL; **[min_is]** and **[first_is]** were not supported in NCS Version 1 NIDL.

User Action: The **[min_is]** attribute is not supported in IDL; remove it. If **[first_is]** is present, either remove it or remove **[v1_array]**.

The attribute **[v1_array]** is invalid for an array with more than 65,535 elements

Explanation: An array with the **[v1_array]** attribute is limited to a total of 65,535 or fewer elements. The declared array has too many elements to be **[v1_array]**.

User Action: Remove the **[v1_array]** attribute from the array declaration.

The attribute **[v1_array]** must be in array, not pointer, syntax

Explanation: The **[v1_array]** attribute is for compatibility with NCS Version 1 arrays. NCS Version 1 NIDL did not allow pointers to represent arrays.

User Action: Define the array using array syntax.

The attributes [*attribute1*] and [*attribute2*] cannot occur together

Explanation: The specified attributes are conflicting and only one or the other can be specified.

User Action: Remove one of the attributes.

The attributes **[in_line]** and **[out_of_line]** apply only to non-scalar types

Explanation: Scalar data types are always marshalled in-line, since there is performance degradation if they are marshalled out-of-line.

User Action: Do not use the **[in_line]** and **[out_of_line]** attributes on scalar types.

The attributes **[last_is]** and **[length_is]** cannot occur together

Explanation: The **[last_is]** and **[length_is]** attributes both specify a field or parameter used to determine the data limit of a varying array. You cannot use both.

User Action: The **[last_is]** attribute specifies the index of the last valid element. The **[length_is]** attribute specifies the total number of elements in the array. Remove one of these attributes.

The attributes **[max_is]** and **[size_is]** cannot occur together

Explanation: The **[max_is]** and **[size_is]** attributes both specify a field or parameter used to determine the upper bound of a conformant array. You cannot use both.

User Action: The **[max_is]** attribute specifies the index of the last possible array element. The **[size_is]** attribute specifies the total number of possible elements in the array. Remove one of the attributes.

The attributes **[max_is,length_is]** or **[size_is,last_is]** used together

Explanation: The **[max_is]** attribute specifies the array's upper bound while the **[size_is]** attribute specifies the total number of array elements. Similarly, **[last_is]** specifies the upper data limit while **[length_is]** specifies the number of valid data elements.

User Action: Mixing the attributes can be incorrect. Make sure the declaration is correct and change if necessary.

The base type of a **pipe** cannot be a conformant type

Explanation: IDL does not allow pipes of any data type of size that is not fixed.

User Action: Change your **pipe** type definition to use a fixed array or some other construct of fixed size.

The base type of a **pipe** cannot be a **[context_handle]** type

Explanation: A **[context_handle]** type cannot be used as the base type of a **pipe**.

User Action: Remove the invalid declaration, or change it so the base type of the **pipe** is not a **[context_handle]** type.

The base type of a **pipe** cannot be a **pipe** type

Explanation: A **pipe** type cannot be used in the definition of another **pipe** type.

User Action: Remove the invalid declaration, or change it so the base type of the **pipe** is not another **pipe** type.

The base type of a **pipe** cannot be a **[transmit_as]** type

Explanation: IDL does not allow the base type of a **pipe** to have the **[transmit_as]** attribute.

User Action: Declare the base type of the **pipe** to be the data type in the **[transmit_as]** clause.

The base type of a **pipe** cannot be **handle_t**

Explanation: Data type **handle_t** is only meaningful when used as the data type of the first parameter in an operation. It is used to establish a binding to a server of the interface.

User Action: Do not declare pipes whose base type is **handle_t**.

The base type of a **pipe** cannot be, or contain, a pointer

Explanation: IDL does not allow the base type of a **pipe** to be a pointer or any data type that contains pointers.

User Action: Change your **pipe** type definition so the base type of the **pipe** is not a pointer and does not contain any pointers.

The **[first_is]** parameter must have the **[in]** attribute

Explanation: The **[first_is]** attribute specifies a parameter that contains the lower data limit of a varying array. Since the array has the **[in]** attribute, the lower data limit parameter must also be **[in]** so the number of array elements to send from client to server is known.

User Action: Change the lower data limit parameter referenced by the **[first_is]** clause to have the **[in]** attribute.

The **[last_is]** parameter must have the **[in]** attribute

Explanation: The **[last_is]** attribute specifies a parameter that contains the upper data limit of a varying array. Since the array has the **[in]** attribute, the upper data limit parameter must also be **[in]** so the number of array elements to send from client to server is known.

User Action: Change the data limit parameter referenced by the **[last_is]** clause to have the **[in]** attribute.

The **[length_is]** parameter must have the **[in]** attribute

Explanation: The **[length_is]** attribute specifies a parameter used to determine the data length of a varying array. Since the array has the **[in]** attribute, the **[length_is]** parameter must also be **[in]** so the number of array elements to send from client to server is known.

User Action: Change the parameter referenced by the **[length_is]** clause to have the **[in]** attribute.

The lower bound must not be greater than the upper bound

Explanation: The syntax of an array requires the lower bound to precede the upper bound.

User Action: Modify the array declaration so the lower bound is first.

The major version number is too large; the maximum is *number*

Explanation: The major version number is too large.

User Action: Replace the major version number (the portion to the left of the period) with a value less than *number*.

The minor version number is too large; the maximum is *number*

Explanation: The minor version number is too large.

User Action: Replace the minor version number (the portion to the right of the period) with a value less than *number*.

The **[represent_as]** type *name* conflicts with previously defined *name*

Explanation: The attribute configuration file (ACF) contains conflicting **[represent_as]** clauses for the same data type.

User Action: Remove one of the **[represent_as]** clauses for that data type.

The size attributes do not match the array dimension

Explanation: There are too many attribute references for the number of dimensions defined for the array.

User Action: Modify the array bound attribute, specifying one reference for each dimension of the array.

The **[v1_string]** attribute can only be applied to a **[v1_array]**

Explanation: A **[v1_string]** is compatible with the NCS Version 1 NIDL **string0** data type. It can be applied only to an array compatible with NCS Version 1. For example, an array with the **[v1_array]** attribute.

User Action: If compatibility with NCS Version 1 NIDL is required, place the **[v1_array]** attribute on the array. Otherwise, change the **[v1_string]** attribute to **[string]**, which is a generalization of **[v1_string]**.

Too many elements in *item*

Explanation: The **enum** *item* contains more than 32,767 elements.

User Action: Reduce the number of elements included in the **enum**.

Too many endpoint specifications; Maximum is *number*

Explanation: There are more endpoint specifications than IDL can process.

User Action: Remove some of the endpoint specifications listed in the **[endpoint]** attribute. Specify at most *number* endpoint specifications for an interface.

Too many scoping levels

Explanation: The input source is too complicated to be parsed. This occurs because of deeply nested **struct** or **union** declarations.

User Action: Simplify the input source by using **typedef**s to represent the nested **struct** or **union** declarations, and building the more complicated **struct** or **union** declarations by referencing the named types instead of in-line specification of the **struct** or **union** declaration.

Type attributes **[in_line]** and **[out_of_line]** cannot occur together

Explanation: The **[in_line]** and **[out_of_line]** attributes are opposite in meaning. You can specify at most one of these attributes on a type.

User Action: Remove one of the conflicting attributes.

Type name *name* referenced in ACF is not defined

Explanation: The context in which a type name is used in the Attribute Configuration File (ACF) requires that the type be defined in the corresponding IDL file.

User Action: See if the referenced type is defined in some other interface. If so, the ACF reference belongs in the ACF for that interface. Check for typographical errors in both the IDL and ACF files. Check that you have not omitted a type definition in the IDL file.

Type *name1* has a **[represent_as]** data type *name2*

Explanation: IDL does not allow a data type that has a **[represent_as]** type to itself be used as a **[represent_as]** type in another type definition.

User Action: The message gives information to help you locate the problem.

Type name: *name* not found

Explanation: The type *name* is not declared at this point in the interface declaration.

User Action: Correct the spelling of *name* if incorrect, and make sure that a definition of *name* precedes the reference.

Types with **[represent_as]** cannot be nested

Explanation: IDL does not allow a data type that has a **[represent_as]** type to itself be used as a **[represent_as]** type in another type definition.

User Action: Do not nest **[represent_as]** types.

Unable to open *filename* for read access

Explanation: The IDL compiler is unable to open a file for processing.

User Action: Make sure the file exists, and that it has the proper access protection for the IDL compiler.

Unable to open *filename* for write access

Explanation: The IDL compiler is unable to create a file.

User Action: Make sure the directory to contain the file exists, and that it has the proper access protection for the IDL compiler.

Unbalanced braces.

Explanation: The numbers of left braces and right braces are not equal.

User Action: Make sure the number of left braces equals the number of right braces and that each brace is in the correct place.

Unbalanced brackets.

Explanation: The numbers of left brackets and right brackets are not equal.

User Action: Make sure the number of left brackets equals the number of right brackets and that each bracket is in the correct place.

Unbalanced parentheses.

Explanation: The numbers of left parentheses and right parentheses are not equal.

User Action: Make sure the number of left parentheses equals the number of right parentheses and that each parenthesis is in the correct place.

Unexpected end-of-file

Explanation: The end of the source file was encountered before the end of the interface definition. The source file may be incomplete.

User Action: Complete the interface definition.

Unexpected end-of-file near *source text*

Explanation: The end of the source file was encountered before the end of the interface definition. The source file may be incomplete.

User Action: Complete the interface definition.

Unknown attribute [*attribute-name*]

Explanation: The attribute specified is not a valid IDL attribute.

User Action: Check for spelling errors or misplaced syntax.

Unknown command line option: *option*

Explanation: You entered an invalid command line option.

User Action: Check the command line for typographical errors. Refer to the documentation for proper command line syntax.

Unterminated comment, end-of-file encountered

Explanation: During the processing of a multiline comment, the end of the source file was reached before the termination characters for the comment.

User Action: Make sure that all multiline comments are correctly terminated.

Unterminated string literal

Explanation: There is a missing " (right double quote) on the string literal.

User Action: Make sure the right double quote for the string literal is on the same source line as the left double quote. Also verify that any double quote characters internal to the string are preceded by the \ (backslash) escape character.

Usage: **idl** *filename* [*options*]

Explanation: Lists the format of the **idl** command that invokes the IDL compiler.

User Action: Use the **-confirm** option to see a list of all to determine those you need.

Use array syntax to declare multidimensional arrays

Explanation: An IDL declaration attempts to use mixed pointer * (an asterisk) and array **[ ]** (brackets) syntax to define a multidimensional array. The interpretation that an * (asterisk) is used to represent an array is due to the presence of one or more of the **[max_is]** or **[size_is]** attributes. It is ambiguous whether size attributes apply to the pointer or the array; thus, IDL does not allow mixing pointer and array syntax when size attributes are present.

User Action: The IDL compiler requires that you make such declarations using only array **[ ]** syntax. If you do not want to declare a multidimensional array, you used the **[max_is]** or **[size_is]** attribute incorrectly. They apply only to arrays with bounds that are not fixed, and the declared array has fixed bounds.

Use *command-option* for list of command options

Explanation: Errors on the command line prevent the IDL compiler from executing.

User Action: Invoke the IDL compiler with the indicated command option to get a list of valid command options, then correct the error.

V1 attributes are incompatible with this type

Explanation: The Version 1 migration attributes are provided for compatibility for applications that were originally written with NCS Version 1 NIDL. These attributes are **[v1_string]**, **[v1_array]**,

[v1_enum], and **[v1_struct]**. In later versions of IDL, strings, conformant and varying arrays, enumerations, and structures are enhanced at the network representation level. A data type with any of the V1 migration attributes cannot contain one of these data types that does not have the corresponding V1 attribute.

User Action: Change the data type declaration so all relevant contained types have the corresponding V1 attribute, or remove V1 attributes if compatibility with NCS Version 1 NIDL is unnecessary.

Variable declarations are not supported; declaration of *variable* ignored

Explanation: IDL does not support the declaration of variables. The types of data that can be declared in IDL are constants, types, and functions. The declaration of *variable* is not a function and is incorrect.

User Action: If intended as a function declaration, correct the declaration so the top-level declaration is a function. Otherwise, remove the declaration.

void * must be used in conjunction with the **[context_handle]** attribute

Explanation: The only valid use of a **void** * data type in an interface definition is on an item with the **[context_handle]** attribute.

User Action: Change the data type in the declaration, or add the **[context_handle]** attribute.

void is valid only in an operation or a pointer declaration

Explanation: The **void** keyword is only valid as the return value of an operation, or as part of a **void** * declaration. Note also that in RPC interfaces, **void** * is only valid if the **[context_handle]** attribute is also specified on the data item.

User Action: You may have missed an * (asterisk) in your declaration. If not, change the **void** reference to some valid data type.

Related Information

Commands: **idl**

nidl_to_idl_messages

Purpose Listing of NIDL to IDL messages

Description

The following **nidl_to_idl_messages** are listed in alphabetical order:

Identifier *name*: named lower bound not adjusted (C arrays are 0-based)

> **Explanation**: A Pascal array whose lower bound is not 0 (zero) has a named constant as a lower data limit. The translator does not automatically adjust it.
>
> **User Action**: Manually correct the declaration in the IDL output file. Replace the name with a constant value that is one less than the value of the name. Otherwise, change the value of the constant name to be one less. The application code may also need adjustment.

Identifier *name*: named upper bound not adjusted (C arrays are 0-based)

> **Explanation**: A Pascal array whose lower bound is not 0 (zero) has a named constant as an upper data limit. The translator does not automatically adjust it.
>
> **User Action**: Manually correct the declaration in the IDL output file. Replace the name with a constant value that is one less than the value of the name. Otherwise, change the value of the constant name to be one less. The application code may also need adjustment.

Identifier *name*: subrange definition omitted, translated as **int**

> **Explanation**: Pascal subranges are translated as integers.
>
> **User Action**: None. This is an informational message.

Invalid **union** case type encountered

> **Explanation**: The **union** case type cannot be translated. Translator uses **enum**, **boolean**, or **int**.
>
> **User Action**: Manually correct the declaration in the generated IDL output file.

Operation *name*: **[comm_status]** requires an ACF

Explanation: In DCE IDL, **[comm_status]** is an attribute in the ACF. The translator generated an ACF.

User Action: Keep the ACF and use it when compiling the generated IDL file under the DCE IDL compiler.

Parameter *name* in operation *name*: **[comm_status]** requires an ACF

Explanation: In DCE IDL, **[comm_status]** is an attribute in the ACF. The translator generated an ACF.

User Action: Keep the ACF and use it when compiling the generated IDL file under the DCE IDL compiler.

Parameter *name* in operation *name*: **[implicit_handle]** requires an ACF

Explanation: In DCE IDL, **[implicit_handle]** is an attribute in the ACF. The translator generated an ACF.

User Action: Keep the ACF and use it when compiling the generated IDL file under the DCE IDL compiler.

Unsupported constant declaration ignored for identifier *name*

Explanation: The translator detected a constant that was not an integer or string.

User Action: Manually correct the constant declaration in the generated IDL file or add it to an application header file.

Unsupported socket address family encountered, substituting **ip**

Explanation: The translator found an unknown socket address family when translating the port attribute. The default protocol, **ip**, as emitted into the translator, is using a default substitute socket address.

User Action: If you do not want **ip** as protocol, edit the generated IDL file and update the value specified in the endpoint attribute.

Variant records embedded in structures are unsupported

Explanation: NIDL Version 1.0 Pascal syntax allows a record definition that includes a variant clause to include other fields. The **nidl_to_idl** command is not capable of providing a translation of this construct.

User Action: Define a record type that consists only of the variant clause. Then replace the variant clause in the original record definition with a field of this type.

Version number too large, must be changed

Explanation: The version number cannot be larger than 65,535. The format for the version number in the new IDL file must be *major_number.minor_number*.

User Action: Modify the generated IDL file by including a new UUID and by resetting the version number to a value less than 65,535.

Related Information

Commands: **nidl_to_idl**.

rpc_status_codes

Purpose Provides a list of RPC status codes

Description

The first section of this reference page documents the RPC status codes in alphabetical order. The documentation for each status code includes the message text, the explanation, and the suggested user action. The second section contains an alphabetical listing of the message texts accompanied by the status code for each.

Note that RPC exceptions are equivalent to RPC status codes. To identify the status code that corresponds to a given exception, replace the **_x_** string of the exception with the string _s_; for example, the exception **rpc_x_comm_failure** is equivalent to the status code **rpc_s_comm_failure**. The RPC exceptions are defined in **dce/rpcexc.h**.

Status Code Explanation and User Actions

The following list provides the RPC status codes (in alphabetical order), an explanation of the status codes, and the suggested user actions:

ept_s_cant_access, cannot access endpoint database

Explanation: The endpoint mapper cannot open the existing database file that holds the endpoint map.

User Action: Check the protection of the database file.

ept_s_cant_create, cannot create endpoint database

Explanation: The endpoint mapper cannot create the database file that holds the endpoint map.

User Action: Check the protection of the database file and the directory that contains the file.

ept_s_cant_perform_op, cannot perform endpoint map operation

Explanation: The endpoint mapper is unable to perform an operation.

User Action: None.

ept_s_database_already_open, endpoint database already open by another process

Explanation: The endpoint mapper cannot open the existing database file that holds the endpoint map because another process has the file locked.

User Action: Make sure no other endpoint mapper is running on the same system.

ept_s_database_invalid, invalid endpoint database

Explanation: The format of the database file that holds the endpoint map is not what the endpoint mapper expects.

User Action: Delete the database file and restart the endpoint mapper.

ept_s_invalid_context, invalid endpoint map or lookup context

Explanation: A context handle supplied as input in a remote call to the endpoint mapper referred to invalid context. This may be an internal error.

User Action: Report it to the vendor.

ept_s_invalid_entry, invalid endpoint entry

Explanation: An entry supplied to the endpoint mapper as input contains invalid data; for example, an invalid tower.

User Action: Correct the contents of the entry.

ept_s_no_memory, no memory for endpoint map service

Explanation: The endpoint mapper is unable to allocate heap storage.

User Action: If the failure is induced by overuse of underlying system resources (for example, address space or swap space), reduce the direct use of these resources by other processes on the system if possible.

ept_s_not_registered, not registered in endpoint map

Explanation: An entry supplied as input to a remote call to the endpoint mapper (for example, for deletion) does not exist in the endpoint map.

User Action: Supply only existing entry when deleting.

ept_s_update_failed, cannot update endpoint database

Explanation: The endpoint mapper is unable to write modifications to the database file that holds the endpoint map.

User Action: Check the protection of the database file.

rpc_s_already_listening, already listening

Explanation: A server application called **rpc_server_listen( )**, but another thread within the process is currently blocked inside a call to this procedure.

User Action: Fix application so that only one thread at a time calls **rpc_server_listen( )**.

rpc_s_already_registered, already registered

Explanation: An application tried to set the type of an object to a value that was already set for that object.

User Action: Remove redundant setting of the object's type.

rpc_s_authn_authz_mismatch, authentication authorization mismatch

Explanation: In a call to **rpc_binding_set_auth_info( )**, the requested authorization service is not supported by the requested authentication service.

User Action: Choose a compatible pair of authentication and authorization services.

rpc_s_authn_challenge_malformed, authentication challenge malformed

Explanation: The client side runtime detected that the authentication challenge it was given by the server is incorrectly formed.

User Action: This usually does not happen. Check for version skew between client and server, or bugs in the client or server runtime.

rpc_s_binding_has_no_auth, not authenticated

Explanation: An application manager routine tried to attain authentication information from a client binding handle, but the client did not establish any authentication on the call.

User Action: The manager routine can either ignore the error or refuse to execute the call. The application writer can change the client to use authentication.

rpc_s_binding_incomplete, binding incomplete (no object ID and no endpoint)

Explanation: The specified server binding information is insufficient. In a local or remote management call to the RPC runtime, the client supplied binding information that lacked an endpoint and an associated object UUID.

User Action: Supply complete binding information and an object UUID to local or remote management calls.

rpc_s_call_cancelled, call canceled

Explanation: A cancel was posted to a thread making a remote call. This error condition occurs at the server, but is usually not seen by the server application.

User Action: None.

rpc_s_call_faulted, call faulted

Explanation: The execution of an application manager routine raised a fault (exception); for example, division by 0 (zero). Applications usually do not see this error as it is intercepted by the client stub and transformed into the specific error condition that occurs in the application manager routine.

User Action: None.

rpc_s_call_orphaned, call orphaned

Explanation: A client application has orphaned (given up waiting for) a manager routine to return. This error occurs at the server, but is usually not seen by the server application.

User Action: None.

rpc_s_call_timeout, call timed out

Explanation: A remote call ran for longer than the limit set by **rpc_mgmt_set_call_timeout**( ).

User Action: None.

rpc_s_calls_too_large_for_wk_ep, calls too large for well-known endpoint

Explanation: The specified value of parameter *max_call_requests* exceeds the maximum allowed when using a well-known endpoint.

User Action: Specify a *max_call_requests* value of **rpc_c_protseq_max_reqs_default** to obtain the maximum value allowed for the specified protocol sequence.

rpc_s_cancel_timeout, cancel time-out

Explanation: A cancel was posted to a thread making a remote call, a noninfinite cancel time-out was previously specified (by the **rpc_mgmt_set_cancel_timeout**( ) routine), and the manager routine did not respond to the cancel within the cancel time-out period.

User Action: None.

rpc_s_cant_bind_socket, cannot bind socket

Explanation: An underlying problem with the local system's network transport service prevented the RPC runtime from assigning an endpoint to a communications socket.

User Action: Make sure the underlying network transport service is working; try non-RPC applications that use this service (for example, file transfer or remote login). Verify that another executing server is not already using the specified endpoint.

rpc_s_cant_create_socket, cannot create socket

Explanation: An underlying problem with the local system's network transport service prevented the RPC runtime from creating a communications socket needed to make or receive remote calls.

User Action: Make sure the underlying network transport service is working; try non-RPC applications that use this service (for example, file transfer or remote login).

rpc_s_cant_get_if_id, cannot get interface id

Explanation: The RPC runtime tried to get information about a communications socket but failed due to an underlying network transport service problem.

User Action: Make sure the underlying network transport service is working; try non-RPC applications that use this service (for example, file transfer or remote login).

rpc_s_cant_inq_socket, cannot inquire socket

Explanation: The RPC runtime tried to get information about a communications socket but failed due to an underlying network transport service problem.

User Action: Make sure the underlying network transport service is working; try non-RPC applications that use this service (for example, file transfer or remote login).

rpc_s_class_version_mismatch, RPC class version mismatch

Explanation: The application attempted to read or modify a name service entry with an incompatible RPC class version. For example, a V1.0 client tried to read a name service entry with a V2.0 version. Only major version incompatibilities are flagged.

User Action: Upgrade either the name service entry or client to the appropriate version.

rpc_s_comm_failure, communications failure

Explanation: The RPC runtime that is attempting to implement a call to a remote procedure gave up waiting for the execution of the procedure to start or complete because the RPC runtime determined that it is not communicating with the remote server.

The RPC runtime may also return this status when a client makes a remote procedure call using a partially bound binding (no endpoint) and the RPC runtime is unable to communicate with the endpoint map service, which is provided by the RPC daemon.

User Action: In the first case, try another server. In the second case, make sure the RPC daemon is running.

rpc_s_cycle_detected, cycle detected

Explanation: A cycle was detected in the course of traversing groups and profiles in the binding import operation.

User Action: Modify the structure of groups and profiles in the name service database to eliminate the cycle.

rpc_s_entry_already_exists, entry already exists

Explanation: The name service entry to that the server or management application is exporting the binding already exists. This is not a problem.

User Action: None.

rpc_s_entry_not_found, entry not found

Explanation: Not visible to the API. The specified name service entry is not found in the name service database. This entry could have been specified directly or indirectly through a profile or group.

User Action: Report it to the vendor.

rpc_s_fault_addr_error, fault addr error

Explanation: An application manager routine running in the server raised a hardware addressing exception.

User Action: Fix the manager routine.

rpc_s_fault_context_mismatch, fault context mismatch

Explanation: A client application passed a context handle into a remote call, but the server detects that the server does not hold the specified context. This error can happen if a server stops and restarts in between remote calls from the client holding the context handle and the client calls the restarted server.

An application will see this status if the Remote Procedure Call Daemon (RPCD) reboots (restarts) during a sequence of application calls to **rpc_mgmt_ep_elt_inq_next( )**. The new instance of RPCD does not know where in the inquiry it was left by the previous RPCD.

User Action: If returned from **rpc_mgmt_ep_elt_inq_next( )**, free the current inquiry context by calling **rpc_mgmt_ep_elt_inq_done( )** and restart the inquiry by calling **rpc_mgmt_ep_elt_inq_begin( )**.

rpc_s_fault_fp_div_by_zero, fault floating-point divide by zero

Explanation: An application manager routine attempted to do a floating-point division with a denominator of 0 (zero).

User Action: Fix the manager routine.

rpc_s_fault_fp_error, fault floating-point error

Explanation: An application manager routine failed in the execution of a floating-point operation.

User Action: Fix the manager routine.

rpc_s_fault_fp_overflow, fault floating-point overflow

Explanation: A floating-point calculation in an application manager routine resulted in an arithmetic overflow.

User Action: Fix the manager routine.

rpc_s_fault_fp_underflow, fault floating-point underflow

Explanation: A floating-point calculation in an application manager routine resulted in an arithmetic underflow.

User Action: Fix the manager routine.

rpc_s_fault_ill_inst, fault illegal instruction

Explanation: An application manager routine attempted to execute an illegal machine instruction.

User Action: Fix the manager routine.

rpc_s_fault_int_div_by_zero, fault integer divide by zero

Explanation: An application manager routine attempted to do an integer division with a denominator of 0 (zero).

User Action: Fix the manager routine.

rpc_s_fault_int_overflow, fault integer overflow

Explanation: An integer calculation in an application manager routine resulted in an arithmetic overflow.

User Action: Fix the manager routine.

rpc_s_fault_invalid_bound, fault invalid bound

Explanation: An application made a remote call that attempted to pass or return an array with a dynamically specified bound that is not appropriate to the declared dimensions of the array.

User Action: Fix the application.

rpc_s_fault_invalid_tag, fault invalid tag

Explanation: An application made a remote call that attempted to pass or return a discriminated union with an invalid tag.

User Action: Fix the application.

rpc_s_fault_pipe_closed, fault pipe closed

Explanation: An application manager routine attempted to write data to a pipe that was already closed by writing a terminator to it.

User Action: Fix the application.

rpc_s_fault_pipe_comm_error, fault pipe communication error

Explanation: A communications error occurred while an application manager routine was reading from or writing to a pipe.

User Action: Client code must recover from an unsuccessful remote call.

rpc_s_fault_pipe_discipline, fault pipe discipline

Explanation: An application manager routine returned control to the server stub while there was still pipe data to be read or written.

User Action: Fix the application.

rpc_s_fault_pipe_empty, fault pipe empty

Explanation: An application manager routine attempted to read data from a pipe from which a terminator had already been received.

User Action: Fix the application.

rpc_s_fault_pipe_memory, fault pipe memory

Explanation: Application code provided insufficient memory to allow the marshalling or unmarshalling of an element of a pipe.

User Action: Fix the application.

rpc_s_fault_pipe_order, fault pipe order

Explanation: An application manager routine attempted to use the pipes in an operation in an order other than that required by the IDL language definition.

User Action: Fix the application.

rpc_s_fault_remote_comm_failure, fault remote communication failure

Explanation: A server stub encountered a communications error.

User Action: Client code must recover from an unsuccessful remote call.

rpc_s_fault_remote_no_memory, fault remote no memory

Explanation: A server stub or application manager routine is unable to allocate heap storage.

User Action: If the failure is induced by overuse of underlying system resources (for example, address space or swap space), reduce the application's direct use of these resources if possible.

rpc_s_fault_unspec, fault unspecified

Explanation: A server stub or application manager routine raised an exception of an unknown kind.

User Action: Fix the application.

rpc_s_group_member_not_found, group member not found

Explanation: The server or management application attempted to remove a group member that does not exist in the name service database.

User Action: Use the RPC control program to see if the group member exists. If it does not, correct the application. If the group member does exist in the name service database, report the problem to the vendor.

rpc_s_helper_aborted, helper process aborted

Explanation: The user-space helper process exited before responding to a request. This indicates that either someone stopped the helper process or that there is a bug in the helper process that is causing it to crash.

User Action: Fix the bug in the helper process.

rpc_s_helper_catatonic, helper process catatonic

Explanation: The user-space helper took longer than 2 to 3 minutes to respond to a request from the kernel. This indicates that the helper process or the services it depends on are malfunctioning or overloaded.

User Action: Ease network congestion, fix bugs, or increase the hard-coded time-out in the kernel

rpc_s_helper_not_running, helper process not running

Explanation: The kernel attempted to issue a request to the user space helper process, but discovered that it was not running.

User Action: Start a helper process and try again.

rpc_s_helper_overflow, helper process too busy

Explanation: Too many outstanding requests in the helper process.

User Action: Increase the table size in the helper process and rebuild.

rpc_s_helper_short_read, short read from kernel helper

Explanation: The kernel attempted to read a request from the user-space DCE helper process, but not enough data was available to satisfy the request. This indicates a bug in the user-space DCE helper process, or version skew between the kernel and the helper process.

User Action: Fix bug or upgrade helper process to match the kernel.

rpc_s_helper_wrong_user, attempting to use credentials belonging to other user

Explanation: Requests from the kernel to the helper process include the user ID and the credentials to use to authenticate a remote operation. The helper process detected that the user ID attached to a request from the kernel is different from the owner of the request.

User Action: This indicates either a kernel bug or an attempt to violate security.

rpc_s_in_args_too_big, input arguments too big

Explanation: The size of the input arguments to a remote call is larger than is allowed in the current context. For example, in broadcast calls the input arguments must fit into a single transport-level packet.

User Action: Reduce size of input arguments.

rpc_s_incomplete_name, incomplete name

Explanation: An incomplete object or directory name was supplied to some NSI operation. The operation failed because the name cannot be expanded.

User Action: Supply a complete name.

rpc_s_interface_not_found, interface not found

Explanation: The unexport operation did not find any binding information for the specified interface. No binding information was unexported.

User Action: Use the RPC control program to find out whether the server entry contains binding information for the specified interface identifier. If the entry contains the binding information, report the problem to the vendor.

rpc_s_invalid_arg, invalid argument

Explanation: An aspect of the arguments supplied as input to the RPC runtime is inappropriate.

In the case of **rpc_mgmt_set_server_stack_size( )**, the underlying thread package does not support the specified value of the *thread_stack_size* parameter.

User Action: Check supplied parameters against the documentation of the call.

rpc_s_invalid_binding, invalid binding

Explanation: An application passed a binding handle to the RPC runtime that is invalid (for example, because it specifies an unsupported protocol).

User Action: This error is frequently caused by an application passing a bad pointer (for example, to random memory or to a binding that was freed) to an RPC runtime routine that takes a binding handle input parameter. If this is the case, the application should be fixed.

rpc_s_invalid_call_opt, invalid call option

Explanation: A call was attempted that is not supported by the underlying RPC protocol. For example, calls to procedures marked **[broadcast]** are not supported by all RPC protocols.

User Action: Change application to not make unsupported calls.

rpc_s_invalid_endpoint_format, invalid endpoint format for remote host

Explanation: An endpoint string with invalid syntax is supplied as input to the RPC runtime.

User Action: Use valid endpoint string syntax.

rpc_s_invalid_inquiry_context, invalid inquiry context

Explanation: An invalid inquiry context was passed to a begin, next, or done operation.

User Action: Verify that the inquiry context is non-**NULL** and was successfully created in a begin operation.

rpc_s_invalid_inquiry_type, invalid inquiry type

Explanation: The application program attempted to perform a lookup in either a profile or an endpoint map using an unsupported lookup key.

User Action: Make sure that the *inquiry_type* parameter passed to **rpc_ns_profile_elt_inq_begin()** or **rpc_mgmt_ep_elt_inq_begin()** is within the set of supported values.

rpc_s_invalid_name_syntax, invalid name syntax

Explanation: An invalid value was specified for the entry name syntax.

User Action: Check the value provided and use one of the API defined constants **rpc_c_ns_syntax_***.

rpc_s_invalid_ns_handle, invalid name service handle

Explanation: An invalid name service handle was passed to a begin, next, or done operation.

User Action: Verify that the name service handle is non-**NULL** and was successfully created in a begin operation.

rpc_s_invalid_object, invalid object

Explanation: An application specified an illegal UUID value or specified a value that was not a valid UUID.

User Action: Verify that the provided value is a UUID and that the called routine allows that value. Some routines do not allow a nil UUID.

rpc_s_invalid_priority, invalid priority

Explanation: The server or management application attempted to add a profile element at an invalid priority.

User Action: Modify the application code.

rpc_s_invalid_rpc_floor, invalid RPC tower floor

Explanation: A tower floor did not contain the expected RPC data.

User Action: Recreate the server entry from which the invalid data was obtained and try again. If the problem persists, report it to the vendor.

rpc_s_invalid_rpc_protseq, invalid RPC protocol sequence

Explanation: An application specified an RPC protocol sequence that is not recognized by the RPC runtime.

User Action: Specify only valid RPC protocol sequences.

rpc_s_invalid_string_binding, invalid string binding

Explanation: An application presented a string binding as input to the RPC runtime and the string binding has invalid syntax.

User Action: Use the correct string binding syntax.

rpc_s_invalid_timeout, invalid time-out

Explanation: An application specified an invalid time-out value to **rpc_mgmt_set_com_timeout**( ).

User Action: Supply a valid time-out value.

rpc_s_invalid_vers_option, invalid interface version option

Explanation: The specified **vers_option** argument value was invalid.

User Action: Check the value provided and use one of the API defined constants **rpc_c_vers_***.

rpc_s_key_func_not_allowed, key function not allowed when default authentication service specified

Explanation: A server application called **rpc_server_register_auth_info( )** with the default authentication service as input but also supplied a non-**NULL** key acquisition function as input.

User Action: Specify either a nondefault authentication function or a **NULL** key function.

rpc_s_max_calls_too_small, max calls (threads) too small

Explanation: A server application passed too small a value as the *max_calls_exec* input parameter to **rpc_server_listen( )**.

User Action: Pass a large enough value for parameter *max_calls_exec*.

rpc_s_max_descs_exceeded, max descriptors exceeded

Explanation: An application caused the RPC runtime to use more file descriptors (for communications sockets) than the runtime is able to store internally.

User Action: The RPC runtime's use of file descriptors can be reduced by making fewer remote calls in parallel, or by calling **rpc_server_use_protseq( )** or one of its variants fewer times.

rpc_s_mgmt_op_disallowed, management operation disallowed

Explanation: A client application called one of the local or remote management RPC runtime functions and the remote server refused to execute it.

User Action: None.

rpc_s_name_service_unavailable, name service unavailable

Explanation: An NSI operation was unable to communicate with the name service server (for example, the CDS server).

User Action: Verify that the name service server is running.

rpc_s_no_bindings, no bindings

Explanation: An application passed an empty or **NULL** binding vector as input to the RPC runtime or requested a binding vector to be returned by the RPC runtime but no bindings exist.

User Action: In the first case, change the application to pass a valid binding vector; the second case may not indicate an error condition.

rpc_s_no_entry_name, no entry name

Explanation: The binding handle does not refer to a name service entry name. Binding handles returned from the import and lookup operations refer to the name of the name service entry where the binding information was found. Binding handles obtained from other sources (for example, from a string binding) do not refer to an entry name.

User Action: If a binding handle returned by the import or lookup operation does not refer to an entry name, report it to the vendor.

rpc_s_no_env_setup, name service environment variable not defined

Explanation: A **NULL** entry name was specified in the import or lookup begin operations and the **RPC_DEFAULT_ENTRY** environment variable was not defined.

User Action: Either define the **RPC_DEFAULT_ENTRY** environment variable or specify a non-**NULL** entry name in import or lookup begin.

rpc_s_no_interfaces, no interfaces

Explanation: An application requested a list of the network interfaces registered by a server, but no interfaces were registered.

User Action: This is generally not an error condition.

rpc_s_no_interfaces_exported, no interfaces exported

Explanation: No interfaces were exported to the specified name service entry. This status code is returned by **rpc_ns_mgmt_entry_inq_if_ids( )**.

User Action: None.

rpc_s_no_memory, no memory for RPC runtime

Explanation: The RPC runtime is unable to allocate heap storage.

User Action: If the failure is induced by overuse of underlying system resources (for example, address space or swap space), reduce the application's direct use of these resources if possible.

rpc_s_no_mepv, no manager EPV available

Explanation: The **rpc_server_register_if( )** routine was called specifying the default manager Entry Point Vector (EPV), but no manager EPV exists (the interface/server stub was generated using **-no_mepv**).

User Action: Regenerate the server stub without specifying **-no_mepv** or provide a manager EPV.

rpc_s_no_more_bindings, no more bindings

Explanation: A client or management application performing a lookup operation on a name service entry exhausted the list of compatible bindings that were exported.

User Action: None.

rpc_s_no_more_elements, no more profile elements

Explanation: No more profile elements are found in the profile lookup. This is usually not reported through the API.

User Action: Report it to the vendor.

rpc_s_no_ns_permission, no permission for name service operation

Explanation: The application program attempted to perform a name service operation that required permissions that the process did not possess.

User Action: Make sure that the application has the requisite name service permission and retry the operation.

rpc_s_no_protseqs, no protocol sequences

Explanation: An application requested a list of the protocol sequences supported by the RPC runtime, but none are supported.

User Action: This may be an internal error. Report it to the vendor.

rpc_s_no_protseqs_registered, no protocol sequences registered

Explanation: A server application called **rpc_server_listen( )**, but did not previously call **rpc_server_use_protseq( )** or one of its variants.

User Action: Fix application to call **rpc_server_use_protseq( )** or one of its variants.

rpc_s_not_all_objs_unexported, not all objects unexported

Explanation: One or more of the object UUIDs specified for unexport were not found in the specified name service entry, and therefore could not be removed.

User Action: Verify that your application is unexporting the object UUIDs that were previously exported.

rpc_s_not_found, not found

Explanation: The specified name service object (profile, group, or entry) does not exist in the name service database.

User Action: Verify that the object or directory name supplied to the NSI operation exists and repeat the operation.

rpc_s_not_in_kernel, feature not supported in kernel

Explanation: Kernel application attempted to use a feature that is not supported in the kernel.

User Action: Modify your application to avoid using that feature.

rpc_s_not_supported, not supported

Explanation: The requested operation is not supported by the RPC runtime.

In the case of **rpc_mgmt_set_server_stack_size( )**, the underlying thread package does not support setting the stack size.

User Action: Do not use the operation.

rpc_s_nothing_to_export, nothing to export

Explanation: The exporting application failed to provide an interface specification or a binding vector, and the object UUID vector is **NULL** (or empty).

User Action: To export binding information, provide an interface specification and a binding vector. To export objects, provide an object UUID vector. To export binding information and objects, provide an interface specification, binding vector, and object UUID vector.

rpc_s_nothing_to_unexport, nothing to unexport

Explanation: The server or management application attempted to unexport binding information for an interface ID that is not present in the target entry or to unexport object UUIDs that are not present.

User Action: None.

rpc_s_object_not_found, object not found

Explanation: Information is requested (for example, through the **rpc_object_inq_type**( ) routine) about an object that is unknown to the RPC runtime.

User Action: Call **rpc_object_set_type**( ) or **rpc_object_set_inq_fn**( ) if appropriate.

rpc_s_op_rng_error, operation out of range

Explanation: A client called the *n*th (zero-based) operation in an interface, but the server supports fewer than *n*-1 operations from the interface.

User Action: Modify server to support the addition operations or arrange for the client to find a server that supports the requested operation.

rpc_s_partial_results, partial results

Explanation: A name service entry was found to exist for a portion of the specified entry name. This status indicates that the resolved and unresolved portions of the name are returned as output arguments.

User Action: If you expect the name to be fully resolved, use the RPC control program to verify that a name service entry of the full name exists. If the entry exists, report the problem to the vendor.

rpc_s_profile_element_not_found, profile element not found

Explanation: The server or management application called **rpc_ns_profile_elt_remove**( ) specifying a profile member name that was not found in the name service database.

User Action: Use the RPC control program to see if the profile element exists. If it does not, correct the application. If the profile element does exist in the name service database, report the problem to the vendor.

rpc_s_protect_level_mismatch, protection level changed unexpectedly

Explanation: The runtime detected an unexpected change to the protection level.

User Action: This usually does not happen. Check for version skew between the client and server, bugs in the client or server runtime, or modifications to packets sent over the network.

rpc_s_proto_unsupp_by_auth, RPC protocol not supported by this auth protocol

Explanation: An application attempted to use a combination of authentication and RPC protocols that do not work together.

User Action: Use RPC and authentication protocols that do work together.

rpc_s_protseq_not_supported, protocol sequence not supported

Explanation: An application specified an RPC protocol sequence that is recognized, but is not supported by the RPC runtime.

User Action: Specify only supported RPC protocol sequences.

rpc_s_rpcd_comm_failure, RPC daemon communications failure

Explanation: The RPC runtime detected a failure while trying to communicate with the RPC daemon.

User Action: Use the RPC control program to verify that the RPC daemon is running.

rpc_s_socket_failure, persistent errors on socket

Explanation: The RPC runtime encountered repeated errors using a communication socket.

User Action: Make sure the underlying network transport service is working; try non-RPC applications that use this service (for example, file transfer or remote login).

rpc_s_ss_char_trans_open_fail, could not open file containing ASCII/EBCDIC translation tables

> **Explanation:** The file named in the environment variable **DCERPCCHARTRANS** is not accessible or does not exist.
>
> **User Action:** Either make the named file available, or unset **DCERPCCHARTRANS** and use the default ASCII/EBCDIC translation tables.

rpc_s_ss_char_trans_short_file, file containing ASCII/EBCDIC translation tables is damaged

> **Explanation:** The file named in the environment variable **DCERPCCHARTRANS** contains less than 512 bytes.
>
> **User Action:** Either make a valid file available, or unset **DCERPCCHARTRANS** and use the default ASCII/EBCDIC translation tables.

rpc_s_ss_context_damaged, a client side context handle has been incorrectly modified

> **Explanation:** The client side representation of a context handle was changed while a remote procedure call was in progress.
>
> **User Action:** Make sure that no client side thread running concurrently with the procedure call modifies the context handle.

rpc_s_ss_in_null_context, null value of **[in]** context handle, or all **[in,out]** context handles

> **Explanation:** If an operation has **[in]** or **[in,out]** context handle parameters, the binding for that operation is determined using those parameters. A **NULL** context handle does not refer to valid binding information.
>
> **User Action:** Make sure that all **[in]** context handles are non-**NULL**. If the operation has **[in,out]** context handle parameters but no **[in]** context handles, make sure that at least one of the **[in,out]** context handles is non-**NULL**.

rpc_s_type_already_registered, type already registered

Explanation: A server application tried to register an interface and type (by means of the **rpc_server_register_if( )** routine) that was previously registered.

User Action: Remove redundant registration or unregister before registering.

rpc_s_underspecified_name, name is underspecified

Explanation: The syntax of a specified entry name indicated a global name. However, the cell name portion does not resolve to a cell. For example, this status code would be returned if the cell name is **/.../c=us/o=osf/ou=dce**, but the cell name portion of the specified entry name is **/.../c=us or /.../c=us/o=osf**.

User Action: Provide the full cell name portion in the specified entry name.

rpc_s_unknown_authn_service, unknown authentication service

Explanation: A client specified an authentication service that is not supported by the RPC runtime.

User Action: The client can be changed to use no authentication or one of the supported authentication services.

rpc_s_unknown_error, unidentified communications error in client stub

Explanation: A communications error detected by the client stub cannot be mapped to an exception. Note that this status is only used as the status value of the **rpc_x_unknown_error exception**.

User Action: Either handle the **rpc_x_unknown_error** exception as a client communications error, or file an SPR/APR; all client communications errors result in identifiable exceptions.

rpc_s_unknown_if, unknown interface

Explanation: A client application tried to make a remote call using an interface that the server being called does not support. This condition also includes the binding, specifying a server that does not support the RPC management service (the **rpc_mgmt_*** routines). This situation can occur if a DCE client is trying to make a **rpc_mgmt_*** call to an NCS V1.5.1 server.

User Action: The client may have bound to an inappropriate server; rebind the client to another server.

rpc_s_unknown_ifspec_vers, interface's version is unknown

Explanation: An application supplied an interface handle that referred to an interface that specified an unknown interface format version. (The interface format version specifies how the interface specification is laid out internally. Do not confuse it with the contents of the IDL version field in an interface definition.) Either the handle is invalid (it does not point to a interface) or there is a version skew between the IDL compiler and RPC runtime used by the application developer.

User Action: Make sure the handle is valid and that correct versions of the IDL compiler and RPC runtime are used.

rpc_s_unknown_mgr_type, unsupported type

Explanation: A client application tried to make a remote call using a binding handle whose associated object UUID has a type that is unsupported for the interface being used.

User Action: Either the client is bound to an inappropriate server (in which case it should rebind to another server) or there is an application error.

rpc_s_unknown_stub_rtl_if_vers, interface's stub/runtime version is unknown

Explanation: An application supplied an interface handle that referred to an interface that specified an unknown stub/runtime interface version. Either the handle is invalid (did not point to a interface) or there is a version skew between the IDL compiler and RPC runtime used by the application developer.

User Action: Make sure the handle is valid and that correct versions of the IDL compiler and RPC runtime are used.

rpc_s_unsupported_auth_subtype, receiver cannot support auth subtype

Explanation: The receiver cannot support the authentication subtype. The connection-oriented protocol supports more than one algorithm for computations performed during security processing. In this case the sender of a remote procedure call requested the receiver to use an algorithm that the receiver (the server system) does not support.

User Action: This may be an attempt to violate system security.

rpc_s_unsupported_name_syntax, unsupported name syntax

Explanation: The value specified for the entry name syntax was valid, but not supported.

User Action: Check the value provided and use one of the supported API defined constants **rpc_c_ns_syntax_***.

rpc_s_unsupported_protect_level, requested protection level is not supported

Explanation: The value for the protection level supplied to **rpc_binding_set_auth_info( )** is unsupported.

User Action: Change application to use the supported value.

rpc_s_unsupported_type, unsupported type

Explanation: A client application tried to make a remote call using a binding handle whose associated object UUID has a type that is unsupported for the interface being used.

User Action: Either the client established a binding with an inappropriate server (and the client should rebind to another server) or an application error exists.

rpc_s_wrong_boot_time, wrong boot time

Explanation: A binding handle that is successfully used to make a remote procedure call using the **ncadg** RPC protocol will be bound to that server instance (identified by remembering the server's boot (start-up) time in the binding handle). A **ncadg** remote procedure call made to a different server instance than the one originally associated with the binding handle results in the remote procedure call failing with this status code (exception).

An application may also see this status code returned from the **rpc_mgmt_ep_elt_inq_begin( )** routine. In this case, the endpoint map service rebooted during the lifetime of the inquiry context.

User Action: For the case of a failed remote procedure call, the client can call **rpc_binding_reset( )** for communications with the new server instance to succeed.

For inquiring endpoint map elements, call **rpc_mgmt_ep_elt_inq_done( )** to delete the failed inquiry context. Next, restart the inquiry by calling **rpc_mgmt_ep_elt_inq_begin( )**.

rpc_s_wrong_kind_of_binding, wrong kind of binding

Explanation: An application specified a client (server) binding handle as input to an RPC runtime routine that expects a server (client) binding handle.

User Action: Change the application to use the correct kind of binding handle.

twr_s_not_implemented, not implemented

Explanation: An application attempted to execute code not yet implemented.

User Action: Check to see that your application uses only the supported protocol sequences. If the problem persists, report it to the vendor.

uuid_s_bad_version, bad UUID version

Explanation: An application passed a UUID as input to the RPC runtime but the UUID was unrecognized.

User Action: Fix the application.

uuid_s_getconf_failure, get_configuration failure

Explanation: The RPC runtime's UUID generator is unable to get hardware interface configuration information.

User Action: Make sure the underlying network transport service is working; try non-RPC applications that use this service (for example, file transfer or remote login).

uuid_s_invalid_string_uuid, invalid string UUID

Explanation: The contents of the string passed to **uuid_from_string( )** is not in the valid UUID string format.

User Action: Supply a correctly formatted UUID.

uuid_s_no_address, no IEEE 802 hardware address

Explanation: The RPC runtime's UUID generator is unable to get the local system's IEEE 802 address.

User Action: Make sure the underlying network transport service is working; try non-RPC applications that use this service (for example, file transfer or remote login).

uuid_s_socket_failure, socket failure

Explanation: The RPC runtime's UUID generator is unable to create a socket it needs in the course of obtaining the local system's IEEE 802 address.

User Action: Make sure the underlying network transport service is working; try non-RPC applications that use this service (for example, file transfer or remote login).

Message Texts and Status Codes

The following list provides the RPC status codes message texts (in alphabetical order) accompanied by the applicable status code:

A client side context handle has been incorrectly modified
rpc_s_ss_context_damaged

Already listening **rpc_s_already_listening**

Already registered **rpc_s_already_registered**

Attempting to use credentials belonging to other user
rpc_s_helper_wrong_user

Authentication authorization mismatch
rpc_s_authn_authz_mismatch

Authentication challenge malformed
rpc_s_authn_challenge_malformed

Bad UUID version **uuid_s_bad_version**

Binding incomplete (no object ID and no endpoint)
rpc_s_binding_incomplete

Call canceled **rpc_s_call_cancelled**

Call faulted **rpc_s_call_faulted**

Call orphaned **rpc_s_call_orphaned**

Call timed out **rpc_s_call_timeout**

Calls too large for well-known endpoint
rpc_s_calls_too_large_for_wk_ep

Cancel timeout **rpc_s_cancel_timeout**

Cannot access endpoint database	**ept_s_cant_access**
Cannot bind socket	**rpc_s_cant_bind_socket**
Cannot create endpoint database	**ept_s_cant_create**
Cannot create socket	**rpc_s_cant_create_socket**
Cannot get interface id	**rpc_s_cant_get_if_id**
Cannot inquire socket	**rpc_s_cant_inq_socket**
Cannot perform endpoint map operation	**ept_s_cant_perform_op**
Cannot update endpoint database	**ept_s_update_failed**
Communications failure	**rpc_s_comm_failure**
Could not open file containing ASCII/EBCDIC translation tables	**rpc_s_ss_char_trans_open_fail**
Cycle detected	**rpc_s_cycle_detected**
Endpoint database already open by another process	**ept_s_database_already_open**
Entry already exists	**rpc_s_entry_already_exists**
Entry not found	**rpc_s_entry_not_found**
Fault addr error	**rpc_s_fault_addr_error**
Fault context mismatch	**rpc_s_fault_context_mismatch**
Fault floating-point divide by zero	**rpc_s_fault_fp_div_by_zero**
Fault floating-point error	**rpc_s_fault_fp_error**
Fault floating-point overflow	**rpc_s_fault_fp_overflow**
Fault floating-point underflow	**rpc_s_fault_fp_underflow**
Fault illegal instruction	**rpc_s_fault_ill_inst**

Fault integer divide by zero	**rpc_s_fault_int_div_by_zero**
Fault integer overflow	**rpc_s_fault_int_overflow**
Fault invalid bound	**rpc_s_fault_invalid_bound**
Fault invalid tag	**rpc_s_fault_invalid_tag**
Fault pipe closed	**rpc_s_fault_pipe_closed**
Fault pipe communication error	**rpc_s_fault_pipe_comm_error**
Fault pipe discipline	**rpc_s_fault_pipe_discipline**
Fault pipe empty	**rpc_s_fault_pipe_empty**
Fault pipe memory	**rpc_s_fault_pipe_memory**
Fault pipe order	**rpc_s_fault_pipe_order**
Fault remote communication failure	**rpc_s_fault_remote_comm_failure**
Fault remote no memory	**rpc_s_fault_remote_no_memory**
Fault unspecified	**rpc_s_fault_unspec**
Feature not supported in kernel	**rpc_s_not_in_kernel**
File containing ASCII/EBCDIC translation tables is damaged	**rpc_s_ss_char_trans_short_file**
Get_configuration failure	**uuid_s_getconf_failure**
Group member not found	**rpc_s_group_member_not_found**
Helper process aborted	**rpc_s_helper_aborted**
Helper process is catatonic	**rpc_s_helper_catatonic**
Helper process not running	**rpc_s_helper_not_running**
Helper process too busy	**rpc_s_helper_overflow**
Incomplete name	**rpc_s_incomplete_name**
Input arguments too big	**rpc_s_in_args_too_big**
Interface not found	**rpc_s_interface_not_found**

Interface's stub/runtime version is unknown	**rpc_s_unknown_stub_rtl_if_vers**
Interface's version is unknown	**rpc_s_unknown_ifspec_vers**
Invalid argument	**rpc_s_invalid_arg**
Invalid binding	**rpc_s_invalid_binding**
Invalid call option	**rpc_s_invalid_call_opt**
Invalid endpoint database	**ept_s_database_invalid**
Invalid endpoint entry	**ept_s_invalid_entry**
Invalid endpoint format for remote host	**rpc_s_invalid_endpoint_format**
Invalid endpoint map or lookup context	**ept_s_invalid_context**
Invalid inquiry context	**rpc_s_invalid_inquiry_context**
Invalid inquiry type	**rpc_s_invalid_inquiry_type**
Invalid interface version option	**rpc_s_invalid_vers_option**
Invalid name service handle	**rpc_s_invalid_ns_handle**
Invalid name syntax	**rpc_s_invalid_name_syntax**
Invalid object	**rpc_s_invalid_object**
Invalid priority	**rpc_s_invalid_priority**
Invalid RPC protocol sequence	**rpc_s_invalid_rpc_protseq**
Invalid RPC tower floor	**rpc_s_invalid_rpc_floor**
Invalid string binding	**rpc_s_invalid_string_binding**
Invalid string UUID	**uuid_s_invalid_string_uuid**
Invalid timeout	**rpc_s_invalid_timeout**
Key function not allowed when default authentication service specified	**rpc_s_key_func_not_allowed**

Management operation disallowed	**rpc_s_mgmt_op_disallowed**
Max calls (threads) too small	**rpc_s_max_calls_too_small**
Max descriptors exceeded	**rpc_s_max_descs_exceeded**
Name is underspecified	**rpc_s_underspecified_name**
Name service environment variable not defined	**rpc_s_no_env_setup**
Name service unavailable	**rpc_s_name_service_unavailable**
No bindings	**rpc_s_no_bindings**
No entry name	**rpc_s_no_entry_name**
No IEEE 802 hardware address	**uuid_s_no_address**
No interfaces	**rpc_s_no_interfaces**
No interfaces exported	**rpc_s_no_interfaces_exported**
No manager EPV available	**rpc_s_no_mepv**
No memory for endpoint map service	**ept_s_no_memory**
No memory for RPC runtime	**rpc_s_no_memory**
No more bindings	**rpc_s_no_more_bindings**
No more profile elements	**rpc_s_no_more_elements**
No permission for name service operation	**rpc_s_no_ns_permission**
No protocol sequences	**rpc_s_no_protseqs**
No protocol sequences registered	**rpc_s_no_protseqs_registered**
Not all objects unexported	**rpc_s_not_all_objs_unexported**
Not authenticated	**rpc_s_binding_has_no_auth**
Not found	**rpc_s_not_found**
Not implemented	**twr_s_not_implemented**

Not registered in endpoint map
ept_s_not_registered

Not supported **rpc_s_not_supported**

Nothing to export **rpc_s_nothing_to_export**

Nothing to unexport **rpc_s_nothing_to_unexport**

Null value of **[in]** context handle or all **[in,out]** context handles
rpc_s_ss_in_null_context

Object not found **rpc_s_object_not_found**

Operation out of range **rpc_s_op_rng_error**

Partial results **rpc_s_partial_results**

Persistent errors on socket **rpc_s_socket_failure**

Profile element not found **rpc_s_profile_element_not_found**

Protection level changed unexpectedly
rpc_s_protect_level_mismatch

Protocol sequence not supported
rpc_s_protseq_not_supported

Receiver cannot support auth subtype
rpc_s_unsupported_auth_subtype

Requested protection level is not supported
rpc_s_unsupported_protect_level

RPC class version mismatch **rpc_s_class_version_mismatch**

RPC daemon communications failure
rpc_s_rpcd_comm_failure

RPC protocol not supported by this auth protocol
rpc_s_proto_unsupp_by_auth

Short read from kernel helper
rpc_s_helper_short_read

Socket failure **uuid_s_socket_failure**

Type already registered **rpc_s_type_already_registered**

Unidentified communications error in client stub
rpc_s_unknown_error

Unknown authentication service	**rpc_s_unknown_authn_service**
Unknown interface	**rpc_s_unknown_if**
Unsupported name syntax	**rpc_s_unsupported_name_syntax**
Unsupported type	**rpc_s_unknown_mgr_type**
Unsupported type	**rpc_s_unsupported_type**
Wrong boot time	**rpc_s_wrong_boot_time**
Wrong kind of binding	**rpc_s_wrong_kind_of_binding**

Related Information

Routines: **dce_***, **rpc_***, **uuid_***.

uuidgen_messages

Purpose Listing of the **uuidgen** command messages

Description

The following **uuidgen** messages are listed in alphabetical order:

A filename must follow the **-o** option

Explanation: The **-o** option must be followed by a filename.

User Action: Specify **-o** followed by a filename indicating the file into which the generated UUID is to be written.

An integer value must follow the **-n** option

Explanation: The **-n** option must be followed by an integer value.

User Action: Specify **-n** followed by an integer value indicating the number of UUIDs to be generated.

An old-style UUID must follow the **-t** option

Explanation: The **-t** option must be followed by an old-style UUID.

User Action: Specify **-t** followed by an old-style UUID. Old-style UUIDs have the following format:
123456789abc.12.34.56.78.9a.bc.de.f0

Cannot open file *filename*

Explanation: The **uuidgen** command cannot open the specified filename.

User Action: Verify that the file name provided on the **-o** option is valid, that you have the appropriate privilege to write into the file, and that the device is not full.

h,? - Display command option summary

Explanation: Describes usage of the **-h** option.

User Action: Specify **-h** to direct **uuidgen** to output a summary of command options.

i - Output UUID in an IDL interface template

Explanation: Describes usage of the **-i** option.

User Action: Specify **-i** if you want the output to be a template IDL interface definition with the generated UUID contained in the **uuid** attribute.

n *#* - Number of UUIDs to generate

Explanation: Describes usage of the **-n** option.

User Action: Specify **-n** followed by an integer number to inform **uuidgen** how many UUID numbers to generate.

NLS message catalog version mismatch in *filename*, Expected: *version*, Actual: *version*

Explanation: The error messages reported by the UUID generator are stored in an NLS message catalog. The catalog *filename* is not the same version as the UUID generator being invoked. The error messages reported may therefore be incorrect or cause the generator to terminate abnormally.

User Action: Check the definition of the NLS environment variable **NLSPATH** and verify that it searches the appropriate directories. The default is *<dceshared>***/nls/msg/***LANG***/%N**.

o *filename* - Redirect output to a file

Explanation: Describes usage of the **-o** option.

User Action: Specify **-o** followed by a filename to direct **uuidgen** to place output in the specified file instead of to the standard output device.

Out of memory

Explanation: The system-defined limit of memory available to **uuidgen** is exceeded.

User Action: Either have the system-defined limit of memory raised, or reduce the number of UUIDs being generated by lowering the value specified with the **-n** option.

Received Error Status: *message-string*

Explanation: A call to the RPC runtime returned an error status. The text is as shown.

User Action: Look up the error message in the RPC runtime documentation for the appropriate action.

Received Error Status: *status-code*

Explanation: A call to the RPC runtime returned the error status specified.

User Action: Look up the error status in the RPC runtime documentation for appropriate action.

s - Output UUID as an initialized C **struct**

Explanation: Describes usage of the **-s** option.

User Action: Specify **-s** if you wish the UUID generated as a **struct** initializer for use in a C application code.

Syntax error in UUID *string*

Explanation: The UUID following the **-t** option is not in the proper syntax.

User Action: Specify **-t** followed by an old-style UUID. Old-style UUIDs have the following format: **123456789abc.12.34.56.78.9a.bc.de.f0**

t *olduuid* - Translate an old-format UUID into new format

Explanation: Describes usage of the **-t** option.

User Action: Specify **-t** followed by an old-format UUID to direct **uuidgen** to translate the UUID into the new format.

usage: **uuidgen [-ihstv?]** [**-on**]

Explanation: An invalid command option is specified.

User Action: For information about the arguments, invoke the **uuidgen** command with the **-h** argument.

v - Display version information about **uuidgen**

Explanation: Describes usage of the **-v** option.

User Action: Specify **-v** to direct **uuidgen** to print the software version number.

version *version-number*

Explanation: Shows the software version of the **uuidgen** utility.

User Action: None. This is an informational message.

Related Information

Commands: **uuidgen**.

Chapter 3

DCE Directory Service

intro

Purpose Introduction to X/OPEN Directory Services (XDS) functions

Synopsis **#include <xom.h>**
#include <xds.h>

Description

This **intro** reference page lists the XDS interface functions in the following table. XDS provides a C language binding.

Service Interface Functions — intro(3xds)	
Function	**Description**
ds_abandon( )	Function not supported.
ds_add_entry( )	Adds a leaf entry to the Directory Information Tree (DIT).
ds_bind( )	Opens a session with a directory user agent.
ds_compare( )	Compares a purported attribute value with the attribute value stored in the directory for a particular entry.
ds_initialize( )	Initializes the interface.
ds_list( )	Enumerates the immediate subordinates of a particular directory entry.
ds_modify_entry( )	Performs an atomic modification of a directory entry.
ds_modify_rdn( )	Changes the Relative Distinguished Name (RDN) of a leaf entry.
ds_read( )	Queries information on a directory entry by name.
ds_receive_result( )	Function not supported.
ds_remove_entry( )	Removes a leaf entry from the DIT.
ds_search( )	Finds entries of interest in a portion of the DIT.
ds_shutdown( )	Shuts down the interface.
ds_unbind( )	Unbinds from a directory session.
ds_version( )	Negotiates features of the interface and service.

The Distributed Computing Environment (DCE) XDS interface does not support asynchronous operations. Thus, **ds_abandon**( ) and **ds_receive_result**( ) are redundant. A **ds_abandon**( ) call returns with a **DS_C_ABANDON_FAILED** (**DS_E_TOO_LATE**) error. A **ds_receive_result**( ) call returns with **DS_status** set to **DS_SUCCESS**, and the *completion_flag_return* parameter set to **DS_NO_OUTSTANDING_OPERATION**.

The following differences exist between Global Directory Service (GDS) and Cell Directory Service (CDS):

- All functions operate on the GDS name space.
- CDS does not support the **ds_modify_rdn**( ) or **ds_search**( ). The error message **DS_C_SERVICE_ERROR** (**DS_E_UNWILLING_TO_PERFORM**) is returned if either of these two functions are attempted on CDS.
- In CDS, no X.500 schema rules apply. There is
    - — No concept of an object class.
    - — No mandatory attributes for a given object.
    - — No set of attributes expressly permitted for a given object.
    - — No predefined definition of single and multivalued attributes.

The absence of these schema rules means that the usual errors, which are returned by GDS for breach of schema rules, are not returned by CDS.

The CDS naming Directory Information Tree (DIT) is modeled on a typical file system architecture, where directories are used for storing objects and directories can contain subdirectories. Leaf objects in the CDS DIT are similar to X.500 naming objects. However, subtree objects are called directories as in a file system directory. All new objects must be added to an existing directory. CDS directory objects cannot be added, removed, modified, or compared using the XDS programming interface.

In CDS, the naming attribute of an object is not stored in the object. Consequently, in CDS, **ds_read**( ) never returns this attribute, and **ds_compare**( ) applied to this attribute returns with **DS_C_ATTRIBUTE_ERROR** (**DS_E_CONSTRAINT_VIOLATION**).

Notes

See the notes in the relevant reference page for function-specific differences.

ds_add_entry

Purpose Adds a leaf entry to the Directory Information Tree (DIT)

Synopsis **#include <xom.h>**
#include <xds.h>

DS_status ds_add_entry(
OM_private_object *session*,
OM_private_object *context*,
OM_object *name*,
OM_object *entry*,
OM_sint **invoke_id_return*);

Parameters

session (Object(**DS_C_SESSION**)). The directory session against which this operation is performed. This must be a private object.

context (Object(**DS_C_CONTEXT**)). The directory context to be used for this operation. This parameter must be a private object or the **DS_DEFAULT_CONTEXT** constant. Note that **DS_DONT_DEREFERENCE_ALIASES** and **DS_SIZE_LIMIT** do not apply to this operation.

name (Object(**DS_C_NAME**)). The name of the entry to be added. The immediate superior of the new entry is determined by removing the last Relative Distinguished Name (RDN) component, which belongs to the new entry. The immediate superior must exist in the same Directory System Agent (DSA); otherwise, the function can fail with **DS_C_UPDATE_ERROR** (**DS_E_AFFECTS_MULTIPLE_DSAS**). Any aliases in the name are *not* dereferenced.

entry (Object(**DS_C_ATTRIBUTE_LIST**)). The attribute information that, together with that from the RDN, constitutes the entry to be created. Note that an instance of Object Management (OM) class **DS_C_ENTRY_INFO** can be supplied as the value of this parameter, since **DS_C_ENTRY_INFO** is a subclass of **DS_C_ATTRIBUTE_LIST**.

Description

The **ds_add_entry**( ) function adds a leaf entry to the Directory. The entry can be either an object or an alias. The Directory checks that the resulting entry conforms to the Directory schema.

Notes

Although the user ideally is not aware whether naming operations are being handled by GDS or CDS, there are some situations where naming results can differ between the two services. (See the **intro** reference page for XDS functions at the beginning of this chapter for general differences between operations on GDS and CDS.)

Note the following issues for the **ds_add_entry**( ) operation:

- Only leaf objects (that is, objects that are not CDS directory objects) can be added to CDS through the XDS interface.
- The **DS_A_OBJECT_CLASS** attribute of an object is single valued in CDS and multivalued in GDS.
- Only the **DS_A_COMMON_NAME** and **DS_A_MEMBER** attributes are valid for the **DS_O_GROUP_OF_NAMES** object in CDS.
- GDS-structured attribute types are not supported by CDS. If an attempt is made to add a GDS-structured attribute type to CDS, then it returns with a **DS_C_ATTRIBUTE_ERROR** (**DS_E_CONSTRAINT_VIOLATION**).

Since CDS does not implement the X.500 schema rules, some CDS objects may not contain mandatory attributes like object class and so on.

Return Values

`DS_status`
: **DS_SUCCESS** is returned if the entry was added; otherwise, an error is returned.

`invoke_id_return`
: (Integer). Not supported.

Errors

This function can return a **DS_C_SYSTEM_ERROR** or one of the following **DS_C_LIBRARY_ERROR**s:

[**DS_E_BAD_ARGUMENT**]

[**DS_E_BAD_CONTEXT**]

[**DS_E_BAD_NAME**]

[**DS_E_BAD_SESSION**]

[**DS_E_MISCELLANEOUS**]

[**DS_E_MISSING_TYPE**]

[**DS_E_TOO_MANY_OPERATIONS**]

The function can return the following directory errors:

[**DS_C_ATTRIBUTE_ERROR**]

[**DS_C_NAME_ERROR**]

[**DS_C_REFERRAL**]

[**DS_C_SECURITY_ERROR**]

[**DS_C_SERVICE_ERROR**]

[**DS_C_UPDATE_ERROR**]

The **DS_C_UPDATE_ERROR** (**DS_E_AFFECTS_MULTIPLE_DSAS**) error, referred to earlier in this reference page, need not be returned if there is local agreement between the DSAs to allow the entry to be added.

This function can return a **DS_C_COMMUNICATIONS_ERROR**, as well as the error constant **DS_NO_WORKSPACE**.

ds_bind

Purpose Opens a session with the Directory

Synopsis

```
#include <xom.h>
#include <xds.h>

DS_status ds_bind(
        OM_object session,
        OM_workspace workspace,
        OM_private_object *bound_session_return);
```

Parameters

session (Object(**DS_C_SESSION**)). Specifies a particular directory service provider, together with other details of the service required. This parameter can be either a public object or a private object. The **DS_DEFAULT_SESSION** constant can also be used as the value of this parameter, causing a new session to be created with default values for all its OM attributes.

workspace Specifies the workspace obtained from a call to **ds_initialize**( ) that is to be associated with the session. All function results from directory operations using this session will be returned as private objects in this workspace. If the *session* parameter is a private object, it must be a private object in this workspace.

Description

The **ds_bind**( ) function sets up a communications link to the DSA.

Notes

Although the user ideally is not aware whether naming operations are being handled by GDS or CDS, there are some situations where naming results can differ between the two services. (See the **intro** reference page for XDS functions at the start of this chapter for general differences between operations on GDS and CDS.)

Note that in order to use CDS when GDS is not active, **ds_bind**( ) must be called with the value of the *session* parameter set to **DS_DEFAULT_SESSION**.

Return Values

`DS_status` **DS_SUCCESS** is returned if the function is completed successfully; otherwise, it indicates the error that has occurred.

`bound_session_return`
(Object(**DS_C_SESSION**)). Upon successful completion, this parameter contains an instance of a directory session that can be used as a parameter to other functions (for example, **ds_read( )**). This is a new private object if the value of the *session* parameter was **DS_DEFAULT_SESSION** or a public object; otherwise, it is that value supplied as a parameter. The function supplies default values for any of the OM attributes that are not present in the *session* parameter instance supplied as a parameter. It also sets the value of the **DS_FILE_DESCRIPTOR** OM attribute to **DS_NO_VALID_FILE_DESCRIPTOR**, since the functionality is not supported.

Errors

This function can return a **DS_C_SYSTEM_ERROR** or one of the following **DS_C_LIBRARY_ERROR**s:

[**DS_E_BAD_SESSION**]

[**DS_E_BAD_WORKSPACE**]

[**DS_E_MISCELLANEOUS**]

[**DS_E_TOO_MANY_SESSIONS**]

The function can return the following directory errors:

[**DS_C_SECURITY_ERROR**]

[**DS_C_SERVICE_ERROR**]

This function can return a **DS_COMMUNICATIONS_ERROR**, as well as the error constant **DS_NO_WORKSPACE**.

Related Information

Functions: **ds_unbind(3xds)**.

ds_compare

Purpose Compares a purported attribute value with the attribute value stored in the directory for a particular entry

Synopsis **#include <xom.h>**
#include <xds.h>

DS_status ds_compare(
OM_private_object *session*,
OM_private_object *context*,
OM_object *name*,
OM_object *ava*,
OM_private_object **result_return*,
OM_sint **invoke_id_return*);

Parameters

session (Object(**DS_C_SESSION**)). The directory session against which this operation is performed. This must be a private object.

context (Object(**DS_C_CONTEXT**)). The directory context to be used for this operation. Note that **DS_SIZE_LIMIT** does not apply to this operation. This parameter must be a private object or the **DS_DEFAULT_CONTEXT** constant.

name (Object(**DS_C_NAME**)). The name of the target object entry. Any aliases in the name are dereferenced unless prohibited by the **DS_DONT_DEREFERENCE_ALIASES** service control attribute of the **DS_C_CONTEXT** object.

ava (Object(**DS_C_AVA**)). The Attribute Value Assertion that specifies the attribute type and value to be compared with those in the entry.

Description

The **ds_compare**( ) function compares the value supplied in the given *ava* parameter with the value or values of the same attribute type in the named entry.

Notes

Although the user ideally is not aware whether naming operations are being handled by GDS or CDS, there are some situations where naming results can differ between the two services. (See the **intro** reference page for XDS functions at the start of this chapter for general differences between operations on GDS and CDS.)

Note the following issues for the **ds_compare()** operation:

- In CDS, the naming attribute of an object is not stored in the attribute list of an object. Thus in CDS, a **ds_compare()** of the purported naming attribute value with the naming attribute value of the directory object always fails to match.
- GDS-structured types are not supported by CDS. If a GDS-structured attribute type is used as a parameter to **ds_compare()** on a CDS object, then it returns with the error **DS_C_ATTRIBUTE_ERROR** (**DS_E_CONSTRAINT_VIOLATION**).
- In CDS, **ds_compare()** can only be used on leaf objects; otherwise, a **DS_C_NAME_ERROR** (**DS_E_NO_SUCH_OBJECT**) is returned.

Return Values

`DS_status`

Indicates whether the comparison is completed or not. If successful, **DS_SUCCESS** is returned. Note that the operation fails and an error is returned either if the target object is not found or if it does not have an attribute of the required type.

`result_return`

(Object(**DS_C_COMPARE_RESULT**)). Upon successful completion, the result contains flags indicating whether the values matched and whether the comparison was made against the original entry. It also contains the distinguished name of the target object if an alias is dereferenced.

`invoke-ID_return`

(Integer). Not supported.

Errors

This function can return a **DS_C_SYSTEM_ERROR** or one of the following **DS_C_LIBRARY_ERROR**s:

[**DS_E_BAD_ARGUMENT**]

[**DS_E_BAD_CONTEXT**]

[**DS_E_BAD_NAME**]

[**DS_E_BAD_SESSION**]

[**DS_E_MISCELLANEOUS**]

[**DS_E_MISSING_TYPE**]

[**DS_E_TOO_MANY_OPERATIONS**]

The following directory errors can be returned:

[**DS_C_ATTRIBUTE_ERROR**]

[**DS_C_NAME_ERROR**]

[**DS_C_REFERRAL**]

[**DS_C_SECURITY_ERROR**]

[**DS_C_SERVICE_ERROR**]

This function can return a **DS_COMMUNICATIONS_ERROR**, as well as the error constant **DS_NO_WORKSPACE**.

ds_initialize

Purpose Initializes the XDS interface

Synopsis

#include <xom.h>
#include <xds.h>

OM_workspace ds_initialize(void);

Description

The **ds_initialize( )** function performs any necessary initialization of the XDS Application Program Interface (API), including the creation of a workspace. It must be called before any other directory interface functions are called. If it is subsequently called before **ds_shutdown( )**, the function returns **NULL**.

Return Values

`OM_workspace`
Upon successful completion, **OM_workspace** contains a handle to a workspace in which OM objects can be created and manipulated. Objects created in this workspace, and only such objects, can be used as parameters to the other directory interface functions. This function returns **NULL** if it fails.

Related Information

Functions: **ds_shutdown(3xds)**.

ds_list

Purpose Enumerates the immediate subordinates of a particular directory entry

Synopsis **#include <xom.h>**
#include <xds.h>

DS_status ds_list(
OM_private_object *session*,
OM_private_object *context*,
OM_object *name*,
OM_private_object **result_return*,
OM_sint **invoke_id_return*);

Parameters

session (Object(**DS_C_SESSION**)). The directory session against which this operation is performed. This must be a private object.

context (Object(**DS_C_CONTEXT**)). The directory context to be used for this operation. This parameter must be a private object or the **DS_DEFAULT_CONTEXT** constant.

name (Object(**DS_C_NAME**)). The name of the object entry whose immediate subordinates are to be listed. Any aliases in the name are dereferenced unless prohibited by the **DS_DONT_DEREFERENCE_ALIASES** service control attribute of the **DS_C_CONTEXT** object.

Description

The **ds_list( )** function is used to obtain a list of the immediate subordinates of the named entry. The list can be incomplete in some circumstances, for example, if the results exceed **DS_SIZE_LIMIT**.

Return Values

`DS_status`
Takes the value **DS_SUCCESS** if the named object is located (even if there are no subordinates) and takes an error value if not.

`result_return`

(Object(**DS_C_LIST_RESULT**)). Upon successful completion, the result contains some information about the target object's immediate subordinates. It also contains the distinguished name of the target object, if an alias was dereferenced to find it. Aliases in the subordinate names are not dereferenced. In addition, there can be a partial outcome qualifier, which indicates that the result is incomplete. It also explains the reason for this (for example, because the time limit expired), and it contains information that can be helpful when attempting to complete the operation.

`invoke_ID_return`

(Integer). Not supported.

Errors

This function can return a **DS_C_SYSTEM_ERROR** or one of the following **DS_C_LIBRARY_ERROR**s:

[**DS_E_BAD_ARGUMENT**]

[**DS_E_BAD_CONTEXT**]

[**DS_E_BAD_NAME**]

[**DS_E_BAD_SESSION**]

[**DS_E_MISCELLANEOUS**]

[**DS_E_MISSING_TYPE**]

[**DS_E_TOO_MANY_OPERATIONS**]

The function can return the following directory errors:

[**DS_C_NAME_ERROR**]

[**DS_C_REFERRAL**]

[**DS_C_SECURITY_ERROR**]

[**DS_C_SERVICE_ERROR**]

This function can return a **DS_COMMUNICATIONS_ERROR**, as well as the error constant **DS_NO_WORKSPACE**.

ds_modify_entry

Purpose Performs an atomic modification on a directory entry

Synopsis

```
#include <xom.h>
#include <xds.h>

DS_status ds_modify_entry(
        OM_private_object session,
        OM_private_object context,
        OM_object name,
        OM_object changes,
        OM_sint *invoke_id_return);
```

Parameters

session (Object(**DS_C_SESSION**)). The directory session against which this operation is performed. This must be a private object.

context (Object(**DS_C_CONTEXT**)). The directory context to be used for this operation. Note that **DS_SIZE_LIMIT** and **DS_DONT_DEREFERENCE_ALIASES** do not apply to this operation. This parameter must be a private object or the **DS_DEFAULT_CONTEXT** constant.

name (Object(**DS_C_NAME**)). The name of the target object entry. Any aliases in the name are *not* dereferenced.

changes (Object(**DS_C_ENTRY_MOD_LIST**)). A sequence of modifications to the named entry.

Description

The **ds_modify_entry( )** function is used to make a series of one or more of the following changes to a single directory entry:

- Add a new attribute (**DS_ADD_ATTRIBUTE**).
- Remove an attribute (**DS_REMOVE_ATTRIBUTE**).

- Add attribute values (**DS_ADD_VALUES**).
- Remove attribute values (**DS_REMOVE_VALUES**).

Values can be replaced by a combination of adding values and removing values in a single operation. The RDN can only be changed using **ds_modify_rdn( )**.

The result of the operation is as if each modification is made in the order specified in the *changes* parameter. If any of the individual modifications fails, then a **DS_C_ATTRIBUTE_ERROR** is reported and the entry is left as it was prior to the whole operation. The operation is atomic; that is, either all or none of the changes are made. The Directory checks that the resulting entry conforms to the Directory schema.

Notes

Although the user ideally is not aware whether naming operations are being handled by GDS or CDS, there are some situations where naming results can differ between the two services. (See the **intro** reference page for XDS functions at the start of this chapter for general differences between operations on GDS and CDS.)

Note the following issues for the **ds_modify_entry( )** operation:

- Naming schema rules do not apply in CDS. Thus, the following attribute errors are never returned by CDS:
  - — **DS_E_NO_SUCH_ATTRIBUTE_OR_VALUE**
  - — **DS_E_ATTRIBUTE_OR_VALUE_ALREADY_EXISTS**
- Naming operations that would normally return these errors succeed in CDS. In particular, the addition of an attribute that already exists does not return with an error. Instead, the values of the attribute to be added are combined with the values of the existing attribute.
- GDS-structured attribute types are not supported by CDS. If a GDS-structured attribute type is used as a parameter to **ds_modify_entry( )** on a CDS object, then it returns with a **DS_C_ATTRIBUTE_ERROR** (**DS_E_CONSTRAINT_VIOLATION**). In CDS, **ds_modify_entry( )** can only be used on leaf objects; otherwise, a **DS_C_NAME_ERROR** (**DS_E_NO_SUCH_OBJECT**) is returned.

Return Values

DS_status
Takes the value **DS_SUCCESS** if all the modifications succeeded and takes an error value if not.

invoke_id_return
(Integer). Not supported.

Errors

This function can return a **DS_C_SYSTEM_ERROR** or one of the following **DS_C_LIBRARY_ERROR**s:

[**DS_E_BAD_ARGUMENT**]

[**DS_E_BAD_CONTEXT**]

[**DS_E_BAD_NAME**]

[**DS_E_BAD_SESSION**]

[**DS_E_MISCELLANEOUS**]

[**DS_E_MISSING_TYPE**]

[**DS_E_TOO_MANY_OPERATIONS**]

The following directory errors can be returned by the function:

[**DS_C_ATTRIBUTE_ERROR**]

[**DS_C_NAME_ERROR**]

[**DS_C_REFERRAL**]

[**DS_C_SECURITY_ERROR**]

[**DS_C_SERVICE_ERROR**]

[**DS_C_UPDATE_ERROR**]

This function can return a **DS_COMMUNICATIONS_ERROR**, as well as the error constant **DS_NO_WORKSPACE**. The following situations apply to GDS:

- An attempt to use **DS_ADD_ATTRIBUTE** to add an existing attribute results in a **DS_C_ATTRIBUTE_ERROR**.
- An attempt to use **DS_ADD_VALUES** to add an existing value results in a **DS_C_ATTRIBUTE_ERROR**, as does an attempt to add a value to a nonexistent attribute type.

- An attempt to use **DS_REMOVE_ATTRIBUTE** to remove a nonexisting attribute results in a **DS_C_ATTRIBUTE_ERROR**, whereas an attempt to remove an attribute that is part of the object's RDN results in a **DS_C_UPDATE_ERROR**.
- An attempt to use **DS_REMOVE_VALUES** to remove a nonexisting value results in a **DS_C_ATTRIBUTE_ERROR**, whereas an attempt to remove a value of an attribute that is part of the object's RDN, or to modify the object class attribute, results in a **DS_C_UPDATE_ERROR**.

ds_modify_rdn

Purpose Changes the Relative Distinguished Name (RDN) of a leaf entry

Synopsis

```
#include <xom.h>
#include <xds.h>

DS_status ds_modify_rdn(
        OM_private_object session,
        OM_private_object context,
        OM_object name,
        OM_object new_RDN,
        OM_boolean delete_old_RDN,
        OM_sint *invoke_id_return);
```

Parameters

session (Object(**DS_C_SESSION**)). The directory session against which this operation is performed. This must be a private object.

context (Object(**DS_C_CONTEXT**)). The directory context to be used for this operation. Note that **DS_SIZE_LIMIT** and **DS_DONT_DEREFERENCE_ALIASES** do not apply to this operation. This parameter must be a private object or the **DS_DEFAULT_CONTEXT** constant.

name (Object(**DS_C_RELATIVE_NAME**)). The current name of the target leaf entry. Any aliases in the name are *not* dereferenced. The immediate superior must *not* have any nonspecific subordinate references; if it does, the function can fail with a **DS_C_UPDATE_ERROR** (**DS_E_AFFECTS_MULTIPLE_DSAS**).

A nonspecific subordinate reference is an indication that another DSA holds some number of children, but does not indicate their RDNs. This means that it is not possible to check the uniqueness of the requested new RDN within a single DSA.

new_RDN
(Object(**DS_C_RELATIVE_NAME**)). The requested new RDN. If an attribute value in the new RDN does not already exist in the entry (either as part of the old RDN or as a nondistinguished value), the new value is added. If it cannot be added, an error is reported.

delete_old_RDN

(Boolean). If this value is **OM_TRUE**, all attribute values that are in the old RDN but not in the new RDN are deleted. If the value is **OM_FALSE**, the old values should remain in the entry (not as part of the RDN). The value must be **OM_TRUE** when a single value attribute in the RDN has its value changed by the operation. If this operation removes the last attribute value of an attribute, that attribute is deleted.

Description

The **ds_modify_rdn( )** function is used to change the RDN of a leaf entry (either an object entry or an alias entry).

Notes

CDS does not support **ds_modify_rdn( )**, and returns with **DS_C_SERVICE_ERROR** (**DS_E_UNWILLING_TO_PERFORM**).

Return Values

`DS_status`

Indicates whether the name of the entry is changed (**DS_SUCCESS** is returned); otherwise, an error is returned.

`invoke_id_return`

(Integer). Not supported.

Errors

This function can return a **DS_C_SYSTEM_ERROR** or one of the following **DS_C_LIBRARY_ERROR**s:

[**DS_E_BAD_ARGUMENT**]

[**DS_E_BAD_CONTEXT**]

[**DS_E_BAD_NAME**]

[**DS_E_BAD_SESSION**]

[**DS_E_MISCELLANEOUS**]

[**DS_E_MISSING_TYPE**]

[**DS_E_TOO_MANY_OPERATIONS**]

The following directory errors can be returned by the function:

[DS_C_ATTRIBUTE_ERROR]

[DS_C_NAME_ERROR]

[DS_C_REFERRAL]

[DS_C_SECURITY_ERROR]

[DS_C_SERVICE_ERROR]

[DS_C_UPDATE_ERROR]

The **DS_C_UPDATE_ERROR** (**DS_E_AFFECTS_MULTIPLE_DSAS**) error, referred to earlier in this reference page, need not be returned if there is local agreement between the DSAs to allow the entry to be modified.

This function can return a **DS_C_COMMUNICATIONS_ERROR**, as well as the error constant **DS_NO_WORKSPACE**.

ds_read

Purpose Queries information on an entry by name

Synopsis

```
#include <xom.h>
#include <xds.h>

DS_status ds_read(
        OM_private_object session,
        OM_private_object context,
        OM_object name,
        OM_object selection,
        OM_private_object *result_return,
        OM_sint *invoke_id_return);
```

Parameters

session (Object(**DS_C_SESSION**)). The directory session against which this operation is performed. This must be a private object.

context (Object(**DS_C_CONTEXT**)). The directory context to be used for this operation. Note that **DS_SIZE_LIMIT** does not apply to this operation. This parameter must be a private object or the **DS_DEFAULT_CONTEXT** constant.

name (Object(**DS_C_NAME**)). The name of the target object entry. Any aliases in the name are dereferenced unless prohibited by the **DS_DONT_DEREFERENCE_ALIASES** service control attribute of the **DS_C_CONTEXT** object.

selection (Object(**DS_C_ENTRY_INFO_SELECTION**)). Specifies what information from the entry is requested. Information about no attributes, all attributes, or just for a named set can be chosen. Attribute types are always returned, but the attribute values need not be returned. The possible values of this parameter are given in the *OSF DCE Application Development Guide*.

Description

The **ds_read()** function is used to extract information from an explicitly named entry. It can also be used to verify a Distinguished Name (DN).

Notes

Although the user ideally is not aware whether naming operations are being handled by GDS or CDS, there are some situations where naming results can differ between the two services. (See the **intro** reference page for XDS functions at the start of this chapter for general differences between operations on GDS and CDS.)

Note the following issues for the **ds_read()** operation:

- Since CDS does not implement the X.500 schema rules, some CDS objects may not contain mandatory attribrutes like object class and so on. In CDS, a read of an alias object fails if the **DS_A_ALIASED_OBJECT_NAME** does not exist. Instead, CDS returns with **DS_C_NAME_ERROR** (**DS_E_NO_SUCH_OBJECT**).
- In CDS, the naming attribute of an object is not stored in the attribute list for the object. Thus in CDS, **ds_read()** does not return this attribute in the attribute list for an object.

Return Values

`DS_status`
: Indicates whether or not the read operation is completed. This is **DS_SUCCESS** if completed.

`result_return`
: (Object(**DS_C_READ_RESULT**)). Upon successful completion, the result contains the DN of the target object, and a flag indicating whether the result came from the original entry or a copy, as well as any requested attribute types and values. Attribute information is only returned if access rights are sufficient.

`invoke_id_return`
: (Integer). Not supported.

Errors

This function can return a **DS_C_SYSTEM_ERROR** or one of the following **DS_C_LIBRARY_ERROR**s:

[**DS_E_BAD_ARGUMENT**]

[**DS_E_BAD_ATTRIBUTE**]

[**DS_E_BAD_CONTEXT**]

[**DS_E_BAD_NAME**]

[**DS_E_BAD_SESSION**]

[**DS_E_MISCELLANEOUS**]

[**DS_E_MISSING_TYPE**]

[**DS_E_TOO_MANY_OPERATIONS**]

The following directory errors can be returned by the function:

[**DS_C_ATTRIBUTE_ERROR**]

[**DS_C_NAME_ERROR**]

[**DS_C_REFERRAL**]

[**DS_C_SECURITY_ERROR**]

[**DS_C_SERVICE_ERROR**]

The directory error **DS_C_ATTRIBUTE_ERROR** (**DS_E_NO_SUCH_ATTRIBUTE_OR_VALUE**) is reported in GDS if an explicit list of attributes is specified by the *selection* parameter, but none of them are present in the entry. This error is not reported if any of the selected attributes are present.

A **DS_C_SECURITY_ERROR** (**DS_E_INSUFFICIENT_ACCESS_RIGHTS**) is only reported where access rights preclude the reading of all requested attribute values.

This function can return a **DS_COMMUNICATIONS_ERROR**, as well as the error constant **DS_NO_WORKSPACE**.

Related Information

Books: *OSF DCE Application Development Guide*.

ds_remove_entry

Purpose Removes a leaf entry from the Directory Information Tree (DIT)

Synopsis **#include <xom.h>**
#include <xds.h>

DS_status ds_remove_entry(
OM_private_object *session*,
OM_private_object *context*,
OM_object *name*,
OM_sint **invoke_id_return*);

Parameters

session (Object(**DS_C_SESSION**). The directory session against which this operation is performed. This must be a private object.

context (Object(**DS_C_CONTEXT**)). The directory context to be used for this operation. Note that **DS_SIZE_LIMIT** and **DS_DONT_DEREFERENCE_ALIASES** do not apply to this operation. This parameter must be a private object or the **DS_DEFAULT_CONTEXT** constant.

name (Object(**DS_C_NAME**)). The name of the target object entry. Any aliases in the name are *not* dereferenced.

Description

The **ds_remove_entry( )** function is used to remove a leaf entry from the Directory (either an object entry or an alias entry).

Return Values

`DS_status`
Indicates whether or not the entry was deleted.

`invoke_id_return`
(Integer). Not supported.

Errors

This function can return a **DS_C_SYSTEM_ERROR** or one of the following **DS_C_LIBRARY_ERROR**s:

[**DS_E_BAD_ARGUMENT**]

[**DS_E_BAD_CONTEXT**]

[**DS_E_BAD_NAME**]

[**DS_E_BAD_SESSION**]

[**DS_E_MISCELLANEOUS**]

[**DS_E_MISSING_TYPE**]

[**DS_E_TOO_MANY_OPERATIONS**]

The function can return the following directory errors:

[**DS_C_NAME_ERROR**]

[**DS_C_REFERRAL**]

[**DS_C_SECURITY_ERROR**]

[**DS_C_SERVICE_ERROR**]

[**DS_C_UPDATE_ERROR**]

This function can return a **DS_C_COMMUNICATIONS_ERROR**, as well as the error constant **DS_NO_WORKSPACE**.

ds_search

Purpose Finds entries of interest in a part of the Directory Information Tree (DIT)

Synopsis

```
#include <xom.h>
#include <xds.h>

DS_status ds_search(
        OM_private_object session,
        OM_private_object context,
        OM_object name,
        OM_sint subset,
        OM_object filter,
        OM_boolean search_aliases,
        OM_object selection,
        OM_private_object *result_return,
        OM_sint *invoke_id_return);
```

Parameters

session (Object(**DS_C_SESSION**)). The directory session against which this operation is performed. This must be a private object.

context (Object(**DS_C_CONTEXT**)). The directory context to be used for this operation. This parameter must be a private object or the **DS_DEFAULT_CONTEXT** constant.

name (Object(**DS_C_NAME**)). The name of the object entry that forms the base of **ds_search( )**. Any aliases in the name are dereferenced, unless that is prohibited by the **DS_DONT_DEREFERENCE_ALIASES** service control attribute of the **DS_C_CONTEXT** object.

subset (Integer). Specifies the portion of the DIT to be searched. Its value must be one of the following:

- **DS_BASE_OBJECT**
  Searches just the given object entry.

- **DS_ONE_LEVEL**
  Searches just the immediate subordinates of the given object entry.

- **DS_WHOLE_SUBTREE**
  Searches the given object and all its subordinates.

filter (Object(**DS_C_FILTER**)). The filter is used to eliminate entries from the search that are not wanted. Information is only returned on entries that satisfy the filter. The **DS_NO_FILTER** constant can be used as the value of this parameter if all entries are searched, and none eliminated. This corresponds to a filter with a **DS_FILTER_TYPE** value of **DS_AND**, and no values of the **DS_FILTER** or **DS_FILTER_ITEM** OM attributes.

search_aliases
(Boolean). Any aliases in the subordinate entries being searched are dereferenced if the value of this parameter is **OM_TRUE**, and are not dereferenced if its value is **OM_FALSE**.

selection (Object(**DS_C_ENTRY_INFO_SELECTION**)). Specifies what information from the entry is requested. Information about no attributes, all attributes, or just for a named set can be chosen. Attribute types are always returned, but the attribute values need not be. The possible values of this parameter are listed in the *OSF DCE Application Development Guide*.

Description

The **ds_search( )** function is used to search a portion of the directory and return selected information from entries of interest. The information may be incomplete in some circumstances, for example, if the results exceed **DS_SIZE_LIMIT**.

Notes

CDS does not support **ds_search( )**, and returns with **DS_C_SERVICE_ERROR** (**DS_E_UNWILLING_TO PERFORM**).

Return Values

`DS_status`
Takes the value **DS_SUCCESS** if the named object is located and takes an error value if not.

`result_return`
(Object(**DS_C_SEARCH_RESULT**)). Upon successful completion, the result contains the requested information from each object in the search space that satisfied the filter. The DN of the target object is present if an alias is dereferenced. In addition, there may be a partial outcome qualifier, which indicates that the result is incomplete. It also explains why it is not complete and how it could be completed.

`invoke_id_return`
(Integer). Not supported.

Errors

This function can return a **DS_C_SYSTEM_ERROR** or one of the following **DS_C_LIBRARY_ERROR**s:

[**DS_E_BAD_ARGUMENT**]

[**DS_E_BAD_CONTEXT**]

[**DS_E_BAD_NAME**]

[**DS_E_BAD_SESSION**]

[**DS_E_MISCELLANEOUS**]

[**DS_E_MISSING_TYPE**]

[**DS_E_TOO_MANY_OPERATIONS**]

The following directory errors can be returned by the function:

[**DS_C_ATTRIBUTE_ERROR**]

[**DS_C_NAME_ERROR**]

[**DS_C_REFERRAL**]

[**DS_C_SECURITY_ERROR**]

[**DS_C_SERVICE_ERROR**]

Note that an unfiltered search of just the base object succeeds even if none of the requested attributes are found, while the **ds_read()** call fails with the same selected attributes.

A **DS_C_SECURITY_ERROR** (**DS_E_INSUFFICIENT_ACCESS_RIGHTS**) is only reported where access rights preclude the reading of all requested attribute values.

This function can return a **DS_C_COMMUNICATIONS_ERROR**, as well as the error constant **DS_NO_WORKSPACE**.

Related Information

Books: *OSF DCE Application Development Guide*.

ds_shutdown

Purpose Shuts down the interface

Synopsis

#include <xom.h>
#include <xds.h>

void ds_shutdown(
  OM_workspace *workspace***);**

Parameters

workspace Specifies the workspace (obtained from a call to **ds_initialize( )**) that is to be deleted.

Description

The **ds_shutdown( )** function deletes the workspace established by **ds_initialize( )**, and enables the service to release resources. All sessions associated with the workspace must be terminated by calling **ds_unbind( )** prior to calling **ds_shutdown( )**. No other directory function may reference the specified workspace after it has been deleted. However, **om_delete( )** and **om_instance( )** may be called if referring to public objects.

Return Values

No value is returned.

Related Information

Functions: **ds_initialize(3xds)**.

ds_unbind

Purpose Unbinds from a directory session

Synopsis

#include <xom.h>
#include <xds.h>

DS_status ds_unbind(
    OM_private_object *session***);**

Parameters

session (Object(**DS_C_SESSION**)). The directory session to be unbound. This must be a private object. The value of the **DS_FILE_DESCRIPTOR** OM attribute is **DS_NO_VALID_FILE_DESCRIPTOR** if the function succeeds. The remaining OM attributes are unchanged.

Description

The **ds_unbind**( ) function terminates the given directory session, and makes the parameter unavailable for use with other interface functions (except **ds_bind**( )). The unbound session can be used again as a parameter to **ds_bind**( ) possibly after modification by the Object Management functions. When it is no longer required, it must be deleted using the Object Management functions.

Return Values

`DS_status` Takes the value **DS_SUCCESS** if the *session* parameter is unbound and takes an error value if not.

Errors This function can return a **DS_C_SYSTEM_ERROR** or one of the following **DS_C_LIBRARY_ERROR**s:

[**DS_E_BAD_SESSION**]

[**DS_E_MISCELLANEOUS**]

This function does not return a **DS_C_COMMUNICATIONS_ERROR** or any directory errors. However, this function can return the error constant **DS_NO_WORKSPACE**.

Related Information

Functions: **ds_bind(3xds)**.

ds_version

Purpose Negotiates features of the interface and service

Synopsis

#include <xom.h>
#include <xds.h>

DS_status ds_version(
DS_feature *feature_list*[ ]**,**
OM_workspace *workspace***);**

Parameters

feature_list[ ] (**DS_feature**). An ordered sequence of features, each represented by an object identifier. The sequence is terminated by an object identifier having no components (a length of 0 (zero) and any value for the data pointer.)

workspace Specifies the workspace obtained from a call to **om_initialize**( ) for which the features are to be negotiated. The features will be in effect for operations that use the workspace or directory sessions associated with the workspace.

Description

The **ds_version**( ) function negotiates features of the interface, which are represented by Object Identifiers. The **DS_BASIC_DIR_CONTENTS_PKG** and the **MHS_DIR_USER_PKG** specified in the *OSF DCE Application Development Guide* are negotiable features in this specification. Features can also include vendor extensions, such as the **DSX_GDS_PKG**, and new features in future versions of the XDS specification. Versions are negotiated after a workspace is initialized with **ds_initialize**( ).

Return Values

`DS_status` Takes the value **DS_SUCCESS** if the function completed successfully.

`activated` (**OM_boolean**). If the function completed successfully, this return value contains an ordered sequence of Boolean values, with the same number of elements as the *feature_list*[ ] parameter. If **OM_TRUE**, each value indicates that the corresponding feature is now part of the interface. If **OM_FALSE**, each value indicates that the corresponding feature is not available.

This result is combined with the *feature_list*[ ] parameter as a single array of structures of type **DS_feature**, which is defined as follows:

```
typedef struct
{
 OM_object_identifier feature;
 OM_boolean           activated;
}
 DS_feature;
```

Errors

This function can return a **DS_C_SYSTEM_ERROR** or the following **DS_C_LIBRARY_ERROR**:

[**DS_E_BAD_WORKSPACE**]

[**DS_E_MISCELLANEOUS**]

This function does not return a **DS_C_COMMUNICATIONS_ERROR** or any directory errors. However, this function can return the error constant **DS_NO_WORKSPACE**.

Related Information

Books: *OSF DCE Application Development Guide*.

intro

Purpose Introduction to XDS header files

Description

There are seven XDS headers, namely **xds.h(4xds)**, **xdsbdcp.h(4xds)**, **xdscds.h(4xds)**, **xdsgds.h(4xds)**, **xdsmdup.h(4xds)**, **xmhp.h(4xds)**, and **xmsga.h(4xds)**.

xds.h Contains definitions for the XDS functions and Directory Service Package.

xdsbdcp.h Contains definitions for the Basic Directory Contents Package.

xdscds.h Contains definitions for the Cell Directory Service.

xdsgds.h Contains definitions for the Global Directory Service Extension Package.

xdsmdup.h Contains definitions for the MHS Directory User Package.

xmhp.h Contains definitions for the MHS Directory objects/attributes.

xmsga.h Contains definitions for the Message Store General attributes.

The **xds.h** header file is a mandatory include for all applications using the XDS API.

The **xdsbdcp.h** and **xdsmdup.h** headers are part of the X/Open XDS specifications. They are required when using the Basic Directory Contents Package and the MHS Directory User Package, respectively.

The **xdsgds.h** and **xdscds.h** headers are DCE extensions to the XDS API. The **xdsgds.h** header is required when using the GDS Extension Package. The **xdscds.h** header is required when using CDS.

The **xmhp.h** and **xmsga.h** headers are required when using the MHS Directory User Package.

xds.h

Purpose Definitions for the Directory Service Package

Synopsis **#include <xom.h>**
#include <xds.h>

Description

The **xds.h** header declares the interface functions, the structures passed to and from those functions, and the defined constants used by the functions and structures.

All application programs that include this header must first include the **xom.h** Object Management header.

```
#ifndef XDS_HEADER
#define XDS_HEADER


/* DS package object identifier */
/* { iso(1) identifier-organization(3) icd-ecma(12) member-company(2)
     dec(1011) xopen(28) dsp(0) } */

#define OMP_O_DS_SERVICE_PKG          "\x2B\x0C\x02\x87\x73\x1C\x00"

/*Defined constants */

/* Intermediate object identifier macro */

#define dsP_c(X)          OMP_O_DS_SERVICE_PKG #X


/* OM class names (prefixed by DS_C_) */

/* Every application program which makes use of a class or other      */
/* Object Identifier must explicitly import it into every             */
/* compilation unit (C source program) which uses it. Each such       */
/* class or Object Identifier name must be explicitly exported        */
/* from just one compilation unit.                                    */

/* In the header file, OM class constants are prefixed with the       */
/* OMP_O prefix to denote that they are OM classes. However,          */
/* when using the OM_IMPORT and OM_EXPORT macros, the base            */
```

```
/* names (without the OMP_O prefix) should be used.                      */
/* For example:                                                          */
/*         OM_IMPORT (DS_C_AVA)                                          */


#define OMP_O_DS_C_ABANDON_FAILED              dsP_c(\x85\x3D)
#define OMP_O_DS_C_ACCESS_POINT                dsP_c(\x85\x3E)
#define OMP_O_DS_C_ADDRESS                     dsP_c(\x85\x3F)
#define OMP_O_DS_C_ATTRIBUTE                   dsP_c(\x85\x40)
#define OMP_O_DS_C_ATTRIBUTE_ERROR             dsP_c(\x85\x41)
#define OMP_O_DS_C_ATTRIBUTE_LIST              dsP_c(\x85\x42)
#define OMP_O_DS_C_ATTRIBUTE_PROBLEM           dsP_c(\x85\x43)
#define OMP_O_DS_C_AVA                         dsP_c(\x85\x44)
#define OMP_O_DS_C_COMMON_RESULTS              dsP_c(\x85\x45)
#define OMP_O_DS_C_COMMUNICATIONS_ERROR        dsP_c(\x85\x46)
#define OMP_O_DS_C_COMPARE_RESULT              dsP_c(\x85\x47)
#define OMP_O_DS_C_CONTEXT                     dsP_c(\x85\x48)
#define OMP_O_DS_C_CONTINUATION_REF            dsP_c(\x85\x49)
#define OMP_O_DS_C_DS_DN                       dsP_c(\x85\x4A)
#define OMP_O_DS_C_DS_RDN                      dsP_c(\x85\x4B)
#define OMP_O_DS_C_ENTRY_INFO                  dsP_c(\x85\x4C)
#define OMP_O_DS_C_ENTRY_INFO_SELECTION        dsP_c(\x85\x4D)
#define OMP_O_DS_C_ENTRY_MOD                   dsP_c(\x85\x4E)
#define OMP_O_DS_C_ENTRY_MOD_LIST              dsP_c(\x85\x4F)
#define OMP_O_DS_C_ERROR                       dsP_c(\x85\x50)
#define OMP_O_DS_C_EXT                         dsP_c(\x85\x51)
#define OMP_O_DS_C_FILTER                      dsP_c(\x85\x52)
#define OMP_O_DS_C_FILTER_ITEM                 dsP_c(\x85\x53)
#define OMP_O_DS_C_LIBRARY_ERROR               dsP_c(\x85\x54)
#define OMP_O_DS_C_LIST_INFO                   dsP_c(\x85\x55)
#define OMP_O_DS_C_LIST_INFO_ITEM              dsP_c(\x85\x56)
#define OMP_O_DS_C_LIST_RESULT                 dsP_c(\x85\x57)
#define OMP_O_DS_C_NAME                        dsP_c(\x85\x58)
#define OMP_O_DS_C_NAME_ERROR                  dsP_c(\x85\x59)
#define OMP_O_DS_C_OPERATION_PROGRESS          dsP_c(\x85\x5A)
#define OMP_O_DS_C_PARTIAL_OUTCOME_QUAL        dsP_c(\x85\x5B)
#define OMP_O_DS_C_PRESENTATION_ADDRESS        dsP_c(\x85\x5C)
#define OMP_O_DS_C_READ_RESULT                 dsP_c(\x85\x5D)
#define OMP_O_DS_C_REFERRAL                    dsP_c(\x85\x5E)
#define OMP_O_DS_C_RELATIVE_NAME               dsP_c(\x85\x5F)
#define OMP_O_DS_C_SEARCH_INFO                 dsP_c(\x85\x60)
#define OMP_O_DS_C_SEARCH_RESULT               dsP_c(\x85\x61)
#define OMP_O_DS_C_SECURITY_ERROR              dsP_c(\x85\x62)
#define OMP_O_DS_C_SERVICE_ERROR               dsP_c(\x85\x63)
```

```
#define OMP_O_DS_C_SESSION                          dsP_c(\x85\x64)
#define OMP_O_DS_C_SYSTEM_ERROR                     dsP_c(\x85\x65)
#define OMP_O_DS_C_UPDATE_ERROR                     dsP_c(\x85\x66)


/* OM attribute names */

#define DS_ACCESS_POINTS                            ((OM_type) 701)
#define DS_ADDRESS                                  ((OM_type) 702)
#define DS_AE_TITLE                                 ((OM_type) 703)
#define DS_ALIASED_RDNS                             ((OM_type) 704)
#define DS_ALIAS_DEREFERENCED                       ((OM_type) 705)
#define DS_ALIAS_ENTRY                              ((OM_type) 706)
#define DS_ALL_ATTRIBUTES                           ((OM_type) 707)
#define DS_ASYNCHRONOUS                             ((OM_type) 708)
#define DS_ATTRIBUTES                               ((OM_type) 709)
#define DS_ATTRIBUTES_SELECTED                      ((OM_type) 710)
#define DS_ATTRIBUTE_TYPE                           ((OM_type) 711)
#define DS_ATTRIBUTE_VALUE                          ((OM_type) 712)
#define DS_ATTRIBUTE_VALUES                         ((OM_type) 713)
#define DS_AUTOMATIC_CONTINUATION                   ((OM_type) 714)
#define DS_AVAS                                     ((OM_type) 715)
#define DS_CHAINING_PROHIB                          ((OM_type) 716)
#define DS_CHANGES                                  ((OM_type) 717)
#define DS_CRIT                                     ((OM_type) 718)
#define DS_DONT_DEREFERENCE_ALIASES                 ((OM_type) 719)
#define DS_DONT_USE_COPY                            ((OM_type) 720)
#define DS_DSA_ADDRESS                              ((OM_type) 721)
#define DS_DSA_NAME                                 ((OM_type) 722)
#define DS_ENTRIES                                  ((OM_type) 723)
#define DS_ENTRY                                    ((OM_type) 724)
#define DS_EXT                                      ((OM_type) 725)
#define DS_FILE_DESCRIPTOR                          ((OM_type) 726)
#define DS_FILTERS                                  ((OM_type) 727)
#define DS_FILTER_ITEMS                             ((OM_type) 728)
#define DS_FILTER_ITEM_TYPE                         ((OM_type) 729)
#define DS_FILTER_TYPE                              ((OM_type) 730)
#define DS_FINAL_SUBSTRING                          ((OM_type) 731)
#define DS_FROM_ENTRY                               ((OM_type) 732)
#define DS_IDENT                                    ((OM_type) 733)
#define DS_INFO_TYPE                                ((OM_type) 734)
#define DS_INITIAL_SUBSTRING                        ((OM_type) 735)
#define DS_ITEM_PARAMETERS                          ((OM_type) 736)
#define DS_LIMIT_PROBLEM                            ((OM_type) 737)
```

```
#define DS_LIST_INFO                        ((OM_type) 738)
#define DS_LOCAL_SCOPE                      ((OM_type) 739)
#define DS_MATCHED                          ((OM_type) 740)
#define DS_MOD_TYPE                         ((OM_type) 741)
#define DS_NAME_RESOLUTION_PHASE            ((OM_type) 742)
#define DS_NEXT_RDN_TO_BE_RESOLVED          ((OM_type) 743)
#define DS_N_ADDRESSES                      ((OM_type) 744)
#define DS_OBJECT_NAME                      ((OM_type) 745)
#define DS_OPERATION_PROGRESS               ((OM_type) 746)
#define DS_PARTIAL_OUTCOME_QUAL             ((OM_type) 747)
#define DS_PERFORMER                        ((OM_type) 748)
#define DS_PREFER_CHAINING                  ((OM_type) 749)
#define DS_PRIORITY                         ((OM_type) 750)
#define DS_PROBLEM                          ((OM_type) 751)
#define DS_PROBLEMS                         ((OM_type) 752)
#define DS_P_SELECTOR                       ((OM_type) 753)
#define DS_RDN                              ((OM_type) 754)
#define DS_RDNS                             ((OM_type) 755)
#define DS_RDNS_RESOLVED                    ((OM_type) 756)
#define DS_REQUESTOR                        ((OM_type) 757)
#define DS_SCOPE_OF_REFERRAL                ((OM_type) 758)
#define DS_SEARCH_INFO                      ((OM_type) 759)
#define DS_SIZE_LIMIT                       ((OM_type) 760)
#define DS_SUBORDINATES                     ((OM_type) 761)
#define DS_S_SELECTOR                       ((OM_type) 762)
#define DS_TARGET_OBJECT                    ((OM_type) 763)
#define DS_TIME_LIMIT                       ((OM_type) 764)
#define DS_T_SELECTOR                       ((OM_type) 765)
#define DS_UNAVAILABLE_CRIT_EXT             ((OM_type) 766)
#define DS_UNCORRELATED_LIST_INFO           ((OM_type) 767)
#define DS_UNCORRELATED_SEARCH_INFO         ((OM_type) 768)
#define DS_UNEXPLORED                       ((OM_type) 769)


/* DS_Filter_Item_Type: */

enum DS_Filter_Item_Type {
        DS_EQUALITY             = 0,
        DS_SUBSTRINGS           = 1,
        DS_GREATER_OR_EQUAL     = 2,
        DS_LESS_OR_EQUAL        = 3,
        DS_PRESENT              = 4,
        DS_APPROXIMATE_MATCH    = 5
};
```

```
/* DS_Filter_Type: */

enum DS_Filter_Type {
        DS_ITEM = 0,
        DS_AND  = 1,
        DS_OR   = 2,
        DS_NOT  = 3
};


/* DS_Information_Type: */

enum DS_Information_Type {
        DS_TYPES_ONLY       = 0,
        DS_TYPES_AND_VALUES = 1
};


/* DS_Limit_Problem: */

enum DS_Limit_Problem {
        DS_NO_LIMIT_EXCEEDED                = -1,
        DS_TIME_LIMIT_EXCEEDED              = 0,
        DS_SIZE_LIMIT_EXCEEDED              = 1,
        DS_ADMIN_LIMIT_EXCEEDED             = 2
};


/* DS_Modification_Type: */

enum DS_Modification_Type {
        DS_ADD_ATTRIBUTE    = 0,
        DS_REMOVE_ATTRIBUTE = 1,
        DS_ADD_VALUES       = 2,
        DS_REMOVE_VALUES    = 3
};


/* DS_Name_Resolution_Phase: */

enum DS_Name_Resolution_Phase {
        DS_NOT_STARTED = 1,
        DS_PROCEEDING  = 2,
        DS_COMPLETED   = 3
```

```
};


/* DS_Priority: */

enum DS_Priority {
        DS_LOW    = 0,
        DS_MEDIUM = 1,
        DS_HIGH   = 2
};


/* DS_Problem: */

enum DS_Problem {
        DS_E_ADMIN_LIMIT_EXCEEDED                    = 1,
        DS_E_AFFECTS_MULTIPLE_DSAS                   = 2,
        DS_E_ALIAS_DEREFERENCING_PROBLEM             = 3,
        DS_E_ALIAS_PROBLEM                           = 4,
        DS_E_ATTRIBUTE_OR_VALUE_EXISTS               = 5,
        DS_E_BAD_ARGUMENT                            = 6,
        DS_E_BAD_CLASS                               = 7,
        DS_E_BAD_CONTEXT                             = 8,
        DS_E_BAD_NAME                                = 9,
        DS_E_BAD_SESSION                             = 10,
        DS_E_BAD_WORKSPACE                           = 11,
        DS_E_BUSY                                    = 12,
        DS_E_CANNOT_ABANDON                          = 13,
        DS_E_CHAINING_REQUIRED                       = 14,
        DS_E_COMMUNICATIONS_PROBLEM                  = 15,
        DS_E_CONSTRAINT_VIOLATION                    = 16,
        DS_E_DIT_ERROR                               = 17,
        DS_E_ENTRY_EXISTS                            = 18,
        DS_E_INAPPROP_AUTHENTICATION                 = 19,
        DS_E_INAPPROP_MATCHING                       = 20,
        DS_E_INSUFFICIENT_ACCESS_RIGHTS              = 21,
        DS_E_INVALID_ATTRIBUTE_SYNTAX                = 22,
        DS_E_INVALID_ATTRIBUTE_VALUE                 = 23,
        DS_E_INVALID_CREDENTIALS                     = 24,
        DS_E_INVALID_REF                             = 25,
        DS_E_INVALID_SIGNATURE                       = 26,
        DS_E_LOOP_DETECTED                           = 27,
        DS_E_MISCELLANEOUS                           = 28,
        DS_E_MISSING_TYPE                            = 29,
```

```
        DS_E_MIXED_SYNCHRONOUS                          = 30,
        DS_E_NAMING_VIOLATION                           = 31,
        DS_E_NO_INFO                                    = 32,
        DS_E_NO_SUCH_ATTRIBUTE_OR_VALUE                 = 33,
        DS_E_NO_SUCH_OBJECT                             = 34,
        DS_E_NO_SUCH_OPERATION                          = 35,
        DS_E_NOT_ALLOWED_ON_NON_LEAF                    = 36,
        DS_E_NOT_ALLOWED_ON_RDN                         = 37,
        DS_E_NOT_SUPPORTED                              = 38,
        DS_E_OBJECT_CLASS_MOD_PROHIB                    = 39,
        DS_E_OBJECT_CLASS_VIOLATION                     = 40,
        DS_E_OUT_OF_SCOPE                               = 41,
        DS_E_PROTECTION_REQUIRED                        = 42,
        DS_E_TIME_LIMIT_EXCEEDED                        = 43,
        DS_E_TOO_LATE                                   = 44,
        DS_E_TOO_MANY_OPERATIONS                        = 45,
        DS_E_TOO_MANY_SESSIONS                          = 46,
        DS_E_UNABLE_TO_PROCEED                          = 47,
        DS_E_UNAVAILABLE                                = 48,
        DS_E_UNAVAILABLE_CRIT_EXT                       = 49,
        DS_E_UNDEFINED_ATTRIBUTE_TYPE                   = 50,
        DS_E_UNWILLING_TO_PERFORM                       = 51
};


/* DS_Scope_Of_Referral: */

enum DS_Scope_Of_Referral {
        DS_DMD     = 0,
        DS_COUNTRY = 1
};


/* Typedefs */

typedef OM_private_object  DS_status;

typedef struct
{
    OM_object_identifier feature;
    OM_boolean           activated;
} DS_feature;
```

```
/* OM_object constants */

#define DS_DEFAULT_CONTEXT                    ((OM_object) 0)
#define DS_DEFAULT_SESSION                    ((OM_object) 0)
#define DS_OPERATION_NOT_STARTED              ((OM_object) 0)
#define DS_NO_FILTER                          ((OM_object) 0)
#define DS_NULL_RESULT                        ((OM_object) 0)
#define DS_SELECT_ALL_TYPES                   ((OM_object) 1)
#define DS_SELECT_ALL_TYPES_AND_VALUES        ((OM_object) 2)
#define DS_SELECT_NO_ATTRIBUTES               ((OM_object) 0)
#define DS_SUCCESS                            ((DS_status) 0)
#define DS_NO_WORKSPACE                       ((DS_status) 1)


/* ds_search() subset */

#define DS_BASE_OBJECT                        ((OM_sint) 0)
#define DS_ONE_LEVEL                          ((OM_sint) 1)
#define DS_WHOLE_SUBTREE                      ((OM_sint) 2)


/* ds_receive_result() completion_flag_return */

#define DS_COMPLETED_OPERATION                ((OM_uint) 1)
#define DS_OUTSTANDING_OPERATIONS             ((OM_uint) 2)
#define DS_NO_OUTSTANDING_OPERATION           ((OM_uint) 3)


/* asynchronous operations limit (implementation-defined) */

#define DS_MAX_OUTSTANDING_OPERATIONS   0   /* no asynchronous */
                                            /* operation       */
/*asynchronous event posting */

#define DS_NO_VALID_FILE_DESCRIPTOR     -1


/* Function Prototypes */

DS_status ds_abandon(
        OM_private_object   session,
        OM_sint             invoke_id
);
```

```
DS_status ds_add_entry(
        OM_private_object   session,
        OM_private_object   context,
        OM_object           name,
        OM_object           entry,
        OM_sint             *invoke_id_return
);

DS_status ds_bind(
        OM_object           session,
        OM_workspace        workspace,
        OM_private_object   *bound_session_return
);

DS_status ds_compare(
        OM_private_object   session,
        OM_private_object   context,
        OM_object           name,
        OM_object           ava,
        OM_private_object   *result_return,
        OM_sint             *invoke_id_return
);

OM_workspace ds_initialize(
        void
);

DS_status ds_list(
        OM_private_object   session,
        OM_private_object   context,
        OM_object           name,
        OM_private_object   *result_return,
        OM_sint             *invoke_id_return
);

DS_status ds_modify_entry(
        OM_private_object   session,
        OM_private_object   context,
        OM_object           name,
        OM_object           changes,
        OM_sint             *invoke_id_return
);

DS_status ds_modify_rdn(
```

```
        OM_private_object   session,
        OM_private_object   context,
        OM_object           name,
        OM_object           new_RDN,
        OM_boolean          delete_old_RDN,
        OM_sint             *invoke_id_return
);

DS_status ds_read(
        OM_private_object   session,
        OM_private_object   context,
        OM_object           name,
        OM_object           selection,
        OM_private_object   *result_return,
        OM_sint             *invoke_id_return
);

DS_status ds_receive_result(
        OM_private_object   session,
        OM_uint             *completion_flag_return,
        DS_status           *operation_status_return,
        OM_private_object   *result_return,
        OM_sint             *invoke_id_return
);

DS_status ds_remove_entry(
        OM_private_object   session,
        OM_private_object   context,
        OM_object           name,
        OM_sint             *invoke_id_return
);

DS_status ds_search(
        OM_private_object   session,
        OM_private_object   context,
        OM_object           name,
        OM_sint             subset,
        OM_object           filter,
        OM_boolean          search_aliases,
        OM_object           selection,
        OM_private_object   *result_return,
        OM_sint             *invoke_id_return
);
```

```
DS_status ds_shutdown(
        OM_workspace        workspace
);

DS_status ds_unbind(
        OM_private_object   session
);

DS_status ds_version(
        DS_feature          feature_list[]
        OM_workspace        workspace
);


#endif  /* XDS_HEADER */
```

Related Information

Books: *X/Open CAE Specification (November 1991), API to Directory Services (XDS),*
X/Open CAE Specification (November 1991), OSI-Abstract-Data Manipulation API (XOM),
OSF DCE Application Development Guide.

xdsbdcp.h

Purpose Definitions for the Basic Directory Contents Package

Synopsis **#include <xom.h>**
#include <xds.h>
#include <xdsbdcp.h>

Description

The **xdsbdcp.h** header defines the object identifiers of directory attribute types and object classes supported by the Basic Directory Contents Package. It also defines OM classes used to represent the values of the attribute types.

All application programs that include this header must first include the **xom.h** Object Management header and the **xds.h** header.

Object identifiers are defined for the (directory) attribute types that are specified in the following list. The actual values of the object identifiers are listed in the *OSF DCE Application Development Guide*.

```
#ifndef XDSBDCP_HEADER
#define XDSBDCP_HEADER

/* BDC package object identifier */
/* { iso(1) identifier-organization(3) icd-ecma(12)
     member-company(2) dec(1011) xopen(28) bdcp(1) } */

#define OMP_O_DS_BASIC_DIR_CONTENTS_PKG \
 "\x2B\x0C\x02\x87\x73\x1c\x01"


/* Intermediate object identifier macros */

#ifndef dsP_attributeType        /* joint-iso-ccitt(2)          */
                                   /* ds(5) attributeType(4) ... */
#define dsP_attributeType (X)     ("\x55\x04" #X)
#endif

#ifndef dsP_objectClass          /* joint-iso-ccitt(2)          */
                                   /* ds(5) objectClass(6) ...   */
#define dsP_objectClass(X)        ("\x55\x06" #X)
#endif
```

```
#define dsP_bdcp_c(X) (OMP_O_DS_BASIC_DIR_CONTENTS_PKG #X)


/* OM class names (prefixed by DS_C_)                          */
/* Directory attribute types (prefixed by DS_A_)               */
/* Directory object classes (prefixed by DS_O_)                */

/* Every application program which makes use of a class or     */
/* other Object Identifier must explicitly import it into      */
/* every compilation unit (C source program) which uses it.    */
/* Each such class or Object Identifier name must be           */
/* explicitly exported from just one compilation unit.         */

/* In the header file, OM class constants are prefixed with    */
/* the OMP_O prefix to denote that they are OM classes.        */
/* However, when using the OM_IMPORT and OM_EXPORT macros,     */
/* the base names (without the OMP_O prefix) should be used.*/
/* For example:                                                */
/*         OM_IMPORT (DS_O_COUNTRY)                            */


/* Directory attribute types */

#define OMP_O_DS_A_ALIASED_OBJECT_NAME      dsP_attributeType(\x01)
#define OMP_O_DS_A_BUSINESS_CATEGORY        dsP_attributeType(\x0F)
#define OMP_O_DS_A_COMMON_NAME              dsP_attributeType(\x03)
#define OMP_O_DS_A_COUNTRY_NAME             dsP_attributeType(\x06)
#define OMP_O_DS_A_DESCRIPTION              dsP_attributeType(\x0D)
#define OMP_O_DS_A_DEST_INDICATOR           dsP_attributeType(\x1B)
#define OMP_O_DS_A_FACSIMILE_PHONE_NBR      dsP_attributeType(\x17)
#define OMP_O_DS_A_INTERNAT_ISDN_NBR        dsP_attributeType(\x19)
#define OMP_O_DS_A_KNOWLEDGE_INFO           dsP_attributeType(\x02)
#define OMP_O_DS_A_LOCALITY_NAME            dsP_attributeType(\x07)
#define OMP_O_DS_A_MEMBER                   dsP_attributeType(\x1F)
#define OMP_O_DS_A_OBJECT_CLASS             dsP_attributeType(\x00)
#define OMP_O_DS_A_ORG_NAME                 dsP_attributeType(\x0A)
#define OMP_O_DS_A_ORG_UNIT_NAME            dsP_attributeType(\x0B)
#define OMP_O_DS_A_OWNER                    dsP_attributeType(\x20)
#define OMP_O_DS_A_PHYS_DELIV_OFF_NAME      dsP_attributeType(\x13)
#define OMP_O_DS_A_POST_OFFICE_BOX          dsP_attributeType(\x12)
#define OMP_O_DS_A_POSTAL_ADDRESS           dsP_attributeType(\x10)
#define OMP_O_DS_A_POSTAL_CODE              dsP_attributeType(\x11)
#define OMP_O_DS_A_PREF_DELIV_METHOD        dsP_attributeType(\x1C)
#define OMP_O_DS_A_PRESENTATION_ADDRESS     dsP_attributeType(\x1D)
```

```
#define OMP_O_DS_A_REGISTERED_ADDRESS      dsP_attributeType(\x1A)
#define OMP_O_DS_A_ROLE_OCCUPANT           dsP_attributeType(\x21)
#define OMP_O_DS_A_SEARCH_GUIDE            dsP_attributeType(\x0E)
#define OMP_O_DS_A_SEE_ALSO                dsP_attributeType(\x22)
#define OMP_O_DS_A_SERIAL_NBR              dsP_attributeType(\x05)
#define OMP_O_DS_A_STATE_OR_PROV_NAME      dsP_attributeType(\x08)
#define OMP_O_DS_A_STREET_ADDRESS          dsP_attributeType(\x09)
#define OMP_O_DS_A_SUPPORT_APPLIC_CONTEXT dsP_attributeType(\x1E)
#define OMP_O_DS_A_SURNAME                 dsP_attributeType(\x04)
#define OMP_O_DS_A_PHONE_NBR               dsP_attributeType(\x14)
#define OMP_O_DS_A_TELETEX_TERM_IDENT      dsP_attributeType(\x16)
#define OMP_O_DS_A_TELEX_NBR               dsP_attributeType(\x15)
#define OMP_O_DS_A_TITLE                   dsP_attributeType(\x0C)
#define OMP_O_DS_A_USER_PASSWORD           dsP_attributeType(\x23)
#define OMP_O_DS_A_X121_ADDRESS            dsP_attributeType(\x18)


/* Directory object classes */

#define OMP_O_DS_O_ALIAS                   dsP_objectClass(\x01)
#define OMP_O_DS_O_APPLIC_ENTITY           dsP_objectClass(\x0C)
#define OMP_O_DS_O_APPLIC_PROCESS          dsP_objectClass(\x0B)
#define OMP_O_DS_O_COUNTRY                 dsP_objectClass(\x02)
#define OMP_O_DS_O_DEVICE                  dsP_objectClass(\x0E)
#define OMP_O_DS_O_DSA                     dsP_objectClass(\x0D)
#define OMP_O_DS_O_GROUP_OF_NAMES          dsP_objectClass(\x09)
#define OMP_O_DS_O_LOCALITY                dsP_objectClass(\x03)
#define OMP_O_DS_O_ORG                     dsP_objectClass(\x04)
#define OMP_O_DS_O_ORG_PERSON              dsP_objectClass(\x07)
#define OMP_O_DS_O_ORG_ROLE                dsP_objectClass(\x08)
#define OMP_O_DS_O_ORG_UNIT                dsP_objectClass(\x05)
#define OMP_O_DS_O_PERSON                  dsP_objectClass(\x06)
#define OMP_O_DS_O_RESIDENTIAL_PERSON      dsP_objectClass(\x0A)
#define OMP_O_DS_O_TOP                     dsP_objectClass(\x00)


/* OM class names */

#define OMP_O_DS_C_FACSIMILE_PHONE_NBR          dsP_bdcp_c(\x86\x21)
#define OMP_O_DS_C_POSTAL_ADDRESS               dsP_bdcp_c(\x86\x22)
#define OMP_O_DS_C_SEARCH_CRITERION             dsP_bdcp_c(\x86\x23)
#define OMP_O_DS_C_SEARCH_GUIDE                 dsP_bdcp_c(\x86\x24)
#define OMP_O_DS_C_TELETEX_TERM_IDENT           dsP_bdcp_c(\x86\x25)
#define OMP_O_DS_C_TELEX_NBR                    dsP_bdcp_c(\x86\x26)
```

```
/* OM attribute names */

#define DS_ANSWERBACK            ((OM_type) 801)
#define DS_COUNTRY_CODE          ((OM_type) 802)
#define DS_CRITERIA              ((OM_type) 803)
#define DS_OBJECT_CLASS          ((OM_type) 804)
#define DS_PARAMETERS            ((OM_type) 805)
#define DS_POSTAL_ADDRESS        ((OM_type) 806)
#define DS_PHONE_NBR             ((OM_type) 807)
#define DS_TELETEX_TERM          ((OM_type) 808)
#define DS_TELEX_NBR             ((OM_type) 809)


/* DS_Preferred_Delivery_Method: */

#define DS_ANY_DELIV_METHOD           0
#define DS_MHS_DELIV                  1
#define DS_PHYS_DELIV                 2
#define DS_TELEX_DELIV                3
#define DS_TELETEX_DELIV              4
#define DS_G3_FACSIMILE_DELIV         5
#define DS_G4_FACSIMILE_DELIV         6
#define DS_IA5_TERMINAL_DELIV         7
#define DS_VIDEOTEX_DELIV             8
#define DS_PHONE_DELIV                9


/* Upper bounds on string lengths and the number of repeated OM */
/* attribute values                                              */

#define DS_VL_A_BUSINESS_CATEGORY          ((OM_value_length) 128)
#define DS_VL_A_COMMON_NAME                ((OM_value_length) 64)
#define DS_VL_A_DESCRIPTION                ((OM_value_length) 1024)
#define DS_VL_A_DEST_INDICATOR             ((OM_value_length) 128)
#define DS_VL_A_INTERNAT_ISDN_NBR          ((OM_value_length) 16)
#define DS_VL_A_LOCALITY_NAME              ((OM_value_length) 128)
#define DS_VL_A_ORG_NAME                   ((OM_value_length) 64)
#define DS_VL_A_ORG_UNIT_NAME              ((OM_value_length) 64)
#define DS_VL_A_PHYS_DELIV_ OFF_NAME       ((OM_value_length) 128)
#define DS_VL_A_POST_OFFICE_BOX            ((OM_value_length) 40)
#define DS_VL_A_POSTAL_CODE                ((OM_value_length) 40)
#define DS_VL_A_SERIAL_NBR                 ((OM_value_length) 64)
#define DS_VL_A_STATE_OR_PROV_NAME         ((OM_value_length) 128)
#define DS_VL_A_STREET_ADDRESS             ((OM_value_length) 128)
```

```
#define DS_VL_A_SURNAME              ((OM_value_length) 64)
#define DS_VL_A_PHONE_NBR            ((OM_value_length) 32)
#define DS_VL_A_TITLE                ((OM_value_length) 64)
#define DS_VL_A_USER_PASSWORD        ((OM_value_length) 128)
#define DS_VL_A_X121_ADDRESS         ((OM_value_length) 15)
#define DS_VL_ANSWERBACK             ((OM_value_length) 8)
#define DS_VL_COUNTRY_CODE           ((OM_value_length) 4)
#define DS_VL_POSTAL_ADDRESS         ((OM_value_length) 30)
#define DS_VL_PHONE_NBR              ((OM_value_length) 32)
#define DS_VL_TELETEX_TERM           ((OM_value_length) 1024)
#define DS_VL_TELEX_NBR              ((OM_value_length) 14)
#define DS_VN_POSTAL_ADDRESS         ((OM_value_length) 6)

#endif  /* XDSBDCP_HEADER */
```

Related Information

Books: *X/Open CAE Specification (November 1991), API to Directory Services (XDS),*
X/Open CAE Specification (November 1991), OSI-Abstract-Data Manipulation API (XOM),
OSF DCE Application Development Guide.

xdscds.h

Purpose Definitions for the Cell Directory Service (CDS)

Synopsis **#include <xom.h>**
#include <xds.h>
#include <xdscds.h>

Description

The **xdscds.h** header declares the object identifiers of directory attribute types supported by the Cell Directory Service (CDS).

All application programs that include this header must first include the **xom.h** Object Management header and the **xds.h** header.

```
#ifndef XDSCDS_HEADER
#define XDSCDS_HEADER

/* iso(1) identified-org(3) osf(22) dce(1) cds(3)
    = "\x2B\x16\x01\x03" */

/* Cell Directory Service attribute types */

#define OMP_O_DSX_A_CDS_Members          "\x2B\x16\x01\x03\x0A"
#define OMP_O_DSX_A_CDS_GroupRevoke      "\x2B\x16\x01\x03\x0B"
#define OMP_O_DSX_A_CDS_CTS              "\x2B\x16\x01\x03\x0C"
#define OMP_O_DSX_A_CDS_UTS              "\x2B\x16\x01\x03\x0D"
#define OMP_O_DSX_A_CDS_ACS              "\x2B\x16\x01\x03\x0E"
#define OMP_O_DSX_A_CDS_Class            "\x2B\x16\x01\x03\x0F"
#define OMP_O_DSX_A_CDS_ClassVersion     "\x2B\x16\x01\x03\x10"
#define OMP_O_DSX_A_CDS_ObjectUID        "\x2B\x16\x01\x03\x11"
#define OMP_O_DSX_A_CDS_Address          "\x2B\x16\x01\x03\x12"
#define OMP_O_DSX_A_CDS_Replicas         "\x2B\x16\x01\x03\x13"
#define OMP_O_DSX_A_CDS_AllUpTo          "\x2B\x16\x01\x03\x14"
#define OMP_O_DSX_A_CDS_Convergence      "\x2B\x16\x01\x03\x15"
#define OMP_O_DSX_A_CDS_InCHName         "\x2B\x16\x01\x03\x16"
#define OMP_O_DSX_A_CDS_ParentPointer    "\x2B\x16\x01\x03\x17"
#define OMP_O_DSX_A_CDS_DirecoryVersion "\x2B\x16\x01\x03\x18"
#define OMP_O_DSX_A_CDS_UpgradeTo        "\x2B\x16\x01\x03\x19"
#define OMP_O_DSX_A_CDS_LinkTarget       "\x2B\x16\x01\x03\x1B"
#define OMP_O_DSX_A_CDS_LinkTimeout      "\x2B\x16\x01\x03\x1C"
#define OMP_O_DSX_A_CDS_Towers           "\x2B\x16\x01\x03\x1E"
```

```
#define OMP_O_DSX_A_CDS_CHName           "\x2B\x16\x01\x03\x20"
#define OMP_O_DSX_A_CDS_CHLastAddress    "\x2B\x16\x01\x03\x22"
#define OMP_O_DSX_A_CDS_CHUpPointers     "\x2B\x16\x01\x03\x23"
#define OMP_O_DSX_A_CDS_CHState          "\x2B\x16\x01\x03\x24"

/* iso(1) identified-org(3) osf(22) dce(1) gds(2)
    = "\x2B\x16\x01\x02" */

#define OMP_O_DSX_UUID                   "\x2B\x16\x01\x01\x01"
#define OMP_O_DSX_TYPELESS_RDN           "\x2B\x16\x01\x01\x02"
#define OMP_O_DSX_NORMAL_SIMPLE_NAME     "\x2B\x16\x01\x03\x00"
#define OMP_O_DSX_BINARY_SIMPLE_NAME     "\x2B\x16\x01\x03\x02"

#endif  /*XDSCDS_HEADER*/
```

Related Information

Books: *X/Open CAE Specification (November 1991), API to Directory Services (XDS),*
X/Open CAE Specification (November 1991), OSI-Abstract-Data Manipulation API (XOM),
OSF DCE Application Development Guide.

xdsgds.h

Purpose Definitions for the Global Directory Service Extension Package

Synopsis **#include <xom.h>**
#include <xds.h>
#include <xdsgds.h>

Description

The **xdsgds.h** header declares the object identifiers of directory attribute types and directory object classes supported by the GDS Extension Package. It also defines OM classes used to represent the values of the attribute types.

All application programs that include this header must first include the **xom.h** Object Management header and the **xds.h** header.

```
#ifndef XDSGDS_HEADER
#define XDSGDS_HEADER


/* GDS package object identifier */
/* iso(1) identified-organization(3) icd-ecma(0012) member-company(2)
   siemens-units(1107) sni(1) directory(3) xds-api(100)gdsp(0) */

#define OMP_O_DSX_GDS_PKG    \
"\x2B\x0C\x02\x88\x53\x01\x03\x64\x00"

/*Intermediate object identifier macros */

/* iso(1) identified-organization(3) icd-ecma(0012) member-company(2)
   siemens-units(1107) sni(1) directory(3) attribute-type(4) ...*/

#define dsP_GDSattributeType(X) \
("\x2B\x0C\x02\x88\x53\x01\x03\x04" #X)

 * iso(1) identified-organization(3) icd-ecma(0012)
   member-company(2) siemens-units(1107) sni(1) directory(3)
   object-class(6) ...*/

#define dsP_GDSobjectClass(X) \
("\x2B\x0C\x02\x88\x53\x01\x03\x06" #X)
```

```
#define dsP_gdsp_c(X)     OMP_O_DSX_GDS_PKG #X

/* OM class names (prefixed by DSX_C_)
   Directory attribute types (prefixed by DSX_A_)
   Directory object classes (prefixed by DSX_O_)
*/


/* Directory attribute types */

#define OMP_O_DSX_A_MASTER_KNOWLEDGE dsP_GDSattributeType(\x00)
#define OMP_O_DSX_A_ACL              dsP_GDSattributeType(\x01)
#define OMP_O_DSX_A_TIME_STAMP       dsP_GDSattributeType(\x02)
#define OMP_O_DSX_A_SHADOWED_BY      dsP_GDSattributeType(\x03)
#define OMP_O_DSX_A_SRT              dsP_GDSattributeType(\x04)
#define OMP_O_DSX_A_OCT              dsP_GDSattributeType(\x05)
#define OMP_O_DSX_A_AT               dsP_GDSattributeType(\x06)
#define OMP_O_DSX_A_CACHE_ATTR       dsP_GDSattributeType(\x07)
#define OMP_O_DSX_A_DEFAULT_DSA      dsP_GDSattributeType(\x08)
#define OMP_O_DSX_A_LOCDSA           dsP_GDSattributeType(\x09)
#define OMP_O_DSX_A_CLIENT           dsP_GDSattributeType(\x0A)
#define OMP_O_DSX_A_DNLIST           dsP_GDSattributeType(\x0B)
#define OMP_O_DSX_A_SHADOWING_JOB    dsP_GDSattributeType(\x0C)
#define OMP_O_DSX_A_CDS_CELL         dsP_GDSattributeType(\x0D)
#define OMP_O_DSX_A_CDS_REPLICA      dsP_GDSattributeType(\x0E)


/* Directory object classes */

#define OMP_O_DSX_O_SCHEMA           dsP_GDSobjectClass(\x00)


/* OM class names */

#define OMP_O_DSX_C_GDS_SESSION         dsP_gdsp_c(\x00)
#define OMP_O_DSX_C_GDS_CONTEXT         dsP_gdsp_c(\x01)
#define OMP_O_DSX_C_GDS_ACL             dsP_gdsp_c(\x02)
#define OMP_O_DSX_C_GDS_ACL_ITEM        dsP_gdsp_c(\x03)


/* OM attribute names */

#define DSX_PASSWORD                    ((OM_type) 850)
#define DSX_DIR_ID                      ((OM_type) 851)
```

```
#define DSX_DUAFIRST                    ((OM_type) 852)
#define DSX_DONT_STORE                  ((OM_type) 853)
#define DSX_NORMAL_CLASS                ((OM_type) 854)
#define DSX_PRIV_CLASS                  ((OM_type) 855)
#define DSX_RESIDENT_CLASS              ((OM_type) 856)
#define DSX_USEDSA                      ((OM_type) 857)
#define DSX_DUA_CACHE                   ((OM_type) 858)
#define DSX_MODIFY_PUBLIC               ((OM_type) 859)
#define DSX_READ_STANDARD               ((OM_type) 860)
#define DSX_MODIFY_STANDARD             ((OM_type) 861)
#define DSX_READ_SENSITIVE              ((OM_type) 862)
#define DSX_MODIFY_SENSITIVE            ((OM_type) 863)
#define DSX_INTERPRETATION              ((OM_type) 864)
#define DSX_USER                        ((OM_type) 865)
#define DSX_PREFER_ADM_FUNCS            ((OM_type) 866)


/* DSX_Interpretation */

enum DSX_Interpretation {
        DSX_SINGLE_OBJECT    = 0,
        DSX_ROOT_OF_SUBTREE  = 1
};

/* OM_object constant */

#define DSX_CACHE_SESSION             ((OM_object)  1)

/* upper bound on string lengths*/

#define DSX_VL_PASSWORD         ((OM_value_length) 16)

#endif  /* XDSGDS_HEADER */
```

Related Information

Books: *X/Open CAE Specification (November 1991), API to Directory Services (XDS),*
X/Open CAE Specification (November 1991), OSI-Abstract-Data Manipulation API (XOM),
OSF DCE Application Development Guide.

xdsmdup.h

Purpose Definitions for the MHS Directory User Package

Synopsis **#include <xom.h>**
#include <xds.h>
#include <xdsmdup.h>

Description

The **xdsmdup.h** header declares the object identifiers of directory attribute types and object classes supported by the MHS Directory User Package. It also defines OM classes used to represent the values of the attribute types.

All application programs that include this header must first include the Object Management header **xom.h** and the **xds.h** header.

```
#ifndef XDSMDUP_HEADER
#define XDSMDUP_HEADER

#ifndef XMHP_HEADER
#include <xmhp.h>
#endif  /* XMHP_HEADER */

/* MDUP package object identifier */
/* { iso(1) identifier-organization(3) icd-ecma(12)
     member-company(2) dec(1011) xopen(28) mdup(3) } */

#define OMP_O_DS_MHS_DIR_USER_PKG \
"\x2B\x0C\x02\x87\x73\x1C\x03"

/* Intermediate object identifier macros */

/* { joint-iso-ccitt(2) mhs-motis(6) arch(5) at(2) } */

#define dsP_MHSattributeType(X) ("\x56\x5\x2" #X)

/* { joint-iso-ccitt(2) mhs-motis(6) arch(5) oc(1) } */

#define dsP_MHSobjectClass(X)    ("\x56\x5\x1" #X)

#define dsP_mdup_c(X)        (OMP_O_DS_MHS_DIR_USER_PKG #X)
```

```
/* OM class names (prefixed DS_C_),                               */
/* Directory attribute types (prefixed DS_A_),                    */
/* and Directory object classes (prefixed DS_O_)                  */

/* Every application program which makes use of a class or        */
/* other Object Identifier must explicitly import it into         */
/* every compilation unit (C source program) which uses it.       */
/* Each such class or Object Identifier name must be              */
/* explicitly exported from just one compilation unit.            */

/* In the header file, OM class constants are prefixed with       */
/* the OMP_O prefix to denote that they are OM classes.           */
/* However, when using the OM_IMPORT and OM_EXPORT macros,        */
/* the base names (without the OMP_O prefix) should be used.      */
/* For example:                                                   */
/*        OM_IMPORT(DS_O_CERT_AUTHORITY)                          */


/* Directory attribute types */

#define OMP_O_DS_A_DELIV_CONTENT_LENGTH        dsP_MHSattributeType(\x00)
#define OMP_O_DS_A_DELIV_CONTENT_TYPES         dsP_MHSattributeType(\x01)
#define OMP_O_DS_A_DELIV_EITS                  dsP_MHSattributeType(\x02)
#define OMP_O_DS_A_DL_MEMBERS                  dsP_MHSattributeType(\x03)
#define OMP_O_DS_A_DL_SUBMIT_PERMS             dsP_MHSattributeType(\x04)
#define OMP_O_DS_A_MESSAGE_STORE               dsP_MHSattributeType(\x05)
#define OMP_O_DS_A_OR_ADDRESSES                dsP_MHSattributeType(\x06)
#define OMP_O_DS_A_PREF_DELIV_METHODS          dsP_MHSattributeType(\x07)
#define OMP_O_DS_A_SUPP_AUTO_ACTIONS           dsP_MHSattributeType(\x08)
#define OMP_O_DS_A_SUPP_CONTENT_TYPES          dsP_MHSattributeType(\x09)
#define OMP_O_DS_A_SUPP_OPT_ATTRIBUTES         dsP_MHSattributeType(\x0A)


/* Directory object classes */

#define OMP_O_DS_O_MHS_DISTRIBUTION_LIST       dsP_MHSobjectClass(\x00)
#define OMP_O_DS_O_MHS_MESSAGE_STORE           dsP_MHSobjectClass(\x01)
#define OMP_O_DS_O_MHS_MESSAGE_TRANS_AG        dsP_MHSobjectClass(\x02)
#define OMP_O_DS_O_MHS_USER                    dsP_MHSobjectClass(\x03)
#define OMP_O_DS_O_MHS_USER_AG                 dsP_MHSobjectClass(\x04)


/* OM class names */
```

```
#define OMP_O_DS_C_DL_SUBMIT_PERMS      dsP_mdup_c(\x87\x05)


/* OM attribute names */

#define DS_PERM_TYPE            ( (OM_type) 901 )
#define DS_INDIVIDUAL           ( (OM_type) 902 )
#define DS_MEMBER_OF_DL         ( (OM_type) 903 )
#define DS_PATTERN_MATCH        ( (OM_type) 904 )
#define DS_MEMBER_OF_GROUP      ( (OM_type) 905 )


/* DS_Permission_Type */

enum DS_Permission_Type {
        DS_PERM_INDIVIDUAL      = 0,
        DS_PERM_MEMBER_OF_DL    = 1,
        DS_PERM_PATTERN_MATCH   = 2,
        DS_PERM_MEMBER_OF_GROUP = 3
};


#endif /* XDSMDUP_HEADER */
```

Related Information

Books: *X/Open CAE Specification (November 1991), API to Directory Services (XDS),*
X/Open CAE Specification (November 1991), OSI-Abstract-Data Manipulation API (XOM),
OSF DCE Application Development Guide,
X/Open CAE Specification (November 1991), API to Electronic Mail (X.400).

xmhp.h

Purpose Definitions for the MHS Directory objects/attributes

Synopsis **#include <xom.h>**
#include <xds.h>
#include <xdsmdup.h>
#include <xmhp.h>

Description

The **xmhp.h** header defines the constants used by the Message Handling Packages. It is required when using the MHS Directory User Package. The **xdsmdup.h** header explicitly includes **xmhp.h**.

xmhp.h contains definitions for the X.400 Message Handling Package. Some of these definitions are needed when negotiating use of the MDUP.
The following four Message Handling classes are referenced:

- **MH_C_G3_FAX_NBPS**
- **MH_C_OR_ADDRESS**
- **MH_C_OR_NAME**
- **MH_C_TELETEX_NBPS**

The only enumerations referenced are **Delivery Mode** and **Terminal Type**. For referenced OM attribute types and OM value lengths see the *OSF DCE Application Development Guide*.

```
/*
 Note that the identifier for the variable name of type OM_STRING
of a class in the Message Handling package can usually be
derived using the name of the class, preceded by "MH_C_", and
replacing a blank space with an underscore. To be in line with the ANSI C
language limitation, some words in the class names are excepted and
are abbreviated as below:

     BILATERAL_INFORMATION is abbreviated to BILATERAL_INFO
     DELIVERED                               DELIV
     CONFIRMATION                            CONFIRM
     CONFIRMATIONS                           CONFIRMS
     PER_RECIPIENT_                          PER_RECIP_
     DELIV_PER_RECIP_REPORT                  DELIV_PER_RECIP_REP
```

```
*/

/* BEGIN MH PORTION OF INTERFACE */

/* SYMBOLIC CONSTANTS */

/* Class */

#define OMP_O_MH_C_ALGORITHM              "\x56\x06\x01\x02\x05\x0B\x00"
#define OMP_O_MH_C_ALGORITHM_AND_RESULT   "\x56\x06\x01\x02\x05\x0B\x01"
#define OMP_O_MH_C_ASYMMETRIC_TOKEN       "\x56\x06\x01\x02\x05\x0B\x02"
#define OMP_O_MH_C_BILATERAL_INFO         "\x56\x06\x01\x02\x05\x0B\x03"
#define OMP_O_MH_C_COMMUNIQUE             "\x56\x06\x01\x02\x05\x0B\x04"
#define OMP_O_MH_C_CONTENT                "\x56\x06\x01\x02\x05\x0B\x05"
#define OMP_O_MH_C_DELIV_MESSAGE          "\x56\x06\x01\x02\x05\x0B\x06"
#define OMP_O_MH_C_DELIV_PER_RECIP_DR     "\x56\x06\x01\x02\x05\x0B\x07"
#define OMP_O_MH_C_DELIV_PER_RECIP_NDR    "\x56\x06\x01\x02\x05\x0B\x08"
#define OMP_O_MH_C_DELIV_PER_RECIP_REP    "\x56\x06\x01\x02\x05\x0B\x09"
#define OMP_O_MH_C_DELIV_REPORT           "\x56\x06\x01\x02\x05\x0B\x0A"
#define OMP_O_MH_C_DELIVERY_CONFIRM       "\x56\x06\x01\x02\x05\x0B\x0B"
#define OMP_O_MH_C_DELIVERY_ENVELOPE      "\x56\x06\x01\x02\x05\x0B\x0C"
#define OMP_O_MH_C_EITS                   "\x56\x06\x01\x02\x05\x0B\x0D"
#define OMP_O_MH_C_EXPANSION_RECORD       "\x56\x06\x01\x02\x05\x0B\x0E"
#define OMP_O_MH_C_EXTENSIBLE_OBJECT      "\x56\x06\x01\x02\x05\x0B\x0F"
#define OMP_O_MH_C_EXTENSION              "\x56\x06\x01\x02\x05\x0B\x10"
#define OMP_O_MH_C_EXTERNAL_TRACE_ENTRY   "\x56\x06\x01\x02\x05\x0B\x11"
#define OMP_O_MH_C_G3_FAX_NBPS            "\x56\x06\x01\x02\x05\x0B\x12"
#define OMP_O_MH_C_GENERAL_CONTENT        "\x56\x06\x01\x02\x05\x0B\x13"
#define OMP_O_MH_C_INTERNAL_TRACE_ENTRY   "\x56\x06\x01\x02\x05\x0B\x14"
#define OMP_O_MH_C_LOCAL_DELIV_CONFIRM    "\x56\x06\x01\x02\x05\x0B\x15"
#define OMP_O_MH_C_LOCAL_DELIV_CONFIRMS   "\x56\x06\x01\x02\x05\x0B\x16"
#define OMP_O_MH_C_LOCAL_NDR              "\x56\x06\x01\x02\x05\x0B\x17"
#define OMP_O_MH_C_LOCAL_PER_RECIP_NDR    "\x56\x06\x01\x02\x05\x0B\x18"
#define OMP_O_MH_C_MESSAGE                "\x56\x06\x01\x02\x05\x0B\x19"
#define OMP_O_MH_C_MESSAGE_RD             "\x56\x06\x01\x02\x05\x0B\x1A"
#define OMP_O_MH_C_MTS_IDENTIFIER         "\x56\x06\x01\x02\x05\x0B\x1B"
#define OMP_O_MH_C_OR_ADDRESS             "\x56\x06\x01\x02\x05\x0B\x1C"
#define OMP_O_MH_C_OR_NAME                "\x56\x06\x01\x02\x05\x0B\x1D"
#define OMP_O_MH_C_PER_RECIP_DR           "\x56\x06\x01\x02\x05\x0B\x1E"
#define OMP_O_MH_C_PER_RECIP_NDR          "\x56\x06\x01\x02\x05\x0B\x1F"
#define OMP_O_MH_C_PER_RECIP_REPORT       "\x56\x06\x01\x02\x05\x0B\x20"
#define OMP_O_MH_C_PROBE                  "\x56\x06\x01\x02\x05\x0B\x21"
#define OMP_O_MH_C_PROBE_RD               "\x56\x06\x01\x02\x05\x0B\x22"
#define OMP_O_MH_C_RD                     "\x56\x06\x01\x02\x05\x0B\x23"
```

```
#define OMP_O_MH_C_REDIRECTION_RECORD    "\x56\x06\x01\x02\x05\x0B\x24"
#define OMP_O_MH_C_REPORT                "\x56\x06\x01\x02\x05\x0B\x25"
#define OMP_O_MH_C_SECURITY_LABEL        "\x56\x06\x01\x02\x05\x0B\x26"
#define OMP_O_MH_C_SESSION               "\x56\x06\x01\x02\x05\x0B\x27"
#define OMP_O_MH_C_SUBMISSION_RESULTS    "\x56\x06\x01\x02\x05\x0B\x28"
#define OMP_O_MH_C_SUBMITTED_COMMUNIQUE "\x56\x06\x01\x02\x05\x0B\x29"
#define OMP_O_MH_C_SUBMITTED_MESSAGE     "\x56\x06\x01\x02\x05\x0B\x2A"
#define OMP_O_MH_C_SUBMITTED_MESSAGE_RD "\x56\x06\x01\x02\x05\x0B\x2B"
#define OMP_O_MH_C_SUBMITTED_PROBE       "\x56\x06\x01\x02\x05\x0B\x2C"
#define OMP_O_MH_C_SUBMITTED_PROBE_RD    "\x56\x06\x01\x02\x05\x0B\x2D"
#define OMP_O_MH_C_TELETEX_NBPS          "\x56\x06\x01\x02\x05\x0B\x2E"
#define OMP_O_MH_C_DELIVERY_REPORT       "\x56\x06\x01\x02\x05\x0B\x2F"
#define OMP_O_MH_C_MT_PUBLIC_DATA        "\x56\x06\x01\x02\x05\x0B\x30"
#define OMP_O_MH_C_TOKEN_PUBLIC_DATA     "\x56\x06\x01\x02\x05\x0B\x31"
#define OMP_O_MH_C_TOKEN                 "\x56\x06\x01\x02\x05\x0B\x32"


/* Enumeration */

/* Action */
#define MH_AC_EXPANDED           ( (OM_enumeration) -2 )
#define MH_AC_REDIRECTED         ( (OM_enumeration) -1 )
#define MH_AC_RELAYED            ( (OM_enumeration) 0 )
#define MH_AC_REROUTED           ( (OM_enumeration) 1 )

/* Builtin EIT */
#define MH_BE_UNDEFINED          ( (OM_enumeration) 0 )
#define MH_BE_TELEX              ( (OM_enumeration) 1 )
#define MH_BE_IA5_TEXT           ( (OM_enumeration) 2 )
#define MH_BE_G3_FAX             ( (OM_enumeration) 3 )
#define MH_BE_G4_CLASS1          ( (OM_enumeration) 4 )
#define MH_BE_TELETEX            ( (OM_enumeration) 5 )
#define MH_BE_VIDEOTEX           ( (OM_enumeration) 6 )
#define MH_BE_MIXED_MODE         ( (OM_enumeration) 9 )
#define MH_BE_ODA                ( (OM_enumeration) 10 )
#define MH_BE_ISO_6937_TEXT      ( (OM_enumeration) 11 )

/* Delivery Mode */
#define MH_DM_ANY                ( (OM_enumeration) 0 )
#define MH_DM_MTS                ( (OM_enumeration) 1 )
#define MH_DM_PDS                ( (OM_enumeration) 2 )
#define MH_DM_TELEX              ( (OM_enumeration) 3 )
#define MH_DM_TELETEX            ( (OM_enumeration) 4 )
#define MH_DM_G3_FAX             ( (OM_enumeration) 5 )
```

```
#define MH_DM_G4_FAX                ( (OM_enumeration) 6 )
#define MH_DM_IA5_TERMINAL          ( (OM_enumeration) 7 )
#define MH_DM_VIDEOTEX              ( (OM_enumeration) 8 )
#define MH_DM_TELEPHONE             ( (OM_enumeration) 9 )

/* Delivery Point */
#define MH_DP_PUBLIC_UA             ( (OM_enumeration) 0 )
#define MH_DP_PRIVATE_UA            ( (OM_enumeration) 1 )
#define MH_DP_MS                    ( (OM_enumeration) 2 )
#define MH_DP_DL                    ( (OM_enumeration) 3 )
#define MH_DP_PDAU                  ( (OM_enumeration) 4 )
#define MH_DP_PDS_PATRON            ( (OM_enumeration) 5 )
#define MH_DP_OTHER_AU              ( (OM_enumeration) 6 )

/* Diagnostic */

#define MH_DG_NO_DIAGNOSTIC                 ( (OM_enumeration) -1 )
#define MH_DG_OR_NAME_UNRECOGNIZED          ( (OM_enumeration) 0 )
#define MH_DG_OR_NAME_AMBIGUOUS             ( (OM_enumeration) 1 )
#define MH_DG_MTS_CONGESTED                 ( (OM_enumeration) 2 )
#define MH_DG_LOOP_DETECTED                 ( (OM_enumeration) 3 )
#define MH_DG_RECIPIENT_UNAVAILABLE         ( (OM_enumeration) 4 )
#define MH_DG_MAXIMUM_TIME_EXPIRED          ( (OM_enumeration) 5 )
#define MH_DG_EITS_UNSUPPORTED              ( (OM_enumeration) 6 )
#define MH_DG_CONTENT_TOO_LONG              ( (OM_enumeration) 7 )
#define MH_DG_IMPRACTICAL_TO_CONVERT        ( (OM_enumeration) 8 )
#define MH_DG_PROHIBITED_TO_CONVERT         ( (OM_enumeration) 9 )
#define MH_DG_CONVERSION_UNSUBSCRIBED       ( (OM_enumeration) 10 )
#define MH_DG_PARAMETERS_INVALID            ( (OM_enumeration) 11 )
#define MH_DG_CONTENT_SYNTAX_IN_ERROR       ( (OM_enumeration) 12 )
#define MH_DG_LENGTH_CONSTRAINT_VIOLATD     ( (OM_enumeration) 13 )
#define MH_DG_NUMBER_CONSTRAINT_VIOLATD     ( (OM_enumeration) 14 )
#define MH_DG_CONTENT_TYPE_UNSUPPORTED      ( (OM_enumeration) 15 )
#define MH_DG_TOO_MANY_RECIPIENTS           ( (OM_enumeration) 16 )
#define MH_DG_NO_BILATERAL_AGREEMENT        ( (OM_enumeration) 17 )
#define MH_DG_CRITICAL_FUNC_UNSUPPORTED     ( (OM_enumeration) 18 )
#define MH_DG_CONVERSION_LOSS_PROHIB        ( (OM_enumeration) 19 )
#define MH_DG_LINE_TOO_LONG                 ( (OM_enumeration) 20 )
#define MH_DG_PAGE_TOO_LONG                 ( (OM_enumeration) 21 )
#define MH_DG_PICTORIAL_SYMBOL_LOST         ( (OM_enumeration) 22 )
#define MH_DG_PUNCTUATION_SYMBOL_LOST       ( (OM_enumeration) 23 )
#define MH_DG_ALPHABETIC_CHARACTER_LOST     ( (OM_enumeration) 24 )
#define MH_DG_MULTIPLE_INFO_LOSSES          ( (OM_enumeration) 25 )
#define MH_DG_REASSIGNMENT_PROHIBITED       ( (OM_enumeration) 26 )
```

```
#define MH_DG_REDIRECTION_LOOP_DETECTED        ( (OM_enumeration) 27 )
#define MH_DG_EXPANSION_PROHIBITED             ( (OM_enumeration) 28 )
#define MH_DG_SUBMISSION_PROHIBITED            ( (OM_enumeration) 29 )
#define MH_DG_EXPANSION_FAILED                 ( (OM_enumeration) 30 )
#define MH_DG_RENDITION_UNSUPPORTED            ( (OM_enumeration) 31 )
#define MH_DG_MAIL_ADDRESS_INCORRECT           ( (OM_enumeration) 32 )
#define MH_DG_MAIL_OFFICE_INCOR_OR_INVD        ( (OM_enumeration) 33 )
#define MH_DG_MAIL_ADDRESS_INCOMPLETE          ( (OM_enumeration) 34 )
#define MH_DG_MAIL_RECIPIENT_UNKNOWN           ( (OM_enumeration) 35 )
#define MH_DG_MAIL_RECIPIENT_DECEASED          ( (OM_enumeration) 36 )
#define MH_DG_MAIL_ORGANIZATION_EXPIRED        ( (OM_enumeration) 37 )
#define MH_DG_MAIL_REFUSED                     ( (OM_enumeration) 38 )
#define MH_DG_MAIL_UNCLAIMED                   ( (OM_enumeration) 39 )
#define MH_DG_MAIL_RECIPIENT_MOVED             ( (OM_enumeration) 40 )
#define MH_DG_MAIL_RECIPIENT_TRAVELLING        ( (OM_enumeration) 41 )
#define MH_DG_MAIL_RECIPIENT_DEPARTED          ( (OM_enumeration) 42 )
#define MH_DG_MAIL_NEW_ADDRESS_UNKNOWN         ( (OM_enumeration) 43 )
#define MH_DG_MAIL_FORWARDING_UNWANTED         ( (OM_enumeration) 44 )
#define MH_DG_MAIL_FORWARDING_PROHIB           ( (OM_enumeration) 45 )
#define MH_DG_SECURE_MESSAGING_ERROR           ( (OM_enumeration) 46 )
#define MH_DG_DOWNGRADING_IMPOSSIBLE           ( (OM_enumeration) 47 )

/* Explicit Conversion */

#define MH_EC_NO_CONVERSION               ( (OM_enumeration) -1 )
#define MH_EC_IA5_TEXT_TO_TELETEX         ( (OM_enumeration) 0 )
#define MH_EC_TELETEX_TO_TELEX            ( (OM_enumeration) 1 )
#define MH_EC_TELEX_TO_IA5_TEXT           ( (OM_enumeration) 2 )
#define MH_EC_TELEX_TO_TELETEX            ( (OM_enumeration) 3 )
#define MH_EC_TELEX_TO_G4_CLASS1          ( (OM_enumeration) 4 )
#define MH_EC_TELEX_TO_VIDEOTEX           ( (OM_enumeration) 5 )
#define MH_EC_IA5_TEXT_TO_TELEX           ( (OM_enumeration) 6 )
#define MH_EC_TELEX_TO_G3_FAX             ( (OM_enumeration) 7 )
#define MH_EC_IA5_TEXT_TO_G3_FAX          ( (OM_enumeration) 8 )
#define MH_EC_IA5_TEXT_TO_G4_CLASS1       ( (OM_enumeration) 9 )
#define MH_EC_IA5_TEXT_TO_VIDEOTEX        ( (OM_enumeration) 10 )
#define MH_EC_TELETEX_TO_IA5_TEXT         ( (OM_enumeration) 11 )
#define MH_EC_TELETEX_TO_G3_FAX           ( (OM_enumeration) 12 )
#define MH_EC_TELETEX_TO_G4_CLASS1        ( (OM_enumeration) 13 )
#define MH_EC_TELETEX_TO_VIDEOTEX         ( (OM_enumeration) 14 )
#define MH_EC_VIDEOTEX_TO_TELEX           ( (OM_enumeration) 15 )
#define MH_EC_VIDEOTEX_TO_IA5_TEXT        ( (OM_enumeration) 16 )
#define MH_EC_VIDEOTEX_TO_TELETEX         ( (OM_enumeration) 17 )
```

```
/* Postal Mode */

#define MH_PM_ORDINARY_MAIL                 ( (OM_enumeration) 0 )
#define MH_PM_SPECIAL_DELIVERY              ( (OM_enumeration) 1 )
#define MH_PM_EXPRESS_MAIL                  ( (OM_enumeration) 2 )
#define MH_PM_CC                            ( (OM_enumeration) 3 )
#define MH_PM_CC_WITH_TELEPHONE_ADVICE      ( (OM_enumeration) 4 )
#define MH_PM_CC_WITH_TELEX_ADVICE          ( (OM_enumeration) 5 )
#define MH_PM_CC_WITH_TELETEX_ADVICE        ( (OM_enumeration) 6 )

/* Postal Report */

#define MH_PR_UNDELIVBLE_MAIL_VIA_PDS       ( (OM_enumeration) 0 )
#define MH_PR_NOTIFICN_VIA_PDS              ( (OM_enumeration) 1 )
#define MH_PR_NOTIFICN_VIA_MTS              ( (OM_enumeration) 2 )
#define MH_PR_NOTIFICN_VIA_MTS_AND_PDS      ( (OM_enumeration) 3 )

/* Priority */

#define MH_PTY_NORMAL    ( (OM_enumeration) 0 )
#define MH_PTY_LOW       ( (OM_enumeration) 1 )
#define MH_PTY_URGENT    ( (OM_enumeration) 2 )

/* Reason */

#define MH_RE_TRANSFER_FAILED                       ( (OM_enumeration) 0 )
#define MH_RE_TRANSFER_IMPOSSIBLE                   ( (OM_enumeration) 1 )
#define MH_RE_CONVERSION_NOT_PERFORMED              ( (OM_enumeration) 2 )
#define MH_RE_PHYSICAL_RENDITN_NOT_DONE             ( (OM_enumeration) 3 )
#define MH_RE_PHYSICAL_DELIV_NOT_DONE               ( (OM_enumeration) 4 )
#define MH_RE_RESTRICTED_DELIVERY                   ( (OM_enumeration) 5 )
#define MH_RE_DIRECTORY_OPERATN_FAILED              ( (OM_enumeration) 6 )

/* Redirection Reason */

#define MH_RR_RECIPIENT_ASSIGNED                    ( (OM_enumeration) 0 )
#define MH_RR_ORIGINATOR_REQUESTED                  ( (OM_enumeration) 1 )
#define MH_RR_RECIPIENT_DOMAIN_ASSIGNED             ( (OM_enumeration) 2 )

/* Registration */

#define MH_RG_UNREGISTERED_MAIL                     ( (OM_enumeration) 0 )
#define MH_RG_REGISTERED_MAIL                       ( (OM_enumeration) 1 )
#define MH_RG_REGISTERED_MAIL_IN_PERSON             ( (OM_enumeration) 2 )
```

```
/* Report Request */

#define MH_RQ_NEVER                 ( (OM_enumeration) 0 )
#define MH_RQ_NON_DELIVERY          ( (OM_enumeration) 1 )
#define MH_RQ_ALWAYS                ( (OM_enumeration) 2 )
#define MH_RQ_ALWAYS_AUDITED        ( (OM_enumeration) 3 )

/* Security Classification */

#define MH_SC_UNMARKED              ( (OM_enumeration) 0 )
#define MH_SC_UNCLASSIFIED          ( (OM_enumeration) 1 )
#define MH_SC_RESTRICTED            ( (OM_enumeration) 2 )
#define MH_SC_CONFIDENTIAL          ( (OM_enumeration) 3 )
#define MH_SC_SECRET                ( (OM_enumeration) 4 )
#define MH_SC_TOP_SECRET            ( (OM_enumeration) 5 )

/* Terminal Type */

#define MH_TT_TELEX                 ( (OM_enumeration) 3 )
#define MH_TT_TELETEX               ( (OM_enumeration) 4 )
#define MH_TT_G3_FAX                ( (OM_enumeration) 5 )
#define MH_TT_G4_FAX                ( (OM_enumeration) 6 )
#define MH_TT_IA5_TERMINAL          ( (OM_enumeration) 7 )
#define MH_TT_VIDEOTEX              ( (OM_enumeration) 8 )


/* Integer */

/* Content Type */

#define MH_CTI_UNIDENTIFIED         ( (OM_integer) 0 )
#define MH_CTI_EXTERNAL             ( (OM_integer) 1 )
#define MH_CTI_P2_1984              ( (OM_integer) 2 )
#define MH_CTI_P2_1988              ( (OM_integer) 22 )


/* Object Identifier (Elements component) */

/* Content Type */
#define OMP_O_MH_CTO_INNER_MESSAGE        "\x56\x03\x03\x01"
#define OMP_O_MH_CTO_UNIDENTIFIED         "\x56\x03\x03\x00"

/* External EITs */
#define OMP_O_MH_EE_G3_FAX                "\x56\x03\x04\x03"
```

```
#define OMP_O_MH_EE_G4_CLASS_1          "\x56\x03\x04\x04"
#define OMP_O_MH_EE_IA5_TEXT            "\x56\x03\x04\x02"
#define OMP_O_MH_EE_MIXED_MODE          "\x56\x03\x04\x09"
#define OMP_O_MH_EE_TELETEX             "\x56\x03\x04\x05"
#define OMP_O_MH_EE_TELEX               "\x56\x03\x04\x01"
#define OMP_O_MH_EE_UNDEFINED           "\x56\x03\x04\x00"
#define OMP_O_MH_EE_VIDEOTEX            "\x56\x03\x04\x06"

/* ODA EIT */
#define OMP_O_MH_ET_ODA_DATA            "\x58\x01\x00\x01"

/* Rendition Attributes */
#define OMP_O_MH_RA_BASIC_RENDITION     "\x56\x03\x05\x00"


/* Type */

#define MH_T_A3_WIDTH                          ( (OM_type) 200 )
#define MH_T_ACTION                            ( (OM_type) 201 )
#define MH_T_ACTUAL_RECIPIENT_NAME             ( (OM_type) 202 )
#define MH_T_ADMD_NAME                         ( (OM_type) 203 )
#define MH_T_ALGORITHM_DATUM                   ( (OM_type) 204 )
#define MH_T_ALGORITHM_ID                      ( (OM_type) 205 )
#define MH_T_ALGORITHM_RESULT                  ( (OM_type) 206 )
#define MH_T_ALTERNATE_RECIP_ALLOWED           ( (OM_type) 207 )
#define MH_T_ALTERNATE_RECIPIENT_NAME          ( (OM_type) 208 )
#define MH_T_ARRIVAL_TIME                      ( (OM_type) 209 )
#define MH_T_ATTEMPTED_ADMD_NAME               ( (OM_type) 210 )
#define MH_T_ATTEMPTED_COUNTRY_NAME            ( (OM_type) 211 )
#define MH_T_ATTEMPTED_MTA_NAME                ( (OM_type) 212 )
#define MH_T_ATTEMPTED_PRMD_IDENTIFIER         ( (OM_type) 213 )
#define MH_T_B4_LENGTH                         ( (OM_type) 214 )
#define MH_T_B4_WIDTH                          ( (OM_type) 215 )
#define MH_T_BILATERAL_INFO                    ( (OM_type) 216 )
#define MH_T_BINARY_CONTENT                    ( (OM_type) 217 )
#define MH_T_BUILTIN_EITS                      ( (OM_type) 218 )
#define MH_T_BUREAU_FAX_DELIVERY               ( (OM_type) 219 )
#define MH_T_COMMON_NAME                       ( (OM_type) 220 )
#define MH_T_CONFIDENTIALITY_ALGORITHM         ( (OM_type) 221 )
#define MH_T_CONFIDENTIALITY_KEY               ( (OM_type) 222 )
#define MH_T_CONTENT                           ( (OM_type) 223 )
#define MH_T_CONTENT_CORRELATOR                ( (OM_type) 224 )
#define MH_T_CONTENT_EXTENSIONS                ( (OM_type) 225 )
#define MH_T_CONTENT_IDENTIFIER                ( (OM_type) 226 )
```

```
#define MH_T_CONTENT_LENGTH                    ( (OM_type) 227 )
#define MH_T_CONTENT_RETURN_REQUESTED          ( (OM_type) 228 )
#define MH_T_CONTENT_TYPE                      ( (OM_type) 229 )
#define MH_T_CONTROL_CHARACTER_SETS            ( (OM_type) 230 )
#define MH_T_CONVERSION_LOSS_PROHIBITED        ( (OM_type) 231 )
#define MH_T_CONVERSION_PROHIBITED             ( (OM_type) 232 )
#define MH_T_CONVERTED_EITS                    ( (OM_type) 233 )
#define MH_T_COUNTRY_NAME                      ( (OM_type) 234 )
#define MH_T_CRITICAL_FOR_DELIVERY             ( (OM_type) 235 )
#define MH_T_CRITICAL_FOR_SUBMISSION           ( (OM_type) 236 )
#define MH_T_CRITICAL_FOR_TRANSFER             ( (OM_type) 237 )
#define MH_T_DEFERRED_DELIVERY_TIME            ( (OM_type) 238 )
#define MH_T_DEFERRED_TIME                     ( (OM_type) 239 )
#define MH_T_DELIVERY_CONFIRMS                 ( (OM_type) 240 )
#define MH_T_DELIVERY_POINT                    ( (OM_type) 241 )
#define MH_T_DELIVERY_TIME                     ( (OM_type) 242 )
#define MH_T_DIRECTORY_NAME                    ( (OM_type) 243 )
#define MH_T_DISCLOSURE_ALLOWED                ( (OM_type) 244 )
#define MH_T_DISTINGUISHED_RECIP_ADDR          ( (OM_type) 245 )
#define MH_T_DOMAIN_TYPE_1                     ( (OM_type) 246 )
#define MH_T_DOMAIN_TYPE_2                     ( (OM_type) 247 )
#define MH_T_DOMAIN_TYPE_3                     ( (OM_type) 248 )
#define MH_T_DOMAIN_TYPE_4                     ( (OM_type) 249 )
#define MH_T_DOMAIN_VALUE_1                    ( (OM_type) 250 )
#define MH_T_DOMAIN_VALUE_2                    ( (OM_type) 251 )
#define MH_T_DOMAIN_VALUE_3                    ( (OM_type) 252 )
#define MH_T_DOMAIN_VALUE_4                    ( (OM_type) 253 )
#define MH_T_ENVELOPES                         ( (OM_type) 254 )
#define MH_T_EVENT_HANDLE                      ( (OM_type) 255 )
#define MH_T_EXPANSION_HISTORY                 ( (OM_type) 256 )
#define MH_T_EXPANSION_PROHIBITED              ( (OM_type) 257 )
#define MH_T_EXPLICIT_CONVERSION               ( (OM_type) 258 )
#define MH_T_EXTENSION_TYPE                    ( (OM_type) 259 )
#define MH_T_EXTENSION_VALUE                   ( (OM_type) 260 )
#define MH_T_EXTENSIONS                        ( (OM_type) 261 )
#define MH_T_EXTERNAL_EITS                     ( (OM_type) 262 )
#define MH_T_EXTERNAL_TRACE_INFO               ( (OM_type) 263 )
#define MH_T_FINE_RESOLUTION                   ( (OM_type) 264 )
#define MH_T_FORWARDING_ADDRESS                ( (OM_type) 265 )
#define MH_T_FORWARDING_ADDR_REQUESTED         ( (OM_type) 266 )
#define MH_T_FORWARDING_PROHIBITED             ( (OM_type) 267 )
#define MH_T_G3_FAX_NBPS                       ( (OM_type) 268 )
#define MH_T_G4_FAX_NBPS                       ( (OM_type) 269 )
#define MH_T_GENERATION                        ( (OM_type) 270 )
```

```
#define MH_T_GIVEN_NAME                         ( (OM_type) 271 )
#define MH_T_GRAPHIC_CHARACTER_SETS             ( (OM_type) 272 )
#define MH_T_INFORMATION                        ( (OM_type) 273 )
#define MH_T_INITIALS                           ( (OM_type) 274 )
#define MH_T_INTEGRITY_CHECK                    ( (OM_type) 275 )
#define MH_T_INTENDED_RECIPIENT_NAME            ( (OM_type) 276 )
#define MH_T_INTENDED_RECIPIENT_NUMBER          ( (OM_type) 277 )
#define MH_T_INTERNAL_TRACE_INFO                ( (OM_type) 278 )
#define MH_T_ISDN_NUMBER                        ( (OM_type) 279 )
#define MH_T_ISDN_SUBADDRESS                    ( (OM_type) 280 )
#define MH_T_LATEST_DELIVERY_TIME               ( (OM_type) 281 )
#define MH_T_LOCAL_IDENTIFIER                   ( (OM_type) 282 )
#define MH_T_MESSAGE_SEQUENCE_NUMBER            ( (OM_type) 283 )
#define MH_T_MISCELLANEOUS_CAPABILITIES         ( (OM_type) 284 )
#define MH_T_MTA_CERTIFICATE                    ( (OM_type) 285 )
#define MH_T_MTA_NAME                           ( (OM_type) 286 )
#define MH_T_MTA_REPORT_REQUEST                 ( (OM_type) 287 )
#define MH_T_MTA_RESPONSIBILITY                 ( (OM_type) 288 )
#define MH_T_MTS_IDENTIFIER                     ( (OM_type) 289 )
#define MH_T_NAME                               ( (OM_type) 290 )
#define MH_T_NON_DELIVERY_DIAGNOSTIC            ( (OM_type) 291 )
#define MH_T_NON_DELIVERY_REASON                ( (OM_type) 292 )
#define MH_T_NUMERIC_USER_IDENTIFIER            ( (OM_type) 293 )
#define MH_T_ORGANIZATION_NAME                  ( (OM_type) 294 )
#define MH_T_ORGANIZATIONAL_UNIT_NAME_1         ( (OM_type) 295 )
#define MH_T_ORGANIZATIONAL_UNIT_NAME_2         ( (OM_type) 296 )
#define MH_T_ORGANIZATIONAL_UNIT_NAME_3         ( (OM_type) 297 )
#define MH_T_ORGANIZATIONAL_UNIT_NAME_4         ( (OM_type) 298 )
#define MH_T_ORIG_AND_EXPANSION_HISTORY         ( (OM_type) 299 )
#define MH_T_ORIGIN_CHECK                       ( (OM_type) 300 )
#define MH_T_ORIGINAL_EITS                      ( (OM_type) 301 )
#define MH_T_ORIGINALLY_INTENDED_RECIP          ( (OM_type) 302 )
#define MH_T_ORIGINATOR_CERTIFICATE             ( (OM_type) 303 )
#define MH_T_ORIGINATOR_NAME                    ( (OM_type) 304 )
#define MH_T_ORIGINATOR_REPORT_REQUEST          ( (OM_type) 305 )
#define MH_T_ORIGINATOR_RETURN_ADDRESS          ( (OM_type) 306 )
#define MH_T_OTHER_RECIPIENT_NAMES              ( (OM_type) 307 )
#define MH_T_PAGE_FORMATS                       ( (OM_type) 308 )
#define MH_T_PER_RECIP_REPORTS                  ( (OM_type) 309 )
#define MH_T_POSTAL_ADDRESS_DETAILS             ( (OM_type) 310 )
#define MH_T_POSTAL_ADDRESS_IN_FULL             ( (OM_type) 311 )
#define MH_T_POSTAL_ADDRESS_IN_LINES            ( (OM_type) 312 )
#define MH_T_POSTAL_CODE                        ( (OM_type) 313 )
#define MH_T_POSTAL_COUNTRY_NAME                ( (OM_type) 314 )
```

```
#define MH_T_POSTAL_DELIVERY_POINT_NAME        ( (OM_type) 315 )
#define MH_T_POSTAL_DELIV_SYSTEM_NAME          ( (OM_type) 316 )
#define MH_T_POSTAL_GENERAL_DELIV_ADDR         ( (OM_type) 317 )
#define MH_T_POSTAL_LOCALE                     ( (OM_type) 318 )
#define MH_T_POSTAL_MODE                       ( (OM_type) 319 )
#define MH_T_POSTAL_OFFICE_BOX_NUMBER          ( (OM_type) 320 )
#define MH_T_POSTAL_OFFICE_NAME                ( (OM_type) 321 )
#define MH_T_POSTAL_OFFICE_NUMBER              ( (OM_type) 322 )
#define MH_T_POSTAL_ORGANIZATION_NAME          ( (OM_type) 323 )
#define MH_T_POSTAL_PATRON_DETAILS             ( (OM_type) 324 )
#define MH_T_POSTAL_PATRON_NAME                ( (OM_type) 325 )
#define MH_T_POSTAL_REPORT                     ( (OM_type) 326 )
#define MH_T_POSTAL_STREET_ADDRESS             ( (OM_type) 327 )
#define MH_T_PREFERRED_DELIVERY_MODES          ( (OM_type) 328 )
#define MH_T_PRESENTATION_ADDRESS              ( (OM_type) 329 )
#define MH_T_PRIORITY                          ( (OM_type) 330 )
#define MH_T_PRIVACY_MARK                      ( (OM_type) 331 )
#define MH_T_PRIVATE_USE                       ( (OM_type) 332 )
#define MH_T_PRMD_IDENTIFIER                   ( (OM_type) 333 )
#define MH_T_PRMD_NAME                         ( (OM_type) 334 )
#define MH_T_PROOF_OF_DELIVERY                 ( (OM_type) 335 )
#define MH_T_PROOF_OF_DELIV_REQUESTED          ( (OM_type) 336 )
#define MH_T_PROOF_OF_SUBMISSION               ( (OM_type) 337 )
#define MH_T_PROOF_OF_SUBMISN_REQUEST          ( (OM_type) 338 )
#define MH_T_PUBLIC_INFORMATION                ( (OM_type) 339 )
#define MH_T_RANDOM_NUMBER                     ( (OM_type) 340 )
#define MH_T_REASON                            ( (OM_type) 341 )
#define MH_T_REASSIGNMENT_PROHIBITED           ( (OM_type) 342 )
#define MH_T_RECIPIENT_CERTIFICATE             ( (OM_type) 343 )
#define MH_T_RECIPIENT_DESCRIPTORS             ( (OM_type) 344 )
#define MH_T_RECIPIENT_NAME                    ( (OM_type) 345 )
#define MH_T_RECIPIENT_NUMBER                  ( (OM_type) 346 )
#define MH_T_RECIP_NUMBER_FOR_ADVICE           ( (OM_type) 347 )
#define MH_T_REDIRECTION_HISTORY               ( (OM_type) 348 )
#define MH_T_REGISTRATION                      ( (OM_type) 349 )
#define MH_T_RENDITION_ATTRIBUTES              ( (OM_type) 350 )
#define MH_T_REPORT_ADDITIONAL_INFO            ( (OM_type) 351 )
#define MH_T_REPORT_DESTINATION                ( (OM_type) 352 )
#define MH_T_REPORTING_DL_NAME                 ( (OM_type) 353 )
#define MH_T_REPORTING_MTA_CERTIFICATE         ( (OM_type) 354 )
#define MH_T_SECRET_INFORMATION                ( (OM_type) 355 )
#define MH_T_SECURITY_CATEGORY_DATA            ( (OM_type) 356 )
#define MH_T_SECURITY_CATEGORY_IDS             ( (OM_type) 357 )
#define MH_T_SECURITY_CLASSIFICATION           ( (OM_type) 358 )
```

```
#define MH_T_SECURITY_LABEL                  ( (OM_type) 359 )
#define MH_T_SECURITY_POLICY_ID              ( (OM_type) 360 )
#define MH_T_SIGNATURE                       ( (OM_type) 361 )
#define MH_T_SUBJECT_EXT_TRACE_INFO          ( (OM_type) 362 )
#define MH_T_SUBJECT_MTS_IDENTIFIER          ( (OM_type) 363 )
#define MH_T_SUBMISSION_TIME                 ( (OM_type) 364 )
#define MH_T_SUPPLEMENTARY_INFO              ( (OM_type) 365 )
#define MH_T_SURNAME                         ( (OM_type) 366 )
#define MH_T_TELETEX_NBPS                    ( (OM_type) 367 )
#define MH_T_TEMPORARY                       ( (OM_type) 368 )
#define MH_T_TERMINAL_IDENTIFIER             ( (OM_type) 369 )
#define MH_T_TERMINAL_TYPE                   ( (OM_type) 370 )
#define MH_T_TIME                            ( (OM_type) 371 )
#define MH_T_TOKEN                           ( (OM_type) 372 )
#define MH_T_TWO_DIMENSIONAL                 ( (OM_type) 373 )
#define MH_T_UNCOMPRESSED                    ( (OM_type) 374 )
#define MH_T_UNLIMITED_LENGTH                ( (OM_type) 375 )
#define MH_T_WORKSPACE                       ( (OM_type) 376 )
#define MH_T_X121_ADDRESS                    ( (OM_type) 377 )

/* Value Length */

#define MH_VL_ADMD_NAME                      ( (OM_value_length) 16 )
#define MH_VL_ATTEMPTED_ADMD_NAME            ( (OM_value_length) 16 )
#define MH_VL_ATTEMPTED_COUNTRY_NAME         ( (OM_value_length) 3 )
#define MH_VL_ATTEMPTED_PRMD_IDENTIFIER      ( (OM_value_length) 16 )
#define MH_VL_COMMON_NAME                    ( (OM_value_length) 64 )
#define MH_VL_CONTENT_CORRELATOR             ( (OM_value_length) 512 )
#define MH_VL_CONTENT_IDENTIFIER             ( (OM_value_length) 16 )
#define MH_VL_COUNTRY_NAME                   ( (OM_value_length) 3 )
#define MH_VL_DOMAIN_TYPE                    ( (OM_value_length) 8 )
#define MH_VL_DOMAIN_VALUE                   ( (OM_value_length) 128 )
#define MH_VL_GENERATION                     ( (OM_value_length) 3 )
#define MH_VL_GIVEN_NAME                     ( (OM_value_length) 16 )
#define MH_VL_INFORMATION                    ( (OM_value_length) 1024 )
#define MH_VL_INITIALS                       ( (OM_value_length) 5 )
#define MH_VL_ISDN_NUMBER                    ( (OM_value_length) 15 )
#define MH_VL_ISDN_SUBADDRESS                ( (OM_value_length) 40 )
#define MH_VL_LATEST_DELIVERY_TIME           ( (OM_value_length) 7 )
#define MH_VL_LOCAL_IDENTIFIER               ( (OM_value_length) 32 )
#define MH_VL_MSG_CONTENT_CORRELATOR         ( (OM_value_length) 16 )
#define MH_VL_MTA_NAME                       ( (OM_value_length) 32 )
#define MH_VL_NUMERIC_USER_IDENTIFIER        ( (OM_value_length) 32 )
#define MH_VL_ORGANIZATION_NAME              ( (OM_value_length) 64 )
```

```
#define MH_VL_ORGANIZATIONAL_UNIT_NAMES        ( (OM_value_length) 32 )
#define MH_VL_POSTAL_ADDRESS_DETAILS           ( (OM_value_length) 30 )
#define MH_VL_POSTAL_ADDRESS_IN_FULL           ( (OM_value_length) 185 )
#define MH_VL_POSTAL_CODE                      ( (OM_value_length) 16 )
#define MH_VL_POSTAL_COUNTRY_NAME              ( (OM_value_length) 32 )
#define MH_VL_POSTAL_DELIV_POINT_NAME          ( (OM_value_length) 30 )
#define MH_VL_POSTAL_DELIV_SYSTEM_NAME         ( (OM_value_length) 16 )
#define MH_VL_POSTAL_GENERAL_DELIV_ADDR        ( (OM_value_length) 30 )
#define MH_VL_POSTAL_LOCALE                    ( (OM_value_length) 30 )
#define MH_VL_POSTAL_OFFICE_BOX_NUMBER         ( (OM_value_length) 30 )
#define MH_VL_POSTAL_OFFICE_NAME               ( (OM_value_length) 30 )
#define MH_VL_POSTAL_OFFICE_NUMBER             ( (OM_value_length) 30 )
#define MH_VL_POSTAL_ORGANIZATION_NAME         ( (OM_value_length) 30 )
#define MH_VL_POSTAL_PATRON_DETAILS            ( (OM_value_length) 30 )
#define MH_VL_POSTAL_PATRON_NAME               ( (OM_value_length) 30 )
#define MH_VL_POSTAL_STREET_ADDRESS            ( (OM_value_length) 30 )
#define MH_VL_PRIVACY_MARK                     ( (OM_value_length) 128 )
#define MH_VL_PRIVATE_USE                      ( (OM_value_length) 126 )
#define MH_VL_PRMD_IDENTIFIER                  ( (OM_value_length) 16 )
#define MH_VL_PRMD_NAME                        ( (OM_value_length) 16 )
#define MH_VL_RECIP_NUMBER_FOR_ADVICE          ( (OM_value_length) 32 )
#define MH_VL_REDIRECTION_TIME                 ( (OM_value_length) 7 )
#define MH_VL_REPORT_ADDITIONAL_INFO           ( (OM_value_length) 1024 )
#define MH_VL_SUPPLEMENTARY_INFO               ( (OM_value_length) 64 )
#define MH_VL_SURNAME                          ( (OM_value_length) 40 )
#define MH_VL_TERMINAL_IDENTIFIER              ( (OM_value_length) 24 )
#define MH_VL_TIME                             ( (OM_value_length) 17 )
#define MH_VL_X121_ADDRESS                     ( (OM_value_length) 15 )

/* Value Number */

#define MH_VN_BILATERAL_INFORMATION            ( (OM_value_number) 8 )
#define MH_VN_ENCODED_INFORMATION_TYPES        ( (OM_value_number) 8 )
#define MH_VN_EXPANSION_HISTORY                ( (OM_value_number) 512 )
#define MH_VN_OTHER_RECIPIENT_NAMES            ( (OM_value_number) 32767 )
#define MH_VN_PREFERRED_DELIVERY_MODES         ( (OM_value_number) 10 )
#define MH_VN_RECIPIENT_DESCRIPTORS            ( (OM_value_number) 32767 )
#define MH_VN_REDIRECTION_HISTORY              ( (OM_value_number) 512 )
#define MH_VN_REPORT_SUBSTANCE                 ( (OM_value_number) 32767 )
#define MH_VN_SECURITY_CATEGORY_DATA           ( (OM_value_number) 64 )
#define MH_VN_SECURITY_CATEGORY_IDS            ( (OM_value_number) 64 )
#define MH_VN_TRACE_INFO                       ( (OM_value_number) 512 )
/* END MH PORTION OF INTERFACE */
```

Related Information

Books: *X/Open CAE Specification (November 1991), API to Directory Services (XDS),*
X/Open CAE Specification (November 1991), OSI-Abstract-Data Manipulation API (XOM),
OSF DCE Application Development Guide,
X/Open CAE Specification (November 1991), API to Electronic Mail (X.400).

xmsga.h

Purpose Definitions for the Message Store General attributes

Synopsis
#include <xom.h>
#include <xds.h>
#include <xdsmdup.h>
#include <xmhp.h>
#include <xmsga.h>

Description

The **xmsga.h** header declares the object identifiers for the Message Store General attributes. They are used with the directory message store object. This header must be included when use of the MHS Directory User Package (MDUP) has been negotiated.

All application programs that include this header must first include the **xom.h** Object Management header, the **xds.h** header, the **xdsmdup.h** and **xmhp.h** headers.

```
#ifndef XMSGA_HEADER
#define XMSGA_HEADER

/* MS General Attributes Package object identifier */

#define OMP_O_MS_GENERAL_ATTRIBUTES_PACKAGE      "\x56\x06\x01\x02\x06\x02"


/* MS General Attributes Types */
/*
 * Note: Every client program must explicitly import into
 * every compilation unit (C source program) the classes or
 * Object Identifiers that it uses. Each of these classes or
 * Object Identifier names must then be explicitly exported from
 * just one compilation unit.
 * Importing and exporting can be done using the OM_IMPORT and
 * OM_EXPORT macros respectively (see [OM API]).
 * For instance, the client program uses
 *                OM_IMPORT( MS_A_CHILD_SEQUENCE_NUMBERS )
 * which in turn will make use of
 *                OMP_O_MS_A_CHILD_SEQUENCE_NUMBERS
 * defined below.
```

```
*/

#define OMP_O_MS_A_CHILD_SEQUENCE_NUMBERS          "\x56\x04\x03\x00"
#define OMP_O_MS_A_CONTENT                         "\x56\x04\x03\x01"
#define OMP_O_MS_A_CONTENT_CONFIDENTL_ALGM_ID      "\x56\x04\x03\x02"
#define OMP_O_MS_A_CONTENT_CORRELATOR              "\x56\x04\x03\x03"
#define OMP_O_MS_A_CONTENT_IDENTIFIER              "\x56\x04\x03\x04"
#define OMP_O_MS_A_CONTENT_INTEGRITY_CHECK         "\x56\x04\x03\x05"
#define OMP_O_MS_A_CONTENT_LENGTH                  "\x56\x04\x03\x06"
#define OMP_O_MS_A_CONTENT_RETURNED                "\x56\x04\x03\x07"
#define OMP_O_MS_A_CONTENT_TYPE                    "\x56\x04\x03\x08"
#define OMP_O_MS_A_CONVERSION_LOSS_PROHIBITED      "\x56\x04\x03\x09"
#define OMP_O_MS_A_CONVERTED_EITS                  "\x56\x04\x03\x0A"
#define OMP_O_MS_A_CREATION_TIME                   "\x56\x04\x03\x0B"
#define OMP_O_MS_A_DELIVERED_EITS                  "\x56\x04\x03\x0C"
#define OMP_O_MS_A_DELIVERY_FLAGS                  "\x56\x04\x03\x0D"
#define OMP_O_MS_A_DL_EXPANSION_HISTORY            "\x56\x04\x03\x0E"
#define OMP_O_MS_A_ENTRY_STATUS                    "\x56\x04\x03\x0F"
#define OMP_O_MS_A_ENTRY_TYPE                      "\x56\x04\x03\x10"
#define OMP_O_MS_A_INTENDED_RECIPIENT_NAME         "\x56\x04\x03\x11"
#define OMP_O_MS_A_MESSAGE_DELIVERY_ENVELOPE       "\x56\x04\x03\x12"
#define OMP_O_MS_A_MESSAGE_DELIVERY_ID             "\x56\x04\x03\x13"
#define OMP_O_MS_A_MESSAGE_DELIVERY_TIME           "\x56\x04\x03\x14"
#define OMP_O_MS_A_MESSAGE_ORIGIN_AUTHEN_CHK       "\x56\x04\x03\x15"
#define OMP_O_MS_A_MESSAGE_SECURITY_LABEL          "\x56\x04\x03\x16"
#define OMP_O_MS_A_MESSAGE_SUBMISSION_TIME         "\x56\x04\x03\x17"
#define OMP_O_MS_A_MESSAGE_TOKEN                   "\x56\x04\x03\x18"
#define OMP_O_MS_A_ORIGINAL_EITS                   "\x56\x04\x03\x19"
#define OMP_O_MS_A_ORIGINATOR_CERTIFICATE          "\x56\x04\x03\x1A"
#define OMP_O_MS_A_ORIGINATOR_NAME                 "\x56\x04\x03\x1B"
#define OMP_O_MS_A_OTHER_RECIPIENT_NAMES           "\x56\x04\x03\x1C"
#define OMP_O_MS_A_PARENT_SEQUENCE_NUMBER          "\x56\x04\x03\x1D"
#define OMP_O_MS_A_PERRECIP_REPORT_DELIV_FLDS      "\x56\x04\x03\x1E"
#define OMP_O_MS_A_PRIORITY                        "\x56\x04\x03\x1F"
#define OMP_O_MS_A_PROOF_OF_DELIVERY_REQUEST       "\x56\x04\x03\x20"
#define OMP_O_MS_A_REDIRECTION_HISTORY             "\x56\x04\x03\x21"
#define OMP_O_MS_A_REPORT_DELIVERY_ENVELOPE        "\x56\x04\x03\x22"
#define OMP_O_MS_A_REPORT_ORIGIN_AUTHEN_CHK        "\x56\x04\x03\x23"
#define OMP_O_MS_A_REPORTING_DL_NAME               "\x56\x04\x03\x24"
#define OMP_O_MS_A_REPORTING_MTA_CERTIFICATE       "\x56\x04\x03\x25"
#define OMP_O_MS_A_SECURITY_CLASSIFICATION         "\x56\x04\x03\x26"
#define OMP_O_MS_A_SEQUENCE_NUMBER                 "\x56\x04\x03\x27"
#define OMP_O_MS_A_SUBJECT_SUBMISSION_ID           "\x56\x04\x03\x28"
```

```
#define OMP_O_MS_A_THIS_RECIPIENT_NAME                  "\x56\x04\x03\x29"


/* Enumeration Constants */

/* for MS_A_ENTRY_STATUS */

#define MS_ES_NEW                          ((OM_enumeration) 0)
#define MS_ES_LISTED                       ((OM_enumeration) 1)
#define MS_ES_PROCESSED                    ((OM_enumeration) 2)


/* for MS_A_ENTRY_TYPE */

#define MS_ET_DELIVERED_MESSAGE            ((OM_enumeration) 0)
#define MS_ET_DELIVERED_REPORT             ((OM_enumeration) 1)
#define MS_ET_RETURNED_CONTENT             ((OM_enumeration) 2)


/* for MS_A_PRIORITY */

#define MS_PTY_NORMAL                      ((OM_enumeration) 0)
#define MS_PTY_LOW                         ((OM_enumeration) 1)
#define MS_PTY_URGENT                      ((OM_enumeration) 2)


/* for MS_A_SECURITY_CLASSIFICATION */

#define MS_SC_UNMARKED                     ((OM_enumeration) 0)
#define MS_SC_UNCLASSIFIED                 ((OM_enumeration) 1)
#define MS_SC_RESTRICTED                   ((OM_enumeration) 2)
#define MS_SC_CONFIDENTIAL                 ((OM_enumeration) 3)
#define MS_SC_SECRET                       ((OM_enumeration) 4)
#define MS_SC_TOP_SECRET                   ((OM_enumeration) 5)


#endif /* XMSGA_HEADER */
```

Related Information

Books: *X/Open CAE Specification (November 1991), API to Directory Services (XDS),*
X/Open CAE Specification (November 1991), OSI-Abstract-Data Manipulation API (XOM),
OSF DCE Application Development Guide,
X/Open CAE Specification (November 1991), API to Electronic Mail (X.400).

intro

Purpose Introduction to X/OPEN OSI-Abstract-Data Manipulation (XOM) functions

Synopsis **#include <xom.h>**

Description

This **intro** reference page defines the functions of the C interface. The following table lists the relevant functions.

Service Interface Functions — intro(3xom)	
Function	**Description**
om_copy()	Copies a private object.
om_copy_value()	Copies a string between private objects.
om_create()	Creates a private object.
om_decode()	This function is not supported by the DCE XOM interface, and returns with an **OM_FUNCTION_DECLINED** error.
om_delete()	Deletes a private or service-generated object.
om_encode()	This function is not supported by the DCE XOM interface, and returns with an **OM_FUNCTION_DECLINED** error.
om_get()	Gets copies of attribute values from a private object.
om_instance()	Tests an object's class.
om_put()	Puts attribute values into a private object.
om_read()	Reads a segment of a string in a private object.
om_remove()	Removes attribute values from a private object.
om_write()	Writes a segment of a string into a private object.

As indicated in the table, the service interface comprises a number of functions whose purpose and range of capabilities are summarized as follows:

om_copy( ) This function creates an independent copy of an existing private object and all its subobjects. The copy is placed in the original's workspace, or in another specified by the XOM application.

om_copy_value( ) This function replaces an existing attribute value or inserts a new value in one private object with a copy of an existing attribute value found in another. Both values must be strings.

om_create( ) This function creates a new private object that is an instance of a particular class. The object can be initialized with the attribute values specified as initial in the class definition.

The service does not permit the API user to explicitly create instances of all classes, but rather only those indicated by a package's definition as having this property.

om_delete( ) This function deletes a service-generated public object, or makes a private object inaccessible.

om_get( ) This function creates a new public object that is an exact but independent copy of an existing private object. The client can request certain exclusions, each of which reduces the copy to a part of the original. The client can also request that values be converted from one syntax to another before they are returned.

The copy can exclude: attributes of types other than those specified, values at positions other than those specified within an attribute, the values of multivalued attributes, copies of (not handles for) subobjects, or all attribute values (revealing only an attribute's presence).

om_instance( ) This function determines whether an object is an instance of a particular class. The client can determine an object's class simply by inspection. This function is useful since it reveals that an object is an instance of a particular class, even if the object is an instance of a subclass of that class.

om_put( ) This function places or replaces in one private object copies of the attribute values of another public or private object.

The source values can be inserted before any existing destination values, before the value at a specified position in the destination attribute, or after any existing destination values. Alternatively, the source values can be substituted for any existing destination values or for the values at specified positions in the destination attribute.

om_read( ) This function reads a segment of a value of an attribute of a private object. The value must be a string. The value can first be converted from one syntax to another. The function enables the client to read an arbitrarily long value without requiring that the service place a copy of the entire value in memory.

om_remove( ) This function removes and discards particular values of an attribute of a private object. The attribute itself is removed if no values remain.

om_write( ) This function writes a segment of a value of an attribute to a private object. The value must be a string. The segment can first be converted from one syntax to another. The written segment becomes the value's last segment since any elements beyond it are discarded. The function enables the client to write an arbitrarily long value without having to place a copy of the entire value in memory.

In the C interface, the functions are realized by macros. The function prototype in the synopsis of a function's specification simply shows the client's view of the function.

The intent of the interface definition is that each function be atomic; that is, either it carries out its assigned task in full and reports success, or it fails to carry out even a part of the task and reports an exception. However, the service does not guarantee that a task is always carried out in full.

Errors

The possible error return values are listed in the function reference pages.

om_copy

Purpose Creates a new private object that is an exact but independent copy of an existing private object

Synopsis **#include <xom.h>**

OM_return_code om_copy(
OM_private_object *original*,
OM_workspace *workspace*,
OM_private_object **copy*);

Parameters

original The original that remains accessible.

workspace The workspace in which the copy is to be created. The original's class must be in a package associated with this workspace.

Description

The **om_copy**( ) function creates a new private object, the copy, that is an exact but independent copy of an existing private object, the original. The function is recursive in that copying the original also copies its subobjects.

Return Values

`OM_return_code`
Indicates whether the function succeeded and, if not, why not. If the function is successful, the value of **OM_return_code** is set to **OM_SUCCESS**; if the function fails, it has one of the error values listed in this reference page.

The exact constants for **OM_return_code** are defined in the **xom.h** header file (see the **xom.h(4xom)** reference page later in this chapter).

`copy` The new copy of the private object. This result is present if and only if the return value for **OM_return_code** is **OM_SUCCESS**.

Errors

[OM_FUNCTION_INTERRUPTED]

[OM_MEMORY_INSUFFICIENT]

[OM_NETWORK_ERROR]

[OM_NO_SUCH_CLASS]

[OM_NO_SUCH_OBJECT]

[OM_NO_SUCH_WORKSPACE]

[OM_NOT_PRIVATE]

[OM_PERMANENT_ERROR]

[OM_POINTER_INVALID]

[OM_SYSTEM_ERROR]

[OM_TEMPORARY_ERROR]

[OM_TOO_MANY_VALUES]

om_copy_value

Purpose Places or replaces a string in one private object with a copy of a string in another private object

Synopsis **#include <xom.h>**

OM_return_code om_copy_value(
  OM_private_object *source*,
  OM_type *source_type*,
  OM_value_position *source_value_position*,
  OM_private_object *destination*,
  OM_type *destination_type*,
  OM_value_position *destination_value_position*);

Parameters

source The source that remains accessible.

source_type Identifies the type of an attribute. One of the attribute values is copied.

source_value_position
The position within the above attribute of the value copied.

destination The destination that remains accessible.

destination_type
Identifies the type of the attribute. One of the attribute values is placed or replaced.

destination_value_position
The position within the above attribute of the value placed or replaced. If the value position exceeds the number of values present in the *destination* attribute, the parameter is taken to be equal to that number.

Description

The **om_copy_value( )** function places or replaces an attribute value in one private object (the destination) with a copy of an attribute value in another private object (the source). The source value is a string. The copy's syntax is that of the original.

Return Values

`OM_return_code`

Indicates whether the function succeeded and, if not, why not. If the function is successful, the value of **OM_return_code** is set to **OM_SUCCESS**; if the function fails, it has one of the error values listed in this reference page.

The exact constants for **OM_return_code** are defined in the **xom.h** header file (see the **xom.h(4xom)** reference page later in this chapter).

Errors

[**OM_FUNCTION_DECLINED**]

[**OM_FUNCTION_INTERRUPTED**]

[**OM_MEMORY_INSUFFICIENT**]

[**OM_NETWORK_ERROR**]

[**OM_NO_SUCH_OBJECT**]

[**OM_NO_SUCH_TYPE**]

[**OM_NOT_PRESENT**]

[**OM_NOT_PRIVATE**]

[**OM_PERMANENT_ERROR**]

[**OM_POINTER_INVALID**]

[**OM_SYSTEM_ERROR**]

[**OM_TEMPORARY_ERROR**]

[**OM_WRONG_VALUE_LENGTH**]

[**OM_WRONG_VALUE_SYNTAX**]

[**OM_WRONG_VALUE_TYPE**]

om_create

Purpose

Creates a new private object that is an instance of a particular class

Synopsis

#include <xom.h>

OM_return_code om_create(
    OM_object_identifier *class*,
    OM_boolean *initialize*,
    OM_workspace *workspace*,
    OM_private_object **object*);

Parameters

class Identifies the class of the object to be created. The specified class shall be concrete.

initialize Determines whether the object created is initialized as specified in the definition of its class. If this parameter is **OM_TRUE**, the object is made to comprise the attribute values specified as initial values in the tabular definitions of the object's class and its superclasses. If this parameter is **OM_FALSE**, the object is made to comprise the **OM_CLASS** attribute alone.

workspace
The workspace in which the object is created. The specified class is in a package associated with this workspace.

Description

The **om_create**( ) function creates a new private object that is an instance of a particular class.

Notes

By subsequently adding new values to the object and replacing and removing existing values, the client can create all conceivable instances of the object's class.

Return Values

`OM_return_code`
Indicates whether the function succeeded and, if not, why not. If the function is successful, the value of **OM_return_code** is set to **OM_SUCCESS**; if the function fails, it has one of the error values listed in this reference page.

`object` The created object. This result is present if and only if the return value for **OM_return_code** is **OM_SUCCESS**.

The exact constants for **OM_return_code** are defined in the **xom.h** header file (see the **xom.h(4xom)** reference page later in this chapter).

Errors

[**OM_FUNCTION_DECLINED**]

[**OM_FUNCTION_INTERRUPTED**]

[**OM_MEMORY_INSUFFICIENT**]

[**OM_NETWORK_ERROR**]

[**OM_NO_SUCH_CLASS**]

[**OM_NO_SUCH_WORKSPACE**]

[**OM_NOT_CONCRETE**]

[**OM_PERMANENT_ERROR**]

[**OM_POINTER_INVALID**]

[**OM_SYSTEM_ERROR**]

[**OM_TEMPORARY_ERROR**]

om_delete

Purpose

Deletes a private or service-generated object

Synopsis

#include <xom.h>

OM_return_code om_delete(
OM_object *subject***);**

Parameters

subject The object to be deleted.

Description

The **om_delete( )** function deletes a service-generated public object, or makes a private object inaccessible. It is not intended for use on client-generated public objects.

If applied to a service-generated public object, the function deletes the object and releases any resources associated with the object, including the space occupied by descriptors and attribute values. The function is applied recursively to any public subobjects. This does not affect any private subobjects.

If applied to a private object, the function makes the object inaccessible. Any existing object handles for the object are invalidated. The function is applied recursively to any private subobjects.

Return Values

`OM_return_code`
Indicates whether the function succeeded and, if not, why not. If the function is successful, the value of **OM_return_code** is set to **OM_SUCCESS**; if the function fails, it has one of the error values listed in this reference page.

Errors

[OM_FUNCTION_INTERRUPTED]

[OM_MEMORY_INSUFFICIENT]

[OM_NETWORK_ERROR]

[OM_NO_SUCH_OBJECT]

[OM_NO_SUCH_SYNTAX]

[OM_NO_SUCH_TYPE]

[OM_NOT_THE_SERVICES]

[OM_PERMANENT_ERROR]

[OM_POINTER_INVALID]

[OM_SYSTEM_ERROR]

[OM_TEMPORARY_ERROR]

om_get

Purpose Creates a public copy of all or particular parts of a private object

Synopsis **#include <xom.h>**

OM_return_code om_get(
OM_private_object *original*,
OM_exclusions *exclusions*,
OM_type_list *included_types*,
OM_boolean *local_strings*,
OM_value_position *initial_value*,
OM_value_position *limiting_value*,
OM_public_object **copy*,
OM_value_position **total_number*);

Parameters

original The original that remains accessible.

exclusions

Explicit requests for zero or more exclusions, each of which reduces the copy to a prescribed portion of the original. The exclusions apply to the attributes of the object, but not to those of its subobjects.

Apart from **OM_NO_EXCLUSIONS**, each value is chosen from the following list. When multiple exclusions are specified, each is applied in the order in which it is displayed in the list with lower numbered exclusions having precedence over higher numbered exclusions. If, after the application of an exclusion, that portion of the object is not returned, no further exclusions need be applied to that portion.

- **OM_EXCLUDE_ALL_BUT_THESE_TYPES**
  The copy includes descriptors comprising only attributes of specified types.

  Note that this exclusion provides a means for determining the values of specified attributes, as well as the syntaxes of those values.

- **OM_EXCLUDE_MULTIPLES**
  The copy includes a single descriptor for each attribute that has two or more values, rather than one descriptor for each value.

None of these descriptors contains an attribute value, and the **OM_S_NO_VALUE** bit of the syntax component is set.

If the attribute has values of two or more syntaxes, the descriptor identifies one of those syntaxes; however, the syntax identified is not specified.

Note that this exclusion provides a means for discerning the presence of multivalued attributes without simultaneously obtaining their values.

- **OM_EXCLUDE_ALL_BUT_THESE_VALUES**
  The copy includes descriptors comprising only values at specified positions within an attribute.

  Note that when this exclusion is used in conjunction with the **OM_EXCLUDE_ALL_BUT_THESE_TYPES** exclusion, it provides a means for determining the values of a specified attribute, as well as the syntaxes of those values, one or more but not all attributes at a time.

- **OM_EXCLUDE_VALUES**
  The copy includes a single descriptor for each attribute value, but the descriptor does not contain the value, and the **OM_S_NO_VALUE** bit of the syntax component is set.

  Note that this exclusion provides a means for determining an object's composition; that is, the type and syntax of each of its attribute values.

- **OM_EXCLUDE_SUBOBJECTS**
  The copy includes, for each value whose syntax is **OM_S_OBJECT**, a descriptor containing an object handle for the original private subobject, rather than a public copy of it. This handle makes that subobject accessible for use in subsequent function calls.

  Note that this exclusion provides a means for examining an object one ''level'' at a time.

- **OM_EXCLUDE_DESCRIPTORS**
  When this exclusion is specified, no descriptors are returned and the copy result is not present. The *total_number* parameter reflects the number of descriptors that would be returned by applying the other inclusion and exclusion specifications.

  Note that this exclusion provides an attribute analysis capability. For instance, the total number of values in a multivalued attribute can be determined by specifying an inclusion of the specific attribute type, and exclusions of **OM_EXCLUDE_DESCRIPTORS**, **OM_EXCLUDE_SUBOBJECTS**, and **OM_EXCLUDE_ALL_BUT_THESE_TYPES**.

The **OM_EXCLUDE_ALL_BUT_THESE_VALUES** exclusion affects the choice of descriptors, while the **OM_EXCLUDE_VALUES** exclusion affects the composition of descriptors.

included_types
This parameter is present if and only if the **OM_EXCLUDE_ALL_BUT_THESE_TYPES** exclusion is requested; it identifies the types of the attributes to be included in the copy (provided that they are displayed in the original).

local_strings
This Boolean parameter is ignored because the functionality is not supported.

initial_value
This parameter is present if and only if the **OM_EXCLUDE_ALL_BUT_THESE_VALUES** exclusion is requested; it specifies the position within each attribute of the first value to be included in the copy.

If it is **OM_ALL_VALUES** or exceeds the number of values present in an attribute, the parameter is taken to be equal to that number.

limiting_value
This parameter is present if and only if the **OM_EXCLUDE_ALL_BUT_THESE_VALUES** exclusion is requested; it specifies the position within each attribute one beyond that of the last value to be included in the copy. If this parameter is not greater than the *initial_value* parameter, no values are included (and no descriptors are returned).

If it is **OM_ALL_VALUES** or exceeds the number of values present in an attribute, the parameter is taken to be equal to that number.

Description

The **om_get( )** function creates a new public object, the *copy* that is an exact but independent copy of an existing private object, the *original* parameter. The client can request certain exclusions, each of which reduces the copy to a part of the original.

One exclusion is always requested implicitly. For each attribute value in the original that is a string whose length exceeds an implementation-defined number, the *copy* parameter includes a descriptor that omits the elements (but not the length) of the string. The *elements* component of the *string* component in the descriptor's *value* component is **OM_ELEMENTS_UNSPECIFIED**, and the **OM_S_LONG_STRING** bit of the *syntax* component is set to **OM_TRUE**.

Note that the client can access long values by means of **om_read( )**.

Return Values

`OM_return_code`
: Indicates whether the function succeeded and, if not, why not. If the function is successful, the value of **OM_return_code** is set to **OM_SUCCESS**; if the function fails, it has one of the error values listed in this reference page.

  The exact constants for **OM_return_code** are defined in the **xom.h** header file (see the **xom.h(4xom)** reference page later in this chapter).

`copy`
: The *copy* parameter is only present if the return value from **OM_return_code** is **OM_SUCCESS** and the **OM_EXCLUDE_DESCRIPTORS** exclusion is not specified.

  The space occupied by the public object and every attribute value that is a string is service provided. If the client alters any part of that space, the effect upon the service's subsequent behavior is unspecified.

`total_number`
: The number of attribute descriptors returned in the public object, but not in any of its subobjects, based on the inclusion and exclusion parameters specified. If the **OM_EXCLUDE_DESCRIPTORS** exclusion is specified, no *copy* result is returned and the *total_number* result reflects the actual number of attribute descriptors that would be returned based on the remaining inclusion and exclusion values.

Note that the total includes only the attribute descriptors in the *copy* parameter. It excludes the special descriptor signaling the end of a public object.

Errors

[**OM_FUNCTION_INTERRUPTED**]

[**OM_MEMORY_INSUFFICIENT**]

[**OM_NETWORK_ERROR**]

[**OM_NO_SUCH_EXCLUSION**]

[**OM_NO_SUCH_OBJECT**]

[**OM_NO_SUCH_TYPE**]

[**OM_NOT_PRIVATE**]

[**OM_PERMANENT_ERROR**]

[**OM_POINTER_INVALID**]

[**OM_SYSTEM_ERROR**]

[**OM_TEMPORARY_ERROR**]

[**OM_WRONG_VALUE_SYNTAX**]

[**OM_WRONG_VALUE_TYPE**]

om_instance

Purpose Determines whether an object is an instance of a particular class or any of its subclasses

Synopsis **#include <xom.h>**

OM_return_code om_instance(
OM_object *subject*,
OM_object_identifier *class*,
OM_boolean **instance*);

Parameters

subject The subject that remains accessible.

class Identifies the class in question.

Description

The **om_instance**( ) function determines whether a service-generated public or private object, the subject, is an instance of a particular class or any of its subclasses.

Notes The client can determine an object's class, **C**, by simply inspecting the object (using programming language constructs if the object is public or **om_get**( ) if it is private). This function is useful in that it reveals that an object is an instance of the specified class, even if **C** is a subclass of that class.

Return Values

`OM_return_code`
Indicates whether the function succeeded and, if not, why not. If the function is successful, the value of **OM_return_code** is set to **OM_SUCCESS**; if the function fails, it has one of the error values listed in this reference page.

The exact constants for **OM_return_code** are defined in the **xom.h** header file (see the **xom.h(4xom)** reference page later in this chapter).

`instance`

Indicates whether the subject is an instance of the specified class or any of its subclasses. This result is present if and only if the value of the **OM_return_code** is set to **OM_SUCCESS**.

Errors

[**OM_FUNCTION_INTERRUPTED**]

[**OM_MEMORY_INSUFFICIENT**]

[**OM_NETWORK_ERROR**]

[**OM_NO_SUCH_CLASS**]

[**OM_NO_SUCH_OBJECT**]

[**OM_NO_SUCH_SYNTAX**]

[**OM_NOT_THE_SERVICES**]

[**OM_PERMANENT_ERROR**]

[**OM_POINTER_INVALID**]

[**OM_SYSTEM_ERROR**]

[**OM_TEMPORARY_ERROR**]

om_put

Purpose Places or replaces in one private object copies of the attribute values of another public or private object

Synopsis **#include <xom.h>**

OM_return_code om_put(
  OM_private_object *destination*,
  OM_modification *modification*,
  OM_object *source*,
  OM_type_list *included_types*,
  OM_value_position *initial_value*,
  OM_value_position *limiting_value*);

Parameters

destination
The destination that remains accessible. The destination's class is unaffected.

modification
The nature of the requested modification. The modification determines how **om_put()** uses the attribute values in the source to modify the object. In all cases, for each attribute present in the source, copies of its values are placed in the object's destination attribute of the same type. The data value is chosen from among the following:

- **OM_INSERT_AT_BEGINNING**
  The source values are inserted before any existing destination values. (The latter are retained.)
- **OM_INSERT_AT_CERTAIN_POINT**
  The source values are inserted before the value at a specified position in the destination attribute. (The latter are retained.)
- **OM_INSERT_AT_END**
  The source values are inserted after any existing destination values. (The latter are retained.)
- **OM_REPLACE_ALL**
  The source values are placed in the *destination* attribute. The existing destination values, if any, are discarded.

- **OM_REPLACE_CERTAIN_VALUES**
  The source values are substituted for the values at specified positions in the destination attribute. (The latter are discarded.)

source The source that remains accessible. The source's class is ignored. However, the attributes being copied from the source must be compatible with the destination's class definition.

included_types
If present, this parameter identifies the types of the attributes to be included in the destination (provided that they are displayed in the source); otherwise, all attributes are to be included.

initial_value
This parameter is present if and only if the *modification* parameter is **OM_INSERT_AT_CERTAIN_POINT** or **OM_REPLACE_CERTAIN_VALUES**. It specifies the position within each destination attribute at which source values are inserted, or of the first value replaced, respectively.

If it is **OM_ALL_VALUES**, or exceeds the number of values present in a destination attribute, the parameter is taken to be equal to that number.

limiting_value
Present if and only if the *modification* parameter is **OM_REPLACE_CERTAIN_VALUES**. It specifies the position within each destination attribute one beyond that of the last value replaced. If this parameter is present, it must be greater than the *initial_value* parameter.

If the *limiting_value* parameter is **OM_ALL_VALUES** or exceeds the number of values present in a destination attribute, the parameter is taken to be equal to that number.

Description

The **om_put()** function places or replaces in one private object (that is, the destination) copies of the attribute values of another public or private object (that is, the source). The client can specify that the source's values replace all or particular values in the destination, or are inserted at a particular position within each attribute. All string values being copied that are in the local representation are first converted into the nonlocal representation for that syntax (which may entail the loss of some information).

Return Values

`OM_return_code`

Indicates whether the function succeeded and, if not, why not. If the function is successful, the value of **OM_return_code** is set to **OM_SUCCESS**; if the function fails, it has one of the error values listed in this reference page.

The exact constants for **OM_return_code** are defined in the **xom.h** header file (see the **xom.h(4xom)** reference page later in this chapter).

Errors

[OM_FUNCTION_DECLINED]

[OM_FUNCTION_INTERRUPTED]

[OM_MEMORY_INSUFFICIENT]

[OM_NETWORK_ERROR]

[OM_NO_SUCH_CLASS]

[OM_NO_SUCH_MODIFICATION]

[OM_NO_SUCH_OBJECT]

[OM_NO_SUCH_SYNTAX]

[OM_NO_SUCH_TYPE]

[OM_NOT_CONCRETE]

[OM_NOT_PRESENT]

[OM_NOT_PRIVATE]

[OM_PERMANENT_ERROR]

[OM_POINTER_INVALID]

[OM_SYSTEM_ERROR]

[OM_TEMPORARY_ERROR]

[OM_TOO_MANY_VALUES]

[OM_VALUES_NOT_ADJACENT]

[OM_WRONG_VALUE_LENGTH]

[OM_WRONG_VALUE_MAKEUP]

[OM_WRONG_VALUE_NUMBER]

[OM_WRONG_VALUE_POSITION]

[OM_WRONG_VALUE_SYNTAX]

[OM_WRONG_VALUE_TYPE]

om_read

Purpose Reads a segment of a string in a private object

Synopsis **#include <xom.h>**

OM_return_code om_read(
  OM_private_object ***subject*,**
  OM_type ***type*,**
  OM_value_position ***value_position*,**
  OM_boolean ***local_string*,**
  OM_string_length ***string_offset*,**
  OM_string ***elements*);**

Parameters

subject The subject that remains accessible.

type Identifies the type of the attribute, one of whose values is read.

value_position
The position within the above attribute of the value read.

local_string
This Boolean parameter is ignored because the functionality is not supported.

string_offset
The offset, in octets, of the start of the string segment to be read. If it exceeds the total length of the string, the parameter is equal to the string length.

elements The space the client provides for the segment to be read. The string's contents are initially unspecified. The string's length is initially the number of octets required to contain the segment that the function is to read.

The service modifies this parameter. The string's elements become the elements actually read. The string's length becomes the number of octets required to hold the segment actually read. This can be less than the initial length if the segment is the last in a long string.

Description

The **om_read( )** function reads a segment of an attribute value in a private object, namely the subject.

The segment returned is a segment of the string value that is returned if the complete value is read in a single call.

Note that this function enables the client to read an arbitrarily long value without requiring that the service place a copy of the entire value in memory.

Return Values

`OM_return_code`
: Indicates whether the function succeeded and, if not, why not. If the function is successful, the value of **OM_return_code** is set to **OM_SUCCESS**; if the function fails, it has one of the error values listed in this reference page.

  The exact constants for **OM_return_code** are defined in the **xom.h** header file (see the **xom.h(4xom)** reference page later in this chapter).

`string_offset`
: The offset, in octets, of the start of the next string segment to be read, or 0 (zero) if the value's final segment is read. The result is present if, and only if, the **OM_return_code** is **OM_SUCCESS**. The value returned can be used as the input *string_offset* parameter in the next call of this function. This enables sequential reading of a value of a long string.

Errors

[**OM_FUNCTION_INTERRUPTED**]

[**OM_MEMORY_INSUFFICIENT**]

[**OM_NETWORK_ERROR**]

[**OM_NO_SUCH_OBJECT**]

[**OM_NO_SUCH_TYPE**]

[**OM_NOT_PRESENT**]

[**OM_NOT_PRIVATE**]

[**OM_PERMANENT_ERROR**]

[**OM_POINTER_INVALID**]

[OM_SYSTEM_ERROR]

[OM_TEMPORARY_ERROR]

[OM_WRONG_VALUE_SYNTAX]

om_remove

Purpose Removes and discards values of an attribute of a private object

Synopsis **#include <xom.h>**

OM_return_code om_remove(
OM_private_object *subject*,
OM_type *type*,
OM_value_position *initial_value*,
OM_value_position *limiting_value*);

Parameters

subject The subject that remains accessible. The subject's class is unaffected.

type Identifies the type of the attribute some of whose values are removed. The type is not **OM_CLASS**.

initial_value
The position within the above attribute of the first value removed.

If it is **OM_ALL_VALUES**, or exceeds the number of values present in the attribute, the parameter is taken to be equal to that number.

limiting_value
The position within the attribute one beyond that of the last value removed. If this parameter is not greater than the *initial_value* parameter, no values are removed.

If it is **OM_ALL_VALUES**, or exceeds the number of values present in an attribute, the parameter is taken to be equal to that number.

Description

The **om_remove()** function removes and discards particular values of an attribute of a private object, the subject. If no values remain, the attribute itself is also removed. If the value is a subobject, the value is first removed and then **om_delete()** is applied to it, thus destroying the object.

Return Values

`OM_return_code`
Indicates whether the function succeeded and, if not, why not. If the function is successful, the value of **OM_return_code** is set to **OM_SUCCESS**; if the function fails, it has one of the error values listed in this reference page.

Errors

[**OM_FUNCTION_DECLINED**]

[**OM_FUNCTION_INTERRUPTED**]

[**OM_MEMORY_INSUFFICIENT**]

[**OM_NETWORK_ERROR**]

[**OM_NO_SUCH_OBJECT**]

[**OM_NO_SUCH_TYPE**]

[**OM_NOT_PRIVATE**]

[**OM_PERMANENT_ERROR**]

[**OM_POINTER_INVALID**]

[**OM_SYSTEM_ERROR**]

[**OM_TEMPORARY_ERROR**]

om_write

Purpose Writes a segment of a string into a private object

Synopsis **#include <xom.h>**

```
OM_return_code om_write(
        OM_private_object subject,
        OM_type type,
        OM_value_position value_position,
        OM_syntax syntax,
        OM_string_length *string_offset,
        OM_string elements);
```

Parameters

subject The subject that remains accessible.

type Identifies the type of the attribute, one of whose values is written.

value_position
The position within the above attribute of the value to be written. The value position can neither be negative nor exceed the number of values present. If it equals the number of values present, the segment is inserted into the attribute as a new value.

syntax If the value being written is not already present in the subject, this identifies the syntax that the value has. It must be a permissible syntax for the attribute of which this is a value. If the value being written is already present in the subject, then that value's syntax is preserved and this parameter is ignored.

string_offset
The offset, in octets, of the start of the string segment to be written. If it exceeds the current length of the string value being written, the parameter is taken to be equal to that current length.

elements The string segment to be written. A copy of this segment occupies a position within the string value being written, starting at the offset given by the *string_offset* input parameter. Any values already at or beyond this offset are discarded.

Description

The **om_write( )** function writes a segment of an attribute value in a private object, the *subject* parameter.

The segment supplied is a segment of the string value that is supplied if the complete value is written in a single call.

The written segment is made the value's last. The function discards any values whose offset equals or exceeds the *string_offset* result. If the value being written is in the local representation, it is converted to the nonlocal representation (which may entail the loss of information and which may yield a different number of elements than that provided).

Note that this function enables the client to write an arbitrarily long value without having to place a copy of the entire value in memory.

Return Values

`OM_return_code`
: Indicates whether the function succeeded and, if not, why not. If the function is successful, the value of **OM_return_code** is set to **OM_SUCCESS**, whereas if the function fails, it has one of the values listed under **ERRORS**.

  The exact constants for **OM_return_code** are defined in the **xom.h** header file (see the **xom.h(4xom)** reference page later in this chapter).

`string_offset`
: The offset, in octets, after the last string segment written. This result is present if, and only if, the **OM_return_code** result is **OM_SUCCESS**. The value returned in *string_offset* can be used as the input *string_offset* parameter the next time this function is called. This enables sequential writing of the value of a long string.

Errors

[OM_FUNCTION_DECLINED]

[OM_FUNCTION_INTERRUPTED]

[OM_MEMORY_INSUFFICIENT]

[OM_NETWORK_ERROR]

[OM_NO_SUCH_OBJECT]

[OM_NO_SUCH_SYNTAX]

[OM_NO_SUCH_TYPE]

[OM_NOT_PRESENT]

[OM_NOT_PRIVATE]

[OM_PERMANENT_ERROR]

[OM_POINTER_INVALID]

[OM_SYSTEM_ERROR]

[OM_TEMPORARY_ERROR]

[OM_WRONG_VALUE_LENGTH]

[OM_WRONG_VALUE_MAKEUP]

[OM_WRONG_VALUE_POSITION]

[OM_WRONG_VALUE_SYNTAX]

xom.h

Purpose Header file for XOM

Synopsis **#include <xom.h>**

Description

The declarations, as assembled here, constitute the contents of a header file made accessible to client programmers. The header file includes by reference a second header file (**xomi.h**) comprising the declarations defining the C workspace interface. The **xomi.h** header file and the workspace interface are only used internally by the service interface, and are not visible to the client programmer.

```
#ifndef XOM_HEADER
#define XOM_HEADER


/* BEGIN SERVICE INTERFACE */

/* INTERMEDIATE DATA TYPES */

typedef  int             OM_sint;
typedef  short           OM_sint16;
typedef  long int        OM_sint32;
typedef  unsigned        OM_uint;
typedef  unsigned short  OM_uint16;
typedef  long unsigned   OM_uint32;

/* PRIMARY DATA TYPES */

/* Boolean */

typedef OM_uint32 OM_boolean;

/* Element Position */

typedef OM_uint32 OM_element_position;

/* String Length */

typedef OM_uint32 OM_string_length;
```

```
/* Enumeration */

typedef OM_sint32 OM_enumeration;

/* Exclusions */

typedef OM_uint OM_exclusions;

/* Integer */

typedef OM_sint32 OM_integer;

/* Modification */

typedef OM_uint OM_modification;

/* Object */

typedef struct OM_descriptor_struct *OM_object;

/* String */

typedef struct {
        OM_string_length      length;
        void   *elements;
} OM_string;

#define OM_STRING(string)         \
         { (OM_string_length)(sizeof(string)-1), string }

/* Workspace */

typedef void *OM_workspace;

/* SECONDARY DATA TYPES */

/* Object Identifier */

typedef OM_string OM_object_identifier;

/* Private Object */

typedef OM_object OM_private_object;
```

```
/* Public Object */

typedef OM_object OM_public_object;

/* Return Code */

typedef OM_uint OM_return_code;

/* Syntax */

typedef OM_uint16 OM_syntax;

/* Type */

typedef OM_uint16 OM_type;

/* Type List */

typedef OM_type *OM_type_list;

/* Value */

typedef struct {
        OM_uint32       padding;
        OM_object       object;
} OM_padded_object;

typedef union OM_value_union {
        OM_string       string;
        OM_boolean      boolean;
        OM_enumeration  enumeration;
        OM_integer      integer;
        OM_padded_object        object;
} OM_value;

/* Value Length */

typedef OM_uint32 OM_value_length;

/* Value Position */

typedef OM_uint32 OM_value_position;

/* TERTIARY DATA TYPES */
```

```
/* Descriptor */

typedef struct OM_descriptor_struct {
        OM_type                    type;
        OM_syntax                  syntax;
        union OM_value_union       value;
} OM_descriptor;


/* SYMBOLIC CONSTANTS */

/* Boolean */

#define OM_FALSE        ((OM_boolean) 0)
#define OM_TRUE         ((OM_boolean) 1)

/* Element Position */

#define OM_LENGTH_UNSPECIFIED   ((OM_string_length) 0xFFFFFFFF)

/* Exclusions */

#define OM_NO_EXCLUSIONS                    ((OM_exclusions) 0)
#define OM_EXCLUDE_ALL_BUT_THESE_TYPES      ((OM_exclusions) 1)
#define OM_EXCLUDE_ALL_BUT_THESE_VALUES     ((OM_exclusions) 2)
#define OM_EXCLUDE_MULTIPLES                ((OM_exclusions) 4)
#define OM_EXCLUDE_SUBOBJECTS               ((OM_exclusions) 8)
#define OM_EXCLUDE_VALUES                   ((OM_exclusions) 16)
#define OM_EXCLUDE_DESCRIPTORS              ((OM_exclusions) 32)

/* Modification */

#define OM_INSERT_AT_BEGINNING              ((OM_modification) 1)
#define OM_INSERT_AT_CERTAIN_POINT          ((OM_modification) 2)
#define OM_INSERT_AT_END                    ((OM_modification) 3)
#define OM_REPLACE_ALL                      ((OM_modification) 4)
#define OM_REPLACE_CERTAIN_VALUES           ((OM_modification) 5)

/* Object Identifiers */

/*  NOTE: These macros rely on the ## token-pasting operator of
 *  ANSI C. On many pre-ANSI compilers the same effect can be
 *  obtained by replacing ## with /**/
```

```
/* Private macro to calculate length of an object identifier
 */
#define OMP_LENGTH(oid_string)  (sizeof(OMP_O_##oid_string)-1)


/* Macro to initialize the syntax and value of an object identifier
 */
#define OM_OID_DESC(type, oid_name)                        \
        { (type), OM_S_OBJECT_IDENTIFIER_STRING,            \
        { { OMP_LENGTH(oid_name) , OMP_D_##oid_name } } }


/* Macro to mark the end of a client-allocated public object
 */
#define OM_NULL_DESCRIPTOR       \
  { OM_NO_MORE_TYPES, OM_S_NO_MORE_SYNTAXES, \
  { { 0, OM_ELEMENTS_UNSPECIFIED } } }


/* Macro to make class constants available within a compilation unit
 */
#define OM_IMPORT(class_name)                              \
                extern char OMP_D_##class_name [];          \
                extern OM_string class_name;


/* Macro to allocate memory for class constants
/* within a compilation unit
 */
#define OM_EXPORT(class_name)                              \
        char OMP_D_##class_name[] = OMP_O_##class_name ;    \
        OM_string class_name =                              \
            { OMP_LENGTH(class_name), OMP_D_##class_name } ;


/* Constant for the OM package
 */
/* { joint-iso-ccitt(2) mhs-motis(6) group(6) white(1)
      api(2) om(4) } */

#define OMP_O_OM_OM              "\x56\x06\x01\x02\x04"

/* Constant for the Encoding class
 */
```

```
#define OMP_O_OM_C_ENCODING      "\x56\x06\x01\x02\x04\x01"

/* Constant for the External class
 */
#define OMP_O_OM_C_EXTERNAL      "\x56\x06\x01\x02\x04\x02"

/* Constant for the Object class
 */
#define OMP_O_OM_C_OBJECT        "\x56\x06\x01\x02\x04\x03"

/* Constant for the BER Object Identifier
 */
#define OMP_O_OM_BER             "\x51\x01"

/* Constant for the Canonical-BER Object Identifier
 */
#define OMP_O_OM_CANONICAL_BER  "\x56\x06\x01\x02\x04\x04"

/* Return Code */

#define OM_SUCCESS                      ((OM_return_code) 0)
#define OM_ENCODING_INVALID             ((OM_return_code) 1)
#define OM_FUNCTION_DECLINED            ((OM_return_code) 2)
#define OM_FUNCTION_INTERRUPTED         ((OM_return_code) 3)
#define OM_MEMORY_INSUFFICIENT          ((OM_return_code) 4)
#define OM_NETWORK_ERROR                ((OM_return_code) 5)
#define OM_NO_SUCH_CLASS                ((OM_return_code) 6)
#define OM_NO_SUCH_EXCLUSION            ((OM_return_code) 7)
#define OM_NO_SUCH_MODIFICATION         ((OM_return_code) 8)
#define OM_NO_SUCH_OBJECT               ((OM_return_code) 9)
#define OM_NO_SUCH_RULES                ((OM_return_code) 10)
#define OM_NO_SUCH_SYNTAX               ((OM_return_code) 11)
#define OM_NO_SUCH_TYPE                 ((OM_return_code) 12)
#define OM_NO_SUCH_WORKSPACE            ((OM_return_code) 13)
#define OM_NOT_AN_ENCODING              ((OM_return_code) 14)
#define OM_NOT_CONCRETE                 ((OM_return_code) 15)
#define OM_NOT_PRESENT                  ((OM_return_code) 16)
#define OM_NOT_PRIVATE                  ((OM_return_code) 17)
#define OM_NOT_THE_SERVICES             ((OM_return_code) 18)
#define OM_PERMANENT_ERROR              ((OM_return_code) 19)
#define OM_POINTER_INVALID              ((OM_return_code) 20)
#define OM_SYSTEM_ERROR                 ((OM_return_code) 21)
#define OM_TEMPORARY_ERROR              ((OM_return_code) 22)
#define OM_TOO_MANY_VALUES              ((OM_return_code) 23)
```

```
#define OM_VALUES_NOT_ADJACENT        ((OM_return_code) 24)
#define OM_WRONG_VALUE_LENGTH         ((OM_return_code) 25)
#define OM_WRONG_VALUE_MAKEUP         ((OM_return_code) 26)
#define OM_WRONG_VALUE_NUMBER         ((OM_return_code) 27)
#define OM_WRONG_VALUE_POSITION       ((OM_return_code) 28)
#define OM_WRONG_VALUE_SYNTAX         ((OM_return_code) 29)
#define OM_WRONG_VALUE_TYPE           ((OM_return_code) 30)

/* String (Elements component) */

#define OM_ELEMENTS_UNSPECIFIED       ((void *) 0)

/* Syntax */

#define OM_S_NO_MORE_SYNTAXES          ((OM_syntax) 0)
#define OM_S_BIT_STRING                ((OM_syntax) 3)
#define OM_S_BOOLEAN                   ((OM_syntax) 1)
#define OM_S_ENCODING_STRING           ((OM_syntax) 8)
#define OM_S_ENUMERATION               ((OM_syntax) 10)
#define OM_S_GENERAL_STRING            ((OM_syntax) 27)
#define OM_S_GENERALISED_TIME_STRING   ((OM_syntax) 24)
#define OM_S_GRAPHIC_STRING            ((OM_syntax) 25)
#define OM_S_IA5_STRING                ((OM_syntax) 22)
#define OM_S_INTEGER                   ((OM_syntax) 2)
#define OM_S_NULL                      ((OM_syntax) 5)
#define OM_S_NUMERIC_STRING            ((OM_syntax) 18)
#define OM_S_OBJECT                    ((OM_syntax) 127)
#define OM_S_OBJECT_DESCRIPTOR_STRING ((OM_syntax) 7)
#define OM_S_OBJECT_IDENTIFIER_STRING ((OM_syntax) 6)
#define OM_S_OCTET_STRING              ((OM_syntax) 4)
#define OM_S_PRINTABLE_STRING          ((OM_syntax) 19)
#define OM_S_TELETEX_STRING            ((OM_syntax) 20)
#define OM_S_UTC_TIME_STRING           ((OM_syntax) 23)
#define OM_S_VIDEOTEX_STRING           ((OM_syntax) 21)
#define OM_S_VISIBLE_STRING            ((OM_syntax) 26)

#define OM_S_LONG_STRING               ((OM_syntax) 0x8000)
#define OM_S_NO_VALUE                  ((OM_syntax) 0x4000)
#define OM_S_LOCAL_STRING              ((OM_syntax) 0x2000)
#define OM_S_SERVICE_GENERATED         ((OM_syntax) 0x1000)
#define OM_S_PRIVATE                   ((OM_syntax) 0x0800)
#define OM_S_SYNTAX                    ((OM_syntax) 0x03FF)

/* Type */
```

```
#define OM_NO_MORE_TYPES              ((OM_type) 0)
#define OM_ARBITRARY_ENCODING         ((OM_type) 1)
#define OM_ASN1_ENCODING              ((OM_type) 2)
#define OM_CLASS                      ((OM_type) 3)
#define OM_DATA_VALUE_DESCRIPTOR      ((OM_type) 4)
#define OM_DIRECT_REFERENCE           ((OM_type) 5)
#define OM_INDIRECT_REFERENCE         ((OM_type) 6)
#define OM_OBJECT_CLASS               ((OM_type) 7)
#define OM_OBJECT_ENCODING            ((OM_type) 8)
#define OM_OCTET_ALIGNED_ENCODING     ((OM_type) 9)
#define OM_PRIVATE_OBJECT             ((OM_type) 10)
#define OM_RULES                      ((OM_type) 11)

/* Value Position */

#define OM_ALL_VALUES         ((OM_value_position) 0xFFFFFFFF)

/* WORKSPACE INTERFACE */

#include <xomi.h>          /* Only for internal use by interface */

/* END SERVICE INTERFACE */
#endif   /* XOM_HEADER */
```

Related Information

Books: *X/Open CAE Specification (November 1991), API to Directory Services (XDS),*
X/Open CAE Specification (November 1991), OSI-Abstract-Data Manipulation API (XOM),
OSF DCE Application Development Guide.

Chapter 4

DCE Distributed Time Service

intro

Purpose Introduction to DCE Distributed Time Service (DTS)

Description

The DCE Distributed Time Service programming routines can obtain timestamps that are based on Coordinated Universal Time (UTC), translate between different timestamp formats, and perform calculations on timestamps. Applications can call the DTS routines from server or clerk systems and use the timestamps that DTS supplies to determine event sequencing, duration, and scheduling.

The DTS routines can perform the following basic functions:

- Retrieve the current (UTC-based) time from DTS.
- Convert binary timestamps expressed in the **utc** time structure to or from **tm** structure components.
- Convert the binary timestamps expressed in the **utc** time structure to or from **timespec** structure components.
- Convert the binary timestamps expressed in the **utc** time structure to or from ASCII strings.
- Compare two binary time values.
- Calculate binary time values.
- Obtain time zone information.

DTS can convert between several types of binary time structures that are based on different calendars and time unit measurements. DTS uses UTC-based time structures, and can convert other types of time structures to its own presentation of UTC-based time.

The following illustration categorizes the DTS portable interface routines by function.

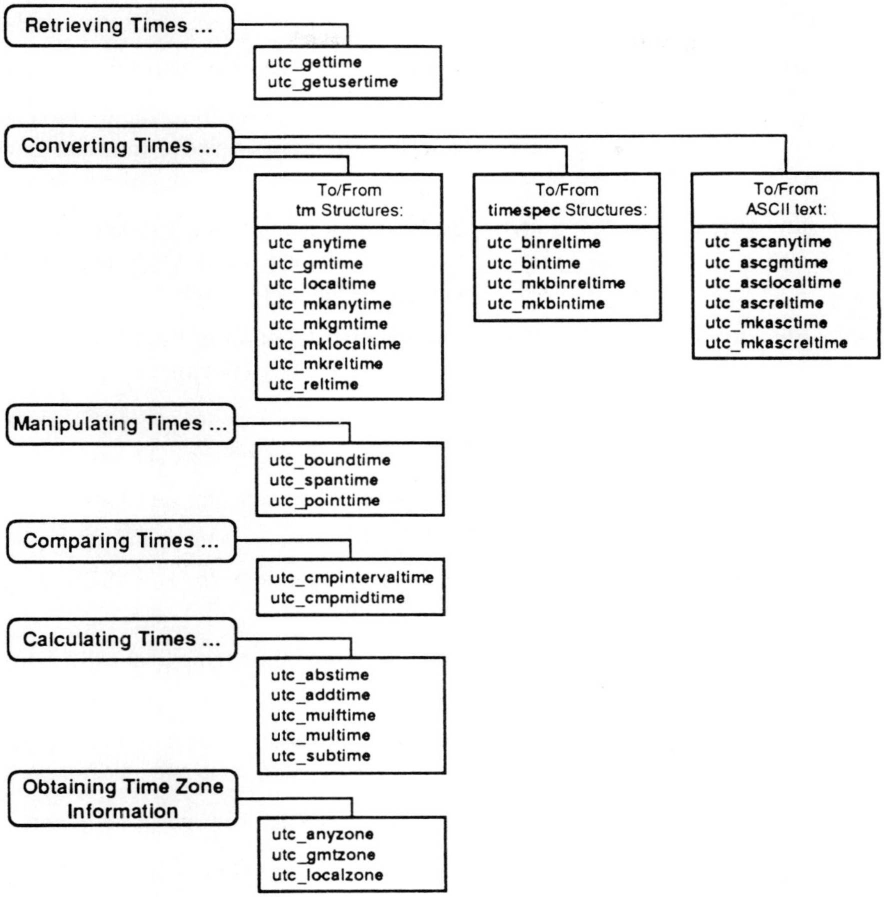
Retrieving Times ...
utc_gettime
utc_getusertime
Converting Times ...
To/From tm Structures:
utc_anytime
utc_gmtime
utc_localtime
utc_mkanytime
utc_mkgmtime
utc_mklocaltime
utc_mkreltime
utc_reltime
To/From timespec Structures:
utc_binreltime
utc_bintime
utc_mkbinreltime
utc_mkbintime
To/From ASCII text:
utc_ascanytime
utc_ascgmtime
utc_asclocaltime
utc_ascreltime
utc_mkasctime
utc_mkascreltime
Manipulating Times ...
utc_boundtime
utc_spantime
utc_pointtime
Comparing Times ...
utc_cmpintervaltime
utc_cmpmidtime
Calculating Times ...
utc_abstime
utc_addtime
utc_mulftime
utc_multime
utc_subtime
Obtaining Time Zone Information
utc_anyzone
utc_gmtzone
utc_localzone

An alphabetical listing of the DTS portable interface routines and a brief description of each one follows:

utc_abstime( ) Computes the absolute value of a relative binary timestamp.

utc_addtime( ) Computes the sum of two binary timestamps; the timestamps can be two relative times or a relative time and an absolute time.

utc_anytime( ) Converts a binary timestamp to a **tm** structure by using the TDF information contained in the timestamp to determine the TDF returned with the **tm** structure.

utc_anyzone( ) Gets the time zone label and offset from GMT by using the TDF contained in the *utc* input parameter.

utc_ascanytime( ) Converts a binary timestamp to an ASCII string that represents an arbitrary time zone.

utc_ascgmtime( ) Converts a binary timestamp to an ASCII string that expresses a GMT time.

utc_asclocaltime( ) Converts a binary timestamp to an ASCII string that represents a local time.

utc_ascreltime( ) Converts a relative binary timestamp to an ASCII string that represents the time.

utc_binreltime( ) Converts a relative binary timestamp to two **timespec** structures that express relative time and inaccuracy.

utc_bintime( ) Converts a binary timestamp to a **timespec** structure.

utc_boundtime( ) Given two UTC times, one before and one after an event, returns a single UTC time whose inaccuracy includes the event.

utc_cmpintervaltime( )
Compares two binary timestamps or two relative binary timestamps.

utc_cmpmidtime( ) Compares two binary timestamps or two relative binary timestamps, ignoring inaccuracies.

utc_gettime( ) Returns the current system time and inaccuracy as a binary timestamp.

utc_getusertime( ) Returns the time and process-specific TDF, rather than the system-specific TDF.

utc_gmtime( ) Converts a binary timestamp to a **tm** structure that expresses GMT or the equivalent UTC.

utc_gmtzone( ) Gets the time zone label for GMT.

utc_localtime( ) Converts a binary timestamp to a **tm** structure that expresses local time.

utc_localzone( ) Gets the local time zone label and offset from GMT, given **utc**.

utc_mkanytime( ) Converts a **tm** structure and TDF (expressing the time in an arbitrary time zone) to a binary timestamp.

utc_mkascreltime( ) Converts a **NULL**-terminated character string that represents a relative timestamp to a binary timestamp.

utc_mkasctime( ) Converts a **NULL**-terminated character string that represents an absolute timestamp to a binary timestamp.

utc_mkbinreltime( ) Converts a **timespec** structure expressing a relative time to a binary timestamp.

utc_mkbintime( ) Converts a **timespec** structure to a binary timestamp.

utc_mkgmtime( ) Converts a **tm** structure that expresses GMT or UTC to a binary timestamp.

utc_mklocaltime( ) Converts a **tm** structure that expresses local time to a binary timestamp.

utc_mkreltime( ) Converts a **tm** structure that expresses relative time to a relative binary timestamp.

utc_mulftime( ) Multiplies a relative binary timestamp by a floating-point value.

utc_multime( ) Multiplies a relative binary timestamp by an integer factor.

utc_pointtime( ) Converts a binary timestamp to three binary timestamps that represent the earliest, most likely, and latest time.

utc_reltime( ) Converts a relative binary timestamp to a **tm** structure.

utc_spantime( ) Given two (possibly unordered) binary timestamps, returns a single UTC time interval whose inaccuracy spans the two input binary timestamps.

utc_subtime( ) Computes the difference between two binary timestamps that express either an absolute time and a relative time, two relative times, or two absolute times.

Notes

Absolute time is a point on a time scale; absolute time measurements are derived from system clocks or external time-providers. For DTS, absolute times reference the UTC standard and include the inaccuracy and other information. When you display an absolute time, DTS converts the time to ASCII text, as shown in the following display:

```
1992-11-21-13:30:25.785-04:00I000.082
```

Relative time is a discrete time interval that is often added to or subtracted from an absolute time. A TDF associated with an absolute time is one example of a relative time. Note that a relative time does not use the calendar date fields, since these fields concern absolute time.

Coordinated Universal Time (UTC) is the international time standard that DTS uses. The zero hour of UTC is based on the zero hour of Greenwich Mean Time (GMT). The documentation consistently refers to the time zone of the Greenwich Meridian as GMT. However, this time zone is also sometimes referred to as UTC.

The Time Differential Factor (TDF) is the difference between UTC and the time in a particular time zone.

The user's environment determines the time zone rule (details are system dependent). For example, on OSF/1 systems, the user selects a time zone by specifying the **TZ** environment variable. (The reference information for the **localtime**( ) system call, which is described in the **ctime(3)** reference page, provides additional information.)

If the user's environment does not specify a time zone rule, the system's rule is used (details of the rule are system dependent). For example, on OSF/1 systems, the rule in **/etc/zoneinfo/localtime** applies.

The *OSF DCE Application Development Guide* provides additional information about UTC and GMT, TDF and time zones, and relative and absolute times.

Unless otherwise specified, the default input and output parameters are as follows:

- If **NULL** is specified for a *utc* input parameter, the current time is used.
- If **NULL** is specified for any output parameter, no result is returned.

Related Information

Books: *OSF DCE Application Development Guide*.

utc_abstime

Purpose Computes the absolute value of a relative binary timestamp

Synopsis **#include <dce/utc.h>**

int utc_abstime(
utc_t *result*,
const utc_t **utc*);

Parameters

Input

utc Relative binary timestamp. Use **NULL** if you want this routine to use the current time for this parameter.

Output

result Absolute value of the input relative binary timestamp.

Description

The **utc_abstime()** routine computes the absolute value of a relative binary timestamp. The input timestamp represents a relative (delta) time.

Return Values

0 Indicates that the routine executed successfully.

-1 Indicates an invalid time parameter or invalid results.

Examples The following example scales a relative time, computes its absolute value, and prints the result.

```
utc_t          relutc, scaledutc;
char           timstr[UTC_MAX_STR_LEN];

/*
 *   Make sure relative timestamp represents a positive interval...
 */
```

```
utc_abstime(&relutc,              /* Out: Abs-value of rel time  */
            &relutc);             /* In:  Relative time to scale */

/*
 *   Scale it by a factor of 17...
 */

utc_multime(&scaledutc,           /* Out: Scaled relative time   */
            &relutc,              /* In:  Relative time to scale */
            17L);                 /* In:  Scale factor           */

utc_ascreltime(timstr,            /* Out: ASCII relative time    */
               UTC_MAX_STR_LEN,   /* In:  Length of input string */
               &scaledutc);       /* In:  Relative time to       */
                                  /*      convert                */

printf("%s\n",timstr);

/*
 *   Scale it by a factor of 17.65...
 */

utc_mulftime(&scaledutc,          /* Out: Scaled relative time   */
             &relutc,             /* In:  Relative time to scale */
             17.65);              /* In:  Scale factor           */

utc_ascreltime(timstr,            /* Out: ASCII relative time    */
               UTC_MAX_STR_LEN,   /* In:  Length of input string */
               &scaledutc);       /* In:  Relative time to       */
                                  /*      convert                */

printf("%s\n",timstr);
```

utc_addtime

Purpose Computes the sum of two binary timestamps

Synopsis **#include <dce/utc.h>**

int utc_addtime(
utc_t *result*,
const utc_t **utc1*,
const utc_t **utc2*);

Parameters

Input

utc1 Binary timestamp or relative binary timestamp. Use **NULL** if you want this routine to use the current time for this parameter.

utc2 Binary timestamp or relative binary timestamp. Use **NULL** if you want this routine to use the current time for this parameter.

Output

result Resulting binary timestamp or relative binary timestamp, depending upon the operation performed:

- *relative time*+*relative time*=**relative time**
- *absolute time*+*relative time*=**absolute time**
- *relative time*+*absolute time*=**absolute time**
- *absolute time*+*absolute time* is undefined. (See the note later in this reference page.)

Description

The **utc_addtime**( ) routine adds two binary timestamps, producing a third binary timestamp whose inaccuracy is the sum of the two input inaccuracies. One or both of the input timestamps typically represents a relative (delta) time. The TDF in the first input timestamp is copied to the output. The timestamps can be two relative times or a relative time and an absolute time.

Notes Although no error is returned, the combination *absolute time+absolute time* should *not* be used.

Return Values

0 Indicates that the routine executed successfully.

-1 Indicates an invalid time parameter or invalid results.

Examples The following example shows how to compute a timestamp that represents a time at least 5 seconds in the future.

```
utc_t                   now, future, fivesec;
reltimespec_t           tfivesec;
timespec_t              tzero;

/*   Construct a timestamp that represents 5 seconds...
 */
tfivesec.tv_sec = 5;
tfivesec.tv_nsec = 0;
tzero.tv_sec = 0;
tzero.tv_nsec = 0;
utc_mkbinreltime(&fivesec,     /* Out: 5 secs in binary timestamp      */
                 &tfivesec,    /* In:  5 secs in timespec              */
                 &tzero);      /* In:  0 secs inaccuracy in timespec   */

/*    Get the maximum possible current time...
 *    (The NULL input parameter is used to specify the current time.)
 */
utc_pointtime((utc_t *)0,      /* Out: Earliest possible current time */
              (utc_t *)0,      /* Out: Midpoint of current time       */
              &now,            /* Out: Latest possible current time   */
              (utc_t *)0);     /* In:  Use current time               */

/*   Add 5 seconds to get future timestamp...
 */
utc_addtime(&future,           /* Out: Future binary timestamp        */
            &now,              /* In:  Latest possible time now       */
            &fivesec);         /* In:  5 secs                         */
```

Related Information

Functions: **utc_subtime(3dts)**.

utc_anytime

Purpose Converts a binary timestamp to a **tm** structure

Synopsis **#include <dce/utc.h>**

int utc_anytime(
  struct tm **timetm*,
  long **tns*,
  struct tm **inacctm*,
  long **ins*,
  long **tdf*,
  const utc_t **utc*);

Parameters

Input

utc Binary timestamp. Use **NULL** if you want this routine to use the current time for this parameter.

Output

timetm Time component of the binary timestamp expressed in the timestamp's local time.

tns Nanoseconds since the Time component of the binary timestamp.

inacctm Seconds of the inaccuracy component of the binary timestamp. If the inaccuracy is finite, then **tm_mday** returns a value of -1 and **tm_mon** and **tm_year** return values of 0 (zero). The field **tm_yday** contains the inaccuracy in days. If the inaccuracy is unspecified, all **tm** structure fields return values of -1.

ins Nanoseconds of the inaccuracy component of the binary timestamp.

tdf TDF component of the binary timestamp in units of seconds east of GMT.

Description

The **utc_anytime()** routine converts a binary timestamp to a **tm** structure by using the TDF information contained in the timestamp to determine the TDF returned with the **tm** structure. The TDF information contained in the timestamp is returned with the time and inaccuracy components; the TDF component determines the offset from GMT and the local time value of the **tm** structure. Additional returns include nanoseconds since Time and nanoseconds of inaccuracy.

Return Values

0 Indicates that the routine executed successfully.

-1 Indicates an invalid time argument or invalid results.

Examples

The following example converts a timestamp by using the TDF information in the timestamp, and then prints the result.

```
utc_t                  evnt;
struct tm              tmevnt;
timespec_t             tevnt, ievnt;
char                   tznam[80];

/*   Assume evnt contains the timestamp to convert...
 *
 *   Get time as a tm structure, using the time zone information in
 *   the timestamp...
 */
utc_anytime(&tmevnt,              /* Out: tm struct of time of evnt    */
            (long *)0,            /* Out: nanosec of time of evnt      */
            (struct tm *)0,       /* Out: tm struct of inacc of evnt   */
            (long *)0,            /* Out: nanosec of inacc of evnt     */
            (int *)0,             /* Out: tdf of evnt                  */
            &evnt);               /* In:  binary timestamp of evnt     */

/*   Get the time and inaccuracy as timespec structures...
 */
utc_bintime(&tevnt,               /* Out: timespec of time of evnt     */
            &ievnt,               /* Out: timespec of inacc of evnt    */
            (int *)0,             /* Out: tdf of evnt                  */
            &evnt);               /* In:  Binary timestamp of evnt     */

/*   Construct the time zone name from time zone information in the
 *   timestamp...
```

```
 */
utc_anyzone(tznam,                 /* Out: Time zone name          */
            80,                    /* In:  Size of time zone name  */
            (long *)0,             /* Out: tdf of event            */
            (long *)0,             /* Out: Daylight saving flag    */
            &evnt);                /* In:  Binary timestamp of evnt */

/*   Print timestamp in the format:
 *
 *          1991-03-05-21:27:50.023I0.140 (GMT-5:00)
 *          1992-04-02-12:37:24.003Iinf (GMT+7:00)
 */

printf("%d-%02d-%02d-%02d:%02d:%02d.%03d",
        tmevnt.tm_year+1900, tmevnt.tm_mon+1, tmevnt.tm_mday,
        tmevnt.tm_hour, tmevnt.tm_min, tmevnt.tm_sec,
        (tevnt.tv_nsec/1000000));

if ((long)ievnt.tv_sec == -1)
    printf("Iinf");
else
    printf("I%d.%03d", ievnt.tv_sec, (ievnt.tv_nsec/1000000));

printf(" (%s)\n", tznam);
```

Related Information

Functions: **utc_mkanytime(3dts), utc_anyzone(3dts), utc_gettime(3dts), utc_getusertime(3dts), utc_gmtime(3dts), utc_localtime(3dts).**

utc_anyzone

Purpose Gets the time zone label and offset from GMT

Synopsis **#include <dce/utc.h>**

int utc_anyzone(
    char ***tzname*****,**
    size_t ***tzlen*****,**
    long ***tdf*****,**
    int ***isdst*****,**
    const utc_t ***utc*****);**

Parameters

Input

tzlen Length of the *tzname* buffer.

utc Binary timestamp. Use **NULL** if you want this routine to use the current time for this parameter.

Output

tzname Character string that is long enough to hold the time zone label.

tdf Longword with differential in seconds east of GMT.

isdst Integer with a value of -1, indicating that no information is supplied as to whether it is standard time or daylight saving time. A value of -1 is always returned.

Description

The **utc_anyzone( )** routine gets the time zone label and offset from GMT by using the TDF contained in the *utc* input parameter. The label returned is always of the form GMT+*n* or GMT-*n* where *n* is the *tdf* expressed in hours:minutes. (The label associated with an arbitrary time zone is not known; only the offset is known.)

Notes

All of the output parameters are optional. No value is returned and no error occurs if the pointer is **NULL**.

Return Values

0 Indicates that the routine executed successfully.

-1 Indicates an invalid time argument or an insufficient buffer.

Examples

See the sample program in the **utc_anytime(3dts)** reference page.

Related Information

Functions: **utc_anytime(3dts)**, **utc_gmtzone(3dts)**, **utc_localzone(3dts)**.

utc_ascanytime

Purpose Converts a binary timestamp to an ASCII string that represents an arbitrary time zone

Synopsis **#include <dce/utc.h>**

int utc_ascanytime(
    char ***cp**,
    size_t *stringlen*,
    const utc_t **utc*);

Parameters

Input

stringlen The length of the *cp* buffer.

utc Binary timestamp. Use **NULL** if you want this routine to use the current time for this parameter.

Output

cp ASCII string that represents the time.

Description

The **utc_ascanytime()** routine converts a binary timestamp to an ASCII string that expresses a time. The TDF component in the timestamp determines the local time used in the conversion.

Return Values

0 Indicates that the routine executed successfully.

-1 Indicates an invalid time parameter or invalid results.

Examples

The following example converts a time to an ASCII string that expresses the time in the time zone where the timestamp was generated.

```
utc_t       evnt;
char        localTime[UTC_MAX_STR_LEN];

/*
 *   Assuming that evnt contains the timestamp to convert, convert
 *   the time to ASCII in the following format:
 *
 *          1991-04-01-12:27:38.37-8:00I2.00
 */

utc_ascanytime(localtime,           /* Out: Converted time    */
               UTC_MAX_STR_LEN,     /* In:  Length of string  */
               &evnt);              /* In:  Time to convert   */
```

Related Information

Functions: **utc_ascgmtime(3dts)**, **utc_asclocaltime(3dts)**.

utc_ascgmtime

Purpose Converts a binary timestamp to an ASCII string that expresses a GMT time

Synopsis **#include <dce/utc.h>**

int utc_ascgmtime(
char ***cp*,**
size_t *stringlen*,
const utc_t ***utc*);**

Parameters

Input

stringlen Length of the *cp* buffer.

utc Binary timestamp.

Output

cp ASCII string that represents the time.

Description

The **utc_ascgmtime()** routine converts a binary timestamp to an ASCII string that expresses a time in GMT.

Return Values

0 Indicates that the routine executed successfully.

-1 Indicates an invalid time parameter or invalid results.

Examples

The following example converts the current time to GMT format.

```
char    gmTime[UTC_MAX_STR_LEN];

/*   Convert the current time to ASCII in the following format:
 *          1991-04-01-12:27:38.37I2.00
 */
utc_ascgmtime(gmTime,                    /* Out: Converted time       */
              UTC_MAX_STR_LEN,           /* In:  Length of string     */
              (utc_t*) NULL);            /* In:  Time to convert      */
                                         /* Default is current time   */
```

Related Information

Functions: **utc_ascanytime(3dts), utc_asclocaltime(3dts)**.

utc_asclocaltime

Purpose Converts a binary timestamp to an ASCII string that represents a local time

Synopsis

#include <dce/utc.h>

int utc_asclocaltime(
 char ******cp*,
 size_t *stringlen*,
 const utc_t ******utc*);

Parameters

Input

stringlen Length of the *cp* buffer.

utc Binary timestamp. Use **NULL** if you want this routine to use the current time for this parameter.

Output

cp ASCII string that represents the time.

Description

The **utc_asclocaltime**( ) routine converts a binary timestamp to an ASCII string that expresses local time.

The user's environment determines the time zone rule (details are system dependent). For example, on OSF/1 systems, the user selects a time zone by specifying the **TZ** environment variable. (The reference information for the **localtime**( ) system call, which is described in the **ctime(3)** reference page, provides additional information.)

If the user's environment does not specify a time zone rule, the system's rule is used (details of the rule are system dependent). For example, on OSF/1 systems, the rule in **/etc/zoneinfo/localtime** applies.

Return Values

0 Indicates that the routine executed successfully.

-1 Indicates an invalid time parameter or invalid results.

Examples

The following example converts the current time to local time.

```
char    localTime[UTC_MAX_STR_LEN];

/*  Convert the current time...
 */

utc_asclocaltime(localTime,         /* Out:  Converted time       */
                 UTC_MAX_STR_LEN,   /* In:   Length of string     */
                 (utc_t*) NULL);    /* In:   Time to convert      */
                                    /* Default is current time    */
```

Related Information

Functions: **utc_ascanytime(3dts)**, **utc_ascgmtime(3dts)**.

utc_ascreltime

Purpose Converts a relative binary timestamp to an ASCII string that represents the time

Synopsis **#include <dce/utc.h>**

int utc_ascreltime(
  char **cp*,
  const size_t *stringlen*,
  const utc_t **utc*);

Parameters

Input

utc Relative binary timestamp. Use **NULL** if you want this routine to use the current time for this parameter.

stringlen Length of the *cp* buffer.

Output

cp ASCII string that represents the time.

Description

The **utc_ascreltime()** routine converts a relative binary timestamp to an ASCII string that represents the time.

Return Values

0 Indicates that the routine executed successfully.

-1 Indicates an invalid time parameter or invalid results.

Examples See the sample program in the **utc_abstime(3dts)** reference page.

Related Information

Functions: **utc_mkascreltime(3dts)**.

utc_binreltime

Purpose Converts a relative binary timestamp to two **timespec** structures that express relative time and inaccuracy

Synopsis **#include <dce/utc.h>**

int utc_binreltime(
reltimespec_t ***timesp*,**
timespec_t ***inaccsp*,**
const utc_t ***utc*);**

Parameters

Input

utc Relative binary timestamp. Use **NULL** if you want this routine to use the current time for this parameter.

Output

timesp Time component of the relative binary timestamp, in the form of seconds and nanoseconds since the base time (1970-01-01:00:00:00.0+00:00I0).

inaccsp Inaccuracy component of the relative binary timestamp, in the form of seconds and nanoseconds.

Description

The **utc_binreltime()** routine converts a relative binary timestamp to two **timespec** structures that express relative time and inaccuracy. These **timespec** structures describe a time interval.

Return Values

0 Indicates that the routine executed successfully.

-1 Indicates an invalid time argument or invalid results.

Examples

The following example measures the duration of a process, then prints the resulting relative time and inaccuracy.

```
utc_t                   before, duration;
reltimespec_t           tduration;
timespec_t              iduration;

/*   Get the time before the start of the operation...
 */
utc_gettime(&before);            /* Out: Before binary timestamp      */

/*    ...Later...
 *    Subtract, getting the duration as a relative time.
 *
 *         NOTE: The NULL argument is used to obtain the current time.
 */

utc_subtime(&duration,           /* Out: Duration rel bin timestamp  */
            (utc_t *)0,          /* In:  After binary timestamp      */
            &before);            /* In:  Before binary timestamp     */

/*   Convert the relative times to timespec structures...
 */

utc_binreltime(&tduration,       /* Out: Duration time timespec      */
               &iduration,       /* Out: Duration inacc timespec     */
               &duration);       /* In:  Duration rel bin timestamp  */

/*   Print the duration...
 */
printf("%d.%04d", tduration.tv_sec, (tduration.tv_nsec/10000));

if ((long)iduration.tv_sec == -1)
    printf("Iinf\n");
else
    printf("I%d.%04d\n", iduration.tv_sec, (iduration.tv_nsec/100000));
```

Related Information

Functions: **utc_mkbinreltime(3dts)**.

utc_bintime

Purpose Converts a binary timestamp to a **timespec** structure

Synopsis **#include <dce/utc.h>**

int utc_bintime(
timespec_t **timesp*,
timespec_t **inaccsp*,
long **tdf*,
const utc_t **utc*);

Parameters

Input

utc Binary timestamp. Use **NULL** if you want this routine to use the current time for this parameter.

Output

timesp Time component of the binary timestamp, in the form of seconds and nanoseconds since the base time.

inaccsp Inaccuracy component of the binary timestamp, in the form of seconds and nanoseconds.

tdf TDF component of the binary timestamp in the form of signed number of seconds east of GMT.

Description

The **utc_bintime( )** routine converts a binary timestamp to a **timespec** structure. The TDF information contained in the timestamp is returned.

Return Values

0 Indicates that the routine executed successfully.

-1 Indicates an invalid time argument or invalid results.

Examples

See the sample program in the **utc_anytime(3dts)** reference page.

Related Information

Functions: **utc_binreltime(3dts)**, **utc_mkbintime(3dts)**.

utc_boundtime

Purpose Given two UTC times, one before and one after an event, returns a single UTC time whose inaccuracy includes the event

Synopsis **#include <dce/utc.h>**

int utc_boundtime(
utc_t ***result*,**
const utc_t ***utc1*,**
const utc_t ***utc2*);**

Parameters

Input

utc1 Before binary timestamp or relative binary timestamp. Use **NULL** if you want this routine to use the current time for this parameter.

utc2 After binary timestamp or relative binary timestamp. Use **NULL** if you want this routine to use the current time for this parameter.

Output

result Spanning timestamp.

Description

Given two UTC times, the **utc_boundtime( )** routine returns a single UTC time whose inaccuracy bounds the two input times. This is useful for timestamping events: the routine gets the **utc** values before and after the event, then calls **utc_boundtime( )** to build a timestamp that includes the event.

Notes The TDF in the output UTC value is copied from the *utc2* input parameter. If one or both input values have unspecified inaccuracies, the returned time value also has an unspecified inaccuracy and is the average of the two input values.

Return Values

0 Indicates that the routine executed successfully.

-1 Indicates an invalid time parameter or invalid parameter order.

Examples

The following example records the time of an event and constructs a single timestamp, which includes the time of the event. Note that the **utc_getusertime( )** routine is called so the time zone information that is included in the timestamp references the user's environment rather than the system's default time zone.

The user's environment determines the time zone rule (details are system dependent). For example, on OSF/1 systems, the user selects a time zone by specifying the **TZ** environment variable. (The reference information for the **localtime**( ) system call, which is described in the **ctime(3)** reference page, provides additional information.)

If the user's environment does not specify a time zone rule, the system's rule is used (details of the rule are system dependent). For example, on OSF/1 systems, the rule in **/etc/zoneinfo/localtime** applies.

```
utc_t                   before, after, evnt;

/*  Get the time before the event...
 */
utc_getusertime(&before);        /* Out: Before binary timestamp      */

/*  Get the time after the event...
 */
utc_getusertime(&after);         /* Out: After binary timestamp       */

/*  Construct a single timestamp that describes the time of the
 *   event...
 */
utc_boundtime(&evnt,             /* Out: Timestamp that bounds event */
              &before,           /* In:  Before binary timestamp     */
              &after);           /* In:  After binary timestamp      */
```

Related Information

Functions: **utc_gettime(3dts)**, **utc_pointtime(3dts)**, **utc_spantime(3dts)**.

utc_cmpintervaltime

Purpose Compares two binary timestamps or two relative binary timestamps

Synopsis **#include <dce/utc.h>**

int utc_cmpintervaltime(
enum utc_cmptype **relation*,
const utc_t **utc1*,
const utc_t **utc2*);

Parameters

Input

utc1 Binary timestamp or relative binary timestamp. Use **NULL** if you want this routine to use the current time for this parameter.

utc2 Binary timestamp or relative binary timestamp. Use **NULL** if you want this routine to use the current time for this parameter.

Output

relation Receives the result of the comparison of *utc1*:*utc2* where the result is an enumerated type with one of the following values:

- **utc_equalTo**
- **utc_lessThan**
- **utc_greaterThan**
- **utc_indeterminate**

Description

The **utc_cmpintervaltime()** routine compares two binary timestamps and returns a flag indicating that the first time is greater than, less than, equal to, or overlapping with the second time. Two times overlap if the intervals (time – inaccuracy, time + inaccuracy) of the two times intersect.

The input binary timestamps express two absolute or two relative times. Do *not* compare relative binary timestamps to absolute binary timestamps. If you do, no meaningful results and no errors are returned.

The following routine does a temporal ordering of the time intervals.

```
utc1 is utc_lessThan utc2 iff
        utc1.time + utc1.inacc < utc2.time - utc2.inacc

utc1 is utc_greaterThan utc2 iff
        utc1.time - utc1.inacc > utc2.time + utc2.inacc

utc1 utc_equalTo utc2 iff
        utc1.time == utc2.time and
        utc1.inacc == 0 and
        utc2.inacc == 0

utc1 is utc_indeterminate with respect to utc2 if the intervals
overlap.
```

Return Values

0 Indicates that the routine executed successfully.

-1 Indicates an invalid time argument.

Examples

The following example checks to see if the current time is definitely after 13:00 local time.

```
struct tm              tmtime, tmzero;
enum utc_cmptype       relation;
utc_t                  testtime;

/*   Zero the tm structure for inaccuracy...
 */
memset(&tmzero, 0, sizeof(tmzero));

/*  Get the current time, mapped to a tm structure...
 *
 *        NOTE: The NULL argument is used to get the current time.
 */
utc_gmtime(&tmtime,          /* Out: Current GMT time in tm struct   */
           (long *)0,        /* Out: Nanoseconds of time             */
           (struct tm *)0,   /* Out: Current inaccuracy in tm struct */
           (long *)0,        /* Out: Nanoseconds of inaccuracy       */
           (utc_t *)0);      /* In:  Current timestamp               */
```

```
/*   Alter the tm structure to correspond to 13:00 local time       */
 */

tmtime.tm_hour = 13;
tmtime.tm_min = 0;
tmtime.tm_sec = 0;

/*  Convert to a binary timestamp...
 */
utc_mkgmtime(&testtime,      /* Out: Binary timestamp of 13:00       */
             &tmtime,        /* In:  1:00 PM in tm struct            */
             0,              /* In:  Nanoseconds of time             */
             &tmzero,        /* In:  Zero inaccuracy in tm struct    */
             0);             /* In:  Nanoseconds of inaccuracy       */

/*   Compare to the current time. Note the use of the NULL argument */
 */
utc_cmpintervaltime(&relation,    /* Out: Comparison relation       */
                    (utc_t *)0,   /* In:  Current timestamp         */
                    &testtime);   /* In:  13:00 PM timestamp        */

/*   If it is not later - wait, print a message, etc.
 */

if (relation != utc_greaterThan) {

/*
 *     Note: It could be earlier than 13:00 local time or it could be
 *           indeterminate. If indeterminate, for some applications
 *           it might be worth waiting.
 */
}
```

Related Information

Functions: **utc_cmpmidtime(3dts)**.

utc_cmpmidtime

Purpose

Compares two binary timestamps or two relative binary timestamps, ignoring inaccuracies

Synopsis

#include <dce/utc.h>

int utc_cmpmidtime(
  enum utc_cmptype **relation*,
  const utc_t **utc1*,
  const utc_t **utc2*);

Parameters

Input

utc1 Binary timestamp or relative binary timestamp. Use **NULL** if you want this routine to use the current time for this parameter.

utc2 Binary timestamp or relative binary timestamp. Use **NULL** if you want this routine to use the current time for this parameter.

Output

relation Result of the comparison of *utc1:utc2* where the result is an enumerated type with one of the following values:

- **utc_equalTo**
- **utc_lessThan**
- **utc_greaterThan**

Description

The **utc_cmpmidtime( )** routine compares two binary timestamps and returns a flag indicating that the first timestamp is greater than, less than, or equal to the second timestamp. Inaccuracy information is ignored for this comparison; the input values are therefore equivalent to the midpoints of the time intervals described by the input binary timestamps.

The input binary timestamps express two absolute or two relative times. Do *not* compare relative binary timestamps to absolute binary timestamps. If you do, no meaningful results and no errors are returned.

The following routine does a lexical ordering on the time interval midpoints.

```
utc1 is utc_lessThan utc2 iff
        utc1.time < utc2.time

utc1 is utc_greaterThan utc2 iff
        utc1.time > utc2.time

utc1 is utc_equalTo utc2 iff
        utc1.time == utc2.time
```

Return Values

0 Indicates that the routine executed successfully.

-1 Indicates an invalid time argument.

Examples

The following example checks if the current time (ignoring inaccuracies) is after 13:00 local time.

```
struct tm           tmtime, tmzero;
enum utc_cmptype    relation;
utc_t               testtime;

/*   Zero the tm structure for inaccuracy...
 */
memset(&tmzero, 0, sizeof(tmzero));

/*   Get the current time, mapped to a tm structure...
 *
 *        NOTE:  The NULL argument is used to get the current time.
 */
utc_localtime(&tmtime,         /* Out: Current local time in tm struct */
             (long *)0,        /* Out: Nanoseconds of time            */
             (struct tm *)0,   /* Out: Current inacc in tm struct     */
             (long *)0,        /* Out: Nanoseconds of inaccuracy      */
             (utc_t *)0);      /* In:  Current timestamp              */
```

```
 /*   Alter the tm structure to correspond to 13:00 local time.
  */
tmtime.tm_hour = 13;
tmtime.tm_min = 0;
tmtime.tm_sec = 0;

 /*   Convert to a binary timestamp...
  */
utc_mklocaltime(&testtime,     /* Out: Binary timestamp of 13:00       */
                &tmtime,       /* In:  13:00 in tm struct              */
                0,             /* In:  Nanoseconds of time             */
                &tmzero,       /* In:  Zero inaccuracy in tm struct    */
                0);            /* In:  Nanoseconds of inaccuracy       */

 /*   Compare to the current time. Note the use of the NULL argument
  */
utc_cmpmidtime(&relation,      /* Out: Comparison relation             */
               (utc_t *)0,     /* In:  Current timestamp               */
               &testtime);     /* In:  13:00 local time timestamp      */

 /*   If the time is not later - wait, print a message, etc.
  */
if (relation != utc_greaterThan) {

 /*          It is not later then 13:00 local time. Note that
  *          this depends on the setting of the user's environment.
  */
}
```

Related Information

Functions: **utc_cmpintervaltime(3dts)**.

utc_gettime

Purpose Returns the current system time and inaccuracy as a binary timestamp

Synopsis

```
#include &lt;dce/utc.h&gt;

int utc_gettime(
        utc_t *utc);
```

Parameters

Input

None.

Output

utc System time as a binary timestamp.

Description

The **utc_gettime**( ) routine returns the current system time and inaccuracy in a binary timestamp. The routine takes the TDF from the operating system's kernel; the TDF is specified in a system-dependent manner.

Return Values

0 Indicates that the routine executed successfully.

-1 Generic error that indicates the time service cannot be accessed.

Examples See the sample program in the **utc_binreltime(3dts)** reference page.

utc_getusertime

Purpose Returns the time and process-specific TDF, rather than the system-specific TDF

Synopsis **#include <dce/utc.h>**

```
int utc_getusertime(
        utc_t *utc);
```

Parameters

Input

None.

Output

utc System time as a binary timestamp.

Description

The **utc_getusertime()** routine returns the system time and inaccuracy in a binary timestamp. The routine takes the TDF from the user's environment, which determines the time zone rule (details are system dependent). For example, on OSF/1 systems, the user selects a time zone by specifying the **TZ** environment variable. (The reference information for the **localtime()** system call, which is described in the **ctime(3)** reference page, provides additional information.)

If the user environment does not specify a TDF, the system's TDF is used. The system's time zone rule is applied (details of the rule are system dependent). For example, on OSF/1 systems, the rule in **/etc/zoneinfo/localtime** applies.

Return Values

0 Indicates that the routine executed successfully.

-1 Generic error that indicates the time service cannot be accessed.

Examples See the sample program in the **utc_boundtime(3dts)** reference page.

Related Information

Functions: **utc_gettime(3dts)**.

utc_gmtime

Purpose Converts a binary timestamp to a **tm** structure that expresses GMT or the equivalent UTC

Synopsis **#include <dce/utc.h>**

```
int utc_gmtime(
        struct tm *timetm,
        long *tns,
        struct tm *inacctm,
        long *ins,
        const utc_t *utc);
```

Parameters

Input

utc Binary timestamp to be converted to **tm** structure components. Use **NULL** if you want this routine to use the current time for this parameter.

Output

timetm Time component of the binary timestamp.

tns Nanoseconds since the Time component of the binary timestamp.

inacctm Seconds of the inaccuracy component of the binary timestamp. If the inaccuracy is finite, then **tm_mday** returns a value of -1 and **tm_mon** and **tm_year** return values of 0 (zero). The field **tm_yday** contains the inaccuracy in days. If the inaccuracy is unspecified, all **tm** structure fields return values of -1.

ins Nanoseconds of the inaccuracy component of the binary timestamp. If the inaccuracy is unspecified, *ins* returns a value of -1.

Description

The **utc_gmtime()** routine converts a binary timestamp to a **tm** structure that expresses GMT (or the equivalent UTC). Additional returns include nanoseconds since Time and nanoseconds of inaccuracy.

Return Values

0 Indicates that the routine executed successfully.

-1 Indicates an invalid time argument or invalid results.

Examples

See the sample program in the **utc_cmpintervaltime(3dts)** reference page.

Related Information

Functions: **utc_anytime(3dts), utc_gmtzone(3dts)**, **utc_localtime(3dts)**, **utc_mkgmtime(3dts)**.

utc_gmtzone

Purpose

Gets the time zone label for GMT

Synopsis

#include <dce/utc.h>

int utc_gmtzone(
char **tzname*,
size_t *tzlen*,
long **tdf*,
int **isdst*,
const utc_t **utc*);

Parameters

Input

tzlen Length of buffer *tzname*.

utc Binary timestamp. This parameter is ignored.

Output

tzname Character string long enough to hold the time zone label.

tdf Longword with differential in seconds east of GMT. A value of 0 (zero) is always returned.

isdst Integer with a value of 0 (zero), indicating that daylight saving time is not in effect. A value of 0 (zero) is always returned.

Description

The **utc_gmtzone( )** routine gets the time zone label and zero offset from GMT. Outputs are always *tdf*=0 and *tzname*=GMT. This routine exists for symmetry with the **utc_anyzone( )** and the **utc_localzone( )** routines. Use **NULL** if you want this routine to use the current time for this parameter.

Notes

All of the output parameters are optional. No value is returned and no error occurs if the *tzname* pointer is **NULL**.

Return Values

0 Indicates that the routine executed successfully (always returned).

Examples

The following example prints out the current time in both local time and GMT time.

```
utc_t         now;
struct tm     tmlocal, tmgmt;
long          tzoffset;
int           tzdaylight;
char          tzlocal[80], tzgmt[80];

/*  Get the current time once, so both conversions use the same
 *    time...
 */
utc_gettime(&now);

/*  Convert to local time, using the process TZ environment
 *    variable...
 */
utc_localtime(&tmlocal,        /* Out: Local time tm structure       */
              (long *)0,       /* Out: Nanosec of time               */
              (struct tm *)0,  /* Out: Inaccuracy tm structure       */
              (long *)0,       /* Out: Nanosec of inaccuracy         */
              (int *)0,        /* Out: TDF of local time             */
              &now);           /* In:  Current timestamp (ignore)    */


/*   Get the local time zone name, offset from GMT, and current
 *   daylight savings flag...
 */
utc_localzone(tzlocal,         /* Out: Local time zone name          */
              80,              /* In:  Length of loc time zone name  */
              &tzoffset,       /* Out: Loc time zone offset in secs  */
              &tzdaylight,     /* Out: Local time zone daylight flag */
              &now);           /* In:  Current binary timestamp      */

/*   Convert to GMT...
 */
```

```
utc_gmtime(&tmgmt,              /* Out: GMT tm structure          */
           (long *)0,           /* Out: Nanoseconds of time       */
           (struct tm *)0,      /* Out: Inaccuracy tm structure   */
           (long *)0,           /* Out: Nanoseconds of inaccuracy */
           &now);               /* In:  Current binary timestamp  */

/*   Get the GMT time zone name...
 */
utc_gmtzone(tzgmt,              /* Out: GMT time zone name        */
            80,                 /* In:  Size of GMT time zone name */
            (long *)0,          /* Out: GMT time zone offset in secs */
            (int *)0,           /* Out: GMT time zone daylight flag */
            &now);              /* In:  Current binary timestamp  */
                                /*      (ignore)                  */

/*   Print out times and time zone information in the following
 *   format:
 *
 *          12:00:37 (EDT) = 16:00:37 (GMT)
 *          EDT is -240 minutes ahead of Greenwich Mean Time.
 *          Daylight savings time is in effect.
 */
printf("%d:%02d:%02d (%s) = %d:%02d:%02d (%s)\n",
       tmlocal.tm_hour, tmlocal.tm_min, tmlocal.tm_sec, tzlocal,
       tmgmt.tm_hour, tmgmt.tm_min, tmgmt.tm_sec, tzgmt);
printf("%s is %d minutes ahead of Greenwich Mean Time\n", tzlocal, tzoffset/60);
if (tzdaylight != 0)
    printf("Daylight savings time is in effect\n");
```

Related Information

Functions: **utc_anyzone(3dts)**, **utc_gmtime(3dts)**, **utc_localzone(3dts)**.

utc_localtime

Purpose

Converts a binary timestamp to a **tm** structure that expresses local time

Synopsis

#include <dce/utc.h>

int utc_localtime(
struct tm **timetm*,
long **tns*,
struct tm **inacctm*,
long **ins*,
const utc_t **utc*);

Parameters

Input

utc Binary timestamp. Use **NULL** if you want this routine to use the current time for this parameter.

Output

timetm Time component of the binary timestamp, expressing local time.

tns Nanoseconds since the Time component of the binary timestamp.

inacctm Seconds of the inaccuracy component of the binary timestamp. If the inaccuracy is finite, then **tm_mday** returns a value of -1 and **tm_mon** and **tm_year** return values of 0 (zero). The field **tm_yday** contains the inaccuracy in days. If the inaccuracy is unspecified, all **tm** structure fields return values of -1.

ins Nanoseconds of the inaccuracy component of the binary timestamp. If the inaccuracy is unspecified, *ins* returns a value of -1.

Description

The **utc_localtime**( ) routine converts a binary timestamp to a **tm** structure that expresses local time.

The user's environment determines the time zone rule (details are system dependent). For example, on OSF/1 systems, the user selects a time zone by specifying the **TZ** environment variable. (The reference information for the

localtime( ) system call, which is described in the **ctime(3)** reference page, provides additional information.)

If the user's environment does not specify a time zone rule, the system's rule is used (details of the rule are system dependent). For example, on OSF/1 systems, the rule in **/etc/zoneinfo/localtime** applies.

Additional returns include nanoseconds since Time and nanoseconds of inaccuracy.

Return Values

0 Indicates that the routine executed successfully.

-1 Indicates an invalid time argument or invalid results.

Examples

See the sample program in the **utc_gmtzone(3dts)** reference page.

Related Information

Functions: **utc_anytime(3dts)**, **utc_gmtime(3dts)**, **utc_localzone(3dts)**, **utc_mklocaltime(3dts)**.

utc_localzone

Purpose Gets the local time zone label and offset from GMT, given **utc**

Synopsis **#include <dce/utc.h>**

int utc_localzone(
  char **tzname*,
  size_t *tzlen*,
  long **tdf*,
  int **isdst*,
  const utc_t **utc*);

Parameters

Input

tzlen Length of the *tzname* buffer.

utc Binary timestamp. Use **NULL** if you want this routine to use the current time for this parameter.

Output

tzname Character string long enough to hold the time zone label.

tdf Longword with differential in seconds east of GMT.

isdst Integer with a value of 0 (zero) if standard time is in effect or a value of 1 if daylight saving time is in effect.

Description

The **utc_localzone**( ) routine gets the local time zone label and offset from GMT, given **utc**.

The user's environment determines the time zone rule (details are system dependent). For example, on OSF/1 systems, the user selects a time zone by specifying the **TZ** environment variable. (The reference information for the **localtime**( ) system call, which is described in the **ctime(3)** reference page, provides additional information.)

If the user's environment does not specify a time zone rule, the system's rule is used (details of the rule are system dependent). For example, on OSF/1 systems, the rule in **/etc/zoneinfo/localtime** applies.

Notes All of the output parameters are optional. No value is returned and no error occurs if the pointer is **NULL**.

Return Values

0 Indicates that the routine executed successfully.

-1 Indicates an invalid time argument or an insufficient buffer.

Examples See the sample program in the **utc_gmtzone(3dts)** reference page.

Related Information

Functions: **utc_anyzone(3dts)**, **utc_gmtzone(3dts)**, **utc_localtime(3dts)**.

utc_mkanytime

Purpose Converts a **tm** structure and TDF (expressing the time in an arbitrary time zone) to a binary timestamp

Synopsis **#include <dce/utc.h>**

int utc_mkanytime(
  utc_t ***utc*,**
  const struct tm ***timetm*,**
  long ***tns*,**
  const struct tm ***inacctm*,**
  long ***ins*,**
  long ***tdf*);**

Parameters

Input

timetm A **tm** structure that expresses the local time; **tm_wday** and **tm_yday** are ignored on input; the value of **tm_isdt** should be -1.

tns Nanoseconds since the Time component.

inacctm A **tm** structure that expresses days, hours, minutes, and seconds of inaccuracy. If **tm_yday** is negative, the inaccuracy is considered to be unspecified; **tm_mday**, **tm_mon**, **tm_wday**, and **tm_isdst** are ignored on input.

ins Nanoseconds of the inaccuracy component.

tdf Time Differential Factor to use in conversion.

Output

utc Resulting binary timestamp.

Description

The **utc_mkanytime()** routine converts a **tm** structure and TDF (expressing the time in an arbitrary time zone) to a binary timestamp. Required inputs include nanoseconds since Time and nanoseconds of inaccuracy.

Return Values

0 Indicates that the routine executed successfully.

-1 Indicates an invalid time argument or invalid results.

Examples

The following example converts a string ISO format time in an arbitrary time zone to a binary timestamp. This may be part of an input timestamp routine, although a real implementation will include range checking.

```
utc_t         utc;
struct tm     tmtime, tminacc;
float         tsec, isec;
double        tmp;
long          tnsec, insec;
int           i, offset, tzhour, tzmin, year, mon;
char          *string;

/*  Try to convert the string...                                    */

if(sscanf(string, "%d-%d-%d-%d:%d:%e+%d:%dI%e",
          &year, &mon, &tmtime.tm_mday, &tmtime.tm_hour,
          &tmtime.tm_min, &tsec, &tzhour, &tzmin, &isec) != 9) {

/*  Try again with a negative TDF...                                */

if (sscanf(string, "%d-%d-%d-%d:%d:%e-%d:%dI%e",
           &year, &mon, &tmtime.tm_mday, &tmtime.tm_hour,
           &tmtime.tm_min, &tsec, &tzhour, &tzmin, &isec) != 9) {

/*  ERROR                                                           */

        exit(1);
    }

/*  TDF is negative                                                 */
```

```
    tzhour = -tzhour;
    tzmin = -tzmin;

}

/*  Fill in the fields...                                         */

tmtime.tm_year = year - 1900;
tmtime.tm_mon = --mon;
tmtime.tm_sec = tsec;
tnsec = (modf(tsec, &tmp)*1.0E9);
offset = tzhour*3600 + tzmin*60;
tminacc.tm_sec = isec;
insec = (modf(isec, &tmp)*1.0E9);

/* Convert to a binary timestamp...                               */

utc_mkanytime(&utc,       /* Out: Resultant binary timestamp      */
              &tmtime,    /* In:  tm struct that represents input */
              tnsec,      /* In:  Nanoseconds from input          */
              &tminacc,   /* In:  tm struct that represents inacc */
              insec,      /* In:  Nanoseconds from input          */
              offset);    /* In:  TDF from input                  */
```

Related Information

Functions: **utc_anytime(3dts)**, **utc_anyzone(3dts)**.

utc_mkascreltime

Purpose Converts a **NULL**-terminated character string that represents a relative timestamp to a binary timestamp

Synopsis **#include <dce/utc.h>**

int utc_mkascreltime(
  utc_t **utc*,
  char **string*);

Parameters

Input

string A **NULL**-terminated string that expresses a relative timestamp in its ISO format.

Output

utc Resulting binary timestamp.

Description

The **utc_mkascreltime**( ) routine converts a **NULL**-terminated string, which represents a relative timestamp, to a binary timestamp.

Notes The ASCII string must be **NULL**-terminated.

Return Values

0 Indicates that the routine executed successfully.

-1 Indicates an invalid time parameter or invalid results.

Examples The following example converts an ASCII relative time string to its binary equivalent.

```
utc_t        utc;
char         str[UTC_MAX_STR_LEN];

/*   Relative time of -333 days, 12 hours, 1 minute, 37.223 seconds
 *   Inaccuracy of 50.22 seconds in the format:  -333-12:01:37.223I50.22
 */
(void)strcpy((void *)str,
             "-333-12:01:37.223I50.22");

utc_mkascreltime(&utc,     /* Out: Binary utc                    */
                 str);     /* In:  String                        */
```

Related Information

Functions: **utc_ascreltime(3dts)**.

utc_mkasctime

Purpose Converts a **NULL**-terminated character string that represents an absolute timestamp to a binary timestamp

Synopsis **#include <dce/utc.h>**

int utc_mkasctime(
utc_t **utc*,
char **string*);

Parameters

Input

string A **NULL**-terminated string that expresses an absolute time.

Output

utc Resulting binary timestamp.

Description

The **utc_mkasctime( )** routine converts a **NULL**-terminated string that represents an absolute time to a binary timestamp.

Notes The ASCII string must be **NULL**-terminated.

Return Values

0 Indicates that the routine executed successfully.

-1 Indicates an invalid time parameter or invalid results.

Examples

The following example converts an ASCII time string to its binary equivalent.

```
utc_t     utc;
char      str[UTC_MAX_STR_LEN];

/*   July 4, 1776, 12:01:37.223 local time
 *   TDF of -5:00 hours
 *   Inaccuracy of 3600.32 seconds
 */
(void)strcpy((void *)str,
             "1776-07-04-12:01:37.223-5:00I3600.32");

utc_mkasctime(&utc,      /* Out: Binary utc           */
              str);      /* In:  String               */
```

Related Information

Functions: **utc_ascanytime(3dts)**, **utc_ascgmtime(3dts)**, **utc_asclocaltime(3dts)**.

utc_mkbinreltime

Purpose Converts a **timespec** structure expressing a relative time to a binary timestamp

Synopsis **#include <dce/utc.h>**

int utc_mkbinreltime(
utc_t **utc*,
const reltimespec_t **timesp*,
const timespec_t **inaccsp*);

Parameters

Input

timesp A **reltimespec** structure that expresses a relative time.

inaccsp A **timespec** structure that expresses inaccuracy. If **tv_sec** is set to a value of -1, the inaccuracy is considered to be unspecified.

Output

utc Resulting relative binary timestamp.

Description

The **utc_mkbinreltime()** routine converts a **timespec** structure that expresses relative time to a binary timestamp.

Return Values

0 Indicates that the routine executed successfully.

-1 Indicates an invalid time argument or invalid results.

Examples See the sample program in the **utc_addtime(3dts)** reference page.

Related Information

Functions: **utc_binreltime(3dts)**, **utc_mkbintime(3dts)**.

utc_mkbintime

Purpose

Converts a **timespec** structure to a binary timestamp

Synopsis

#include <dce/utc.h>

int utc_mkbintime(
  utc_t **utc*,
  const timespec_t **timesp*,
  const timespec_t **inaccsp*,
  long *tdf*);

Parameters

Input

timesp A **timespec** structure that expresses time since 1970-01-01:00:00:00.0+0:00I0.

inaccsp A **timespec** structure that expresses inaccuracy. If **tv_sec** is set to a value of -1, the inaccuracy is considered to be unspecified.

tdf TDF component of the binary timestamp.

Output

utc Resulting binary timestamp.

Description

The **utc_mkbintime()** routine converts a **timespec** structure time to a binary timestamp. The TDF input is used as the TDF of the binary timestamp.

Return Values

0 Indicates that the routine executed successfully.

-1 Indicates an invalid time argument or invalid results.

Examples

The following example obtains the current time from **time(3)**, converts it to a binary timestamp with an inaccuracy of 5.2 seconds, and specifies GMT.

```
timespec_t   ttime, tinacc;
utc_t        utc;

/*   Obtain the current time (without the inaccuracy)...
 */

ttime.tv_sec = time((time_t *)0);
ttime.tv_nsec = 0;

/*   Specify the inaccuracy...
 */

tinacc.tv_sec = 5;
tinacc.tv_nsec = 200000000;

/*   Convert to a binary timestamp...
 */

utc_mkbintime(&utc,         /* Out: Binary timestamp          */
              &ttime,       /* In:  Current time in timespec  */
              &tinacc,      /* In:  5.2 seconds in timespec   */
              0);           /* In:  TDF of GMT                */
```

Related Information

Functions: **utc_bintime(3dts)**, **utc_mkbinreltime(3dts)**.

utc_mkgmtime

Purpose Converts a **tm** structure that expresses GMT or UTC to a binary timestamp

Synopsis **#include <dce/utc.h>**

int utc_mkgmtime(
utc_t ******utc*,
const struct tm ******timetm*,
long *tns*,
const struct tm ******inacctm*,
long *ins***);**

Parameters

Input

timetm A **tm** structure that expresses GMT. On input, **tm_wday** and **tm_yday** are ignored; the value of **tm_isdt** should be -1.

tns Nanoseconds since the Time component.

inacctm A **tm** structure that expresses days, hours, minutes, and seconds of inaccuracy. If **tm_yday** is negative, the inaccuracy is considered to be unspecified. On input, **tm_mday**, **tm_mon**, **tm_wday**, and **tm_isdst** are ignored.

ins Nanoseconds of the inaccuracy component.

Output

utc Resulting binary timestamp.

Description

The **utc_mkgmtime( )** routine converts a **tm** structure that expresses GMT or UTC to a binary timestamp. Additional inputs include nanoseconds since the last second of Time and nanoseconds of inaccuracy.

Return Values

0 Indicates that the routine executed successfully.

-1 Indicates an invalid time argument or invalid results.

See the sample program in the **utc_cmpintervaltime(3dts)** reference page.

Related Information

Functions: **utc_gmtime(3dts)**.

utc_mklocaltime

Purpose Converts a **tm** structure that expresses local time to a binary timestamp

Synopsis **#include <dce/utc.h>**

int utc_mklocaltime(
  utc_t **utc*,
  const struct tm **timetm*,
  long *tns*,
  const struct tm **inacctm*,
  long *ins***);**

Parameters

Input

timetm A **tm** structure that expresses the local time. On input, **tm_wday** and **tm_yday** are ignored; the value of **tm_isdst** should be -1.

tns Nanoseconds since the Time component.

inacctm A **tm** structure that expresses days, hours, minutes, and seconds of inaccuracy. If **tm_yday** is negative, the inaccuracy is considered to be unspecified. On input, **tm_mday**, **tm_mon**, **tm_wday**, and **tm_isdst** are ignored.

ins Nanoseconds of the inaccuracy component.

Output

utc Resulting binary timestamp.

Description

The **utc_mklocaltime**( ) routine converts a **tm** structure that expresses local time to a binary timestamp.

The user's environment determines the time zone rule (details are system dependent). For example, on OSF/1 systems, the user selects a time zone by specifying the **TZ** environment variable. (The reference information for the **localtime**( ) system call, which is described in the **ctime(3)** reference page, provides additional information.)

If the user's environment does not specify a time zone rule, the system's rule is used (details of the rule are system dependent). For example, on OSF/1 systems, the rule in **/etc/zoneinfo/localtime** applies.

Additional inputs include nanoseconds since the last second of Time and nanoseconds of inaccuracy.

Return Values

0 Indicates that the routine executed successfully.

-1 Indicates an invalid time argument or invalid results.

Examples

See the sample program in the **utc_cmpmidtime(3dts)** reference page.

Related Information

Functions: **utc_localtime(3dts)**.

utc_mkreltime

Purpose Converts a **tm** structure that expresses relative time to a relative binary timestamp

Synopsis **#include <dce/utc.h>**

int utc_mkreltime(
    utc_t **utc*,
    const struct tm **timetm*,
    long *tns*,
    const struct tm **inacctm*,
    long *ins*);

Parameters

Input

timetm A **tm** structure that expresses a relative time. On input, **tm_wday** and **tm_yday** are ignored; the value of **tm_isdst** should be -1.

tns Nanoseconds since the Time component.

inacctm A **tm** structure that expresses seconds of inaccuracy. If **tm_yday** is negative, the inaccuracy is considered to be unspecified. On input, **tm_mday**, **tm_mon**, **tm_year**, **tm_wday**, **tm_isdst**, and **tm_zone** are ignored.

ins Nanoseconds of the inaccuracy component.

Output

utc Resulting relative binary timestamp.

Description

The **utc_mkreltime()** routine converts a **tm** structure that expresses relative time to a relative binary timestamp. Additional inputs include nanoseconds since the last second of Time and nanoseconds of inaccuracy.

Return Values

0 Indicates that the routine executed successfully.

-1 Indicates an invalid time argument or invalid results.

Examples

The following example converts the relative time: 125-03:12:30.1I120.25 to a relative binary timestamp.

```
utc_t         utc;
struct tm     tmtime,tminacc;
long          tnsec,insec;

    /* Fill in the fields
     */
    memset((void *)&tmtime,0,sizeof(tmtime));
    tmtime.tm_mday = 125;
    tmtime.tm_hour = 3;
    tmtime.tm_min  = 12;
    tmtime.tm_sec  = 30;
    tnsec = 100000000;      /* .1 * 1.0E9 */

    memset((void *)&tminacc,0,sizeof(tminacc));
    tminacc.tm_sec = 120;
    tnsec = 250000000;      /* .25 * 1.0E9 */

/* Convert to a relative binary timestamp...
 */
utc_mkreltime(&utc,         /* Out: Resultant relative binary timestamp */
              &tmtime,      /* In:  tm struct that represents input     */
              tnsec,        /* In:  Nanoseconds from input              */
              &tminacc,     /* In:  tm struct that represents inacc     */
              insec);       /* In:  Nanoseconds from input              */
```

utc_mulftime

Purpose Multiplies a relative binary timestamp by a floating-point value.

Synopsis **#include <dce/utc.h>**

int utc_mulftime(
utc_t ***result*,**
const utc_t ***utc1*,**
const double *factor***);**

Parameters

Input

utc1 Relative binary timestamp. Use **NULL** if you want this routine to use the current time for this parameter.

factor Real scale factor (double-precision, floating-point value).

Output

result Resulting relative binary timestamp.

Description

The **utc_mulftime( )** routine multiplies a relative binary timestamp by a floating-point value. Either or both may be negative; the resulting relative binary timestamp has the appropriate sign. The unsigned inaccuracy in the relative binary timestamp is also multiplied by the absolute value of the floating-point value.

Return Values

0 Indicates that the routine executed successfully.

-1 Indicates an invalid time argument or invalid results.

Examples

The following example scales a relative time by a floating-point factor and prints the result.

```
utc_t         relutc, scaledutc;
struct tm     scaledreltm;
char          timstr[UTC_MAX_STR_LEN];

/*    Assume relutc contains the time to scale.
 */
utc_mulftime(&scaledutc,                  /* Out: Scaled rel time      */
             &relutc,                     /* In:  Rel time to scale    */
             17.65);                      /* In:  Scale factor         */

utc_ascreltime(timstr,                    /* Out: ASCII rel time       */
               UTC_MAX_STR_LEN,           /* In:  Input buffer length */
               &scaledutc);               /* In:  Rel time to convert */

printf("%s\n",timstr);

/*     Convert it to a tm structure and print it.
 */
utc_reltime(&scaledreltm,                 /* Out: Scaled rel tm        */
            (long *)0,                    /* Out: Scaled rel nano-sec */
            (struct tm *)0,               /* Out: Scaled rel inacc tm */
            (long *)0,                    /* Out: Scd rel inacc nanos */
            &scaledutc);                  /* In:  Rel time to convert */

printf("Approximately %d days, %d hours and %d minutes\n",
       scaledreltm.tm_yday, scaledreltm.tm_hour, scaledreltm.tm_min);
```

Related Information

Functions: **utc_multime(3dts)**.

utc_multime

Purpose

Multiplies a relative binary timestamp by an integer factor

Synopsis

#include <dce/utc.h>

int utc_multime(
utc_t ***result*,**
const utc_t ***utc1*,**
long *factor***);**

Parameters

Input

utc1 Relative binary timestamp.

factor Integer scale factor.

Output

result Resulting relative binary timestamp.

Description

The **utc_multime()** routine multiplies a relative binary timestamp by an integer. Either or both may be negative; the resulting binary timestamp has the appropriate sign. The unsigned inaccuracy in the binary timestamp is also multiplied by the absolute value of the integer.

Return Values

0 Indicates that the routine executed successfully.

-1 Indicates an invalid time argument or invalid results.

Examples

The following example scales a relative time by an integral value and prints the result.

```
utc_t        relutc, scaledutc;

char         timstr[UTC_MAX_STR_LEN];

/*   Assume relutc contains the time to scale. Scale it by a factor
 *   of 17 ...
 */
utc_multime(&scaledutc,          /* Out: Scaled rel time       */
                  &relutc,       /*  In: Rel time to scale     */
                      17L);      /*  In: Scale factor          */

utc_ascreltime(timstr,           /* Out: ASCII rel time        */
      UTC_MAX_STR_LEN,           /*  In: Input buffer length   */
           &scakedutc);          /*  In: Rel time to convert   */

printf("Scaled result is %s0, timstr);
```

Related Information

Functions: **utc_mulftime(3dts)**.

utc_pointtime

Purpose Converts a binary timestamp to three binary timestamps that represent the earliest, most likely, and latest time

Synopsis **#include <dce/utc.h>**

int utc_pointtime(
  utc_t ***utclp*,**
  utc_t ***utcmp*,**
  utc_t ***utchp*,**
  const utc_t ***utc*);**

Parameters

Input

utc Binary timestamp or relative binary timestamp. Use **NULL** if you want this routine to use the current time for this parameter.

Output

utclp Lowest (earliest) possible absolute time or shortest possible relative time that the input timestamp can represent.

utcmp Midpoint of the input timestamp.

utchp Highest (latest) possible absolute time or longest possible relative time that the input timestamp can represent.

Description

The **utc_pointtime()** routine converts a binary timestamp to three binary timestamps that represent the earliest, latest, and most likely (midpoint) times. If the input is a relative binary time, the outputs represent relative binary times.

Notes

All outputs have zero inaccuracy. An error is returned if the input binary timestamp has an unspecified inaccuracy.

Return Values

0 Indicates that the routine executed successfully.

-1 Indicates an invalid time argument.

Examples

See the sample program in the **utc_addtime(3dts)** reference page.

Related Information

Functions: **utc_boundtime(3dts)**, **utc_spantime(3dts)**.

utc_reltime

Purpose Converts a relative binary timestamp to a **tm** structure

Synopsis **#include <dce/utc.h>**

int utc_reltime(
struct tm ****timetm*,**
long ****tns*,**
struct tm ****inacctm*,**
long ****ins*,**
const utc_t ****utc*);**

Parameters

Input

utc Relative binary timestamp. Use **NULL** if you want this routine to use the current time for this parameter.

Output

timetm Relative time component of the relative binary timestamp. The field **tm_mday** returns a value of -1 and the fields **tm_year** and **tm_mon** return values of 0 (zero). The field **tm_yday** contains the number of days of relative time.

tns Nanoseconds since the Time component of the relative binary timestamp.

inacctm Seconds of the inaccuracy component of the relative binary timestamp. If the inaccuracy is finite, then **tm_mday** returns a value of -1 and **tm_mon** and **tm_year** return values of 0 (zero). The field **tm_yday** contains the inaccuracy in days. If the inaccuracy is unspecified, all **tm** structure fields return values of -1.

ins Nanoseconds of the inaccuracy component of the relative binary timestamp.

Description

The **utc_reltime( )** routine converts a relative binary timestamp to a **tm** structure. Additional returns include nanoseconds since Time and nanoseconds of inaccuracy.

Return Values

0 Indicates that the routine executed successfully.

-1 Indicates an invalid time argument or invalid results.

Examples

See the sample program in the **utc_mulftime(3dts)** reference page.

Related Information

Functions: **utc_mkreltime(3dts)**.

utc_spantime

Purpose Given two (possibly unordered) binary timestamps, returns a single UTC time interval whose inaccuracy spans the two input binary timestamps

Synopsis **#include <dce/utc.h>**

int utc_spantime(
utc_t ***result*,**
const utc_t ***utc1*,**
const utc_t ***utc2*);**

Parameters

Input

utc1 Binary timestamp. Use **NULL** if you want this routine to use the current time for this parameter.

utc2 Binary timestamp. Use **NULL** if you want this routine to use the current time for this parameter.

Output

result Spanning timestamp.

Description

Given two binary timestamps, the **utc_spantime()** routine returns a single UTC time interval whose inaccuracy spans the two input timestamps (that is, the interval resulting from the earliest possible time of either timestamp to the latest possible time of either timestamp).

Notes The *tdf* parameter in the output UTC value is copied from the *utc2* input. If either input binary timestamp has an unspecified inaccuracy, an error is returned.

Return Values

0 Indicates that the routine executed successfully.

-1 Indicates an invalid time argument.

Examples

The following example computes the earliest and latest times for an array of 10 timestamps.

```
utc_t                  time_array[10], testtime, earliest, latest;
int                    i;

/*    Set the running timestamp to the first entry...
 */
testtime = time_array[0];

for (i=1; i<10; i++) {

    /*    Compute the minimum and the maximum against the next
     *    element...
     */
utc_spantime(&testtime,          /* Out: Resultant interval          */
             &testtime,          /* In:  Largest previous interval   */
             &time_array[i]);    /* In:  Element under test          */
}

/*    Compute the earliest and latest possible times
 */

utc_pointtime(&earliest,         /* Out: Earliest poss time in array */
              (utc_t *)0,        /* Out: Midpoint                    */
              &latest,           /* Out: Latest poss time in array   */
              &testtime);        /* In:  Spanning interval           */
```

Related Information

Functions: **utc_boundtime(3dts)**, **utc_gettime(3dts)**, **utc_pointtime(3dts)**.

utc_subtime

Purpose

Computes the difference between two binary timestamps

Synopsis

#include <dce/utc.h>

int utc_subtime(
utc_t ****result*,**
const utc_t ****utc1*,**
const utc_t ****utc2*);**

Parameters

Input

utc1 Binary timestamp or relative binary timestamp. Use **NULL** if you want this routine to use the current time for this parameter.

utc2 Binary timestamp or relative binary timestamp. Use **NULL** if you want this routine to use the current time for this parameter.

Output

result Resulting binary timestamp or relative binary timestamp, depending upon the operation performed:

- *absolute time–absolute time*=**relative time**
- *relative time–relative time*=**relative time**
- *absolute time–relative time*=**absolute time**
- *relative time–absolute time* is undefined. (See the note later in this reference page.)

Description

The **utc_subtime( )** routine subtracts one binary timestamp from another. The two binary timestamps express either an absolute time and a relative time, two relative times, or two absolute times. The resulting timestamp is *utc1* minus *utc2*. The inaccuracies of the two input timestamps are combined and included in the output timestamp. The TDF in the first timestamp is copied to the output.

Notes

Although no error is returned, the combination *relative time–absolute time* should *not* be used.

Return Values

0 Indicates that the routine executed successfully.

-1 Indicates an invalid time argument or invalid results.

Examples

See the sample program in the **utc_binreltime(3dts)** reference page.

Related Information

Functions: **utc_addtime(3dts)**.

Chapter 5

DCE Security Service

intro

Purpose Application Program Interface to the DCE Security Service

Description

The Distributed Computing Environment (DCE) Security Service Application Program Interface (API) allows developers to create network services with complete access to all the authentication and authorization capabilities of DCE Security Service and facilities.

The transaction of a network service generally consists of a client process requesting some action from a server process. The client may itself be a server, or a user, and the server may also be a client of other servers. Before the targeted server executes the specified action, it must be sure of the client's identity, and it must know whether the client is authorized to request the service.

The Security Service API consists of the following five sets of Remote Procedure Calls (RPCs) used to communicate with various security-related services and facilities:

login Validates a principal's network identity.

rgy Maintains the network registry of principal identities.

acl Implements an Access Control List (ACL) protocol for the authorization of a principal to network access and services.

key Provides facilities for the maintenance of account keys for daemon principals.

id Maps file system names to Universal Unique IDs (UUIDs).

All the calls in this API have names beginning with the **sec_** prefix. These are the same calls used by various user-level tools provided as part of the DCE. For example, the **rgy_create(1)** tool is written with **sec_rgy** calls, **acl_edit(1)** is written with **sec_acl** calls, and the **login(1)** program, with which a user logs in to a DCE system, is written using **sec_login** calls. Most sites will find the user-level tools adequate for their needs, and only must use the Security Service API to customize or replace the functionality of these tools.

Though most of the calls in the Security Service API represent RPC transactions, code has been provided on the client side to handle much of the overhead involved with making remote calls. These ''stubs'' handle binding to the requested security server site, the marshalling of data into whatever form is needed for transmission, and other bookkeeping involved with these remote calls. An application programmer can use the Security Service interfaces as if they were composed of simple C functions.

This reference page introduces each of the following APIs:

- Registry APIs
- Login APIs
- ACL APIs
- Key Management APIs
- ID Mapping APIs

The section for each API is organized as follows:

- Synopsis
- Data Types
- Constants
- Status Codes
- Files

REGISTRY API DATA TYPES

Synopsis

#include <dce/rgybase.h>

Data Types

The following data types are used in **sec_rgy_** calls:

sec_rgy_handle_t
A pointer to the registry server handle. The registry server is bound to a handle with the **sec_rgy_site_open( )** routine.

sec_timeval_sec_t
A 32-bit integer containing the seconds portion of a UNIX **timeval_t**, to be used when expressing absolute dates.

sec_timeval_t
A structure containing the full UNIX time. The structure contains two 32-bit integers that indicate seconds (**sec**) and microseconds (**usec**) since 0:00, January 1, 1970.

sec_timeval_period_t
A 32-bit integer expressing seconds relative to some well-known time.

sec_rgy_acct_key_t
Specifies how many parts (person, group, organization) of an account login name will be enough to specify a unique abbreviation for that account.

sec_rgy_cursor_t
A structure providing a pointer into a registry database. This type is used for iterative operations on the registry information. For example, a call to **sec_rgy_pgo_get_members( )** might return the 10 account names following the input **sec_rgy_cursor_t** position. Upon return, the cursor position will have been updated, so the next call to that routine will return the next 10 names. The components of this structure are not used by application programs.

sec_rgy_pname_t
A character string of length **sec_rgy_pname_t_size**.

sec_rgy_name_t
A character string of length **sec_rgy_name_t_size**.

sec_rgy_login_name_t
A struct representing an account login name. It contains three strings of type **sec_rgy_name_t**:

pname The person name for the account.

gname The group name for the account.

oname The organization name for the account.

sec_rgy_member_t
A character string of length **sec_rgy_name_t_size**.

sec_rgy_foreign_id_t
The representation of a foreign ID. This structure contains two components:

cell A string of type **uuid_t** representing the UUID of the foreign cell.

principal A string of type **uuid_t** representing the UUID of the principal.

sec_rgy_sid_t
A structure identifying an account. It contains three fields:

person The UUID of the person part of the account.

group The UUID of the group part of the account.

org The UUID of the organization part of the account.

sec_rgy_unix_sid_t
A structure identifying an account with UNIX ID numbers. It contains three fields:

person The UNIX ID of the person part of the account.

group The UNIX ID of the group part of the account.

org The UNIX ID of the organization part of the account.

sec_rgy_domain_t
This 32-bit integer specifies which naming domain a character string refers to: person, group, or organization.

sec_rgy_pgo_flags_t
A 32-bit bitset containing flags pertaining to registry entries. This type contains the following three flags:

sec_rgy_pgo_is_an_alias
If set, indicates the registry entry is an alias of another entry.

sec_rgy_pgo_is_required
If set, the registry item is required and cannot be deleted. An example of a required account is the one for the registry server itself.

sec_rgy_pgo_projlist_ok
If the accompanying item is a person entry, this flag indicates the person may have concurrent group sets. If the item is a group entry, the flag means this group can appear in a concurrent group set. The flag is undefined for organization items.

sec_rgy_pgo_item_t
The structure identifying a registry item. It contains five components:

id The UUID of the registry item, in **uuid_t** form.

unix_num A 32-bit integer containing the UNIX ID number of the registry item.

quota A 32-bit integer representing the maximum number of user-defined groups the account owner can create.

flags A **sec_rgy_pgo_flags_t** bitset containing information about the entry.

fullname A **sec_rgy_pname_t** character string containing a full name for the registry entry. For a person entry, this field might contain the real name of the account owner. For a group, it might contain a description of the group. This is just a data field, and registry queries cannot search on the **fullname** entry.

sec_rgy_acct_admin_flags_t

A 32-bit bitset containing administration flags used as part of the administrator's information for any registry account. The set contains three flags:

sec_rgy_acct_admin_valid

Specifies that the account is valid for login.

sec_rgy_acct_admin_server

If set, the account's name can be used as a server name in a ticket-granting ticket.

sec_rgy_acct_admin_client

If set, the account's name can be used as a client name in a ticket-granting ticket.

Note that you can prevent the principal from being authenticated, by turning off both the **sec_rgy_acct_admin_server** and the **sec_rgy_acct_admin_client flags**.

sec_rgy_acct_auth_flags_t

A 32-bit bitset containing account authorization flags used to implement authentication policy as defined by the Kerberos Version 5 protocol. The set contains six flags:

sec_rgy_acct_auth_post_dated

Allows issuance of post-dated certificates.

sec_rgy_acct_auth_forwardable

Allows issuance of forwardable certificates.

sec_rgy_acct_auth_tgt
Allows issuance of certificates based on Ticket-Granting Ticket (TGT) authentication. If this flag is not set, a client requesting a service may have to supply a password directly to the server.

sec_rgy_acct_auth_renewable
Allows issuance of renewable certificates.

sec_rgy_acct_auth_proxiable
Allows issuance of proxiable certificates.

sec_rgy_acct_auth_dup_session_key
Allows issuance of duplicate session keys.

sec_rgy_acct_admin_t
The portion of a registry account item that is only directly modifiable by an administrator. This structure consists of the following components:

creator The first four fields are all set by the server. This field, in **foreign_id_t format**, identifies the administrator who created the registry account.

creation_date
Specifies the creation date of the account, in **sec_timeval_sec_t** format.

last_changer Identifies the last person to change any of the account information, in **foreign_id_t** format.

change_date Specifies the date of the last modification of the account information, in **sec_timeval_sec_t** format.

expiration_date
The date after which the account will no longer be valid. In **sec_timeval_sec_t** format.

good_since_date
The Kerberos Version 5 TGT revocation date. TGTs issued before this date will not be honored. In **sec_timeval_sec_t** format.

flags Administrative flags in **sec_rgy_acct_admin_flags_t** format.

authentication_flags
Authentication flags in **sec_rgy_acct_auth_flags_t** format.

sec_rgy_acct_user_flags_t
A 32-bit bitset containing flags controlling user-modifiable information. There is only one flag currently implemented. If **sec_rgy_acct_user_passwd_valid** is set, it indicates the user password is valid. If it is not set, this flag prompts the user to change the password on the next login attempt.

sec_rgy_acct_user_t
A structure containing registry account information that can be modified by the account owner, or other authorized user. It contains seven components:

gecos This is a character string (in **sec_rgy_pname_t** format) containing information about the account user. It generally consists of everything after the full name in the UNIX **gecos** format.

homedir The login directory for the account user, in **sec_rgy_pname_t** format.

shell The default shell for the account user, in **sec_rgy_pname_t** format.

passwd_version_number
An unsigned 32-bit integer, indicating the password version number.

passwd The encrypted account password, in **sec_rgy_unix_passwd_buf_t** format.

passwd_dtm The date the password was established, in **sec_timeval_sec_t** format.

flags Account user flags, in **sec_rgy_acct_user_flags_t** format.

sec_rgy_plcy_pwd_flags_t
A 32-bit bitset containing two flags about password policy:

sec_rgy_plcy_pwd_no_spaces
If set, will not allow spaces in a password.

sec_rgy_plcy_pwd_non_alpha
If set, requires at least one nonalphanumeric character in the password.

sec_rgy_plcy_t
A structure defining aspects of registry account policy. It contains five components:

passwd_min_len
A 32-bit integer describing the minimum number of characters in the account password.

passwd_lifetime
The number of seconds after a password's creation until it expires, in **sec_timeval_period_t** format.

passwd_exp_date
The expiration date of the account password, in **sec_timeval_sec_t** format.

acct_lifespan The number of seconds after the creation of an account before it expires, in **sec_timeval_period_t** format.

passwd_flags Account password policy flags, in **sec_rgy_plcy_pwd_flags_t** format.

sec_rgy_plcy_auth_t
This type describes authentication policy. It is a structure containing two time periods, in **sec_timeval_period_t** format. One, **max_ticket_lifetime**, specifies the maximum length of the period during which a Ticket-Granting Ticket (TGT) will be valid. The other, **max_renewable_lifetime**, specifies the maximum length of time for which such a ticket may be renewed. This authentication policy applies both to the registry as a whole as well as individual accounts. The effective policy for a given account is defined to be the more restrictive of the site and principal authentication policy.

sec_rgy_properties_t
A structure describing some registry properties. It contains the following:

read_version A 32-bit integer describing the earliest version of the **secd** software that can read this registry.

write_version
A 32-bit integer describing the version of the **secd** software that wrote this registry.

minimum_ticket_lifetime
The minimum lifetime of an authentication certificate, in **sec_timeval_period_t** format.

default_certificate_lifetime
The ''normal'' lifetime of an an authentication certificate (ticket-granting ticket in Kerberos parlance), in **sec_timeval_period_t** format. Processes may request authentication certificates with longer lifetimes up to, but not in excess of, the maximum allowable lifetime as determined by the effective policy for the account.

low_unix_id_person
The lowest UNIX number permissible for a person item in the registry.

low_unix_id_group
The lowest UNIX number permissible for a group item in the registry.

low_unix_id_org
The lowest UNIX number permissible for an organization item in the registry.

max_unix_id The largest UNIX number permissible for any registry entry.

flags Property flags, in **sec_rgy_properties_flags_t** format.

realm The name of the cell, in **sec_rgy_name_t** form, for which this registry is the authentication service.

realm_uuid The UUID of the same cell.

sec_rgy_properties_flags_t
A 32-bit bitset, containing flags concerning registry properties:

sec_rgy_prop_readonly
If set (TRUE), indicates that this registry is a query site.

sec_rgy_prop_auth_cert_unbound
If set (TRUE), the registry server will accept requests from any site.

sec_rgy_prop_shadow_passwd
If the shadow password flag is set (TRUE), the registry server will not include the account password when responding to a request for the user data from a specified account. This helps minimize the risk of an account password being intercepted while traveling over the network.

sec_rgy_prop_embedded_unix_id
Indicates that all UUIDs in this registry contain a UNIX number embedded. This implies that the UNIX numbers of objects in the registry cannot be changed, since UUIDs are immutable.

sec_rgy_override_t
A 32-bit integer used as a flag for registry override mode. Currently, its possible values are the constants **sec_rgy_no_override** and **sec_rgy_override**. When this mode is enabled, override data supplied by the node administrator will replace some of the data gotten from the registry for a given person/account under certain conditions. These conditions are as follows:

1. The registry permits the requested overrides to be set for this machine.
2. The override data is intended for person/account at hand.

When the mode is ''override off,'' data from the registry is returned to the end user or the application remains untouched.

sec_rgy_mode_resolve_t
A 32-bit integer used as a flag for resolve mode. Currently, its possible values are the constants **sec_rgy_no_resolve_pname** and **sec_rgy_resolve_pname**. When the mode is enabled, pathnames containing leading // (slashes) will be translated into a form understandable by the local machine's NFS.

sec_rgy_unix_passwd_buf_t
A character array of UNIX password strings.

Constants

The following constants are used in **sec_rgy_** calls:

sec_rgy_default_handle
The value of an unbound registry server handle.

The following 32-bit integer constants are used with the **sec_rgy_acct_key_t** data type:

sec_rgy_acct_key_none
Invalid key.

sec_rgy_acct_key_person
The person name alone is enough.

sec_rgy_acct_key_group
The person and group names are both necessary for the account abbreviation.

sec_rgy_acct_key_org
The person, group, and organization names are all necessary.

sec_rgy_acct_key_last
Key values must be less than this constant.

sec_rgy_pname_t_size
The maximum number of characters in a **sec_rgy_pname_t**.

sec_rgy_name_t_size
The maximum number of characters in a **sec_rgy_name_t**.

sec_rgy_domain_t
The following 32-bit integer constants are the possible values of the **sec_rgy_domain_t** data type:

sec_rgy_domain_person
The name in question refers to a person.

sec_rgy_domain_group
The name in question refers to a group.

sec_rgy_domain_org
The name in question refers to an organization.

sec_rgy_pgo_flags_t
A 32-bit constant equal to a variable of type **sec_rgy_pgo_flags_t** with no flags set.

sec_rgy_quota_unlimited
A 32-bit integer. Set the **quota** field of the **sec_rgy_pgo_item_t** type to this constant to override the registry quota limitation.

sec_rgy_acct_admin_flags_t
A 32-bit integer. This is the value of the **sec_rgy_acct_admin_flags_t** bitset when none of its flags are set.

sec_rgy_acct_auth_flags_none
A 32-bit integer. This is the value of the **sec_rgy_acct_auth_flags_t** bitset when none of its flags are set.

sec_rgy_acct_user_flags_t
A 16-bit integer. This is the value of the **sec_rgy_acct_user_flags_t** bitset when none of its flags are set.

sec_rgy_plcy_pwd_flags_t
A 16-bit integer. This is the value of the **sec_rgy_policy_pwd_flags_t** bitset when none of its flags are set.

sec_rgy_properties_flags_t
A 16-bit integer. This is the value of the **sec_rgy_properties_flags_t** bitset when none of its flags are set.

sec_rgy_override
A 32-bit integer, which turns registry override mode on. When this mode is enabled, override data supplied by the node administrator will replace some of the data gotten from the registry for a given person/account under certain conditions.

sec_rgy_no_override
A 32-bit integer, which turns off registry override mode.

sec_rgy_resolve_pname
A 32-bit integer, which turns on registry resolve mode. When the mode is enabled, pathnames containing leading *//* (slashes) will be translated into a form understandable by the local machine's NFS.

sec_rgy_no_resolve_pname
A 32-bit integer, which turns off registry resolve mode.

Status Codes

The following status codes are used in **sec_rgy_** calls:

sec_rgy_not_implemented
Operation not yet implemented.

sec_rgy_bad_domain
Operation not supported on specified domain.

sec_rgy_object_exists
Object already exists.

sec_rgy_name_exists
Name already exists.

sec_rgy_unix_id_changed
UNIX ID changed on an alias add.

sec_rgy_is_an_alias
Query returned an alias and **allow_aliases** was not set.

sec_rgy_no_more_entries
No more matching entries.

sec_rgy_object_not_found
Registry object not found.

sec_rgy_server_unavailable
Registry server unavailable.

sec_rgy_not_member_group
User is not a member of specified group.

sec_rgy_not_member_org
User is not a member of specified organization.

sec_rgy_not_member_group_org
User is not a member of specified group and organization.

sec_rgy_incomplete_login_name
Incomplete login name specification.

sec_rgy_passwd_invalid
Invalid password.

sec_rgy_not_authorized
User is not authorized to update record.

sec_rgy_read_only
Registry is read-only; updates are not allowed.

sec_rgy_bad_alias_owner
PGO alias entry has an invalid owner.

sec_rgy_bad_data
Invalid data record.

sec_rgy_cant_allocate_memory
Unable to allocate memory.

sec_rgy_dir_not_found
Directory not found.

sec_rgy_dir_not_empty
Directory not empty.

sec_rgy_bad_name
Illegal PGO or directory name.

sec_rgy_dir_could_not_create
Unable to create directory.

sec_rgy_dir_move_illegal
Directory move not allowed.

sec_rgy_quota_exhausted
Principal quota exhausted.

sec_rgy_foreign_quota_exhausted
Foreign quota for realm exhausted.

sec_rgy_no_more_unix_ids
UNIX ID space for domain has been exhausted.

sec_rgy_uuid_bad_version
UUID version invalid.

sec_rgy_key_bad_version
Key version number out of range.

sec_rgy_key_version_in_use
Key version number currently in use.

sec_rgy_key_bad_type
Key type not supported.

sec_rgy_crypt_bad_type
The (de)encryption type is not supported.

sec_rgy_bad_scope
Scope doesn't name existing directory or PGO.

sec_rgy_object_not_in_scope
Object found was not in scope.

sec_rgy_cant_authenticate
Can't establish authentication to security server.

sec_rgy_alias_not_allowed
Can't add alias for this name or principal (e.g., **krbtgt**).

sec_rgy_bad_chksum_type
Checksum type not supported.

sec_rgy_bad_integrity
Data integrity error.

sec_rgy_key_bad_size
Invalid size for key data.

sec_rgy_mkey_cant_read_stored
Can't read stored master key.

sec_rgy_mkey_bad_stored
Stored master key is bad.

sec_rgy_mkey_bad
Supplied master key is bad.

sec_rgy_bad_handle
Bad security context handle.

sec_rgy_s_pgo_is_required
PGO/account is required and can't be deleted.

Files

/usr/include/dce/rgybase.idl
The **idl** file from which **rgybase.h** was derived.

LOGIN API DATA TYPES

Synopsis

#include <dce/sec_login.h>

Data Types

The following data types are used in **sec_login_** calls:

sec_login_handle_t
This is an opaque pointer to a data structure representing a complete login context. The context includes a principal's network credentials, as well as other account information. The network credentials are also referred to as the principal's ''ticket-granting ticket.''

sec_login_flags_t
A 32-bit set of flags describing restrictions on the use of a principal's validated network credentials. Currently, only one flag is implemented, and the set can take on the following two values:

sec_login_no_flags
No special flags are set.

sec_login_credentials_private
Restricts the validated network credentials to the current process. If this flag is not set, it is permissible to share credentials with descendents of current process.

sec_login_auth_src_t
An enumerated set describing how the login context was authorized. There are two possible values:

sec_login_auth_src_network
Authentication accomplished through the normal network authority. A login context authenticated this way will have all the network credentials it ought to have.

sec_login_auth_src_local
Authentication accomplished via local data. Authentication occurs locally if a principal's account is tailored for the local machine, or if the network authority is unavailable. Since login contexts authenticated locally have no network credentials, they may not be used for network operations.

sec_login_passwd_t
The **sec_login_get_pwent( )** call will return a pointer to a ''password'' structure, which depends on the underlying registry structure. In most cases, the structure will look like that supported by Berkeley 4.4BSD and OSF/1, which looks like this:

```
struct passwd {
   char   *pw_name;       * user name *
   char   *pw_passwd;     * encrypted password *
   int    pw_uid;         * user uid *
   int    pw_gid;         * user gid *
   time_t pw_change;      * password change time *
   char   *pw_class;      * user access class *
   char   *pw_gecos;      * Honeywell login info *
   char   *pw_dir;        * home directory *
   char   *pw_shell;      * default shell *
   time_t pw_expire;      * account expiration *
};
```

sec_passwd_rec_t
A structure containing either a plaintext password or a preencrypted buffer of password data. The **sec_passwd_rec_t** structure consists of three components:

version_number
The version number of the password.

pepper
A character string combined with the password before an encryption key is derived from the password.

key_type
The key type can be the following:

sec_passwd_plain
Indicates that a printable string of data is stored in **plain**.

sec_passwd_des_key_t
Indicates that an array of data is stored in **des_key.**

Constants

The following constants are used in **sec_login_** calls:

sec_login_default_handle
The value of a login context handle before setup or validation.

The next two constants are for use with the **sec_login_flags_t** type.

sec_login_no_flags
No special flags are set.

sec_login_credentials_private
Restricts the validated network credentials to the current process. If this flag is not set, it is permissible to share credentials with descendents of current process.

sec_login_remote_uid
Used in the **sec_login_passwd_t** structure for users from remote cells.

sec_login_remote_gid
Used in the **sec_login_passwd_t** structure for users from remote cells.

Status Codes

The following status codes are used in **sec_login_** calls:

error_status_ok
Routine completed successfully.

sec_s_not_implemented
Operation not yet implemented.

sec_s_no_memory
No memory available.

sec_login_s_auth_local
Operation not valid on local context.

sec_login_s_handle_invalid
Context handle not valid.

sec_login_s_context_invalid
Context has not been validated.

sec_login_s_no_current_context
No currently established network identity for which context exists.

sec_login_s_groupset_invalid
The group set is not valid.

sec_login_s_info_not_avail
Information not available.

sec_login_s_default_use
Illegal use of default **sec_login** handle.

sec_login_s_already_valid
Login context has already been validated.

sec_login_s_privileged
User is not a privileged user (effective UNIX ID is not 0).

sec_login_s_not_certified
The Ticket Granting Ticket (TGT) is not certified.

sec_login_s_config
Bad configuration file (or **sec_clientd** could not validate the TGT).

sec_login_s_internal_error
Internal error.

sec_login_s_no_override_info
No override information.

sec_login_s_acct_invalid
Account is invalid.

sec_login_s_null_password
Password is a null password.

sec_login_s_unsupp_passwd_type
The password is an unsupported type.

sec_login_s_no_identity
There is no login identity.

sec_login_s_refresh_ident_bad
The identity to be refreshed is bad (changed).

sec_login_s_override_failure
Unable to determine if override exists.

sec_login_s_ovrd_ent_not_found
No matching override entry found.

sec_login_s_invalid_password
Invalid password.

sec_login_s_incomplete_ovrd_ent
Incomplete override entry, cannot proceed.

Files **/usr/include/dce/sec_login.idl**
The **idl** file from which **sec_login.h** was derived.

ACL API DATA TYPES

Synopsis **#include <dce/aclbase.h>**

Data Types

The following data types are used in **sec_acl_** calls:

sec_acl_handle_t
A pointer to an opaque handle bound to an ACL that is the subject of a test or examination. The handle is bound to the ACL with **sec_acl_bind**( ). An unbound handle has the value **sec_acl_default_handle**.

sec_acl_t
This data type is the fundamental type for the ACL manager interfaces. The **sec_acl_t** type contains a complete access control list, made up of a list of entry fields (type **sec_acl_entry_t**). The default cell identifies the authentication authority for simple ACL entries (foreign entries identify their own foreign cells). The **sec_acl_manager_type** identifies the manager to interpret this ACL.

The **sec_acl_t** type is a structure containing the following fields:

default_realm
A structure of type **sec_acl_id_t**, this identifies the UUID and (optionally) the name of the default cell.

sec_acl_manager_type
Contains the UUID of the ACL manager type.

num_entries An unsigned 32-bit integer containing the number of ACL entries in this ACL.

sec_acl_entries
An array containing **num_entries** pointers to different ACL entries, each of type **sec_acl_entry_t**.

sec_acl_p_t
This data type, simply a pointer to a **sec_acl_t**, is for use with the **sec_acl_list_t** data type.

sec_acl_list_t
This data type is a structure containing an unsigned 32-bit integer **num_acls** that describes the number of ACLs indicated by its companion array of pointers, **sec_acls**, of type **sec_acl_p_t**.

sec_acl_entry_t
The **sec_acl_entry_t** type is a structure made up of the following components:

perms A set of flags of type **sec_acl_permset_t** that describe the permissions granted for the principals identified by this ACL entry. Note that if a principal matches more than one ACL entry, the effective permissions will be the most restrictive combination of all the entries.

entry_info A structure containing two members:

entry_type A flag of type **sec_acl_entry_type_t**, indicating the type of ACL entry.

tagged_union
A tagged union whose contents depend on the type of the entry.

The types of entries indicated by **entry_type** can be the following:

sec_acl_e_type_user_obj
The entry contains permissions for the implied user object. This type is described in the POSIX 1003.6 standard.

sec_acl_e_type_group_obj
The entry contains permissions for the implied group object. This type is described in the POSIX 1003.6 standard.

sec_acl_e_type_other_obj
The entry contains permissions for principals not otherwise named through user or group entries. This type is described in the POSIX 1003.6 standard.

sec_acl_e_type_user
The entry contains a key that identifies a user. This type is described in the POSIX 1003.6 standard.

sec_acl_e_type_group
The entry contains a key that identifies a group. This type is described in the POSIX 1003.6 standard.

sec_acl_e_type_mask_obj
The entry contains the maximum permissions for all entries other than **mask_obj**, **unauthenticated**, **user_obj**, **other_obj**.

sec_acl_e_type_foreign_user
The entry contains a key that identifies a user and the foreign realm.

sec_acl_e_type_foreign_group
The entry contains a key that identifies a group and the foreign realm.

sec_acl_e_type_foreign_other
The entry contains a key that identifies a foreign realm. Any user that can authenticate to the foreign realm will be allowed access.

sec_acl_e_type_any_other
The entry contains permissions to be applied to any accessor who can authenticate to any realm, but is not identified in any other entry (except **sec_acl_e_type_unauthenticated**).

sec_acl_e_type_unauthenticated
The entry contains permissions to be applied when the accessor does not pass authentication procedures. A privilege attribute

certificate will indicate that the caller's identity is not authenticated. The identity is used to match against the standard entries, but the access rights are masked by this mask. If this mask does not exist in an ACL, the ACL is assumed to grant no access and all unauthenticated access attempts will be denied.

Great care should be exercised when allowing unauthenticated access to an object. Almost by definition, unauthenticated access is very easy to spoof. The presence of this mask on an ACL essentially means that anyone can get at least as much access as allowed by the mask.

sec_acl_e_type_extended
The entry contains additional ''pickled'' data. This kind of entry cannot be interpreted, but can be used by an out-of-date client when copying an ACL from one manager to another (assuming that the two managers each understand the data).

The contents of the tagged union depend on the entry type.

For the following entry types, the union contains a UUID and an optional print string (called **entry_info.tagged_union.id** with type **sec_id_t**) for an identified local principal, or for an identified foreign realm.

- **sec_acl_e_type_user**
- **sec_acl_e_type_group**
- **sec_acl_type_foreign_other**

For the following entry types, the union contains two UUIDs and optional print strings (called **entry_info.tagged_union.foreign_id** with type **sec_id_foreign_t**) for an identified foreign principal and its realm.

- **sec_acl_e_type_foreign_user**
- **sec_acl_e_type_foreign_group**

For an extended entry (**sec_acl_e_type_extended**), the union contains **entry_info.tagged_union.extended_info**, a pointer to an information block of type **sec_acl_extend_info_t**.

sec_acl_permset_t
A 32-bit set of permission flags. The flags currently represent the conventional file system permissions (read, write, execute) and the extended DFS permissions (owner, insert, delete). The ''unused'' flags represent permissions that can only be interpreted by the manager for the

object. For example, **sec_acl_perm_unused_00000080** may mean to one ACL manager that withdrawals are allowed, and to another ACL manager that rebooting is allowed.

The following constants are defined for use with the **sec_acl_permset_t** data type:

sec_acl_perm_read
The ACL allows read access to the protected object.

sec_acl_perm_write
The ACL allows write access to the protected object.

sec_acl_perm_execute
The ACL allows execute access to the protected object.

sec_acl_perm_control
The ACL allows the ACL itself to be modified.

sec_acl_perm_insert
The ACL allows insert access to the protected object.

sec_acl_perm_delete
The ACL allows delete access to the protected object.

sec_acl_perm_test
The ACL allows access to the protected object only to the extent of being able to test for existence.

The bits from 0x00000080 to 0x80000000 are not used by the conventional ACL permission set. Constants of the form **sec_acl_perm_unused_00000080** have been defined so application programs can easily use these bits for extended ACLs.

sec_acl_extend_info_t
This is an extended information block, provided for future extensibility. Primarily, this allows an out-of-date client to read an ACL from a newer manager and apply it to another (up-to-date) manager. The data cannot be interpreted by the out-of-date client without access to the appropriate ''pickling'' routines (that presumably are unavailable to such a client).

In general, ACL managers should not accept ACLs that contain entries the manager does not understand. The manager clearly cannot perform the security service requested by an uninterpretable entry, and it is considered a security breach to lead a client to believe that the manager is performing a particular class of service if the manager cannot do so.

The data structure is made up of the following components:

extension_type
The UUID of the extension type.

format_label The format of the label, in **ndr_format_t** form.

num_bytes An unsigned 32-bit integer indicating the number of bytes containing the ''pickled'' data.

pickled_data The byte array containing the ''pickled'' data.

sec_acl_type_t

The **sec_acl_type_t** type differentiates among the various types of ACLs an object can possess. Most file system objects will only have one ACL controlling the access to that object, but objects that control the creation of other objects (sometimes referred to as ''containers'') may have more. For example, a directory can have three different ACLs: the directory ACL, controlling access to the directory; the initial object (or default object) ACL, which serves as a mask when creating new objects in the directory; and the initial directory (or default directory) ACL, which serves as a mask when creating new directories (containers).

The **sec_acl_type_t** is an enumerated set containing one of the following values:

sec_acl_type_object
The ACL refers to the specified object.

sec_acl_type_default_object
The ACL is to be used when creating objects in the container.

sec_acl_type_default_container
The ACL is to be used when creating nested containers.

The following values are defined but not currently used. They are available for application programs that may create an application-specific ACL definition.

sec_acl_type_unspecified_3

sec_acl_type_unspecified_4

sec_acl_type_unspecified_5

sec_acl_type_unspecified_6

sec_acl_type_unspecified_7

sec_acl_printstring_t
A **sec_acl_printstring_t** structure contains a printable representation for a permission in a **sec_acl_permset_t** permission set. This allows a generic ACL editing tool to be used for application-specific ACLs. The tool need not know the printable representation for each permission bit in a given permission set. The following functions will query an ACL manager for the print strings of the permissions it supports: **sec_acl_get_printstring()** or **sec_acl_mgr_get_printstring()**.

The structure consists of three components:

printstring A character string of maximum length **sec_acl_printstring_len** describing the printable representation of a specified permission.

helpstring A character string of maximum length **sec_acl_printstring_help_len** containing some text that may be used to describe the specified permission.

permissions A **sec_acl_permset_t** permission set describing the permissions that will be represented with the specified print string.

sec_acl_component_name_t
This type is a pointer to a character string, to be used to specify the entity a given ACL is protecting.

Constants

The following constants are used in **sec_acl_** calls:

sec_acl_default_handle
The value of an unbound ACL manager handle.

The following 32-bit integer constants are used with the **sec_rgy_acct_key_t** data type:

sec_rgy_acct_key_none
Invalid key.

sec_rgy_acct_key_person
The person name alone is enough.

sec_rgy_acct_key_group
The person and group names are both necessary for the account abbreviation.

sec_rgy_acct_key_org
The person, group, and organization names are all necessary.

sec_rgy_acct_key_last
Key values must be less than this constant.

sec_rgy_pname_t_size
The maximum number of characters in a **sec_rgy_pname_t**.

The following constants are defined for use with the **sec_acl_permset_t** data type:

sec_acl_perm_read
The ACL allows read access to the protected object.

sec_acl_perm_write
The ACL allows write access to the protected object.

sec_acl_perm_execute
The ACL allows execute access to the protected object.

sec_acl_perm_owner
The ACL allows owner-level access to the protected object.

sec_acl_perm_insert
The ACL allows insert access to the protected object.

sec_acl_perm_delete
The ACL allows delete access to the protected object.

sec_acl_perm_test
The ACL allows access to the protected object only to the extent of being able to test for existence.

sec_acl_perm_unused_00000080 - **sec_acl_perm_unused_0x80000000**
The bits from 0x00000080 to 0x80000000 are not used by the conventional ACL permission set. Constants have been defined so application programs can easily use these bits for extended ACLs.

sec_acl_printstring_len
The maximum length of the printable representation of an ACL permission. (See **sec_acl_printstring_t**.)

sec_acl_printstring_help_len
The maximum length of a help message to be associated with a supported ACL permission. (See **sec_acl_printstring_t**.)

Status Codes

The following status codes are used in **sec_acl_** calls:

sec_rgy_status_ok
Generic status ok.

sec_acl_not_implemented
The requested operation has not yet been implemented.

sec_acl_cant_allocate_memory
The requested operation requires more memory than is available.

sec_acl_invalid_site_name
The site name is not valid.

sec_acl_unknown_manager_type
The manager type selected is not an available option.

sec_acl_object_not_found
The requested object could not be found.

sec_acl_no_acl_found
The requested ACL was not present.

sec_acl_invalid_entry_name
The requested entry name is invalid.

sec_acl_expected_user_obj
The ACL entry is not type **user_obj**.

sec_acl_expected_group_obj
The ACL entry is not of type **group_obj**.

sec_acl_invalid_entry_type
The ACL entry type is not valid.

sec_acl_invalid_type
The ACL type is not valid.

sec_acl_bad_key
The ACL entry key is not valid.

sec_acl_invalid_manager_type
The manager type is not valid.

sec_acl_read_only
The ACL is read-only.

sec_acl_site_read_only
The site ACL is read-only.

sec_acl_invalid_permission
The permissions for this ACL are invalid.

sec_acl_bad_acl_syntax
The syntax of the ACL entry is invalid.

sec_acl_no_owner
The requested operation requires owner permission.

sec_acl_unable_to_authenticate
The requested operation requires authentication.

sec_acl_name_resolution_failed
The name requested in the operation cannot be resolved.

sec_acl_rpc_error
The operation requested failed in RPC.

sec_acl_bind_error
Unable to get ACL binding.

sec_invalid_acl_handle
The ACL binding handle is invalid.

sec_acl_no_update sites
No update site for this ACL operation.

sec_acl_mgr_file_open_error
The ACL manager could not open the data file.

sec_acl_missing_required_entry
The ACL is missing a required entry.

sec_acl_duplicate_entry
The ACL has duplicate entries.

sec_acl_bad_parameter
Parameter passed is invalid.

sec_acl_not_authorized
The requested operation is not allowed.

Files

/usr/include/dce/aclbase.idl
The **idl** file from which **aclbase.h** was derived.

KEY MANAGEMENT API DATA TYPES

Notes

Key management operations that take a keydata argument expect a pointer to a **sec_passwd_rec_t** structure, and those that take a keytype argument (**void** *) expect a pointer to a **sec_passwd_type_t**. Key management operations that yield a keydata argument as output set the pointer to an array of **sec_passwd_rec_t**. (The array is terminated by an element with a key type of **sec_passwd_none**.)

Operations that take a keydata argument expect a pointer to a **sec_passwd_rec_t** structure. Operations that yield a keydata argument as output set the pointer to an array of **sec_passwd_rec_t**. (The array is terminated by an element with key type **sec_passwd_none**.) Operations that take a keytype argument (**void** *) expect a pointer to a **sec_passwd_type_t**.

Synopsis

#include <dce/keymgmt.h>

Data Types

The only data type defined for the key management API is **sec_key_mgmt_authn_service**, a 32-bit unsigned integer whose purpose is to indicate the authentication service in use, since a server may have different keys for different levels of security. The possible values of this data type and their meanings are as follows:

rpc_c_authn_none
No authentication.

rpc_c_authn_dce_private
DCE private key authentication (an implementation of the Kerberos system).

rpc_c_authn_dce_public
DCE public key authentication (reserved for future use).

Constants There are no constants specially defined for use with the key management API.

Status Codes

The following status codes are used in **sec_key_mgmt** calls:

sec_key_mgmt_e_key_unavailable
The principal's current key is unavailable.

sec_key_mgmt_e_authn_invalid
The authentication service is invalid.

sec_key_mgmt_e_auth_unavailable
The authentication service is unavailable.

sec_key_mgmt_e_unauthorized
The caller is unauthorized to perform operation.

sec_key_mgmt_e_key_unsupported
A requested key type is not supported.

sec_key_mgmt_e_key_version_ex
The specified key already exists in key store.

sec_key_mgmt_e_not_implemented
The operation is not implemented.

Files **/usr/include/dce/keymgmt.idl**
The **idl** file from which **keymgmt.h** was derived.

ID MAPPING API DATA TYPES

Synopsis **#include <dce/secidmap.h>**

Data Types

No special data types are defined for the ID Mapping API.

Constants No special constants are defined for the ID Mapping API.

Status Codes

The following status codes are used in **sec_id** calls:

sec_id_e_name_too_long
The name is too long for current implementation.

sec_id_e_bad_cell_uuid
The cell UUID is not a valid cell name.

sec_id_e_foreign_cell_referral
The global name yields a principal in foreign cell, use referral.

Files

/usr/include/dce/secidmap.idl
The **idl** file from which **secidmap.h** was derived.

rdacl_get_access

Purpose Reads a privilege attribute certificate

Synopsis **#include <dce/rdaclif.h>**

void rdacl_get_access(
handle_t *h*,
sec_acl_component_name_t *component_name*,
uuid_t **manager_type*,
sec_acl_permset_t **net_rights*,
error_status_t **status*);

Parameters

Input

h A handle referring to the object whose ACL is to be accessed. Use **sec_acl_bind( )** to create this handle.

component_name A character string containing the name of the target object.

manager_type A pointer to the UUID identifying the type of the ACL manager in question. There may be more than one type of ACL manager protecting the object whose ACL is bound to the input handle. Use this parameter to distinguish them. Use **sec_acl_get_manager_types( )** to acquire a list of the manager types protecting a given object.

Output

net_rights The output list of access rights, in **sec_acl_permset_t** form. This is a 32-bit set of permission flags supported by the manager type.

status A pointer to the completion status. On successful completion, the routine returns **error_status_ok**. Otherwise, it returns an error.

Description

The **rdacl_get_access( )** routine determines the complete extent of access to the specified object by the calling process. Although the **rdacl_test_access( )** routines are the preferred method of testing access, this routine is useful for implementing operations like the conventional UNIX access function.

Notes

This call is not intended to be used by application programs. The **sec_acl** Application Programming Interface (API) provides all the functionality necessary to use the ACL facility. This reference page is provided for programmers who wish to write an ACL manager. In order to write an ACL manager, a programmer must implement the entire **rdacl** interface. The **sec_acl_mgr** reference pages are provided as an example of a successful implementation. (See **intro(3sec)** for more information about writing an ACL manager.)

This network interface is called on the client side via the **sec_acl** local interface. Developers are responsible for implementing the server side of this interface. Test server code is included as a sample implementation.

Files

/usr/include/dce/rdaclif.idl
The **idl** file from which **dce/rdaclif.h** was derived.

Errors

error_status_ok The call was successful.

Related Information

Functions: **intro(3sec)**, **rdacl_test_access(3sec)**.

rdacl_get_manager_types

Purpose Lists the types of ACLs protecting an object

Synopsis **#include <dce/rdaclif.h>**

void rdacl_get_manager_types(
handle_t *h*,
sec_acl_component_name_t *component_name*,
sec_acl_type_t *sec_acl_type*,
unsigned32 *size_avail*,
unsigned32 **size_used*,
unsigned32 **num_types*,
uuid_t *manager_types*[ ],
error_status_t **status*);

Parameters

Input

h A handle referring to the target object. Use **sec_acl_bind**( ) to create this handle.

component_name
A character string containing the name of the target object.

sec_acl_type The ACL type. The **sec_acl_type_t** data type distinguishes the various types of ACLs an object can possess for a given manager type. The possible values are as follows:

- **sec_acl_type_object**
- **sec_acl_type_default_object**
- **sec_acl_type_default_container**

size_avail An unsigned 32-bit integer containing the allocated length of the *manager_types*[ ] array.

Output

size_used An unsigned 32-bit integer containing the number of output entries returned in the *manager_types*[ ] array.

num_types An unsigned 32-bit integer containing the number of types returned in the *manager_types*[ ] array. This is always equal to *size_used*.

manager_types[ ]
An array of length *size_avail* to contain UUIDs (of type **uuid_t**) identifying the different types of ACL managers protecting the target object.

status A pointer to the completion status. On successful completion, the routine returns **error_status_ok**. Otherwise, it returns an error.

Description

The **rdacl_get_manager_types( )** routine returns a list of the types of ACLs protecting an object. For example, in addition to the regular file system ACL, a file representing the stable storage of some database could have an ACL manager that supported permissions allowing database updates only on certain days of the week.

ACL editors and browsers can use this operation to determine the ACL manager types that a particular reference monitor is using to protect a selected entity. Then, using the **rdacl_get_printstring( )** routine, they can determine how to format for display the permissions supported by a specific manager.

Notes

This call is not intended to be used by application programs. The **sec_acl** Application Programming Interface (API) provides all the functionality necessary to use the ACL facility. This reference page is provided for programmers who wish to write an ACL manager. In order to write an ACL manager, a programmer must implement the entire **rdacl** interface. The **sec_acl_mgr** reference pages are provided as an example of a successful implementation. (See **intro(3sec)** for more information about writing an ACL manager.)

This network interface is called on the client side via the **sec_acl** local interface. Developers are responsible for implementing the server side of this interface. Test server code is included as a sample implementation.

Files

/usr/include/dce/rdaclif.idl The **idl** file from which **dce/rdaclif.h** was derived.

Errors

error_status_ok	The call was successful.

Related Information

Functions: **intro(3sec)**, **rdacl_get_printstring(3sec)**.

rdacl_get_printstring

Purpose Returns printable ACL strings

Synopsis **#include <dce/rdaclif.h>**

void rdacl_get_printstring(
handle_t *h*,
uuid_t **manager_type*,
unsigned32 *size_avail*,
uuid_t **manager_type_chain*,
sec_acl_printstring_t **manager_info*,
boolean32 **tokenize*,
unsigned32 **total_num_printstrings*,
unsigned32 **size_used*,
sec_acl_printstring_t *printstrings*[ ],
error_status_t **status*);

Parameters

Input

h A handle referring to the target object. Use **sec_acl_bind**( ) to create this handle.

manager_type
A pointer to the UUID identifying the type of the ACL manager in question. There may be more than one type of ACL manager protecting the object whose ACL is bound to the input handle. Use this parameter to distinguish them. Use **rdacl_get_manager_types**( ) to acquire a list of the manager types protecting a given object.

size_avail An unsigned 32-bit integer containing the allocated length of the *printstrings*[ ] array.

Output

manager_type_chain
If the target object ACL contains more than 32 permission bits, multiple manager types are used, one for each 32-bit wide ''slice'' of permissions. The UUID returned in *manager_type_chain* refers

to the next ACL manager in the chain. If there are no more ACL managers for this ACL, **uuid_nil** is returned.

manager_info Provides a name and helpstring for the given ACL manager.

tokenize When FALSE this variable indicates that the returned permission printstrings are unambiguous and therefore may be concatenated when printed without confusion. When TRUE, however, this property does not hold, and the strings need to be separated when printed or passed.

total_num_printstrings
An unsigned 32-bit integer containing the total number of permission printstrings supported by this ACL manager type.

size_used An unsigned 32-bit integer containing the number of permission entries returned in the *printstrings*[ ] array.

printstrings[ ] An array of permission printstrings of type **sec_acl_printstring_t**. Each entry of the array is a structure containing three components:

printstring A character string of maximum length **sec_acl_printstring_len** containing the printable representation of a specified permission.

helpstring A character string of maximum length **sec_acl_printstring_help_len** containing some text that can be used to describe the specified permission.

permissions A **sec_acl_permset_t** permission set describing the permissions that are to be represented with the companion printstring.

The array consists of one such entry for each permission supported by the ACL manager identified by *manager_type*.

status A pointer to the completion status. On successful completion, the routine returns **error_status_ok**. Otherwise, it returns an error.

Description

The **rdacl_get_printstring( )** routine returns an array of printable representations (called printstrings) for each permission bit or combination of permission bits the specified ACL manager will support. The ACL manager type specified must be one of the types indicated by the ACL handle.

In addition to returning the printstrings, this routine also returns instructions about how to print the strings. When the *tokenize* variable is set to FALSE, a print string might be `r` or `w`, which could be concatenated in the display as `rw` without any confusion. However, when the *tokenize* variable is TRUE, it implies the printstrings might be of a form like `read` or `write`, which must be displayed separated by spaces or colons or something.

In any list of permission printstrings, there may appear to be some redundancy. ACL managers often define aliases for common permission combinations. By convention, however, simple entries need to appear at the beginning of the *printstrings*[ ] array, and combinations need to appear at the end.

Notes

This call is not intended to be used by application programs. The **sec_acl** Application Programming Interface (API) provides all the functionality necessary to use the ACL facility. This reference page is provided for programmers who wish to write an ACL manager. In order to write an ACL manager, a programmer must implement the entire **rdacl** interface. The **sec_acl_mgr** reference pages are provided as an example of a successful implementation. (See **intro(3sec)** for more information about writing an ACL manager.)

This network interface is called on the client side via the **sec_acl** local interface. Developers are responsible for implementing the server side of this interface. Test server code is included as a sample implementation.

Files

/usr/include/dce/rdaclif.idl The **idl** file from which **dce/rdaclif.h** was derived.

Errors

sec_acl_unknown_manager_type
The manager type selected is not among those referenced by the input handle.

error_status_ok
The call was successful.

Related Information

Functions: **intro(3sec)**, **sec_acl_bind(3sec)**, **rdacl_get_manager_types(3sec)**.

rdacl_get_referral

Purpose Gets a referral to an ACL update site

Synopsis **#include <dce/rdaclif.h>**

void rdacl_get_referral(
handle_t *h*,
sec_acl_component_name_t *component_name*,
uuid_t **manager_type*,
sec_acl_type_t *sec_acl_type*,
sec_acl_tower_set_t **towers*[ ],
error_status_t **status*);

Parameters

Input

h A handle referring to the target object. Use **sec_acl_bind()** to create this handle.

component_name
A character string containing the name of the target object.

manager_type A pointer to the UUID identifying the type of the ACL manager in question. There may be more than one type of ACL manager protecting the object whose ACL is bound to the input handle. Use this parameter to distinguish them. Use **sec_acl_get_manager_types()** to acquire a list of the manager types protecting a given object.

sec_acl_type The ACL type. The **sec_acl_type_t** data type distinguishes the various types of ACLs an object can possess for a given manager type. The possible values are as follows:

- **sec_acl_type_object**
- **sec_acl_type_default_object**
- **sec_acl_type_default_container**

Output

towers[ ] A pointer to address information indicating an ACL update site. This information, obtained from the RPC runtime, is used by the client-side code to construct a new ACL binding handle indicating a site that will not return the **sec_acl_site_readonly** error.

The **sec_acl_tower_set_t** structure contains an array of towers (called *towers*[ ]) and an unsigned 32-bit integer indicating the number of array elements (called *count*). This type enables the client to pass in an unallocated array of towers and have the server allocate the correct amount.

status A pointer to the completion status. On successful completion, the routine returns **error_status_ok**. Otherwise, it returns an error.

Description

The **rdacl_get_referral( )** routine obtains a referral to an ACL update site. This function is used when the current ACL site yields a **sec_acl_site_readonly** error. Some replication managers will require all updates for a given object to be directed to a given replica. If clients of the generic ACL interface know they are dealing with an object that is replicated in this way, this function allows them to recover from the problem and rebind to the proper update site. The DCE network registry, for example, is replicated this way.

Notes

This call is not intended to be used by application programs. The **sec_acl** Application Programming Interface (API) provides all the functionality necessary to use the ACL facility. This reference page is provided for programmers who wish to write an ACL manager. In order to write an ACL manager, a programmer must implement the entire **rdacl** interface. The **sec_acl_mgr** reference pages are provided as an example of a successful implementation. (See **intro(3sec)** for more information about writing an ACL manager.)

This network interface is called on the client side via the **sec_acl** local interface. Developers are responsible for implementing the server side of this interface. Test server code is included as a sample implementation.

Files

/usr/include/dce/rdaclif.idl The **idl** file from which **dce/rdaclif.h** was derived.

Errors

sec_acl_unknown_manager_type
The manager type selected is not an available option.

error_status_ok
The call was successful.

Related Information

Functions: **intro(3sec)**.

rdacl_lookup

Purpose Returns the ACL for an object

Synopsis **#include <dce/rdaclif.h>**

void rdacl_lookup(
handle_t *h*,
sec_acl_component_name_t *component_name*,
uuid_t **manager_type*,
sec_acl_type_t *sec_acl_type*,
sec_acl_result_t **result*);

Parameters

Input

h A handle referring to the target object. Use **sec_acl_bind( )** to create this handle.

component_name A character string containing the name of the target object.

manager_type A pointer to the UUID identifying the type of the ACL manager in question. There may be more than one type of ACL manager protecting the object whose ACL is bound to the input handle. Use this parameter to distinguish them. Use **sec_acl_get_manager_types( )** to acquire a list of the manager types protecting a given object.

sec_acl_type The ACL type. The **sec_acl_type_t** data type distinguishes the various types of ACLs an object can possess for a given manager type. The possible values are as follows:

- **sec_acl_type_object**
- **sec_acl_type_default_object**
- **sec_acl_type_default_container**

Output

result — A pointer to a tagged union of type **sec_acl_result_t**. The tag is the completion status, *result.st*, and if equal to **error_status_ok**, the union contains an ACL. Otherwise, the completion status indicates an error, and the union is empty. This strategy avoids pointlessly sending an ACL across the network when there has been an error.

If the call returned successfully, the **result.sec_acl** (type **sec_acl_t**) structure contains a complete Access Control List. An ACL contains a list of ACL entries, the UUID of the default cell where authentication will take place (foreign entries in the ACL contain the name of their parent cell), and the UUID of the ACL manager to interpret the list.

Description

The **rdacl_lookup()** routine loads into memory a copy of an object's ACL corresponding to the specified manager type. The routine returns a pointer to the ACL. This routine is only used by ACL editors and browsers; an application would use **sec_acl_test_access()** or **sec_acl_test_access_on_behalf()** to process the contents of an ACL.

Notes

This call is not intended to be used by application programs. The **sec_acl** Application Programming Interface (API) provides all the functionality necessary to use the ACL facility. This reference page is provided for programmers who wish to write an ACL manager. In order to write an ACL manager, a programmer must implement the entire **rdacl** interface. The **sec_acl_mgr** reference pages are provided as an example of a successful implementation. (See **intro(3sec)** for more information about writing an ACL manager.)

This network interface is called on the client side via the **sec_acl** local interface. Developers are responsible for implementing the server side of this interface. Test server code is included as a sample implementation.

Files

/usr/include/dce/rdaclif.idl — The **idl** file from which **dce/rdaclif.h** was derived.

Errors

sec_acl_unknown_manager_type
The manager type selected is not an available option.

sec_acl_cant_allocate_memory
The requested operation requires more memory than is available.

error_status_ok
The call was successful.

Related Information

Functions: **intro(3sec)**, **sec_acl_bind(3sec)**, **sec_acl_test_access(3sec)**, **sec_acl_test_access_on_behalf(3sec)**.

rdacl_replace

Purpose

Replaces an ACL

Synopsis

#include <dce/rdaclif.h>

void rdacl_replace(
handle_t *h*,
sec_acl_component_name_t *component_name*,
uuid_t **manager_type*,
sec_acl_type_t *sec_acl_type*,
sec_acl_list_t **sec_acl_list*,
error_status_t **status*);

Parameters

Input

h A handle referring to the target object. Use **sec_acl_bind**( ) to create this handle.

component_name
A character string containing the name of the target object.

manager_type A pointer to the UUID identifying the type of the ACL manager in question. There may be more than one type of ACL manager protecting the object whose ACL is bound to the input handle. Use this parameter to distinguish them. Use **sec_acl_get_manager_types**( ) to acquire a list of the manager types protecting a given object.

sec_acl_type The ACL type. The **sec_acl_type_t** data type distinguishes the various types of ACLs an object can possess for a given manager type. The possible values are as follows:

- **sec_acl_type_object**
- **sec_acl_type_default_object**
- **sec_acl_type_default_container**

sec_acl_list The new ACL to use for the target object. This is represented by a pointer to the **sec_acl_list_t** structure containing the complete Access Control List. An ACL contains a list of ACL entries, the

UUID of the default cell where authentication takes place (foreign entries in the ACL contain the name of their parent cell), and the UUID of the ACL manager to interpret the list.

Output

status A pointer to the completion status. On successful completion, the routine returns **error_status_ok**. Otherwise, it returns an error.

Description

The **rdacl_replace**( ) routine replaces the ACL indicated by the input handle with the information in the *sec_acl_list* parameter. ACLs are thought of as immutable, and in order to modify them, an editing application must read an entire ACL (using the **sec_acl_lookup**( ) routine), modify it as needed, and replace it using this routine.

Notes

This call is not intended to be used by application programs. The **sec_acl** Application Programming Interface (API) provides all the functionality necessary to use the ACL facility. This reference page is provided for programmers who wish to write an ACL manager. In order to write an ACL manager, a programmer must implement the entire **rdacl** interface. The **sec_acl_mgr** reference pages are provided as an example of a successful implementation. (See **intro(3sec)** for more information about writing an ACL manager.)

This network interface is called on the client side via the **sec_acl** local interface. Developers are responsible for implementing the server side of this interface. Test server code is included as a sample implementation.

Cautions

There is no authorization checking performed on this operation; it is strictly local. The application needs to call **sec_acl_mgr_test_access**( ) with *desired_permset* set to ''permission setting'' or ''owner'' or something indicating permission to set the ACL before actually attempting the replace.

Files

/usr/include/dce/rdaclif.idl The **idl** file from which **dce/rdaclif.h** was derived.

Errors

sec_acl_unknown_manager_type
The manager type selected is not an available option.

error_status_ok
The call was successful.

Related Information

Functions: **intro(3sec)**, **sec_acl_bind(3sec)**, **sec_acl_lookup(3sec)**.

rdacl_test_access

Purpose Tests access to an object

Synopsis **#include <dce/rdaclif.h>**

boolean32 rdacl_test_access(
  handle_t *h*,
  sec_acl_component_name_t *component_name*,
  uuid_t **manager_type*,
  sec_acl_permset_t *desired_permset*,
  error_status_t **status*);

Parameters

Input

h A handle referring to the target object. Use **sec_acl_bind**( ) to create this handle.

component_name
A character string containing the name of the target object.

manager_type A pointer to the UUID identifying the type of the ACL manager in question. There may be more than one type of ACL manager protecting the object whose ACL is bound to the input handle. Use this parameter to distinguish them. Use **sec_acl_get_manager_types**( ) to acquire a list of the manager types protecting a given object.

desired_permset A permission set in **sec_acl_permset_t** form containing the desired privileges. This is a 32-bit set of permission flags supported by the manager type.

Output

status A pointer to the completion status. On successful completion, the routine returns **error_status_ok**. Otherwise, it returns an error.

Description

The **rdacl_test_access( )** routine determines if the specified ACL contains entries granting privileges to the calling process matching those in *desired_permset*. An application generally only inquires after the minimum set of privileges needed to accomplish a specific task.

Notes

This call is not intended to be used by application programs. The **sec_acl** Application Programming Interface (API) provides all the functionality necessary to use the ACL facility. This reference page is provided for programmers who wish to write an ACL manager. In order to write an ACL manager, a programmer must implement the entire **rdacl** interface. The **sec_acl_mgr** reference pages are provided as an example of a successful implementation. (See **intro(3sec)** for more information about writing an ACL manager.)

This network interface is called on the client side via the **sec_acl** local interface. Developers are responsible for implementing the server side of this interface. Test server code is included as a sample implementation.

Files

/usr/include/dce/rdaclif.idl The **idl** file from which **dce/rdaclif.h** was derived.

Errors

sec_acl_unknown_manager_type
The manager type selected is not an available option.

error_status_ok The call was successful.

Related Information

Functions: **intro(3sec)**, **rdacl_test_access_on_behalf(3sec)**.

rdacl_test_access_on_behalf

Purpose Tests access to an object on behalf of another process

Synopsis **#include <dce/rdaclif.h>**

boolean rdacl_test_access_on_behalf(
    handle_t *h*,
    sec_acl_component_name_t *component_name*,
    uuid_t **manager_type*,
    sec_id_pac_t **subject*,
    sec_acl_permset_t *desired_permset*,
    error_status_t **status*);

Parameters

Input

h A handle referring to the target object. Use **sec_acl_bind**( ) to create this handle.

component_name
A character string containing the name of the target object.

manager_type A pointer to the UUID identifying the type of the ACL manager in question. There may be more than one type of ACL manager protecting the object whose ACL is bound to the input handle. Use this parameter to distinguish them. Use **sec_acl_get_manager_types**( ) to acquire a list of the manager types protecting a given object.

subject A Privilege Attribute Certificate (PAC) for the subject process. The PAC contains the name and UUID of the principal and parent cell of the subject process, as well as a list of any groups to which it belongs. The PAC also contains a flag (named **authenticated**). When set, it indicates that the certificate was obtained from an authenticated source. When not set, the certificate must not be trusted. (The field is FALSE when it was obtained from the **rpc_auth** layer and the protect level was set to **rpc_c_protect_level_none**. This indicates that no authentication protocol was actually used in the remote procedure call; the identity was simply transmitted from the caller to the callee. If an authentication protocol was used, then the flag is set to TRUE.) A server uses **rpc_binding_inq_auth_client( )** to acquire a certificate for the client process.

desired_permset A permission set in **sec_acl_permset_t** form containing the desired privileges. This is a 32-bit set of permission flags supported by the manager type.

Output

status A pointer to the completion status. On successful completion, the routine returns **error_status_ok**. Otherwise, it returns an error.

Description

The **rdacl_test_access_on_behalf( )** routine determines if the specified ACL contains entries granting privileges to the subject, a process besides the calling process, matching those in *desired_permset*. This routine succeeds only if the access is available to both the caller process as well as the subject identified in the call. An application will generally only inquire after the minimum set of privileges needed to accomplish a specific task.

Notes

This call is not intended to be used by application programs. The **sec_acl** Application Programming Interface (API) provides all the functionality necessary to use the ACL facility. This reference page is provided for programmers who wish to write an ACL manager. In order to write an ACL manager, a programmer must implement the entire **rdacl** interface. The **sec_acl_mgr** reference pages are provided as an example of a successful implementation. (See **intro(3sec)** for more information about writing an ACL manager.)

This network interface is called on the client side via the **sec_acl** local interface. Developers are responsible for implementing the server side of this interface. Test server code is included as a sample implementation.

Files

/usr/include/dce/rdaclif.idl The **idl** file from which **dce/rdaclif.h** was derived.

Errors

sec_acl_unknown_manager_type
The manager type selected is not an available option.

error_status_ok The call was successful.

Related Information

Functions: **intro(3sec)**, **rdacl_test_access(3sec)**, **rpc_binding_inq_auth_client(3rpc)**.

sec_acl_bind

Purpose Returns a handle for an object's ACL

Synopsis **#include <dce/daclif.h>**

void sec_acl_bind(
  unsigned_char_p_t *entry_name***,**
  boolean32 *bind_to_entry***,**
  sec_acl_handle_t **h***,**
  error_status_t **status***);**

Parameters

Input

entry_name The name of the target object. Subsequent ACL operations using the returned handle will affect the ACL of this object.

bind_to_entry Bind indicator, for use when *entry_name* identifies both an entry in the global namespace and an actual object. A TRUE value binds the handle to the entry in the namespace, while FALSE binds the handle to the actual object.

Output

h A pointer to the **sec_acl_handle_t** variable to receive the returned ACL handle. The other **sec_acl** routines use this handle to refer to the ACL for the object specified with *entry_name*.

status A pointer to the completion status. On successful completion, the routine returns **error_status_ok**. Otherwise, it returns an error.

Description

The **sec_acl_bind**( ) routine returns a handle bound to the indicated object's ACL. This routine is central to all the other **sec_acl** routines, each of which requires this handle to identify the ACL on which to operate.

Notes

If the specified name is both an actual object, and an entry in the global namespace, there are two ACLs associated with it. For example, in addition to the ACL normally attached to file system objects, the root directory of a file system has an ACL corresponding to its entry in the global namespace. This controls access by outsiders to the entire file system, whereas the resident ACL for the root directory only controls access to the directory and, by inheritance, its subdirectories. The ambiguity must be resolved with the *bind_to_entry* parameter.

Files

/usr/include/dce/daclif.idl The **idl** file from which **dce/daclif.h** was derived.

Errors

sec_acl_object_not_found The requested object could not be found.

sec_acl_no_acl_found There is no ACL associated with the specified object.

error_status_ok The call was successful.

Related Information

Functions: **intro(3sec)**.

sec_acl_bind_to_addr

Purpose Returns a handle to an object identified by its network address

Synopsis **#include <dce/daclif.h>**

```
void sec_acl_bind_to_addr(
        unsigned_char_p_t entry_name,
        sec_acl_component_name_t component_name,
        sec_acl_handle_t *h,
        error_status_t *status);
```

Parameters

Input

site_addr A pointer to the fully qualified network address of the target object.

component_name The name of the target object. Subsequent ACL operations using the returned handle will affect the ACL of this object.

Output

h A pointer to the **sec_acl_handle_t** variable to receive the returned ACL handle. The other **sec_acl** routines use this handle to refer to the ACL for the object specified with *entry_name*.

status A pointer to the completion status. On successful completion, the routine returns **error_status_ok**. Otherwise, it returns an error.

Description

The **sec_acl_bind_to_addr()** routine returns a handle bound to the indicated object's ACL manager. This routine and the **sec_acl_bind()** routine are central to all the other **sec_acl** routines, each of which requires a handle to identify the ACL on which to operate.

This routine differs from **sec_acl_bind()** in that it binds to the network address of the target object, rather than to a cell namespace entry. Therefore, unlike **sec_acl_bind()**, it is possible to pass **sec_acl_bind_to_addr()** a null string as a component name and to bind with a nonexistent name. The purpose of this call is to eliminate the necessity of looking up an object's name. To validate the name, use **sec_acl_bind( )**.

Files

/usr/include/dce/daclif.idl The **idl** file from which **dce/daclif.h** was derived.

Errors

sec_acl_object_not_found The requested object could not be found.

sec_acl_no_acl_found There is no ACL associated with the specified object.

error_status_ok The call was successful.

Related Information

Functions: **intro(3sec)**.

sec_acl_calc_mask

Purpose Returns the **sec_acl_type_mask_obj** entry for the specified ACL list

Synopsis **#include <dce/daclif.h>**

void sec_acl_calc_mask(
  sec_acl_list_t *sec_acl_list*,
  error_status_t **status*);

Parameters

Input/Output

sec_acl_list The number of ACLs of each ACL type. The **sec_acl_type_t** data type distinguishes between the various types of ACLs an object can possess for a given manager. In the file system, for example, most objects have only one ACL, controlling the access to that object, but objects that control the creation of other objects (sometimes referred to as ‘‘containers’’) may have more. A directory, for example, can have ACLs to be used as initial values when member objects are created.

Do not confuse ACL types with the permissions corresponding to different ACL manager types or with the ACL manager types themselves.

Output

status A pointer to the completion status. On successful completion, the routine returns **error_status_ok**. Otherwise, it returns an error.

Description

The **sec_acl_calc_mask()** routine calculates and sets the **sec_acl_e_type_mask_obj** entry of the specified ACL list. The value of the **sec_acl_e_type_mask_obj** entry is the union of the permissions of all ACL entries that refer to members of the File Group Class.

This operation is performed locally, within the client. The function does not check to determine if the manager to which the specified ACL list will be submitted supports the **sec_acl_e_type_mask_obj** entry type. The calling application must determine whether to call this routine, after obtaining the required, if any, POSIX semantics, via the **sec_acl_get_mgr_types_semantics( )** routine.

Notes

This call is provided in source code form.

Files

/usr/include/dce/daclif.idl The **idl** file from which **dce/daclif.h** was derived.

Errors

sec_acl_cant_allocate_memory
Requested operation requires more memory than is available.

error_status_ok The call was successful.

Related Information

Functions: **intro(3sec)**, **sec_acl_mgr_configure(3sec)**, **sec_acl_mgr_get_access(3sec)**, **sec_acl_mgr_get_access(3sec)**.

sec_acl_get_access

Purpose Lists the access (permission set) that the caller has for an object

Synopsis **#include <dce/daclif.h>**

void sec_acl_get_access(
sec_acl_handle_t *h*,
uuid_t **manager_type*,
sec_acl_permset_t **net_rights*,
error_status_t **status*);

Parameters

Input

h A handle referring to the object whose ACL is to be accessed. Use **sec_acl_bind( )** to create this handle.

manager_type A pointer to the UUID identifying the manager type of the ACL in question. There may be more than one type of ACL manager protecting the object whose ACL is bound to the input handle. Use this parameter to distinguish them. Use **sec_acl_get_manager_types( )** to acquire a list of the manager types protecting a given object.

Output

net_rights The output list of access rights in **sec_acl_permset_t** form. This is a 32-bit set of permission flags supported by the manager type.

status A pointer to the completion status. On successful completion, the routine returns **error_status_ok**. Otherwise, it returns an error.

Description

The **sec_acl_get_access( )** routine determines the complete extent of access to the specified object by the calling process. Although the **sec_acl_test_access( )** and **sec_acl_test_access_on_behalf( )** routines are the preferred method of testing access, this routine is useful for implementing operations like the conventional UNIX access function.

Permissions Required

The **sec_acl_get_access( )** routine requires at least one permission of any kind on the object for which the access is to be returned.

Files

/usr/include/dce/daclif.idl The **idl** file from which **dce/daclif.h** was derived.

Errors

error_status_ok The call was successful.

Related Information

Functions: **sec_acl_test_access(3sec)**, **sec_acl_test_access_on_behalf(3sec)**.

sec_acl_get_error_info

Purpose Returns error information from an ACL handle

Synopsis **#include <dce/daclif.h>**

error_status_t sec_acl_get_error_info(
 sec_acl_handle_t *h*);

Parameters

Input

h A handle referring to the target ACL. The handle is bound to the ACL with the **sec_acl_bind( )** routine, which also specifies the name of the object to which the target ACL belongs.

Description

The **sec_acl_get_error_info( )** routine returns error information from the specified ACL handle.

During a call to a routine in the **sec_acl** Application Programming Interface (API), error codes received from the NCS runtime or other APIs are saved in the ACL handle and a corresponding error code from the **sec_acl** set is passed back by the ACL API. The **sec_acl_get_error_info( )** routine returns the last error code stored in the ACL handle for those clients who need to know exactly what went wrong.

Files **/usr/include/dce/daclif.idl** The **idl** file from which **dce/daclif.h** was derived.

Return Values

This routine returns a value of type **error_status_t**, indicating the cause of the last error issued by the NCS runtime.

Errors

This routine has no provision for issuing its own error codes, only the transcription of errors issued by other routines.

Related Information

Functions: **intro(3sec)**, **sec_acl_bind(3sec)**, **sec_acl_lookup(3sec)**.

sec_acl_get_manager_types

Purpose Lists the manager types of the ACLs protecting an object

Synopsis **#include <dce/daclif.h>**

void sec_acl_get_manager_types(
    sec_acl_handle_t *h*,
    sec_acl_type_t *sec_acl_type*,
    unsigned32 *size_avail*,
    unsigned32 **size_used*,
    unsigned32 **num_types*,
    uuid_t *manager_types*[ ],
    error_status_t **status*);

Parameters

Input

h — A handle referring to the target object. Use **sec_acl_bind( )** to create this handle.

sec_acl_type — The ACL type. The **sec_acl_type_t** data type distinguishes the various types of ACLs an object can possess for a given manager type. The possible values are as follows:

- **sec_acl_type_object**
- **sec_acl_type_default_object**
- **sec_acl_type_default_container**

size_avail — An unsigned 32-bit integer containing the allocated length of the *manager_types*[ ] array.

Output

size_used — An unsigned 32-bit integer containing the number of output entries returned in the *manager_types*[ ] array.

num_types — An unsigned 32-bit integer containing the number of types returned in the *manager_types*[ ] array. This may be greater than *size_used* if there was not enough space allocated in the *manager_types*[ ] array for all the manager types.

manager_types[ ]
An array of length *size_avail* to contain UUIDs (of type **uuid_t**) identifying the different types of ACL managers protecting the target object.

status A pointer to the completion status. On successful completion, the routine returns **error_status_ok**. Otherwise, it returns an error.

Description

The **sec_acl_get_manager_types( )** routine returns a list of the manager types of ACLs of type *sec_acl_type* that are protecting the object identified by *h*. For example, in addition to the regular file system ACL, a file representing the stable storage of some database could have an ACL manager that supported permissions allowing database updates only on certain days of the week.

ACL editors and browsers can use this operation to determine the ACL manager types that a particular reference monitor is using to protect a selected entity. Then, using the **sec_acl_get_printstring( )** routine, they can determine how to format for display the permissions supported by a specific manager.

Permissions Required

The **sec_acl_get_manager_types( )** routine requires at least one permission of any kind on the object for which the ACL manager types are to be returned.

Files

/usr/include/dce/daclif.idl The **idl** file from which **dce/daclif.h** was derived.

Errors

error_status_ok The call was successful.

Related Information

Functions: **intro(3sec)**, **sec_acl_bind(3sec)**, **sec_acl_get_printstring(3sec)**.

sec_acl_get_manager_types_semantics

Purpose Lists the manager types of the ACLs protecting an object

Synopsis **#include <dce/daclif.h>**

void sec_acl_get_manager_types_semantics(
    sec_acl_handle_t *h*,
    sec_acl_type_t *sec_acl_type*,
    unsigned32 *size_avail*,
    unsigned32 **size_used*,
    unsigned32 **num_types*,
    uuid_t *manager_types*[ ],
    sec_acl_posix_semantics_t *posix_semantics*[ ],
    error_status_t **status*);

Parameters

Input

h A handle referring to the target object. Use **sec_acl_bind**( ) to create this handle.

sec_acl_type The ACL type. The **sec_acl_type_t** data type distinguishes the various types of ACLs an object can possess for a given manager type. The possible values are as follows:

- **sec_acl_type_object**
- **sec_acl_type_default_object**
- **sec_acl_type_default_container**

size_avail An unsigned 32-bit integer containing the allocated length of the *manager_types*[ ] array.

Output

size_used An unsigned 32-bit integer containing the number of output entries returned in the *manager_types*[ ] array.

num_types An unsigned 32-bit integer containing the number of types returned in the *manager_types*[ ] array. This may be greater than *size_used* if there was not enough space allocated in the *manager_types*[ ] array for all the manager types.

manager_types[ ] — An array of length *size_avail* to contain UUIDs (of type **uuid_t**) identifying the different types of ACL managers protecting the target object.

posix_semantics[ ] — An array of POSIX semantics supported by each manager type with entries of type **sec_acl_posix_semantics_t**.

status — A pointer to the completion status. On successful completion, the routine returns **error_status_ok**. Otherwise, it returns an error.

Description

The **sec_acl_get_manager_types_semantics( )** routine returns a list of the manager types of ACLs of type *sec_acl_type* that are protecting the object identified by *h*. For example, in addition to the regular file system ACL, a file representing the stable storage of some database could have an ACL manager that supported permissions allowing database updates only on certain days of the week.

ACL editors and browsers can use this operation to determine the ACL manager types that a particular reference monitor is using to protect a selected entity. Then, using the **sec_acl_get_printstring( )** routine, they can determine how to format for display the permissions supported by a specific manager.

Permissions Required

The **sec_acl_get_manager_types_semantics( )** routine requires at least one permission of any kind on the object for which the ACL manager types are to be returned.

Files

/usr/include/dce/daclif.idl — The **idl** file from which **dce/daclif.h** was derived.

Errors

error_status_ok — The call was successful.

Related Information

Functions: **intro(3sec)**, **sec_acl_bind(3sec)**, **sec_acl_get_printstring(3sec)**.

sec_acl_get_printstring

Purpose Returns printable ACL strings

Synopsis **#include <dce/daclif.h>**

void sec_acl_get_printstring(
 sec_acl_handle_t *h*,
 uuid_t **manager_type*,
 unsigned32 *size_avail*,
 uuid_t **manager_type_chain*,
 sec_acl_printstring_t **manager_info*,
 boolean32 **tokenize*,
 unsigned32 **total_num_printstrings*,
 unsigned32 **size_used*,
 sec_acl_printstring_t *printstrings*[ ],
 error_status_t **status*);

Parameters

Input

h A handle referring to the target object. Use **sec_acl_bind**( ) to create this handle.

manager_type A pointer to the UUID identifying the type of the ACL manager in question. There may be more than one type of ACL manager protecting the object whose ACL is bound to the input handle. Use this parameter to distinguish them. Use **sec_acl_get_manager_types**( ) to acquire a list of the manager types protecting a given object.

size_avail An unsigned 32-bit integer containing the allocated length of the *printstrings*[ ] array.

Output

manager_type_chain
If the target object ACL contains more than 32 permission bits, multiple manager types are used, one for each 32-bit wide ''slice'' of permissions. The UUID returned in *manager_type_chain* refers to the next ACL manager in the

chain. If there are no more ACL managers for this ACL, **uuid_nil** is returned.

manager_info Provides a name and helpstring for the given ACL manager.

tokenize When FALSE, this variable indicates that the returned permission printstrings are unambiguous and therefore may be concatenated when printed without confusion. When TRUE, however, this property does not hold, and the strings need to be separated when printed or passed.

total_num_printstrings
An unsigned 32-bit integer containing the total number of permission printstrings supported by this ACL manager type.

size_used An unsigned 32-bit integer containing the number of permission entries returned in the *printstrings*[ ] array.

printstrings[ ] An array of permission printstrings of type **sec_acl_printstring_t**. Each entry of the array is a structure containing the following three components:

printstring A character string of maximum length **sec_acl_printstring_len** describing the printable representation of a specified permission.

helpstring A character string of maximum length **sec_acl_printstring_help_len** containing some text that can be used to describe the specified permission.

permissions A **sec_acl_permset_t** permission set describing the permissions that are represented with the companion printstring.

The array consists of one such entry for each permission supported by the ACL manager identified by *manager_type*.

status A pointer to the completion status. On successful completion, the routine returns **error_status_ok**. Otherwise, it returns an error.

Description

The **sec_acl_get_printstring( )** routine returns an array of printable representations (called ''printstrings'') for each permission bit or combination of permission bits the specified ACL manager supports. The ACL manager type specified must be one of the types protecting the object indicated by *h*.

In addition to returning the printstrings, this routine also returns instructions about how to print the strings. When the *tokenize* variable is set to FALSE, a printstring might be `r` or `w`, which could be concatenated in the display as `rw` without any confusion. However, when the *tokenize* variable is TRUE, it implies the printstrings might be of a form like `read` or `write`, which must be displayed separated by spaces or colons or something.

In any list of permission printstrings, there may appear to be some redundancy. ACL managers often define aliases for common permission combinations. By convention, however, simple entries should appear at the beginning of the *printstrings*[ ] array, and combinations should appear at the end.

Files

/usr/include/dce/daclif.idl The **idl** file from which **dce/daclif.h** was derived.

Errors

sec_acl_unknown_manager_type
The manager type selected is not among those referenced by the input handle.

error_status_ok The call was successful.

Related Information

Functions: **intro(3sec)**, **sec_acl_bind(3sec)**, **sec_acl_get_manager_types(3sec)**.

sec_acl_lookup

Purpose Returns the ACL for an object

Synopsis **#include <dce/daclif.h>**

void sec_acl_lookup(
    sec_acl_handle_t *h*,
    uuid_t **manager_type*,
    sec_acl_type_t *sec_acl_type*,
    sec_acl_list_t **sec_acl_list*,
    error_status_t **status*);

Parameters

Input

h A handle referring to the target object. Use **sec_acl_bind( )** to create this handle.

manager_type A pointer to the UUID identifying the type of the ACL manager in question. There may be more than one type of ACL manager protecting the object whose ACL is bound to the input handle. Use this parameter to distinguish them. Use **sec_acl_get_manager_types( )** to acquire a list of the manager types protecting a given object.

sec_acl_type The ACL type. The **sec_acl_type_t** data type distinguishes the various types of ACLs an object can possess for a given manager type. The possible values are as follows:

- **sec_acl_type_object**
- **sec_acl_type_default_object**
- **sec_acl_type_default_container**

Output

sec_acl_list A pointer to the **sec_acl_list_t** structure to receive the complete Access Control List. An ACL contains a list of ACL entries, the UUID of the default cell where authentication takes place (foreign entries in the ACL contain the name of their home cell), and the UUID of the ACL manager to interpret the list.

status A pointer to the completion status. On successful completion, the routine returns **error_status_ok**. Otherwise, it returns an error.

Description

The **sec_acl_lookup( )** routine loads into memory a copy of an object's ACL corresponding to the specified manager type. The routine returns a pointer to the ACL. This routine is only used by ACL editors and browsers; an application would use **sec_acl_test_access( )** or **sec_acl_test_access_on_behalf( )** to process the contents of an ACL.

Permissions Required

The **sec_acl_lookup( )** routine requires at least one permission of any kind on the object for which the ACL is to be returned.

Notes

The memory containing the **sec_acl_t** structure for each ACL is dynamically allocated. Use the **sec_acl_release( )** routine to return each ACL's memory block to the pool when an application is finished with the ACLs.

Files

/usr/include/dce/daclif.idl The **idl** file from which **dce/daclif.h** was derived.

Errors

sec_acl_unknown_manager_type
The manager type selected is not an available option.

sec_acl_cant_allocate_memory
The requested operation requires more memory than is available.

Related Information

Functions: **intro(3sec)**, **sec_acl_bind(3sec)**, **sec_acl_test_access(3sec)**, **sec_acl_test_access_on_behalf(3sec)**.

sec_acl_mgr_configure

Purpose Configures an ACL manager

Synopsis **#include <dce/daclmgr.h>**

void sec_acl_mgr_configure(
sec_acl_mgr_config_t *config_info*,
unsigned_char_p_t *db_name*,
sec_acl_mgr_handle_t **sec_acl_mgr*,
error_status_t **status*);

Parameters

Input

config_info An unsigned 32-bit set of flags containing miscellaneous information about how to treat the specified ACL database. Currently, only the following two flags are used:

sec_acl_mgr_config_create Creates a new database with the given name. If one with the input name already exists, an error is returned.

sec_acl_mgr_config_stable Provides stable storage for the database state. If not set, **sec_acl_mgr_configure**( ) assumes that the calling program takes care of storing the ACL database, and does not save it.

db_name Identifies which ACL database to use. The name generally refers to the file system object that represents the persistent storage for the database.

Output

sec_acl_mgr A pointer to a handle for an ACL manager and the storage configuration chosen with the *config_info* parameter. Having a distinct handle for the combination of ACL manager and configuration allows the application to use different storage strategies for different types of objects.

status A pointer to the completion status. On successful completion, the routine returns **error_status_ok**. Otherwise, it returns an error.

Description

The **sec_acl_mgr_configure( )** routine provides a handle to refer to the particular ACL database in use and which is necessary for all other ACL manager operations.

The only storage model supported by the current ACL manager interface is one with a separate stable storage file.

Notes

This call is provided in source code form. It is not intended to be used by application programs. The **sec_acl** Application Programming Interface (API) provides all the functionality necessary to use the ACL facility. This reference page is provided for programmers who wish to write an ACL manager. In order to write an ACL manager, a programmer must implement the entire **rdacl** interface. The **sec_acl_mgr** reference pages are provided as an example of a successful implementation. (See **intro(3sec)** for more information about writing an ACL manager.)

Files

/usr/include/dce/daclmgr.idl
The **idl** file from which **dce/daclmgr.h** was derived.

Errors

sec_acl_mgr_error_exists The call requested the creation of a database that already exists.

error_status_ok The call was successful.

Examples

Here is an example of the common usage of the ACL manager routines. The application uses **rpc_binding_inq_auth_client( )** to acquire a privilege attribute certificate.

```
application_op(handle_t h, ... ) {
  ...
  sec_acl_mgr_configure(<configuration info>,
                        <name of acl file system object>,
                        &sec_acl_mgr_handle, &status);
  ...
  rpc_binding_inq_auth_client(h, &PAC, &server_name, &lvl,
          &authn_svc, &authz_svc, &status);
```

```
rpc_binding_inq_object(h, &object, &status);
if (sec_acl_mgr_is_authorized(acl_mgr_handle,
                   <needed permissions>,
                   &PAC, (sec_acl_key_t) &object,
                   sec_acl_type_object, NULL, NULL, &status)) {
    /* Application code to perform operation */
 } else {
    /* Caller is not authorized to have the desired permissions
     * over the indicated object.  Act accordingly...
     */
     . . .
} }
```

Related Information

Functions: **intro(3sec)**.

sec_acl_mgr_get_access

Purpose Reads a privilege attribute certificate

Synopsis **#include <dce/daclmgr.h>**

void sec_acl_mgr_get_access(
sec_acl_mgr_handle_t *sec_acl_mgr*,
sec_id_pac_t **accessor_info*,
sec_acl_key_t *sec_acl_key*,
uuid_t **manager_type*,
sec_id_t **user_obj*,
sec_id_t **group_obj*,
sec_acl_permset_t **net_rights*,
error_status_t **status*);

Parameters

Input

sec_acl_mgr A pointer to a handle for an ACL manager and the storage configuration chosen with **sec_acl_mgr_configure()**. Having a distinct handle for the combination of ACL manager and configuration allows the application to use different storage strategies for different types of objects.

accessor_info The Privilege Attribute Certificate (PAC) of the calling process. The PAC contains the identity and group membership of the calling process, which can then be compared with entries in the ACL to determine whether it is authorized to have indicated desired privileges. Use **rpc_binding_inq_auth_client()** to acquire a certificate for the caller process.

sec_acl_key A pointer indicating the object whose ACL is in question. The type of the pointer depends on the ACL manager involved. For file system ACLs, it points to a **uuid_t** variable, containing the UUID and name of the file system object.

manager_type A pointer to the UUID identifying the type of the ACL manager in question. There may be more than one type of ACL manager protecting the object whose ACL is bound to the input handle. Use this parameter to distinguish them. Use

sec_acl_get_manager_types( ) to acquire a list of the manager types protecting a given object.

user_obj Contains the identity of the caller. This is to be used when the ACL manager encounters a **USER_OBJ** field in an ACL. The identity used is generally the person field of the caller account. This parameter may be **NULL**, although this produces an error and denial of access to the object if the ACL contains a **USER_OBJ** entry.

group_obj Identical in use to the *user_obj* parameter, except this refers to the caller account's group and any potential **GROUP_OBJ** entry in the target object's ACL.

Output

net_rights The output list of access rights in **sec_acl_permset_t** form. This is a 32-bit set of permission flags. The flags may represent the conventional file system permissions (read, write, and execute), the extended AFS permissions (owner, insert, and delete), or some other permissions supported only by the specific ACL manager. For example, a bit that is unused for file system permissions may mean ''withdrawals'' are allowed for a ''bank'' ACL manager, while it may mean ''rebooting'' is allowed for a ''CPU'' ACL manager.

status A pointer to the completion status. On successful completion, the routine returns **error_status_ok**. Otherwise, it returns an error.

Description

The **sec_acl_mgr_get_access**( ) routine determines the complete extent of access to the specified object by the process described in the input privilege attribute certificate (called a PAC and passed in the *accessor_info* parameter). Although the **sec_acl_mgr_is_authorized**( ) routine is the preferred method of testing access, this routine is useful for implementing operations like the conventional UNIX access function.

The actual ACL to be compared against the input PAC is not passed directly to this routine, but is referred to by the *sec_acl_key* and the *manager_type* parameters.

Notes

This call is provided in source code form. It is not intended to be used by application programs. The **sec_acl** Application Programming Interface (API) provides all the functionality necessary to use the ACL facility. This reference page is provided for programmers who wish to write an ACL manager. In order to write an ACL manager, a programmer must implement the entire **rdacl** interface. The **sec_acl_mgr** reference pages are provided as an example of a successful implementation. (See **intro(3sec)** for more information about writing an ACL manager.)

Files

/usr/include/dce/daclmgr.idl The **idl** file from which **dce/daclmgr.h** was derived.

Errors

error_status_ok The call was successful.

Related Information

Functions: **intro(3sec)**, **sec_acl_mgr_configure(3sec)**, **sec_acl_mgr_is_authorized(3sec)**.

sec_acl_mgr_get_manager_types

Purpose Returns the types of ACLs that are protecting an object

Synopsis **#include <dce/daclmgr.h>**

void sec_acl_mgr_get_manager_types(
sec_acl_mgr_handle_t *sec_acl_mgr*,
sec_acl_key_t *sec_acl_key*,
sec_acl_type_t *sec_acl_type*,
unsigned32 *size_avail*,
unsigned32 **size_used*,
unsigned32 **num_types*,
uuid_t *manager_types*[ ],
error_status_t **status*);

Parameters

Input

sec_acl_mgr A pointer to a handle for an ACL manager and the storage configuration chosen with **sec_acl_mgr_configure( )**. Having a distinct handle for the combination of ACL manager and configuration allows the application to use different storage strategies for different types of objects.

sec_acl_key A pointer indicating the object whose ACL is in question. The type of the pointer depends on the ACL manager involved. For file system ACLs, it points to a **uuid_t** variable, containing the UUID and name of the file system object.

sec_acl_type The ACL type. It is generally **sec_acl_type_object**. The **sec_acl_type_t** data type distinguishes between the various types of ACLs an object can possess for a given manager. In the file system, for example, most objects have only one ACL controlling the access to that object, but objects that control the creation of other objects (sometimes referred to as ‘‘containers’’) may have more. A directory, for example, can have ACLs to be used as initial values when member objects are created.

Do not confuse ACL types with the permissions corresponding to different ACL manager types or with the ACL manager types themselves.

size_avail An unsigned 32-bit integer containing the allocated length of the *manager_types*[ ] array.

Output

size_used An unsigned 32-bit integer containing the actual length of the *manager_types*[ ] array.

num_types An unsigned 32-bit integer containing the actual number of manager types returned in the *manager_types*[ ] array.

manager_types[ ]
An array of manager types in which each entry is of type **uuid_t**.

status A pointer to the completion status. On successful completion, the routine returns **error_status_ok**. Otherwise, it returns an error.

Description

The **sec_acl_mgr_get_manager_types( )** routine returns the types of ACLs that are protecting an object. ACL editors and browsers can use this routine to determine the ACL manager types that a particular reference monitor is using to manage the ACLs of *sec_acl_type* on the object identified by *sec_acl_key*.

The number of the ACL manager types supported by the object for the specified *sec_acl_type* is returned in *num_types*. The actual ACL manager types are returned as entries in the *manager_types*[ ] array.

If the returned size is greater than the specified *size_avail*, invoke the routine again with a buffer large enough to hold the returned information.

Note that if *num_types* is greater than 1, it means that the object is polymorphic and supports ACL manager types for each of its forms.

This call is provided in source code form.

Files

/usr/include/dce/daclmgr.idl The **idl** file from which **dce/daclmgr.h** was derived.

Errors

sec_acl_cant_allocate_memory
The requested operation requires more memory than is available.

error_status_ok The call was successful.

Related Information

Functions: **intro(3sec)**, **sec_acl_mgr_configure(3sec)**, **sec_acl_mgr_get_access(3sec)**, **sec_acl_mgr_is_authorized(3sec)**.

sec_acl_mgr_get_types_semantics

Purpose Returns the types of ACLs and the POSIX semantics that are protecting an object

Synopsis **#include <dce/daclmgr.h>**

void sec_acl_mgr_get_types_semantics(
sec_acl_handle_t *sec_acl_mgr*,
sec_acl_key_t *sec_acl_key*,
sec_acl_type_t *sec_acl_type*,
unsigned32 *size_avail*,
unsigned32 **size_used*,
unsigned32 **num_types*,
uuid_t *manager_types*[ ],
sec_acl_posix_semantics *posix_semantics[ ]*,
error_status_t **status*);

Parameters

Input

sec_acl_mgr A pointer to a handle for an ACL manager and the storage configuration chosen with **sec_acl_mgr_configure**( ). Having a distinct handle for the combination of ACL manager and configuration allows the application to use different storage strategies for different types of objects.

sec_acl_key A pointer indicating the object whose ACL is in question. The type of the pointer depends on the ACL manager involved. For file system ACLs, it points to a **uuid_t** variable, containing the UUID and name of the file system object.

sec_acl_type The ACL type. It is generally **sec_acl_type_object**. The **sec_acl_type_t** data type distinguishes between the various types of ACLs an object can possess for a given manager. In the file system, for example, most objects have only one ACL controlling the access to that object, but objects that control the creation of other objects (sometimes referred to as ''containers'') may have more. A directory, for example, can have ACLs to be used as initial values when member objects are created.

Do not confuse ACL types with the permissions corresponding to different ACL manager types or with the ACL manager types themselves.

size_avail — An unsigned 32-bit integer containing the allocated length of the *manager_types*[ ] array.

Output

size_used — An unsigned 32-bit integer containing the actual length of the *manager_types*[ ] array.

num_types — An unsigned 32-bit integer containing the actual number of manager types returned in the *manager_types*[ ] array.

manager_types[ ] — An array of manager types in which each entry is of type **uuid_t**.

posix_semantics[ ] — An array of POSIX semantics supported by each manager type with entries of type **sec_acl_posix_semantics**.

status — A pointer to the completion status. On successful completion, the routine returns **error_status_ok**. Otherwise, it returns an error.

Description

The **sec_acl_mgr_get_types_semantics**( ) routine returns the types of ACLs that are protecting an object. ACL editors and browsers can use this routine to determine the ACL manager types that a particular reference monitor is using to manage the ACLs of *sec_acl_type* on the object identified by *sec_acl_key*.

The number of the ACL manager types supported by the object for the specified *sec_acl_type* is returned in *num_types*. The actual ACL manager types are returned as entries in the *manager_types*[ ] array.

If the returned size is greater than the specified *size_avail*, invoke the routine again, with a buffer large enough to hold the returned information.

Note that if *num_types* is greater than 1, it means that the object is polymorphic and supports ACL manager types for each of its forms.

This call is provided in source code form.

Files

/usr/include/dce/daclmgr.idl The **idl** file from which **dce/daclmgr.h** was derived.

Errors

sec_acl_cant_allocate_memory
The requested operation requires more memory than is available.

error_status_ok The call was successful.

Related Information

Functions: **intro(3sec)**, **sec_acl_mgr_configure(3sec)**, **sec_acl_mgr_get_access(3sec)**, **sec_acl_mgr_is_authorized(3sec)**.

sec_acl_mgr_get_printstring

Purpose Returns printable ACL strings

Synopsis **#include <dce/daclmgr.h>**

void sec_acl_mgr_get_printstring(
sec_acl_mgr_handle_t *sec_acl_mgr*,
uuid_t **manager_type*,
unsigned32 *size_avail*,
uuid_t **manager_type_chain*,
sec_acl_printstring_t **manager_info*,
boolean32 **tokenize*,
unsigned32 **total_num_printstrings*,
unsigned32 **size_used*,
sec_acl_printstring_t *printstrings*[ ],
error_status_t **status*);

Parameters

Input

sec_acl_mgr A pointer to a handle for an ACL manager and the storage configuration chosen with **sec_acl_mgr_configure**( ). Having a distinct handle for the combination of ACL manager and configuration allows the application to use different storage strategies for different types of objects.

manager_type The ACL manager type.

size_avail An unsigned 32-bit integer containing the allocated length of the *printstrings*[ ] array.

Output

manager_type_chain
If the target object ACL contains more than 32 permission bits, multiple manager types are used, one for each 32-bit wide ''slice'' of permissions. The UUID returned in *manager_type_chain* refers to the next ACL manager in the chain. If there are no more ACL managers for this ACL, **uuid_nil** is returned.

manager_info A printstring (**sec_acl_printstring_t**) providing a name and helpstring for the given ACL manager.

tokenize When FALSE, this variable indicates that the returned permission printstrings are unambiguous and therefore may be concatenated when printed without confusion. When TRUE, however, this property does not hold, and the strings need to be separated when printed or passed.

total_num_printstrings
An output pointer to an unsigned 32-bit integer indicating the total number of printstrings supported by this ACL manager. If *size_avail* is smaller than *total_num_printstrings*, multiple calls to **sec_acl_mgr_get_printstring( )** are necessary to retrieve all the supported printstrings.

size_used An unsigned 32-bit integer containing the number of permission entries returned in the *printstrings*[ ] array.

printstrings[ ] An array of permission printstrings of type **sec_acl_printstring_t**. Each entry of the array is a structure containing three components:

printstring A character string of maximum length **sec_acl_printstring_len** describing the printable representation of a specified permission.

helpstring A character string of maximum length **sec_acl_printstring_help_len** containing some text that can be used to describe the specified permission.

permissions A **sec_acl_permset_t** permission set describing the permissions that are represented with the companion printstring.

The array consists of one such entry for each permission supported by the target ACL manager.

status A pointer to the completion status. On successful completion, the routine returns **error_status_ok**. Otherwise, it returns an error.

Description

The **sec_acl_mgr_get_printstring**( ) routine returns an array of printable representations (called ''printstrings'') for each permission bit or combination of permission bits the ACL manager will support.

In addition to returning the printstrings, this routine also returns instructions about how to print the strings. When the *tokenize* variable is set to FALSE, a printstring might be `r` or w, which could be concatenated in the display as `rw` without any confusion. However, when the *tokenize* variable is TRUE, it implies the printstrings might be of a form like `read` or `write`, which must be displayed separated by spaces or colons or something.

In any list of permission printstrings, there may appear to be some redundancy. ACL managers often define aliases for common permission combinations. By convention, however, simple entries should appear at the beginning of the *printstrings*[ ] array, and combinations should appear at the end.

Notes

This call is not intended to be used by application programs. The **sec_acl** Application Programming Interface (API) provides all the functionality necessary to use the ACL facility. This reference page is provided for programmers who wish to write an ACL manager. In order to write an ACL manager, a programmer must implement the entire **rdacl** interface. The **sec_acl_mgr** reference pages are provided as an example of a successful implementation. (See **intro(3sec)** for more information about writing an ACL manager.)

This call is provided in source code form.

Files

/usr/include/dce/daclmgr.idl The **idl** file from which **dce/daclmgr.h** was derived.

Errors

error_status_ok The call was successful.

Related Information

Functions: **intro(3sec)**, **sec_acl_mgr_configure(3sec)**.

sec_acl_mgr_is_authorized

Purpose Compares a privilege attribute certificate with an ACL

Synopsis **#include <dce/daclmgr.h>**

boolean32 sec_acl_mgr_is_authorized(
    sec_acl_mgr_handle_t *sec_acl_mgr***,**
    sec_acl_permset_t *desired_permset***,**
    sec_id_pac_t **accessor_info***,**
    sec_acl_key_t *sec_acl_key***,**
    uuid_t **manager_type***,**
    sec_id_t **user_obj***,**
    sec_id_t **group_obj***,**
    error_status_t **status***);**

Parameters

Input

sec_acl_mgr A pointer to a handle for an ACL manager and the storage configuration chosen with **sec_acl_mgr_configure( )**. Having a distinct handle for the combination of ACL manager and configuration allows the application to use different storage strategies for different types of objects.

desired_permset A permission set in **sec_acl_permset_t** form containing the desired privileges. This is a 32-bit set of permission flags. The flags may represent the conventional file system permissions (read, write, and execute), the extended AFS permissions (owner, insert, and delete), or some other permissions supported only by the specific ACL manager. For example, a bit that is unused for file system permissions may mean ''withdrawals'' are allowed for a ''bank'' ACL manager, while it may mean ''rebooting'' is allowed for a ''CPU'' ACL manager.

accessor_info The Privilege Attribute Certificate (PAC) of the calling process. The PAC contains the identity and group membership of the calling process, which can then be compared with entries in the ACL to determine whether it is authorized to have indicated desired privileges. Use **rpc_binding_inq_auth_client( )** to acquire a certificate for the caller process.

sec_acl_key A pointer indicating the object whose ACL is in question. The type of the pointer depends on the ACL manager involved. For file system ACLs, it points to a **uuid_t** variable, containing the UUID and name of the file system object.

manager_type The ACL manager type.

user_obj Contains the identity of the caller. This is to be used when the ACL manager encounters a **USER_OBJ** field in an ACL. The identity used is generally the person field of the caller account. This parameter may be **NULL**, although this produces an error and denial of access to the object if the ACL contains a **USER_OBJ** entry.

group_obj Identical in use to the *user_obj* parameter, except this refers to the caller account's group and any potential **GROUP_OBJ** entry in the target object's ACL.

Output

status A pointer to the completion status. On successful completion, the routine returns **error_status_ok**. Otherwise, it returns an error.

Description

The **sec_acl_mgr_is_authorized**( ) routine interprets an ACL, compares it to a privilege attribute certificate (called a PAC and passed in the *accessor_info* parameter) for a process, and declares whether that process is permitted to have the access implied by the privileges in *desired_permset*. This is the basic function of an ACL manager. Applications that provide controlled access to objects must acquire a PAC and submit that certificate to the ACL manager through this function.

The actual ACL to be compared against the input PAC is not passed directly to this routine, but is referred to by the *sec_acl_key* and the *manager_type* parameters.

This call is provided in source code form.

Notes

This call is not intended to be used by application programs. The **sec_acl** Application Programming Interface (API) provides all the functionality necessary to use the ACL facility. This reference page is provided for programmers who wish to write an ACL manager. In order to write an ACL manager, a programmer must implement the entire **rdacl** interface. The **sec_acl_mgr** reference pages are provided as an example of a successful implementation. (See **intro(3sec)** for more information about writing an ACL manager.)

Return Values

The routine returns TRUE if the caller process is authorized to perform the operations implied by the privileges specified in *desired_permset*.

Files

/usr/include/dce/daclmgr.idl The **idl** file from which **dce/daclmgr.h** was derived.

Errors

error_status_ok The call was successful.

Examples

Following is an example of the common usage of the ACL manager routines. The application uses **rpc_binding_inq_auth_client( )** to acquire a privilege attribute certificate, and **sec_acl_mgr_configure( )** to acquire the ACL manager handle.

```
application_op(handle_t h, ... ) {
  ...
  sec_acl_mgr_configure(<configuration info>,
             <name of acl file system object>,
             &sec_acl_mgr_handle, &status);
  ...
  rpc_binding_inq_auth_client(h, &PAC, &server_name,
              &lvl, &authn_svc, &authz_svc, &status);
  rpc_binding_inq_object(h, &object, &status);
  if (sec_acl_mgr_is_authorized(acl_mgr_handle,
                  <needed permissions>,
                  &PAC, (sec_acl_key_t) &object,
                  sec_acl_type_object, NULL, NULL, &status)) {
   /* Application code to perform operation */
  } else {
   /* Caller is not authorized to have the desired permissions over
    * the indicated object.  Act accordingly...
    */
      . . .
  }
}
```

Related Information

Functions: **intro(3sec)**, **sec_acl_mgr_configure(3sec)**, **sec_acl_mgr_get_access(3sec)**.

sec_acl_mgr_lookup

Purpose Finds an ACL using its key

Synopsis **#include <dce/daclmgr.h>**

void sec_acl_mgr_lookup(
sec_acl_mgr_handle_t *sec_acl_mgr*,
sec_acl_key_t *sec_acl_key*,
uuid_t **manager_type*,
sec_acl_type_t *sec_acl_type*,
sec_acl_list_t ***sec_acl_list*,
error_status_t **status***);**

Parameters

Input

sec_acl_mgr A pointer to a handle for an ACL manager and the storage configuration chosen with **sec_acl_mgr_configure( )**. Having a distinct handle for the combination of ACL manager and configuration allows the application to use different storage strategies for different types of objects.

sec_acl_key A pointer indicating the object whose ACL is in question. The type of the pointer depends on the ACL manager involved. For file system ACLs, it points to a **uuid_t** variable, containing the UUID and name of the file system object.

manager_type
The ACL manager type.

sec_acl_type The ACL type. It is generally **sec_acl_type_object**. The **sec_acl_type_t** data type distinguishes between the various types of ACLs an object can possess for a given manager. In the file system, for example, most objects have only one ACL controlling the access to that object, but objects that control the creation of other objects (sometimes referred to as ‘‘containers’’) may have more. A directory, for example, can have ACLs to be used as initial values when member objects are created.

Do not confuse ACL types with the permissions corresponding to different ACL manager types or with the ACL manager types themselves.

Output

sec_acl_list A pointer to the **sec_acl_list_t** structure to receive the complete Access Control List. An ACL contains a list of ACL entries, the UUID of the default cell where authentication takes place (foreign entries in the ACL contain the name of their parent cell), and the UUID of the ACL manager to interpret the list.

status A pointer to the completion status. On successful completion, the routine returns **error_status_ok**. Otherwise, it returns an error.

Description

The **sec_acl_mgr_lookup( )** routine loads into memory a copy of the ACL corresponding to the *sec_acl_key*. The routine returns a pointer to the ACL. This routine is only used by ACL editors and browsers; an application uses **sec_acl_mgr_get_access( )** or **sec_acl_mgr_is_authorized( )** to process the contents of an ACL.

Notes

This call is provided in source code form. It is not intended to be used by application programs. The **sec_acl** Application Programming Interface (API) provides all the functionality necessary to use the ACL facility. This reference page is provided for programmers who wish to write an ACL manager. In order to write an ACL manager, a programmer must implement the entire **rdacl** interface. The **sec_acl_mgr** reference pages are provided as an example of a successful implementation. (See **intro(3sec)** for more information about writing an ACL manager.)

Files

/usr/include/dce/daclmgr.idl The **idl** file from which **dce/daclmgr.h** was derived.

Errors

sec_acl_cant_allocate_memory
The requested operation requires more memory than is available.

error_status_ok The call was successful.

Related Information

Functions: **intro(3sec)**, **sec_acl_mgr_configure(3sec)**, **sec_acl_mgr_get_access(3sec)**, **sec_acl_mgr_is_authorized(3sec)**.

sec_acl_mgr_replace

Purpose Replaces an ACL

Synopsis **#include <dce/daclmgr.h>**

void sec_acl_mgr_replace(
sec_acl_mgr_handle_t *sec_acl_mgr*,
sec_acl_key_t *sec_acl_key*,
uuid_t **manager_type*,
sec_acl_type_t *sec_acl_type*,
sec_acl_list_t **sec_acl_list*,
error_status_t **status*);

Parameters

Input

sec_acl_mgr A pointer to a handle for an ACL manager and the storage configuration chosen with **sec_acl_mgr_configure**( ). Having a distinct handle for the combination of ACL manager and configuration allows the application to use different storage strategies for different types of objects.

sec_acl_key A pointer indicating the object whose ACL is in question. The type of the pointer depends on the ACL manager involved. For file system ACLs, it points to a **uuid_t** variable, containing the UUID and name of the file system object.

manager_type
A pointer indicating the ACL manager type.

sec_acl_type The ACL type. It is generally **sec_acl_type_object**. The **sec_acl_type_t** data type distinguishes between the various types of ACLs an object can possess for a given manager. In the file system, for example, most objects will have only one ACL controlling the access to that object, but objects that control the creation of other objects (sometimes referred to as ''containers'') may have more. A directory, for example, can have ACLs to be used as initial values when member objects are created.

Do not confuse ACL types with the permissions corresponding to different ACL manager types or with the ACL manager types themselves.

sec_acl_list The new ACL to use for the target object. This is represented by a pointer to the **sec_acl_list_t** structure containing the complete Access Control List. An ACL contains a list of ACL entries, the UUID of the default cell where authentication will take place (foreign entries in the ACL contain the name of their parent cell), and the UUID of the ACL manager to interpret the list.

Output

status A pointer to the completion status. On successful completion, the routine returns **error_status_ok**. Otherwise, it returns an error.

Description

The **sec_acl_mgr_replace( )** routine replaces the ACL indicated by the input handle with the information in the *sec_acl_list* parameter. This package treats ACLs as immutable, and in order to modify them, an editing application must read an entire ACL (using the **sec_acl_mgr_lookup( )** routine), modify it as needed, and replace it using this routine.

Notes

This call is not intended to be used by application programs. The **sec_acl** Application Programming Interface (API) provides all the functionality necessary to use the ACL facility. This reference page is provided for programmers who wish to write an ACL manager. In order to write an ACL manager, a programmer must implement the entire **rdacl** interface. The **sec_acl_mgr** reference pages are provided as an example of a successful implementation. (See **intro(3sec)** for more information about writing an ACL manager.)

Cautions

There is no authorization checking performed on this operation; it is strictly local. The application needs to call **sec_acl_mgr_is_authorized( )** with *desired_permset* set to ‘‘permission setting’’ or ‘‘owner’’ or something indicating permission to set the ACL before actually attempting the replace.

This call is provided in source code form.

Files	**/usr/include/dce/daclmgr.idl**	The **idl** file from which **dce/daclmgr.h** was derived.

Errors	**error_status_ok**	The call was successful.

Related Information

Functions: **intro(3sec)**, **sec_acl_mgr_configure(3sec)**.

sec_acl_release

Purpose

Releases ACL storage

Synopsis

#include <dce/daclif.h>

void sec_acl_release(
  sec_acl_handle_t *h*,
  sec_acl_t **sec_acl*,
  error_status_t **status*);

Parameters

Input

h — A handle referring to the target object. Use **sec_acl_bind**( ) to create this handle.

sec_acl — A pointer to the complete ACL associated with the target object.

Output

status — A pointer to the completion status. On successful completion, the routine returns **error_status_ok**. Otherwise, it returns an error.

Description

The **sec_acl_release**( ) routine releases any local storage associated with the ACL object, returning it to the pool. This is strictly a local operation (since the storage in question is local), and has no effect on the remote object or its ACL. The ACL handle is in the argument list only for consistency with other **sec_acl** routines.

Files

/usr/include/dce/daclif.idl — The **idl** file from which **dce/daclif.h** was derived.

Errors

error_status_ok — The call was successful.

Related Information

Functions: **intro(3sec)**, **sec_acl_bind(3sec)**, **sec_acl_lookup(3sec)**.

sec_acl_release_handle

Purpose Removes an ACL handle

Synopsis **#include <dce/daclif.h>**

void sec_acl_release_handle(
    sec_acl_handle_t ******h*,
    error_status_t ******status*);

Parameters

Input

h The handle to be removed. The handle is bound to the object to which the ACL belongs with the **sec_acl_bind( )** routine.

Output

status A pointer to the completion status. On successful completion, the routine returns **error_status_ok**. Otherwise, it returns an error.

Description

The **sec_acl_release_handle( )** routine removes the specified handle. This is strictly a local operation, and has no effect on the remote object or its ACL.

Files **/usr/include/dce/daclif.idl** The **idl** file from which **dce/daclif.h** was derived.

Errors **error_status_ok** The call was successful.

Related Information

Functions: **intro(3sec)**, **sec_acl_bind(3sec)**.

sec_acl_replace

Purpose Replaces an ACL

Synopsis **#include <dce/daclif.h>**

void sec_acl_replace(
sec_acl_handle_t *h*,
uuid_t **manager_type*,
sec_acl_type_t *sec_acl_type*,
sec_acl_list_t **sec_acl_list*,
error_status_t **status*);

Parameters

Input

h A handle referring to the target object. Use **sec_acl_bind( )** to create this handle.

manager_type
A pointer to the UUID identifying the type of the ACL manager in question. There may be more than one type of ACL manager protecting the object whose ACL is bound to the input handle. Use this parameter to distinguish them. Use **sec_acl_get_manager_types( )** to acquire a list of the manager types protecting a given object.

sec_acl_type The ACL type. The **sec_acl_type_t** data type distinguishes the various types of ACLs an object can possess for a given manager type. The possible values are as follows:

- **sec_acl_type_object**
- **sec_acl_type_default_object**
- **sec_acl_type_default_container**

sec_acl_list The new ACL to use for the target object. This is represented by a pointer to the **sec_acl_list_t** structure containing the complete Access Control List. An ACL contains a list of ACL entries, the UUID of the default cell where authentication will take place (foreign entries in the ACL contain the name of their parent cell), and the UUID of the ACL manager to interpret the list.

Output

status A pointer to the completion status. On successful completion, the routine returns **error_status_ok**. Otherwise, it returns an error.

Description

The **sec_acl_replace**( ) routine replaces the ACL indicated by the input handle with the information in the *sec_acl_list* parameter. ACLs are thought of as immutable, and in order to modify them, an editing application must read an entire ACL (using the **sec_acl_lookup**( ) routine), modify it as needed, and replace it using this routine.

Permissions Required

The **sec_acl_replace**( ) routine requires the **c** (control) permission on the object for which the ACL is to be replaced.

Files

/usr/include/dce/daclif.idl The **idl** file from which **dce/daclif.h** was derived.

Errors

sec_acl_unknown_manager_type
The manager type selected is not an available option.

error_status_ok The call was successful.

Related Information

Functions: **intro(3sec)**, **sec_acl_bind(3sec)**, **sec_acl_lookup(3sec)**.

sec_acl_test_access

Purpose Tests access to an object

Synopsis **#include <dce/daclif.h>**

boolean32 sec_acl_test_access(
 sec_acl_handle_t *h*,
 uuid_t **manager_type*,
 sec_acl_permset_t *desired_permset*,
 error_status_t **status*);

Parameters

Input

h A handle referring to the target object. Use **sec_acl_bind()** to create this handle.

manager_type A pointer to the UUID identifying the type of the ACL manager in question. There may be more than one type of ACL manager protecting the object whose ACL is bound to the input handle. Use this parameter to distinguish them. Use **sec_acl_get_manager_types()** to acquire a list of the manager types protecting a given object.

desired_permset A permission set in **sec_acl_permset_t** form containing the desired privileges. This is a 32-bit set of permission flags supported by the manager type.

Output

status A pointer to the completion status. On successful completion, the routine returns **error_status_ok**. Otherwise, it returns an error.

Description

The **sec_acl_test_access( )** routine determines if the specified ACL contains entries granting privileges to the calling process matching those in *desired_permset*. An application generally only inquires after the minimum set of privileges needed to accomplish a specific task.

Permissions Required

The **sec_acl_test_access( )** routine requires at least one permission of any kind on the object for which the privileges are to be tested.

Files

/usr/include/dce/daclif.idl The **idl** file from which **dce/daclif.h** was derived.

Return Values

The routine returns TRUE if the calling application program is authorized to access the target object with the privileges in *desired_permset*.

Errors

sec_acl_unknown_manager_type
The manager type selected is not an available option.

error_status_ok The call was successful.

Related Information

Functions: **intro(3sec)**, **sec_acl_bind(3sec)**, **sec_acl_test_access_on_behalf(3sec)**.

sec_acl_test_access_on_behalf

Purpose

Tests access to an object on behalf of another process

Synopsis

#include <dce/daclif.h>

boolean32 sec_acl_test_access_on_behalf(
sec_acl_handle_t *h*,
uuid_t **manager_type*,
sec_id_pac_t **subject*,
sec_acl_permset_t *desired_permset*,
error_status_t **status***);**

Parameters

Input

h — A handle referring to the target object. Use **sec_acl_bind**( ) to create this handle.

manager_type — A pointer to the UUID identifying the type of the ACL manager in question. There may be more than one type of ACL manager protecting the object whose ACL is bound to the input handle. Use this parameter to distinguish them. Use **sec_acl_get_manager_types**( ) to acquire a list of the manager types protecting a given object.

subject — A Privilege Attribute Certificate (PAC) for the subject process. The PAC contains the name and UUID of the principal and cell of the subject process, as well as a list of any groups to which it belongs. The PAC also contains a flag (named **authenticated**). When set, it indicates that the certificate was obtained from an authenticated source. When not set, the certificate must not be trusted. (The field is FALSE when it was obtained from the **rpc_auth(3rpc)** layer and the protect level was set to **rpc_c_protect_level_none**. This indicates that no authentication protocol was actually used in the remote procedure call; the identity was simply transmitted from the caller to the callee. If an authentication protocol was used, then the flag is set to TRUE.)

If a null PAC is passed, the subject is treated as an ''anonymous user,'' matching only the **any_other** and **unauthenticated** entries (if they exist) on the ACL.

A server uses **rpc_binding_inq_auth_client( )** to acquire a certificate for the client process.

desired_permset A permission set in **sec_acl_permset_t** form containing the desired privileges. This is a 32-bit set of permission flags supported by the manager type.

Output

status A pointer to the completion status. On successful completion, the routine returns **error_status_ok**. Otherwise, it returns an error.

Description

The **sec_acl_test_access_on_behalf( )** routine determines if the specified ACL contains entries that grant the privileges specified in *desired_permset* to the subject process. An application generally inquires about only the minimum set of privileges needed to accomplish a specific task.

Permissions Required

The **sec_acl_test_access_on_behalf( )** routine requires at least one permission of any kind on the object for which the privileges are to be tested. Both the calling process and the identified subject must have permission on the object.

Files

/usr/include/dce/daclif.idl The **idl** file from which **dce/daclif.h** was derived.

Return Values

If the routine completes successfully (with a completion status of **error_status_ok**) it returns a value of

- TRUE if the caller has any access (at least one permission of any kind), and the subject has the *desired_permset* privileges.
- FALSE if both the caller and the subject have any access, but the subject does not have the *desired_permset* privileges.

If the routine does not complete successfully, it returns a bad completion status code and a return value of FALSE.

Errors

sec_acl_unknown_manager_type
The manager type selected is not an available option.

error_status_ok
The call was successful.

Related Information

Functions: **intro(3sec)**, **sec_acl_bind(3sec)**, **sec_acl_test_access(3sec)**, **rpc_binding_inq_auth_client(3rpc)**.

sec_id_gen_group

Purpose Generates a global name from cell and group UUIDs

Synopsis **#include <dce/secidmap.h>**

void sec_id_gen_group(
sec_rgy_handle_t *context*,
uuid_t **cell_idp*,
uuid_t **group_idp*,
sec_rgy_name_t *global_name*,
sec_rgy_name_t *cell_namep*,
sec_rgy_name_t *group_namep*,
error_status_t **status*);

Parameters

Input

context A pointer to an opaque handle bound to a registry server. Use **sec_rgy_site_open**( ) to acquire a bound handle.

cell_idp A pointer to the UUID of the home cell of the group whose name is in question.

group_idp A pointer to the UUID of the group whose name is in question.

Output

global_name The global (full) name of the group in **sec_rgy_name_t** form.

cell_namep The name of the group's home cell in **sec_rgy_name_t** form.

group_namep The local (with respect to the home cell) name of the group in **sec_rgy_name_t** form.

status A pointer to the completion status. On successful completion, the function returns **error_status_ok**. Otherwise, it returns an error.

Description

The **sec_id_gen_group( )** routine generates a global name from input cell and group UUIDs. For example, given a UUID specifying the cell **/.../world/hp/brazil**, and a UUID specifying a group resident in that cell named **writers**, the routine would return the global name of that group, in this case, **/.../world/hp/brazil/writers**. It also returns the simple names of the cell and group, translated from the UUIDs.

The routine will not produce translations to any name for which a **NULL** pointer has been supplied.

Files

/usr/include/dce/secidmap.idl The **idl** file from which **dce/secidmap.h** was derived.

Errors

sec_id_e_name_too_long The name is too long for current implementation.

sec_id_e_bad_cell_uuid The cell UUID is not valid.

sec_id_e_foreign_cell_referral
The global name yields a group in foreign cell use referral.

error_status_ok The call was successful.

Related Information

Functions: **intro(3sec)**, **sec_id_gen_name(3sec)**, **sec_id_parse_group(3sec)**, **sec_id_parse_name(3sec)**.

sec_id_gen_name

Purpose Generates a global name from cell and principal UUIDs

Synopsis **#include <dce/secidmap.h>**

void sec_id_gen_name(
    sec_rgy_handle_t *context*,
    uuid_t **cell_idp*,
    uuid_t **princ_idp*,
    sec_rgy_name_t *global_name*,
    sec_rgy_name_t *cell_namep*,
    sec_rgy_name_t *princ_namep*,
    error_status_t **status*);

Parameters

Input

context A pointer to an opaque handle bound to a registry server. Use **sec_rgy_site_open**( ) to acquire a bound handle.

cell_idp A pointer to the UUID of the home cell of the principal whose name is in question.

princ_idp A pointer to the UUID of the principal whose name is in question.

Output

global_name The global (full) name of the principal in **sec_rgy_name_t** form.

cell_namep The name of the principal's home cell in **sec_rgy_name_t** form.

princ_namep The local (with respect to the home cell) name of the principal in **sec_rgy_name_t** form.

status A pointer to the completion status. On successful completion, the function returns **error_status_ok**. Otherwise, it returns an error.

Description

The **sec_id_gen_name()** routine generates a global name from input cell and principal UUIDs. For example, given a UUID specifying the cell **/.../world/hp/brazil**, and a UUID specifying a principal resident in that cell named **writers/tom**, the routine would return the global name of that principal, in this case, **/.../world/hp/brazil/writers/tom**. It also returns the simple names of the cell and principal, translated from the UUIDs.

The routine will not produce translations to any name for which a **NULL** pointer has been supplied.

Permissions Required

The **sec_id_gen_name()** routine requires at least one permission of any kind on the account associated with the input cell and principal UUIDs.

Files

/usr/include/dce/secidmap.idl The **idl** file from which **dce/secidmap.h** was derived.

Errors

sec_id_e_name_too_long The name is too long for current implementation.

sec_id_e_bad_cell_uuid The cell UUID is not valid.

sec_id_e_foreign_cell_referral
The global name yields a principal in foreign cell use referral.

error_status_ok The call was successful.

Related Information

Functions: **intro(3sec)**, **sec_id_gen_group(3sec)**, **sec_id_parse_group(3sec)**, **sec_id_parse_name(3sec)**.

sec_id_parse_group

Purpose Translates a global name into group and cell names and UUIDs

Synopsis **#include <dce/secidmap.h>**

void sec_id_parse_group(
sec_rgy_handle_t *context*,
sec_rgy_name_t *global_name*,
sec_rgy_name_t *cell_namep*,
uuid_t **cell_idp*,
sec_rgy_name_t *group_namep*,
uuid_t **group_idp*,
error_status_t **status*);

Parameters

Input

context A pointer to an opaque handle bound to a registry server. Use **sec_rgy_site_open( )** to acquire a bound handle.

global_name The global (full) name of the group in **sec_rgy_name_t** form.

Output

cell_namep The output name of the group's home cell in **sec_rgy_name_t** form.

cell_idp A pointer to the UUID of the home cell of the group whose name is in question.

group_namep The local (with respect to the home cell) name of the group in **sec_rgy_name_t** form.

group_idp A pointer to the UUID of the group whose name is in question.

status A pointer to the completion status. On successful completion, the function returns **error_status_ok**. Otherwise, it returns an error.

Description

The **sec_id_parse_group( )** routine translates a global group name into a cell name and a cell-relative group name. It also returns the UUIDs associated with the group and its home cell.

The routine will not produce translations to any name for which a **NULL** pointer has been supplied.

Files

/usr/include/dce/secidmap.idl The **idl** file from which **dce/secidmap.h** was derived.

Errors

sec_id_e_name_too_long The name is too long for current implementation.

sec_id_e_bad_cell_uuid The cell UUID is not valid.

sec_id_e_foreign_cell_referral
The global name yields a group in foreign cell use referral.

error_status_ok The call was successful.

Related Information

Functions: **intro(3sec)**, **sec_id_gen_group(3sec)**, **sec_id_gen_name(3sec)**, **sec_id_parse_group(3sec)**, **sec_id_parse_name(3sec)**.

sec_id_parse_name

Purpose Translates a global name into principal and cell names and UUIDs

Synopsis **#include <dce/secidmap.h>**

```
void sec_id_parse_name(
        sec_rgy_handle_t context,
        sec_rgy_name_t global_name,
        sec_rgy_name_t cell_namep,
        uuid_t *cell_idp,
        sec_rgy_name_t princ_namep,
        uuid_t *princ_idp,
        error_status_t *status);
```

Parameters

Input

context A pointer to an opaque handle bound to a registry server. Use **sec_rgy_site_open( )** to acquire a bound handle.

global_name The global (full) name of the principal in **sec_rgy_name_t** form.

Output

cell_namep The output name of the principal's home cell in **sec_rgy_name_t** form.

cell_idp A pointer to the UUID of the home cell of the principal whose name is in question.

princ_namep The local (with respect to the home cell) name of the principal in **sec_rgy_name_t** form.

princ_idp A pointer to the UUID of the principal whose name is in question.

status A pointer to the completion status. On successful completion, the function returns **error_status_ok**. Otherwise, it returns an error.

Description

The **sec_id_parse_name( )** routine translates a global principal name into a cell name and a cell-relative principal name. It also returns the UUIDs associated with the principal and its home cell.

The routine will not produce translations to any name for which a **NULL** pointer has been supplied.

Permissions Required

Only if *princ_idp* is requested as output does the **sec_id_parse_name( )** routine require a permission. In this case, the routine requires at least one permission of any kind on the account whose global principal name is to be translated.

Files

/usr/include/dce/secidmap.idl The **idl** file from which **dce/secidmap.h** was derived.

Errors

sec_id_e_name_too_long The name is too long for current implementation.

sec_id_e_bad_cell_uuid The cell UUID is not valid.

sec_id_e_foreign_cell_referral
The global name yields a principal in foreign cell use referral.

error_status_ok The call was successful.

Related Information

Functions: **intro(3sec)**, **sec_id_gen_name(3sec)**.

sec_key_mgmt_change_key

Purpose Changes a principal's key

Synopsis **#include <dce/keymgmt.h>**

void sec_key_mgmt_change_key(
    sec_key_mgmt_authn_service *authn_service*,
    void **arg*,
    char **principal_name*,
    unsigned32 *key_vno*,
    void **keydata*,
    sec_timeval_period_t **garbage_collect_time*,
    error_status_t **status*);

Parameters

Input

authn_service Identifies the authentication protocol using this key. The possible authentication protocols are as follows:

rpc_c_authn_dce_secret DCE shared-secret key authentication.

rpc_c_authn_dce_public DCE public key authentication (reserved for future use).

arg An alternative local key file. This is the same value as the *arg* parameter passed to the **rpc_server_register_auth_info( )** routine.

principal_name A pointer to a character string indicating the name of the principal whose key is to be changed.

key_vno The version number of the new key. If 0 (zero) is specified, the routine will select the next appropriate key version number.

keydata A pointer to the new key value.

Output

garbage_collect_time
The number of seconds that must elapse before all currently valid tickets (which are encoded with the current or previous keys) expire. At that time, all obsolete keys may be ''garbage collected,'' since no valid tickets encoded with those keys will remain outstanding on the network.

status
A pointer to the completion status. On successful completion, the routine returns **error_status_ok**. Otherwise, it returns an error.

Description

The **sec_key_mgmt_change_key( )** routine performs all activities necessary to update a principal's key to the specified value. This includes updating any local storage for the principal's key and also performing any remote operations needed to keep the authentication protocol (or network registry) current. Old keys for the principal are garbage collected if appropriate.

Files

/usr/include/dce/keymgmt.idl The **idl** file from which **dce/keymgmt.h** was derived.

Errors

Any error condition will leave the key state unchanged.

sec_key_mgmt_e_key_unavailable
The old key is not present and therefore cannot be used to set a client side authentication context.

sec_key_mgmt_e_authn_invalid
The authentication protocol is not valid.

sec_key_mgmt_e_auth_unavailable
The authentication protocol is not available to update the network database or to obtain the necessary network credentials.

sec_key_mgmt_e_unauthorized
The caller is not authorized to perform the operation.

sec_key_mgmt_e_key_unsupported
The key type is not supported.

sec_key_mgmt_e_key_version_ex
A key with this version number already exists.

error_status_ok The call was successful.

Related Information

Functions: **intro(3sec)**, **sec_key_mgmt_generate_key(3sec)**, **sec_key_mgmt_set_key(3sec)**.

sec_key_mgmt_delete_key

Purpose Deletes a key from the local storage

Synopsis **#include <dce/keymgmt.h>**

void sec_key_mgmt_delete_key(
sec_key_mgmt_authn_service *authn_service*,
void **arg*,
char **principal_name*,
unsigned32 *key_vno*,
error_status_t **status*);

Parameters

Input

authn_service Identifies the authentication protocol using this key. The possible authentication protocols are as follows:

rpc_c_authn_dce_secret DCE shared-secret key authentication.

rpc_c_authn_dce_public DCE public key authentication (reserved for future use).

arg An alternative local key file. This is the same value as the *arg* parameter passed to the **rpc_server_register_auth_info()** routine.

principal_name A pointer to a character string indicating the name of the principal whose key is to be deleted.

key_vno The version number of the desired key. If 0 (zero) is specified, the function will select the most recent key version number.

Output

status A pointer to the completion status. On successful completion, the routine returns **error_status_ok**. Otherwise, it returns an error.

Description

The **sec_key_mgmt_delete_key( )** routine deletes the specified key from the local key store. If an administrator ever discovers or suspects that the security of a server's key has been compromised, the administrator should delete the key immediately with **sec_key_mgmt_delete_key( )**. This routine removes the key from the local key storage, which invalidates all extant tickets encoded with the key. If the compromised key is the current one, the principal should change the key with **sec_key_mgmt_change_key( )** before deleting it. It is not an error for a process to delete the current key (as long as it is done *after* the network context has been established), but it may seriously inconvenience legitimate clients of a service.

This routine deletes all key types that have the specified key version number. A key type identifies the data encryption algorithm being used (for example, DES). This routine differs from **sec_key_mgmt_delete_key_type( )** in that **sec_key_mgmt_delete_key_type( )** deletes only the specified key version of the specified key type from the local key store.

Files

/usr/include/dce/keymgmt.idl The **idl** file from which **dce/keymgmt.h** was derived.

Errors

Any error condition will leave the key state unchanged.

sec_key_mgmt_e_key_unavailable
The requested key is not present.

sec_key_mgmt_e_authn_invalid
The authentication protocol is not valid.

sec_key_mgmt_e_unauthorized
The caller is not authorized to perform the operation.

error_status_ok The call was successful.

Related Information

Functions: **intro(3sec)**, **sec_key_mgmt_delete_key_type(3sec)**, **sec_key_mgmt_garbage_collect(3sec)**.

sec_key_mgmt_delete_key_type

Purpose Deletes a key version of a key type from the local key storage

Synopsis **#include <dce/keymgmt.h>**

```
void sec_key_mgmt_delete_key_type(
        sec_key_mgmt_authn_service authn_service,
        void *arg,
        char *principal_name,
        void *keytype,
        unsigned32 key_vno,
        error_status_t *status);
```

Parameters

Input

authn_service Identifies the authentication protocol using this key. The possible authentication protocols are as follows:

rpc_c_authn_dce_secret DCE shared-secret key authentication.

rpc_c_authn_dce_public DCE public key authentication (reserved for future use).

arg An alternative local key file. This is the same value as the *arg* parameter passed to the **rpc_server_register_auth_info()** routine.

principal_name A pointer to a character string indicating the name of the principal whose key type is to be deleted.

keytype The key type to be deleted. The key type identifies the data encryption algorithm that is being used (for example, DES).

key_vno The version number of the desired key. If 0 (zero) is specified, the function will select the most recent key version number.

Output

status A pointer to the completion status. On successful completion, the routine returns **error_status_ok**. Otherwise, it returns an error.

Description

The **sec_key_mgmt_delete_key_type( )** routine deletes the specified key version of the specified key type from the local key store. It differs from **sec_key_mgmt_delete_key( )** in that **sec_key_mgmt_delete_key( )** deletes all key types that have the same key version number.

This routine removes the key from the local key storage, which invalidates all extant tickets encoded with the key. If the key in question is the current one, the principal should change the key with **sec_key_mgmt_change_key( )** before deleting it. It is not an error for a process to delete the current key (as long as it is done *after* the network context has been established), but it may seriously inconvenience legitimate clients of a service.

Files

/usr/include/dce/keymgmt.idl The **idl** file from which **dce/keymgmt.h** was derived.

Errors

Any error condition will leave the key state unchanged.

sec_key_mgmt_e_key_unavailable
The requested key is not present.

sec_key_mgmt_e_authn_invalid
The authentication protocol is not valid.

sec_key_mgmt_e_unauthorized
The caller is not authorized to perform the operation.

error_status_ok The call was successful.

Related Information

Functions: **intro(3sec)**, **sec_key_mgmt_delete_key(3sec)**, **sec_key_mgmt_garbage_collect(3sec)**.

sec_key_mgmt_free_key

Purpose Frees the memory used by a key value

Synopsis **#include <dce/keymgmt.h>**

void sec_key_mgmt_free_key(
void **keydata***,**
error_status_t **status***);**

Parameters

Input

keydata A pointer to the storage that is to be returned to the pool.

Output

status A pointer to the completion status. On successful completion, the routine returns **error_status_ok**.

Description

The **sec_key_mgmt_free_key( )** routine releases any storage allocated for the indicated key data by **sec_key_mgmt_get_key( )**. The storage for the key data returned by **sec_key_mgmt_get_key( )** is dynamically allocated.

Files **/usr/include/dce/keymgmt.idl** The **idl** file from which **dce/keymgmt.h** was derived.

Errors **error_status_ok** The call was successful.

Related Information

Functions: **intro(3sec)**, **sec_key_mgmt_get_key(3sec)**.

sec_key_mgmt_garbage_collect

Purpose Deletes obsolete keys

Synopsis **#include <dce/keymgmt.h>**

void sec_key_mgmt_garbage_collect(
sec_key_mgmt_authn_service *authn_service*,
void **arg*,
char **principal_name*,
error_status_t **status*);

Parameters

Input

authn_service Identifies the authentication protocol using this key. The possible authentication protocols are as follows:

rpc_c_authn_dce_secret DCE shared-secret key authentication.

rpc_c_authn_dce_public DCE public key authentication (reserved for future use).

arg An alternative local key file. This is the same value as the *arg* parameter passed to the **rpc_server_register_auth_info( )** routine.

principal_name A pointer to a character string indicating the name of the principal whose key information is to be garbage collected.

Output

status A pointer to the completion status. On successful completion, the routine returns **error_status_ok**. Otherwise, it returns an error.

Description

The **sec_key_mgmt_garbage_collect**( ) routine discards any obsolete key information for this principal. An obsolete key is one that can only decode invalid tickets. As an example, consider a key that was in use on Monday, and was only used to encode tickets whose maximum lifetime was 1 day. If that key was changed at 8:00 a.m. Tuesday morning, then it would become obsolete by 8:00 a.m. Wednesday morning, at which time there could be no valid tickets outstanding.

Files

/usr/include/dce/keymgmt.idl The **idl** file from which **dce/keymgmt.h** was derived.

Errors

sec_key_mgmt_e_authn_invalid
The authentication protocol is not valid.

sec_key_mgmt_e_unauthorized
The caller is not authorized to perform the operation.

sec_key_mgmt_e_key_unavailable
Requested key not present.

error_status_ok The call was successful.

Related Information

Functions: **intro(3sec)**, **sec_key_mgmt_delete_key(3sec)**.

sec_key_mgmt_gen_rand_key

Purpose Generates a new random key of a specified key type

Synopsis **#include <dce/keymgmt.h>**

void sec_key_mgmt_gen_rand_key(
sec_key_mgmt_authn_service *authn_service*,
void **arg*,
char **principal_name*,
void **keytype*,
unsigned32 *key_vno*,
void ***keydata*,
error_status_t **status*);

Parameters

Input

authn_service Identifies the authentication protocol using this key. The possible authentication protocols are as follows:

rpc_c_authn_dce_secret DCE shared-secret key authentication.

rpc_c_authn_dce_public DCE public key authentication (reserved for future use).

arg An alternative local key file. This is the same value as the *arg* parameter passed to the **rpc_server_register_auth_info**( ) routine.

principal_name A pointer to a character string indicating the name of the principal for whom the key is to be generated.

keytype The key type for the new key. The key type identifies the data encryption algorithm to be used for the key (for example, DES).

key_vno The version number of the new key. If 0 (zero) is specified, the routine will select the next appropriate key version number.

Output

keydata — The returned key value. The storage for this key is allocated dynamically, so the returned pointer actually indicates a pointer to the key value. The storage for this data may be freed with the **sec_key_mgmt_free_key**( ) function.

status — A pointer to the completion status. On successful completion, the routine returns **error_status_ok**. Otherwise, it returns an error.

Description

The **sec_key_mgmt_gen_rand_key( )** routine generates a new random key for a specified principal and of a specified key type. The generated key can be used with the **sec_key_mgmt_change_key**( ) and **sec_key_mgmt_set_key**( ) routines.

Note that to initialize the random keyseed, the process must first make an authenticated call such as **sec_rgy_site_open**( ).

Files

/usr/include/dce/keymgmt.idl The **idl** file from which **dce/keymgmt.h** was derived.

Errors

sec_key_mgmt_e_authn_invalid
The authentication protocol is not valid.

sec_key_mgmt_e_unauthorized
The caller is not authorized to perform the operation.

error_status_ok The call was successful.

Related Information

Functions: **intro(3sec)**, **sec_key_mgmt_change_key(3sec)**, **sec_key_mgmt_generate_key(3sec)**, **sec_key_mgmt_set_key(3sec)**.

sec_key_mgmt_get_key

Purpose

Retrieves a key from local storage

Synopsis

#include <dce/keymgmt.h>

void sec_key_mgmt_get_key(
sec_key_mgmt_authn_service *authn_service*,
void **arg*,
char **principal_name*,
unsigned32 *key_vno*,
void ***keydata*,
error_status_t **status*);

Parameters

Input

authn_service Identifies the authentication protocol using this key. The possible authentication protocols are as follows:

rpc_c_authn_dce_secret DCE shared-secret key authentication.

rpc_c_authn_dce_public DCE public key authentication (reserved for future use).

arg An alternative local key file. This is the same value as the *arg* parameter passed to the **rpc_server_register_auth_info**( ) routine.

principal_name A pointer to a character string indicating the name of the principal to whom the key belongs.

key_vno The version number of the desired key. If 0 (zero) is specified, the function will select the most recent key version.

Output

keydata The returned key value. The storage for this key is allocated dynamically, so the returned pointer actually indicates a pointer to the key value. The storage for this data may be freed with the **sec_key_mgmt_free_key**( ) routine.

status A pointer to the completion status. On successful completion, the routine returns **error_status_ok**. Otherwise, it returns an error.

Description

The **sec_key_mgmt_get_key( )** routine extracts the specified key from the local key store.

Files

/usr/include/dce/keymgmt.idl The **idl** file from which **dce/keymgmt.h** was derived.

Errors

sec_key_mgmt_e_key_unavailable
The requested key is not present.

sec_key_mgmt_e_authn_invalid
The authentication protocol is not valid.

sec_key_mgmt_e_unauthorized
The caller is not authorized to perform the operation.

error_status_ok The call was successful.

Related Information

Functions: **intro(3sec)**.

sec_key_mgmt_get_next_key

Purpose Retrieves successive keys from the local key storage

Synopsis **#include <dce/keymgmt.h>**

void sec_key_mgmt_get_next_key(
void **cursor*,
char ***principal_name*,
unsigned32 **key_vno*,
void ***keydata*,
error_status_t **status*);

Parameters

Input

cursor A pointer to the current cursor position in the local key storage. The cursor position is set via the routine **sec_key_mgmt_initialize_cursor**( ).

Output

principal_name A pointer to a character string indicating the name of the principal associated with the extracted key.

key_vno The version number of the extracted key.

keydata The extracted key value. The storage for this key is allocated dynamically, so the returned pointer actually indicates a pointer to the key value. The storage for this data may be freed with the **sec_key_mgmt_free_key**( ) function.

status A pointer to the completion status. On successful completion, the routine returns **error_status_ok**. Otherwise, it returns an error.

Description

The **sec_key_mgmt_get_next_key( )** routine extracts the key pointed to by the cursor in the local key store and updates the cursor to point to the next key. By repeatedly calling this routine you can scan all the keys in the local store.

Files

/usr/lib/dce/keymgmt.idl — The **idl** file from which **dce/keymgmt.h** was derived.

Errors

sec_key_mgmt_e_key_unavailable
The requested key is not present.

sec_key_mgmt_e_unauthorized
The caller is not authorized to perform the operation.

error_status_ok — The call was successful.

Related Information

Functions: **intro(3sec)**, **sec_key_mgmt_get_key(3sec)**, **sec_key_mgmt_initialize_cursor(3sec)**.

sec_key_mgmt_get_next_kvno

Purpose Retrieves the next eligible key version number for a key

Synopsis **#include <dce/keymgmt.h>**

void sec_key_mgmt_get_next_kvno(
sec_key_mgmt_authn_service *authn_service*,
void **arg*,
char **principal_name*,
void **keytype*,
unsigned32 **key_vno*,
unsigned32 **next_key_vno*,
error_status_t **status*);

Parameters

Input

authn_service Identifies the authentication protocol using this key. The possible authentication protocols are as follows:

rpc_c_authn_dce_secret DCE shared-secret key authentication.

rpc_c_authn_dce_public DCE public key authentication (reserved for future use).

arg An alternative local key file. This is the same value as the *arg* parameter passed to the **rpc_server_register_auth_info( )** routine.

principal_name A pointer to a character string indicating the name of the principal associated with the key.

keytype The key type for the key. The key type identifies the data encryption algorithm (for example, DES) being used for the key.

Output

key_vno The current version number of the key. Specify **NULL** if you do not need this value to be returned.

next_key_vno The next eligible version number for the key. Specify **NULL** if you do not need this value to be returned.

status A pointer to the completion status. On successful completion, the routine returns **error_status_ok**. Otherwise, it returns an error.

Description

The **sec_key_mgmt_get_next_kvno( )** routine returns the current and next eligible version numbers for a key. The key is identified via its associated authentication protocol, principal name, and key type. The *arg* value associated with the key is also specified.

Files

/usr/include/dce/keymgmt.idl The **idl** file from which **dce/keymgmt.h** was derived.

Errors

sec_key_mgmt_e_key_unavailable
The requested key is not present.

sec_key_mgmt_e_authn_invalid
The authentication protocol is not valid.

sec_key_mgmt_e_unauthorized
The caller is not authorized to perform the operation.

error_status_ok The call was successful.

Related Information

Functions: **intro(3sec)**.

sec_key_mgmt_initialize_cursor

Purpose Repositions the cursor in the local key store

Synopsis **#include <dce/keymgmt.h>**

```
void sec_key_mgmt_initialize_cursor(
        sec_key_mgmt_authn_service authn_service,
        void *arg,
        char *principal_name,
        void *keytype,
        void **cursor,
        error_status_t *status);
```

Parameters

Input

authn_service Identifies the authentication protocol using this key. The possible authentication protocols are as follows:

rpc_c_authn_dce_secret DCE shared-secret key authentication.

rpc_c_authn_dce_public DCE public key authentication (reserved for future use).

arg An alternative local key file. This is the same value as the *arg* parameter passed to the **rpc_server_register_auth_info( )** routine.

principal_name A pointer to a character string indicating the name of the principal whose key is to be changed.

keytype A pointer to the data encryption algorithm (for example, DES) being used for the key.

Output

cursor The returned cursor value. The storage for the cursor information is allocated dynamically, so the returned pointer actually indicates a pointer to the cursor value. The storage for this data may be freed with the **sec_key_mgmt_release_cursor( )** routine.

status A pointer to the completion status. On successful completion, the routine returns **error_status_ok**. Otherwise, it returns an error.

Description

The **sec_key_mgmt_initialize_cursor()** routine resets the cursor in the local key store.

Use this routine to reposition the cursor before performing a scan of the local store via **sec_key_mgmt_get_next_key()**. The returned cursor value is supplied as input to **sec_key_mgmt_get_next_key()**.

Files

/usr/include/dce/keymgmt.idl The **idl** file from which **dce/keymgmt.h** was derived.

Errors

sec_key_mgmt_e_authn_invalid
The authentication protocol is not valid.

sec_key_mgmt_e_unauthorized
The caller is not authorized to perform the operation.

error_status_ok The call was successful.

Related Information

Functions: **intro(3sec)**, **sec_key_mgmt_get_next_key(3sec)**, **sec_key_mgmt_release_cursor(3sec)**.

sec_key_mgmt_manage_key

Purpose Automatically changes a principal's key before it expires

Synopsis **#include <dce/keymgmt.h>**

```
void sec_key_mgmt_manage_key(
        sec_key_mgmt_authn_service authn_service,
        void *arg,
        char *principal_name,
        error_status_t *status);
```

Parameters

Input

authn_service Identifies the authentication protocol using this key. The possible authentication protocols are as follows:

rpc_c_authn_dce_secret DCE shared-secret key authentication.

rpc_c_authn_dce_public DCE public key authentication (reserved for future use).

arg An alternative local key file. This is the same value as the *arg* parameter passed to the **rpc_server_register_auth_info( )** routine.

principal_name A pointer to a character string indicating the name of the principal whose key is to be managed.

Output

status A pointer to the completion status. On successful completion, the routine returns **error_status_ok**. Otherwise, it returns an error.

Description

The **sec_key_mgmt_manage_key( )** routine changes the specified principal's key on a regular basis, as determined by the local cell's policy. It will run indefinitely, never returning during normal operation, and therefore should be invoked only from a thread that has been devoted to managing keys.

This routine queries the DCE Registry to determine the password expiration policy that applies to the named principal. It then idles until a short time before the current key is due to expire and then uses the **sec_key_mgmt_gen_rand_key( )** to produce a new random key, updating both the local key store and the DCE Registry. This routine also invokes **sec_key_mgmt_garbage_collect( )** as needed.

Files

/usr/include/dce/keymgmt.idl The **idl** file from which **dce/keymgmt.h** was derived.

Errors

sec_key_mgmt_e_key_unavailable
The old key is not present and therefore cannot be used to set a client side authentication context.

sec_key_mgmt_e_authn_invalid
The authentication protocol is not valid.

sec_key_mgmt_e_unauthorized
The caller is not authorized to perform the operation.

error_status_ok
The call was successful.

Related Information

Functions: **intro(3sec)**, **sec_key_mgmt_gen_rand_key(3sec)**, **sec_key_mgmt_garbage_collect(3sec)**.

sec_key_mgmt_release_cursor

Purpose Releases the memory used by an initialized cursor value

Synopsis **#include <dce/keymgmt.h>**

void sec_key_mgmt_release_cursor(
void *****cursor*,**
error_status_t ****status*);**

Parameters

Input

cursor A pointer to the cursor value for which the storage is to be released.

Output

status A pointer to the completion status. On successful completion, the routine returns **error_status_ok**.

Description

The **sec_key_mgmt_release_cursor( )** routine releases any storage allocated for the indicated cursor value by **sec_key_mgmt_initialize_cursor( )**. The storage for the cursor value returned by **sec_key_mgmt_initialize_cursor( )** is dynamically allocated.

Files **/usr/include/dce/keymgmt.idl** The **idl** file from which **dce/keymgmt.h** was derived.

Errors

sec_key_mgmt_e_unauthorized
The caller is not authorized to perform the operation.

error_status_ok The call was successful.

Related Information

Functions: **intro(3sec)**, **sec_key_mgmt_initialize_cursor(3sec)**.

sec_key_mgmt_set_key

Purpose Inserts a key value into the local storage

Synopsis **#include <dce/keymgmt.h>**

void sec_key_mgmt_set_key(
sec_key_mgmt_authn_service *authn_service*,
void **arg*,
char **principal_name*,
unsigned32 *key_vno*,
void **keydata*,
error_status_t **status*);

Parameters

Input

authn_service Identifies the authentication protocol using this key. The possible authentication protocols are as follows:

rpc_c_authn_dce_secret DCE shared-secret key authentication.

rpc_c_authn_dce_public DCE public key authentication (reserved for future use).

arg An alternative local key file. This is the same value as the *arg* parameter passed to the **rpc_server_register_auth_info( )** routine.

principal_name A pointer to a character string indicating the name of the principal associated with the key to be set.

key_vno The version number of the key to be set. If 0 (zero) is specified, the routine will select the next appropriate key version number.

keydata A pointer to the key value to be set.

Output

status A pointer to the completion status. On successful completion, the routine returns **error_status_ok**. Otherwise, it returns an error.

Description

The **sec_key_mgmt_set_key()** routine performs all local activities necessary to update a principal's key to the specified value. This routine will not update the authentication protocol's value for the principal's key.

In some circumstances, a server may only wish to change its key in the local key storage, and not in the DCE Registry. For example, a database system may have several replicas of a master database, managed by servers running on independent machines. Since these servers together represent only one service, they should all share the same key. This way, a user with a ticket to use the database can choose whichever server is least busy. To change the database key, the master server would signal all the replica (slave) servers to change the current key in their local key storage. They would use the **sec_key_mgmt_set_key()** routine, which does not communicate with the DCE Registry. Once all the slaves have complied, the master server can then change the Registry key and its own local storage.

Files

/usr/include/dce/keymgmt.idl The **idl** file from which **dce/keymgmt.h** was derived.

Errors

sec_key_mgmt_e_key_unavailable
The old key is not present and therefore cannot be used to set a client side authentication context.

sec_key_mgmt_e_authn_invalid
The authentication protocol is not valid.

sec_key_mgmt_e_unauthorized
The caller is not authorized to perform the operation.

sec_key_mgmt_e_key_unsupported
The key type is not supported.

sec_key_mgmt_e_key_version_ex
A key with this version number already exists.

error_status_ok The call was successful.

Related Information

Functions: **intro(3sec)**, **sec_key_mgmt_change_key(3sec)**, **sec_key_mgmt_gen_rand_key(3sec)**.

sec_login_certify_identity

Purpose Certifies the network authentication service

Synopsis **#include <dce/sec_login.h>**

boolean32 sec_login_certify_identity(
sec_login_handle_t *login_context*,
error_status_t **status*);

Parameters

Input

login_context An opaque handle to login context data. The login context contains, among other data, the account principal name and UUID, account restrictions, records of group membership, the process home directory, and the encrypted password. (See **intro(3sec)** for more details about the login context.)

Output

status A pointer to the completion status. On successful completion, the routine returns **error_status_ok**. Otherwise, it returns an error.

Description

The **sec_login_certify_identity( )** routine certifies that the Security Server used to set up and validate a login context is legitimate. A legitimate server is one that knows the host machine's secret key. On some systems, this may be a privileged operation.

Information may be retrieved via **sec_login_get_pwent( )**, **sec_login_get_groups( )**, and **sec_login_get_expiration( )** from an uncertified login context, but such information cannot be trusted. All system login programs that use the **sec_login** interface must call **sec_login_certify_identity( )** to certify the Security Server. If they do not, they open the local file system to attacks by imposter Security servers returning suspect local process credentials (UUID and group IDs). This operation updates the local registry with the login context credentials if the certification check succeeds.

Files

/usr/include/dce/sec_login.idl The **idl** file from which **dce/sec_login.h** was derived.

Return Values

The routine returns a **boolean32** value that is TRUE if the certification was successful, and FALSE otherwise.

Errors

sec_login_s_not_certified The operation failed, the authentication service is not authentic.

sec_login_s_context_invalid The input context is invalid.

sec_login_s_default_use It is an error to try to certify the default context.

error_status_ok The call was successful.

Examples

Applications wishing to perform a straightforward login could use the **sec_login** package as follows:

```
if (sec_login_setup_identity(user_name, sec_login_no_flags, &login_context,
                             &st)) {
   ... get password from user...

   if (sec_login_validate_identity(login_context, password,
                             &reset_passwd, &auth_src, &st)) {

      if (!sec_login_certify_identity(login_context, &st))
          exit(error_weird_auth_svc);

      sec_login_set_context(login_context, &st);

      if (auth_src != sec_login_auth_src_network)
         printf("no network credentials");

      if (reset_passwd) {
         ... get new password from user, reset registry record ...
      };

      sec_login_get_pwent(login_context, &pw_entry, &st);

      if (pw_entry.pw_expire < todays_date) {
         sec_login_purge_context(&login_context, &st);
         exit(0)
```

```
        }

        ... any other application specific login valid actions ...
        }

    } else {
        sec_login_purge_context(&login_context, &st);

        ... application specific login failure actions ...
    }
}
```

Related Information

Functions: **intro(3sec)**, **sec_login_get_pwent(3sec)**, **sec_login_get_groups(3sec)**, **sec_login_get_expiration(3sec)**.

sec_login_export_context

Purpose Creates an exportable login context

Synopsis **#include <dce/sec_login.h>**

void sec_login_export_context(
    sec_login_handle_t *login_context*,
    unsigned32 *buf_len*,
    byte *buf*[ ],
    unsigned32 **len_used*,
    unsigned32 **len_needed*,
    error_status_t **status*);

Parameters

Input

login_context An opaque handle to login context data. The login context contains, among other data, the account principal name and UUID, account restrictions, records of group membership, the process home directory, and the encrypted password. (See **intro(3sec)** for more details about the login context.)

buf_len An unsigned 32-bit integer containing the allocated length (in bytes) of the buffer that is to contain the login context.

Output

buf[ ] A byte array that contains the exportable login context upon return.

len_used A pointer to an unsigned 32-bit integer indicating the number of bytes needed for the entire login context, up to *buf_len*.

len_needed If the allocated length of the buffer is too short, an error is issued (**sec_login_s_no_memory**), and on return this pointer indicates the number of bytes necessary to contain the login context.

status A pointer to the completion status. On successful completion, the routine returns **error_status_ok**. Otherwise, it returns an error.

Description

The **sec_login_export_context**( ) routine obtains an exportable version of the login context information. This information may be passed to another process running on the same machine.

Files

/usr/include/dce/sec_login.idl The **idl** file from which **dce/sec_login.h** was derived.

Errors

sec_login_s_no_memory Not enough space was allocated for the *buf*[ ] array. The *len_needed* parameter will point to the needed length.

sec_login_s_handle_invalid The login context handle is invalid.

sec_login_s_context_invalid The login context specified by the input handle is invalid.

Related Information

Functions: **intro(3sec)**, **sec_login_import_context(3sec)**.

sec_login_free_net_info

Purpose Frees storage allocated for a principal's network information

Synopsis **#include <dce/sec_login.h>**

void sec_login_free_net_info(
sec_login_net_info_t ***net_info*);**

Parameters

Input/Output

net_info A pointer to the **sec_login_net_info_t** structure to be freed.

Description

The **sec_login_free_net_info( )** routine frees any memory allocated for a principal's network information. Network information is returned by a previous successful call to **sec_login_inquire_net_info( )**.

Cautions This routine does not return any completion codes. Make sure that you supply a valid **sec_login_net_info_t** address. The routine simply frees a range of storage beginning at the supplied address, without regard to the actual contents of the storage.

Files **/usr/include/dce/sec_login.idl** The **idl** file from which **dce/sec_login.h** was derived.

Related Information

Functions: **intro(3sec)**, **sec_login_inquire_net_info(3sec)**.

sec_login_get_current_context

Purpose Returns a handle to the current login context

Synopsis **#include <dce/sec_login.h>**

void sec_login_get_current_context(
sec_login_handle_t **login_context*,
error_status_t **status*);

Parameters

Output

login_context A pointer to an opaque handle to login context data. The login context contains, among other data, the account principal name and UUID, account restrictions, records of group membership, the process home directory, and the encrypted password. (See **intro(3sec)** for more details about the login context.)

status A pointer to the completion status. On successful completion, the routine returns **error_status_ok**. Otherwise, it returns an error.

Description

The **sec_login_get_current_context**( ) routine retrieves a handle to the login context for the currently established network identity. The context returned is created from locally cached data so subsequent data extraction operations may return some **NULL** values.

Files **/usr/include/dce/sec_login.idl** The **idl** file from which **dce/sec_login.h** was derived.

Errors **sec_login_s_no_current_context**
There was no current context to retrieve. (See **sec_login_setup_identity(3sec)** for information about how to set up, validate, and implement a login context.)

error_status_ok The call was successful.

Examples

The following example illustrates use of the **sec_login_get_current_context()** routine as part of a process to change the groupset:

```
sec_login_get_current_context(&login_context, &st);

sec_login_get_groups(login_context, &num_groups, &groups, &st);

   ...the group IDs have to be converted from the returned UNIX
   numbers into UUIDs (use sec_rgy_pgo_unix_num_to_id(3sec)...

for (i=0; i < num_groups; i++) {
   ... query whether the user wants to discard any of the current
   group memberships. Copy new groupset to the new_groups array ...
}

if ( !sec_login_newgroups(sec_login_no_flags, num_new_groups,
        new_groups, &login_context, &st)) {
   if (st == sec_login_s_groupset_invalid)
        printf("New groupset invalid0);

   ... application specific error handling ...
}
```

Related Information

Functions: **intro(3sec)**, **sec_login_setup_identity(3sec)**.

sec_login_get_expiration

Purpose Returns the TGT lifetime for an authenticated identity

Synopsis **#include <dce/sec_login.h>**

```
void sec_login_get_expiration(
        sec_login_handle_t login_context,
        signed32 *identity_expiration,
        error_status_t *status);
```

Parameters

Input

login_context An opaque handle to login context data. The login context contains, among other data, the account principal name and UUID, account restrictions, records of group membership, the process home directory, and the encrypted password. (See **intro(3sec)** for more details about the login context.)

Output

identity_expiration
The lifetime of the Ticket-Granting Ticket (TGT) belonging to the authenticated identity identified by *login_context*.

status A pointer to the completion status. On successful completion, the routine returns **error_status_ok**. Otherwise, it returns an error.

Description

The **sec_login_get_expiration()** routine extracts the lifetime for the TGT belonging to the authenticated identity contained in the login context. The liftime value is filled in if available; otherwise, it is set to 0 (zero). This routine allows an application to tell an interactive user how long the user's network login (and authenticated identity) will last before having to be refreshed.

The routine works only on previously certified contexts.

Files

/usr/include/dce/sec_login.idl The **idl** file from which **dce/sec_login.h** was derived.

Errors

sec_login_s_context_invalid The login context itself is invalid.

sec_login_s_default_use There was illegal use of the default login handle.

sec_login_s_not_certified The login context has not been certified.

error_status_ok The call was successful.

Examples

Since the authenticated network identity for a process has a finite lifetime, there is a risk it will expire during some long network operation, preventing the operation from completing. To avoid this situation, an application might, before initiating a long operation, use the **sec_login** package to check the expiration time of its identity and refresh it if there is not enough time remaining to complete the operation. After refreshing the identity, the process must validate it again with **sec_login_validate_identity( )**.

```
sec_login_get_expiration(login_context, &expire_time, &st);

if (expire_time < (current_time + operation_duration)) {

   if (!sec_login_refresh_identity(login_context, &st)) {
      if (st == sec_login_s_refresh_ident_change) {
         ... identity has changed ...
      } else {
         ... login context cannot be renewed ...
         exit(error_context_expired);
      }

    if (sec_login_validate_identity(login_context, password,
                              &reset_passwd, &auth_src, &st)) {
         ... identity validated ...
      } else {
         ... validation failed ...
         exit(error_validation_failure);
      }
   }
}

operation();
```

Related Information

Functions: **intro(3sec)**, **sec_login_get_current_context(3sec)**.

sec_login_get_groups

Purpose Returns the groupset from a login context

Synopsis **#include <dce/sec_login.h>**

```
void sec_login_get_groups(
        sec_login_handle_t login_context,
        unsigned32 *num_groups,
        signed32 **group_set,
        error_status_t *status);
```

Parameters

Input

login_context An opaque handle to login context data. The login context contains, among other data, the account principal name and UUID, account restrictions, records of group membership, the process home directory, and the encrypted password. (See **intro(3sec)** for more details about the login context.)

Output

num_groups An unsigned 32-bit integer indicating the total number of groups returned in the *group_set* array.

group_set The list of groups to which the user belongs.

status A pointer to the completion status. On successful completion, the routine returns **error_status_ok**. Otherwise, it returns an error.

Description

The **sec_login_get_groups( )** routine returns the groups contained in the supplied login context. Part of a network identity is a list of the various groups to which the principal belongs. The groups are used to determine a user's access to various objects and services. This routine extracts from the login context a list of the groups for which the user has established network privileges.

The routine works only on previously validated contexts.

Files

/usr/include/dce/sec_login.idl The **idl** file from which **dce/sec_login.h** was derived.

Errors

sec_login_s_context_invalid The login context itself is not valid.

sec_login_s_info_not_avail The login context has no UNIX information.

sec_login_s_default_use Illegal use of the default login handle occurred.

sec_login_s_not_certified The login context has not been certified.

error_status_ok The call was successful.

Examples

The following example illustrates use of the **sec_login_get_groups**( ) routine as part of a process to change the groupset:

```
sec_login_get_current_context(&login_context, &st);

sec_login_get_groups(login_context, &num_groups, &groups, &st);

   ...the group IDs have to be converted from the returned UNIX
   numbers into UUIDs (use sec_rgy_pgo_unix_num_to_id(3sec)...

for (i=0; i < num_groups; i++) {
   ... query whether the user wants to discard any of the current
   group memberships. Copy new groupset to the new_groups array ...
}

if ( !sec_login_newgroups(sec_login_no_flags, num_new_groups,
        new_groups, &login_context, &st)) {
   if (st == sec_login_s_groupset_invalid)
        printf("New groupset invalid0);

   ... application specific error handling ...
}
```

Related Information

Functions: **intro(3sec)**, **sec_rgy_acct_get_projlist(3sec)**.

sec_login_get_pwent

Purpose Returns a **passwd**-style entry for a login context

Synopsis **#include <dce/sec_login.h>**

void sec_login_get_pwent(
  sec_login_handle_t *login_context***,**
  sec_login_passwd_t **pwent***,**
  error_status_t **status***);**

Parameters

Input

login_context An opaque handle to login context data. The login context contains, among other data, the account principal name and UUID, account restrictions, records of group membership, the process home directory, and the encrypted password. (See **intro(3sec)** for more details about the login context.)

Output

pwent The returned **passwd**-style file entry. The particular **passwd**-style file entry depends on the underlying system. In most cases, the structure looks like that supported by 4.4BSD and OSF/1:

```
struct passwd {
   char   *pw_name;    /* user name */
   char   *pw_passwd; /* encrypted password */
   int    pw_uid;      /* user uid */
   int    pw_gid;      /* user gid */
   time_t pw_change;   /* password change time */
   char   *pw_class;   /* user access class */
   char   *pw_gecos;   /* miscellaneous account info */
   char   *pw_dir;     /* home directory */
   char   *pw_shell;   /* default shell */
   time_t pw_expire;   /* account expiration */
};
```

status A pointer to the completion status. On successful completion, the routine returns **error_status_ok**. Otherwise, it returns an error.

Description

The **sec_login_get_pwent( )** routine creates a **passwd**-style file entry for the current network login context. This is generally useful for establishing the local operating system context. Applications that require all of the data normally extracted via **getpwnam( )** should extract that data from the login context with this call.

This routine works only on explicitly created (not inherited or imported) contexts.

Cautions

The returned **sec_login_passwd_t** structure points to data stored in the structure indicated by the *login_context* pointer and must be treated as read-only data. Writing to these data objects may cause unexpected failures.

Files

/usr/include/dce/sec_login.idl The **idl** file from which **dce/sec_login.h** was derived.

Errors

sec_login_s_context_invalid The login context itself is invalid.

sec_login_s_not_certified The login context has not been certified.

sec_login_s_default_use Illegal use of the default login handle occurred.

sec_login_s_info_not_avail The login context has no UNIX information.

error_status_ok The call was successful.

Related Information

Functions: **intro(3sec)**.

sec_login_import_context

Purpose Imports a login context

Synopsis **#include <dce/sec_login.h>**

void sec_login_import_context(
unsigned32 *buf_len*,
byte *buf*[ ],
sec_login_handle_t **login_context*,
error_status_t **status*);

Parameters

Input

buf_len The allocated length (in bytes) of the buffer containing the login context.

buf[ ] A byte array containing the importable login context.

Output

login_context An opaque handle to login context data. The login context contains, among other data, the account principal name and UUID, account restrictions, records of group membership, the process home directory, and the encrypted password. (See **intro(3sec)** for more details about the login context.)

status A pointer to the completion status. On successful completion, the routine returns **error_status_ok**. Otherwise, it returns an error.

Description

The **sec_login_import_context()** routine imports a context obtained via a call to **sec_login_export_context()** performed on the same machine. This routine is generally reserved to the privileged user.

Files

/usr/include/dce/sec_login.idl	The **idl** file from which **dce/sec_login.h** was derived.

Errors

sec_login_s_context_invalid	The login context itself is not valid.
sec_login_s_default_use	Illegal use of the default login handle occurred.
error_status_ok	The call was successful.

Related Information

Functions: **intro(3sec)**, **sec_login_export_context(3sec)**.

sec_login_init_first

Purpose

Initializes the default context

Synopsis

#include <dce/sec_login.h>

void sec_login_init_first(
    error_status_t **status***);**

Parameters

Output

status — A pointer to the completion status. On successful completion, the routine returns **error_status_ok**. Otherwise, it returns an error.

Description

The **sec_login_init_first( )** routine initializes the default context inheritance mechanism. If the default inheritance mechanism is already initialized, the operation fails. Typically, this routine is called by the initial process at machine boot time to initialize the default context inheritance mechanism for the host machine process hierarchy.

Files

/usr/include/dce/sec_login.idl The **idl** file from which **dce/sec_login.h** was derived.

Errors

sec_login_s_default_use	The default context is already initialized.
sec_login_s_privileged	An unprivileged process was called in.
error_status_ok	The call was successful.

Related Information

Functions: **intro(3sec)**, **sec_login_setup_first(3sec)**, **sec_login_validate_first(3sec)**.

sec_login_inquire_net_info

Purpose Returns a principal's network information

Synopsis **#include <dce/sec_login.h>**

void sec_login_inquire_net_info(
sec_login_handle_t *login_context*,
sec_login_net_info_t **net_info*,
error_status_t **status*);

Parameters

Input

login_context An opaque handle to the login context for the desired principal. (See **intro(3sec)** for more details about the login context.)

Output

net_info A pointer to the returned **sec_login_net_info_t** data structure that contains the principal's network information. The **sec_login_net_info_t** structure is defined as follows:

```
typedef struct {
  sec_id_pac_t  pac;
  unsigned32   acct_expiration_date;
  unsigned32   passwd_expiration_date;
  unsigned32   identity_expiration_date;
} sec_login_net_info_t;
};
```

status A pointer to the completion status. On successful completion, the routine returns **error_status_ok**. Otherwise, it returns an error.

Description

The **sec_login_inquire_net_info( )** routine returns network information for the principal identified by the specified login context. The network information consists of the following:

- The Privilege Attribute Certificate (PAC) that describes the identity and group memberships of the principal.
- The expiration date for the principal's account in the DCE Registry.
- The expiration date for the principal's password in the DCE Registry.
- The lifetime for the principal's authenticated network identity. This is the lifetime of the principal's TGT (see the **sec_login_get_expiration( )** routine).

A value of 0 (zero) for an expiration date means there is no expiration date. In other words, the principal's account, password, or authenticated identity is good indefinitely.

To remove the returned **net_info** structure when it is no longer needed, use **sec_login_free_net_info( )**.

Files

/usr/include/dce/sec_login.idl The **idl** file from which **dce/sec_login.h** was derived.

Errors

sec_login_s_not_certified The login context is not certified.

sec_login_s_context_invalid The login context is not valid.

sec_login_s_no_current_context
The default context was specified, but none exists.

error_status_ok The call was successful.

Related Information

Functions: **intro(3sec)**, **sec_login_get_expiration(3sec)**, **sec_login_free_net_info(3sec)**.

sec_login_newgroups

Purpose Changes the group list for a login context

Synopsis **#include <dce/sec_login.h>**

boolean32 sec_login_newgroups(
  sec_login_handle_t *login_context*,
  sec_login_flags_t *flags*,
  unsigned32 *num_local_groups*,
  sec_id_t *local_groups*[ ],
  sec_login_handle_t **restricted_context*,
  error_status_t **status*);

Parameters

Input

login_context An opaque handle to login context data. The login context contains, among other data, the account principal name and UUID, account restrictions, records of group membership, the process home directory, and the encrypted password. (See **intro(3sec)** for more details about the login context.)

flags A set of flags of type **sec_login_flags_t**. These contain information about how the new network credentials will be used. Currently, the only flag used is **sec_login_credentials_private**, that, when set, implies that the new context is only to be used by the calling process. If this flag is not set (*flags* = **sec_login_no_flags**), descendants of the calling process may also use the new network credentials.

num_local_groups
An unsigned 32-bit integer containing the number of local group identities to include in the new context.

local_groups[ ] An array of **sec_id_t** elements. Each element contains the UUID of a local group identity to include in the new context. These identities are local to the cell. Optionally, each element may also contain a pointer to a character string containing the name of the local group.

Output

restricted_context
An opaque handle to the login context containing the changed group list.

status
A pointer to the completion status. On successful completion, the routine returns **error_status_ok**. Otherwise, it returns an error.

Description

The **sec_login_newgroups( )** routine changes the group list for the specified login context. Part of a network identity is a list of the various groups to which a principal belongs. The groups are used to determine a user's access to various objects and services. This routine returns a new login context that contains the changed group list. To remove the new login context when it is no longer needed, use **sec_login_purge_context( )**.

This operation does not need to be validated as the user identity does not change. Consequently, knowledge of the password is not needed.

Notes

Currently you can have only groups from the local cell.

Files

/usr/include/dce/sec_login.idl The **idl** file from which **dce/sec_login.h** was derived.

Return Values

This routine returns TRUE when the new login context is successfully established.

Errors

sec_login_s_default_use It is an error to try to certify the default context.

sec_login_s_groupset_invalid The input list of group names is invalid. There may be groups to which the caller does not belong, or the list may contain groups that do not exist.

error_status_ok The call was successful.

Examples

The following example illustrates use of the **sec_login_newgroups**( ) routine as part of a process to change the groupset:

```
sec_login_get_current_context(&login_context, &st);

sec_login_get_groups(login_context, &num_groups, &groups, &st);

   ...the group IDs have to be converted from the returned UNIX
   numbers into UUIDs (use sec_rgy_pgo_unix_num_to_id(3sec)...

for (i=0; i < num_groups; i++) {
   ... query whether the user wants to discard any of the current
   group memberships. Copy new groupset to the new_groups array ...
}

if ( !sec_login_newgroups(sec_login_no_flags, num_new_groups,
         new_groups, &login_context, &st)) {
   if (st == sec_login_s_groupset_invalid)
         printf("New groupset invalid0);

   ... application specific error handling ...
}
```

Related Information

Functions: **intro(3sec)**, **sec_login_get_groups(3sec)**, **sec_login_purge_context(3sec)**.

sec_login_purge_context

Purpose Destroys a login context and frees its storage

Synopsis **#include <dce/sec_login.h>**

void sec_login_purge_context(
sec_login_handle_t **login_context*,
error_status_t **status*);

Parameters

Input

login_context A pointer to an opaque handle to login context data. The login context contains, among other data, the account principal name and UUID, account restrictions, records of group membership, the process home directory, and the encrypted password. (See **intro(3sec)** for more details about the login context.) Note that a pointer to the handle is submitted, so the handle may be reset to **NULL** upon successful completion.

Output

status A pointer to the completion status. On successful completion, the routine returns **error_status_ok**. Otherwise, it returns an error.

Description

The **sec_login_purge_context()** routine frees any storage allocated for the specified login context and destroys the associated network credentials, if any exist.

Cautions

Applications must be cautious when purging the current context as this destroys network credentials for all processes that share the credentials.

Files

/usr/include/dce/sec_login.idl The **idl** file from which **dce/sec_login.h** was derived.

Errors

sec_login_s_default_use Illegal use of the default login handle occurred.

sec_login_s_context_invalid The login context itself is not valid.

error_status_ok The call was successful.

Examples

The following example illustrates use of the **sec_login_purge_context( )** routine as part of a straightforward login process:

```
if (sec_login_setup_identity(user_name, sec_login_no_flags, &login_context,
                             &st)) {
   ... get password from user...

   if (sec_login_validate_identity(login_context, password,
                             &reset_passwd, &auth_src, &st)) {

      if (!sec_login_certify_identity(login_context, &st))
          exit(error_wierd_auth_svc);

      sec_login_set_context(login_context, &st);

      if (auth_src != sec_login_auth_src_network)
         printf("no network credentials");

      if (reset_passwd) {
         ... get new password from user, reset registry record ...
      };

      sec_login_get_pwent(login_context, &pw_entry, &st);

      if (pw_entry.pw_expire < todays_date) {
         sec_login_purge_context(&login_context, &st);
         exit(0)
      }

      ... any other application specific login valid actions ...
      }

   } else {
      sec_login_purge_context(&login_context, &st);
```

```
        ... application specific login failure actions ...
    }
}
```

Related Information

Functions: **intro(3sec)**, **sec_login_set_context(3sec)**, **sec_login_setup_identity(3sec)**, **sec_login_validate_identity(3sec)**.

sec_login_refresh_identity

Purpose Refreshes an authenticated identity for a login context

Synopsis **#include <dce/sec_login.h>**

boolean32 sec_login_refresh_identity(
sec_login_handle_t **login_context*,
error_status_t **status*);

Parameters

Input

login_context An opaque handle to login context data. The login context contains, among other data, the account principal name and UUID, account restrictions, records of group membership, the process home directory, and the encrypted password. (See **intro(3sec)** for more details about the login context.)

Output

status A pointer to the completion status. On successful completion, the routine returns **error_status_ok**. Otherwise, it returns an error.

Description

The **sec_login_refresh_identity()** routine refreshes a previously established identity. It operates on an existing valid context, and cannot be used to change credentials associated with that identity.

If any administrative changes to the principal's identity have occurred since the identity was established or last refreshed (for example, the principal's membership in one or more groups may have been revoked), the refreshed identity reflects these changes, and a warning status is returned. In this case, the refreshed identity must be validated with **sec_login_validate_identity()** before it can be used.

It is an error to refresh a locally authenticated context.

Notes

The routine returns TRUE even if the context had to be changed. In this case, the *status* parameter contains the **sec_login_s_refresh_ident_change** warning. This warning indicates that the principal account has changed since the login context was first established. This means the refreshed context is different from the input context, and will need to be validated again with **sec_login_validate_identity( )**.

Files

/usr/include/dce/sec_login.idl The **idl** file from which **dce/sec_login.h** was derived.

Errors

sec_rgy_object_not_found The principal no longer exists.

sec_rgy_server_unavailable The network registry is not available.

sec_login_s_context_invalid The login context itself is not valid.

sec_login_s_default_use Illegal use of the default login handle occurred.

error_status_ok The call was successful.

Examples

Since the authenticated network identity for a process has a finite lifetime, there is a risk it will expire during some long network operation, preventing the operation from completing. To avoid this situation, an application might, before initiating a long operation, use the **sec_login** package to check the expiration time of its identity and refresh it if there is not enough time remaining to complete the operation. After refreshing the identity, the process must validate it again with **sec_login_validate_identity( )**.

```
sec_login_get_expiration(login_context, &expire_time, &st);

if (expire_time < (current_time + operation_duration)) {

   if (!sec_login_refresh_identity(login_context, &st)) {
      if (st == sec_login_s_refresh_ident_change) {
         ... identity has changed ...
      } else {
         ... login context cannot be renewed ...
         exit(error_context_expired);
      }

      if (sec_login_validate_identity(login_context, password,
                                  &reset_passwd, &auth_src, &st)) {
         ... identity validated ...
      } else {
         ... validation failed ...
```

```
            exit(error_validation_failure);
        }
    }
}

operation();
```

Related Information

Functions: **intro(3sec)**, **sec_login_validate_identity(3sec)**.

sec_login_release_context

Purpose Frees storage allocated for a login context

Synopsis **#include <dce/sec_login.h>**

void sec_login_release_context(
  sec_login_handle_t ***login_context*,**
  error_status_t ***status*);**

Parameters

Input/Output

login_context A pointer to an opaque handle to login context data. The login context contains, among other data, the account principal name and UUID, account restrictions, records of group membership, the process home directory, and the encrypted password. (See **intro(3sec)** for more details about the login context.)

Output

status A pointer to the completion status. On successful completion, the routine returns **error_status_ok**. Otherwise, it returns an error.

Description

The **sec_login_release_context( )** routine frees any memory allocated for a login context. Unlike **sec_login_purge_context( )**, it does not destroy the associated network credentials that still reside in the credential cache.

Files **/usr/include/dce/sec_login.idl** The **idl** file from which **dce/sec_login.h** was derived.

Errors

sec_login_s_default_use	Illegal use of the default login handle occurred.
sec_login_s_context_invalid	The login context itself is invalid.
error_status_ok	The call was successful.

Related Information

Functions: **intro(3sec)**, **sec_login_purge_context(3sec)**.

sec_login_set_context

Purpose Creates network credentials for a login context

Synopsis **#include <dce/sec_login.h>**

void sec_login_set_context(
    sec_login_handle_t *login_context***,**
    error_status_t **status***);**

Parameters

Input

login_context An opaque handle to login context data. The login context contains, among other data, the account principal name and UUID, account restrictions, records of group membership, the process home directory, and the encrypted password. (See **intro(3sec)** for more details about the login context.)

Output

status A pointer to the completion status. On successful completion, the routine returns **error_status_ok**. Otherwise, it returns an error.

Description

The **sec_login_set_context( )** routine sets the network credentials to those specified by the login context. This context must have been previously validated. Contexts acquired through **sec_login_get_current_context( )** or **sec_login_newgroups( )** do not need to be validated since those routines return previously validated contexts.

Files **/usr/include/dce/sec_login.idl** The **idl** file from which **dce/sec_login.h** was derived.

Errors

sec_login_s_context_invalid The login context itself is invalid.

sec_login_s_default_use Illegal use of the default login handle occurred.

error_status_ok The call was successful.

Examples

The following example illustrates use of the **sec_login_set_context()** routine as part of a straightforward login process:

```
if (sec_login_setup_identity(user_name, sec_login_no_flags, &login_context,
                             &st)) {
   ... get password from user...

   if (sec_login_validate_identity(login_context, password,
                             &reset_passwd, &auth_src, &st)) {

      if (!sec_login_certify_identity(login_context, &st))
          exit(error_weird_auth_svc);

      sec_login_set_context(login_context, &st);

      if (auth_src != sec_login_auth_src_network)
         printf("no network credentials");

      if (reset_passwd) {
         ... get new password from user, reset registry record ...
      };

      sec_login_get_pwent(login_context, &pw_entry, &st);

      if (pw_entry.pw_expire < todays_date) {
         sec_login_purge_context(&login_context, &st);
         exit(0)
      }

      ... any other application specific login valid actions ...
      }

   } else {
      sec_login_purge_context(&login_context, &st);

      ... application specific login failure actions ...
   }
}
```

Related Information

Functions: **intro(3sec)**, **sec_login_setup_identity(3sec)**, **sec_login_validate_identity(3sec)**.

sec_login_setup_first

Purpose Sets up the default network context

Synopsis **#include <dce/sec_login.h>**

boolean32 sec_login_setup_first(
sec_login_handle_t **init_context*,
error_status_t **status***);**

Parameters

Output

init_context A pointer to an opaque handle to login context data. The login context contains, among other data, the account principal name and UUID, account restrictions, records of group membership, the process home directory, and the encrypted password. In this call, the context will be that of the host machine initial process. (See **intro(3sec)** for more details about the login context.)

status A pointer to the completion status. On successful completion, the routine returns **error_status_ok**. Otherwise, it returns an error.

Description

The **sec_login_setup_first**( ) routine sets up the default context network identity. If the default context already contains valid credentials, the routine fails. Typically, this routine is called from the **sec_clientd** helper process to breathe life into the default credentials for the host machine process hierarchy.

This routine uses the hostname available via the local **dce_config** interface as the principal name for the setup, so it does need a principal name as input.

Return Values

The routine returns a **boolean32** value that is TRUE if the setup was successful, and FALSE otherwise.

Files

/usr/include/dce/sec_login.idl The **idl** file from which **dce/sec_login.h** was derived.

Errors

sec_login_s_default_use The default context is already in use and does not need to be set up again.

sec_login_s_no_current_context The calling process has no context of its own.

sec_login_s_privileged An unprivileged process was called in.

sec_login_s_config The DCE configuration (**dce_config**) information is not available.

sec_rgy_object_not_found The principal does not exist.

sec_rgy_server_unavailable The network registry is not available.

sec_login_s_no_memory A memory allocation error occurred.

error_status_ok The call was successful.

Related Information

Functions: **intro(3sec)**, **sec_login_init_first(3sec)**, **sec_login_validate_first(3sec)**.

sec_login_setup_identity

Purpose Sets up the user's network identity

Synopsis **#include <dce/sec_login.h>**

boolean32 sec_login_setup_identity(
unsigned_char_p_t *principal*,
sec_login_flags_t *flags*,
sec_login_handle_t **login_context*,
error_status_t **status*);

Parameters

Input

principal A pointer (type **unsigned_char_p_t**) indicating a character string containing the principal name on the registry account corresponding to the calling process.

flags A set of flags of type **sec_login_flags_t**. These contain information about how the new network credentials are to be used.

Output

login_context A pointer to an opaque handle to login context data. The login context contains, among other data, the account principal name and UUID, account restrictions, records of group membership, the process home directory, and the encrypted password. (See **intro(3sec)** for more details about the login context.)

status A pointer to the completion status. On successful completion, the routine returns **error_status_ok**. Otherwise, it returns an error.

Description

The **sec_login_setup_identity( )** routine creates any local context necessary to perform authenticated network operations. It does not establish any local operating system context; that is the responsibility of the caller. It is the standard network login function. The network identity set up by this operation cannot be used until it is validated via **sec_login_validate_identity( )**.

This routine retrieves sealed network credentials (or certificates), that are unsealed during the operation of validating an identity.

The **sec_login_setup_identity( )** operation and the **sec_login_validate_identity( )** operation are two halves of a single logical operation. Together they collect the identity data needed to establish an authenticated identity. The operations are independent so the user's password need not be sent across the network.

Notes

Neither **sec_login_setup_identity( )** nor **sec_login_validate_identity( )** check for account or identity expiration. The application program using this interface is responsible for such checks.

Return Values

The routine returns TRUE if the identity has been successfully established.

Files

/usr/include/dce/sec_login.idl The **idl** file from which **dce/sec_login.h** was derived.

Errors

sec_rgy_object_not_found The principal does not exist.

sec_rgy_server_unavailable The network registry is not available.

sec_login_s_no_memory Not enough memory is available to complete the operation.

error_status_ok The call was successful.

Examples

The following example illustrates use of the **sec_login_setup_identity( )** routine as part of a straightforward login process:

```
if (sec_login_setup_identity(user_name, sec_login_no_flags, &login_context,
                              &st)) {
    ... get password from user...

    if (sec_login_validate_identity(login_context, password,
                                     &reset_passwd, &auth_src, &st)) {
```

```
            if (!sec_login_certify_identity(login_context, &st))
                exit(error_weird_auth_svc);

            sec_login_set_context(login_context, &st);

            if (auth_src != sec_login_auth_src_network)
               printf("no network credentials");

            if (reset_passwd) {
               ... get new password from user, reset registry record ...
            };

            sec_login_get_pwent(login_context, &pw_entry, &st);

            if (pw_entry.pw_expire < todays_date) {
               sec_login_purge_context(&login_context, &st);
               exit(0)
            }

            ... any other application specific login valid actions ...
            }

        } else {
            sec_login_purge_context(&login_context, &st);

            ... application specific login failure actions ...
        }
    }
```

Related Information

Functions: **intro(3sec)**, **sec_login_validate_identity(3sec)**, **sec_login_set_context(3sec)**.

sec_login_valid_and_cert_ident

Purpose Validates and certifies a login context

Synopsis **#include <dce/sec_login.h>**

boolean32 sec_login_valid_and_cert_ident(
 sec_login_handle_t *login_context*,
 sec_passwd_rec_t **passwd*,
 boolean32 **reset_passwd*,
 sec_login_auth_src_t **auth_src*,
 error_status_t **status*);

Parameters

Input

login_context An opaque handle to login context data. The login context contains, among other data, the account principal name and UUID, account restrictions, records of group membership, the process home directory, and the encrypted password. (See **intro(3sec)** for more details about the login context.)

passwd A password record to be checked against the password in the principal's registry account. The routine returns TRUE if the two match.

Output

reset_passwd A pointer to a 32-bit **boolean32** value. The routine returns TRUE if the account password has expired and must be reset.

auth_src A 32-bit set of flags identifying the source of the authentication. Upon return after successful authentication, the flags in *auth_src* indicate what authority was used to validate the login context. If the authentication was accomplished with the network authority, the **sec_login_auth_src_network** flag is set, and the process login context has credentials to use the network. If the authentication was accomplished with local data only (either the principal's account is tailored for the local machine with overrides, or the network authority is unavailable), the **sec_login_auth_src_local** flag is set. Login contexts that are authenticated locally may not be used to establish network credentials because they have none.

status — A pointer to the completion status. On successful completion, the routine returns **error_status_ok**. Otherwise, it returns an error.

Description

The **sec_login_valid_and_cert_ident**( ) routine validates and certifies a login context established with **sec_login_setup_identity**( ). The caller must know the user's password for this operation to succeed.

This routine combines the operations of the **sec_login_validate_identity**( ) and **sec_login_certify_identity**( ) routines. It is intended for use by system login programs that need to extract trustworthy operating system credentials for use in setting the local identity for a process. This operation destroys the contents of the *passwd* input parameter.

If the network security service is unavailable or if the user's password has been overridden on the host, a locally authenticated context is created, and the *auth_src* parameter is set to **sec_login_auth_src_local**. Data extracted from a locally authenticated context may be used to set the local OS identity, but it cannot be used to establish network credentials.

This routine is a privileged operation.

Return Values

The routine returns TRUE if the login identity has been successfully validated.

Files

/usr/include/dce/sec_login.idl — The **idl** file from which **dce/sec_login.h** was derived.

Errors

sec_rgy_passwd_invalid — The input string does not match the account password.

sec_rgy_server_unavailable — The DCE Registry Server is unavailable.

sec_login_s_acct_invalid — The account is invalid or has expired.

sec_login_s_privileged — This is a privileged operation and was invoked by an unprivileged process.

sec_login_s_null_password — The input string is **NULL**.

sec_login_s_default_use The input context was the default context, which cannot be validated.

sec_login_s_already_valid The login context has already been validated.

sec_login_s_unsupp_passwd_type
The password type is not supported.

error_status_ok The call was successful.

Examples

The following example illustrates use of the **sec_login_valid_and_cert_ident()** routine as part of a system login process:

```
if (sec_login_setup_identity(<user>,
     sec_login_no_flags, &login_context, &st)) {
          ... get password ...
          if (sec_login_valid_and_cert_ident(login_context,
               password, &st)) {
                if (auth_src == sec_login_auth_src_network) {
                   if (GOOD_STATUS(&st)
                   sec_login_set_context(login_context);
                   }
          }
          if (reset_passwd) {
             ... reset the user's password ...
             if (passwd_reset_fails) {
                 sec_login_purge_context(login_context)
                 ... application login failure actions ...
          }
          ... application specific login valid actions ...
     }
}
```

Related Information

Functions: **intro(3sec)**, **sec_login_certify_identity(3sec)**, **sec_login_setup_identity(3sec)**, **sec_login_validate_identity(3sec)**.

sec_login_validate_first

Purpose Validates the initial login context

Synopsis **#include <dce/sec_login.h>**

boolean32 sec_login_validate_first(
sec_login_handle_t *init_context*,
boolean32 **reset_passwd*,
sec_login_auth_src_t **auth_src*,
error_status_t **status*);

Parameters

Input

init_context An opaque handle to login context data. The login context contains, among other data, the account principal name and UUID, account restrictions, records of group membership, the process home directory, and the encrypted password. In this call, the context will be that of the host machine initial process. (See **intro(3sec)** for more details about the login context.)

Output

reset_passwd A pointer to a 32-bit **boolean32** value. The routine returns TRUE if the account password has expired and must be reset.

auth_src A 32-bit set of flags identifying the source of the authentication. Upon return after successful authentication, the flags in *auth_src* indicate what authority was used to validate the login context. If the authentication was accomplished with the network authority, the **sec_login_auth_src_network** flag is set, and the process login context has credentials to use the network. If the authentication was accomplished with local data only (either the principal's account is tailored for the local machine with overrides, or the network authority is unavailable), the **sec_login_auth_src_local** flag is set. Login contexts that are authenticated locally may not be used to establish network credentials because they have none.

status A pointer to the completion status. On successful completion, the routine returns **error_status_ok**. Otherwise, it returns an error.

Description

The **sec_login_validate_first( )** routine validates the default login context established via **sec_login_setup_first( )**. Typically, this operation is called from the **sec_clientd** helper process to validate the default credentials for the host machine process hierarchy. This operation uses the password for the local host, and therefore does not require a password parameter.

Return Values

The routine returns a **boolean32** value that is TRUE if the setup was successful, and FALSE otherwise.

Files

/usr/include/dce/sec_login.idl The **idl** file from which **dce/sec_login.h** was derived.

Errors

sec_login_s_privileged An unprivileged process was called in.

sec_rgy_server_unavailable The network authentication service was unavailable.

error_status_ok The call was successful.

Related Information

Functions: **intro(3sec)**, **sec_login_init_first(3sec)**, **sec_login_setup_first(3sec)**.

sec_login_validate_identity

Purpose Validates a login context's identity

Synopsis **#include <dce/sec_login.h>**

boolean32 sec_login_validate_identity(
sec_login_handle_t *login_context*,
sec_passwd_rec_t **passwd*,
boolean32 **reset_passwd*,
sec_login_auth_src_t **auth_src*,
error_status_t **status*);

Parameters

Input

login_context An opaque handle to login context data. The login context contains, among other data, the account principal name and UUID, account restrictions, records of group membership, the process home directory, and the encrypted password. (See **intro(3sec)** for more details about the login context.)

passwd A password record to be checked against the password in the principal's registry account. The routine returns TRUE if the two match.

Output

reset_passwd A pointer to a 32-bit **boolean32** value. The routine returns TRUE if the account password has expired and must be reset.

auth_src A 32-bit set of flags identifying the source of the authentication. Upon return after successful authentication, the flags in *auth_src* indicate what authority was used to validate the login context. If the authentication was accomplished with the network authority, the **sec_login_auth_src_network** flag is set, and the process login context has credentials to use the network. If the authentication was accomplished with local data only (either the principal's account is tailored for the local machine with overrides, or the network authority is unavailable), the **sec_login_auth_src_local** flag is set. Login contexts that are authenticated locally may not be used to establish network credentials because they have none.

status A pointer to the completion status. On successful completion, the routine returns **error_status_ok**. Otherwise, it returns an error.

Description

The **sec_login_validate_identity( )** routine validates the login context established with **sec_login_setup_identity( )**. The caller must know the user's password for this operation to succeed. This operation must be invoked before the network credentials can be used.

When a network identity is set, only state information for network operations has been established. The local operating system identity has not been modified. It is the responsibility of the caller to establish any local operating identity state.

The **sec_login_setup_identity( )** operation and the **sec_login_validate_identity( )** operation are two halves of a single logical operation. Together they collect the identity data needed to establish an authenticated identity. The operations are independent so the user's password need not be sent across the network. The identity validation performed by **sec_login_validate_identity( )** is a local operation.

Notes

A context is not secure and must not be set or exported until the authentication service is itself authenticated with the **sec_login_certify_identity( )** call.

System login programs that set local operating system identity using data extracted from a login context should use **sec_login_valid_and_cert_ident( )** instead of **sec_login_validate_identity( )**.

Return Values

The routine returns TRUE if the login identity has been successfully validated.

Files

/usr/include/dce/sec_login.idl The **idl** file from which **dce/sec_login.h** was derived.

Errors

sec_rgy_passwd_invalid The input string does not match the account password.

sec_rgy_server_unavailable There is no data with which to compare the input string.

sec_login_s_acct_invalid The account is invalid or has expired.

sec_login_s_null_password The input string is **NULL**.

sec_login_s_default_use The input context was the default context, which cannot be validated.

sec_login_s_already_valid The login context has already been validated.

sec_login_s_unsupp_passwd_type The password type is not supported.

error_status_ok The call was successful.

Examples

The following example illustrates use of the **sec_login_validate_identity( )** routine as part of a straightforward login process:

```
if (sec_login_setup_identity(user_name, sec_login_no_flags, &login_context,
                             &st)) {
   ... get password from user...

   if (sec_login_validate_identity(login_context, password,
                             &reset_passwd, &auth_src, &st)) {

      if (!sec_login_certify_identity(login_context, &st))
          exit(error_weird_auth_svc);

      sec_login_set_context(login_context, &st);

      if (auth_src != sec_login_auth_src_network)
         printf("no network credentials");

      if (reset_passwd) {
         ... get new password from user, reset registry record ...
      };

      sec_login_get_pwent(login_context, &pw_entry, &st);

      if (pw_entry.pw_expire < todays_date) {
         sec_login_purge_context(&login_context, &st);
```

```
            exit(0)
         }

         ... any other application specific login valid actions ...
         }

      } else {
         sec_login_purge_context(&login_context, &st);

         ... application specific login failure actions ...
      }
   }
```

Related Information

Functions: **intro(3sec)**, **sec_login_certify_identity(3sec)**, **sec_login_setup_identity(3sec)**, **sec_login_valid_and_cert_ident(3sec)**.

sec_rgy_acct_add

Purpose Adds an account for a login name

Synopsis **#include <dce/acct.h>**

void sec_rgy_acct_add(
sec_rgy_handle_t *context*,
sec_rgy_login_name_t **login_name*,
sec_rgy_acct_key_t **key_parts*,
sec_rgy_acct_user_t **user_part*,
sec_rgy_acct_admin_t **admin_part*,
sec_passwd_rec_t **caller_key*,
sec_passwd_rec_t **new_key*,
sec_passwd_type_t *new_keytype*,
sec_passwd_version_t **new_key_version*,
error_status_t **status*);

Parameters

Input

context A pointer to an opaque handle bound to a registry server. Use **sec_rgy_site_open( )** to acquire a bound handle.

login_name A pointer to the account login name. A login name is composed of three character strings, containing the person, group, and organization (PGO) names corresponding to the account. All three names must be completely specified.

key_parts A pointer to the minimum abbreviation allowed when logging in to the account. Abbreviations are not currently implemented and the only legal value is **sec_rgy_acct_key_person**.

user_part A pointer to the **sec_rgy_acct_user_t** structure containing the user part of the account data. This represents such information as the account password, home directory, and default shell.

admin_part A pointer to the **sec_rgy_acct_admin_t** structure containing the administrative part of an account's data. This information includes the account creation and expiration dates and flags describing limits to the use of privilege attribute certificates, among other information.

caller_key A key to use to encrypt *new_key* for transmission to the registry server.

new_key The password for the new account. During transmission to the registry server, it is encrypted with *caller_key*.

new_keytype The type of the new key. The server uses this parameter to decide how to encode *new_key* if it is sent as plaintext.

Output

new_key_version
The key version number returned by the server. If the client requests a particular key version number (via the **version_number** field of the *new_key* input parameter), the server returns the requested version number back to the client.

status A pointer to the completion status. On successful completion, the routine returns **error_status_ok**. Otherwise, it returns an error.

Description

The **sec_rgy_acct_add()** routine adds an account with the specified login name. The login name is given in three parts, corresponding to the person, group, and organization names for the account.

The *key_parts* variable specifies the minimum login abbreviation for the account. If the requested abbreviation duplicates an existing abbreviation for another account, the routine supplies the next shortest unique abbreviation and returns this abbreviation in *key_parts*. Abbreviations are not currently implemented.

Permissions Required

The **sec_rgy_acct_add()** routine requires the following permissions on the account (principal) that is to be added:

- The **m** (**mgmt_info**) permission to change management information.
- The **a** (**auth_info**) permission to change authentication information.
- The **u** (**user_info**) permission to change user information.

Notes The constituent person, group, and organization (PGO) items for an account must be added before the account can be created. (See the **sec_rgy_pgo_add( )** routine). Also, the person must have been added as a member of the specified group and organization. (See the **sec_rgy_pgo_add_member( )** routine).

Files

/usr/include/dce/acct.idl	The **idl** file from which **dce/acct.h** was derived.

Errors

sec_rgy_not_authorized	The client program is not authorized to add an account to the registry.
sec_rgy_not_member_group	The indicated person is not a member of the indicated group.
sec_rgy_not_member_org	The indicated person is not a member of the indicated organization.
sec_rgy_not_member_group_org	The indicated person is not a member of the indicated group or organization.
sec_rgy_object exists	The account to be added already exists.
error_status_ok	The call was successful.

Related Information

Functions: **intro(3sec)**, **sec_rgy_acct_delete(3sec)**, **sec_rgy_login_get_info(3sec)**, **sec_rgy_pgo_add(3sec)**, **sec_rgy_pgo_add_member(3sec)**, **sec_rgy_site_open(3sec)**.

sec_rgy_acct_admin_replace

Purpose Replaces administrative account data

Synopsis **#include <dce/acct.h>**

void sec_rgy_acct_admin_replace(
sec_rgy_handle_t *context*,
sec_rgy_login_name_t **login_name*,
sec_rgy_acct_key_t **key_parts*,
sec_rgy_acct_admin_t **admin_part*,
error_status_t **status*);

Parameters

Input

context A pointer to an opaque handle bound to a registry server. Use **sec_rgy_site_open( )** to acquire a bound handle.

login_name A pointer to the account login name. A login name is composed of three character strings, containing the person, group, and organization (PGO) names corresponding to the account. Blank strings serve as wildcards, matching any entry.

key_parts A pointer to the minimum abbreviation allowed when logging in to the account. Abbreviations are not currently implemented and the only legal value is **sec_rgy_acct_key_person**.

admin_part A pointer to the **sec_rgy_acct_admin_t** structure containing the administrative part of an account's data. This information includes the account creation and expiration dates and flags describing limits to the use of privilege attribute certificates, among other information, and can be modified only by an administrator. The **sec_rgy_acct_admin_t** structure contains the following fields:

creator The identity of the principal who created this account in **sec_rgy_foreign_id_t** form. This field is set by the registry server.

creation_date The date (**sec_timeval_sec_t**) the account was created. This field is set by the registry server.

last_changer The identity of the principal who last modified any of the account information (user or administrative). This field is set by the registry server.

change_date The date (**sec_timeval_sec_t**) the account was last modified (either user or administrative data). This field is set by the registry server.

expiration_date The date (**sec_timeval_sec_t**) the account will cease to be valid.

good_since_date This date (**sec_timeval_sec_t**) is for Kerberos-style, ticket-granting ticket revocation. Ticket-granting tickets issued before this date will not be honored by authenticated network services.

flags Contains administration flags used as part of the administrator's information for any registry account. This field is in **sec_rgy_acct_admin_flags_t** form. (See **intro(3sec)** for a complete description of these flags.)

authentication_flags
Contains flags controlling use of authentication services. This field is in **sec_rgy_acct_auth_flags_t** form. (See **intro(3sec)** for a complete description of these flags.)

Output

status A pointer to the completion status. On successful completion, the routine returns **error_status_ok**. Otherwise, it returns an error.

Description

The **sec_rgy_acct_admin_replace()** routine replaces the administrative information in the account record specified by the input login name. The administrative information contains limitations on the account's use and privileges. It can be modified only by a registry administrator; that is, a user with the **admin_info** (abbreviated as **a**) privilege for an account.

The *key_parts* variable identifies how many of the *login_name* parts to use as the unique abbreviation for the account. If the requested abbreviation duplicates an existing abbreviation for another account, the routine supplies the next shortest unique abbreviation and returns this abbreviation using *key_parts*.

Permissions Required

The **sec_rgy_acct_admin_replace()** routine requires the following permissions on the account principal:

- The **m** (**mgmt_info**) permission, if **flags** or **expiration_date** is to be changed.
- The **a** (**auth_info**) permission, if **authentication_flags** or **good_since_date** is to be changed.

Notes

All users need the **w** (**write**) privilege in the appropriate ACL entry to modify any account information.

Files

/usr/include/dce/acct.idl The **idl** file from which **dce/acct.h** was derived.

Errors

sec_rgy_not_authorized The client program is not authorized to change the administrative information for the specified account.

error_status_ok The call was successful.

Related Information

Functions: **intro(3sec)**, **sec_rgy_acct_user_replace(3sec)**, **sec_rgy_acct_replace_all(3sec)**, **sec_rgy_acct_lookup(3sec)**.

sec_rgy_acct_delete

Purpose Deletes an account

Synopsis **#include <dce/acct.h>**

```
void sec_rgy_acct_delete(
        sec_rgy_handle_t context,
        sec_rgy_login_name_t *login_name,
        error_status_t *status);
```

Parameters

Input

context A pointer to an opaque handle bound to a registry server. Use **sec_rgy_site_open( )** to acquire a bound handle.

login_name A pointer to the account login name. A login name is composed of three character strings, containing the person, group, and organization (PGO) names corresponding to the account. All three strings must be completely specified.

Output

status A pointer to the completion status. On successful completion, the routine returns **error_status_ok**. Otherwise, it returns an error.

Description

The **sec_rgy_acct_delete( )** routine deletes from the registry the account corresponding to the specified login name.

Permissions Required

The **sec_rgy_acct_delete( )** routine requires the following permissions on the account principal:

- The **m** (**mgmt_info**) permission to remove management information.
- The **a** (**auth_info**) permission to remove authentication information.
- The **u** (**user_info**) permission to remove user information.

Notes

Even though the account is deleted, the PGO items corresponding to the account remain. These must be deleted with separate calls to **sec_rgy_pgo_delete( )**.

Files

/usr/include/dce/acct.idl The **idl** file from which **dce/acct.h** was derived.

Errors

sec_rgy_not_authorized The client program is not authorized to delete the specified account.

sec_rgy_object_not_found No PGO item was found with the given name.

error_status_ok The call was successful.

Related Information

Functions: **intro(3sec)**, **sec_rgy_acct_add(3sec)**, **sec_rgy_pgo_delete(3sec)**.

sec_rgy_acct_get_projlist

Purpose Returns the projects in an account's project list

Synopsis **#include <dce/acct.h>**

void sec_rgy_acct_get_projlist(
  sec_rgy_handle_t *context*,
  sec_rgy_login_name_t **login_name*,
  sec_rgy_cursor_t **projlist_cursor*,
  long *max_number*,
  long **supplied_number*,
  uuid_t *id_projlist*[ ],
  long *unix_projlist*[ ],
  long **num_projects*,
  error_status_t **status*);

Parameters

Input

context A pointer to an opaque handle bound to a registry server. Use **sec_rgy_site_open**( ) to acquire a bound handle.

login_name A pointer to the account login name. A login name is composed of three character strings, containing the person, group, and organization (PGO) names corresponding to the account. Blank strings serve as wildcards, matching any entry.

max_number The maximum number of projects to be returned by the call. This must be no larger than the allocated size of the *projlist*[ ] arrays.

Input/Output

projlist_cursor An opaque pointer indicating a specific project in an account's project list. The **sec_rgy_acct_get_projlist**( ) routine returns the project indicated by *projlist_cursor*, and advances the cursor to point to the next project in the list. When the end of the list is reached, the routine returns the value **sec_rgy_no_more_entries** in the *status* parameter. Use **sec_rgy_cursor_reset**( ) to reset the cursor.

Output

supplied_number
A pointer to the actual number of projects returned. This will always be less than or equal to the *max_number* supplied on input. If there are more projects in the account list, **sec_rgy_acct_get_projlist( )** sets *projlist_cursor* to point to the next entry after the last one in the returned list.

id_projlist[ ]
An array to receive the UUID of each project returned. The size allocated for the array is given by *max_number*. If this value is less than the total number of projects in the account project list, multiple calls must be made to return all of the projects.

unix_projlist[ ]
An array to receive the UNIX number of each project returned. The size allocated for the array is given by *max_number*. If this value is less than the total number of projects in the account project list, multiple calls must be made to return all of the projects.

num_projects
A pointer indicating the total number of projects in the specified account's project list.

status
A pointer to the completion status. On successful completion, the routine returns **error_status_ok**. Otherwise, it returns an error.

Description

The **sec_rgy_acct_get_projlist( )** routine returns members of the project list for the specified account. It returns the project information in two arrays. The *id_projlist*[ ] array contains the UUIDs for the returned projects. The *unix_projlist*[ ] array contains the UNIX numbers for the returned projects.

The project list cursor, *projlist_cursor*, provides an automatic place holder in the project list. The **sec_rgy_acct_get_projlist( )** routine automatically updates this variable to point to the next project in the project list. To return an entire project list, reset *projlist_cursor* with **sec_rgy_cursor_reset( )** on the initial call and then issue successive calls until all the projects are returned.

Permissions Required

The **sec_rgy_acct_get_projlist( )** routine requires the **r** (**read**) permission on the account principal for which the project list data is to be returned.

Cautions

There are several different types of cursors used in the registry Application Programmer Interface (API). Some cursors point to PGO items, others point to members in a membership list, and others point to account data. Do not use a cursor for one sort of object in a call expecting another sort of object. For example, you cannot use the same cursor on a call to **sec_rgy_acct_get_projlist( )** and **sec_rgy_pgo_get_next( )**. The behavior in this case is undefined.

Furthermore, cursors are specific to a server. A cursor pointing into one replica of the registry database is useless as a pointer into another replica.

Use **sec_rgy_cursor_reset( )** to refresh a cursor for use with another call or for another server.

Files

/usr/include/dce/acct.idl — The **idl** file from which **dce/acct.h** was derived.

Errors

sec_rgy_no_more_entries — The cursor is at the end of the list of projects.

sec_rgy_not_authorized — The client program is not authorized to see a project list for this principal.

sec_rgy_object exists — The account to be added already exists.

error_status_ok — The call was successful.

Related Information

Functions: **intro(3sec)**, **sec_rgy_cursor_reset(3sec)**, **sec_rgy_pgo_get_next(3sec)**.

sec_rgy_acct_lookup

Purpose

Returns data for a specified account

Synopsis

#include <dce/acct.h>

void sec_rgy_acct_lookup(
sec_rgy_handle_t *context*,
sec_rgy_login_name_t **name_key*,
sec_rgy_cursor_t **account_cursor*,
sec_rgy_login_name_t **name_result*,
sec_rgy_sid_t **id_sid*,
sec_rgy_unix_sid_t **unix_sid*,
sec_rgy_acct_key_t **key_parts*,
sec_rgy_acct_user_t **user_part*,
sec_rgy_acct_admin_t **admin_part*,
error_status_t **status*);

Parameters

Input

context — A pointer to an opaque handle bound to a registry server. Use **sec_rgy_site_open**( ) to acquire a bound handle.

name_key — A pointer to the account login name. A login name is composed of three character strings, containing the person, group, and organization (PGO) names corresponding to the account. Blank strings serve as wildcards, matching any entry.

Input/Output

account_cursor — An opaque pointer to a specific account in the registry database. If *name_key* is blank, **sec_rgy_acct_lookup**( ) returns information about the account to which the cursor is pointing. On return, the cursor points to the next account in the database after the returned account. If *name_key* is blank and the *account_cursor* has been reset with **sec_rgy_cursor_reset**( ), **sec_rgy_acct_lookup**( ) returns information about the first account in the database. When the end of the list of accounts in the database is reached, the routine returns the value

sec_rgy_no_more_entries in the *status* parameter. Use **sec_rgy_cursor_reset( )** to refresh the cursor.

Output

name_result A pointer to the full login name of the account (including all three names) for which the information is returned. The remaining parameters contain the information belonging to the returned account.

id_sid A structure containing the three UUIDs of the person, group, and organization for the account.

unix_sid A structure containing the three UNIX numbers of the person, group, and organization for the account.

key_parts A pointer to the minimum abbreviation allowed when logging in to the account. Abbreviations are not currently implemented and the only legal value is **sec_rgy_acct_key_person**.

user_part A pointer to the **sec_rgy_acct_user_t** structure containing the user part of the account data. This represents such information as the account password, home directory, and default shell, all of which are accessible to, and may be modified by, the account owner.

admin_part A pointer to the **sec_rgy_acct_admin_t** structure containing the administrative part of an account's data. This information includes the account creation and expiration dates and flags describing limits to the use of privilege attribute certificates, among other information, and can be modified only by an administrator.

status A pointer to the completion status. On successful completion, the routine returns **error_status_ok**. Otherwise, it returns an error.

Description

The **sec_rgy_acct_lookup( )** routine returns all the information about an account in the registry database. The account can be specified either with *name_key* or *account_cursor*. If *name_key* is completely blank, the routine uses the *account_cursor* value instead.

For *name_key*, a zero-length person, group, or organization key serves as a wildcard. For example, a login name key with the person and organization fields blank returns the next (possibly first) account whose group matches the input group field. The full login name of the returned account is passed back in *name_result*.

The *account_cursor* provides an automatic place holder in the registry database. The routine automatically updates this variable to point to the next account in the database, after the account for which the information was returned. If *name_key* is blank and the *account_cursor* has been reset with **sec_rgy_cursor_reset( )*O, sec_rgy_acct_lookup( )** returns information about the first account in the database.

Permissions Required

The **sec_rgy_acct_lookup( )** routine requires the **r** (**read**) permission on the account principal to be viewed.

Cautions

There are several different types of cursors used in the registry Application Programmer Interface (API). Some cursors point to PGO items, others point to members in a membership list, and others point to account data. Do not use a cursor for one sort of object in a call expecting another sort of object. For example, you cannot use the same cursor on a call to **sec_rgy_acct_get_projlist( )** and **sec_rgy_pgo_get_next( )**. The behavior in this case is undefined.

Furthermore, cursors are specific to a server. A cursor pointing into one replica of the registry database is useless as a pointer into another replica.

Use **sec_rgy_cursor_reset( )** to renew a cursor for use with another call or for another server.

Files

/usr/include/dce/acct.idl — The **idl** file from which **dce/acct.h** was derived.

Errors

sec_rgy_no_more_entries — The cursor is at the end of the accounts in the registry.

sec_rgy_object_not_found — The input account could not be found by the registry server.

error_status_ok — The call was successful.

Related Information

Functions: **intro(3sec)**, **sec_rgy_cursor_reset(3sec)**, **sec_rgy_acct_replace_all(3sec)**, **sec_rgy_acct_admin_replace(3sec)**, **sec_rgy_acct_user_replace(3sec)**.

sec_rgy_acct_passwd

Purpose Changes the password for an account

Synopsis **#include <dce/acct.h>**

void sec_rgy_acct_passwd(
sec_rgy_handle_t *context*,
sec_rgy_login_name_t **login_name*,
sec_passwd_rec_t **caller_key*,
sec_passwd_rec_t **new_key*,
sec_passwd_type_t *new_keytype*,
sec_passwd_version_t **new_key_version*,
error_status_t **status*);

Parameters

Input

context A pointer to an opaque handle bound to a registry server. Use **sec_rgy_site_open( )** to acquire a bound handle.

login_name A pointer to the account login name. A login name is composed of three character strings, containing the person, group, and organization (PGO) names corresponding to the account. All three strings must be completely specified.

caller_key A key to use to encrypt the key for transmission to the registry server. If communications secure to the **rpc_c_authn_level_pkt_privacy** level are available on a system, then this parameter is not necessary, and the packet encryption is sufficient to ensure security.

new_key The password for the new account. During transmission to the registry server, it is encrypted with *caller_key*.

new_keytype The type of the new key. The server uses this parameter to decide how to encode *new_key* if it is sent as plaintext.

Output

new_key_version
: The key version number returned by the server. If the client requests a particular key version number (via the **version_number** field of the *new_key* input parameter), the server returns the requested version number back to the client.

status
: A pointer to the completion status. On successful completion, the routine returns **error_status_ok**. Otherwise, it returns an error.

Description

The **sec_rgy_acct_passwd**( ) routine changes an account password to the input password character string. Wildcards (blank fields) are not permitted in a specified account name; the account names must completely specify the person, group, and organization names of the account.

Permissions Required

The **sec_rgy_acct_passwd**( ) routine requires the **u** (**user_info**) permission on the account principal whose password is to be changed.

Files

/usr/include/dce/acct.idl — The **idl** file from which **dce/acct.h** was derived.

Errors

sec_rgy_not_authorized — The client program is not authorized to change the password of this account.

sec_rgy_object_not_found — The account to be modified was not found by the registry server.

error_status_ok — The call was successful.

Related Information

Functions: **intro(3sec)**.

sec_rgy_acct_rename

Purpose Changes an account login name

Synopsis **#include <dce/acct.h>**

void sec_rgy_acct_rename(
  sec_rgy_handle_t *context*,
  sec_rgy_login_name_t **old_login_name*,
  sec_rgy_login_name_t **new_login_name*,
  sec_rgy_acct_key_t **new_key_parts*,
  error_status_t **status*);

Parameters

Input

context A pointer to an opaque handle bound to a registry server. Use **sec_rgy_site_open( )** to acquire a bound handle.

old_login_name A pointer to the current account login name. The login name is composed of three character strings, containing the person, group, and organization (PGO) names corresponding to the account. All three strings must be completely specified.

new_login_name
A pointer to the new account login name. Again, all three component names must be completely specified.

Input/Output

new_key_parts A pointer to the minimum abbreviation allowed when logging in to the account. Abbreviations are not currently implemented and the only legal value is **sec_rgy_acct_key_person**.

Output

status A pointer to the completion status. On successful completion, the routine returns **error_status_ok**. Otherwise, it returns an error.

Description

The **sec_rgy_acct_rename( )** routine changes an account login name from *old_login_name* to *new_login_name*. Wildcards (empty fields) are not permitted in either input name; both the old and new login names must completely specify their component person, group, and organization names. Note, though, that the person component in a login name cannot be changed.

The *new_key_parts* variable identifies how many of the *new_login_name* parts to use as the unique abbreviation for the account. If the requested abbreviation duplicates an existing abbreviation for another account, the routine identifies the next shortest unique abbreviation and returns this abbreviation using *new_key_parts*.

Permissions Required

The **sec_rgy_acct_rename( )** routine requires the **m** (**mgmt_info**) permission on the account principal to be renamed.

Notes

The **sec_rgy_acct_rename( )** routine does not affect any of the registry PGO data. The constituent person, group, and organization items for an account must be added before the account can be created. (See the **sec_rgy_pgo_add( )** routine). Also, the person must have been added as a member of the specified group and organization. (See the **sec_rgy_pgo_add_member( )** routine).

Files

/usr/include/dce/acct.idl The **idl** file from which **dce/acct.h** was derived.

Errors

sec_rgy_not_authorized The client program is not authorized to make the changes.

sec_rgy_object_not_found The account to be modified was not found by the registry server.

sec_rgy_name_exists The new account name is already in use by another account.

error_status_ok The call was successful.

Related Information

Functions: **intro(3sec)**, **sec_rgy_acct_add(3sec)**.

sec_rgy_acct_replace_all

Purpose Replaces all account data for an account

Synopsis **#include <dce/acct.h>**

void sec_rgy_acct_replace_all(
sec_rgy_handle_t *context*,
sec_rgy_login_name_t **login_name*,
sec_rgy_acct_key_t **key_parts*,
sec_rgy_acct_user_t **user_part*,
sec_rgy_acct_admin_t **admin_part*,
boolean32 *set_password*,
sec_passwd_rec_t **caller_key*,
sec_passwd_rec_t **new_key*,
sec_passwd_type_t *new_keytype*,
sec_passwd_version_t **new_key_version*,
error_status_t **status*);

Parameters

Input

context A pointer to an opaque handle bound to a registry server. Use **sec_rgy_site_open()** to acquire a bound handle.

login_name A pointer to the account login name. A login name is composed of three character strings, containing the person, group, and organization (PGO) names corresponding to the account. Blank strings serve as wildcards, matching any entry.

user_part A pointer to the **sec_rgy_acct_user_t** structure containing the user part of the account data. This represents such information as the account password, home directory, and default shell, all of which are accessible to, and may be modified by, the account owner.

admin_part A pointer to the **sec_rgy_acct_admin_t** structure containing the administrative part of an account's data. This information includes the account creation and expiration dates and flags describing limits to the use of privilege attribute certificates, among other information, and can be modified only by an administrator.

set_passwd The password reset flag. If TRUE, the password key will be reset. This will require the user to change the account password on the next login attempt.

caller_key A key to use to encrypt the key for transmission to the registry server. If communications secure to the **rpc_c_authn_level_pkt_privacy** level are available on a system, then this parameter is not necessary, and the packet encryption is sufficient to ensure security.

new_key The password for the new account. During transmission to the registry server, it is encrypted with *caller_key*.

new_keytype The type of the new key. The server uses this parameter to decide how to encode the plaintext key.

Input/Output

key_parts A pointer to the minimum abbreviation allowed when logging in to the account. Abbreviations are not currently implemented and the only legal value is **sec_rgy_acct_key_person**.

Output

new_key_version
The key version number returned by the server. If the client requests a particular key version number (via the **version_number** field of the *new_key* input parameter), the server returns the requested version number back to the client.

status A pointer to the completion status. On successful completion, the routine returns **error_status_ok**. Otherwise, it returns an error.

Description

The **sec_rgy_acct_replace_all( )** routine replaces both the user and administrative information in the account record specified by the input login name. The administrative information contains limitations on the account's use and privileges. The user information contains such information as the account home directory and default shell. Typically, the administrative information can only be modified by a registry administrator (users with **admin_info** (**a**) privileges for an account), while the user information can be modified by the account owner (users with **user_info** (**u**) privileges for an account).

The *set_passwd* parameter indicates whether to reset the password. If TRUE, the account user will be prompted to supply a new password at the next login.

The *key_parts* variable identifies how many of the *login_name* parts to use as the unique abbreviation for the replaced account. If the requested abbreviation duplicates an existing abbreviation for another account, the routine identifies the next shortest unique abbreviation and returns this abbreviation using *key_parts*.

Permissions Required

The **sec_rgy_acct_replace_all( )** routine requires the following permissions on the account principal:

- The **m** (**mgmt_info**) permission, if **flags** or **expiration_date** is to be changed.
- The **a** (**auth_info**) permission, if **authentication_flags** or **good_since_date** is to be changed.
- The **u** (**user_info**) permission, if user **flags**, **gecos**, **homedir** (home directory), **shell**, or **passwd** (password) are to be changed.

Notes

All users need the **w** (**write**) privilege to modify any account information.

Files

/usr/include/dce/acct.idl The **idl** file from which **dce/acct.h** was derived.

Errors

sec_rgy_not_authorized	The client program is not authorized to change account information.
sec_rgy_object_not_found	The specified account could not be found.
error_status_ok	The call was successful.

Related Information

Functions: **intro(3sec)**, **sec_rgy_acct_add(3sec)**, **sec_rgy_acct_admin_replace(3sec)**, **sec_rgy_acct_rename(3sec)**, **sec_rgy_acct_user_replace(3sec)**.

sec_rgy_acct_user_replace

Purpose Replaces user account data

Synopsis **#include <dce/acct.h>**

void sec_rgy_acct_user_replace(
sec_rgy_handle_t *context*,
sec_rgy_login_name_t **login_name*,
sec_rgy_acct_user_t **user_part*,
boolean32 *set_passwd*,
sec_passwd_rec_t **caller_key*,
sec_passwd_rec_t **new_key*,
sec_passwd_type_t *new_keytype*,
sec_passwd_version_t **new_key_version*,
error_status_t **status*);

Parameters

Input

context A pointer to an opaque handle bound to a registry server. Use **sec_rgy_site_open**( ) to acquire a bound handle.

login_name A pointer to the account login name. A login name is composed of three character strings, containing the person, group, and organization (PGO) names corresponding to the account. Blank strings serve as wildcards, matching any entry.

user_part A pointer to the **sec_rgy_acct_user_t** structure containing the user part of the account data. This represents such information as the account password, home directory, and default shell, all of which are accessible to, and may be modified by, the account owner. The structure contains the following fields:

gecos A character string containing information about the account owner. This often includes such information as their name and telephone number.

homedir The default directory upon login for the account.

shell The default shell to use upon login.

passwd_version_number
The password version number, a 32-bit unsigned integer, set by the registry server.

passwd_dtm The date and time of the last password change (in **sec_timeval_sec_t** form), also set by the registry server.

flags A flag set of type **sec_rgy_acct_user_flags_t**.

passwd The account's encrypted password.

set_passwd The password reset parameter. If TRUE, the password key will be reset. This will require the user to change the account password on the next login attempt.

caller_key A key to use to encrypt the key for transmission to the registry server. If communications secure to the **rpc_c_authn_level_pkt_privacy** level are available on a system, then this parameter is not necessary, and the packet encryption is sufficient to ensure security.

new_key The password for the new account. During transmission to the registry server, it is encrypted with *caller_key*.

new_keytype The type of the new key. The server uses this parameter to decide how to encode the plaintext key.

Output

new_key_version
The key version number returned by the server. If the client requests a particular key version number (via the **version_number** field of the *new_key* input parameter), the server returns the requested version number back to the client.

status A pointer to the completion status. On successful completion, the routine returns **error_status_ok**. Otherwise, it returns an error.

Description

The **sec_rgy_acct_user_replace**( ) routine replaces the user information in the account record specified by the input login name. The user information contains such information as the account home directory and default shell. Typically, the the user information can be modified by the account owner (users with **user_info** (**u**) privileges for an account).

The *set_passwd* parameter indicates whether to reset the password. If TRUE, the account user will be prompted to supply a new password at the next login.

Permissions Required

The **sec_rgy_acct_user_replace( )** routine requires the **u** (**user_info**) permission on the account principal.

Notes

All users need the **w** (**write**) privilege to modify any account information.

Files

/usr/include/dce/acct.idl	The **idl** file from which **dce/acct.h** was derived.

Errors

sec_rgy_not_authorized	The client program is not authorized to modify the account data.
sec_rgy_object_not_found	The specified account could not be found.
error_status_ok	The call was successful.

Related Information

Functions: **intro(3sec)**, **sec_rgy_acct_add(3sec)**, **sec_rgy_acct_admin_replace(3sec)**, **sec_rgy_acct_rename(3sec)**, **sec_rgy_acct_replace_all(3sec)**.

sec_rgy_auth_plcy_get_effective

Purpose Returns the effective authentication policy for an account

Synopsis **#include <dce/policy.h>**

void sec_rgy_auth_plcy_get_effective(
  sec_rgy_handle_t *context*,
  sec_rgy_login_name_t **account*,
  sec_rgy_plcy_auth_t **auth_policy*,
  error_status_t **status*);

Parameters

Input

context A pointer to an opaque handle bound to a registry server. Use **sec_rgy_site_open( )** to acquire a bound handle.

account A pointer to the account login name (type **sec_rgy_login_name_t**). A login name is composed of three character strings, containing the person, group, and organization (PGO) names corresponding to the account. If all three fields contain empty strings, the authentication policy returned is that of the registry.

Output

auth_policy A pointer to the **sec_rgy_plcy_auth_t** structure to receive the authentication policy. The authentication policy structure contains the maximum lifetime for an authentication ticket, and the maximum amount of time for which one can be renewed.

status A pointer to the completion status. On successful completion, the routine returns **error_status_ok**. Otherwise, it returns an error.

Description

The **sec_rgy_auth_plcy_get_effective( )** routine returns the effective authentication policy for the specified account. The authentication policy in effect is the more restrictive of the registry and the account policies for each policy category. If no account is specified, the registry's authentication policy is returned.

Permissions Required

The **sec_rgy_auth_plcy_get_effective( )** routine requires the **r** (**read**) permission on the policy object from which the data is to be returned. If an account is specified and an account policy exists, the routine also requires the **r** (**read**) permission on the account principal.

Files

/usr/include/dce/policy.idl The **idl** file from which **dce/policy.h** was derived.

Errors

sec_rgy_object_not_found The specified account could not be found.

error_status_ok The call was successful.

Related Information

Functions: **intro(3sec)**, **sec_rgy_auth_plcy_get_info(3sec)**, **sec_rgy_auth_plcy_set_info(3sec)**.

sec_rgy_auth_plcy_get_info

Purpose Returns the authentication policy for an account

Synopsis **#include <dce/policy.h>**

void sec_rgy_auth_plcy_get_info(
    sec_rgy_handle_t *context*,
    sec_rgy_login_name_t **account*,
    sec_rgy_plcy_auth_t **auth_policy*,
    error_status_t **status*);

Parameters

Input

context A pointer to an opaque handle bound to a registry server. Use **sec_rgy_site_open**( ) to acquire a bound handle.

account A pointer to the account login name (type **sec_rgy_login_name_t**). A login name is composed of three character strings, containing the person, group, and organization (PGO) names corresponding to the account.

Output

auth_policy A pointer to the **sec_rgy_plcy_auth_t** structure to receive the authentication policy. The authentication policy structure contains the maximum lifetime for an authentication ticket, and the maximum amount of time for which one can be renewed.

status A pointer to the completion status. On successful completion, the routine returns **error_status_ok**. Otherwise, it returns an error.

Description

The **sec_rgy_auth_plcy_get_info( )** routine returns the authentication policy for the specified account. If no account is specified, the registry's authentication policy is returned.

Permissions Required

The **sec_rgy_auth_plcy_get_info( )** routine requires the **r** (**read**) permission on the policy object or account principal from which the data is to be returned.

Notes

The actual policy in effect will not correspond precisely to what is returned by this call if the overriding registry authentication policy is more restrictive than the policy for the specified account. Use **sec_rgy_auth_plcy_get_effective( )** to return the policy currently in effect for the given account.

Files

/usr/include/dce/policy.idl	The **idl** file from which **dce/policy.h** was derived.

Errors

sec_rgy_object_not_found	No account with the given login name could be found.
error_status_ok	The call was successful.

Related Information

Functions: **intro(3sec)**, **sec_rgy_auth_plcy_get_effective(3sec)**, **sec_rgy_auth_plcy_set_info(3sec)**.

sec_rgy_auth_plcy_set_info

Purpose Sets the authentication policy for an account

Synopsis **#include <dce/policy.h>**

void sec_rgy_auth_plcy_set_info(
    sec_rgy_handle_t *context*,
    sec_rgy_login_name_t **account*,
    sec_rgy_plcy_auth_t **auth_policy*,
    error_status_t **status*);

Parameters

Input

context A pointer to an opaque handle bound to a registry server. Use **sec_rgy_site_open( )** to acquire a bound handle.

account A pointer to the account login name (type **sec_rgy_login_name_t**). A login name is composed of three character strings, containing the person, group, and organization (PGO) names corresponding to the account. All three names must be completely specified.

auth_policy A pointer to the **sec_rgy_plcy_auth_t** structure containing the authentication policy. The authentication policy structure contains the maximum lifetime for an authentication ticket, and the maximum amount of time for which one can be renewed.

Output

status A pointer to the completion status. On successful completion, the routine returns **error_status_ok**. Otherwise, it returns an error.

Description

The **sec_rgy_auth_plcy_set_info( )** routine sets the indicated authentication policy for the specified account. If no account is specified, the authentication policy is set for the registry as a whole.

Permissions Required

The **sec_rgy_auth_plcy_set_info( )** routine requires the **a** (**auth_info**) permission on the policy object or account principal for which the data is to be set.

Notes

The policy set on an account may be less restrictive than the policy set for the registry as a whole. In this case, the change in policy has no effect, since the effective policy is the most restrictive combination of the principal and registry authentication policies. (See the **sec_rgy_auth_plcy_get_effective( )** routine).

Files

/usr/include/dce/policy.idl	The **idl** file from which **dce/policy.h** was derived.

Errors

sec_rgy_object_not_found	No account with the given login name could be found.
sec_rgy_not_authorized	The user is not authorized to update the specified record.
error_status_ok	The call was successful.

Related Information

Functions: **intro(3sec)**, **sec_rgy_auth_plcy_get_effective(3sec)**, **sec_rgy_auth_plcy_get_info(3sec)**.

sec_rgy_cell_bind

Purpose Binds to a registry in a cell

Synopsis **#include <dce/binding.h>**

void sec_rgy_cell_bind(
unsigned_char_t **cell_name*,
sec_rgy_bind_auth_info_t **auth_info*,
sec_rgy_handle_t **context*,
error_status_t **status*);

Parameters

Input

cell_name A character string (type **unsigned_char_t**) containing the name of the cell in question. Upon return, a Security Server for that cell is associated with *context*, the registry server handle. The cell must be specified completely and precisely. This routine offers none of the pathname resolving services of **sec_rgy_site_bind**( ).

auth_info A pointer to the **sec_rgy_bind_auth_info_t** structure that identifies the authentication protocol, protection level, and authorization protocol to use in establishing the binding. (See the **rpc_binding_set_auth_info**( ) routine).

Output

context A pointer to a **sec_rgy_handle_t** variable. Upon return, this contains a registry server handle indicating (''bound to'') the desired registry site.

status A pointer to the completion status. On successful completion, the routine returns **error_status_ok**. Otherwise, it returns an error.

Description

The **sec_rgy_cell_bind( )** routine establishes a relationship with a registry site at an arbitrary level of security. The *cell_name* parameter identifies the target cell.

Files

/usr/include/dce/binding.idl The **idl** file from which **dce/binding.h** was derived.

Errors

error_status_ok The call was successful.

Related Information

Functions: **intro(3sec)**, **sec_rgy_site_bind(3sec)**.

sec_rgy_cursor_reset

Purpose

Resets the registry database cursor

Synopsis

#include <dce/misc.h>

void sec_rgy_cursor_reset(
  sec_rgy_cursor_t ***cursor*);**

Parameters

Input/Output

cursor A pointer into the registry database.

Description

The **sec_rgy_cursor_reset( )** routine resets the database cursor to return the first suitable entry. A cursor is a pointer into the registry. It serves as a place holder when returning successive items from the registry.

A cursor is bound to a particular server. In other words, a cursor that is in use with one replica of the registry has no meaning for any other replica. If a calling program attempts to use a cursor from one replica with another, the cursor is reset and the routine for which the cursor was specified returns the first item in the database.

A cursor that is in use with one call cannot be used with another. For example, you cannot use the same cursor on a call to **sec_rgy_acct_get_projlist( )** and **sec_rgy_pgo_get_next( )**. The behavior in this case is undefined.

Files

/usr/include/dce/misc.idl The **idl** file from which **dce/misc.h** was derived.

Examples

The following example illustrates use of the cursor within a loop. The initial **sec_rgy_cursor_reset( )** call resets the cursor to point to the first item in the registry. Successive calls to **sec_rgy_pgo_get_next( )** return the next PGO item and update the cursor to reflect the last item returned. When the end of the list of PGO items is reached, the routine returns the value **sec_rgy_no_more_entries** in the *status* parameter.

```
sec_rgy_cursor_reset(&cursor);
do {
    sec_rgy_pgo_get_next(context, domain, scope, &cursor,
                    &item, name &status);
    if (status == error_status_ok) {
         /* Print formatted PGO item info */
    }
}while (status == error_status_ok);
```

Related Information

Functions: **intro(3sec)**, **sec_rgy_acct_get_projlist(3sec)**, **sec_rgy_acct_lookup(3sec)**, **sec_rgy_pgo_get_by_id(3sec)**, **sec_rgy_pgo_get_by_name(3sec)**, **sec_rgy_pgo_get_by_unix_num(3sec)**, **sec_rgy_pgo_get_members(3sec)**, **sec_rgy_pgo_get_next(3sec)**.

sec_rgy_login_get_effective

Purpose Returns the effective login data for an account

Synopsis **#include <dce/misc.h>**

void sec_rgy_login_get_effective(
    sec_rgy_handle_t *context*,
    sec_rgy_login_name_t **login_name*,
    sec_rgy_acct_key_t **key_parts*,
    sec_rgy_sid_t **sid*,
    sec_rgy_unix_sid_t **unix_sid*,
    sec_rgy_acct_user_t **user_part*,
    sec_rgy_acct_admin_t **admin_part*,
    sec_rgy_plcy_t **policy_data*,
    signed32 *max_number*,
    signed32 **supplied_number*,
    uuid_t *id_projlist*[ ],
    signed32 *unix_projlist*[ ],
    signed32 **num_projects*,
    sec_rgy_name_t *cell_name*,
    uuid_t **cell_uuid*,
    sec_override_fields_t **overridden*,
    error_status_t **status*);

Parameters

Input

context The registry server handle.

max_number The maximum number of projects to be returned by the call. This must be no larger than the allocated size of the *projlist*[ ] arrays.

Input/Output

login_name A pointer to the account login name. A login name is composed of the names for the account's person, group, and organization (PGO) items.

Output

key_parts A pointer to the minimum abbreviation allowed when logging in to the account. Abbreviations are not currently implemented and the only legal value is **sec_rgy_acct_key_person**.

sid A pointer to a **sec_rgy_sid_t** structure to receive the returned Subject Identifier (SID) for the account. This structure consists of the UUIDs for the account's PGO items.

unix_sid A pointer to a **sec_rgy_unix_sid_t** structure to receive the returned UNIX Subject Identifier (SID) for the account. This structure consists of the UNIX numbers for the account's PGO items.

user_part A pointer to a **sec_rgy_acct_user_t** structure to receive the returned user data for the account.

admin_part A pointer to a **sec_rgy_acct_admin_t** structure to receive the returned administrative data for the account.

policy_data A pointer to a **sec_rgy_policy_t** structure to receive the policy data for the account. The policy data is associated with the account's organization, as identified in the login name.

supplied_number
A pointer to the actual number of projects returned. This will always be less than or equal to the *max_number* supplied on input.

id_projlist[ ] An array to receive the UUID of each project returned. The size allocated for the array is given by *max_number*. If this value is less than the total number of projects in the account project list, multiple calls must be made to return all of the projects.

unix_projlist[ ] An array to receive the UNIX number of each project returned. The size allocated for the array is given by *max_number*. If this value is less than the total number of projects in the account project list, multiple calls must be made to return all of the projects.

num_projects A pointer indicating the total number of projects in the specified account's project list.

cell_name The name of the account's cell.

cell_uuid The UUID for the account's cell.

overridden A pointer to a 32-bit set of flags identifying the local overrides, if any, for the account login information.

status A pointer to the completion status. On successful completion, the routine returns **error_status_ok**. Otherwise, it returns an error.

Description

The **sec_rgy_login_get_effective**( ) routine returns effective login information for the specified account. Login information is extracted from the account's entry in the registry database. Effective login information is a combination of the login information from the registry database and any login overrides defined for the account on the local machine.

The *overridden* parameter indicates which, if any, of the following local overrides have been defined for the account:

- The UNIX user ID
- The group ID
- The encrypted password
- The account's miscellaneous information (**gecos**) field
- The account's home directory
- The account's login shell

Local overrides for account login information are defined in the **/etc/passwd_override** file and apply only to the local machine.

Files

/usr/include/dce/misc.idl The **idl** file from which **dce/misc.h** was derived.

/etc/passwd_override The file that defines local overrides for account login information.

Errors

sec_rgy__object_not_found The specified account could not be found.

error_status_ok The call was successful.

Related Information

Functions: **intro(3sec)**, **sec_rgy_acct_add(3sec)**, **sec_rgy_login_get_info(3sec)**.

Files: **passwd_override(5sec)**.

sec_rgy_login_get_info

Purpose Returns login information for an account

Synopsis **#include <dce/misc.h>**

void sec_rgy_login_get_info(
sec_rgy_handle_t *context*,
sec_rgy_login_name_t **login_name*,
sec_rgy_acct_key_t **key_parts*,
sec_rgy_sid_t **sid*,
sec_rgy_unix_sid_t **unix_sid*,
sec_rgy_acct_user_t **user_part*,
sec_rgy_acct_admin_t **admin_part*,
sec_rgy_plcy_t **policy_data*,
signed32 *max_number*,
signed32 **supplied_number*,
uuid_t *id_projlist*[ ],
signed32 *unix_projlist*[ ],
signed32 **num_projects*,
sec_rgy_name_t *cell_name*,
uuid_t **cell_uuid*,
error_status_t **status*);

Parameters

Input

context The registry server handle.

max_number The maximum number of projects to be returned by the call. This must be no larger than the allocated size of the *projlist*[ ] arrays.

Input/Output

login_name A pointer to the account login name. A login name is composed of the names for the account's person, group, and organization (PGO) items.

Output

key_parts A pointer to the minimum abbreviation allowed when logging in to the account. Abbreviations are not currently implemented and the only legal value is **sec_rgy_acct_key_person**.

sid A pointer to a **sec_rgy_sid_t** structure to receive the returned Subject Identifier (SID) for the account. This structure consists of the UUIDs for the account's PGO items.

unix_sid A pointer to a **sec_rgy_unix_sid_t** structure to receive the returned UNIX Subject Identifier (SID) for the account. This structure consists of the UNIX numbers for the account's PGO items.

user_part A pointer to a **sec_rgy_acct_user_t** structure to receive the returned user data for the account.

admin_part A pointer to a **sec_rgy_acct_admin_t** structure to receive the returned administrative data for the account.

policy_data A pointer to a **sec_rgy_policy_t** structure to receive the policy data for the account. The policy data is associated with the account's organization, as identified in the login name.

supplied_number
A pointer to the actual number of projects returned. This will always be less than or equal to the *max_number* supplied on input.

id_projlist[ ] An array to receive the UUID of each project returned. The size allocated for the array is given by *max_number*. If this value is less than the total number of projects in the account project list, multiple calls must be made to return all of the projects.

unix_projlist[ ] An array to receive the UNIX number of each project returned. The size allocated for the array is given by *max_number*. If this value is less than the total number of projects in the account project list, multiple calls must be made to return all of the projects.

num_projects A pointer indicating the total number of projects in the specified account's project list.

cell_name The name of the account's cell.

cell_uuid The UUID for the account's cell.

status A pointer to the completion status. On successful completion, the routine returns **error_status_ok**. Otherwise, it returns an error.

Description

The **sec_rgy_login_get_info( )** routine returns login information for the specified account. This information is extracted from the account's entry in the registry database. To return any local overrides for the account's login data, use **sec_rgy_login_get_effective( )**.

Permissions Required

The **sec_rgy_login_get_info( )** routine requires the **r** (**read**) permission on the account principal from which the data is to be returned.

Files

/usr/lib/dce/misc.idl The **idl** file from which **dce/misc.h** was derived.

Errors

sec_rgy_object_not_found The specified account could not be found.

error_status_ok The call was successful.

Related Information

Functions: **intro(3sec)**, **sec_rgy_acct_add(3sec)**, **sec_rgy_login_get_effective(3sec)**.

sec_rgy_pgo_add

Purpose Adds a PGO item to the registry database

Synopsis **#include <dce/pgo.h>**

void sec_rgy_pgo_add(
sec_rgy_handle_t *context*,
sec_rgy_domain_t *name_domain*,
sec_rgy_name_t *name*,
sec_rgy_pgo_item_t **pgo_item*,
error_status_t **status*);

Parameters

Input

context A pointer to an opaque handle bound to a registry server. Use **sec_rgy_site_open**( ) to acquire a bound handle.

name_domain This variable identifies the type of the person, group, or organization (PGO) item identified by the given name. The valid values are as follows:

sec_rgy_domain_person The name identifies a person.

sec_rgy_domain_group The name identifies a group.

sec_rgy_domain_org The name identifies an organization.

name A pointer to a **sec_rgy_name_t** character string containing the name of the new PGO item.

pgo_item A pointer to a **sec_rgy_pgo_item_t** structure containing the data for the new PGO item. The data in this structure includes the PGO item's name, UUID, UNIX number (if any), and administrative data, such as whether the item may have (or belong to) a concurrent group set.

Output

status A pointer to the completion status. On successful completion, the routine returns **error_status_ok**. Otherwise, it returns an error.

Description

The **sec_rgy_pgo_add**( ) routine adds a PGO item to the registry database.

The PGO data consists of the following:

- The Universal Unique Identifier (UUID) of the PGO item. Specify **NULL** to have the registry server create a new UUID for an item.
- The UNIX number for the PGO item. If the registry uses embedded UNIX IDs (where a subset of the UUID bits represent the UNIX ID), then the specified ID must match the UUID, if both are specified. Use a value of -1 for the UNIX number to match any value.
- The quota for subaccounts allowed for this item entry.
- The full name of the PGO item.
- Flags (in the **sec_rgy_pgo_flags_t** format) indicating whether
  - — A person item is an alias.
  - — The PGO item can be deleted from the registry.
  - — A person item can have a concurrent group set.
  - — A group item can appear in a concurrent group set.

Permissions Required

The **sec_rgy_pgo_add**( ) routine requires the **i** (**insert**) permission on the parent directory in which the the PGO item is to be created.

Notes

An account can be added to the registry database only when all its constituent PGO items are already in the database, and the appropriate membership relationships between them are established. For example, to establish an account with person name **tom**, group name **writers**, and organization name **hp**, all three names must exist as independent PGO items in the database. Furthermore, **tom** must be a member of **writers**, which must be a member of **hp**. (See **sec_rgy_acct_add( )** to add an account to the registry.)

Files

/usr/include/dce/pgo.idl — The **idl** file from which **dce/pgo.h** was derived.

Errors

sec_rgy_not_authorized — The client program is not authorized to add the specified PGO item.

sec_rgy_object_already_exists — A PGO item already exists with the name given in *name*.

error_status_ok — The call was successful.

Related Information

Functions: **intro(3sec)**, **sec_rgy_pgo_delete(3sec)**, **sec_rgy_pgo_rename(3sec)**, **sec_rgy_pgo_replace(3sec)**, **sec_rgy_acct_add(3sec)**.

sec_rgy_pgo_add_member

Purpose Adds a person to a group or organization

Synopsis **#include <dce/pgo.h>**

void sec_rgy_pgo_add_member(
  sec_rgy_handle_t *context*,
  sec_rgy_domain_t *name_domain*,
  sec_rgy_name_t *go_name*,
  sec_rgy_name_t *person_name*,
  error_status_t **status*);

Parameters

Input

context A pointer to an opaque handle bound to a registry server. Use **sec_rgy_site_open**( ) to acquire a bound handle.

name_domain This variable identifies the type of the person, group, or organization (PGO) item identified by the given name. The valid values are as follows:

sec_rgy_domain_group The *go_name* parameter identifies a group.

sec_rgy_domain_org The *go_name* parameter identifies an organization.

go_name A character string (type **sec_rgy_name_t**) containing the name of the group or organization to which the specified person will be added.

person_name A character string (type **sec_rgy_name_t**) containing the name of the person to be added to the membership list of the group or organization specified by *go_name*.

Output

status A pointer to the completion status. On successful completion, the routine returns **error_status_ok**. Otherwise, it returns an error.

Description

The **sec_rgy_pgo_add_member( )** routine adds a member to the membership list of a group or organization in the registry database.

Permissions Required

The **sec_rgy_pgo_add_member( )** routine requires the **M** (**Member_list**) permission on the group or organization item specified by *go_name*. If *go_name* specifies a group, the routine also requires the **g** (**groups**) permission on the principal *person_name*.

Notes

An account can be added to the registry database only when all its constituent PGO items are already in the database, and the appropriate membership relationships between them are established. For example, to establish an account with person name **tom**, group name **writers**, and organization name **hp**, all three names must exist as independent PGO items in the database. Furthermore, **tom** must be a member of **writers**, which must be a member of **hp**. (See the **sec_rgy_acct_add( )** routine to add an account to the registry.)

Files

/usr/include/dce/pgo.idl The **idl** file from which **dce/pgo.h** was derived.

Errors

sec_rgy_not_authorized The client program is not authorized to add members to the specified group or organization.

sec_rgy_bad_domain An invalid domain was specified. A member can be added only to a group or organization, not a person.

error_status_ok The call was successful.

Related Information

Functions: **intro(3sec)**, **sec_rgy_pgo_add(3sec)**, **sec_rgy_pgo_delete_member(3sec)**, **sec_rgy_pgo_get_members(3sec)**, **sec_rgy_pgo_is_member(3sec)**.

sec_rgy_pgo_delete

Purpose Deletes a PGO item from the registry database

Synopsis **#include <dce/pgo.h>**

void sec_rgy_pgo_delete(
 sec_rgy_handle_t *context*,
 sec_rgy_domain_t *name_domain*,
 sec_rgy_name_t *name*,
 error_status_t **status*);

Parameters

Input

context A pointer to an opaque handle bound to a registry server. Use **sec_rgy_site_open( )** to acquire a bound handle.

name_domain This variable identifies the type of person, group, or organization (PGO) item identified by the given name. The valid values are as follows:

sec_rgy_domain_person The name identifies a person.

sec_rgy_domain_group The name identifies a group.

sec_rgy_domain_org The name identifies an organization.

name A pointer to a **sec_rgy_name_t** character string containing the name of the PGO item to be deleted.

Output

status A pointer to the completion status. On successful completion, the routine returns **error_status_ok**. Otherwise, it returns an error.

Description

The **sec_rgy_pgo_delete( )** routine deletes a PGO item from the registry database. Any account depending on the deleted PGO item is also deleted.

Permissions Required

The **sec_rgy_pgo_delete( )** routine requires the following permissions:

- The **d** (**delete**) permission on the parent directory that contains the the PGO item to be deleted.
- The **D** (**Delete_object**) permission on the PGO item itself.

Files

/usr/include/dce/pgo.idl The **idl** file from which **dce/pgo.h** was derived.

Errors

sec_rgy_not_authorized The client program is not authorized to delete the specified item.

error_status_ok The call was successful.

Related Information

Functions: **intro(3sec)**, **sec_rgy_pgo_add(3sec)**.

sec_rgy_pgo_delete_member

Purpose Deletes a member of a group or organization

Synopsis **#include <dce/pgo.h>**

void sec_rgy_pgo_delete_member(
sec_rgy_handle_t *context*,
sec_rgy_domain_t *name_domain*,
sec_rgy_name_t *go_name*,
sec_rgy_name_t *person_name*,
error_status_t **status*);

Parameters

Input

context A pointer to an opaque handle bound to a registry server. Use **sec_rgy_site_open( )** to acquire a bound handle.

name_domain This variable identifies the type of the person, group, or organization (PGO) item identified by the given name. The valid values are as follows:

sec_rgy_domain_group The *go_name* parameter identifies a group.

sec_rgy_domain_org The *go_name* parameter identifies an organization.

go_name A character string (type **sec_rgy_name_t**) containing the name of the group or organization from which the specified person will be deleted.

person_name A character string (type **sec_rgy_name_t**) containing the name of the person to be deleted from the membership list of the group or organization specified by *go_name*.

Output

status A pointer to the completion status. On successful completion, the routine returns **error_status_ok**. Otherwise, it returns an error.

Description

The **sec_rgy_pgo_delete_member( )** routine deletes a member from the membership list of a group or organization. Any accounts in which the person holds the deleted group or organization membership are also deleted.

Permissions Required

The **sec_rgy_pgo_delete_member( )** routine requires the **M** (**Member_list**) permission on the group or organization item specified by *go_name*.

Files

/usr/include/dce/pgo.idl	The **idl** file from which **dce/pgo.h** was derived.

Errors

sec_rgy_not_authorized	The client program is not authorized to delete the specified member.
sec_rgy_bad_domain	An invalid domain was specified. Members can exist only for groups and organizations, not for persons.
sec_rgy_not_member_group	The specified person is not a member of the specified group.
sec_rgy_not_member_org	The specified person is not a member of the specified organization.
sec_rgy_object_not_found	The specified group or organization was not found.
error_status_ok	The call was successful.

Related Information

Functions: **intro(3sec)**, **sec_rgy_pgo_add(3sec)**, **sec_rgy_pgo_add_member**.

sec_rgy_pgo_get_by_id

Purpose Returns the name and data for a PGO item identified by its UUID

Synopsis **#include <dce/pgo.h>**

void sec_rgy_pgo_get_by_id(
  sec_rgy_handle_t *context*,
  sec_rgy_domain_t *name_domain*,
  sec_rgy_name_t *scope*,
  uuid_t **item_id*,
  boolean32 *allow_aliases*,
  sec_rgy_cursor_t **item_cursor*,
  sec_rgy_pgo_item_t **pgo_item*,
  sec_rgy_name_t *name*,
  error_status_t **status*);

Parameters

Input

context A pointer to an opaque handle bound to a registry server. Use **sec_rgy_site_open( )** to acquire a bound handle.

name_domain This variable identifies the type of the person, group, or organization (PGO) item identified by the given name. The valid values are as follows:

sec_rgy_domain_person	The UUID identifies a person.
sec_rgy_domain_group	The UUID identifies a group.
sec_rgy_domain_org	The UUID identifies an organization.

scope A character string (type **sec_rgy_name_t**) containing the scope of the desired search. The registry database is designed to accommodate a tree-structured name hierarchy. The scope of a search is the name of the branch under which the search takes place. For example, all names in a registry might start with **/alpha**, and be divided further into **/beta** or **/gamma**. To search only the part of the database under **/beta**, the scope of the search would be **/alpha/beta**, and any resulting PGO items would have names beginning with this string. Note that these naming conventions need not have anything to do with group or organization PGO item membership lists.

item_id A pointer to the **uuid_t** variable containing the UUID (Unique Universal Identifier) of the desired PGO item.

allow_aliases A **boolean32** value indicating whether to search for a primary PGO item, or whether the search can be satisfied with an alias. If TRUE, the routine returns the next entry found for the PGO item. If FALSE, the routine returns only the primary entry.

Input/Output

item_cursor An opaque pointer indicating a specific PGO item entry in the registry database. The **sec_rgy_pgo_get_next( )** routine returns the PGO item indicated by *item_cursor*, and advances the cursor to point to the next item in the database. When the end of the list of entries is reached, the routine returns **sec_rgy_no_more_entries** in the *status* parameter. Use **sec_rgy_cursor_reset( )** to reset the cursor.

Output

pgo_item A pointer to a **sec_rgy_pgo_item_t** structure to receive the data for the returned PGO item. The data in this structure includes the PGO item's name, UUID, UNIX number (if any), and administrative data, such as whether the item, if a person, may have a concurrent group set.

name A pointer to a **sec_rgy_name_t** character string containing the returned name for the PGO item.

status A pointer to the completion status. On successful completion, the routine returns **error_status_ok**. Otherwise, it returns an error.

Description

The **sec_rgy_pgo_get_by_id( )** routine returns the name and data for a PGO item. The desired item is identified by its type (domain) and its UUID.

The *item_cursor* parameter specifies the starting point for the search through the registry database. It provides an automatic place holder in the database. The routine automatically updates this variable to point to the next PGO item after the returned item. The returned cursor location can be supplied on a subsequent database access call that also uses a PGO item cursor.

Permissions Required

The **sec_rgy_pgo_get_by_id( )** routine requires the **r** (**read**) permission on the PGO item to be viewed.

Cautions

There are several different types of cursors used in the registry Application Programmer Interface (API). Some cursors point to PGO items, others point to members in a membership list, and others point to account data. Do not use a cursor for one sort of object in a call expecting another sort of object. For example, you cannot use the same cursor on a call to **sec_rgy_acct_get_projlist( )** and **sec_rgy_pgo_get_next( )**. The behavior in this case is undefined.

Furthermore, cursors are specific to a server. A cursor pointing into one replica of the registry database is useless as a pointer into another replica.

Use **sec_rgy_cursor_reset( )** to renew a cursor for use with another call or for another server.

Files

/usr/include/dce/pgo.idl The **idl** file from which **dce/pgo.h** was derived.

Errors

sec_rgy_no_more_entries The cursor is at the end of the list of PGO items.

sec_rgy_object_not_found The specified PGO item was not found.

error_status_ok The call was successful.

Related Information

Functions: **intro(3sec)**, **sec_rgy_pgo_add(3sec)**, **sec_rgy_pgo_get_by_name(3sec)**, **sec_rgy_pgo_get_by_unix_num(3sec)**, **sec_rgy_pgo_get_next(3sec)**, **sec_rgy_pgo_id_to_name(3sec)**, **sec_rgy_pgo_id_to_unix_num(3sec)**, **sec_rgy_pgo_name_to_id(3sec)**, **sec_rgy_pgo_unix_num_to_id(3sec)** **sec_rgy_cursor_reset(3sec)**.

sec_rgy_pgo_get_by_name

Purpose Returns the data for a named PGO item

Synopsis **#include <dce/pgo.h>**

void sec_rgy_pgo_get_by_name(
sec_rgy_handle_t *context*,
sec_rgy_domain_t *name_domain*,
sec_rgy_name_t *pgo_name*,
sec_rgy_cursor_t **item_cursor*,
sec_rgy_pgo_item_t **pgo_item*,
error_status_t **status*);

Parameters

Input

context A pointer to an opaque handle bound to a registry server. Use **sec_rgy_site_open( )** to acquire a bound handle.

name_domain This variable identifies the type of the person, group, or organization (PGO) item identified by the given name. The valid values are as follows:

sec_rgy_domain_person The name identifies a person.

sec_rgy_domain_group The name identifies a group.

sec_rgy_domain_org The name identifies an organization.

pgo_name A character string (type **sec_rgy_name_t**) containing the name of the person, group, or organization to search for. The name must not duplicate the directory name set by the **scope** command. (For example, if the scope is **/alpha/beta**, and the search is for the PGO item **/alpha/beta/fred**, the *pgo_name* parameter must only contain **fred**.)

Output

item_cursor An opaque pointer indicating a specific PGO item entry in the registry database. The **sec_rgy_pgo_get_next( )** routine returns the PGO item indicated by *item_cursor*, and advances the cursor to point to the next item in the database. When the end of the list of entries is reached, the routine returns the value **sec_rgy_no_more_entries** in the *status* parameter. Use **sec_rgy_cursor_reset( )** to reset the cursor.

pgo_item — A pointer to a **sec_rgy_pgo_item_t** structure to receive the data for the returned PGO item. The data in this structure includes the PGO item's name, UUID, UNIX number (if any), and administrative data, such as whether the item, if a person, may have a concurrent group set.

status — A pointer to the completion status. On successful completion, the routine returns **error_status_ok**. Otherwise, it returns an error.

Description

The **sec_rgy_pgo_get_by_name( )** routine returns the data for a named PGO item from the registry database. The desired item is identified by its type (*name_domain*) and name.

The *item_cursor* parameter specifies the starting point for the search through the registry database. It provides an automatic place holder in the database. The routine automatically updates this variable to point to the next PGO item after the returned item. The returned cursor location can be supplied on a subsequent database access call that also uses a PGO item cursor.

Permissions Required

The **sec_rgy_pgo_get_by_name( )** routine requires the **r** (**read**) permission on the PGO item to be viewed.

Cautions

There are several different types of cursors used in the registry Application Programmer Interface (API). Some cursors point to PGO items, others point to members in a membership list, and others point to account data. Do not use a cursor for one sort of object in a call expecting another sort of object. For example, you cannot use the same cursor on a call to **sec_rgy_acct_get_projlist( )** and **sec_rgy_pgo_get_next( )**. The behavior in this case is undefined.

Furthermore, cursors are specific to a server. A cursor pointing into one replica of the registry database is useless as a pointer into another replica.

Use **sec_rgy_cursor_reset( )** to renew a cursor for use with another call or for another server.

Files

/usr/include/dce/pgo.idl The **idl** file from which **dce/pgo.h** was derived.

Errors

sec_rgy_no_more_entries The cursor is at the end of the list of PGO items.

sec_rgy_object_not_found The specified PGO item was not found.

error_status_ok The call was successful.

Related Information

Functions: **intro(3sec)**, **sec_rgy_pgo_add(3sec)**, **sec_rgy_pgo_get_by_id(3sec)**, **sec_rgy_pgo_get_by_unix_num(3sec)**, **sec_rgy_pgo_get_next(3sec)**, **sec_rgy_pgo_id_to_name(3sec)**, **sec_rgy_pgo_id_to_unix_num(3sec)**, **sec_rgy_pgo_name_to_id(3sec)**, **sec_rgy_pgo_unix_num_to_id(3sec)**, **sec_rgy_cursor_reset(3sec)**.

sec_rgy_pgo_get_by_unix_num

Purpose

Returns the name and data for a PGO item identified by its UNIX ID

Synopsis

#include <dce/pgo.h>

void sec_rgy_pgo_get_by_unix_num(
sec_rgy_handle_t *context*,
sec_rgy_domain_t *name_domain*,
sec_rgy_name_t *scope*,
long *unix_id*,
boolean32 *allow_aliases*,
sec_rgy_cursor_t **item_cursor*,
sec_rgy_pgo_item_t **pgo_item*,
sec_rgy_name_t *name*,
error_status_t **status*);

Parameters

Input

context — A pointer to an opaque handle bound to a registry server. Use **sec_rgy_site_open**( ) to acquire a bound handle.

name_domain — This variable identifies the type of the person, group, or organization (PGO) item identified by the given name. The valid values are as follows:

sec_rgy_domain_person	The UNIX number identifies a person.
sec_rgy_domain_group	The UNIX number identifies a group.
sec_rgy_domain_org	The UNIX number identifies an organization.

scope — A character string (type **sec_rgy_name_t**) containing the scope of the desired search. The registry database is designed to accommodate a tree-structured name hierarchy. The scope of a search is the name of the branch under which the search takes place. For example, all names in a registry might start with **/alpha**, and be divided further into **/beta** or **/gamma**. To search only the part of the database under **/beta**, the scope of the search would be **/alpha/beta**, and any resulting PGO items would have names beginning with this string. Note that these naming conventions need not have anything to do with group or organization PGO item membership lists.

unix_id The UNIX number of the desired registry PGO item.

allow_aliases A **boolean32** value indicating whether to search for a primary PGO item, or whether the search can be satisfied with an alias. If TRUE, the routine returns the next entry found for the PGO item. If FALSE, the routine returns only the primary entry.

Input/Output

item_cursor An opaque pointer indicating a specific PGO item entry in the registry database. The **sec_rgy_pgo_get_next( )** routine returns the PGO item indicated by *item_cursor*, and advances the cursor to point to the next item in the database. When the end of the list of entries is reached, the routine returns the value **sec_rgy_no_more_entries** in the *status* parameter. Use **sec_rgy_cursor_reset( )** to reset the cursor.

Output

pgo_item A pointer to a **sec_rgy_pgo_item_t** structure to receive the data for the returned PGO item. The data in this structure includes the PGO item's name, UUID, UNIX number (if any), and administrative data, such as whether the item, if a person, may have a concurrent group set.

name A pointer to a **sec_rgy_name_t** character string containing the returned name for the PGO item.

status A pointer to the completion status. On successful completion, the routine returns **error_status_ok**. Otherwise, it returns an error.

Description

The **sec_rgy_pgo_get_by_unix_num( )** routine returns the name and data for a PGO item. The desired item is identified by its type (domain) and its UNIX number.

The *item_cursor* parameter specifies the starting point for the search through the registry database. It provides an automatic place holder in the database. The routine automatically updates this variable to point to the next PGO item after the returned item. The returned cursor location can be supplied on a subsequent database access call that also uses a PGO item cursor.

Permissions Required

The **sec_rgy_pgo_get_by_unix_num( )** routine requires the **r** (**read**) permission on the PGO item to be viewed.

Cautions

There are several different types of cursors used in the registry Application Programmer Interface (API). Some cursors point to PGO items, others point to members in a membership list, and others point to account data. Do not use a cursor for one sort of object in a call expecting another sort of object. For example, you cannot use the same cursor on a call to **sec_rgy_acct_get_projlist( )** and **sec_rgy_pgo_get_next( )**. The behavior in this case is undefined.

Furthermore, cursors are specific to a server. A cursor pointing into one replica of the registry database is useless as a pointer into another replica.

Use **sec_rgy_cursor_reset( )** to renew a cursor for use with another call or for another server.

Files

/usr/include/dce/pgo.idl The **idl** file from which **dce/pgo.h** was derived.

Errors

sec_rgy_no_more_entries The cursor is at the end of the list of PGO items.

sec_rgy_object_not_found The specified PGO item was not found.

error_status_ok The call was successful.

Related Information

Functions: **intro(3sec)**, **sec_rgy_pgo_add(3sec)**, **sec_rgy_pgo_get_by_id(3sec)**, **sec_rgy_pgo_get_by_name(3sec)**, **sec_rgy_pgo_get_next(3sec)**, **sec_rgy_pgo_id_to_name(3sec)**, **sec_rgy_pgo_id_to_unix_num(3sec)**, **sec_rgy_pgo_name_to_id(3sec)**, **sec_rgy_pgo_unix_num_to_id(3sec)**, **sec_rgy_cursor_reset(3sec)**.

sec_rgy_pgo_get_members

Purpose Returns the membership list for a group or organization

Synopsis **#include <dce/pgo.h>**

void sec_rgy_pgo_get_members(
  sec_rgy_handle_t *context*,
  sec_rgy_domain_t *name_domain*,
  sec_rgy_name_t *go_name*,
  sec_rgy_cursor_t **member_cursor*,
  long *max_members*,
  sec_rgy_member_t *member_list*[ ],
  long **number_supplied*,
  long **number_members*,
  error_status_t **status*);

Parameters

Input

context A pointer to an opaque handle bound to a registry server. Use **sec_rgy_site_open**( ) to acquire a bound handle.

name_domain This variable identifies the type of the person, group, or organization (PGO) item identified by the given name. The valid values are as follows:

sec_rgy_domain_group The *go_name* parameter identifies a group.

sec_rgy_domain_org The *go_name* parameter identifies an organization.

go_name A character string (type **sec_rgy_name_t**) that contains the name of the group or organization whose members are to be returned.

max_members A **long** variable containing the allocated dimension of the *member_list*[ ] array. This is the maximum number of members returned by a single call.

Input/Output

member_cursor An opaque pointer indicating a specific member entry in the membership list of the specified group or organization. The returned list of members begins with the entry specified by *member_cursor*. Upon return, the cursor points to the next entry after the last one returned. If there are no more entries in the specified membership list, the routine returns the value **sec_rgy_no_more_entries** in the *status* parameter. Use **sec_rgy_cursor_reset( )** to reset the cursor to the beginning of the list.

Output

member_list[ ] An array of character strings to receive the returned member names. The size allocated for the array is given by *max_number*. If this value is less than the total number of members in the membership list, multiple calls must be made to return all of the members.

number_supplied
A pointer to a **long** variable to receive the number of members actually returned in *member_list*[ ].

number_members
A pointer to a **long** variable to receive the total number of members in the specified group or organization. If this number is greater than *number_supplied*, multiple calls to **sec_rgy_pgo_get_members( )** are necessary to return the entire membership list. Use the *member_cursor* parameter to coordinate successive calls.

status A pointer to the completion status. On successful completion, the routine returns **error_status_ok**. Otherwise, it returns an error.

Description

The **sec_rgy_pgo_get_members( )** routine returns a list of the members in the specified group or organization.

The *member_cursor* parameter specifies the starting point for the search through the registry database. It provides an automatic place holder in the database. The routine automatically updates this variable to point to the next member (if any) after the returned list. If not all of the members are returned, the updated cursor can be supplied on successive calls to return the remainder of the list.

Permissions Required

The **sec_rgy_pgo_get_members( )** routine requires the **r** (**read**) permission on the group or organization item specified by *go_name*.

Cautions

There are several different types of cursors used in the registry Application Programmer Interface (API). Some cursors point to PGO items, others point to members in a membership list, and others point to account data. Do not use a cursor for one sort of object in a call expecting another sort of object. For example, you cannot use the same cursor on a call to **sec_rgy_acct_get_projlist( )** and **sec_rgy_pgo_get_next( )**. The behavior in this case is undefined.

Furthermore, cursors are specific to a server. A cursor pointing into one replica of the registry database is useless as a pointer into another replica.

Use **sec_rgy_cursor_reset( )** to renew a cursor for use with another call or for another server.

Return Values

The routine returns the members in the specified group or organization in *member_list*[ ]. The *member_list*[ ] entries consist of the names of person PGO items previously added to the group or organization. The routine also returns the number of members actually returned (in *number_supplied*) and the total number of members in the group or organization (in *number_members*).

Files

/usr/include/dce/pgo.idl — The **idl** file from which **dce/pgo.h** was derived.

Errors

sec_rgy_no_more_entries — The cursor points to the end of the membership list for the group or organization.

sec_rgy_object_not_found — The specified group or organization could not be found.

error_status_ok — The call was successful.

Related Information

Functions: **intro(3sec)**, **sec_rgy_pgo_add_member(3sec)**, **sec_rgy_cursor_reset(3sec)**, **sec_rgy_pgo_is_member(3sec)**.

sec_rgy_pgo_get_next

Purpose Returns the next PGO item in the registry database

Synopsis **#include <dce/pgo.h>**

void sec_rgy_pgo_get_next(
sec_rgy_handle_t *context*,
sec_rgy_domain_t *name_domain*,
sec_rgy_name_t *scope*,
sec_rgy_cursor_t **item_cursor*,
sec_rgy_pgo_item_t **pgo_item*,
sec_rgy_name_t *name*,
error_status_t **status*);

Parameters

Input

context A pointer to an opaque handle bound to a registry server. Use **sec_rgy_site_open**( ) to acquire a bound handle.

name_domain This variable identifies the type of the person, group, or organization (PGO) item identified by the given name. The valid values are as follows:

sec_rgy_domain_person	Returns the next person item.
sec_rgy_domain_group	Returns the next group item.
sec_rgy_domain_org	Returns the next organization item.

scope A character string (type **sec_rgy_name_t**) containing the scope of the desired search. The registry database is designed to accommodate a tree-structured name hierarchy. The scope of a search is the name of the branch under which the search takes place. For example, all names in a registry might start with **/alpha**, and be divided further into **/beta** or **/gamma**. To search only the part of the database under **/beta**, the scope of the search would be **/alpha/beta**, and any resulting PGO items would have names beginning with this string. Note that these naming conventions need not have anything to do with group or organization PGO item membership lists.

Input/Output

item_cursor
: An opaque pointer indicating a specific PGO item entry in the registry database. The **sec_rgy_pgo_get_next( )** routine returns the PGO item indicated by *item_cursor*, and advances the cursor to point to the next item in the database. When the end of the list of entries is reached, the routine returns the value **sec_rgy_no_more_entries** in the *status* parameter. Use **sec_rgy_cursor_reset( )** to reset the cursor.

Output

pgo_item
: A pointer to a **sec_rgy_pgo_item_t** structure to receive the data for the returned PGO item. The data in this structure includes the PGO item's name, UUID, UNIX number (if any), and administrative data, such as whether the item, if a person, may have a concurrent group set.

name
: A pointer to a **sec_rgy_name_t** character string containing the name of the returned PGO item.

status
: A pointer to the completion status. On successful completion, the routine returns **error_status_ok**. Otherwise, it returns an error.

Description

The **sec_rgy_pgo_get_next( )** routine returns the data and name for the PGO in the registry database indicated by *item_cursor*. It also advances the cursor to point to the next PGO item in the database. Successive calls to this routine return all the PGO items in the database of the specified type (given by *name_domain*), in storage order.

The PGO data consists of the following:

- The Universal Unique Identifier (UUID) of the PGO item.
- The UNIX number for the PGO item.
- The quota for subaccounts.
- The full name of the PGO item.
- Flags indicating whether
  - — A person item is an alias.

— The PGO item can be deleted.

— A person item can have a concurrent group set.

— A group item can appear on a concurrent group set.

Permissions Required

The **sec_rgy_pgo_get_next( )** routine requires the **r** (**read**) permission on the PGO item to be viewed.

Cautions

There are several different types of cursors used in the registry Application Programmer Interface (API). Some cursors point to PGO items, others point to members in a membership list, and others point to account data. Do not use a cursor for one sort of object in a call expecting another sort of object. For example, you cannot use the same cursor on a call to **sec_rgy_acct_get_projlist( )** and **sec_rgy_pgo_get_next( )**. The behavior in this case is undefined.

Furthermore, cursors are specific to a server. A cursor pointing into one replica of the registry database is useless as a pointer into another replica.

Use **sec_rgy_cursor_reset( )** to renew a cursor for use with another call or for another server.

Return Values

The routine returns the data for the returned PGO item in *pgo_item* and the name in *name*.

Files

/usr/include/dce/pgo.idl The **idl** file from which **dce/pgo.h** was derived.

Errors

sec_rgy_no_more_entries The cursor is at the end of the list of PGO items.

error_status_ok The call was successful.

Related Information

Functions: **intro(3sec)**, **sec_rgy_pgo_add(3sec)**, **sec_rgy_cursor_reset(3sec)**, **sec_rgy_pgo_get_by_id(3sec)**, **sec_rgy_pgo_get_by_name(3sec)**, **sec_rgy_pgo_get_by_unix_num(3sec)**, **sec_rgy_pgo_id_to_unix_num(3sec)**, **sec_rgy_pgo_unix_num_to_id(3sec)**.

sec_rgy_pgo_id_to_name

Purpose Returns the name for a PGO item identified by its UUID

Synopsis **#include <dce/pgo.h>**

void sec_rgy_pgo_id_to_name(
  sec_rgy_handle_t *context*,
  sec_rgy_domain_t *name_domain*,
  uuid_t **item_id*,
  sec_rgy_name_t *pgo_name*,
  error_status_t **status*);

Parameters

Input

context A pointer to an opaque handle bound to a registry server. Use **sec_rgy_site_open( )** to acquire a bound handle.

name_domain This variable identifies the type of the person, group, or organization (PGO) item identified by the given name. The valid values are as follows:

sec_rgy_domain_person The *item_id* parameter identifies a person.

sec_rgy_domain_group The *item_id* parameter identifies a group.

sec_rgy_domain_org The *item_id* parameter identifies an organization.

item_id A pointer to the **uuid_t** variable containing the input UUID (Unique Universal Identifier).

Output

pgo_name A character string (type **sec_rgy_name_t**) containing the name of the person, group, or organization with the input UUID.

status A pointer to the completion status. On successful completion, the routine returns **error_status_ok**. Otherwise, it returns an error.

Description

The **sec_rgy_pgo_id_to_name**( ) routine returns the name of the PGO item having the specified UUID.

Permissions Required

The **sec_rgy_pgo_id_to_name**( ) routine requires at least one permission of any kind on the PGO item to be viewed.

Files

/usr/include/dce/pgo.idl The **idl** file from which **dce/pgo.h** was derived.

Errors

sec_rgy_object_not_found No item with the specified UUID could be found.

error_status_ok The call was successful.

Related Information

Functions: **intro(3sec)**, **sec_rgy_pgo_add(3sec)**, **sec_rgy_pgo_get_by_id(3sec)**, **sec_rgy_pgo_get_by_name(3sec)**, **sec_rgy_pgo_get_by_unix_num(3sec)**, **sec_rgy_pgo_id_to_unix_num(3sec)**, **sec_rgy_pgo_name_to_id(3sec)**, **sec_rgy_pgo_unix_num_to_id(3sec)**.

sec_rgy_pgo_id_to_unix_num

Purpose Returns the UNIX number for a PGO item identified by its UUID

Synopsis **#include <dce/pgo.h>**

void sec_rgy_pgo_id_to_unix_num(
sec_rgy_handle_t *context*,
sec_rgy_domain_t *name_domain*,
uuid_t **item_id*,
long **item_unix_id*,
error_status_t **status*);

Parameters

Input

context A pointer to an opaque handle bound to a registry server. Use **sec_rgy_site_open**( ) to acquire a bound handle.

name_domain This variable identifies the type of the person, group, or organization (PGO) item identified by the given name. The valid values are as follows:

sec_rgy_domain_person The *item_id* parameter identifies a person.

sec_rgy_domain_group The *item_id* parameter identifies a group.

sec_rgy_domain_org The *item_id* parameter identifies an organization.

item_id A pointer to the **uuid_t** variable containing the input UUID (Unique Universal Identifier).

Output

item_unix_id A pointer to the **long** variable to receive the returned UNIX number for the PGO item.

status A pointer to the completion status. On successful completion, the routine returns **error_status_ok**. Otherwise, it returns an error.

Description

The **sec_rgy_pgo_id_to_unix_num**( ) routine returns the UNIX number for the PGO item having the specified UUID.

Files

/usr/include/dce/pgo.idl The **idl** file from which **dce/pgo.h** was derived.

Errors

sec_rgy_object_not_found No item with the specified UUID could be found.

error_status_ok The call was successful.

Related Information

Functions: **intro(3sec)**, **sec_rgy_pgo_add(3sec)**, **sec_rgy_pgo_get_by_id(3sec)**, **sec_rgy_pgo_get_by_name(3sec)**, **sec_rgy_pgo_get_by_unix_num(3sec)**, **sec_rgy_pgo_id_to_name(3sec)**, **sec_rgy_pgo_name_to_id(3sec)**, **sec_rgy_pgo_unix_num_to_id(3sec)**.

sec_rgy_pgo_is_member

Purpose

Checks group or organization membership

Synopsis

#include <dce/pgo.h>

boolean32 sec_rgy_pgo_is_member(
sec_rgy_handle_t *context***,**
sec_rgy_domain_t *name_domain***,**
sec_rgy_name_t *go_name***,**
sec_rgy_name_t *person_name***,**
error_status_t ****status*);**

Parameters

Input

context
: A pointer to an opaque handle bound to a registry server. Use **sec_rgy_site_open( )** to acquire a bound handle.

name_domain
: This variable identifies the type of the person, group, or organization (PGO) item identified by the given name. The valid values are as follows:

sec_rgy_domain_group — The *go_name* parameter identifies a group.

sec_rgy_domain_org — The *go_name* parameter identifies an organization.

go_name
: A character string (type **sec_rgy_name_t**) containing the name of the group or organization whose membership list is in question.

person_name
: A character string (type **sec_rgy_name_t**) containing the name of the person whose membership in the group or organization specified by *go_name* is in question.

Output

status
: A pointer to the completion status. On successful completion, the routine returns **error_status_ok**. Otherwise, it returns an error.

Description

The **sec_rgy_pgo_is_member( )** routine tests whether the specified person is a member of the named group or organization.

Permissions Required

The **sec_rgy_pgo_is_member( )** routine requires the **t** (**test**) permission on the group or organization item specified by *go_name*.

Return Values

The routine returns TRUE if the person is a member of the named group or organization. If the person is not a member, the routine returns FALSE and sets *status* to either **sec_rgy_status_not_member_group** or **sec_rgy_status_not_member_org**.

Files

/usr/include/dce/pgo.idl The **idl** file from which **dce/pgo.h** was derived.

Errors

sec_rgy_object_not_found The named group or organization was not found.

sec_rgy_not_member_group The person is not a member of the specified group.

sec_rgy_not_member_org The person is not a member of the specified organization.

error_status_ok The call was successful.

Related Information

Functions: **intro(3sec)**, **sec_rgy_pgo_add_member(3sec)**, **sec_rgy_pgo_get_members(3sec)**.

sec_rgy_pgo_name_to_id

Purpose Returns the UUID for a named PGO item

Synopsis **#include <dce/pgo.h>**

void sec_rgy_pgo_name_to_id(
sec_rgy_handle_t *context*,
sec_rgy_domain_t *name_domain*,
sec_rgy_name_t *pgo_name*,
uuid_t **item_id*,
error_status_t **status*);

Parameters

Input

context A pointer to an opaque handle bound to a registry server. Use **sec_rgy_site_open( )** to acquire a bound handle.

name_domain This variable identifies the type of the person, group, or organization (PGO) item identified by the given name. The valid values are as follows:

sec_rgy_domain_person The name identifies a person.

sec_rgy_domain_group The name identifies a group.

sec_rgy_domain_org The name identifies an organization.

pgo_name A character string (type **sec_rgy_name_t**) containing the name of the person, group, or organization whose UUID is desired.

Output

item_id A pointer to the **uuid_t** variable containing the UUID (Unique Universal Identifier) of the resulting PGO item.

status A pointer to the completion status. On successful completion, the routine returns **error_status_ok**. Otherwise, it returns an error.

Description

The **sec_rgy_pgo_name_to_id**( ) routine returns the UUID associated with the named PGO item.

Files

/usr/include/dce/pgo.idl The **idl** file from which **dce/pgo.h** was derived.

Errors

sec_rgy_object_not_found The specified PGO item could not be found.

error_status_ok The call was successful.

Related Information

Functions: **intro(3sec)**, **sec_rgy_pgo_add(3sec)**, **sec_rgy_pgo_get_by_id(3sec)**, **sec_rgy_pgo_get_by_name(3sec)**, **sec_rgy_pgo_get_by_unix_num(3sec)**, **sec_rgy_pgo_id_to_name(3sec)**, **sec_rgy_pgo_id_to_unix_num(3sec)**, **sec_rgy_pgo_unix_num_to_id(3sec)**.

sec_rgy_pgo_name_to_unix_num

Purpose Returns the UNIX number for a PGO item identified by its name

Synopsis **#include <dce/pgo.h>**

void sec_rgy_pgo_name_to_unix_num(
  sec_rgy_handle_t *context*,
  sec_rgy_domain_t *name_domain*,
  sec_rgy_name_t *pgo_name*,
  long **item_unix_id*,
  error_status_t **status*);

Parameters

Input

context A pointer to an opaque handle bound to a registry server. Use **sec_rgy_site_open( )** to acquire a bound handle.

name_domain This variable identifies the type of the person, group, or organization (PGO) item identified by the given name. The valid values are as follows:

sec_rgy_domain_person The name identifies a person.

sec_rgy_domain_group The name identifies a group.

sec_rgy_domain_org The name identifies an organization.

pgo_name A character string containing the name of the PGO item in question.

Output

item_unix_id A pointer to the **long** variable to receive the returned UNIX number for the PGO item.

status A pointer to the completion status. On successful completion, the routine returns **error_status_ok**. Otherwise, it returns an error.

Description

The **sec_rgy_pgo_name_to_unix_num( )** routine returns the UNIX number for the PGO item having the specified name.

Files

/usr/include/dce/pgo.idl	The **idl** file from which **dce/pgo.h** was derived.

Errors

sec_rgy_object_not_found	No item with the specified UUID could be found.
error_status_ok	The call was successful.

Related Information

Functions: **intro(3sec)**, **sec_rgy_pgo_add(3sec)**, **sec_rgy_pgo_get_by_id(3sec)**, **sec_rgy_pgo_get_by_name(3sec)**, **sec_rgy_pgo_get_by_unix_num(3sec)**, **sec_rgy_pgo_id_to_name(3sec)**, **sec_rgy_pgo_name_to_id(3sec)**, **sec_rgy_pgo_unix_num_to_id(3sec)**.

sec_rgy_pgo_rename

Purpose Changes the name of a PGO item in the registry database

Synopsis **#include <dce/pgo.h>**

void sec_rgy_pgo_rename(
sec_rgy_handle_t *context*,
sec_rgy_domain_t *name_domain*,
sec_rgy_name_t *old_name*,
sec_rgy_name_t *new_name*,
error_status_t **status*);

Parameters

Input

context A pointer to an opaque handle bound to a registry server. Use **sec_rgy_site_open**( ) to acquire a bound handle.

name_domain This variable identifies the type of the person, group, or organization (PGO) item identified by the given name. The valid values are as follows:

sec_rgy_domain_person The name identifies a person.

sec_rgy_domain_group The name identifies a group.

sec_rgy_domain_org The name identifies an organization.

old_name A pointer to a **sec_rgy_name_t** character string containing the existing name of the PGO item.

new_name A pointer to a **sec_rgy_name_t** character string containing the new name for the PGO item.

Output

status A pointer to the completion status. On successful completion, the routine returns **error_status_ok**. Otherwise, it returns an error.

Description

The **sec_rgy_pgo_rename( )** routine renames a PGO item in the registry database.

Permissions Required

If the **sec_rgy_pgo_rename( )** routine is performing a rename within a directory, it requires the **n** (**name**) permission on the old name of the PGO item. If the routine is performing a move between directories, it requires the following permissions:

- The **d** (**delete**) permission on the parent directory that contains the PGO item.
- The **n** (**name**) permission on the old name of the PGO item.
- The **i** (**insert**) permission on the parent directory in which the PGO item is to be added under the new name.

Files

/usr/include/dce/pgo.idl The **idl** file from which **dce/pgo.h** was derived.

Errors

sec_rgy_not_authorized The client program is not authorized to change the name of the specified PGO item.

error_status_ok The call was successful.

Related Information

Functions: **intro(3sec)**, **sec_rgy_pgo_add(3sec)**, **sec_rgy_pgo_replace(3sec)**.

sec_rgy_pgo_replace

Purpose Replaces the data in an existing PGO item

Synopsis **#include <dce/pgo.h>**

void sec_rgy_pgo_replace(
    sec_rgy_handle_t *context***,**
    sec_rgy_domain_t *name_domain***,**
    sec_rgy_name_t *pgo_name***,**
    sec_rgy_pgo_item_t **pgo_item***,**
    error_status_t **status***);**

Parameters

Input

context — A pointer to an opaque handle bound to a registry server. Use **sec_rgy_site_open( )** to acquire a bound handle.

name_domain — This variable identifies the type of the person, group, or organization (PGO) item identified by the given name. The valid values are as follows:

sec_rgy_domain_person — The name identifies a person.

sec_rgy_domain_group — The name identifies a group.

sec_rgy_domain_org — The name identifies an organization.

pgo_name — A character string (type **sec_rgy_name_t**) containing the name of the person, group, or organization whose data is to be replaced.

pgo_item — A pointer to a **sec_rgy_pgo_item_t** structure containing the new data for the PGO item. The data in this structure includes the PGO item's name, UUID, UNIX number (if any), and administrative data, such as whether the item, if a person, may have a concurrent group set.

Output

status	A pointer to the completion status. On successful completion, the routine returns **error_status_ok**. Otherwise, it returns an error.

Description

The **sec_rgy_pgo_replace**( ) routine replaces the data associated with a PGO item in the registry database.

The UNIX ID and UUID of a PGO item cannot be replaced. To change the UNIX ID or UUID, the existing PGO item must be deleted and a new PGO item added in its place. The one exception to this rule is that the UNIX ID can be replaced in the PGO item for a cell principal. The reason for this exception is that the UUID for a cell principal does not contain an embedded UNIX ID.

Permissions Required

The **sec_rgy_pgo_replace**( ) routine requires at least one of the following permissions:

- The **m** (**mgmt_info**) permission on the PGO item, if **quota** or **flags** is being set.
- The **f** (**fullname**) permission on the PGO item, if **fullname** is being set.

Files

/usr/include/dce/pgo.idl	The **idl** file from which **dce/pgo.h** was derived.

Errors

sec_rgy_not_authorized	The client program is not authorized to replace the specified PGO item.
sec_rgy_object_not_found	No PGO item was found with the given name.
sec_rgy_unix_id_changed	The UNIX number of the PGO item was changed.
error_status_ok	The call was successful.

Related Information

Functions: **intro(3sec)**, **sec_rgy_pgo_add(3sec)**, **sec_rgy_pgo_delete(3sec)**, **sec_rgy_pgo_rename(3sec)**.

sec_rgy_pgo_unix_num_to_id

Purpose Returns the UUID for a PGO item identified by its UNIX number

Synopsis **#include <dce/pgo.h>**

void sec_rgy_pgo_unix_num_to_id(
sec_rgy_handle_t *context*,
sec_rgy_domain_t *name_domain*,
long *item_unix_id*,
uuid_t **item_id*,
error_status_t **status*);

Parameters

Input

context A pointer to an opaque handle bound to a registry server. Use **sec_rgy_site_open**( ) to acquire a bound handle.

name_domain This variable identifies the type of the person, group, or organization (PGO) item identified by the given name. The valid values are as follows:

sec_rgy_domain_person The *item_unix_id* parameter identifies a person.

sec_rgy_domain_group The *item_unix_id* parameter identifies a group.

sec_rgy_domain_org The *item_unix_id* parameter identifies an organization.

item_unix_id The **long** variable containing the UNIX number for the PGO item.

Output

item_id A pointer to the **uuid_t** variable containing the UUID (Unique Universal Identifier) of the resulting PGO item.

status A pointer to the completion status. On successful completion, the routine returns **error_status_ok**. Otherwise, it returns an error.

Description

The **sec_rgy_pgo_unix_num_to_id**( ) routine returns the Universal Unique Identifier (UUID) for a PGO item that has the specified UNIX number.

Files

/usr/include/dce/pgo.idl	The **idl** file from which **dce/pgo.h** was derived.

Errors

sec_rgy_object_not_found	No item with the specified UNIX number could be found.
error_status_ok	The call was successful.

Related Information

Functions: **intro(3sec)**, **sec_rgy_pgo_add(3sec)**, **sec_rgy_pgo_get_by_id(3sec)**, **sec_rgy_pgo_get_by_name(3sec)**, **sec_rgy_pgo_get_by_unix_num(3sec)**, **sec_rgy_pgo_id_to_name(3sec)**, **sec_rgy_pgo_id_to_unix_num(3sec)**, **sec_rgy_pgo_name_to_id(3sec)**.

sec_rgy_pgo_unix_num_to_name

Purpose Returns the name for a PGO item identified by its UNIX number

Synopsis **#include <dce/pgo.h>**

void sec_rgy_pgo_to_unix_num_to_id(
sec_rgy_handle_t *context***,**
sec_rgy_domain_t *name_domain***,**
long *item_unix_id***,**
sec_rgy_name_t *pgo_name***,**
error_status_t ****status*);

Parameters

Input

context A pointer to an opaque handle bound to a registry server. Use **sec_rgy_site_open**( ) to acquire a bound handle.

name_domain The type of the person, group, or organization (PGO) item identified by *item_unix_id*. Valid values are as follows:

sec_rgy_domain_person The *item_unix_id* parameter identifies a person.

sec_rgy_domain_group The *item_unix_id* parameter identifies a group.

sec_rgy_domain_org The *item_unix_id* parameter identifies an organization.

item_unix_id The **long** variable containing the UNIX number for the PGO item.

Output

pgo_name A character string containing the name of the PGO item in question.

status A pointer to the completion status. On successful completion, the routine returns **error_status_ok**. Otherwise, it returns an error.

Description

The **sec_rgy_pgo_unix_num_to_name( )** routine returns the name for a PGO item that has the specified UNIX number.

Permissions Required

The **sec_rgy_pgo_unix_num_to_name( )** routine requires at least one permission of any kind on the PGO item identified by *item_unix_id*.

Files

/usr/include/dce/pgo.idl The **idl** file from which **dce/pgo.h** was derived.

Errors

sec_rgy_object_not_found No item with the specified UNIX number could be found.

error_status_ok The call was successful.

Related Information

Functions: **intro(3sec)**, **sec_rgy_pgo_add(3sec)**, **sec_rgy_pgo_get_by_id(3sec)**, **sec_rgy_pgo_get_by_name(3sec)**, **sec_rgy_pgo_get_by_unix_num(3sec)**, **sec_rgy_pgo_id_to_name(3sec)**, **sec_rgy_pgo_id_to_unix_num(3sec)**, **sec_rgy_pgo_name_to_id(3sec)**.

sec_rgy_plcy_get_effective

Purpose Returns the effective policy for an organization

Synopsis **#include <dce/policy.h>**

void sec_rgy_plcy_get_effective(
  sec_rgy_handle_t *context*,
  sec_rgy_name_t *organization*,
  sec_rgy_plcy_t **policy_data*,
  error_status_t **status*);

Parameters

Input

context A pointer to an opaque handle bound to a registry server. Use **sec_rgy_site_open( )** to acquire a bound handle.

organization A character string (type **sec_rgy_name_t**) containing the name of the organization for which the policy data is to be returned. If this string is empty, the routine returns the registry's policy data.

Output

policy_data A pointer to the **sec_rgy_plcy_t** structure to receive the authentication policy. This structure contains the minimum length of a user's password, the lifetime of a password, the expiration date of a password, the lifetime of the entire account, and some flags describing limitations on the password spelling.

status A pointer to the completion status. On successful completion, the routine returns **error_status_ok**. Otherwise, it returns an error.

Description

The **sec_rgy_plcy_get_effective( )** routine returns the effective policy for the specified organization.

The effective policy data is the most restrictive combination of the registry and the organization policies.

The policy data consists of the following:

- The password expiration date. This is the date on which account passwords will expire.
- The minimum length allowed for account passwords.
- The period of time (life span) for which account passwords will be valid.
- The period of time (life span) for which accounts will be valid.
- Flags indicating whether account passwords can consist entirely of spaces or entirely of alphanumeric characters.

Permissions Required

The **sec_rgy_plcy_get_effective( )** routine requires the **r** (**read**) permission on the policy object from which the data is to be returned. If an organization is specified, the routine also requires the **r** (**read**) permission on the organization.

Notes

If no organization is specified, the routine returns the registry's policy data. To return the effective policy, an organization must be specified. This is because the routine compares the registry's policy data with that of the organization to determine which is more restrictive.

Files

/usr/include/dce/policy.idl The **idl** file from which **dce/policy.h** was derived.

Errors

sec_rgy_object_not_found The registry server could not find the specified organization.

error_status_ok The call was successful.

Related Information

Functions: **intro(3sec)**, **sec_rgy_plcy_get_info(3sec)**, **sec_rgy_plcy_set_info(3sec)**.

sec_rgy_plcy_get_info

Purpose Returns the policy for an organization

Synopsis **#include <dce/policy.h>**

void sec_rgy_plcy_get_info(
sec_rgy_handle_t *context*,
sec_rgy_name_t *organization*,
sec_rgy_plcy_t **policy_data*,
error_status_t **status*);

Parameters

Input

context A pointer to an opaque handle bound to a registry server. Use **sec_rgy_site_open()** to acquire a bound handle.

organization A character string (type **sec_rgy_name_t**) containing the name of the organization for which the policy data is to be returned. If this string is empty, the routine returns the registry's policy data.

Output

policy_data A pointer to the **sec_rgy_plcy_t** structure to receive the authentication policy. This structure contains the minimum length of a user's password, the lifetime of a password, the expiration date of a password, the lifetime of the entire account, and some flags describing limitations on the password spelling.

status A pointer to the completion status. On successful completion, the routine returns **error_status_ok**. Otherwise, it returns an error.

Description

The **sec_rgy_plcy_get_info()** routine returns the policy data for the specified organization. If no organization is specified, the registry's policy data is returned.

The policy data consists of the following:

- The password expiration date. This is the date on which account passwords will expire.

- The minimum length allowed for account passwords.
- The period of time (life span) for which account passwords will be valid.
- The period of time (life span) for which accounts will be valid.
- Flags indicating whether account passwords can consist entirely of spaces or entirely of alphanumeric characters.

Permissions Required

The **sec_rgy_plcy_get_info()** routine requires the **r** (**read**) permission on the policy object or organization from which the data is to be returned.

Notes

The returned policy may not be in effect if the overriding registry authorization policy is more restrictive. (See the **sec_rgy_auth_plcy_get_effective()** routine.)

Files

/usr/include/dce/policy.idl The **idl** file from which **dce/policy.h** was derived.

Errors

sec_rgy_object_not_found The registry server could not find the specified organization.

error_status_ok The call was successful.

Related Information

Functions: **intro(3sec)**, **sec_rgy_plcy_get_effective_info(3sec)**, **sec_rgy_plcy_set_info(3sec)**.

sec_rgy_plcy_set_info

Purpose Sets the policy for an organization

Synopsis **#include <dce/policy.h>**

void sec_rgy_plcy_set_info(
sec_rgy_handle_t *context***,**
sec_rgy_name_t *organization***,**
sec_rgy_plcy_t **policy_data***,**
error_status_t **status***);**

Parameters

Input

context A pointer to an opaque handle bound to a registry server. Use **sec_rgy_site_open( )** to acquire a bound handle.

organization A character string (type **sec_rgy_name_t**) containing the name of the organization for which the policy data is to be returned. If this string is empty, the routine sets the registry's policy data.

policy_data A pointer to the **sec_rgy_plcy_t** structure containing the authentication policy. This structure contains the minimum length of a user's password, the lifetime of a password, the expiration date of a password, the lifetime of the entire account, and some flags describing limitations on the password spelling.

Output

status A pointer to the completion status. On successful completion, the routine returns **error_status_ok**. Otherwise, it returns an error.

Description

The **sec_rgy_plcy_set_info( )** routine sets the authentication policy for a specified organization. If no organization is specified, the registry's policy data is set.

Policy data can be returned or set for individual organizations and for the registry as a whole.

Permissions Required

The **sec_rgy_plcy_set_info( )** routine requires the **m** (**mgmt_info**) permission on the policy object or organization for which the data is to be set.

Notes

The policy set on an account may be less restrictive than the policy set for the registry as a whole. In this case, the changes in policy have no effect, since the effective policy is the most restrictive combination of the organization and registry authentication policies. (See the **sec_rgy_auth_plcy_get_effective( )** routine.)

Files

/usr/include/dce/policy.idl The **idl** file from which **dce/policy.h** was derived.

Errors

sec_rgy_not_authorized The user is not authorized to perform this operation.

sec_rgy_object_not_found The registry server could not find the specified organization.

error_status_ok The call was successful.

Related Information

Functions: **intro(3sec)**, **sec_rgy_plcy_get_effective(3sec)**, **sec_rgy_plcy_get_info(3sec)**.

sec_rgy_properties_get_info

Purpose

Returns registry properties

Synopsis

#include <dce/policy.h>

void sec_rgy_properties_get_info(
sec_rgy_handle_t *context*,
sec_rgy_properties_t **properties*,
error_status_t **status*);

Parameters

Input

context — A pointer to an opaque handle bound to a registry server. Use **sec_rgy_site_open( )** to acquire a bound handle.

Output

properties — A pointer to a **sec_rgy_properties_t** structure to receive the returned property information. A registry's property information contains information such as the default and minimum lifetime and other restrictions on privilege attribute certificates, the realm authentication name, and whether or not this replica of the registry supports updates.

status — A pointer to the completion status. On successful completion, the routine returns **error_status_ok**. Otherwise, it returns an error.

Description

The **sec_rgy_properties_get_info( )** routine returns a list of the registry properties.

The property information consists of the following:

read_version — A stamp specifying the earliest version of the registry server software that can read from this registry.

write_version — A stamp specifying the earliest version of the registry server software that can write to this registry.

minimum_ticket_lifetime
The minimum period of time for which an authentication ticket remains valid.

default_certificate_lifetime
The default period of time for which an authentication certificate (ticket-granting ticket) remains valid. A process can request an authentication certificate with a longer lifetime. Note that the maximum lifetime for an authentication certificate cannot exceed the lifetime established by the effective policy for the requesting account.

low_unix_id_person
The lowest UNIX ID that can be assigned to a person in the registry.

low_unix_id_group
The lowest UNIX ID that can be assigned to a group in the registry.

low_unix_id_org
The lowest UNIX ID that can be assigned to an organization in the registry.

max_unix_id The maximum UNIX ID that can be used for any item in the registry.

realm A character string naming the cell controlled by this registry.

realm_uuid The UUID of the cell controlled by this registry.

flags Flags indicating whether

sec_rgy_prop_readonly If TRUE, the registry database is read-only.

sec_rgy_prop_auth_cert_unbound
If TRUE, privilege attribute certificates can be generated for use at any site.

sec_rgy_prop_shadow_password
: If FALSE, passwords can be distributed over the network. If this flag is TRUE, passwords will be stripped from the returned data to the **sec_rgy_acct_lookup( )**, and other calls that return an account's encoded password.

sec_rgy_prop_embedded_unix_id
: All registry UUIDs contain embedded UNIX IDs. This implies that the UNIX ID of any registry object cannot be changed, since UUIDs are immutable.

Permissions Required

The **sec_rgy_properties_get_info( )** routine requires the **r** (**read**) permission on the policy object from which the property information is to be returned.

Files

/usr/include/dce/policy.idl — The **idl** file from which **dce/policy.h** was derived.

Errors

error_status_ok — The call was successful.

Related Information

Functions: **intro(3sec)**, **sec_rgy_properties_set_info(3sec)**.

sec_rgy_properties_set_info

Purpose Sets registry properties

Synopsis **#include <dce/policy.h>**

void sec_rgy_properties_set_info(
sec_rgy_handle_t *context*,
sec_rgy_properties_t **properties*,
error_status_t **status*);

Parameters

Input

context The registry server handle. A pointer to an opaque handle bound to a registry server. Use **sec_rgy_site_open( )** to acquire a bound handle.

properties A pointer to a **sec_rgy_properties_t** structure containing the registry property information to be set. A registry's property information contains information such as the default and minimum lifetime and other restrictions on privilege attribute certificates, the realm authentication name, and whether or not this replica of the registry supports updates.

Output

status A pointer to the completion status. On successful completion, the routine returns **error_status_ok**. Otherwise, it returns an error.

Description

The **sec_rgy_properties_set_info( )** routine sets the registry properties.

The property information consists of the following:

read_version A stamp specifying the earliest version of the registry server software that can read from this registry.

write_version A stamp specifying the earliest version of the registry server software that can write to this registry.

minimum_ticket_lifetime
The minimum period of time for which an authentication ticket remains valid.

default_certificate_lifetime
The default period of time for which an authentication certificate (ticket-granting ticket) remains valid. A process can request an authentication certificate with a longer lifetime. Note that the maximum lifetime for an authentication certificate cannot exceed the lifetime established by the effective policy for the requesting account.

low_unix_id_person
The lowest UNIX ID that can be assigned to a person in the registry.

low_unix_id_group
The lowest UNIX ID that can be assigned to a group in the registry.

low_unix_id_org
The lowest UNIX ID that can be assigned to an organization in the registry.

max_unix_id The maximum UNIX ID that can be used for any item in the registry.

realm A character string naming the cell controlled by this registry.

realm_uuid The UUID of the cell controlled by this registry.

flags Flags indicating whether

sec_rgy_prop_readonly If TRUE, the registry database is read-only.

sec_rgy_prop_auth_cert_unbound
If TRUE, privilege attribute certificates can be generated for use at any site.

sec_rgy_prop_shadow_password
If FALSE, passwords can be distributed over the network. If this flag is TRUE, passwords will be stripped from the returned data to the **sec_rgy_acct_lookup( )**, and other calls that return an account's encoded password.

sec_rgy_prop_embedded_unix_id
All registry UUIDs contain embedded UNIX IDs. This implies that the UNIX ID of any registry object cannot be changed, since UUIDs are immutable.

Permissions Required

The **sec_rgy_properties_set_info( )** routine requires the **m** (**mgmt_info**) permission on the policy object for which the property information is to be set.

Files

/usr/include/dce/policy.idl The **idl** file from which **dce/policy.h** was derived.

Errors

sec_rgy_not_authorized The user is not authorized to change the registry properties.

error_status_ok The call was successful.

Related Information

Functions: **intro(3sec)**, **sec_rgy_properties_get_info(3sec)**.

sec_rgy_site_bind

Purpose Binds to a registry site

Synopsis **#include <dce/binding.h>**

void sec_rgy_site_bind(
 unsigned_char_t **site_name*,
 sec_rgy_bind_auth_info_t **auth_info*,
 sec_rgy_handle_t **context*,
 error_status_t **status*);

Parameters

Input

site_name A character string (type **unsigned_char_t**) containing the name of the registry site to bind to. Upon return, this site is associated with *context*, the registry server handle. If the specified name is in any way incomplete, or if it refers to a registry item (rather than the registry itself), the routine tries to complete the pathname, or call **sec_id_parse_name**( ). In this case, upon return, the *site_name* parameter will contain the proper name.

auth_info A pointer to the **sec_rgy_bind_auth_info_t** structure that identifies the authentication protocol, protection level, and authorization protocol to use in establishing the binding. (See the **rpc_binding_set_auth_info**( ) routine).

Output

context A pointer to a **sec_rgy_handle_t** variable. Upon return, this contains a registry server handle indicating (''bound to'') the desired registry site.

status A pointer to the completion status. On successful completion, the routine returns **error_status_ok**. Otherwise, it returns an error.

Description

The **sec_rgy_site_bind( )** routine establishes a relationship with a registry site at an arbitrary level of security. The *site_name* parameter identifies the registry to use. If *site_name* is **NULL**, or a zero-length string, a registry site is selected by the client agent.

Files

/usr/include/dce/binding.idl The **idl** file from which **dce/binding.h** was derived.

Errors

error_status_ok The call was successful.

Related Information

Functions: **intro(3sec)**, **sec_rgy_site_open(3sec)** **sec_rgy_cell_bind(3sec)**.

sec_rgy_site_bind_query

Purpose Binds to a registry query site

Synopsis **#include <dce/binding.h>**

void sec_rgy_site_bind_query(
  unsigned_char_t **site_name*,
  sec_rgy_bind_auth_info_t **auth_info*,
  sec_rgy_handle_t **context*,
  error_status_t **status*);

Parameters

Input

site_name A character string (type **unsigned_char_t**) containing the name of the registry site to bind to. Upon return, this site is associated with *context*, the registry server handle. If the specified name is in any way incomplete, or if it refers to a registry item (rather than the registry itself), the routine tries to complete the pathname, or call **sec_id_parse_name**( ). In this case, upon return, the *site_name* parameter will contain the proper name.

auth_info A pointer to the **sec_rgy_bind_auth_info_t** structure that identifies the authentication protocol, protection level, and authorization protocol to use in establishing the binding. (See the **rpc_binding_set_auth_info**( ) routine).

Output

context A pointer to a **sec_rgy_handle_t** variable. Upon return, this contains a registry server handle indicating (''bound to'') the desired registry site.

status A pointer to the completion status. On successful completion, the routine returns **error_status_ok**. Otherwise, it returns an error.

Description

The **sec_rgy_site_bind_query**( ) routine establishes a relationship with a registry query site at an arbitrary level of security. The *site_name* parameter identifies the registry to use. If *site_name* is **NULL**, or a zero-length string, a registry site is selected by the client agent.

Files

/usr/include/dce/binding.idl The **idl** file from which **dce/binding.h** was derived.

Errors

error_status_ok The call was successful.

Related Information

Functions: **intro(3sec)**, **sec_rgy_site_open(3sec)**, **sec_rgy_site_bind(3sec)**.

sec_rgy_site_bind_update

Purpose Binds to a registry update site

Synopsis **#include <dce/binding.h>**

void sec_rgy_site_bind_update(
    unsigned_char_t **site_name*,
    sec_rgy_bind_auth_info_t **auth_info*,
    sec_rgy_handle_t **context*,
    error_status_t **status*);

Parameters

Input

site_name A character string (type **unsigned_char_t**) containing the name of the registry site to bind to. Upon return, this site is associated with *context*, the registry server handle. If the specified name is in any way incomplete, or if it refers to a registry item (rather than the registry itself), the routine tries to complete the pathname, or call **sec_id_parse_name**( ). In this case, upon return, the *site_name* parameter will contain the proper name.

auth_info A pointer to the **sec_rgy_bind_auth_info_t** structure that identifies the authentication protocol, protection level, and authorization protocol to use in establishing the binding. (See the **rpc_binding_set_auth_info**( ) routine).

Output

context A pointer to a **sec_rgy_handle_t** variable. Upon return, this contains a registry server handle indicating (''bound to'') the desired registry site.

status A pointer to the completion status. On successful completion, the routine returns **error_status_ok**. Otherwise, it returns an error.

Description

The **sec_rgy_site_bind_update**( ) routine establishes a relationship with a master registry site at an arbitrary level of security. The *site_name* parameter identifies the registry site to use. If *site_name* is **NULL**, or a zero-length string, a registry site is selected by the client agent.

Files

/usr/include/dce/binding.idl The **idl** file from which **dce/binding.h** was derived.

Errors

error_status_ok The call was successful.

Related Information

Functions: **intro(3sec)**, **sec_rgy_site_open(3sec)**, **sec_rgy_site_bind(3sec)**, **sec_rgy_site_open(3sec)**.

sec_rgy_site_binding_get_info

Purpose Returns information from the registry binding handle

Synopsis **#include <dce/binding.h>**

void sec_rgy_site_binding_get_info(
sec_rgy_handle_t *context*,
unsigned_char_t *******cell_name*,
unsigned_char_t *******server_name*,
unsigned_char_t *******string_binding*,
sec_rgy_bind_auth_info_t **auth_info*,
error_status_t **status*);

Parameters

Input

context A pointer to a **sec_rgy_handle_t** variable that contains a registry server handle indicating (''bound to'') the desired registry site.

Output

cell_name The name of the home cell for this registry.

server_name The name of the node on which the server is resident.

string_binding A string containing binding information from **sec_rgy_handle_t**.

auth_info A pointer to the **sec_rgy_bind_auth_info_t** structure that identifies the authentication protocol, protection level, and authorization protocol to use in establishing the binding. (See the **rpc_binding_set_auth_info( )** routine).

status A pointer to the completion status. On successful completion, the routine returns **error_status_ok**. Otherwise, it returns an error.

Description

The **sec_rgy_site_binding_get_info( )** routine returns the site name and authentication information associated with the *context* parameter. If the context is the default context, the information for the default binding is returned. Passing in a **NULL** value for any of the output values (except for *status*) will prevent that value from being returned.

Files

/usr/include/dce/binding.idl The **idl** file from which **dce/binding.h** was derived.

Errors

error_status_ok The call was successful.

Related Information

Functions: **intro(3sec)**, **sec_rgy_site_open(3sec)**, **sec_rgy_site_bind(3sec)**.

sec_rgy_site_close

Purpose Frees the binding handle for a registry server

Synopsis **#include <dce/binding.h>**

void sec_rgy_site_close(
sec_rgy_handle_t *context*,
error_status_t **status*);

Parameters

Input

context A pointer to an opaque handle indicating (''bound to'') a registry server. Use **sec_rgy_site_open**( ) to acquire a bound handle.

Output

status A pointer to the completion status. On successful completion, the routine returns **error_status_ok**. Otherwise, it returns an error.

Description

The **sec_rgy_site_close**( ) routine frees the memory occupied by the specified handle and destroys its binding with the registry server.

Notes A handle cannot be used after it is freed.

Files **/usr/include/dce/binding.idl** The **idl** file from which **dce/binding.h** was derived.

Errors

sec_rgy_server_unavailable The requested registry server is not available.

error_status_ok The call was successful.

Related Information

Functions: **intro(3sec)**, **sec_rgy_site_get(3sec)**, **sec_rgy_site_is_readonly(3sec)**, **sec_rgy_site_open(3sec)**, **sec_rgy_site_open_query(3sec)**, **sec_rgy_site_open_update(3sec)**.

sec_rgy_site_get

Purpose Returns the string representation for a bound registry site

Synopsis **#include <dce/binding.h>**

void sec_rgy_site_get(
sec_rgy_handle_t *context*,
unsigned_char_t *******site_name*,
error_status_t **status*);

Parameters

Input

context A pointer to an opaque handle indicating (''bound to'') a registry server. Use **sec_rgy_site_open( )** to acquire a bound handle.

Output

site_name A pointer to a character string (type **unsigned_char_t**) containing the returned name of the registry site associated with *context*, the given registry server handle.

status A pointer to the completion status. On successful completion, the routine returns **error_status_ok**. Otherwise, it returns an error.

Description

The **sec_rgy_site_get( )** routine returns the name of the registry site associated with the specified handle. If the handle is the default handle (as supplied by the **sec_rgy_site_open( )** routine), the routine returns the name of the default site.

Files **/usr/include/dce/binding.idl** The **idl** file from which **dce/binding.h** was derived.

Errors

sec_rgy_server_unavailable	The requested registry server is not available.
error_status_ok	The call was successful.

Related Information

Functions: **intro(3sec)**, **sec_rgy_site_open(3sec)**.

sec_rgy_site_is_readonly

Purpose Checks whether a registry site is read-only

Synopsis **#include <dce/binding.h>**

boolean32 sec_rgy_site_is_readonly(
sec_rgy_handle_t *context***);**

Parameters

Input

context A pointer to an opaque handle indicating (''bound to'') a registry server. Use **sec_rgy_site_open( )** to acquire a bound handle.

Description

The **sec_rgy_site_is_readonly( )** routine checks whether the registry site associated with the specified handle is a query site or an update site. A query site is a read-only replica of a master registry database. The update site accepts changes to the registry database, and duplicates the changes in its associated query sites.

Return Values

The routine returns TRUE if the registry site is read-only and FALSE if it is an update site.

Files **/usr/include/dce/binding.idl** The **idl** file from which **dce/binding.h** was derived.

Related Information

Functions: **intro(3sec)**, **sec_rgy_site_open(3sec)**, **sec_rgy_site_open_query(3sec)**.

sec_rgy_site_open

Purpose Binds to a registry site

Synopsis **#include <dce/binding.h>**

void sec_rgy_site_open(
    unsigned_char_t **site_name*,
    sec_rgy_handle_t **context*,
    error_status_t **status*);

Parameters

Input/Output

site_name A pointer to a character string (type **unsigned_char_t**) containing the name of the registry site to bind to. Upon return, this site is associated with *context*, the registry server handle. If the specified name is in any way incomplete, or if it refers to a registry item (rather than the registry itself), the routine tries to complete the pathname, or call **sec_id_parse_name( )**. In this case, upon return, the *site_name* parameter will contain the proper name.

Output

context A pointer to a **sec_rgy_handle_t** variable. Upon return, this contains a registry server handle indicating (''bound to'') the desired registry site.

status A pointer to the completion status. On successful completion, the routine returns **error_status_ok**. Otherwise, it returns an error.

Description

The **sec_rgy_site_open( )** routine binds an RPC handle to the registry server at the indicated site. The returned handle is for use in subsequent calls that communicate with the registry server.

If *site_name* is a zero-length string, the client agent supplies a default. If *site_name* is a partial *site_name*, the client agent supplies the complete name. In either case, the routine returns the site name actually used.

Notes

If the input *site_name* is blank, causing **sec_rgy_site_open( )** to choose a registry site to bind to, there is no way to control whether it is a query or an update registry site. Use **sec_rgy_site_open_query( )** or **sec_rgy_site_open_update( )** to control which sort of registry server to bind to.

Currently, the routine returns only a bound-to-host handle. Fully bound handles are not implemented yet.

Files

/usr/include/dce/binding.idl The **idl** file from which **dce/binding.h** was derived.

Errors

sec_rgy_server_unavailable The requested registry server is not available.

error_status_ok The call was successful.

Related Information

Functions: **intro(3sec)**, **sec_rgy_site_close(3sec)**, **sec_rgy_site_is_readonly(3sec)**, **sec_rgy_site_open_query(3sec)**, **sec_rgy_site_open_update(3sec)**.

sec_rgy_site_open_query

Purpose Binds to a registry query site

Synopsis **#include <dce/binding.h>**

void sec_rgy_site_open_query(
  unsigned_char_t **site_name*,
  sec_rgy_handle_t **context*,
  error_status_t **status*);

Parameters

Output

site_name A pointer to a character string (type **unsigned_char_t**) containing the returned name of the registry query site associated with *context*, the returned registry server handle.

context A pointer to a **sec_rgy_handle_t** variable. Upon return, this contains a registry server handle indicating (''bound to'') the desired registry site.

status A pointer to the completion status. On successful completion, the routine returns **error_status_ok**. Otherwise, it returns an error.

Description

The **sec_rgy_site_open_query( )** routine binds to a registry query site. A registry query site is a satellite server that operates on a periodically updated copy of the main registry database. To change the registry database, it is necessary to change a registry update site, which then automatically updates its associated query sites. No changes can be made directly to a registry query database.

The name of the bound site is returned in *site_name*. The handle for the associated registry server is returned in *context*. The handle is only for use in subsequent calls that query the registry database. Use of this registry context handle with calls that change the registry database (for example, the **sec_rgy_pgo_add( )** and **sec_rgy_acct_delete( )** calls) returns a **sec_rgy_read_only** error.

Files

/usr/include/dce/binding.idl The **idl** file from which **dce/binding.h** was derived.

Errors

error_status_ok The call was successful.

Related Information

Functions: **intro(3sec)**, **sec_rgy_site_close(3sec)**, **sec_rgy_site_get(3sec)**, **sec_rgy_site_is_readonly(3sec)**, **sec_rgy_site_open(3sec)**, **sec_rgy_site_open_update(3sec)**.

sec_rgy_site_open_update

Purpose Binds to a registry update site

Synopsis **#include <dce/binding.h>**

void sec_rgy_site_open_update(
    unsigned_char_t **site_name*,
    sec_rgy_handle_t **context*,
    error_status_t **status*);

Parameters

Output

site_name A pointer to a character string (type **unsigned_char_t**) containing the returned name of the registry site associated with *context*, the given registry server handle.

context A pointer to a **sec_rgy_handle_t** variable. Upon return, this contains a registry server handle indicating (''bound to'') the desired registry site.

status A pointer to the completion status. On successful completion, the routine returns **error_status_ok**. Otherwise, it returns an error.

Description

The **sec_rgy_site_open_update**( ) routine binds to a registry update site. A registry update site is a master server that may control several satellite (query) servers. To change the registry database, it is necessary to change a registry update site, which then automatically updates its associated query sites. No changes can be made directly to a registry query database.

The name of the bound site is returned in *site_name*. The handle for the associated registry server is returned in *context*. The handle is for use in subsequent calls that update or query the registry database. Use this registry context handle with calls that change the registry database (for example, the **sec_rgy_pgo_add**( ) and **sec_rgy_acct_delete**( ) calls).

Files

/usr/include/dce/binding.idl The **idl** file from which **dce/binding.h** was derived.

Errors

error_status_ok The call was successful.

Related Information

Functions: **intro(3sec)**, **sec_rgy_site_close(3sec)**, **sec_rgy_site_get(3sec)**, **sec_rgy_site_is_readonly(3sec)**, **sec_rgy_site_open(3sec)**, **sec_rgy_site_open_query(3sec)**.

sec_rgy_unix_getgrgid

Purpose Returns a UNIX style group entry for the account matching the specified group ID

Synopsis **#include <dce/rgynbase.h>**

void sec_rgy_unix_getgrent(
sec_rgy_handle_t *context*,
signed32 *gid*,
signed32 *max_number*,
sec_rgy_cursor_t **item_cursor*,
sec_rgy_unix_group_t **group_entry*,
signed32 **number_members*,
sec_rgy_member_t *member_list*[ ],
error_status_t **status*);

Parameters

Input

context A pointer to an opaque handle bound to a registry server. Use **sec_rgy_site_open( )** to acquire a bound handle.

gid A 32-bit integer specifying the group ID to match.

max_number The maximum number of members to be returned by the call. This must be no larger than the allocated size of the *member_list*[ ] array.

Input/Output

item_cursor An opaque pointer indicating a specific PGO item entry in the registry database. The **sec_rgy_pgo_get_next( )** routine returns the PGO item indicated by *item_cursor*, and advances the cursor to point to the next item in the database. When the end of the list of entries is reached, the routine returns **sec_rgy_nomore_entries**. Use **sec_rgy_cursor_reset( )** to refresh the cursor.

Output

group_entry A UNIX style group entry structure returned with information about the account matching *gid*.

number_members
An signed 32-bit integer containing the total number of member names returned in the *member_list*[ ] array.

member_list[ ] An array of character strings to receive the returned member names. The size allocated for the array is given by *max_number*. If this value is less than the total number of members in the membership list, multiple calls must be made to return all of the members.

status On successful completion, the routine returns **error_status_ok**. Otherwise, it returns an error.

Description

The **sec_rgy_unix_getgrgid( )** routine returns the next UNIX group structure that matches the input UNIX group ID. The structure is in the following form:

```
typedef struct {
  sec_rgy_name_t          name;
  signed32            gid;
  sec_rgy_member_buf_t      members;
}      sec_rgy_unix_group_t;
```

The structure includes

- The name of the group.
- The group's UNIX ID.
- A string containing the names of the group members. This string is limited in size by the size of the **sec_rgy_member_buf_t** type defined in **rgynbase.idl**.

The routine also returns an array of member names, limited in size by the *number_members* parameter.

This call is supplied in source code form.

Files

/usr/include/dce/rgynbase.idl The **idl** file from which **dce/rgybase.h** was derived.

Errors

error_status_ok The call was successful.

sec_rgy_nomore_entries The end of the list of entries has been reached.

Related Information

Functions: **intro(3sec)**.

sec_rgy_unix_getgrnam

Purpose Returns a UNIX style group entry for the account matching the specified group name

Synopsis **#include <dce/rgynbase.h>**

void sec_rgy_unix_getgrnam(
  sec_rgy_handle_t *context*,
  sec_rgy_name_t *name*,
  signed32 *name_length*,
  signed32 *max_num_members*,
  sec_rgy_cursor_t *item_cursor*,
  sec_rgy_group_t *group_entry*,
  signed32 *number_members*,
  sec_rgy_member_t *member_list*[ ],
  error_status_t **status*);

Parameters

Input

context A pointer to an opaque handle bound to a registry server. Use **sec_rgy_site_open( )** to acquire a bound handle.

name A character string (of type **sec_rgy_name_t**) specifying the group name to be matched.

name_length An signed 32-bit integer specifying the length of *name* in characters.

max_num_members
The maximum number of members to be returned by the call. This must be no larger than the allocated size of the *member_list*[ ] array.

Input/Output

item_cursor An opaque pointer indicating a specific PGO item entry in the registry database. The **sec_rgy_pgo_get_next( )** routine returns the PGO item indicated by *item_cursor*, and advances the cursor to point to the next item in the database. When the end of the list of entries is reached, the routine returns

sec_rgy_nomore_entries. Use **sec_rgy_cursor_reset( )** to refresh the cursor.

Output

group_entry A UNIX style group entry structure returned with information about the account matching *name*.

number_members
An signed 32-bit integer containing the total number of member names returned in the *member_list*[ ] array.

member_list[ ] An array of character strings to receive the returned member names. The size allocated for the array is given by *max_number*. If this value is less than the total number of members in the membership list, multiple calls must be made to return all of the members.

status On successful completion, the routine returns **error_status_ok**. Otherwise, it returns an error.

Description

The **sec_rgy_unix_getgrnam**( ) routine looks up the next group entry in the registry that matches the input group name and returns the corresponding UNIX style group structure. The structure is in the following form:

```
typedef struct {
  sec_rgy_name_t          name;
  signed32                gid;
  sec_rgy_member_buf_t    members;
}           sec_rgy_unix_group_t;
```

The structure includes

- The name of the group.
- The group's UNIX ID.
- A string containing the names of the group members. This string is limited in size by the size of the **sec_rgy_member_buf_t** type defined in **rgynbase.idl**.

The routine also returns an array of member names, limited in size by the *number_members* parameter.

This call is provided in source code form.

Files

/usr/include/dce/rgynbase.idl The **idl** file from which **dce/rgybase.h** was derived.

Errors

sec_rgy bad_data The name supplied as input was too long.

error_status_ok The call was successful.

sec_rgy_nomore_entries The end of the list of entries has been reached.

Related Information

Functions: **intro(3sec)**.

sec_rgy_unix_getpwuid

Purpose Returns a UNIX style **passwd** entry for the account matching the specified UID

Synopsis **#include <dce/rgynbase.h>**

void sec_rgy_unix_getpwuid(
sec_rgy_handle_t *context*,
signed32 *uid*,
sec_rgy_cursor_t **item_cursor*,
sec_rgy_unix_passwd_t **passwd_entry*,
error_status_t **status*);

Parameters

Input

context A pointer to an opaque handle bound to a registry server. Use **sec_rgy_site_open( )** to acquire a bound handle.

uid A 32-bit integer UNIX ID.

Input/Output

item_cursor An opaque pointer indicating a specific PGO item entry in the registry database. The **sec_rgy_pgo_get_next( )** routine returns the PGO item indicated by *item_cursor*, and advances the cursor to point to the next item in the database. When the end of the list of entries is reached, the routine returns **sec_rgy_nomore_entries**. Use **sec_rgy_cursor_reset( )** to refresh the cursor.

Output

passwd_entry A UNIX style password structure returned with information about the account matching *uid*.

status On successful completion, the routine returns **error_status_ok**. Otherwise, it returns an error.

Description

The **sec_rgy_unix_getpwuid**( ) routine looks up the next **passwd** entry in the registry that matches the input UNIX ID and returns the corresponding **sec_rgy_passwd** structure. The structure is in the following form:

```
typedef struct {
    sec_rgy_unix_login_name_t  name;
    sec_rgy_unix_passwd_buf_t  passwd;
    signed32                   Vuid;
    signed32                   Vgid;
    signed32                   oid;
    sec_rgy_unix_gecos_t       gecos;
    sec_rgy_pname_t            homedir;
    sec_rgy_pname_t            shell;
}       sec_rgy_unix_passwd_t;
```

The structure includes

- The account's login name.
- The account's password.
- The account's UNIX ID.
- The UNIX ID of group and organization associated with the account.
- The account's GECOS information.
- The account's home directory.
- The account's login shell

Files

/usr/include/dce/rgynbase.idl The **idl** file from which **dce/rgynbase.h** was derived.

This call is provided in source code form.

Errors

error_status_ok The call was successful.

sec_rgy_nomore_entries The end of the list of entries has been reached.

Related Information

Functions: **intro(3sec)**.

sec_rgy_wait_until_consistent

Purpose Blocks updates while propagating prior updates to registry replicas

Synopsis **#include <dce/misc.h>**

boolean32 sec_rgy_wait_until_consistent(
sec_rgy_handle_t *context*,
error_status_t **status***);**

Parameters

Input

context The registry server handle associated with the master registry.

Output

status A pointer to the completion status. On successful completion, the routine returns **error_status_ok**. Otherwise, it returns an error.

Description

The **sec_rgy_wait_until_consistent( )** routine blocks updates to the master registry until all prior updates have been propagated to all active registry replicas.

Return Values

The routine returns TRUE when all replicas have received the prior updates. It returns FALSE if at least one replica did not receive the updates.

Files **/usr/include/dce/misc.idl** The **idl** file from which **dce/misc.h** was derived.

Errors

sec_rgy_server_unavailable	The server for the master registry is not available.
sec_rgy_read_only	Either the master site is in maintenance mode or the site associated with the handle is a read-only (query) site.
error_status_ok	The call was successful.

Related Information

Functions: **intro(3sec)**.

Chapter 6

DCE Distributed File Service

intro

Purpose

Introduction to the DFS Cache Manager

Libraries

The **afs_syscall( )**, **ioctl( )**, and **pioctl( )** calls are defined in the library **libdcedfs.a**.

Description

The DFS Cache Manager runs on client machines, and maintains a copy of data that has been obtained from the server in the recent past. If the file or information requested is already present in the cache, no remote call is necessary. If the information requested by the application is not already present in the cache, the Cache Manager makes calls to the File Exporter on the appropriate file server to retrieve that information, and stores it.

DFS provides calls to manipulate the Cache Manager. There are three classes of calls. First, there are changes to the **ioctl( )** call to add DFS functionality. Second, there is a new call, **pioctl( )**, which is like **ioctl( )** in most respects. The **pioctl( )** call uses pathnames instead of file descriptors, and specifically implements Cache Manager operations. Third, there is a new call, **afs_syscall( )**, to handle Access Control Lists.

Related Information

Functions: **intro(3dfs), afs_syscall(2dfs), ioctl(2dfs), pioctl(2dfs)**.

afs_syscall

Purpose Sets, changes, or modifies the Access Control List on a file or directory

Synopsis **#include<dce/syscall.h>**
#include<dce/aclint.h>

int afs_syscall(
  int AFSCALL_VNODE_OPS,
  int VNX_OPCODE_GETACL,
  char ***pathname*,**
  char ***acl*,**
  int ***length*,**
  int *whichacl*)

int afs_syscall(
  int AFSCALL_VNODE_OPS,
  int VNX_OPCODE_SETACL,
  char ***pathname*,**
  char ***acl*,**
  int *length*,
  int *whichacl*)

int afs_syscall(
  int AFSCALL_VNODE_OPS,
  int VNX_OPCODE_COPYACL,
  char ***dest_pathname*,**
  char ***source_pathname*,**
  int *dest_whichacl*
  int *source_whichacl*)

Parameters

Input

pathname The file or directory affected.

whichacl Specifies which of three ACLs to set on a directory.

dest_pathname The target file or directory for the ACL.

source_pathname The file or directory whose ACL is to be copied.

dest_whichacl The ACL to set in the destination object.

source_whichacl The ACL to use from the source object.

Input/Output

acl The ACL (see the following for the format).

length The length of *acl*.

Description

The **afs_syscall**( ) system call gets, sets, and copies DFS ACLs. A directory can have up to three ACLs, as follows:

VNX_ACL_REGULAR_ACL
The directory itself.

VNX_ACL_INITIAL_ACL The files created in the directory.

VNX_ACL_DEFAULT_ACL The directories created in the directory.

A file can have only one ACL. The *whichacl* parameter determines which of these ACLs is affected; for files, use **VNX_ACL_REGULAR_ACL**. For the **VNX_OPCODE_COPYACL** call, *dest_whichacl* specifies the ACL to set in the destination file, and *source_whichacl* specifies which ACL in the source to copy.

The *pathname, dest_pathname,* and *source_pathname* parameters are all full pathnames for the file or directory to be affected. *acl* is the ACL string, and its length is *length*.

The ACL is a character array with the following components:

- The manager type, the length of a **uuid_t**. For DFS ACLs this is always **episodeAclMgmtUuid**.
- The default realm UUID, the length of a **uuid_t**.
- The number of ACL entries, the length of a 32-bit unsigned integer.
- For each ACL entry, the following components:

    — The permission bits, represented by 4 bytes.

    — The entry type, represented by 4 bytes.

    — Type-dependent information.

The permission bits are represented as a mask of the desired values from the following list:

- **sec_acl_perm_read**
- **sec_acl_perm_write**
- **sec_acl_perm_execute**
- **sec_acl_perm_control**
- **sec_acl_perm_insert**
- **sec_acl_perm_delete**

The entry type is one of the following:

- **sec_acl_e_type_user_obj**
- **sec_acl_e_type_group_obj**
- **sec_acl_e_type_other_obj**
- **sec_acl_e_type_user**
- **sec_acl_e_type_group**
- **sec_acl_e_type_mask_obj**
- **sec_acl_e_type_foreign_user**
- **sec_acl_e_type_foreign_group**
- **sec_acl_e_type_foreign_other**
- **sec_acl_e_type_unauthenticated**
- **sec_acl_e_type_extended**
- **sec_acl_e_type_any_other**

The last items in an ACL entry depend on the type of the entry. If the type is **sec_acl_e_type_user**, **sec_acl_e_type_group**, or **sec_acl_e_type_foreign_other**, then the remaining data is a UUID of the length of a **uuid_t**.

If the type is **sec_acl_e_type_foreign_user** or **sec_acl_e_type_foreign_group**, then the remaining data is a UUID indicating the ID of the foreign user or group (length of a **uuid_t**), followed by a UUID indicating the realm of the foreign user or group (length of a **uuid_t**).

If the type is **sec_acl_e_type_extended**, then the data is the following, in the order shown:

- Extension type UUID (**uuid_t**)
- Format label, consisting of the following:
  - — Integer byte order (**short int**)
  - — Character format (**short int**)
  - — Floating-point format (**short int**)
  - — Reserved bytes (**char**)
- The number of bytes of data following (unsigned 32-bit integer)
- The data
- Whatever padding is necessary to get to a 4-byte boundary

For more information about the various components of an ACL, see the *OSF DCE Application Development Guide*, and Chapter 5 of this manual.

Errors

The following are possible values for **errno**:

[**EPERM**] Calling process doesn't own the specified entry.

[**ENOTDIR**] Specified entry is not a directory.

[**ENOENT**] No such file or directory was found.

[**EACCES**] Permission was denied.

[**EROFS**] The entry specifies a read-only file system.

[**EMFILE**] Too many files are open.

[**ENXIO**] A nonexistent pathname was specified.

[**EFAULT**] A bad pathname was specified.

[**ELOOP**] The pathname involves too many levels of symbolic links.

[**EINVAL**] Bad syscall number or ACL cannot be validated.

[**EIO**] File is not exported, or error in storing ACL.

[**ERANGE**] ACL does not fit into an 8188-byte buffer.

[ESPIPE] ACL is malformed and ordinary permission bits cannot be determined.

[ENOMEM] Out of memory.

[EDQUOT] Fileset full; cannot write ACL.

[ENOSPC] Aggregate full; cannot write ACL.

[ENOSYS] File is not exported, or is an exported AIX file.

[EFBIG] ACL is too large for file system.

Related Information

Functions: **syscall(2)**.

Books: *OSF DCE Application Development Guide*.

ioctl

Purpose

Executes a call on a file descriptor

Synopsis

#include <dce/ioctl.h>

long ioctl(
int *des*,
int *request*,
struct blob *******arg*)

Parameters

Input

des The file descriptor.

request The call to execute.

Input/Output

arg A data structure representing the input and output parameters (see **ioctl(2)**).

Description

The **ioctl**( ) call is a standard (BSD) UNIX call. DFS extends it in the following way:

The **VIOCIGETCELL**( ) call gets the cell name associated with an open descriptor, *des*. If the file is not in the DCE Distributed File Service, this call returns an error ([**ENOTTY**]). Otherwise, it returns one output parameter, a **NULL**-terminated string that is the name of the cell containing the file associated with *des*. This is the recommended method of determining whether a file is stored in the DCE File System.

Errors

The following are possible values for **errno**:

[**EFAULT**] Outside address space, or not enough room for result.

[**ENOTTY**] No cell associated with file.

[**EINVAL**] Bad ioctl request.

Related Information

Functions: **intro(2dfs), ioctl(2)**.

pioctl

Purpose

Executes a call on a pathname

Synopsis

#include <dce/ioctl.h>

long pioctl(
  char **pathname*,
  int *command*,
  struct afs_ioctl **arg*,
  int *follow_links*)

Parameters

Input

pathname The pathname for any file or directory affected by this call.

command The specific **pioctl( )** call to invoke.

follow_links Specifies whether to follow symbolic links in paths.

Input/Output

arg The data to be passed to and from the call.

Description

The **pioctl( )** system call is very similar to the **ioctl( )** system call, with two exceptions. First, the relevant file is passed via a pathname (rather than a file descriptor) as the first parameter. Second, there is a fourth parameter, which determines what file is used if the file specified is a symbolic link. If this parameter is 1, the symbolic link is followed to its destination and **pioctl( )** is applied to that destination file. If the parameter is 0 (zero), **pioctl( )** is applied to the symbolic link itself. Note that this fourth parameter only applies to a symbolic link if it is the last component of the pathname; links encountered in intermediate components are always followed.

All **pioctl( )** calls take a single input for the third parameter, but sometimes more than one piece of information needs to be passed in. This is handled by passing in a single chunk of data that is ''dissected'' by **pioctl( )**. For instance, **VIOCCKSERV( )** takes a **long** followed by a **sockaddr**; the way to provide this is to provide a pointer to a section of memory that contains the **long** followed immediately by the **sockaddr**. The **pioctl()** call knows how much of the memory contains each object.

For those calls that do not affect a file, supply a pathname of **NULL**. For those calls that do not take an input parameter, use **NULL**.

All calls either return 0 (zero) to indicate the call was successful, or return -1 and set **errno** to an error flag.

The data is passed via the **afs_ioctl** structure, defined as follows:

```
struct afs_ioctl {
        char * in, out;     /* Data to be transferred in, or out */
        short in_size;      /* Size of in buffer (<= AFSIO_BUFSIZE) */
        short out_size;     /* Max size of out buffer (<= AFSIO_BUFSIZE) */
}
```

The rest of this reference page describes the specific **pioctl()** calls.

In the following descriptions, **Path** indicates what the path argument (the first argument) to **pioctl()** represents, if anything. **In** is a description of the contents of the input buffer, and **Out** describes the output buffer. **Access** describes the access needed to make the call to **pioctl()**.

VIOCACCESS() - Requests access to a file or directory

Path: Identifies a file
In: **long** *access_bits*
Out: None
Access: ACL controlled

The input describes the kind of access desired (read, write, and so on). It is a **long**, and is a mask of the following values:

- **sec_acl_perm_read**
- **sec_acl_perm_write**
- **sec_acl_perm_execute**
- **sec_acl_perm_owner**
- **sec_acl_perm_insert**
- **sec_acl_perm_delete**

These are DFS ACLs, not UNIX protection bits; UNIX protection bits do not work correctly with DFS. Eight user-defined bits (a through h) are also reserved for applications. This call fails if any of the accesses requested for the file or directory is denied.

VIOC_AFS_DELETE_MT_PT( ) - Removes the mount point

Path: Identifies a directory in which the mount point exists
In: **char** *mtPtName*[ ]
Out: None
Access: ACL controlled

The input is a string giving the name of a file (the pathname is that file's directory). This call removes the mount point for the input file.

VIOC_AFS_STAT_MT_PT( ) - Gets the mount object status

Path: Identifies a directory in which the mount point exists
In: **char** *mtPtName*[ ]
Out: **char** *mtPtTarget*[ ]
Access: ACL controlled

This call returns information about the mount object. The output is the type of mount point (a character), an optional colon-terminated name of a cell, and the name of the fileset to be mounted at this point in the tree (a string). If no cell is specified, the fileset is presumed to reside in the cell in which the mount point resides. The name can optionally be given as the ASCII representation of the fileset's number. The type character can be **#** (number sign), **%** (percent sign), or **!** (exclamation point), described as follows:

- A type of **#** tells the file system to use the latest read-only fileset corresponding to the named fileset, if the mount point is part of a read-only file system. Otherwise, the mount point functions as a mount point to the named fileset.

- A type of **%** indicates that the read/write version of the named fileset is to be mounted at this point.

- A type of **!** indicates a mount point for the global namespace; such mount points are used mainly for diskless support.

The mount point string is not **NULL**-terminated.

The input is a name, as in **VIOC_AFS_DELETE_MT_PT( )**.

VIOC_AFS_SYSNAME( ) - Sets the **@sys** string

Path: Ignored
In: **long** *setFlag*, **char** *newName*[ ]
Out: **long** *foundName*, **char** *oldName*[ ]
Access: Superuser to set

This call sets the string that the **@sys** variable expands to. If *setFlag* is 0 (zero), a 1 is returned in *foundName* and the old **@sys** name is returned as *oldName*. If *setFlag* is nonzero, *newName* is set as the new **@sys** name and the old name is not returned.

VIOC_CLOCK_MGMT( ) - Reads or sets clock management

Path: Ignored
In: Data block (see the description)
Out: Data block (see the description)
Access: Open to read, superuser to set

This **pioctl( )** call controls the Cache Manager's setting of the machine's local clock. It also fetches and stores kernel values that describe the clock's accuracy. The Cache Manager has an optional feature, typically used only on client-only machines, by which it sets the machine's clock based on the time as set on a local file server machine. This feature is initialized with **dfsd** and is controllable with this **pioctl( )** call.

The data block is formatted the same for reading and setting. Some values may be read and written; others may only be read. The entries in this data block follow:

- **long** *clock_style* - This currently must be 0 (zero).
- **long** *read_or_write* - This is 0 (zero) to read values, nonzero to set values.
- **long** *CM_clockset* - This may be read and written. It is 1 if the Cache Manager sets the local clock based on File Exporter calls, and 0 (zero) if not.
- **struct afsTimeval** *currTime* - This may only be read. It is the time when the call is made.
- **long** *synchDistance* - This may be read and written. It is the clock accuracy parameter.
- **long** *synchDispersion* - This may be read and written. It is the clock accuracy parameter.
- **struct afsNetAddr** *last_set_addr* - This may only be read. It is the address of the Fileset Server from which the time has been set.
- **struct afsTimeval** *last_set_time* - This may only be read. It is the time to which the Cache Manager last set the machine's clock.
- **long** *residue* - This may only be read. It is the number of seconds fast that the Cache Manager's last clock-set operation left the

clock, because it did not want to back the clock up more than a few seconds at once.

VIOCCKBACK( ) - Flushes the fileset name and ID mappings

Path: Ignored
In: None
Out: None
Access: Open

This call flushes the mappings between fileset names and IDs, and between the ID of the read/write fileset and its read-only (replicated) copies, if any. Normally this flushing is done once an hour. The call has no input or output.

VIOCCKSERV( ) - Checks for functioning servers

Path: Ignored
In: **long** *flagword,* [optional] **char** *cellName*[ ] (**NULL**-terminated)
Out: **long** *returnCode,* **struct sockaddr** *serverAddresses*[ ]
Access: Open

This call optionally checks a set of servers for reachability. It returns the addresses of the servers that are considered ''down.'' If there is text following the input *flagword*, it is viewed as the name of a cell whose servers are to be reported, after the optional check. If the name does not correspond to an already known cell, -1 is returned as the *returnCode*, and no *serverAddresses* are returned. If there is no text after the input *flagword*, and bit 2 (0x2) is set in the input *flagword*, the servers corresponding to the ''local'' cell are considered. Otherwise, all servers known to the Cache Manager are considered.

If bit 1 (0x1) is clear in *flagword*, the set of servers is actually checked (by trying a trivial RPC call). If bit 1 (0x1) is set in *flagword*, no immediate check is done.

The servers from the indicated set (named cell, local cell, all servers) are then scanned, and all servers that are currently marked as ''down'' have their network addresses passed out as the set of *serverAddresses*[ ]. In this case, 0 (zero) is returned as the value of *returnCode*.

The last item in the list of *serverAddresses*[ ] has its **sa_family** field set to **AF_UNSPEC**.

VIOC_EXPORTAFS - Exports DFS to NFS clients

Path: Ignored
In: **long** *handleValue*
Out: **long** *exportedFlag*
Access: Superuser to set, open to read

The high-order 8 bits of *handleValue* define an exporter type, and thus define a File Exporter, or the call fails with **errno** set to [**ENODEV**]. The next 8 bits of *handleValue* define the *changeState* flag. The low 8 bits of *handleValue* define the *export* flag.

If the *changeState* flag is 0 (zero), the call returns 1 (in *exportedFlag*) if the identified File Exporter is set to export files, or it returns 0 (in *exportedFlag*) if this is disabled for the identified exporter. If *changeState* is nonzero, the identified file exporter is enabled to, or disabled from, exporting files depending on whether the *export* flag is nonzero or zero, respectively.

VIOC_FILE_CELL_NAME( ) - Gets the cell for *pathname*

Path: Identifies a file
In: None
Out: **char** *cellName*[ ]
Access: ACL controlled

This call takes no input. Its output is the name of the cell that the file (given as the *pathname* argument to the **pioctl( )** call) is part of (a string).

VIOCFLUSH( ) - Flushes the cache entry

Path: Identifies a file to flush
In: None
Out: None
Access: Open

This call flushes the cache entry for the pathname; the next time the pathname is accessed, the server is queried. It has no input or output parameters.

VIOC_FLUSHVOLUME( ) - Flushes all cached data for a fileset

Path: Identifies a file (really a fileset in which a file is located)
In: None
Out: None
Access: Open

This call flushes all cached data for a fileset, but not any of the other cached information.

VIOCGETCACHEPARMS( ) - Gets the size of the local cache

Path: Ignored
In: None
Out: **long** *words***[16]**
Access: Open

This call returns status information from the Cache Manager. *words***[0]** is set to the number of 1024-byte units that the Cache Manager is permitted to use. *words***[1]** is set to the number of 1024-byte units that the Cache Manager is currently using. Bit 1 (0x1) of *words***[2]** is set to 1 if the cache is in memory (the Cache Manager is running without a disk cache); otherwise, it is set to 0 (zero).

VIOCGETCELL( ) - Lists the cell configuration

Path: Ignored
In: **long** *index*
Out: **long** *count,* **struct sockaddr** *serverAddresses*[*count*], **char** *cellName*[ ]
Access: Open

This call returns information about the *index*th cell that the Cache Manager understands, starting with a value of 0 (zero). Call this **pioctl( )** repeatedly with larger *index* values, until -1 is returned and **[EDOM]** is placed in **errno**.

The returned data is a count of Fileset Location Server addresses, the addresses of the Fileset Location Servers, and the **NULL**-terminated text name of the cell.

VIOC_GETCELLSTATUS( ) - Gets information about cell status

Path: Ignored
In: **char** *cellName*[ ]
Out: **long** *cellStates*
Access: Open

This cell returns the **states** field in the cell structure for the cell whose name is given as an input parameter. The only defined state bit at present is bit 1 (0x1), which is set if and only if the cell is the local one.

VIOCGETFID( ) - Gets the file handle for the file or directory

Path: Identifies a file
In: None
Out: **struct afsFid** *fileFid*
Access: ACL controlled

This call takes no inputs. The output is the file handle associated with the file or directory. It contains the cell ID, fileset ID, file slot number, and a uniquifier. The structure is internal to DFS.

VIOCGETREQUEST( ) - Announces that a process is ready to receive calls

Path: Ignored
In: None
Out: **long** *count,* **char** *outBytes*[*count*]
Access: Superuser

Because not everything can be stored in the kernel, the kernel needs to be able to make calls to functions in user space. This could be used to call DCE components that are not kernel resident, for example.

This **pioctl( )** call is issued by a process in user space to announce to the kernel that it is ready to receive calls to be executed by the local helper process. When the kernel is ready to issue such a call, the request is returned in *outBytes*.

The **pioctl( )** calls, **VIOCGETREQUEST( )** and **VIOCSENDRESPONSE( )**, are typically used in the following way. A user process announces its availability by issuing a call to **VIOCGET-REQUEST( )**. This process then waits until the kernel returns from the call. (The kernel itself, of course, does not hang.) When the call returns, the output buffer contains a request to take some action. The process takes this action and then calls **VIOCSENDRESPONSE( )** with the result. The process may then call **VIOCGETREQUEST( )** again and wait for the next request.

VIOCGETVOLSTAT( ) - Gets status information about a fileset

Path: Identifies a file (really a fileset in which a file is located)
In: None
Out: **long** *status*
Access: Open

The low-order bit, **VIOC_DEF_SGIDOK**, if set, means that executions of the set-group-ID and set-user-ID files will set the group and user ID fields for the executed process (the **setgid** and **setuid** bits will be honored). If this bit is off, neither group nor user IDs will be altered in the executing process, and the **setgid** and **setuid** bits will be masked away. The second bit, **VIOC_DEF_DEVOK**, if set, means that special device files will be honored when found in a fileset with this bit on.

VIOC_GET_WS_CELL( ) - Gets a cell for a workstation

Path: Ignored
In: None
Out: **char** *cellName*[ ]
Access: Open

This call takes no input. Its output is the cell name with which the current workstation is associated.

VIOCLISTSTORES( ) - Lists files waiting to be written

Path: Ignored
In: None
Out: **long** *fileCount*, **long** *hyperCount*, **struct afsHyper** *fsIds*[*hyperCount*]
Access: Open

This call produces information about the files waiting to be written that are being blocked by quota problems (see the **VIOCRESETSTORES( )** call). *fileCount* is the number of files awaiting store-back. *hyperCount* is the number of fileset IDs, and *fsIds* are the IDs of the filesets for which stores have been queued.

VIOCPREFETCH( ) - Prefetches a file

Path: Identifies a file to prefetch
In: None
Out: None
Access: ACL controlled

This call prefetches a file into the cache. This allows the programmer some control over when the delay caused by fetching a file occurs. (Prefetching, for example, could be done while the application is busy with other things, improving perceived response time.)

VIOCRESETSTORES( ) - Stops trying file stores

Path: Ignored
In: None
Out: None
Access: Open

If a fileset is over quota when a file write is attempted, the Cache Manager keeps trying the write about once a minute. **VIOCRESETSTORES( )** tells the Cache Manager to give up on all of these delayed write-backs.

VIOCSENDRESPONSE( ) - Makes a call to a helper function in user space

Path: Ignored
In: **char** *inBytes*[ ]
Out: None
Access: Superuser

This call sends a response back to the kernel as a result of a kernel request (made by way of the **VIOCGETREQUEST( )** call). (See the description of **VIOCGETREQUEST( )** for more information.)

VIOCSETCACHESIZE( ) - Changes cache size

Path: Ignored
In: **long int** *numUnits*
Out: None
Access: Superuser only, and only if not diskless

The input is a **long int** (4 bytes) indicating the number of 1024-byte units to use for the cache. This call sets the cache to that size. There is no output.

VIOC_SETCELLSTATUS( ) - Sets status information for a cell

Path: Ignored
In: **long** *newStates*, **long** *spare*, **char** *cellName*[ ]
Out: None
Access: Superuser

The input is the name of a cell (a string) and a **long** representing some status bits (as described under the **VIOC_GETCELLSTATUS( )** call). The call sets the cell to have that status.

VIOCSETVOLSTAT( ) - Sets status information about a fileset

Path: Identifies a file (really a fileset in which a file is located)
In: **long** *status*
Out: None
Access: Superuser

The *pathname* parameter is the fileset in question. This call sets the bits described previously under **VIOCGETVOLSTAT( )**.

VIOCWHEREIS( ) - Finds addresses of servers containing fileset

Path: Identifies a file (really a fileset in which a file is located)
In: None
Out: **long** *numSockaddrs,*
struct sockaddr *serverAddresses*[*numSockaddrs*],
char *filesetName*[ ]
Access: Open

The fileset on which the pathnamed file is located is identified by this call. The output buffer is filled with a long integer representing the number of **sockaddr** structures to follow, that number of **sockaddr** structures on which the fileset is located, and finally the **NULL**-terminated name of the fileset.

This call is used to find all the places where replicated copies of the fileset are being kept.

Errors

The following are possible values for **errno**:

[**EPERM**] Calling process doesn't own the specified entry. Typically, this error is encountered if the calling process doesn't have *root* privileges.

[**ENOTDIR**] Specified entry is not a directory.

[**ENOENT**] No such file or directory was found.

[**EACCES**] Permission was denied.

[**EROFS**] The entry specifies a read-only file system.

[**EMFILE**] Too many files are open.

[**ENXIO**] A nonexistent pathname was specified.

[**EFAULT**] A bad pathname was specified.

[**ELOOP**] The pathname involves too many levels of symbolic links.

[**EINVAL**] Bad **pioctl** number.

[**E2BIG**] Result too large for buffer.

[**ENODEV**] **VIOCWHEREIS**( ) can't find volume for **fdesc**.

[**EDOM**] Parameter to **VIOCGETCELL**( ) is past known number of cells.

[**ESRCH**] **VIOC_FILE_CELL_NAME**( ) can't find cell for file.

[**EWOULDBLOCK**] **VIOCPREFETCH**( ) can't get a background thread immediately.

In addition, several calls make server RPCs and return **errno** values based on their RPC results.

Related Information

Functions: **intro(2dfs), ioctl(2dfs)**.

intro

Purpose

Introduction to the Distributed File Service

Libraries

All **BOSSVR**( ), **FTSERVER**( ), **VC**( ), and **VL**( ) functions are defined in the library **libdcedfs.a**.

Description

Each node, or system, in a DFS installation is either a file server machine, maintaining local file systems on disk and exporting them to other nodes, or a client, running applications that access files that are exported by servers. (A client node can also act as a server if it exports a local file system.) The DFS functions described in this section are for use by those client applications.

The DFS function sets are as follows:

- **VC**( ) (Volume Call): These functions perform operations on filesets. When appropriate, the FLDB (Fileset Location Database) is automatically updated. These functions are implemented on top of the **FTSERVER**( ) and **VL**( ) functions.
- **VL**( ) (Fileset Location Server interface): These functions examine and modify the FLDB, which maintains information about all filesets in the cell.
- **FTSERVER**( ) (Fileset Server interface): These functions perform basic operations on filesets, such as creating, deleting, moving, and replicating them. Operations are carried out within transactions.
- **BOSSVR**( ): These functions perform the basic process monitoring and system software installation operations used for maintaining the DFS file server machines.

In addition to these functions, DFS provides system calls to manipulate the Cache Manager. (See the **intro(2dfs)** reference page).

Related Information

Functions: **BOSSVR(3dfs), intro(2dfs), FTSERVER(3dfs), VC(3dfs), VL(3dfs)**.

BOSSVR

Purpose Introduction to file server monitoring functions

Synopsis **#include <dce/bbos_ncs_interface.h>**
#include <dce/rpc.h>

Libraries All **BOSSVR**( ) functions are defined in the library **libdcedfs.a**.

Description

The **BOSSVR**( ) (BOS Server interface) functions provide the basic process monitoring and system software installation tools used for maintaining the DFS file server machines. The functions fall into several categories.

- Process Monitoring: Monitoring processes and restarting them on failure.
- Server Key Maintenance: Maintaining the set of authentication keys used by the various DFS servers.
- Binary Maintenance: Installing new binaries on the server machines and scheduling server restarts to pick up the newly installed binaries.
- Authorization: Ensuring that only authorized users reconfigure the servers. Authentication of these users is handled by the DCE authentication system.

Process Monitoring

Processes that are run under the BOS Server are specified by the term ''bnodes.'' The process monitoring routines create, delete, and alter these processes and start and stop the BOS Server. Bnodes have types, and for each type of bnode, the BOS Server has embedded code defining how those processes are managed. There are two types of bnodes: **simple** bnodes and **cron** bnodes.

All bnodes are parameterizable at bnode creation time. Bnode parameters are character strings, and each type of bnode has its own specific set of parameters.

A **simple** bnode manages a single process, and manages it with a simple goal: to keep the process running. If a process managed by a **simple** bnode crashes, it is restarted, and any resulting core file is saved for future reference. If the process restarts too often in a given period, the bnode instance is marked as damaged and is shut down pending an operator's intervention. Most bnode instances in a file server installation are **simple** bnodes.

A **simple** bnode has only one parameter, the command string to be used to start the process. The command string is parsed by the BOS Server itself, and thus cannot contain the usual shell-provided expansions (such as those containing asterisks), but otherwise resembles a typical UNIX command. This command is reexecuted whenever the process needs to be restarted.

A **cron** bnode manages a single process that is to be run either once-only or periodically. Essentially, this is a generalization of the **simple** bnode that runs a process, but leaves it shut down after it exits until the next time that the process is scheduled to be executed. After a process's last scheduled execution (assuming that it *has* a last execution), a **cron** bnode deletes itself; this generally only occurs with once-only bnodes.

A **cron** bnode has two parameters. The first is the command to be used to start the process to be managed, and the second is a string that can be parsed as a periodically recurring date, giving the times that the process should be run.

The date format is one of the following (all are strings):

- **never**
- **now**
- A day of the week and a time (in 24-hour notation), separated by spaces, such as **wed 16:00**.
  Such processes run once per week. The day must come first and be in lowercase. Use either the entire day name or the first three letters.
- A time, in 24-hour notation. The process runs once per day.

Server Key Maintenance

The server key maintenance functions maintain the authentication keys used by DFS servers. More information about server keys can be found in the Security chapters of the *OSF DCE Application Development Guide*.

Binary Maintenance

There are several functions for installing system binaries and recovering to earlier versions when necessary.

Authorization

There are functions to maintain DFS server administration lists.

Structures

A number of functions in this section return strings in the **bossvr_out_string** structure. This structure is defined as follows:

```
struct bossvr_out_string {
        unsigned long strLen;
        char *theString;
}
```

Related Information

Functions: **intro(3dfs)**.

Books: *OSF DCE Applications Development Guide*.

BOSSVR_AddKey

Purpose

Adds a new server key to the database

Synopsis

long BOSSVR_AddKey(
handle_t *bosserverBinding,*
char *prinName*[*BOSSVR_BSSIZE*]**,**
long *kvno,*
char *passwdP*[*BOSSVR_BSSIZE*]**,**
long *localOnly***,**
error_status_t **theCommStatus***)**

Parameters

Input

bosserverBinding The RPC handle.

prinName The principal name.

kvno The key's DCE key version number.

passwdP The password to use.

localOnly A flag indicating whether to only update the local keyfile (the value is 1) or to both update the local keyfile and notify the Registry Server (the value is 0).

Output

theCommStatus An RPC error is returned, if an error occurred.

Description

BOSSVR_AddKey() adds a new key to the DFS server key database. The principal is specified by *prinName*, the key data by *passwdP*, and the key's DCE key version number by *kvno*. The recorded key modification time is set to the current time. If *localOnly* is nonzero, the BOS Server only updates the local keyfile on the BOS Server's machine. If its value is 0 (zero), the BOS Server calls a security routine that updates not only the local keyfile but also the Registry Server.

The caller must be on the BOS Server's administration list to execute this routine.

Errors

BZACCESS The user is not authorized to perform this operation.

BZ_ERROR_INTERNAL_ERROR
An unexpected internal error occurred; check the BOS Server log.

BZ_SEC_KEY_MGMT_ERROR
An error from an underlying DCE key management system occurred; check the BOS Server log.

Related Information

Functions: **BOSSVR_DeleteKey(3dfs), BOSSVR_GarbageCollectKeys(3dfs), BOSSVR_GenerateKey(3dfs), BOSSVR_ListKeys(3dfs)**.

BOSSVR_AddSUser

Purpose Adds a user to the named administration list

Synopsis
long BOSSVR_AddSUser(
handle_t *bosserverBinding*,
char *filename*[*BOSSVR_BSSIZE*],
char *typeStr*[*BOSSVR_BSSIZE*],
char *name*[*BOSSVR_BSSIZE*],
char *permsStr*[*BOSSVR_BSSIZE*],
long *createFile*,
error_status_t **theCommStatus*)

Parameters

Input

bosserverBinding The RPC handle.

filename The administration list to update.

typeStr The type of user: **user**, **group**, **foreign_user**, **foreign_group**, or **foreign_other**.

name The user's or group's DCE Registry identity.

permsStr Reserved for future use.

createFile Specifies whether to create *filename* if it does not exist; 0 (zero) means do not create, and any other value means create.

Output

theCommStatus An RPC error is returned, if an error occurred.

Description

BOSSVR_AddSUser( ) adds a user to the superuser list contained in file *filename*. If *filename* contains any **/** (slash) characters, it is used as an absolute pathname. Otherwise, the pathname *dcelocal***/var/dfs/** is prepended to the name and the resultant filename is used as the name of the file containing the user list.

The user's or group's DCE Registry identity is passed in as the *name* parameter. The *typeStr* parameter must be one of **user**, **group**, or **foreign_user**,

foreign_group, **foreign_other**, as appropriate. The *permsStr* parameter is for future expansion and is currently ignored.

The caller must be on the BOS Server's administration list to execute this routine.

Errors

BZ_ILLEGAL_ENTRY_TYPE
The string given as *typeStr* is not a legal user list entry type.

BZACCESS The user is not authorized to perform this operation.

BZEXISTS The user is already on the administration list.

BZ_ERROR_INTERNAL_ERROR
An unexpected internal error occurred; check the BOS Server log.

BZ_SEC_RGY_PGO_ERROR
The DCE Security Registry reported an unexpected error.

Related Information

Functions: **BOSSVR_DeleteSUser(3dfs), BOSSVR_ListSUsers(3dfs)**.

BOSSVR_CreateBnode

Purpose Creates a new process bnode instance

Synopsis **long BOSSVR_CreateBnode(**
handle_t *bosserverBindin*,
char *type*[*BOSSVR_BSSIZE*],
char *instance*[*BOSSVR_BSSIZE*],
char *p1*[*BOSSVR_BSSIZE*],
char *p2*[*BOSSVR_BSSIZE*],
char *p3*[*BOSSVR_BSSIZE*],
char *p4*[*BOSSVR_BSSIZE*],
char *p5*[*BOSSVR_BSSIZE*],
char *p6*[*BOSSVR_BSSIZE*],
error_status_t **theCommStatus*)

Parameters

Input

bosserverBinding The RPC handle.

type The bnode type, **simple** or **cron**.

instance The name of the bnode instance.

p1, p2, p3, p4, p5, p6 The parameters to be used in bnode creation.

Output

theCommStatus An RPC error is returned, if an error occurred.

Description

BOSSVR_CreateBnode() creates a new bnode instance on the server, representing a new process to be run. The instance name is specified by the *instance* parameter, and is used by various commands to name the process after its creation; it must be unique on the server. The *type* parameter gives the type of the process, and must be one of **simple** or **cron**. The remaining parameters are type-specific strings. Generally, they name the program to be run by this bnode instance, among other things.

The largest number of parameters for a bnode is currently 2; 6 strings are provided for future expansion. Pass "" (the empty string) for the unused parameters.

The caller must be on the BOS Server's administration list to execute this routine.

Errors

BZEXISTS A bnode with this name already exists.

BZBADTYPE The type specified for this bnode is not one of the known bnode types.

BZACCESS The user is not authorized to perform this operation.

BZNOCREATE
Some other failure occurred while creating the bnode.

BZ_ERROR_INTERNAL_ERROR
An unexpected internal error occurred; check the BOS Server log.

Related Information

Functions: **BOSSVR_DeleteBnode(3dfs), BOSSVR_EnumerateInstance(3dfs), BOSSVR_GetInstanceInfo(3dfs), BOSSVR_GetInstanceParm(3dfs)**.

BOSSVR_DeleteBnode

Purpose

Deletes a bnode instance

Synopsis

long BOSSVR_DeleteBnode(
handle_t *bosserverBinding*,
char *instance*[*BOSSVR_BSSIZE*],
error_status_t **theCommStatus*)

Parameters

Input

bosserverBinding The RPC handle.

instance The name of the instance to delete.

Output

theCommStatus An RPC error is returned, if an error occurred.

Description

BOSSVR_DeleteBnode( ) deletes the named bnode from the server. The process associated with the bnode must not be running when this call is made, or the call fails with the code **BZBUSY**.

The caller must be on the BOS Server's administration list to execute this routine.

Errors

BZBUSY The server is running the instance at present.

BZACCESS The user is not authorized to perform this operation.

BZNOENT The named instance does not exist.

BZ_ERROR_INTERNAL_ERROR
An unexpected internal error occurred; check the BOS Server log.

Related Information

Functions: **BOSSVR_CreateBnode(3dfs)**, **BOSSVR_EnumerateInstance(3dfs)**, **BOSSVR_GetInstanceInfo(3dfs)**, **BOSSVR_GetInstanceParm(3dfs)**.

BOSSVR_DeleteKey

Purpose Deletes the named server key

Synopsis **long BOSSVR_DeleteKey(**
handle_t *bosserverBinding***,**
char *prinName*[*BOSSVR_BSSIZE*]**,**
long *kvno***,**
error_status_t **theCommStatus***)**

Parameters

Input

bosserverBinding The RPC handle.

prinName The principal name.

kvno The key version number.

Output

theCommStatus An RPC error is returned, if an error occurred.

Description

BOSSVR_DeleteKey( ) removes the key with key version number *kvno* for principal *prinName* from the DFS key database on the server.

The caller must be on the BOS Server's administration list to execute this routine.

Errors

BZACCESS The user is not authorized to perform this operation.

BZ_ERROR_INTERNAL_ERROR
An unexpected internal error occurred; check the BOS Server log.

BZ_SEC_KEY_MGMT_ERROR
An error from an underlying DCE key management system occurred; check the BOS Server log.

Related Information

Functions: **BOSSVR_AddKey(3dfs)**, **BOSSVR_ListKeys(3dfs)**, **BOSSVR_GarbageCollectKeys(3dfs)**, **BOSSVR_GenerateKey(3dfs)**.

BOSSVR_DeleteSUser

Purpose Deletes a user from the named administration list

Synopsis **long BOSSVR_DeleteSUser(**
handle_t *bosserverBinding*,
char *filename*[*BOSSVR_BSSIZE*],
char *typeStr*[*BOSSVR_BSSIZE*],
char *name*[*BOSSVR_BSSIZE*],
long *removeFile*,
error_status_t **theCommStatus*)

Parameters

Input

bosserverBinding The RPC handle.

filename The administration list.

typeStr The entry type.

name The user's DCE Registry identity.

removeFile If *name* is the last entry in *filename*, *removeFile* specifies whether to delete the file; 0 (zero) means not to delete the file.

Output

theCommStatus An RPC error is returned, if an error occurred.

Description

BOSSVR_DeleteSUser( ) removes a user from the administration list in file *filename*. (See the **BOSSVR_AddSUser( )** reference page for a description of filename interpretation.) The user's DCE Registry identity is passed as the *name* parameter. The *typeStr* string must match the user list entry type in order for the deletion to be performed.

This change takes effect immediately.

The caller must be on the BOS Server's administration list to execute this routine.

Errors

BZACCESS The user is not authorized to perform this operation.

BZNOENT The user is not on the administration list.

BZ_ERROR_INTERNAL_ERROR
An unexpected internal error occurred; check the BOS Server log.

BZIO An I/O error occurred within the BOS Server.

BZ_ERROR_UNKNOWN_USER_OR_GROUP
The user or group name was not recognized by the DCE Security Registry.

BZ_ADMIN_FILE_NOT_FOUND
The named administration list file was not found.

BZ_SEC_RGY_PGO_ERROR
The DCE Security Registry reported an unexpected error.

Related Information

Functions: **BOSSVR_AddSUser(3dfs), BOSSVR_ListSUsers(3dfs)**.

BOSSVR_EnumerateInstance

Purpose Enumerates all bnode instances on a server

Synopsis **long BOSSVR_EnumerateInstance(**
handle_t *bosserverBinding*,
long *instanceNum*,
bossvr_out_string **result*,
error_status_t **theCommStatus*)

Parameters

Input

bosserverBinding The RPC handle.

instanceNum The iterator value.

Output

result The returned instance.

theCommStatus An RPC error is returned, if an error occurred.

Description

BOSSVR_EnumerateInstance( ) is used to enumerate all of the bnode instances on a server. To enumerate all instances, call this function with *instanceNum* values starting at 0 (zero) and increasing by 1 on each call until the error code **BZDOM** is returned. On each call, the function returns the name of the instance specified by *instanceNum* in the *result* parameter.

No authorization is required to execute this routine.

Errors **BZDOM** There are no more bnode instances to list.

BZ_ERROR_INTERNAL_ERROR
An unexpected internal error occurred; check the BOS Server log.

Related Information

Functions: **BOSSVR_CreateBnode(3dfs), BOSSVR_DeleteBnode(3dfs), BOSSVR_GetInstanceInfo(3dfs), BOSSVR_GetInstanceParm(3dfs)**.

BOSSVR_Exec

Purpose Executes a command from the BOS Server

Synopsis

long BOSSVR_Exec(
handle_t *bosserverBinding*,
char *cmd*[*BOSSVR_BSSIZE*],
error_status_t **theCommStatus*)

Parameters

Input

bosserverBinding The RPC handle.

cmd The shell command to be executed.

Output

theCommStatus An RPC error is returned, if an error occurred.

Description

BOSSVR_Exec( ) takes one parameter, a string representing a shell command to be executed in a subprocess of the **bosserver** process. The call returns after executing the program and the program exits. Any output produced by the command is discarded. The command or program runs as root.

The caller must be on the BOS Server's administration list to execute this routine.

Errors

BZACCESS The user is not authorized to perform this operation.

BZ_ERROR_INTERNAL_ERROR
An unexpected internal error occurred; check the BOS Server log.

BZNOTACTIVE
The execution of the command or routine or call returned some error.

BOSSVR_GarbageCollectKeys

Purpose Gets rid of obsolete keys

Synopsis **long BOSSVR_GarbageCollectKeys(**
handle_t *bosserverBinding*,
char *prinName*[*BOSSVR_BSSIZE*],
error_status_t **theCommStatus*)

Parameters

Input

bosserverBinding The RPC handle.

prinName The principal name for which obsolete keys are to be removed.

Output

theCommStatus An RPC error is returned, if an error occurred.

Description

BOSSVR_GarbageCollectKeys( ) removes obsolete keys for the named principal in the local key file. Obsolete keys are any that are no longer being used by the server.

The caller must be on the BOS Server's administration list to execute this routine.

Errors

BZACCESS The user is not authorized to perform this operation.

BZ_ERROR_INTERNAL_ERROR
An unexpected internal error occurred; check the BOS Server log.

BZ_SEC_KEY_MGMT_ERROR
An error from an underlying DCE key management system occurred; check the BOS Server log.

Related Information

Functions: **BOSSVR_AddKey(3dfs), BOSSVR_DeleteKey(3dfs), BOSSVR_GenerateKey(3dfs), BOSSVR_ListKeys(3dfs)**.

BOSSVR_GenerateKey

Purpose

Generates and adds a key to the server key database

Synopsis

long BOSSVR_GenerateKey(
handle_t *bosserverBinding***,**
char *prinName*[*BOSSVR_BSSIZE*]**,**
long *kvno***,**
error_status_t **theCommStatus***)**

Parameters

Input

bosserverBinding The RPC handle.

prinName The principal name.

kvno The key version number.

Output

theCommStatus An RPC error is returned, if an error occurred.

Description

BOSSVR_GenerateKey( ) is like **BOSSVR_AddKey( )**, except that it randomly generates a key to put into the local database, and it contacts the Registry Server to install the new, random key in the Registry Server's database.

The caller must be on the BOS Server's administration list to execute this routine.

Errors

BZACCESS The user is not authorized to perform this operation.

BZ_ERROR_INTERNAL_ERROR
An unexpected internal error occurred; check the BOS Server log.

BZ_SEC_KEY_MGMT_ERROR
An error from an underlying DCE key management system occurred; check the BOS Server log.

Related Information

Functions: **BOSSVR_AddKey(3dfs)**, **BOSSVR_DeleteKey(3dfs)**, **BOSSVR_GarbageCollectKeys(3dfs)**, **BOSSVR_ListKeys(3dfs)**.

BOSSVR_GetCellName

Purpose Gets the server's cell name

Synopsis

long BOSSVR_GetCellName(
handle_t *bosserverBinding*,
bossvr_out_string **name*,
error_status_t **theCommStatus*)

Parameters

Input

bosserverBinding The RPC handle.

Output

name The cell name.

theCommStatus An RPC error is returned, if an error occurred.

Description

BOSSVR_CetCellName( ) returns the server's cell name (a string) in the *name* parameter.

No authorization is required to execute this routine.

Errors

BZIO The routine failed to open the **config** file.

BZ_NOMEM An internal memory allocation error occurred.

BZNOENT No cell name was specified in the local configuration file.

BZ_ERROR_INTERNAL_ERROR
An unexpected internal error occurred; check the BOS Server log.

All standard locking error codes also apply.

BOSSVR_GetDates

Purpose Gets the modification times of a program and its backups

Synopsis

long BOSSVR_GetDates(
handle_t *bosserverBinding***,**
char *path*[*BOSSVR_BSSIZE*]**,**
long **newtime***,**
long **baktime***,**
long **oldtime***,**
error_status_t **theCommStatus*)

Parameters

Input

bosserverBinding The RPC handle.

path The pathname for the program to check.

Output

newtime The modification time for the program.

baktime The modification time for the backup version (**.BAK**).

oldtime The modification time for the previous version (**.OLD**).

theCommStatus An RPC error is returned, if an error occurred.

Description

BOSSVR_GetDates(**) returns the modification time of a program and its backup files, if any exist. It returns the UNIX modification times for the program, its backup file (*filename*.BAK**), and its previous version file (*filename***.OLD**), or 0 (zero) for those files that do not exist.

No authorization is required to execute this routine.

Errors

BZ_ERROR_INTERNAL_ERROR
An unexpected internal error occurred; check the BOS Server log.

BOSSVR_GetInstanceInfo

Purpose Gets a basic bnode instance description

Synopsis **long BOSSVR_GetInstanceInfo(**
handle_t *bosserverBinding*,
char *instance[BOSSVR_BSSIZE]*,
bossvr_out_string **type*,
struct bossvr_status **status*
error_status_t **theCommStatus*)

Parameters

Input

bosserverBinding The RPC handle.

instance The name of the bnode instance.

Output

type The type of the named instance.

status The status of the named instance.

theCommStatus An RPC error is returned, if an error occurred.

Description

BOSSVR_GetInstanceInfo( ) returns the type (as a character string) and current status of the named bnode instance. Status is set by calling **BOSSVR_SetStatus( )**.

The **bossvr_status** structure describes the information recorded for a process monitored by the BOS Server. It is defined as follows:

```
struct bossvr_status{
  long int goal;              /* the short-term goal */
  long int fileGoal;          /* the goal field in file */
  long int procStartTime;     /* last time a process was started */
  long int procStarts;        /* process starts */
  long int lastAnyExit;       /* time process exited, any reason */
  long int lastErrorExit;     /* time process exited unexpectedly */
  long int errorCode;         /* last exit return code */
  long int errorSignal;       /* last proc terminating signal */
```

```
    long int flags;                 /* status flags (see below) */
    unsigned long spare1;
    unsigned long spare2;
    unsigned long spare3;
    unsigned long spare4;
    unsigned long spare5;
    unsigned long spare6;
    unsigned long spare7;
    unsigned long spare8;
};
```

The **goal** field gives the short-term goal (a value of 1 means run this process, a value of 0 (zero) means do not run this process) for the specified process. The **fileGoal** field gives the permanent goal for this collection; this field usually has the same value as the **goal** field. The **procStartTime** field gives the time that the BOS Server last started the process, and the **procStarts** field gives the total number of times the BOS Server has started this process since the BOS Server began running.

The **lastAnyExit** field gives the time that a process exited for any reason, while the **lastErrorExit** field gives the time that a process exited not in response to a request from the BOS Server.

The **errorCode** field gives the exit return code from the last process exit, and, if this return code indicates that the process was terminated due to an uncaught signal, the uncaught signal is provided in **errorSignal**. The **flags** field is one of the following:

```
const BOSSVR_HASCORE = 1;           /* core file exists */
const BOSSVR_ERRORSTOP = 2;         /* stopped due to too many errors */
const BOSSVR_BADDIRACCESS = 4;      /* bad mode bits */
```

No authorization is required to execute this routine.

Errors

BZNOENT The bnode instance specified does not exist.

BZ_ERROR_INTERNAL_ERROR
An unexpected internal error occurred; check the BOS Server log.

Related Information

Functions: **BOSSVR_CreateBnode(3dfs), BOSSVR_DeleteBnode(3dfs), BOSSVR_EnumerateInstance(3dfs), BOSSVR_GetInstanceParm(3dfs)**.

BOSSVR_GetInstanceParm

Purpose Gets the parameters for a bnode instance

Synopsis **long BOSSVR_GetInstanceParm(**
handle_t *bosserverBinding*,
char *instance*[*BOSSVR_BSSIZE*],
long *num*,
bossvr_out_string **parm*,
error_status_t **theCommStatus*)

Parameters

Input

bosserverBinding	The RPC handle.
instance	The name of the bnode instance.
num	Specifies which parameter to return (a zero-based counter).

Output

parm	The returned parameter.
theCommStatus	An RPC error is returned, if an error occurred.

Description

BOSSVR_GetInstanceParm( ) returns a particular parameter from the creation parameters for a particular bnode instance. The parameter *num* is a zero-based counter used to specify which parameter is desired from the *instance* bnode. The desired parameter string is returned in *parm*.

No authorization is required to execute this routine.

Errors

BZDOM There are no more parameters to enumerate.

BZNOENT The specified instance does not exist.

BZ_ERROR_INTERNAL_ERROR
An unexpected internal error occurred; check the BOS Server log.

Related Information

Functions: **BOSSVR_CreateBnode(3dfs), BOSSVR_DeleteBnode(3dfs).**

BOSSVR_GetLog

Purpose Retrieves a text log file

Synopsis **long BOSSVR_GetLog(**
handle_t *bosserverBinding*,
char *name*[*BOSSVR_BSSIZE*],
pipe_t **thePipeP*,
error_status_t **theCommStatus*)

Parameters

Input

bosserverBinding	The RPC handle.
name	The filename of the log.

Output

thePipeP	The contents of the log.
theCommStatus	An RPC error is returned, if an error occurred.

Description

BOSSVR_GetLog( ) returns the contents of a text log file from the server. It takes one input parameter, a filename; the caller must provide a function that handles the output pipe. The **pipe_t** type is defined by DCE RPC.

This function could, in theory, retrieve any ASCII file, but it is usually used to retrieve log files generated by server processes managed by the BOS Server.

If the filename contains the / (slash) character, the caller must be on the BOS Server's administration list to execute this routine. Otherwise, no authorization is required.

Errors

BZACCESS The user is not authorized to perform this operation.

BZNOENT The log file was not found.

BZ_ERROR_INTERNAL_ERROR
An unexpected internal error occurred; check the BOS Server log.

DCE RPC may also generate exceptions during pipe processing; see the documentation of that component for more information.

BOSSVR_GetRestartTime

Purpose Returns the BOS Server restart time

Synopsis **long BOSSVR_GetRestartTime(**
handle_t *bosserverBinding*,
long *type*,
struct bossvr_netKTime **restartTime*,
error_status_t **theCommStatus*)

Parameters

Input

bosserverBinding The RPC handle.

type The type of restart time to get: the value 1 is the whole system, 2 is a periodic new binary check.

Output

restartTime The returned restart time.

theCommStatus An RPC error is returned, if an error occurred.

Description

BOSSVR_GetRestartTime( ) retrieves the specified restart time from the **bosserver** process on a particular host. The desired restart time is specified by the *type* parameter, which has the same values as in the **BOSSVR_SetRestartTime( )** call.

The **bossvr_netKTime** structure is described under **BOSSVR_SetRestartTime( )**.

No authorization is required to execute this routine.

Errors

BZDOM The *type* parameter is out-of-bounds.

BZ_ERROR_INTERNAL_ERROR
An unexpected internal error occurred; check the BOS Server log.

Related Information

Functions: **BOSSVR_SetRestartTime(3dfs)**.

BOSSVR_GetStatus

Purpose

Gets the run status of a bnode instance

Synopsis

long BOSSVR_GetStatus(
handle_t *bosserverBinding*,
char *instance*[*BOSSVR_BSSIZE*],
long **status*,
bossvr_out_string **statdescr*,
error_status_t **theCommStatus*)

Parameters

Input

bosserverBinding The RPC handle.

instance The name of the bnode instance.

Output

status The returned status information.

statdescr The auxiliary status, for **cron** bnodes.

theCommStatus An RPC error is returned, if an error occurred.

Description

BOSSVR_GetStatus( ) returns an integer giving the state of the bnode instance, and an optional string description of the instance, for those cases where the defined integer does not provide a complete description.

The possible values for *status* are **BSTAT_SHUTDOWN**, **BSTAT_NORMAL**, **BSTAT_STARTINGUP** and **BSTAT_SHUTTINGDOWN**. **BSTAT_SHUTDOWN** means that the process is not currently running, while **BSTAT_NORMAL** means that the process is running normally. **BSTAT_SHUTTINGDOWN** means that a signal has been sent to the process, but that it has not yet exited. **BSTAT_STARTINGUP** means that the BOS Server is still starting up the process; this code is almost never seen.

For **cron** bnode instances, *statdescr* is used to provide a description of the process collection's auxiliary status. Processes of type **simple** have no auxiliary status, but *statdescr* should still have a non-**NULL** value.

No authorization is required to execute this routine.

Errors

BZNOENT The specified instance does not exist on the server.

BZ_ERROR_INTERNAL_ERROR
An unexpected internal error occurred; check the BOS Server log.

Related Information

Functions: **BOSSVR_SetStatus(3dfs), BOSSVR_SetTStatus(3dfs)**.

BOSSVR_Install

Purpose Installs a server binary on a server

Synopsis **long BOSSVR_Install(**
handle_t *bosserverBinding*,
char *path*[*BOSSVR_BSSIZE*],
long *size*,
long *flags*,
long *date*,
pipe_t **thePipeP*,
error_status_t **theCommStatus*)

Parameters

Input

bosserverBinding The RPC handle.

path The pathname (on the destination machine) for the server binary to be installed.

size The size of the program in bytes.

flags Reserved for future use.

date The last write date for the file.

thePipeP The contents of the file to be installed.

Output

theCommStatus An RPC error is returned, if an error occurred.

Description

BOSSVR_Install( ) takes a pathname of a program to install, along with the contents, and creates a new instance of the file, creating **.BAK** and **.OLD** files as appropriate. The *size* parameter is used by the server to check the number of bytes read from the pipe parameter, and the *date* parameter is used to stamp the file with a date. The *flags* parameter is reserved for future use, and must be 0 (zero).

The caller must be on the BOS Server's administration list to execute this routine.

Errors

BZINSTALLFAILED
The specified file could not be created.

BZACCESS The user is not authorized to perform this operation.

BZ_ERROR_INTERNAL_ERROR
An unexpected internal error occurred; check the BOS Server log.

Related Information

Functions: **BOSSVR_Prune(3dfs), BOSSVR_UnInstall(3dfs)**.

BOSSVR_ListKeys

Purpose Lists all known server keys

Synopsis

long BOSSVR_ListKeys(
handle_t *bosserverBinding***,**
char *prinName*[*BOSSVR_BSSIZE*]**,**
long *an***,**
long **kvno***,**
struct bossvr_key **key***,**
struct bossvr_keyInfo **keyinfo***,**
error_status_t **theCommStatus***)**

Parameters

Input

bosserverBinding	The RPC handle.
prinName	The principal name.
an	The iterator.

Output

kvno	The key version number.
key	The key.
keyinfo	The auxiliary key information.
theCommStatus	An RPC error is returned, if an error occurred.

Description

BOS_ListKeys( ) returns the key specified by *an* for the principal specified by *prinName*, which has DCE principal key version number *kvno*. The *an* parameter is a zero-based counter that should be incremented by 1 repeatedly until the call fails with the error code **BZDOM** in order to enumerate all of the keys for the named principal in the server key database.

The **bossvr_key** structure defines an encryption key as it is passed to the BOS Server.

```
struct bossvr_key{
    char data[8];
}
```

The **bossvr_keyInfo** structure defines the auxiliary information that is computed for DFS server keys by the BOS Server. In DCE 1.0, the only parts of this structure that are used are the **mod_usec** and **keyCheckSum** fields.

```
struct bossvr_keyInfo{
    long int mod_sec;
    long int mod_usec;
    unsigned long keyCheckSum;
    unsigned long spare1;
    unsigned long spare2;
    unsigned long spare3;
    unsigned long spare4;
}
```

If the BOS Server is running in **NoAuth** mode, the key itself is returned. If not, only the key checksum and modification time are returned.

The caller must be on the BOS Server's administration list to execute this routine.

Errors

BZDOM There are no more keys left to enumerate.

BZACCESS The user is not authorized to perform this operation.

BZ_ERROR_INTERNAL_ERROR
An unexpected internal error occurred; check the BOS Server log.

BZ_SEC_KEY_MGMT_ERROR
An error returned from an underlying DCE key management system occurred; check the BOS Server log.

Related Information

Functions: **BOSSVR_AddKey(3dfs), BOSSVR_DeleteKey(3dfs), BOSSVR_GarbageCollectKeys(3dfs), BOSSVR_GenerateKey(3dfs)**.

BOSSVR_ListSUsers

Purpose Gets the list of all administrative users in the specified list

Synopsis **long BOSSVR_ListSUsers(**
handle_t *bosserverBinding*,
char *filename*[*BOSSVR_BSSIZE*],
long *an*,
bossvr_out_string **nameP*,
bossvr_out_string **typeStrP*,
bossvr_out_string **permStrP*,
error_status_t **theCommStatus*)

Parameters

Input

bosserverBinding The RPC handle.

filename The administration list filename.

an The iterator value.

Output

nameP The name of the user or group in the administration list.

typeStrP The user list entry type.

permStrP Reserved for future use.

theCommStatus An RPC error is returned, if an error occurred.

Description

BOSSVR_ListSUsers( ) returns the DCE Registry name of the *an*th member of the administration list from *filename* in the *nameP* parameter and the type of the user list entry in the *typeStrP* parameter. The first member is obtained by calling this function with an *an* parameter of 0 (zero). To enumerate the entire list, continue incrementing *an* in successive calls until the function returns the error code **BZDOM**.

The *permStrP* parameter is for future expansion and is currently ignored, although it must be non-**NULL**.

For an explanation of filename resolution, see **BOSSVR_AddSUser( )**.

No authorization is required to execute this routine.

Errors

BZDOM There are no more administrative users to enumerate.

BZ_ERROR_INTERNAL_ERROR
An unexpected internal error occurred; check the BOS Server log.

Related Information

Functions: **BOSSVR_AddSUser(3dfs), BOSSVR_DeleteSUser(3dfs)**.

BOSSVR_Prune

Purpose Deletes old and unnecessary binaries

Synopsis **long BOSSVR_Prune(**
handle_t *bosserverBinding*,
long *flags*,
error_status_t **theCommStatus*)

Parameters

Input

bosserverBinding	The RPC handle.
flags	The flags indicating what to purge.

Output

theCommStatus	An RPC error is returned, if an error occurred.

Description

BOSSVR_Prune( ) deletes all of the **.BAK** or **.OLD** files or both from *dcelocal*/**bin**, and removes all of the saved core files from *dcelocal*/**var/dfs/adm**, depending upon the actual flags passed. If **BOSSVR_PRUNEOLD** is set, all **.OLD** files are removed. If **BOSSVR_PRUNEBAK** is set, all **.BAK** files are removed, and if **BOSSVR_PRUNECORE** is set, all saved core files are removed (these have the name **core.***instance* where *instance* names the process that aborted, producing the core file). This call does not allow the caller to selectively remove individual **.BAK** or **.OLD** files.

The flags have the following numeric values. To specify the flags, add the values for the specific flags you wish to set:

BOSSVR_PRUNEOLD	A value of 1.
BOSSVR_PRUNEBAK	A value of 2.
BOSSVR_PRUNECORE	A value of 4.

The caller must be on the BOS Server's administration list to execute this routine.

Errors

BZACCESS The user is not authorized to perform this operation.

BZ_ERROR_INTERNAL_ERROR
An unexpected internal error occurred; check the BOS Server log.

Related Information

Functions: **BOSSVR_Install(3dfs), BOSSVR_UnInstall(3dfs)**.

BOSSVR_ReBossvr

Purpose Restarts all servers, including the BOS Server

Synopsis **long BOSSVR_ReBossvr(**
handle_t *bosserverBinding*,
error_status_t **theCommStatus*)

Parameters

Input

bosserverBinding The RPC handle.

Output

theCommStatus An RPC error is returned, if an error occurred.

Description

BOSSVR_ReBossvr( ) restarts all of the bnode instances at a server that are marked as runnable in the BOS Server's initialization file, just as in the **BOSSVR_RestartAll**( ) call. This call also forces the BOS Server to reexecute itself, thus picking up a new version of the BOS Server binary if one exists.

The caller must be on the BOS Server's administration list to execute this routine.

Errors **BZACCESS** The user does not have rights to perform this operation.

BZ_ERROR_INTERNAL_ERROR
An unexpected internal error occurred; check the BOS Server log.

BOSSVR_Restart

Purpose Restarts a given BOS process

Synopsis **long BOSSVR_Restart(**
handle_t *bosserverBinding*,
char *instance*[*BOSSVR_BSSIZE*],
error_status_t **theCommStatus*)

Parameters

Input

bosserverBinding The RPC handle.

instance The bnode instance to restart.

Output

theCommStatus An RPC error is returned, if an error occurred.

Description

BOSSVR_Restart( ) shuts down and restarts the bnode named by *instance*.

The caller must be on the BOS Server's administration list to execute this routine.

Errors

BZACCESS The user does not have the rights to perform this operation.

BZNOENT The bnode instance specified by *instance* does not exist on the server.

BZ_ERROR_INTERNAL_ERROR
An unexpected internal error occurred; check the BOS Server log.

Related Information

Functions: **BOSSVR_RestartAll(3dfs)**.

BOSSVR_RestartAll

Purpose

Restarts all BOS processes

Synopsis

long BOSSVR_RestartAll(
handle_t *bosserverBinding*,
error_status_t **theCommStatus*)

Parameters

Input

bosserverBinding The RPC handle.

Output

theCommStatus An RPC error is returned, if an error occurred.

Description

BOSSVR_RestartAll( ) shuts down all of the bnode instances at a server, including the BOS Server itself, and then restarts all of them. It does not change the BOS Server **init** file, or do anything to those bnode instances marked in the **init** file as not runnable. It is not necessary to call **BOSSVR_ShutdownAll**( ) before calling **BOSSVR_RestartAll**( ).

Calling **BOSSVR_RestartAll**( ) is equivalent to calling **BOSSVR_Restart**( ) for every bnode instance.

The caller must be on the BOS Server's administration list to execute this routine.

Errors

BZACCESS The user does not have the rights to perform this operation.

BZ_ERROR_INTERNAL_ERROR
An unexpected internal error occurred; check the BOS Server log.

Related Information

Functions: **BOSSVR_Restart(3dfs)**.

BOSSVR_SetNoAuthFlag

Purpose Sets the flag that controls whether servers check authorization

Synopsis **long BOSSVR_SetNoAuthFlag(**
handle_t *bosserverBinding*,
long *flag*,
error_status_t **theCommStatus*)

Parameters

Input

bosserverBinding The RPC handle.

flag The flag indicating whether to check authorization.

Output

theCommStatus An RPC error is returned, if an error occurred.

Description

BOSSVR_SetNoAuthFlag( ) controls the flag specifying whether the various DFS servers check authorization. A *flag* parameter of 1 disables authorization checking, and a *flag* parameter of 0 (zero) enables authorization checking again.

The caller must be on the BOS Server's administration list to make this call, unless authorization is already disabled.

Errors **BZACCESS** The user is not authorized to perform this operation.

BZ_ERROR_INTERNAL_ERROR
An unexpected internal error occurred; check the BOS Server log.

BOSSVR_SetRestartTime

Purpose Sets the BOS Server process restart times

Synopsis **long BOSSVR_SetRestartTime(**
handle_t *bosserverBinding*,
long *type*,
struct bossvr_netKTime **restartTime*,
error_status_t **theCommStatus*)

Parameters

Input

bosserverBinding The RPC handle.

type Specifies which restart time to set.

restartTime The new restart time.

Output

theCommStatus An RPC error is returned, if an error occurred.

Description

BOS_SetRestartTime( ) sets one of the **bosserver** process's restart times to the value specified by the *restartTime* parameter. A *type* value of 1 directs the **bosserver** to set the periodic whole-system restart time to the indicated value. A *type* value of 2 directs the **bosserver** to set the periodic new binary check time to the specified value.

The **bossvr_netKTime** structure represents a restart time or period to the BOS Server. Periodic times are represented as a set of fields (day, hour, minute, and second) and a set of flags specifying which fields must match. In addition, other flags specify special time sets; **now** represents the present time, and **never** represents the empty set of times.

```
struct bossvr_netKTime{
    long int mask;
    short int hour;  /* 0 - 23 */
    short int min;   /* 0 - 60 */
    short int sec;   /* 0 - 60 */
    short int day;   /* 0 is sunday */
};
```

The following flags for the restart time's mask are not defined by the BOS Server but facilitate the use of this function. These are defined in **afs/ktime.h**.

```
const KTIME_HOUR = 1;     /* hour should match */
const KTIME_MIN = 2;      /* minute should match */
const KTIME_SEC = 4;      /* second should match */
const KTIME_TIME = 7;     /* all times should match */
const KTIME_DAY = 8;      /* day should match */
const KTIME_NEVER = 0x10; /* special case: never */
const KTIME_NOW = 0x20;   /* special case: right now */
```

If **KTIME_NOW** is specified, the BOS Server uses the current time as the restart time. Otherwise, the requested restart would occur repeatedly without any time between restarts.

The caller must be on the BOS Server's administration list to execute this routine.

Errors

BZDOM: The *type* field is out-of-bounds.

BZACCESS: The user is not authorized to perform this operation.

BZ_ERROR_INTERNAL_ERROR:
An unexpected internal error occurred; check BOS Server log.

BZDATEPARSINGERROR:
The **now** flag was specified and the BOS Server had trouble setting up a restart time structure representing the current time.

Related Information

Functions: **BOSSVR_GetRestartTime(3dfs)**.

BOSSVR_SetStatus

Purpose

Sets the run status of a bnode instance

Synopsis

long BOSSVR_SetStatus(
handle_t *bosserverBinding***,**
char *instance*[*BOSSVR_BSSIZE*]**,**
long *status***,**
error_status_t **theCommStatus***)**

Parameters

Input

bosserverBinding The RPC handle.

instance The bnode instance to set the status of.

status The new status.

Output

theCommStatus An RPC error is returned, if an error occurred.

Description

BOS_SetStatus( ) sets the running status of the bnode named by *instance* to *status*. If *status* is 0 (zero), the process collection *instance* is stopped from running, and this state is recorded in the BOS Server's **init** file. If the *status* field is 1, the *instance* is marked as runnable in the **init** file, and the process is started if it is not already running.

The caller must be on the BOS Server's administration list to execute this routine.

Errors

BZNOENT The named instance does not exist.

BZACCESS The user is not authorized to perform this operation.

BZ_ERROR_INTERNAL_ERROR
An unexpected internal error occurred; check the BOS Server log.

Related Information

Functions: **BOSSVR_SetTStatus(3dfs)**, **BOSSVR_GetStatus(3dfs)**, **BOSSVR_WaitAll(3dfs)**.

BOSSVR_SetTStatus

Purpose

Temporarily sets the run status of a bnode instance

Synopsis

long BOSSVR_SetTStatus(
handle_t *bosserverBinding***,**
char *instance*[*BOSSVR_BSSIZE*]**,**
long *status***,**
error_status_t **theCommStatus*)

Parameters

Input

bosserverBinding The RPC handle.

instance The bnode instance to set the status of.

status The new status.

Output

theCommStatus An RPC error is returned, if an error occurred.

Description

BOSSVR_SetTStatus( ) sets the temporary process status to runnable (if *status* is 1) or not runnable (if *status* is 0 (zero)), and starts or stops the named process if the state has changed. The BOS Server's initialization file is not changed, so if the system crashes and restarts, the process reverts to its initial state. To change the initialization file as well, use **BOSSVR_SetStatus( )**.

The caller must be on the BOS Server's administration list to execute this routine.

Errors

BZNOENT The named instance does not exist.

BZACCESS The user is not authorized to perform this operation.

BZ_ERROR_INTERNAL_ERROR
An unexpected internal error occurred; check the BOS Server log.

Related Information

Functions: **BOSSVR_SetStatus(3dfs)**, **BOSSVR_GetStatus(3dfs)**, **BOSSVR_WaitAll(3dfs)**.

BOSSVR_ShutdownAll

Purpose Shuts down all BOS processes

Synopsis **long BOSSVR_ShutdownAll(**
handle_t *bosserverBinding*,
error_status_t **theCommStatus*)

Parameters

Input

bosserverBinding The RPC handle.

Output

theCommStatus An RPC error is returned, if an error occurred.

Description

BOSSVR_ShutdownAll( ) shuts down all of the bnode instances at a server. It does not change the BOS Server **init** file, so all BOS processes marked as runnable in the initialization file start up again when BOS is restarted.

The caller must be on the BOS Server's administration list to execute this routine.

Errors **BZACCESS** The user does not have the rights to perform this operation.

BZ_ERROR_INTERNAL_ERROR
An unexpected internal error occurred; check the BOS Server log.

BOSSVR_StartupAll

Purpose Starts all BOS processes

Synopsis **long BOSSVR_StartupAll(**
handle_t *bosserverBinding***,**
error_status_t **theCommStatus***)**

Parameters

Input

bosserverBinding The RPC handle.

Output

theCommStatus An RPC error is returned, if an error occurred.

Description

BOSSVR_StartupAll( ) starts all of the bnode instances at a server that are not running and that are marked as runnable in the BOS Server's initialization file. This call does not change the initialization file, or do anything to those bnode instances marked in the file as not runnable.

It is not necessary to call **BOS_ShutdownAll( )** before calling **BOSSVR_StartupAll( )** because the latter only starts processes that are not already running.

The caller must be on the BOS Server's administration list to execute this routine.

Errors

BZACCESS The user does not have the rights to perform this operation.

BZ_ERROR_INTERNAL_ERROR
An unexpected internal error occurred; check the BOS Server log.

BOSSVR_UnInstall

Purpose

Reverts to an older copy of a program

Synopsis

long BOSSVR_UnInstall(
handle_t *bosserverBinding***,**
char *path*[*BOSSVR_BSSIZE*]**,**
error_status_t **theCommStatus*)

Parameters

Input

bosserverBinding The RPC handle.

path The pathname of the program to uninstall.

Output

theCommStatus An RPC error is returned, if an error occurred.

Description

BOSSVR_UnInstall( ) deletes the current binary, *path*, renames any existing **.BAK** file to be the currently installed program, and renames any existing **.OLD** file to be the new **.BAK** file. If there is no **.BAK** file, it installs the **.OLD** file as the current version.

The caller must be on the BOS Server's administration list to execute this routine.

Errors

BZNOENT There is no **.BAK** file or **.OLD** file to uninstall.

BZACCESS The user is not authorized to perform this operation.

BZ_ERROR_INTERNAL_ERROR
An unexpected internal error occurred; check the BOS Server log.

Related Information

Functions: **BOSSVR_Install(3dfs), BOSSVR_Prune(3dfs)**.

BOSSVR_WaitAll

Purpose Waits for all BOS processes to stabilize their status

Synopsis **long BOSSVR_WaitAll(**
handle_t *bosserverBinding*,
error_status_t **theCommStatus***)**

Parameters

Input

bosserverBinding The RPC handle.

Output

theCommStatus An RPC error is returned, if an error occurred.

Description

BOSSVR_WaitAll( ) waits until all of the bnode instances that are changing state from running to not running, or vice versa, complete their state change. The call does not return until all state changes are complete.

The caller must be on the BOS Server's administration list to execute this routine.

Errors

BZACCESS The user does not have the rights to perform this operation.

BZ_ERROR_INTERNAL_ERROR
An unexpected internal error occurred; check the BOS Server log.

Related Information

Functions: **BOSSVR_SetStatus(3dfs), BOSSVR_SetTStatus(3dfs)**.

FTSERVER

Purpose

Introduction to Fileset Server interface functions

Synopsis

#include <dce/ftserver_proc.h>
#include <dce/sysincludes.h>
#include <dce/fldb_data.h>
#include <dce/flserver.h>
#include <dce/ftserver.h>
#include <dce/ftserver_trans.h>
#include <dce/rpc.h>

Libraries

All **FTSERVER** functions are defined in the library **libdcedfs.a**.

Description

The **FTSERVER( )** call functions are used to do basic operations on filesets, such as creating, deleting, moving, and replicating them. These functions are similar to the **VC( )** functions, but are at a lower level. The **VC( )** functions do general operations and do all of the appropriate bookkeeping, such as maintaining the Fileset Location Database (FLDB) and bringing new filesets online. The **FTSERVER( )** functions do not do this bookkeeping, but let you manipulate filesets at a much lower level. If you are unsure of which functions to use, you should probably be using **VC( )**.

Each operation is carried out as a *transaction*, which can be logically viewed as an ''open fileset'' operation with an exclusive lock on the affected fileset. Atomicity is not guaranteed, however. Opening a transaction signals to other servers that may be interested in accessing a fileset that it is unavailable while the Fileset Server is manipulating it. This prevents the corruption that could result from multiple simultaneous operations on a fileset.

Before calling any function except **FTSERVER_CreateVolume( )** or **FTSERVER_GetOneVolStatus( )**, the programmer must open a transaction by calling **FTSERVER_CreateTrans( )**, or the function fails. (**FTSERVER_CreateVolume( )** and **FTSERVER_GetOneVolStatus( )** open their own transactions automatically.) The programmer then must explicitly close every transaction, even those created by **FTSERVER_CreateVolume( )**, with **FTSERVER_DeleteTrans( )**, or the affected fileset remains locked.

Transactions time out after a short while to prevent filesets from becoming permanently unavailable should the crash of a File Server machine or other problem interrupt a transaction before **FTSERVER_DeleteTrans( )** is called. In the absence of network or other problems, transactions are able to complete within the time-out period.

Every call to the Fileset Server requires a Remote Procedure Call (RPC) connection parameter that implicitly specifies which server to contact. It is defined here rather than in the reference page for each call:

RpcBinding A pointer to an RPC connection (of type **rpc_binding_handle_t**), which is a connection to an authenticated path that allows multiple asynchronous conversations. This structure is completely opaque to the application programmer, and is simply passed around. The RPC function that opens a connection returns this pointer.

A commonly used data structure in the **FTSERVER( )** functions is **afsHyper**. It is defined as follows:

```
struct afsHyper {
    unsigned long high;
    unsigned long low;
};
```

This structure simply represents a 64-bit counter.

Errors

In addition to the error messages listed with each function in this set, all functions can return lower level errors from other DCE components or from within DFS.

Related Information

Functions: **intro(3dfs), VC(3dfs), VL(3dfs)**.

FTSERVER_AggregateInfo

Purpose Provides specific information about an aggregate

Synopsis **long FTSERVER_AggregateInfo(**
rpc_binding_handle_t *RpcBinding*,
unsigned long *aggrID*,
struct ftserver_aggrInfo **aggrDesc*)

Parameters

Input

RpcBinding The RPC handle.

aggrID The ID of the aggregate.

Output

aggrDesc The aggregate attributes.

Description

FTSERVER_AggregateInfo( ) returns the attributes of an aggregate *aggrID* on the server specified in *RpcBinding*.

The attributes are represented by the following structure.

```
struct ftserver_aggrInfo{
    char name[32];                  /* Mounted partition name */
    char devName[32];               /* raw partition name */
    unsigned long type;             /* Type (UFS, DCE LFS, etc) */
    unsigned long totalUsable;      /* usable 1024-byte blocks */
    unsigned long curFree;          /* total space free (in K) */
    unsigned long minFree;          /* reserved space */
    unsigned long spare1;
    unsigned long spare2;
    unsigned long spare3;
    unsigned long spare4;
    unsigned long spare5;
    unsigned long spare6;
    char cspare[64];
};
```

Errors

ENOENT The aggregate ID is not an ID for an attached aggregate.

FTSERVER_Clone

Purpose

Creates a read-only copy of a fileset

Synopsis

long FTSERVER_Clone(
rpc_binding_handle_t *RpcBinding*,
unsigned long *transID*,
unsigned long *newType*,
char **newName*,
struct afsHyper **newfilesetID*)

Parameters

Input

RpcBinding — The RPC handle.

transID — The transaction ID.

newType — The type of the clone (**VOLTIX_TO_VOLTYPE(ROVOL)** or **VOLTIX_TO_VOLTYPE(BACKVOL)**).

newName — The name of the clone.

Input/Output

newfilesetID — The fileset ID of the clone.

Description

FTSERVER_Clone( ) creates a clone of a read/write fileset. The variables *newType*, *newfilesetID*, and *newName* specify the clone's type, fileset ID, and name, respectively.

The possible types are read-only (**VOLTIX_TO_VOLTYPE(ROVOL)**) and backup (**VOLTIX_TO_VOLTYPE(BACKVOL)**). Clones cannot be read/write, so **VOLTIX_TO_VOLTYPE(RWVOL)** is not an appropriate type for this parameter.

The fileset is inaccessible until **FTSERVER_SetFlags( )** is called to bring it online.

For a discussion of clones and their uses, see the *OSF DCE Application Development Guide*.

This function only applies to DCE LFS filesets.

Related Information

Functions: **FTSERVER_ReClone(3dfs), FTSERVER_SetFlags(3dfs)**.

Books: *OSF DCE Application Development Guide*.

FTSERVER_CreateTrans

Purpose Opens a transaction on a fileset

Synopsis **long FTSERVER_CreateTrans(**
rpc_binding_handle_t *RpcBinding*,
struct afsHyper **filesetIDp*,
unsigned long *aggregateID*,
unsigned long *flags*,
unsigned long ***transID*)

Parameters

Input

RpcBinding The RPC handle.

filesetIDp The fileset on which to create the transaction.

aggregateID The aggregate housing *filesetIDp*.

flags The operations and status flags.

Output

transID The ID of the new transaction.

Description

FTSERVER_CreateTrans( ) creates a transaction for the fileset with fileset ID number *filesetIDp*, housed on aggregate *aggregateID* of the File Server machine specified in *RpcBinding*.

The *flags* parameter represents the operations that will be performed while the fileset is open and the status codes to report to other processes attempting to access the same fileset. The flags are combined via bitwise OR.

The following flags represent operations that will be performed on the fileset during the transaction:

- **FTSERVER_OP_DELETE**
- **FTSERVER_OP_DUMP**

- **FTSERVER_OP_RESTORE**
- **FTSERVER_OP_CLONE**
- **FTSERVER_OP_RECLONE**
- **FTSERVER_OP_GETFLAGS**
- **FTSERVER_OP_SETFLAGS**
- **FTSERVER_OP_SETSTATUS**
- **FTSERVER_OP_GETSTATUS**

The following flags represent the error codes that can be reported:

VOLERR_PERS_LOWEST The lowest bound for persistent errors occurred.

VOLERR_PERS_DELETED The fileset was already deleted or moved.

VOLERR_PERS_BADDUMPOPCODE
A bad opcode was passed to a dump.

VOLERR_PERS_BADDUMP There was a bad dump format.

VOLERR_PERS_BADFTSOPSVECTOR
A bad **ftserver** ops vector was passed in.

VOLERR_PERS_REPDESTROY
The fileset was deleted by the **repserver**.

VOLERR_PERS_DAMAGED The fileset is inconsistent.

VOLERR_PERS_BADVOLOPSVECTOR
A bad fileset ops vector was passed in.

VOLERR_TRANS_LOWEST The lowest bound for transient errors occurred.

VOLERR_TRANS_DELETE The fileset was being deleted or moved.

VOLERR_TRANS_DUMP The fileset was being dumped.

VOLERR_TRANS_RESTORE
The fileset was being restored.

VOLERR_TRANS_CLONE The fileset was being cloned.

VOLERR_TRANS_RECLONE
The fileset was being recloned.

VOLERR_TRANS_LIST Lists filesets.

VOLERR_TRANS_GETSTATUS
Gets the status of the fileset.

VOLERR_TRANS_CREATEFILESET
Creates a new fileset.

VOLERR_TRANS_RELEASE Releases a fileset.

VOLERR_TRANS_SETQUOTA
Sets a quota on the fileset.

VOLERR_TRANf_FILESETEXISTS
The fileset already exists.

VOLERR_TRANS_SETFLAGS
Sets flags on the fileset.

VOLERR_TRANS_MOVE The fileset was being moved.

VOLERR_TRANS_SETSTATUS
Sets the status on the fileset.

VOLERR_TRANS_COPYCLONE
Copies the clone to a new location.

VOLERR_TRANS_FORWARD
Copies the fileset to a different server or aggregate.

VOLERR_TRANS_BACKUPDUMP
Dumps a fileset to tape.

VOLERR_TRANS_BACKUPRESTORE
Restores a fileset from tape.

VOLERR_TRANS_REPGETSTATUS
The **repserver** gets the status on the fileset.

VOLERR_TRANS_REPSETSTATUS
The **repserver** sets the status on the fileset.

VOLERR_TRANS_REPSETFILESETVERSION
The **repserver** sets the fileset version.

VOLERR_TRANS_REPCLONE
The **repserver** clones the fileset.

VOLERR_TRANS_REPEDITSTATUS
The **repserver** edits the fileset status.

VOLERR_TRANS_REPCLEARSTATUS
The **repserver** clears the fileset status.

VOLERR_TRANS_REPUNCLONE
The **repserver** unclones the fileset.

VOLERR_TRANS_REPSWITCHFILESETS
The **repserver** switches filesets.

VOLERR_TRANS_REPGETFILESETCHANGES
The **repserver** gets the fileset changes.

VOLERR_TRANS_REPFORWARD
The **repserver** forwards the fileset.

VOLERR_PERS_NOMEM There is no more memory.

VOLERR_PERS_IO A pipe I/O failure occurred.

VOLERR_TRANS_QUOTA The fileset is over quota.

VOLERR_TRANS_HIGHEST The upper bound for transient errors occurred.

Additional **VOLERR** codes are allocated as spares to provide for future expansion.

If no flag is set, the fileset is available.

Any number of operation flags can be specified, but only one error code may be given. The operation flags are used by DFS to determine what operations may occur concurrently with this one; the error code is returned to any process that attempts to open the fileset for an incompatable operation.

Errors

FTSERVER_ERR_TRELE A transaction was not properly released.

FTSERVER_ERR_TRANSEXISTS A transaction on the fileset already exists.

DAUT_ERROR_ACCESS_DENIED Access was denied.

Related Information

Functions: **FTSERVER_DeleteTrans(3dfs)**.

FTSERVER_CreateVolume

Purpose Creates a new fileset

Synopsis **long FTSERVER_CreateVolume(**
rpc_binding_handle_t *RpcBinding*,
unsigned long *aggregateID*,
char **name*,
unsigned long *type*,
unsigned long *flags*,
struct afsHyper **parentID*,
struct afsHyper **filesetID*,
unsigned long **transID*)

Parameters

Input

RpcBinding The RPC handle.

aggregateID The aggregate on which to create the fileset.

name The name of the fileset.

type The type of the fileset.

flags The operations and status flags.

parentID The ID of the read/write copy of this fileset, or **NULL** for read/write filesets.

Input/Output

filesetID The ID of the fileset.

Output

transID The transaction ID.

Description

FTSERVER_CreateVolume( ) creates a fileset called *name* of type *type* on the aggregate *aggregateID* of the File Server machine specified in *RpcBinding*. It also opens an associated transaction whose identifier is returned as *transID*.

The following fileset types are possible:

read/write (**VOLTIX_TO_VOLTYPE(RWVOL)**),
read-only (**VOLTIX_TO_VOLTYPE(ROVOL)**), and
backup (**VOLTIX_TO_VOLTYPE(BACKVOL)**).

The *flags* parameter represents the operations that will be performed while the fileset is open and the status codes to report to other processes attempting to access the same fileset. The flags are combined via bitwise OR. The list of flags is provided under **FTSERVER_CreateTrans( )**.

The *parentID* is the ID of the parent fileset, not the mount point. For read-only and backup filesets, the parent is the read/write copy. Read/write filesets have no parents.

The fileset is not actually accessible until **FTSERVER_SetFlags( )** is called to bring it online. Also, be sure to call **FTSERVER_DeleteTrans( )** to close *transID* when you are done with the fileset, or the fileset remains unavailable until the transaction times out.

This function applies only to DCE LFS filesets.

Errors

DAUT_ERROR_ACCESS_DENIED Access was denied.

Related Information

Functions: **FTSERVER_SetFlags(3dfs), FTSERVER_DeleteTrans(3dfs)**.

FTSERVER_DeleteTrans

Purpose Closes a transaction on a fileset

Synopsis **long FTSERVER_DeleteTrans(**
rpc_binding_handle_t *RpcBinding*,
unsigned long *transID*)

Parameters

Input

RpcBinding The RPC handle.

transID The ID of the transaction to delete.

Description

FTSERVER_DeleteTrans( ) ends the transaction *transID*. (The identifier of the transaction is returned by **FTSERVER_CreateTrans( )** or **FTSERVER_CreateVolume( )**.) *RpcBinding* points to the File Server.

Errors **DAUT_ERROR_ACCESS_DENIED** Access was denied.

Related Information

Functions: **FTSERVER_CreateTrans(3dfs)**, **FTSERVER_CreateVolume(3dfs)**.

FTSERVER_DeleteVolume

Purpose

Deletes a fileset

Synopsis

long FTSERVER_DeleteVolume(
rpc_binding_handle_t *RpcBinding***,**
unsigned long *transID***)**

Parameters

Input

RpcBinding The RPC handle.

transID The ID of the transaction on the fileset to be deleted.

Description

FTSERVER_DeleteVolume( ) deletes the specified fileset from the file system. There must be an open transaction on this fileset; *transID* is returned by **FTSERVER_CreateTrans( )** and **FTSERVER_CreateVolume( )**.

This function only applies to DCE LFS filesets.

Errors

DAUT_ERROR_ACCESS_DENIED Access was denied.

FTSERVER_Dump

Purpose Dumps a fileset to a character stream

Synopsis **long FTSERVER_Dump(**
rpc_binding_handle_t *RpcBinding*,
unsigned long *transID*,
struct ftserver_Date **dumpDate*,
struct pipe_t **dataPipeP*)

Parameters

Input

RpcBinding The RPC handle.

transID The ID of the transaction on the fileset to be dumped.

dumpDate The dump type (full or incremental) and if incremental, the reference date. This *struct* consists of three active and three spare (unused) fields, namely *dumpDate->mask* (of type **long**), *dumpDate->dumpDate* (an **afsHyper** 64-bit counter), and *dumpDate->dumpVersion*.

Output

dataPipeP The dumped data.

Description

Dumping refers to the conversion of a fileset into an output stream suitable for storage on tape, or as an intermediate format when moving filesets between File Server machines that store filesets in different formats. Restoring refers to conversion of a fileset back into the appropriate fileset format from this representation, and to its placement back into the file system.

FTSERVER_Dump( ) dumps the specified fileset into dump format. The dump can be either full or incremental, depending on the value of *dumpDate->fromDate* (which must be expressed as a UNIX date).

To get a full dump, specify 0 (zero) for *dumpDate->fromDate*. To get an incremental dump, specify the UNIX date from which you want the incremental dump to begin. Version numbers can also be specified as the reference point. The *dumpDate->mask* value determines which of the subfields to use.

The dump itself is returned as an output stream parameter. (See **dump(5dfs)** for a description of the dump format.)

The **ftserver_Date** structure is defined as follows:

```
struct ftserver_Date {
    long mask;        /* 0=none, 1=fromDate, 2=fromVersion */
    struct afsTimeval fromDate;
    struct afsHyper fromVersion;
    struct afsHyper spare1;
    struct afsHyper spare2;
    struct afsHyper spare3;
};
```

The **afsTimeval** structure is defined as follows:

```
struct afsTimeval {
    unsigned long sec;    /* seconds */
    unsigned long usec;   /* microseconds */
};
```

The **sec** field is represented in the standard UNIX way (number of seconds elapsed since January 1, 1970).

Errors

DAUT_ERROR_ACCESS_DENIED Access was denied.

Related Information

Functions: **FTSERVER_Forward(3dfs), FTSERVER_Restore(3dfs), dump(5dfs)**.

FTSERVER_Forward

Purpose Dumps a fileset from one File Server and restore it to another (DCE LFS filesets only)

Synopsis **long FTSERVER_Forward(**
rpc_binding_handle_t *RpcBinding*,
unsigned long *fromTrans*,
struct ftserver_Date **fromDate*,
struct ftserver_dest **destAddress*,
unsigned long *destTrans***)**

Parameters

Input

RpcBinding The RPC handle.

fromTrans The transaction for the source fileset.

fromDate The type and reference date for the dump. This *struct* consists of three active and three spare (unused) fields, namely *fromDate->mask* (of type **long**), *fromDate->fromDate* (an **afsHyper** 64-bit counter), and *fromDate->fromVersion*.

destAddress The address of the destination machine.

destTrans The transaction for the destination fileset.

Description

FTSERVER_Forward( ) dumps the fileset associated with transaction *fromTrans* and currently residing on the File Server machine specified in *RpcBinding*, and then restores the fileset on the File Server machine specified in *destAddress*, where transaction *destTrans* has been established. The dump may be full (if both fields in *fromDate->fromDate* are 0 (zero)) or incremental (if *fromDate->fromDate* represents a number of seconds since 1 January 1970). *fromDate->fromVersion* can also be used as a reference point for the incremental dump. *fromDate->mask* determines which field to use as a reference.

The destination fileset must exist before carrying out this operation, and the invoking process must start transactions on both of the participating filesets first.

The same effect can be achieved by calling **FTSERVER_Dump( )** and **FTSERVER_Restore( )**, except that the data is transferred through the calling machine, which may be considerably slower than a direct point-to-point transfer.

The **ftserver_Date** structure definition is given under **FTSERVER_Dump( )**. The **ftserver_dest** structure is defined as follows:

```
struct ftserver_dest {
   struct afsNetAddr address;
   unsigned long destSSID;
   unsigned long spare1;
   unsigned long spare2;
   unsigned long spare3;
   char prinName[FTSERVER_MAXPRINNAME];
};
```

Use 1 for the value of **destSSID**.

This function applies only to DCE LFS filesets.

Errors

FTSERVER_ERR_NOTRANS	The transaction was not found.
FTSERVER_ERR_IO	The operation cannot write to the disk.
FTSERVER_ERR_BADDUMP	The dump is incorrectly formatted.
DAUT_ERROR_ACCESS_DENIED	Access was denied.

Related Information

Functions: **FTSERVER_Dump(3dfs), FTSERVER_Restore(3dfs)**.

FTSERVER_GetFlags

Purpose Gets the current availability of a fileset

Synopsis **long FTSERVER_GetFlags(**
rpc_binding_handle_t *RpcBinding*,
unsigned long *transID*,
unsigned long **flags*)

Parameters

Input

RpcBinding The RPC handle.

transID The transaction ID on the target fileset.

Output

flags The address of the returned flags.

Description

FTSERVER_GetFlags( ) returns, by way of *flags*, the status flags for the fileset associated with transaction *transID* and residing on the File Server machine specified in *RpcBinding*. The *flags* parameter is a bitwise OR of the following values:

- **VOL_RW** indicates that the fileset allows both read and write access.
- **VOL_READONLY** indicates that the fileset is read-only. Writes to this fileset fail.
- **VOL_DELONSALVAGE** indicates that the fileset is not usable; it will be deleted upon reboot. This is an intermediate state used to guarantee correctness for large operations such as cloning a fileset.
- **VOL_OFFLINE** indicates that the fileset is offline. Reads and writes to this fileset fail.
- **VOL_BUSY** indicates that the fileset is temporarily unavailable.
- **VOL_OUTOFSERVICE** indicates that the fileset is not usable; it will not be deleted upon reboot.

- **VOL_DEADMEAT** indicates that the fileset is in the process of being deleted.
- **VOL_OK** is the bitwise negation of **VOL_BUSY**, **VOL_OFFLINE**, **VOL_DELONSALVAGE**, and **VOL_OUTOFSERVICE**. It is used to mark a fileset as usable.
- **VOL_REPFIELD** is used for replication and should never be modified by applications.
- **VOL_IS_COMPLETE** is used as a flag by the Replication Server.
- **VOL_HAS_TOKEN** is used for communications between the Replication Server and the File Exporter.
- **VOL_KNOWDALLY** is used by the File Exporter to prevent files from being deleted prematurely.
- **VOL_TYPEFIELD** is a record of more specific fileset uses.

Errors

DAUT_ERROR_ACCESS_DENIED Access was denied.

FTSERVER_GetOneVolStatus

Purpose Gets the full status of a fileset without establishing a transaction

Synopsis **long FTSERVER_GetOneVolStatus(**
rpc_binding_handle_t *RpcBinding*,
struct afsHyper **filesetID*,
unsigned long *aggrID*,
unsigned long *spare1*,
struct ftserver_status **status*)

Parameters

Input

RpcBinding The RPC handle.

filesetID The fileset identifier.

aggrID The aggregate identifier.

spare1 This is not currently used.

Output

status The returned status.

Description

FTSERVER_GetOneVolStatus( ) returns, in *status*, the status information associated with the fileset *filesetID* on aggregate *aggrID*. The function does not require a previous call to **FTSERVER_CreateTrans( )**, and does not take a transaction ID.

The **ftserver_status** structure is defined under **FTSERVER_GetStatus( )**.

Errors

VOLS_ERR_NOTRANS The transaction was not found.

VOLS_ERR_TOOBIG Too much space is required for the returned fileset name.

Related Information

Functions: **FTSERVER_GetStatus(3dfs)**, **FTSERVER_ListVolumes(3dfs)**, **FTSERVER_SetStatus(3dfs)**, **VC_VolserStatus(3dfs)**.

FTSERVER_GetStatus

Purpose Gets the full status of a fileset

Synopsis **long FTSERVER_GetStatus(**
rpc_binding_handle_t *RpcBinding***,**
unsigned long *transID***,**
struct ftserver_status **status***)**

Parameters

Input

RpcBinding The RPC handle.

transID The transaction ID on the target fileset.

Output

status The returned status.

Description

FTSERVER_GetStatus( ) returns, by way of *status*, the status information associated with the fileset associated with the transaction *transID*. The structure definitions and descriptions of the fields follow.

```
struct ftserver_status {
    ftserver_status_static vss;
    ftserver_status_dynamic vsd;
    }

struct ftserver_status_static {
    struct afsHyper volId;
    struct afsHyper parentId;
    struct afsTimeval cloneTime;
    struct afsTimeval vvCurrentTime;
    struct afsTimeval vvPingCurrentTime;
    unsigned long type;
    unsigned long accStatus;
    unsigned long accError;
    unsigned long states;
```

```
        unsigned long reclaimDally;
        long static_spare1;
        long static_spare2;
        long static_spare3;
        long static_spare4;
        long static_spare5;
        long static_spare6;
        long static_spare7;
        char volName[FTSERVER_MAXFSNAME];
        char static_cspares[16];
        }

    struct ftserver_status_dynamic {
        struct afsTimeval creationDate;
        struct afsTimeval updateDate;
        struct afsTimeval accessDate;
        struct afsTimeval backupDate;
        struct afsTimeval copyDate;
        struct afsHyper volversion;
        struct afsHyper backupId;
        struct afsHyper cloneId;
        long fileCount;
        long maxQuota;
        long minQuota;
        long size;
        long owner;
        long unique;
        long index;
        long rwindex;
        long backupIndex;
        long parentIndex;
        long cloneIndex;
        struct afsHyper llBackId;
        struct afsHyper llFwdId;
        long dynamic_spare1;
        long dynamic_spare2;
        long dynamic_spare3;
        long dynamic_spare4;
        long dynamic_spare5;
        long dynamic_spare6;
        char statusMsg[128];
        char dynamic_cspares[16];
        }
```

The fields of these structures are as follows.

- **ftserver_status_static**

  — **volId**: The ID of the fileset, which should be unique throughout this DFS cell.

  — **parentId**: Fileset ID of the read/write source, if this is a read-only or backup clone.

  — **cloneTime**: The time the last clone was made of this fileset.

  — **vvCurrentTime**: The most recent time that the fileset version number was known to be current on the read/write site. Applications should not modify this field.

  — **vvPingCurrentTime**: The most recent time that a read-only site tried to contact a read/write site to determine how current the fileset version number is. Applications should not modify this field.

  — **type**: The fileset's type.

  — **accStatus**: The access status on the fileset; the status will be one of the codes described under **FTSERVER_CreateTrans( )**. This field should never be modified by an application program.

  — **accError**: The access error on a fileset; this will be one of the codes described under **FTSERVER_CreateTrans( )**. This field should never be modified by an application program.

  — **states**: The status flag, as set by **FTSERVER_SetFlags( )**.

  — **reclaimDally**: The time, in seconds, between keep-alive messages sent by the Cache Manager.

  — **static_spare1** through **static_spare3**: Spares reserved for future use.

  — **volName**: The name of the fileset.

  — **static_cspares**: Reserved for future use.

- **ftserver_status_dynamic**

  — **creationDate**: The date of the fileset's creation.

  — **updateDate**: The timestamp of the last modification by a user.

  — **accessDate**: The last access time by a user.

— **backupDate**: The date at which the last backup clone was made.

— **copyDate**: The time that this copy of the fileset was created.

— **volVersion**: The current version number of the fileset.

— **backupId**: The fileset ID of the latest backup version of this fileset.

— **cloneId**: The fileset ID of the clone.

— **llBackId** and **llFwdId**: The links for all related filesets in a doubly linked list; used to find the correct fileset to unclone when deleting a fileset.

— **fileCount**: The number of files in the fileset.

— **maxQuota**: The maximum amount of disk space the fileset is allowed to take up, expressed in units of 1024 bytes. Somewhat paradoxically, a value of 0 (zero) means there is no limit.

— **minQuota**: The amount of disk space guaranteed to be available for the fileset, expressed in 1024-byte units. Other filesets on the partition are prevented from growing if their growth would impinge on this limit.

— **size**: The size of the fileset, in 1024-byte units.

— **owner**: The DFS ID of the owner of the fileset.

— **unique**: The uniquifier, a value combined with other IDs to guarantee uniqueness (do not modify this).

— **index**, **rwindex**, **backupIndex**, **parentIndex**, and **cloneIndex**: Information about where other related filesets are located within an aggregate; for the remote application user they are meaningless. They cannot be set remotely.

— **dynamic_spare1** through **dynamic_spare6**: Spares reserved for future use.

— **statusMsg**: Message field used by low-level code to transmit error messages back up to the caller (across the Fileset Server-to-kernel interface). Applications should not use this field.

— **dynamic_cspares**: Reserved for future use.

Errors

FTSERVER_ERR_NOTRANS	The transaction was not found.
DAUT_ERROR_ACCESS_DENIED	Access was denied.

Related Information

Functions: **FTSERVER_ListVolumes(3dfs)**, **FTSERVER_SetStatus(3dfs)**, **VC_VolserStatus(3dfs)**.

FTSERVER_ListAggregates

Purpose Identifies all valid aggregates on a server

Synopsis **long FTSERVER_ListAggregates(**
rpc_binding_handle_t *RpcBinding*,
ftserver_iterator *inCookie*,
ftserver_iterator *outCookie*,
struct ftserver_aggrEntries **aggrList*)

Parameters

Input

RpcBinding The RPC handle.

inCookie The position at which to start: an index into the aggregate list.

Output

aggrList Descriptions of all the aggregates on the server.

outCookie The next position at which to start: an index into the aggregate list.

Description

FTSERVER_ListAggregates( ) returns, in *aggrList*, the name, ID, and type of the next valid aggregate on the called server. The input and output iterators are used to move through the list.

The **ftserver_aggrEntries** structure is defined as follows:

```
struct ftserver_aggrEntries{
  unsigned long ftserver_aggrList_len;
  struct ftserver_aggrList ftserver_aggrEntries_val[FTSERVER_MAXAGGR];
}
```

The **ftserver_aggrList** structure is defined as follows:

```
struct ftserver_aggrList{
    char name[32];      /* aggregate name */
    char dvname[32];    /* device name */
    unsigned long Id;   /* aggregate Id */
    unsigned long type; /* aggregate type */
    unsigned long spare1;
    unsigned long spare2;
    unsigned long spare3;
    unsigned long spare4;
};
```

FTSERVER_ListVolumes

Purpose Lists the filesets on a File Server

Synopsis

long FTSERVER_ListVolumes(
rpc_binding_handle_t *RpcBinding*,
unsigned long *aggrID*,
struct ftserver_iterator **inCookie*,
struct ftserver_iterator **outCookie*,
struct ftserver_statEntries **statEntries*[ ])

Parameters

Input

RpcBinding The RPC handle.

aggrID The aggregate to list.

inCookie The iterator value: an index into the volume list.

Output

outCookie The iterator to use for the next call: an index into the volume list.

statEntries[ ] The output.

Description

FTSERVER_ListVolumes( ) returns a list by way of *statEntries*[ ] of all the filesets on the aggregate *aggrID* of the server specified in *RpcBinding*. This is a heavyweight operation because it reads the fileset headers for all the filesets on that aggregate on the disk. The parameters *inCookie* and *outCookie* are used to break up large arrays of data; if all of the information does not fit in *statEntries*[ ], **FTSERVER_ListVolumes( )** returns, by way of *outCookie*, a number that should be used as the value for *inCookie* on a subsequent call. Repeat this process until the return error code is **VOL_ERR_EOF** or the **index** field in *outCookie* is the same as the **index** field passed in through *inCookie*.

The **ftserver_iterator** structure is defined as follows:

```
struct ftserver_iterator{
    unsigned long index;
    struct afsUUID uuid;
}
```

The **ftserver_statEntries** structure is defined as follows:

```
struct ftserver_statEntries{
    unsigned long ftserver_status_len;
    struct ftserver_status ftserver_status_val[FTSERVER_MAXENTRIES];
}
```

Information about the **ftserver_status** structure can be found in the description of **FTSERVER_GetStatus( )**.

Errors

DAUT_ERROR_ACCESS_DENIED There is insufficient permission.

Related Information

Functions: **FTSERVER_GetStatus(3dfs)**.

FTSERVER_Monitor

Purpose Identifies all active transactions involving a given File Server

Synopsis **long FTSERVER_Monitor(**
rpc_binding_handle_t *RpcBinding*,
struct ftserver_transEntries **aggrInfoP*)

Parameters

Input

RpcBinding The RPC handle.

Output

aggrInfoP Information about all active transactions.

Description

FTSERVER_Monitor( ) returns a list in *aggrInfoP* of all the active transactions involving the fileset server process running on the File Server machine specified in *RpcBinding*. The status of remote procedure calls associated with each transaction is also indicated. This function enables processes to monitor the progress of a transaction as well as debug the system remotely.

The **ftserver_transEntries** structure is defined as follows:

```
struct ftserver_transEntries {
  unsigned long ftserver_status_len;
  struct ftserver_transStatus ftserver_status_val[FTSERVER_MAXENTRIES];
}
```

The **ftserver_transStatus** structure is defined as follows:

```
struct ftserver_transStatus{
    unsigned long transId;        /* transaction id */
    unsigned long aggrId;         /* open fileset's aggregate */
    afsHyper volId;               /* open fileset's Id */
    unsigned long vDesc;          /* fileset's desc to VOP_* calls */
    unsigned long lastTime;       /* time trans was last active */
    struct afsTimeval creationTime; /* time transaction started */
    unsigned long returnCode;     /* transaction error code */
    unsigned long states;         /* transaction's status bits */
    unsigned long spare0;
    unsigned long spare1;
    unsigned long spare2;
    unsigned long spare3;
    unsigned long spare4;
    unsigned long spare5;
}
```

Errors

DAUT_ERROR_ACCESS_DENIED There is insufficient permission.

FTSERVER_ReClone

Purpose Brings a clone up-to-date with the read/write copy

Synopsis **long FTSERVER_ReClone(**
rpc_binding_handle_t *RpcBinding*,
unsigned long *transID*,
struct afsHyper **cloneID*)

Parameters

Input

RpcBinding The RPC handle.

transID The transaction for the source fileset.

Input/Output

cloneID The fileset ID of the clone to be updated.

Description

FTSERVER_ReClone( ) brings a preexisting clone (*cloneID*) up-to-date with the fileset associated with *transID*.

This function only applies to DCE LFS filesets.

Errors **DAUT_ERROR_ACCESS_DENIED** Access was denied.

Related Information

Functions: **FTSERVER_Clone(3dfs)**.

FTSERVER_Restore

Purpose Restores a fileset from a character stream (DCE LFS filesets only)

Synopsis **long FTSERVER_Restore(**
rpc_binding_handle_t *RpcBinding*,
unsigned long *transID*,
unsigned long *flags*,
pipe_t **dataPipeP*)

Parameters

Input

RpcBinding The RPC handle.

transID The transaction for the target fileset.

flags Reserved for future use.

dataPipeP The data.

Description

Dumping refers to the conversion of a fileset into a data stream suitable for storage on tape, or as an intermediate format when moving filesets. Restoring refers to conversion of a data stream back into the appropriate fileset format, and to its placement back into the file system.

FTSERVER_Restore( ) reads the stream of a fileset dump from *dataPipeP* and passes it to the fileset associated with the active transaction *transID*. The effect of this call is to convert a fileset dump into proper fileset format. The dump format is described under **FTSERVER_Dump( )**.

The *flags* parameter is currently ignored.

This function applies only to DCE LFS filesets.

Errors

FTSERVER_ERR_NOTRANS	The transaction was not found.
FTSERVER_ERR_IO	The operation could not write to the disk.
FTSERVER_ERR_BADDUMP	The dump is incorrectly formatted.
DAUT_ERROR_ACCESS_DENIED	Access was denied.

Related Information

Functions: **FTSERVER_Dump(3dfs)**, **FTSERVER_Forward(3dfs)**.

FTSERVER_SetFlags

Purpose Sets the current availability of a fileset

Synopsis **long FTSERVER_SetFlags(**
rpc_binding_handle_t *RpcBinding*,
unsigned long *transID*,
unsigned long *flags*)

Parameters

Input

RpcBinding The RPC handle.

transID The transaction for the fileset to be changed.

flags The new status flag.

Description

FTSERVER_SetFlags( ) sets the fileset's flags to *flags*, which may be one of those listed for **FTSERVER_GetFlags( )**.

Call **FTSERVER_SetFlags( )** with a *flags* value of **VOL_RW** (read/write) or **VOL_READONLY** after calling **FTSERVER_CreateVolume( )** or **FTSERVER_Clone( )** to bring the newly created fileset online. If you do not do this, the fileset is left offline and other operations on it fail.

Errors **DAUT_ERROR_ACCESS_DENIED** Access was denied.

Related Information

Functions: **FTSERVER_CreateVolume(3dfs), FTSERVER_Clone(3dfs).**

FTSERVER_SetStatus

Purpose Sets the various status information for a fileset

Synopsis

long FTSERVER_SetStatus(
rpc_binding_handle_t *RpcBinding*,
unsigned long *transID*,
unsigned long *mask*,
struct ftserver_status **status*,
unsigned long *spare1*)

Parameters

Input

RpcBinding The RPC handle.

transID The transaction on the fileset to be altered.

mask A mask of the status information to be set.

status The actual status information.

spare1 Reserved for future use.

Description

FTSERVER_SetStatus( ) sets the status information on the fileset associated with the transaction *transID*, according to the values in *status*. Status information includes the fileset name and ID, type, IDs of parent and clones, quota information, and dates of access, creation, expiration, and backup. Complete information about fileset status can be found in the **FTSERVER_GetStatus( )** reference page.

The mask is the bitwise OR of identifiers for the fields to be set. The fields are defined by the following constants:

- **VOL_STAT_VOLNAME**
- **VOL_STAT_VOLID**
- **VOL_STAT_VERSION**
- **VOL_STAT_UNIQUE**

- **VOL_STAT_OWNER**
- **VOL_STAT_TYPE**
- **VOL_STAT_STATES**
- **VOL_STAT_ACCSTATUS**
- **VOL_STAT_BACKUPID**
- **VOL_STAT_PARENTID**
- **VOL_STAT_CLONEID**
- **VOL_STAT_CREATEDATE**
- **VOL_STAT_UPDATEDATE**
- **VOL_STAT_ACCESSDATE**
- **VOL_STAT_COPYDATE**
- **VOL_STAT_FILECOUNT**
- **VOL_STAT_MAXQUOTA**
- **VOL_STAT_MINQUOTA**
- **VOL_STAT_SIZE**
- **VOL_STAT_INDEX**
- **VOL_STAT_BACKVOLINDEX**
- **VOL_STAT_STATUSMSG**
- **VOL_STAT_CLONETIME**
- **VOL_STAT_VVCURRTIME**
- **VOL_STAT_VVPINGCURRTIME**
- **VOL_STAT_ACCERROR**
- **VOL_STAT_BACKUPDATE**
- **VOL_STAT_RECLAIMDALLY**
- **VOL_STAT_LLBACKID**
- **VOL_STAT_LLFWDID**

Errors

DAUT_ERROR_ACCESS_DENIED Access was denied.

Related Information

Functions: **FTSERVER_GetStatus(3dfs)**.

VC

Purpose Introduction to the Fileset Server interface functions

Synopsis

#include <dce/common_data.h>
#include <dce/rpc.h>
#include <dce/pthread.h>
#include <dce/pthread_exc.h>
#include <dce/compat.h>
#include <dce/nubik.h>
#include <dce/fldb_proc.h>
#include <dce/flserver.h>
#include <dce/flclient.h>
#include <fcntl.h>
#include <dce/ftserver_proc.h>
#include <dce/volume.h>
#include <dce/fldb_data.h>
#include <dce/ftserver.h>
#include <dce/ftserver_trans.h>
#include <dce/aggr.h>
#include <dce/volc.h>

Libraries All **VC( )** functions are defined in the library **libdcedfs.a**.

Description

The **VC( )** (Volume Call) functions obtain information and perform actions on File Server machines. These functions are distinct from those that talk to the various databases for server information.

Most of these functions manipulate filesets. They operate at a high level and do all of the necessary bookkeeping, such as maintaining the Fileset Location Database (FLDB), bringing new filesets online, and so on. To operate at lower levels, use the **FTSERVER( )** and **VL( )** functions to do these things manually.

Many of these functions take the same basic set of parameters. These common parameters are as follows:

RpcBinding A pointer to an RPC connection, which is a connection to an authenticated path that allows multiple asynchronous conversations (type **rpc_binding_handle_t**, a structure). This structure is completely opaque to the application programmer, and is simply passed around. The RPC function that opens a connection returns this pointer.

servAddrp A pointer to the address of the target server (type **sockaddr**, a structure).

aggrID A long integer that identifies the fileset's location on the specified aggregate (typically, a disk number).

volNamep A pointer to a string that gives the fileset's name.

volIDp A pointer to a unique fileset identifier (type **afsHyper**, a structure).

Unless otherwise specified, all **VC( )** functions return 0 (zero) if the function completes successfully, or an error otherwise. These functions do not follow the UNIX convention of returning -1 when there are errors and setting **errno** to the specific flag.

All functions that return a structure (as opposed to an integer) have as the final argument a pointer to a structure of the appropriate type. You do not need to worry about creating that structure; this is just a pointer to a chunk of memory into which RPC writes the resulting data. It is up to you to dispose of this memory when it is no longer needed.

During most function calls, the FLDB entry for a fileset is locked. Locks are purely advisory; they do not actually prevent other processes from modifying the fileset or the FLDB entry. The lock does prevent other locks, however, so if you are careful to always lock the fileset before modifying it, you do not cause conflicts.

A *volIDp* is a pointer to an **afsHyper** structure, which represents a 64-bit counter:

```
struct afsHyper {
    unsigned long high;
    unsigned long low;
  };
```

Errors

The following Fileset Server errors can be returned by the **VC( )** functions:

VL_IDEXIST A fileset ID entry exists in the FLDB.

VL_IO An I/O error occurred.

VL_NAMEEXIST A fileset name entry exists in the FLDB.

VL_CREATEFAIL An internal creation failure occurred.

VL_NOENT There is no such entry.

VL_EMPTY	The FLDB is empty.
VL_ENTDELETED	The entry is deleted (soft delete).
VL_BADNAME	The fileset name is illegal.
VL_BADINDEX	The index is out of range.
VL_BADVOLTYPE	A bad fileset type was encountered.
VL_BADSERVER	There is an illegal server number (out of range).
VL_BADPARTITION	A bad partition number was encountered.
VL_REPSFULL	The operation ran out of space for replication sites.
VL_NOREPSERVER	No such replication server site exists.
VL_DUPREPSERVER	The replication site already exists.
VL_RWNOTFOUND	The parent read/write entry was not found.
VL_BADREFCOUNT	An illegal reference count number was encountered.
VL_SIZEEXCEEDED	The FLDB size for attributes was exceeded.
VL_BADENTRY	A bad incoming FLDB entry was encountered.
VL_BADVOLIDBUMP	An illegal maximum fileset ID increment was encountered.
VL_IDALREADYHASHED	The RO/BACK ID was already hashed.
VL_ENTRYLOCKED	The FLDB entry is already locked.
VL_BADVOLOPER	A bad fileset operation code was encountered.
VL_BADRELLOCKTYPE	A bad release lock type was encountered.
VL_RERELEASE	Status Report: The last release was aborted.
VL_BADSERVERFLAG	An invalid replication site server flag was encountered.
VL_PERM	There is no permission access.
VL_NOMEM	The **malloc( )** (**realloc( )**) function failed to allocate enough memory.

VL_SITESCORRUPTED The site table is corrupted.

VL_LASTADDRESS The last address for a site cannot be removed.

VL_ADDRESSFULL The operation ran out of space for addresses for a site.

VL_ADDRESSEXISTS The address already exists in this site.

VL_ADDRESSELSEWHERE FLDB: The address already exists in another site.

VL_NOTYETIMPLEMENTED
The facility is not yet implemented.

VL_ENDOFLIST The operation is at the end of the list.

VL_OUTOFQUOTA FLDB: There is no remaining quota for creations on a server.

VL_NOSUCHSERVER FLDB: The given server does not exist.

VL_BADCOOKIE FLDB: A bad site *Cookie* value given.

VL_INCONSISTENT FLDB: An internal inconsistency was detected.

VL_NOSERVER FLDB: There is no such server in the FLDB.

VL_BADID FLDB: The fileset ID was not reserved.

FTS_ERR_ATTACH A fileset could not be attached.

FTS_ERR_DETACH A fileset could not be detached.

FTS_ERR_BADAGGREGATE
An illegal aggregate was encountered.

FTS_ERR_BADNAME A bad fileset name was encountered.

FTS_ERR_BADACCESS There is insufficient privilege for the fileset operation.

FTS_ERR_VLDB An error from the fileset location database occurred.

FTS_ERR_MOVED The fileset moved.

FTS_ERR_BADOP An illegal fileset operation was encountered.

FTS_ERR_DUMP A badly formatted dump was encountered.

FTS_ERR_BADDUMP The operation is restoring a bad format dump.

FTS_ERR_BADRELEASE The fileset release failed.

FTS_ERR_BUSY The fileset is still in use by **FTSERVER( )**.

FTS_ERR_NOMEM The operation ran out of virtual memory in **FTSERVER( )**.

FTS_ERR_NOVOL There is no such fileset.

FTS_ERR_MULTIRWVOL More than one read/write fileset exists.

FTS_ERR_FAILEDOP Not all entries were successfully processed.

FTS_ERR_IO An I/O error was encountered.

FTS_ERR_NOTIMP The operation is not yet implemented.

FTS_ERR_INTERNAL_FLDB
The FLDB client was not initialized.

FTSERVER_ERR_ATTACH The fileset could not be attached.

FTSERVER_ERR_DETACH The fileset could not be detached.

FTSERVER_ERR_BADAGGREGATE
An illegal aggregate was encountered.

FTSERVER_ERR_BADNAME
A bad fileset name was encountered.

FTSERVER_ERR_BADACCESS
There is insufficient privilege for the fileset operation.

FTSERVER_ERR_VLDB An error from the fileset location database occurred.

FTSERVER_ERR_MOVED The fileset moved.

FTSERVER_ERR_BADOP An illegal fileset operation occurred.

FTSERVER_ERR_DUMP A badly formatted dump was encountered.

FTSERVER_ERR_BADDUMP
The operation is restoring a bad format dump.

FTSERVER_ERR_BADRELEASE
The fileset release failed.

FTSERVER_ERR_BUSY The fileset is still in use by **FTSERVER( )**.

FTSERVER_ERR_OFFLINE The fileset is offline.

FTSERVER_ERR_NOMEM The operation ran out of virtual memory in **FTSERVER( )**.

FTSERVER_ERR_NOVOL There is no such fileset.

FTSERVER_ERR_MULTIRWVOL
More than one read/write fileset exists.

FTSERVER_ERR_IO An I/O error occurred.

FTSERVER_ERR_TRANSEXISTS
The transaction already exists.

FTSERVER_ERR_NOTRANS
The transaction does not exist.

FTSERVER_ERR_TRELE An internal error releasing transaction occurred.

FTSERVER_ERR_DELETED The fileset is already deleted.

FTSERVER_ERR_LCLMOUNT
The fileset is locally mounted.

In addition, all errors that can be returned by the DCE RPC component can appear.

Related Information

Functions: **FTSERVER(3dfs)**, **intro(3dfs)**, **VL(3dfs)**.

VC_BackupVolume

Purpose Makes a backup copy of a fileset (DCE LFS filesets only)

Synopsis **long VC_BackupVolume(**
rpc_binding_handle_t *RpcBinding*,
struct sockaddr **servAddrp*,
unsigned long *aggrID*,
struct afsHyper **filesetIDp*)

Parameters

Input

RpcBinding The RPC handle.

servAddrp The server address.

aggrID The aggregate on which the fileset lives.

filesetIDp The fileset ID.

Description

VC_BackupVolume( ) makes a copy (clone) of the specified fileset and registers this copy in the FLDB as a backup. This copy is stored on the same aggregate as the original fileset. **VC_BackupVolume( )** gives the new fileset the name *fileset*.**backup** and brings it online. If a backup fileset already exists, **VC_BackupVolume( )** updates it.

The FLDB entry for the original fileset is locked during this operation.

This function applies only to DCE LFS filesets.

VC_CreateVolume

Purpose Creates a new fileset (DCE LFS filesets only)

Synopsis **long VC_CreateVolume(**
rpc_binding_handle_t *RpcBinding*,
struct sockaddr **servAddrp*,
unsigned long *aggrID*,
char **filesetNamep*,
struct afsHyper **filesetIDp*)

Parameters

Input

RpcBinding The RPC handle.

servAddrp The server address.

aggrID The ID of the aggregate on which to create the fileset.

filesetNamep The name of the fileset.

Output

filesetIDp The ID of the fileset.

Description

VC_CreateVolume( ) creates a fileset on the specified server and aggregate and returns the ID of the read/write copy.

This function applies only to DCE LFS filesets.

VC_DeleteVolume

Purpose

Deletes a fileset (DCE LFS filesets only)

Synopsis

long VC_DeleteVolume(
rpc_binding_handle_t *RpcBinding***,**
struct sockaddr **servAddrp***,**
unsigned long *aggrID***,**
struct afsHyper **filesetIDp***)**

Parameters

Input

RpcBinding	The RPC handle.
servAddrp	The server address.
aggrID	The ID of the aggregate from which to delete the fileset.
filesetIDp	The ID of the fileset to delete.

Description

VC_DeleteVolume( ) deletes the specified fileset and updates the FLDB. If there is an error, it returns the appropriate error code.

This function applies only to DCE LFS filesets.

Related Information

Functions: **VC_VolumeZap(3dfs)**.

VC_DumpVolume

Purpose

Dumps recent changes to a fileset

Synopsis

long VC_DumpVolume(
rpc_binding_handle_t *RpcBinding***,**
struct sockaddr **servAddrp***,**
struct afsHyper **filesetIDp***,**
unsigned long *fromAggrID***,**
struct ftserver_Date **dumpDatep***,**
char **filename***)**

Parameters

Input

RpcBinding — The RPC handle.

servAddrp — The server address.

filesetIDp — The ID of the fileset to dump.

fromAggrID — The source aggregate.

dumpDateP — The reference date for the dump.

filename — The name of the file in which to dump the output.

Description

VC_DumpVolume( ) makes a copy of the changes to the specified fileset since the date specified. *filename* is a string naming the output file, or **NULL**, signaling that the dump output is to be sent to **stdout**.

The date is specified by the **ftserver_Date** structure, described under **FTSERVER_Dump( )**.

Related Information

Functions: **FTSERVER_Dump(3dfs), VC_RestoreVolume(3dfs)**.

VC_ListVolumes

Purpose Gets a list of filesets on a particular aggregate

Synopsis **long VC_ListVolumes(**
rpc_binding_handle_t *RpcBinding*,
struct sockaddr **servAddrp*,
unsigned long *aggrId*,
int *allFlag*,
struct ftserver_status ***resultPtr*,
long **sizep*)

Parameters

RpcBinding	The RPC handle.
servAddrp	The server address.
aggrId	The aggregate to examine.
allFlag	Flag indicating whether all fileset fields are returned.
resultPtr	The returned data.
sizep	The size, in bytes, of the result.

Description

VC_ListVolumes( ) returns an array of pointers to all the filesets on the given aggregate. If there are no filesets, **VC_ListVolumes( )** returns 0 (zero) in *sizep*.

If *allFlag* is 1, then all the relevant fields of the fileset are also returned; otherwise, only the IDs are returned. The result pointer (*resultPtr*) is specified by the **ftserver_status** structure; this structure is described under **FTSERVER_GetStatus( )**. A successful call allocates storage for the result with **malloc( )**. When you are finished with the result, you should free it.

The **afsTimeval** structure is defined in the reference page for **FTSERVER_Dump( )**.

Related Information

Functions: **VC_VolserStatus(3dfs), VC_VolumeStatus(3dfs)**.

VC_MoveVolume

Purpose Moves a fileset from one aggregate to another (DCE LFS filesets only)

Synopsis **long VC_MoveVolume(**
struct afsHyper ***filesetIDp*****,**
struct sockaddr ***fromservAddrp*****,**
unsigned long ***fromaggrID*****,**
struct sockaddr ***toservAddrp*****,**
unsigned long *toaggrID***)**

Parameters

Input

filesetIDp	The fileset to move.
fromservAddrp	The source server address.
fromaggrID	The source aggregate.
toservAddrp	The destination server address.
toaggrID	The destination aggregate.

Description

VC_MoveVolume( ) moves the fileset *filesetIDp* from one aggregate to another. If the fileset does not exist in the source aggregate, or if the destination aggregate does not exist, **VC_MoveVolume( )** returns **FTS_ERR_MOVED.** Otherwise, once the fileset is transferred, the function deletes any existing backups of the fileset from the source aggregate. No backups are made in the new aggregate.

The FLDB entry for the fileset is locked for the duration of the call.

This function applies only to DCE LFS filesets.

VC_RenameVolume

Purpose Renames a fileset

Synopsis **long VC_RenameVolume(**
struct vldbentry **entryp*,
char **oldNamep*,
char **newNamep*)

Parameters

Input

entryp	The FLDB entry for the fileset.
oldNamep	The old fileset name.
newNamep	The new fileset name.

Description

VC_RenameVolume( ) renames the fileset from the old name to the new name. It also renames all associated backup and replicated copies. The caller must provide the FLDB entry for the fileset; **VC_RenameVolume**( ) does not look up this information. The caller can get this entry by using **VL_GetEntryByName( )** or **VL_GetEntryByID**( ).

The FLDB entry is locked during the operation.

Related Information

Functions: **VL_GetEntryByID(3dfs), VL_GetEntryByName(3dfs)**.

VC_RestoreVolume

Purpose Restores previously saved changes to a fileset (DCE LFS filesets only)

Synopsis **long VC_RestoreVolume(**
rpc_binding_handle_t **toRpcBinding***,**
struct sockaddr **toservAddrp***,**
unsigned long *toaggrID***,**
struct afsHyper **filesetIDp***,**
char **filesetNamep***,**
int *override***,**
char **filename***)**

Parameters

Input

toRpcBinding The RPC handle.

toservAddrp The destination server address.

toaggrID The destination aggregate.

filesetIDp The ID of the fileset to restore.

filesetNamep The name of the fileset to restore.

override A flag indicating whether to overwrite any preexisting copy of the fileset.

filename The name of the file containing the dump, or **NULL**, to indicate that the fileset data may be found on **stdout**.

Description

VC_RestoreVolume( ) restores a fileset from a data stream produced by **VC_DumpVolume( )**. The *override* parameter says what to do with any preexisting copy of the fileset; the value 1 means to overwrite it, and 0 (zero) means to cancel the restore if a fileset already exists with that name.

This function applies only to DCE LFS filesets.

VC_SetQuota

Purpose

Sets the disk space quota for a fileset (DCE LFS filesets only)

Synopsis

long VC_SetQuota(
rpc_binding_handle_t *RpcBinding***,**
struct sockaddr **servAddrp***,**
unsigned long *aggrID***,**
struct afsHyper **filesetIDp***,**
unsigned long *quota***)**

Parameters

Input

RpcBinding	The RPC handle.
servAddrp	The fileset's server.
aggrID	The fileset's aggregate.
filesetIDp	The fileset on which to set quota.
quota	The new quota.

Description

VC_SetQuota( ) sets the disk quota of the fileset named by *filesetIDp* on aggregate *aggrID* on server *servAddrp* to be *quota* 1024-byte units. If the fileset is already using more space than that, the change succeeds and writes to the fileset will fail until the quota is changed or usage is reduced below the new quota.

This function applies only to DCE LFS filesets.

VC_SyncServer

Purpose Removes filesets from an aggregate that are not listed as being there in the Fileset Location Database

Synopsis
long VC_SyncServer(
rpc_binding_handle_t *RpcBinding*,
struct sockaddr **servAddrp*,
unsigned long *aggrId*)

Parameters

Input

RpcBinding The RPC handle.

servAddrp The server address.

aggrId The aggregate to be affected.

Description

VC_SyncServer( ) synchronizes the server with the FLDB. Filesets that do not have FLDB entries are given entries, unless they are corrupted, in which case they are removed. If *aggrId* is -1, this is done for all aggregates on the server.

This function should not be called unless **VC_SyncVldb( )** is called first; if **VC_SyncVldb( )** is not called and there are things on disk that are not in the FLDB, then **VC_SyncServer( )** concludes that they are garbage and deletes them.

This function applies only to DCE LFS filesets.

Related Information

Functions: **VC_SyncVldb(3dfs)**.

VC_SyncVldb

Purpose Synchronizes the Fileset Location Database with the actual state of an aggregate

Synopsis **long VC_SyncVldb(**
rpc_binding_handle_t *RpcBinding*,
struct sockaddr **servAddrp*,
unsigned long *aggrId*)

Parameters

Input

RpcBinding	The RPC handle.
servAddrp	The server address.
aggrId	The source aggregate.

Description

VC_SyncVldb( ) makes sure that everything in the specified aggregate is also represented in the FLDB. If FLDB entries are found for filesets that do not actually exist on the aggregate, this function removes the entries. If *aggrId* is -1, this is done for all aggregates on the server. This function should always be called before calling **VC_SyncServer( )**.

Related Information

Functions: **VC_SyncServer(3dfs)**.

VC_VolserStatus

Purpose Reports the status of a Fileset Server

Synopsis **long VC_VolserStatus(**
rpc_binding_handle_t *RpcBinding*,
struct sockaddr **servAddrp*,
struct ftserver_transEntries ***rstatusp*)

Parameters

Input

RpcBinding The RPC handle.

servAddrp The server address.

Output

rstatusp The transaction status information.

Description

VC_VolserStatus( ) returns a list of all of the active transactions on the specified server. These transactions cover all file server operations, such as rename, delete, create, move, and copy.

Related Information

Functions: **FTSERVER_GetStatus(3dfs), VC_DumpVolume(3dfs), VC_ListVolumes(3dfs)**.

VC_VolumeStatus

Purpose Reports the status of a particular fileset

Synopsis **long VC_VolumeStatus(**
rpc_binding_handle_t *RpcBinding***,**
struct sockaddr ***servAddrp*,**
unsigned long *aggrID***,**
struct afsHyper ***filesetIDp*,**
struct ftserver_status ***statusp*)**

Parameters

Input

RpcBinding The RPC handle.

servAddrp The server address.

aggrID The aggregate on which the fileset is stored.

filesetIDp The fileset ID.

Output

statusp The status information.

Description

VC_VolumeStatus( ) returns the status of the specified fileset. The fileset status is represented by the **fileset_status** structure, which is described in **VC_ListVolumes( )**.

Related Information

Functions: **VC_ListVolumes(3dfs)**.

VC_VolumeZap

Purpose Deletes a fileset without updating the Fileset Location Database (DCE LFS filesets only)

Synopsis **long VC_VolumeZap(**
rpc_binding_handle_t *RpcBinding*,
struct sockaddr **servAddrp*,
unsigned long *aggrID*,
struct afsHyper **filesetIDp*)

Parameters

Input

RpcBinding The RPC handle.

servAddrp The server address.

aggrID The aggregate on which the fileset resides.

filesetIDp The fileset ID.

Description

VC_VolumeZap( ) deletes a fileset. Unlike **VC_DeleteVolume( )**, **VC_VolumeZap( )** does not update the FLDB.

You should use **VC_VolumeZap( )** instead of **VC_DeleteVolume( )** if the FLDB entry is corrupted or does not exist, or if you have multiple copies of a fileset and some of them are garbage.

Cautions Because **VC_VolumeZap( )** does not update the FLDB, the FLDB may believe that the fileset exists when it does not after this call. You should exercise care in the use of this function.

This function applies only to DCE LFS filesets.

Related Information

Functions: **VC_DeleteVolume(3dfs)**.

VL

Purpose Introduction to the Fileset Location Database server functions

Synopsis

#include <dce/common_data.h>
#include <dce/rpc.h>
#include <dce/pthread.h>
#include <dce/pthread_exc.h>
#include <dce/compat.h>
#include <dce/nubik.h>
#include <dce/fldb_proc.h>
#include <dce/flserver.h>
#include <dce/flclient.h>

Libraries All **VL( )** functions are defined in the library **libdcedfs.a**.

Description

The **VL( )** fileset location call functions are used by remote clients to interact with the Fileset Location Server. These procedures are the basic means by which DFS Cache Managers locate filesets in a DCE File System cell. The prime resource located is the fileset (formerly volume), the collection of files that is the unit of backup, quota enforcement, and replication. The locations of filesets are listed in the Fileset Location Database (FLDB), and it is this database that the Fileset Location Server primarily reads and updates.

The functions provided fall into several categories.

- Fileset Location: These functions determine the location of a fileset by its (64-bit) identifier or by its (character string) name.
- Fileset Maintenance: These functions create, delete, and change attributes of filesets, enumerate entries in the FLDB, report statistics, and change attributes of fileset-bearing servers. In order to modify the FLDB, the caller must be the cell administrator.
- Configuration Discovery: This function allows a Cache Manager to get information about a cell from the Fileset Location Server.

There are several types of descriptor blocks passed between the Fileset Location Server and its clients. The simplest clients retrieve a fileset-descriptor block called a **vldbentry**.

```
/* defines for convenience of vl users */
#define VLF_RWEXISTS    0x01000 /* flags for whole fldb entry */
#define VLF_ROEXISTS    0x02000
#define VLF_BACKEXISTS  0x04000
#define VLF_LAZYREP     0x08000 /* Replication of RO filesets by sched rep */
#define VLF_LAZYRELE    0x10000 /* even if LAZYREP, one R/O is vos-released */
#define VLSF_NEWREPSITE 0x01    /* flags for indiv. server entry */
#define VLSF_SAMEASPREV 0x10
#define VLSF_DEFINED    0x20
#define VLSF_ZEROIXHERE ((unsigned long) 0x80000000)

/* External (visible) representation of an individual fldb entry */
struct vldbentry{
    char name[MAXNAMELEN];
    unsigned long volumeType;
    unsigned long nServers;
    struct afsNetAddr siteAddr[MAXNSERVERS];
    unsigned long sitePartition[MAXNSERVERS];
    unsigned long siteFlags[MAXNSERVERS];
    unsigned long sitemaxReplicaLatency[MAXNSERVERS];
    struct kerb_princ_name sitePrincipal[MAXNSERVERS];
    struct afsUUID siteOwner[MAXNSERVERS];
    struct afsUUID siteObjID[MAXNSERVERS];
    struct afsHyper VolIDs[MAXVOLTYPES];
    unsigned long VolTypes[MAXVOLTYPES];
    struct afsHyper cloneId;
    unsigned long flags;
    unsigned long maxTotalLatency;
    unsigned long hardMaxTotalLatency;
    unsigned long minimumPounceDally;
    unsigned long defaultMaxReplicaLatency;
    unsigned long reclaimDally;
    unsigned long WhenLocked;
    unsigned long spare1;
    unsigned long spare2;
    unsigned long spare3;
    unsigned long spare4;
    char LockerName[MAXLOCKNAMELEN];
    char charSpares[50];
  }
```

The fields of this structure are as follows:

name The string naming the fileset.

volumeType
The fileset type, one of the following:

- **VOLTIX_TO_VOLTYPE(RWVOL)** (read/write)
- **VOLTIX_TO_VOLTYPE(ROVOL)** (read-only)
- **VOLTIX_TO_VOLTYPE(BACKVOL)** (backup)

The macro **VOLTIX_TO_VOLTYPE** takes one of the three types as its argument and produces the actual type representation, which is internal.

nServers The number of servers that contain this fileset, up to **MAXNSERVERS**.

siteAddr An array of server addresses; everything after the *nServers*th entry is meaningless.

sitePartition
An array, as in the previous example, listing aggregate identifiers for the fileset on each server.

siteFlags Flags for each server.

sitemaxReplicaLatency
The maximum age, in seconds, that a fileset replica can be without the Replication Server attempting to update it.

sitePrincipal
The name of the DCE principal.

siteOwner
The UUID of the authentication group that can modify site information.

siteObjId The UUID of the site.

VolIDs The fileset IDs for all related filesets.

VolTypes The types of those related filesets. This array and the previous one are paired.

cloneId IDs of cloned copies of a fileset.

flags General flags, as opposed to site flags.

maxTotalLatency
The maximum age, in seconds, a cached copy of data from a fileset can be before the DFS Cache Manager seeks to refresh it.

hardMaxTotalLatency
The replica age at which the Cache Manager refuses to use cached data.

minimumPounceDally
The amount of time, in seconds, for the Replication Server to wait before attempting to retrieve a new token after losing one.

defaultMaxReplicaLatency
The age, in seconds, a replica can be, before the Replication Server will not trust it.

reclaimDally
The time, in seconds, between keep-alive messages sent by the Cache Manager.

WhenLocked
The time at which this entry was locked, if it is currently locked.

LockerName
The name of the user holding the current lock on the entry, if any.

The **VLSF_SAMEASPREV** flag is set in an indexed entry in *siteFlags* when its index represents an additional network address for the server listed with the previous index.

The **VLSF_DEFINED** flag is set in *siteFlags* for only those indices where the corresponding fields are meaningful, and is cleared otherwise.

The **VLSF_ZEROIXHERE** flag, right-shifted between 0 and 7 bits, is set in *siteFlags* to say which fileset instances are on which servers. Multiple fileset instances can be on a single server, such as read/write and backup instances. The rule is as follows: **VLSF_ZEROIXHERE**, right-shifted by *k* bits, is set in the *siteFlags* entry for a server on which the fileset with identifier *VolIDs*[*k*] and type *VolTypes*[*k*] is present. Thus:

VLSF_ZEROIXHERE: indicates a fileset with ID VolIDs[0], type VolTypes[0]
VLSF_ZEROIXHERE >> 1: indicates a fileset with ID VolIDs[1], type VolTypes[1]
VLSF_ZEROIXHERE >> 2: indicates a fileset with ID VolIDs[2], type VolTypes[2]
.....
VLSF_ZEROIXHERE >> 7: indicates a fileset with ID VolIDs[7], type VolTypes[7]

In many cases, a complete **vldbentry** structure is not necessary, and a **compactvldbentry** structure can be used instead. Its definition follows.

```
struct compactvldbentry {
    char name[MAXNAMELEN];
    unsigned long volumeType;
    unsigned long nServers;
```

```
    unsigned long siteCookies[MAXNSERVERS];
    unsigned long sitePartition[MAXNSERVERS];
    unsigned long siteFlags[MAXNSERVERS];
    unsigned long sitemaxReplicaLatency[MAXNSERVERS];
    afsHyper VolIDs[MAXVOLTYPES];
    unsigned long VolTypes[MAXVOLTYPES];
    afsHyper cloneId;
    unsigned long flags;
    unsigned long maxTotalLatency;
    unsigned long hardMaxTotalLatency;
    unsigned long minimumPounceDally;
    unsigned long defaultMaxReplicaLatency;
    unsigned long reclaimDally;
    unsigned long WhenLocked;
    unsigned long spare1;
    unsigned long spare2;
    unsigned long spare3;
    unsigned long spare4;
    char LockerName[MAXLOCKNAMELEN];
    char charSpares[50];
}
```

The fields in this structure have the same meanings as the corresponding fields in the **vldbentry** structure.

Calls that update the server-specific information add or remove **afsNetAddr** structures from the set of attributes of servers, or set the name of the DCE principal that is authoritative for that server. The **afsNetAddr** structure is a copy of the BSD **sockaddr**; the name of a DFS principal is simply an array of 64 characters terminated by a **NULL**.

```
struct kerb_princ_name {
    char text[MAXKPRINCIPALLEN];
};
```

Calls that obtain information about the set of servers known to the FLDB (the **VL_GetSiteInfo( )** and **VL_GenerateSites( )** calls) do so by returning a **siteDesc** structure. This structure describes a single server, and contains up to four **afsNetAddr** (**sockaddr**) structures and a DCE principal structure.

```
struct siteDesc {
    struct afsNetAddr Addr[ADDRSINSITE];
    char KerbPrin[MAXPRINCIPALLEN];
    afsUUID owner;
    afsUUID ObjID;
    unsigned long CreationQuota;
```

```
    unsigned long CreationUses;
    unsigned long spare1;
    unsigned long spare2;
    unsigned long spare3;
    unsigned long spare4;
    unsigned long spare5;
};
```

The **VL_GenerateSites( )** call potentially returns information about many servers at once. It does so by returning the **bulkSites** structure, which is simply a fixed-size array of **siteDesc** structures.

```
struct bulkSites {
    struct siteDesc Sites[9];
};
```

Errors

In addition to the error messages listed with each function in this set, all functions can return lower level errors from other DCE components or from within DFS.

Related Information

Functions: **intro(3dfs), VC(3dfs), FTSERVER(3dfs)**.

VL_AddAddress

Purpose Declares another net address for a server

Synopsis **long VL_AddAddress(**
rpc_binding_handle_t *rpcBinding*,
struct afsNetAddr **OldAddr*,
struct afsNetAddr **AddrToAdd*,
error_status_t **theCommStatus*)

Parameters

Input

rpcBinding The RPC handle.

OldAddr A current address for the server.

AddrToAdd The new address.

Output

theCommStatus An error is returned, if one occurred.

Description

The FLDB can store multiple network addresses per server machine. If a server entry has been created with **VL_CreateServer( )**, additional network addresses can be added to the FLDB's representation for that server. Such additional addresses will be returned in the **siteAddr** array in **vldbentry** structures returned from the FLDB whenever that server is listed as the repository for a fileset.

File servers are represented in the FLDB as equivalence classes of network addresses, and the internal representation of the FLDB entry lists only the pointers to these equivalence classes. The **VL_AddAddress( )** call, like the related calls **VL_RemoveAddress( )**, **VL_ChangeAddress( )**, and **VL_AlterServer( )**, alters the equivalence class represented in the FLDB. The **VL_GetSiteInfo( )** call is used to obtain the other addresses associated with a given file server, and the **VL_GenerateSites( )** call is used to enumerate all file servers known to the FLDB.

Cache Managers use the multiple addresses given for a particular file server in routing their packets to that server.

OldAddr is any of the current network addresses of the server, and *AddrToAdd* is the address to be added.

Errors

VL_PERM	The caller is not the superuser.
VL_BADENTRY	A bad *AddrToAdd* parameter exists.
VL_ADDRESSELSEWHERE	FLDB: The address already exists in another site.
VL_NOENT	FLDB: There is no such entry.
VL_BADINDEX	Internal corruption in the table of equivalence classes occurred.
VL_SITESCORRUPTED	Another sort of internal corruption in the table of equivalence classes occurred.
VL_IO	An error from an underlying database system occurred.
VL_ADDRESSEXISTS	This *AddrToAdd* value is already in this equivalence class.
VL_ADDRESSFULL	There is no more room to store additional addresses in the equivalence class.

Related Information

Functions: **VL_RemoveAddress(3dfs), VL_ChangeAddress(3dfs), VL_AlterServer(3dfs), VL_GetSiteInfo(3dfs), VL_GenerateSites(3dfs), VL_CreateServer(3dfs)**.

VL_AlterServer

Purpose Alters server information in the FLDB

Synopsis **long VL_AlterServer(**
rpc_binding_handle_t *rpcBinding*,
struct afsNetAddr **Addr*,
struct siteAlter **Attrs*,
error_status_t **theCommStatus*)

Parameters

Input

rpcBinding The RPC handle.

Addr The address of the server.

Attrs The changes to make.

Output

theCommStatus An error is returned, if one occurred.

Description

VL_AlterServer() changes some information about the server identified by *Addr*. It takes a **siteAlter** structure describing the changes to make. This structure is defined as follows.

```
struct siteAlter {
    unsigned long Mask;
    char KerbPrin[MAXKPRINCIPALLEN];
    afsUUID Owner;
    afsUUID ObjID;
    unsigned long CreationQuota;
    unsigned long CreationUses;
    unsigned long spare1;
    unsigned long spare2;
}
```

Mask is the bitwise OR of the flags for the fields to be altered; the new values for those fields are taken from the rest of this structure. The flags are

SITEALTER_PRINCIPAL, **SITEALTER_OWNER**, **SITEALTER_OBJID**, **SITEALTER_CREATIONQUOTA**, **SITEALTER_CREATIONUSES**, and **SITEALTER_DELETEME**.

If **CreationQuota** is 0 (zero), there is no limit to the number of filesets that may point to that server.

If **SITEALTER_DELETEME** is specified, the server is deleted from the FLDB. It is an error to combine this bit with any other, or to delete a server that is still in use. In the first case, **VL_BADINDEX** is returned; in the latter case, **VL_INCONSISTENT** is returned. If the **CreationUses** field is nonzero, **VL_SITEINUSE** is returned.

Once a site is deleted, there is no way to retrieve it. The memory used to store the data is zeroed and reused by the next site creation.

The paradigm for equivalence classes of network addresses is explained more fully in the discussion of **VL_AddAddress( )**.

Related Information

Functions: **intro(3dfs)**, **VL_CreateServer(3dfs)**.

VL_ChangeAddress

Purpose Alters a network address entry for a server

Synopsis **long VL_ChangeAddress(**
rpc_binding_handle_t *rpcBinding*,
struct afsNetAddr **OldAddr*,
struct afsNetAddr **NewAddr*,
error_status_t **theCommStatus*)

Parameters

Input

rpcBinding The RPC handle.

OldAddr The old address.

NewAddr The address to change it to.

Output

theCommStatus An error is returned, if one occurred.

Description

VL_ChangeAddress( ) changes one of the network addresses in an equivalence class for a file server to a new value. It is comparable to **VL_AddAddress(OldAddr, NewAddr)**, followed by **VL_RemoveAddress(OldAddr)**, but does not require that the equivalence class have space available.

The paradigm for equivalence classes of network addresses is explained more fully in the discussion of **VL_AddAddress( )**.

OldAddr is the address to be changed, and *NewAddr* is the new value to which it should be changed.

Errors

VL_PERM	The caller is not the superuser.
VL_BADENTRY	A bad value for *NewAddr* exists.
VL_IO	An error from an underlying database occurred.
VL_NOENT	FLDB: There is no such entry.
VL_BADINDEX	Internal corruption in the table of equivalence classes occurred.
VL_SITESCORRUPTED	Another sort of internal corruption in the table of equivalence classes occurred.
VL_ADDRESSELSEWHERE	FLDB: The address already exists in another site.

Related Information

Functions: **VL_AddAddress(3dfs)**.

VL_CreateEntry

Purpose Creates a new FLDB entry

Synopsis

long VL_CreateEntry(
rpc_binding_handle_t *rpcBinding***,**
struct vldbentry ***new*,**
error_status_t ***theCommStatus*)**

Parameters

Input

rpcBinding	The RPC handle.
new	The new entry.

Output

theCommStatus	An error is returned, if one occurred.

Description

VL_CreateEntry( ) enters the given FLDB entry into the database. It is assumed to be formatted correctly; a few syntactic checks are made on the entry, but the correctness and completeness of the entry are ultimately up to the caller.

Errors

VL_PERM	The caller is not the superuser.
VL_BADNAME	The name has illegal characters.
VL_BADSERVER	The given number of servers is out of bounds.
VL_BADPARTITION	The partition value is out of bounds for some server.
VL_BADSERVERFLAG	The *siteFlags* value is out of bounds for some server.
VL_BADVOLTYPE	A bad *VolTypes* value was given.
VL_IDEXIST	A fileset of this ID already exists in the FLDB.

VL_NAMEEXIST	A fileset of this name already exists in the FLDB.
VL_CREATEFAIL	There is some underlying error in database manipulation.
VL_IO	There is a different underlying error in database manipulation.
VL_IDALREADYHASHED	A fileset of this ID has already been partially added to the FLDB.

VL_CreateServer

Purpose Declares another server machine to the FLDB

Synopsis **long VL_CreateServer(**
rpc_binding_handle_t *rpcBinding*,
struct siteDesc **FullSiteInfo*,
error_status_t **theCommStatus*)

Parameters

Input

rpcBinding The RPC handle.

FullSiteInfo A description of the new server.

Output

theCommStatus An error is returned, if one occurred.

Description

VL_CreateServer( ) informs the FLDB of the existence of a new server. If you deploy a server and put filesets on it without informing the FLDB, those filesets will be inaccessible as far as the FLDB is concerned; the information is not automatically added. *FullSiteInfo* contains a network address and DCE principal. The **siteDesc** structure is described under **VL( )**.

If there are deleted servers in the FLDB, the first one is used for the new server, and its status is changed from deleted to active. This is done to conserve space in the FLDB.

The paradigm for equivalence classes of network addresses is explained more fully in the discussion of **VL_AddAddress( )**.

Related Information

Functions: **VL_AlterServer(3dfs)**.

VL_DeleteEntry

Purpose Deletes an entry from the FLDB

Synopsis

long VL_DeleteEntry(
rpc_binding_handle_t *rpcBinding***,**
struct afsHyper ***filesetID***,**
unsigned long *filesetType***,**
error_status_t ***theCommStatus*)

Parameters

Input

rpcBinding The RPC handle.

filesetID The ID of the fileset to delete.

filesetType The type of the fileset.

Output

theCommStatus An error is returned, if one occurred.

Description

The *filesetID* parameter is the 64-bit identifier for the fileset to be deleted. *filesetType* is the type of fileset. More information about fileset types can be found in the reference page for **VL_GetEntryByID( )**.

VL_DeleteEntry( ) deletes the FLDB entry for the given fileset. The *filesetType* parameter may be a wildcard, as in **VL_GetEntryByID( )**.

Errors

VL_PERM The caller is not the superuser.

VL_BADFILESETTYPE
The *filesetType* parameter is not comprehensible.

VL_NOENT FLDB: There is no such entry.

VL_ENTDELETED The fileset is already deleted.

VL_BADINDEX	An internal error occurred; the index is out of bounds.
VL_IO	An I/O error in an underlying system occurred.

Related Information

Functions: **VL_GetEntryByID(3dfs)**.

VL_ExpandSiteCookie

Purpose

Expands compacted site representation

Synopsis

long VL_ExpandSiteCookie(
rpc_binding_handle_t *rpcBinding***,**
unsigned long *Cookie***,**
struct siteDesc **FullSiteInfo***,**
error_status_t **theCommStatus***)**

Parameters

Input

rpcBinding The RPC handle.

Cookie An index into the compact representation.

Output

FullSiteInfo The full site description.

theCommStatus An error is returned, if one occurred.

Description

VL_ExpandSiteCookie( ) takes *Cookie*, a field in the **compactvldbentry** structure representing site information, and produces *FullSiteInfo*, a **siteDesc** structure that contains information such as the network address and DCE principal for the site.

Related Information

Functions: **VL_GetCEntryByID(3dfs), VL_GetCEntryByName(3dfs), VL_GetCNextServersByID(3dfs), VL_GetCNextServersByName(3dfs).**

VL_GenerateSites

Purpose Lists all file servers known to the FLDB

Synopsis **long VL_GenerateSites(**
rpc_binding_handle_t *rpcBinding*,
unsigned long *startHere*,
unsigned long **nextStartP*,
struct bulkSites **TheseSites*,
long **nSites*,
error_status_t **theCommStatus*)

Parameters

Input

rpcBinding The RPC handle.

startHere The iterator.

Output

nextStartP The next iterator.

TheseSites The site information.

nSites Specifies how many entries are contained in *TheseSites*.

theCommStatus An error is returned, if one occurred.

Description

VL_GenerateSites() provides information about all file servers known to the FLDB (in other words, any servers mentioned in it).

Successive calls to **VL_GenerateSites()** return all the descriptions for file servers stored in the FLDB. Use 0 (zero) for the value of the *startHere* parameter the first time, and in subsequent calls, pass as *startHere* the value returned in the previous call via *nextStartP*. The *TheseSites* parameter is a fixed-size array of **siteDesc** structures, and the value of the *nSites* parameter indicates how many of the elements in *TheseSites* are valid.

Servers that are flagged as being deleted are skipped by this function.

The **bulkSites** structure is:

```
struct bulkSites {
    struct siteDesc Sites[9];
};
```

Errors

VL_BADINDEX	A bad value for *startHere* was passed in, or there is internal corruption in the table of equivalence classes.
VL_IO	An error from an underlying database occurred.
VL_SITESCORRUPTED	Another sort of internal corruption in the table of equivalence classes occurred.
VL_ENDOFLIST	No further site descriptions are present.

Related Information

Functions: **VL_AddAddress(3dfs)**.

VL_GetCEntryByID

Purpose Gets the compact FLDB entry corresponding to a fileset ID

Synopsis **long VL_GetCEntryByID(**
rpc_binding_handle_t *rpcBinding*,
struct afsHyper **filesetID*,
unsigned long *filesetType*,
struct compactvldbentry **entry*,
error_status_t **theCommStatus*)

Parameters

Input

rpcBinding The RPC handle.

filesetID The fileset ID.

filesetType The fileset type.

Output

entry The compact entry.

theCommStatus An error is returned, if one occurred.

Description

VL_GetCEntryByID( ) retrieves the **compactvldbentry** information about the fileset identified by the 64-bit fileset ID, *filesetID*. If *filesetType* is -1, it indicates that the fileset should be found regardless of the type, but if *filesetType* is some other value, it indicates that the fileset ID must be of the given type or it is not found. At present, the *filesetType* parameter should be **VOLTIX_TO_FILESETTYPE(***x***)**, where *x* is one of **RWVOL** (the read/write fileset), **ROVOL** (the read-only fileset), or **BACKVOL** (the backup fileset).

The resulting **compactvldbentry** structure is copied to *entry*.

Errors

VL_BADFILESETTYPE Indicates that there is no legal value for *filesetType*.

VL_NOENT FLDB: There is no such entry.

VL_ENTDELETED The entry exists but is marked ''deleted.''

VL_IO There is some problem reading or writing the database.

Related Information

Functions: **VL_ExpandSiteCookie(3dfs)**, **VL_GetEntryByID(3dfs)**, **VL_GetCEntryByName(3dfs)**, **VL_GetCNextServersByID(3dfs)**.

VL_GetCEntryByName

Purpose Gets the compact FLDB entry corresponding to a fileset name

Synopsis

long VL_GetCEntryByName(
rpc_binding_handle_t *rpcBinding*,
char **filesetName*,
struct compactvldbentry **entry*,
error_status_t **theCommStatus*)

Parameters

Input

rpcBinding The RPC handle.

filesetName The fileset name.

Output

entry The compact entry.

theCommStatus An error is returned, if one occurred.

Description

VL_GetCEntryByName( ) looks up the **compactvldbentry** for a fileset given its name, *filesetName*, and returns the result via the *entry* parameter.

If the name contains only characters that are either digits or periods or commas, this function returns the result of **VL_GetEntryByID( )** instead, with a wildcard value for *filesetType*.

Errors

VL_BADNAME The *filesetName* parameter contains illegal characters.

VL_NOENT FLDB: There is no such entry.

VL_ENTDELETED The fileset was found but it is marked as "deleted."

VL_IO A low-level error manipulating the database occurred.

Related Information

Functions: **VL_ExpandSiteCookie(3dfs), VL_GetEntryByName, VL_GetCEntryByID(3dfs)**.

VL_GetCNextServersByID

Purpose Returns the next set of servers from a compact FLDB entry for a fileset (using the ID for lookup)

Synopsis **long VL_GetCNextServersByID(**
rpc_binding_handle_t *rpcBinding*,
struct afsHyper **filesetID*,
unsigned long *filesetType*,
unsigned long *startHere*,
unsigned long **nextStartP*,
struct compactvldbentry **entry*,
unsigned long **flags*,
error_status_t **theCommStatus*)

Parameters

Input

rpcBinding	The RPC handle.
filesetID	The fileset ID.
filesetType	The fileset type.
startHere	The iterator.

Output

nextStartP	The next iterator.
entry	The compact entry.
flags	Indicates whether there are more entries.
theCommStatus	An error is returned, if one occurred.

Description

VL_GetCNextServersByID( ) and the related **VL_GetCNextServersByName( )** circumvent a limitation of the fixed-size arrays in the **compactvldbentry** type. That is, there may be more information in the FLDB about a fileset than can fit into a fixed-size **compactvldbentry** structure. In particular, the **compactvldbentry** structure lists the file servers on which the given fileset may be found, in the *siteAddr, sitePartition, siteFlags*, and *sitemaxReplicaLatency* arrays, each of which is **MAXNSERVERS** elements long. **VL_GetCNextServersByID( )** is exactly analogous to **VL_GetCEntryByID( )**, except that it can return many successive **compactvldbentry** structures that can each refer to up to 16 additional machine addresses where file servers containing the fileset may be found. The caller first initializes the *startHere* parameter to 0 (zero), and if the function returns successfully, the parameter *nextStartP* is set to a nonzero value to be used as the next value for *startHere*. The other parameters, *filesetID*, *filesetType*, and *entry*, are exactly as in **VL_GetCEntryByID( )**. The low order bit in *flags* is set to 1 if there are no further addresses to return.

Errors

In addition to the codes that can be returned by **VL_GetEntryByID( )**, **VL_GetNextServersByID( )** returns the following:

VL_ENDOFLIST There are no further servers to be returned.

Related Information

Functions: **VL_GetCEntryByID(3dfs), VL_GetCNextServersByName(3dfs), VL_ExpandSiteCookie(3dfs), VL_GetEntryByID(3dfs).**

VL_GetCNextServersByName

Purpose Returns the next set of servers from a compact FLDB entry for a fileset (using the name for lookup)

Synopsis **long VL_GetCNextServerByName(**
rpc_binding_handle_t *rpcBinding*,
char **filesetName*,
unsigned long *startHere*,
unsigned long **nextStartP*,
struct compactvldbentry **entry*,
unsigned long **flags*,
error_status_t **theCommStatus*)

Parameters

Input

rpcBinding The RPC handle.

filesetName The fileset name.

startHere The iterator.

Output

nextStartP The next iterator.

entry The compact entry.

flags Indicates whether there are more entries.

theCommStatus An error is returned, if one occurred.

Description

VL_GetCNextServersByName( ) is to **VL_GetCEntryByName( )** as **VL_GetCNextServersByID( )** is to **VL_GetCEntryByID( )**. That is, **VL_GetCNextServersByName( )** helps circumvent the limitation on the number of file server addresses that can be listed in a single return from **VL_GetCEntryByName( )**. Pass 0 (zero) as the value for *startHere* in the first call, and on successive calls, pass the value returned via *nextStartP*. The **compactvldbentry** structures successively returned via *entry* have a succession of server descriptions, until the error code **VL_ENDOFLIST** is returned to indicate that there are no more servers to return. The low-order bit in *flags* will be set to 1 if there are no more addresses to return (after the ones currently being returned).

Errors

In addition to **VL_ENDOFLIST**, **VL_GetNextServersByName( )** returns all the error codes returned by **VL_GetEntryByName( )**.

Related Information

Functions: **VL_GetCNextServersByID(3dfs)**, **VL_GetEntryByName(3dfs)**, **VL_ExpandSiteCookie(3dfs)**, **VL_GetNextServersByName(3dfs)**.

VL_GetCellInfo

Purpose Gets configuration information for the server's cell

Synopsis **long VL_GetCellInfo(**
rpc_binding_handle_t *rpcBinding*,
struct vlconf_cell **MyCell*,
error_status_t **theCommStatus*)

Parameters

Input

rpcBinding The RPC handle.

Output

MyCell The cell configuration information.

theCommStatus An error is returned, if one occurred.

Description

VL_GetCellInfo( ) lets an application learn all the configuration information about a cell, simply by contacting one of the Fileset Location Server instances for that cell.

The only errors returned from this call reflect internal errors.

The return structure is as follows.

```
/* Complete server info for one cell.  An RPC mimic of ''struct afsconf_cell''. */

struct hostnam {char hstnam[MAXVLHOSTCHARS];};

struct vlconf_cell {
  char name[MAXVLCELLCHARS];         /* Cell name */
  struct afsHyper CellID;            /* identifier for that cell */
  long numServers;                   /* Num active servers for the cell */
  struct afsNetAddr hostAddr[MAXVLHOSTSPERCELL]; /* IP addrs for DB servers */
  struct hostnam hostName[MAXVLHOSTSPERCELL]; /* Names for DB servers */
  unsigned long spare1;
  unsigned long spare2;
```

```
unsigned long spare3;
unsigned long spare4;
unsigned long spare5;};
```

VL_GetEntryByID

Purpose Gets the FLDB entry corresponding to a fileset ID

Synopsis

long VL_GetEntryByID(
rpc_binding_handle_t *rpcBinding***,**
struct afsHyper **filesetID***,**
unsigned long *filesetType***,**
struct vldbentry **entry***,**
error_status_t **theCommStatus***)**

Parameters

Input

rpcBinding The RPC handle.

filesetID The fileset identifier.

filesetType The fileset type.

Output

entry The returned FLDB entry.

theCommStatus An error is returned, if one occurred.

Description

VL_GetEntryByID( ) retrieves the **vldbentry** information about the fileset identified by the 64-bit fileset ID, *filesetID*. If *filesetType* is -1, it indicates that the fileset should be found regardless of the type, but if *filesetType* is some other value, it indicates that the fileset ID must be of the given type or it is not found. At present, the *filesetType* parameter should be **VOLTIX_TO_FILESETTYPE(***x***)**, where *x* is one of **RWVOL** (the read/write fileset), **ROVOL** (the read-only fileset), or **BACKVOL** (the backup fileset).

The resulting **vldbentry** structure is copied to *entry*.

Errors

VL_BADFILESETTYPE Indicates that there is no legal value for *filesetType*.

VL_NOENT FLDB: There is no such entry.

VL_ENTDELETED	The entry exists but it is marked ''deleted.''
VL_IO	There is some problem reading or writing the database.

Related Information

Functions: **VC_RenameVolume(3dfs), VL_DeleteEntry(3dfs), VL_GetCEntryByID(3dfs), VL_GetEntryByName(3dfs), VL_GetCNextSeversByID(3dfs)**.

VL_GetEntryByName

Purpose Gets the FLDB entry corresponding to a fileset name

Synopsis
long VL_GetEntryByName(
rpc_binding_handle_t *rpcBinding*,
char **name*,
struct vldbentry **entry*,
error_status_t **theCommStatus*)

Parameters

Input

rpcBinding The RPC handle.

name The fileset name.

Output

entry The returned FLDB entry.

theCommStatus An error is returned, if one occurred.

Description

VL_GetEntryByName( ) looks up the **vldbentry** for a fileset given its name, *name*, and returns the result via the *entry* parameter.

If the name, in fact, contains only characters that are either digits or periods or commas, this function returns the result of **VL_GetEntryByID( )** instead, with a wildcard value for *filesetType*.

Errors

VL_BADNAME The *name* parameter contains illegal characters.

VL_NOENT FLDB: There is no such entry.

VL_ENTDELETED The fileset was found but it is marked as ''deleted.''

VL_IO A low-level error manipulating the database occurred.

Related Information

Functions: **VC_RenameVolume(3dfs)**, **VL_GetEntryByID(3dfs)**, **VL_GetCEntryByName(3dfs)**, **VL_GetCNextServersByName(3dfs)**.

VL_GetNewVolumeId

Purpose Allocates some fileset IDs

Synopsis

long VL_GetNewVolumeId(
rpc_binding_handle_t *rpcBinding*,
unsigned long *BumpCount*,
struct afsNetAddr **servAddrp*,
struct afsHyper **NewfilesetID*,
error_status_t **theCommStatus*)

Parameters

Input

rpcBinding	The RPC handle.
BumpCount	The number of fileset IDs to allocate.
servAddrp	The address of a server that you administer.

Output

NewfilesetID	The IDs.
theCommStatus	An error is returned, if one occurred.

Description

VL_GetNewVolumeId( ) reserves *BumpCount* 64-bit fileset IDs. It puts the first one into *NewfilesetID*. These new IDs can be used, for example, to identify newly created filesets in a **VL_CreateEntry**( ) call.

While the limit on the total number of fileset IDs is very large, these IDs need to be good for all time in a cell. They should therefore not be consumed rapidly or in large quantities unless they are actually needed.

If you are not in the administration file but are in the group that owns a server, you may still allocate IDs by referring to that server as *servAddrp*.

Errors

VL_PERM The caller is not the cell administrator.

VL_BADVOLIDBUMP The operation is asking for too many fileset IDs at a time.

VL_IO Some error in an underlying system occurred.

Related Information

Functions: **VL_CreateEntry(3dfs)**.

VL_GetNewVolumeIds

Purpose Allocates several fileset IDs

Synopsis **long VL_GetNewVolumeId(**
rpc_binding_handle_t *rpcBinding*,
unsigned long *numWanted*,
struct afsNetAddr **servAddrp*,
struct bulkIds **newIDs*,
error_status_t **theCommStatus*)

Parameters

Input

rpcBinding The RPC handle.

numWanted The number of fileset IDs to allocate.

servAddrp The address of a server that you administer.

Output

NewIDs The IDs.

theCommStatus An error is returned, if one occurred.

Description

VL_GetNewVolumeIds(), like **VL_GetNewVolumeId()**, reserves several fileset IDs, but this function returns them explicitly in a bulk format.

The **bulkIds** structure is defined as follows:

```
struct bulkIDs{
    unsigned long bulkID_len;
    struct afsHyper bulkIDs_val[MAXBULKLEN];
}
```

While the limit on the total number of fileset IDs is very large, these IDs need to be good for all time in a cell. They should therefore not be consumed rapidly or in large quantities unless they are actually needed.

If you are not in the administration file but are in the group that owns a server, you may still allocate IDs by referring to that server as *servAddrp*.

Errors

VL_PERM The caller is not the cell administrator.

VL_BADVOLIDBUMP The operation is asking for too many fileset IDs at a time.

VL_IO Some error in an underlying system occurred.

Related Information

Functions: **VL_CreateEntry(3dfs)**.

VL_GetNextServersByID

Purpose Returns the next set of servers for a fileset (using the ID for lookup)

Synopsis

long VL_GetNextServersByID(
rpc_binding_handle_t *rpcBinding*,
struct afsHyper **filesetID*,
unsigned long *filesetType*,
unsigned long *startHere*,
unsigned long **nextStartP*,
struct vldbentry **entry*,
unsigned long **flags*,
error_status_t **theCommStatus*)

Parameters

Input

rpcBinding The RPC handle.

filesetID The identifier of the fileset being looked up.

filesetType The fileset type.

startHere The input iterator value; start with 0 (zero).

Output

nextStartP The returned iterator value; use this in the next call for *startHere*.

entry The returned FLDB entry.

flags Specifies whether there are any more entries to return.

theCommStatus An error is returned, if one occurred.

Description

VL_GetNextServersByID( ) and the related call **VL_GetNextServersByName( )** circumvent a limitation of the fixed-size arrays in the **vldbentry** type. That is, there may be more information in the FLDB about a fileset than can fit into a fixed-size **vldbentry** structure. In particular, the **vldbentry** structure lists the file servers on which the given fileset may be found, in the *siteAddr, sitePartition, siteFlags*, and *sitemaxReplicaLatency* arrays, each of which is 16 elements long. Thus, the **VL_GetEntryByID( )** call is limited to listing only 16 different machine addresses at a time. **VL_GetNextServersByID( )** is exactly analogous to **VL_GetEntryByID( )**, except that it can return many successive **vldbentry** structures that can each contain up to 16 additional machine addresses where file servers containing the fileset may be found. The caller first initializes the *startHere* parameter to 0 (zero), and if the function returns successfully, the parameter *nextStartP* is set to a nonzero value to be used as the next value for *startHere*. The other parameters, *filesetID*, *filesetType*, and *entry*, are exactly as in **VL_GetEntryByID( )**. The low-order bit in *flags* is set to 1 if there are no further addresses to return.

Errors

In addition to the codes that can be returned by **VL_GetEntryByID( )**, **VL_GetNextServersByID( )** returns the following:

VL_ENDOFLIST There are no further servers to be returned.

Related Information

Functions: **VL_GetEntryByID(3dfs), VL_GetCEntryByID(3dfs), VL_GetCNextServersByName(3dfs)**.

VL_GetNextServersByName

Purpose Returns the next set of servers for a fileset (using the name for lookup)

Synopsis **long VL_GetNextServerByName(**
rpc_binding_handle_t *rpcBinding***,**
char ****name*,**
unsigned long *startHere***,**
unsigned long ****nextStartP*,**
struct vldbentry ****entry*,**
unsigned long ****flags*,**
error_status_t ****theCommStatus*)**

Parameters

Input

rpcBinding The RPC handle.

name The name of the fileset being looked up.

startHere The input iterator value; start with 0 (zero).

Output

nextStartP The returned iterator value; use this in the next call for *startHere*.

entry The returned FLDB entry.

flags Specifies whether there are any more entries to return.

theCommStatus An error is returned, if one occurred.

Description

VL_GetNextServersByName( ) is to **VL_GetEntryByName( )** as **VL_GetNextServersByID( )** is to **VL_GetEntryByID( )**. That is, **VL_GetNextServersByName( )** helps circumvent the limitation on the number of file server addresses that can be listed in a single return from **VL_GetEntryByName( )**. Pass 0 (zero) as the value for *startHere* in the first call, and on successive calls, pass the value returned via *nextStartP*. The **vldbentry** structures successively returned via *entry* have a succession of server descriptions, until the error code **VL_ENDOFLIST** is returned to indicate that there are no further servers to be returned. The low-order bit in *flags* will be set to 1 if there are no further addresses to return (after the ones currently being returned).

Errors In addition to **VL_ENDOFLIST**, **VL_GetNextServersByName( )** returns all the codes returned by **VL_GetEntryByName( )**.

Related Information

Functions: **VL_GetNextServersByID(3dfs), VL_GetEntryByName(3dfs), VL_GetCNextServersByName(3dfs)**.

VL_GetSiteInfo

Purpose Finds out a server's addresses and principal

Synopsis

long VL_GetSiteInfo(
rpc_binding_handle_t *rpcBinding*,
struct afsNetAddr **OldAddr*,
struct siteDesc **FullSiteInfo*,
error_status_t **theCommStatus*)

Parameters

Input

rpcBinding	The RPC handle.
OldAddr	One address for a server.

Output

FullSiteInfo	The addresses and principal.
theCommStatus	An error is returned, if one occurred.

Description

VL_GetSiteInfo( ) returns the full equivalence class of addresses stored in the FLDB for a file server, given any one of the addresses. It also returns the DCE principal associated with the file server. The paradigm for equivalence classes of network addresses is explained more fully in the discussion of **VL_AddAddress( )**.

Errors

VL_NOENT	FLDB: There is no such entry.
VL_IO	An error from an underlying database occurred.
VL_BADINDEX	Internal corruption in the table of equivalence classes occurred.
VL_SITESCORRUPTED	Another sort of internal corruption in the table of equivalence classes occurred.

Related Information

Functions: **VL_AddAddress(3dfs)**.

VL_GetStats

Purpose Gets the FLDB and server statistics

Synopsis
long VL_GetStats(
rpc_binding_handle_t *rpcBinding*,
struct vldstats **stats*,
struct vital_vlheader **vital_header*,
error_status_t **theCommStatus*)

Parameters

Input

rpcBinding The RPC handle.

Output

stats The operational statistics.

vital_header The basic FLDB statistics.

theCommStatus An error is returned, if one occurred.

Description

VL_GetStats( ) returns two data structures that describe both the specific operational statistics that are gathered by this Fileset Location Server instance and the basic information describing the FLDB as a whole.

The operational statistics are described in the following structure:

```
/* General stats on opcode hit frequency */
struct vldstats {
    unsigned long start_time;
    unsigned long requests[MAX_NUMBER_OPCODES];
    unsigned long aborts[MAX_NUMBER_OPCODES];
    unsigned long reserved[5];
};
```

The **start_time** parameter indicates when this server instance started up in the standard UNIX way (seconds since January 1, 1970). The **requests** and **aborts** arrays count the number of times that this server has begun processing, or aborted, each different RPC procedure. The index to these arrays is the well-known number of the RPC call, offset by the lowest of the well-known RPC call numbers. For example, the statistics for the **VL_GetEntryByID( )** call are found in **requests[2]** and **aborts[2]** because the RPC call number for the **VL_GetEntryByID** procedure is two higher than the smallest RPC call number, **VLCREATEENTRY**. The call numbers are defined as constants in the installed file **afs/fl_opcodes.h**.

The basic FLDB information is returned in the following structure:

```
/* the leading section of the fldb header (vlheader);
  contains frequently used globals and general statistics
  information */
struct vital_vlheader {
     unsigned long vldbversion;
     unsigned long headersize;
     unsigned long freePtr;
     unsigned long eofPtr;
     unsigned long allocs;
     unsigned long frees;
     struct afsHyper MaxVolumeId;
     unsigned long sitesPtr;
     unsigned long numSites;
     unsigned long totalEntries[MAXVOLTYPES];
     unsigned long Reserv[15];
};
```

Most of these values have meaning only in reference to the Fileset Location Server implementation. One exception is that the current value of **vldbversion** is 2, while its predecessor (which had, for instance, 32-bit fileset IDs, 31 maximum file server addresses, 4-byte network addresses, and the like) had a **vldbversion** of 1.

Errors

VL_PERM The caller is not the superuser.

VL_IO Some error in an underlying database occurred.

VL_ListByAttributes

Purpose Returns selected FLDB entries

Synopsis **long VL_ListByAttributes(**
rpc_binding_handle_t *rpcBinding*,
struct VldbListByAttributes **attributes*,
unsigned long *Cookie*,
unsigned long **nentries*,
bulkentries **blkentries*,
unsigned long **nextcookiep*,
unsigned long **flagsp*,
error_status_t **theCommStatus*)

Parameters

Input

rpcBinding The RPC handle.

attributes The attributes to search for.

Cookie The iterator; start with 0 (zero).

Output

nentries The number of entries contained in *blkentries*.

blkentries The entries.

nextcookiep The next iterator value to use.

flagsp A flag indicating whether there are more entries to return.

theCommStatus An error is returned, if one occurred.

Description

VL_ListByAttributes( ) addresses two limitations in the **VL_ListEntry( )** mechanism: that each FLDB entry is returned in individual RPC calls, and that no selection of FLDB entries is done at the database site itself. **VL_ListByAttributes( )** uses a selector structure (**VldbListByAttributes**) that describes the subset of the FLDB entries that should be returned. The results are returned as a bulk array (*blkentries*).

As usual, the *Cookie* parameter (the iterator) should be 0 (zero) for the first call and the value returned via *nextcookiep* on subsequent calls. The low-order bit of the **unsigned long** returned via *flagsp* is 0 (zero) if there are more entries to return, and 1 if this return includes the last matching entry.

The **VldbListByAttributes** structure is as follows:

```
/* Structure used by the VL_ListByAttributes routine */
struct VldbListByAttributes {
      unsigned long Mask;
      struct afsNetAddr site;
      unsigned long partition;
      unsigned long volumetype;
      struct afsHyper volumeid;
      unsigned long flag;
      unsigned long spare1;
      unsigned long spare2;
      unsigned long spare3;
      unsigned long spare4;
      unsigned long spare5;
};

/* struct VldbListByAttributes Mask bit values */
const  VLLIST_SITE=           0x1;
const  VLLIST_PARTITION=      0x2;
const  VLLIST_VOLUMETYPE=     0x4;
const  VLLIST_VOLUMEID=       0x8;
const  VLLIST_FLAG=           0x10;

typedef     vldbentry bulkentries<>;
```

The **Mask** field of the structure contains the bitwise OR of a selection of **VLLIST**_*xxx* flag bits. For each flag bit that is set, the value of the corresponding field further limits the selection of FLDB entries. Thus, all the FLDB entries that are on a particular site and a particular aggregate may be selected by specifying a **Mask** value of **VLLIST_SITE** compared by a bitwise OR with **VLLIST_PARTITION** and placing in the **site** and **partition** fields the values that are to be matched.

Selection by **VLLIST_VOLUMEID** overrides all other selections. That is, if a search is being done by fileset ID, all the other search criteria are ignored.

Errors

VL_IO Some error from an underlying database occurred.

VL_NOMEM The operation ran out of room allocating space for the results.

VL_SIZEEXCEEDED The operation ran out of room allocating space for the results.

VL_BADVOLTYPE There is a bad *volumetype* value in the **attributes** structure.

VL_ENDOFLIST The *Cookie* parameter points past the end of the FLDB.

Related Information

Functions: **VL_ListEntry(3dfs)**.

VL_ListEntry

Purpose Lists the contents of the FLDB

Synopsis **long VL_ListEntry(**
rpc_binding_handle_t *rpcBinding*,
unsigned long *previous_index*,
unsigned long **count*,
unsigned long **next_index*,
struct vldbentry **entry*,
error_status_t **theCommStatus*)

Parameters

Input

rpcBinding The RPC handle.

previous_index The iterator value; start with 0 (zero).

Output

count The approximate number of entries remaining.

next_index The next iterator value to use.

entry The entry.

theCommStatus An error is returned, if one occurred.

Description

VL_ListEntry( ) allows a caller to retrieve all **vldbentry** structures in the entire FLDB. Passing 0 (zero) as the value for *previous_index* results in the first **vldbentry** structure being returned. Thereafter, using the returned value for *next_index* as a subsequent value for *previous_index* results in the next **vldbentry** structure being returned. The *count* parameter returns an estimate for the number of entries yet to be returned.

When the *count* parameter is returned as 0 (zero), the last entry is returned. However, even if the *count* parameter is returned as larger than 0 (zero), the last entry may still have been returned already (if, for instance, all physically subsequent entries are marked as ‘‘deleted.’’) Thus, when **VL_ListEntry( )**

dynamically determines that the last entry has already been returned, it returns a 0 (zero) *count* and a 0 (zero) *next_index*, and does not overwrite *entry*. Thus, if a 0 (zero) *count* is returned, a 0 (zero) value for *next_index* means that the last entry has already been returned, and a nonzero value for *next_index* means that the entry just returned is in fact the last entry (and a subsequent call to **VL_ListEntry( )** will return a 0 (zero) *next_index*).

The *count* parameter is returned as -1 if a bad *previous_index* value is given or if there is some underlying error in reading the FLDB, and the return value from the **VL_ListEntry( )** procedure may still be 0 (zero).

Errors

VL_IO An error in an underlying database occurred.

Related Information

Functions: **VL_ListByAttributes(3dfs)**.

VL_Probe

Purpose Checks whether the Fileset Location Server is reachable

Synopsis **long VL_Probe(**
rpc_binding_handle_t *rpcBinding*,
error_status_t **theCommStatus*)

Parameters

Input

rpcBinding The RPC handle.

Output

theCommStatus An error is returned, if one occurred.

Description

VL_Probe( ) simply checks for any communications problems with the Fileset Location Server. There are no Fileset Location Server-specific error conditions, although the underlying communications mechanism may encounter errors; thus, there are no error codes specific to this call.

VL_ReleaseLock

Purpose Releases a previously held lock on an FLDB entry

Synopsis **long VL_ReleaseLock(**
rpc_binding_handle_t *rpcBinding*,
struct afsHyper **filesetID*,
unsigned long *filesetType*,
long *ReleaseType*,
error_status_t **theCommStatus*)

Parameters

Input

rpcBinding	The RPC handle.
filesetID	The identifier of the fileset for which an entry has been locked.
filesetType	The type of fileset.
ReleaseType	Specifies how many FLDB lock bits should be cleared.

Output

theCommStatus	An error is returned, if one occurred.

Description

VL_ReleaseLock( ) releases a lock previously acquired by **VL_SetLock( )**. *ReleaseType* specifies how many FLDB lock bits should be cleared. *filesetID* is the fileset identifier, and *filesetType* is the fileset type.

Errors

VL_PERM	The caller is not the superuser.
VL_BADFILESETTYPE	The *filesetType* is not recognized.
VL_BADRELLOCKTYPE	There is a bad value for *ReleaseType*.
VL_NOENT	FLDB: There is no such entry.

VL_ENTDELETED	The fileset is marked as ''deleted.''
VL_IO	The problem is in an underlying system.

Related Information

Functions: **VL_SetLock(3dfs)**.

VL_RemoveAddress

Purpose Removes a network address for a server

Synopsis **long VL_RemoveAddress(**
rpc_binding_handle_t *rpcBinding*,
struct afsNetAddr *AddrToRemove*,
error_status_t **theCommStatus*)

Parameters

Input

rpcBinding	The RPC handle.
AddrToRemove	The server address to remove.

Output

theCommStatus	An error is returned, if one occurred.

Description

VL_RemoveAddress( ) removes a network address from the equivalence class of network addresses that describes a file server. This structure is described more fully under **VL_AddAddress( )**.

Errors

VL_PERM	The caller is not the superuser.
VL_IO	An error from an underlying database system occurred.
VL_LASTADDRESS	The given address is the only one in its equivalence class and cannot be removed, or else a server would be left with no address at all.
VL_BADINDEX	Internal corruption in the table of equivalence classes occurred.

VL_SITESCORRUPTED
Another sort of internal corruption in the table of equivalence classes occurred.

VL_NOENT FLDB: There is no such entry.

Related Information

Functions: **VL_AddAddress(3dfs)**.

VL_ReplaceEntry

Purpose Replaces an FLDB entry for a fileset

Synopsis

long VL_ReplaceEntry(
rpc_binding_handle_t *rpcBinding*,
struct afsHyper **filesetID*,
unsigned long *filesetType*,
struct vldbentry **new*,
long *ReleaseType*,
error_status_t **theCommStatus*)

Parameters

Input

rpcBinding	The RPC handle.
filesetID	The identifier of the fileset being affected.
filesetType	The fileset type.
new	The new FLDB entry.
ReleaseType	Specifies which FLDB lock bits are to be cleared.

Output

theCommStatus	An error is returned, if one occurred

Description

VL_ReplaceEntry( ) replaces the **vldbentry** structure for *filesetID* (with *filesetType*) in the FLDB with *new*. *ReleaseType*, if nonzero, gives a mask of **LOCKREL_***xxx* bits that specify what **vldbentry** lock bits are to be cleared.

Errors

VL_PERM	The caller is not the superuser.
VL_BADNAME	The name has illegal characters.
VL_BADSERVER	The given number of servers is out of bounds.
VL_BADPARTITION	The partition value is out of bounds for some server.
VL_BADSERVERFLAG	The *siteFlags* value is out of bounds for some server.
VL_BADFILESETTYPE	A bad *filesetType* value is given in the new entry.
VL_BADRELLOCKTYPE	A bad *ReleaseType* value is given.
VL_IO	Some problem with an underlying database occurred.
VL_NOENT	FLDB: There is no such entry.
VL_BADENTRY	The operation is not allowed to change the read/write fileset ID.

VL_SetLock

Purpose Marks an FLDB entry as locked

Synopsis **long VL_SetLock(**
rpc_binding_handle_t *rpcBinding*,
struct afsHyper **filesetID*,
unsigned long *filesetType*,
long *fsOper*,
error_status_t **theCommStatus*)

Parameters

Input

rpcBinding	The RPC handle.
filesetID	The identifier of the fileset whose entry is to be locked.
filesetType	The fileset type.
fsOper	The lock flags that should be set.

Output

theCommStatus	An error is returned, if one occurred.

Description

VL_SetLock() sets an advisory lock on an FLDB entry for use by cooperating updaters of a fileset. *fsOper* specifies the flags that should be set in the FLDB while the lock is in force. The possible values are **VLOP_MOVE, VLOP_RELEASE, VLOP_BACKUP, VLOP_DELETE, VLOP_DUMP, VLOP_RESTORE,** and **VLOP_ADDSITE**.

Errors

VL_PERM	The caller is not the superuser.
VL_BADFILESETTYPE	The *filesetType* is not recognized.
VL_IO	An problem in an underlying system occurred.
VL_NOENT	FLDB: There is no such entry.

VL_ENTDELETED	The fileset is marked ''deleted.''
VL_ENTRYLOCKED	The fileset is already marked ''locked.''

Related Information

Functions: **VL_ReleaseLock(3dfs)**.

dump

Purpose The fileset dump format

Description

A fileset dump consists of a fileset header dump followed by a set of individual vnode dumps, followed by an end-of-fileset opcode. Individual vnode dumps consist of a vnode start opcode, many vnode descriptor opcodes, and an end-of-vnode opcode.

A field is generally represented as a 2-byte opcode followed by a 2-byte or 6-byte field length (with the length not including the opcode and length fields), followed by data. The length field is 6 bytes if the opcode represents a data opcode. A data opcode is recognized as such if the test **(opcode & 0xf000) == 0xf000** is TRUE. These opcodes are followed by a 48-bit length that follows the 16-bit opcode. The length bytes are represented MSB (Most Significant Byte) to LSB (Least Significant Byte).

Some fields contain **short** words, which are represented as 2 bytes, MSB first. **long** words are represented as 4 bytes, MSB first. **hyper** words are represented as 8 bytes, MSB first. Strings are represented as **NULL**-terminated arrays of bytes. In many cases the null terminator is redundant, as the overall field length implies where the null-terminator must appear in the string.

The various opcodes that are part of the dump are listed here in the order in which they can appear, along with the legal values associated with them.

- *Start of dump* is represented by the opcode **VOLS_DUMP_HEADER_START** (0x80), followed by a long number **VOLS_DUMP_HEADER_STARTMAGIC** (0x343833af). The length field is set to 4 bytes.

- *Maximum uniquifier* is the value of the highest uniquifier that is used. It is represented by the opcode **VOLS_DUMP_HEADER_UNIQUEGEN** (0x100). The length field is 32 bytes. Currently only 8 bytes of these (MSB) are filled.

- *Maximum quota* is represented by the opcode **VOLS_DUMP_HEADER_MAXQUOTA** (0x101). Its length is 4 bytes. The value (a **long**) indicates the maximum number of 1-KB blocks that the fileset can grow to. If it is 0 (zero), there is no limit.

- *Minimum quota* is represented by the opcode **VOLS_DUMP_HEADER_MINQUOTA** (0x102). Its length is 4 bytes. The value (a **long**) indicates the minimum number of 1-KB blocks that the fileset has reserved. If it is 0 (zero), there is no reservation.

- *Disk usage* is represented by the opcode **VOLS_DUMP_HEADER_DISKUSED** (0x103). Its length is 4 bytes. The value (a **long**) indicates the number of 1-KB blocks actually used by the fileset.
- *File count* is represented by the opcode **VOLS_DUMP_HEADER_FILECOUNT** (0x104). The length is 4 bytes. The value (a **long**) indicates the number of files in the fileset.
- *Owner* is represented by the opcode **VOLS_DUMP_HEADER_OWNER** (0x105). The length is 4 bytes. The value (a **long**) indicates the ID of the owner of the fileset.
- *Creation date* is represented by the opcode **VOLS_DUMP_HEADER_CREATION_DATE** (0x106). The length is 8 bytes. The value (2 **long** words) represents the date that the fileset ID was first used by this fileset, in seconds and microseconds since January 1, 1970.
- *Access date* is represented by the opcode **VOLS_DUMP_HEADER_ACCESS_DATE** (0x107). The length is 8 bytes. The value (2 **long** words) represents the date that the fileset was last accessed, in seconds and microseconds since January 1, 1970.
- *Update date* is represented by the opcode **VOLS_DUMP_HEADER_UPDATE_DATE** (0x108). The length is 8 bytes. The value (2 **long** words) represents the date that the fileset was last updated, in seconds and milliseconds since January 1, 1970.
- *Message of the day* is represented by the opcode **VOLS_DUMP_HEADER_MOTD** (0x109). The length is the length of the message string. The fileset message of the day is a string that gives human readable information about the particular state of this fileset (why the fileset is unavailable, when it is to be back, and so forth).
- *Fileset version* is represented by the opcode **VLS_DUMP_HEADER_VOLVERSION** (0x10c), an 8-byte value.
- *Dump source style* is represented by the opcode **VOLS_DUMP_HEADER_DUMP_STYLE** (0x10e). The value is a 32-byte structure indicating how the server was selected, and is essentially a **ftserver_Date** structure.
- *Source type* for a fileset dump is represented by the opcode **VOLS_DUMP_HEADER_BASETYPE** (0x10d). Its length is 8 bytes, organized as 2 **long** words. The first **long** is the aggregate type

(**AG_TYPE_EPI** or **AG_TYPE_UFS**), as in the **FTSERVER_AggregateInfo** call. The second **long** is reserved to indicate a subtype.

- *Vnode* is represented by the opcode **VOLS_DUMP_HEADER_VNODE** (0x10a). The length is 8 bytes. It contains the vnode of the file. This opcode introduces a vnode. The end of a vnode dump is indicated by the opcode **VOLS_DUMP_VNODE_EOF** (0x2ff).
- *Deleted vnode* is represented by the opcode **VOLS_DUMP_HEADER_NOVNODE** (0x10b). The length is 8 bytes. The content is the vnode of the file that has been deleted.
- *Vnode type* is represented by the opcode **VOLS_DUMP_VNODE_TYPE** (0x200). The length is 4 bytes. The value represents the type of the vnode.
- *Vnode link count* is represented by the opcode **VOLS_DUMP_VNODE_LINKCOUNT** (0x201). The length is 4 bytes. The value is a **long** and represents the link count of the vnode.
- *Vnode data version* is represented by the opcode **VOLS_DUMP_VNODE_DATAVERSION** (0x202). The length is 8 bytes. The value is a **hyper** and represents the data version number of the file corresponding to the vnode.
- *Vnode fileset version* is represented by the opcode **VOLS_DUMP_VNODE_VOLVERSION** (0x203). The length is 8 bytes. The value is a **hyper** and represents the data version number of the fileset that was current when this vnode was last updated. This is a monotonically increasing quantity that changes with every update to the file's data or status.
- *Vnode access time* is represented by the opcode **VOLS_DUMP_VNODE_ACCESSTIME** (0x204). The length is 8 bytes. The value is a **timeval** structure and represents the time the file was last accessed. This opcode corresponds to **atime** under UNIX.
- *Vnode modify time* is represented by the opcode **VOLS_DUMP_VNODE_MODIFYTIME** (0x205). The length is 8 bytes. The value is a **timeval** structure and represents the time the file was last modified. It corresponds to **mtime** under UNIX.
- *Vnode change time* is represented by the opcode **VOLS_DUMP_VNODE_CHANGETIME** (0x206). The length is 8 bytes. The value is a **timeval** structure and represents the time the file's status was last changed. It corresponds to **ctime** under UNIX.
- *Vnode true modify time* is represented by the opcode **VOLS_DUMP_VNODE_SERVERMODTIME** (0x207). The length is 8

bytes. The value is a **timeval** and represents the true time the file was last modified, as opposed to the value stored in the **mtime** field. The value stored in the **mtime** field is written when the *client*, not the *server*, records that the file has been modified; the actual modification time could be different by a small amount, or the client could supply an incorrect time. This modification time can only be written by the server.

- *Vnode group* is represented by the opcode **VOLS_DUMP_VNODE_GROUP** (0x208). The length is 4 bytes. The value is a 32-bit integer, representing the UNIX group owner of the file.

- *Vnode author* is represented by the opcode **VOLS_DUMP_VNODE_AUTHOR** (0x209). The length is 4 bytes. The value is a 32 bit integer, representing the identity of the person who last changed the file's status or data, except for implicit changes to an inode's access time.

- *Vnode owner* is represented by the opcode **VOLS_DUMP_VNODE_OWNER** (0x20a). The length is 4 bytes. The value is a 32 bit integer, representing the UNIX owner of the file.

- *Vnode mode* is represented by the opcode **VOLS_DUMP_VNODE_UNIXMODE** (0x20b). The length is 4 bytes. The value is a **long**, representing the UNIX mode bits for the file.

- *Vnode ACLs* are represented either by opcode **VOLS_DUMP_VNODE_ACL_INLINE** (0x20e) or **VOLS_DUMP_VNODE_ACL_COPY** (0x20f). The date for the former is a **long** indicating which ACL is to be set, followed by the external representation of the ACL itself. The data for the latter is 16 bytes, organized as 2 **long** words and a **hyper**. The first word indicates which ACL of the current vnode is to be set; the second indicates which ACL of another vnode is to be copied. The **hyper** gives the vnode index and uniquifier value for a vnode, one of whose ACLs is to be copied as the ACL of the current vnode.

- *Vnode size* is represented by the opcode **VOLS_DUMP_VNODE_SIZE** (0x20d). The length is 8 bytes. The value is a **hyper** giving the size of the file in bytes.

- *Vnode data* is represented by the opcode **VOLS_DUMP_VNODE_DATA** (0xf001). The length is the size of the chunk of data, plus 8 bytes. Data follows the length. The first 8 bytes of the data are a **hyper** and indicate the offset within the file of the data. (Large files can be broken into smaller chunks; the offset is used to properly ''position'' this chunk of data within the file.) The rest are file data.

- *Vnode end marker* is represented by the opcode **VOLS_DUMP_VNODE_EOF** (0x2ff). The length is 0 bytes; no data follows the opcode.
- *End of dump marker* is represented by the opcode **VOLS_DUMP_HEADER_END** (0x81). The length is 4 bytes. The value is a magic number **VOLSS_DUMP_HEADER_ENDMAGIC** (0x4383faf7), which is a **long**. Occurrence of this opcode signals the end of the dump.

Related Information

Functions: **FTSERVER_Dump(3dfs), VC_DumpVolume(3dfs)**.

Chapter 7

DCE Routines

intro

Purpose Introduction to the DCE configuration routines

Description

The DCE configuration routines return information based on the contents of the local DCE configuration file, which is created during the DCE cell-configuration or machine-configuration process. A configuration file is located on each DCE machine; it contains the host's name, as well as the name of the cell in which the host is located. The configuration routines can also be used to get some additional information corollary to the hostname, namely:

- The host's principal name.
- Binding information to the host.

The Security Service component on each DCE machine must be able to find out, by strictly local means, its machine's hostname, the host machine's principal name, and its cell's name. The DCE configuration routines exist primarily to enable Security components to do these things. But because this information can be useful to DCE applications as well, these routines are made available as part of the general application programming interface.

Note that ''hostname'' as used throughout this section refers to the *DCE hostname* (that is, the machine's */.../cellname/host_directory/hostname* entry in the CDS namespace), and not, for example, its DNS (Domain Name Service) hostname, which could be quite different from the DCE name.

Note: Cell names are case insensitive. Cell names returned by DCE routines default to lowercase. If you are doing string comparisons on cell names returned by DCE routines, you must convert your strings to lowercase before performing the comparisons.

Overview of the DCE Configuration Routines

The DCE configuration routines are listed below:

dce_cf_binding_entry_from_host( )
Returns the host binding entry name.

dce_cf_get_cell_name( ) Returns the local cell name.

dce_cf_get_host_name( ) Returns the hostname relative to a local cell.

dce_cf_prin_name_from_host( ) Returns the host's principal name.

dce_cf_find_name_by_key( ) Returns a string tagged by key (this is a lower-level utility routine that is used by the others).

Cautions

The DCE 1.0 implementations of the DCE configuration routines will accept only lines (in the configuration file) whose length is less than 1024 characters. If a tag occurs more than once in the input, the routines will recognize only the first occurrence.

Files

dcelocal/**dce_cf.db** The machine's local DCE configuration file (where *dcelocal* is usually something like **/opt/dcelocal**).

The format of the configuration file is as follows.

Each of the entries is tagged with its own identifier, which must be the first nonblank token on a line that does not begin with a # (number sign) comment character. The second token on a line is assumed to be the name associated with the tag that was detected in front of it.

For example, **cellname** and **hostname** are tags, identifying the cellname and hostname, respectively, for the machine on which the configuration file is located. A sample configuration file could have the following contents:

```
cellname /.../osf.org
hostname hosts/brazil
```

which would identify the host **brazil** in the **osf.org** cell.

Text characterized by the following is ignored:

- Garbage lines; that is, lines that do not conform to the previously described format.
- Leading and trailing spaces in lines.
- Additional tokens appearing on a line after the second token.

The configuration file should be writable only by privileged users, and readable by all.

Output

The DCE configuration routines return relative names (without global or cell-local prefixes), such as:

host_directory/hostname

or:

principalname

where:

host_directory is usually **hosts**.

However, the DCE NSI (Name Service Interface) routines require names passed to them to be expressed either in a cell-local form, such as:

/.:/*host_directory/hostname*

or as global names, with the global root prefix **/.../** and the cell name, such as:

/.../*cellname/host_directory/hostname*

Therefore, either the cell-local (**/.:/**) or correct global (**/.../***cellname*) prefix must be added by an application to any name it receives from a DCE configuration routine, before passing the name to an NSI routine. (NSI routines all have names beginning with **rpc_ns_**.) For example, the name *host_directory/hostname* would become, if expressed in cell-local form:

/.:/*hosts/hostname*

The cell-local form of the name *principalname* would be:

/.:/sec/principals/*principalname*

where:

hostname and *principalname* are the host's name and principal name, respectively.

Related Information

Functions: **dce_cf_binding_entry_from_host(3dce)**, **dce_cf_find_name_by_key(3dce)**, **dce_cf_get_cell_name(3dce)**, **dce_cf_get_host_name(3dce)**, **dce_cf_prin_name_from_host(3dce)**.

Books: *OSF DCE Administration Guide*.

dce_cf_binding_entry_from_host

Purpose Returns the host binding entry name

Library **libdce.a**

Synopsis **#include <dce/dce_cf.h>**

public void dce_cf_binding_entry_from_host(
char **hostname*,
char ***entry_name*,
unsigned long **status*);

Parameters

Input

hostname Specifies the name of the host. If **NULL**, the configuration file is searched for the hostname, and that name, if found, is used.

Output

entry_name The binding entry name associated with the specified host.

status Returns the status code from this operation. The status code is a value that indicates whether the routine completed successfully and if not, why not.

Possible status codes and their meanings are as follows:

dce_cf_st_ok Operation completed successfully.

dce_cf_e_file_open File open error.

dce_cf_e_no_mem No memory available.

dce_cf_e_no_match No hostname entry in the DCE configuration file.

Description

The **dce_cf_binding_entry_from_host**( ) routine returns the binding entry name string associated with the *hostname* passed to it. If *hostname* is **NULL**, the binding entry name associated with the name returned by **dce_cf_get_host_name**( ) is returned.

Note: Cell names are case insensitive. Cell names returned by DCE routines default to lowercase. If you are doing string comparisons on cell names returned by DCE routines, you must convert your strings to lowercase before performing the comparisons.

Files

dcelocal/**dce_cf.db** The machine's local DCE configuration file (where *dcelocal* is usually something like **/opt/dcelocal**).

Return Values

No value is returned.

Related Information

Functions: **dce_cf_find_name_by_key(3dce)** , **dce_cf_get_cell_name(3dce)**, **dce_cf_get_host_name(3dce)**, **dce_cf_prin_name_from_host(3dce)**.

Books: *OSF DCE Administration Guide*.

dce_cf_find_name_by_key

Purpose Returns a string tagged by a character string key

Library **libdce.a**

Synopsis **#include <dce/dce_cf.h>**

public void dce_cf_find_name_by_key(
FILE **fp*,
char **key*,
char ***name*,
unsigned long **status);*

Parameters

Input

fp A file pointer to a correctly formatted text file opened for reading.

key A character string key that will be used to find *name*.

Input/Output

name A pointer to a string (**char ****) in which a string containing the name found will be placed. The name string will be allocated by **malloc( )**.

Output

status Returns the status code from this operation. The status code is a value that indicates whether the routine completed successfully and if not, why not.

Possible status codes and their meanings are as follows:

dce_cf_st_ok	Operation completed succesfully.
dce_cf_e_no_mem	No memory available.
dce_cf_e_no_match	No match for *key* in the file.

Description

The **dce_cf_find_name_by_key( )** routine searches a text file for the first occurrence of a string tag identical to the string passed in *key*. The tag string, in order to be found, must be the first non-white space string on an uncommented line. If the tag string is found, **dce_cf_find_name_by_key( )** allocates (by a call to **malloc( )**) a buffer for the next string found on the same line as the tag string, copies this second string into the buffer, and returns its address in the *name* input parameter.

This routine is called by **dce_cf_get_host_name( )** and by **dce_cf_get_cell_name( )**.

Note: Cell names are case insensitive. Cell names returned by DCE routines default to lowercase. If you are doing string comparisons on cell names returned by DCE routines, you must convert your strings to lowercase before performing the comparisons.

Cautions

The memory for a returned name string is allocated by **malloc( )**, and must be freed by the original caller of the configuration routine that called **dce_cf_find_name_by_key( )**.

The DCE 1.0 version of this routine is limited to processing lines of text whose length is less than 1024 characters.

Files

dcelocal/**dce_cf.db** — The machine's local DCE configuration file (where *dcelocal* is usually something like **/opt/dcelocal**).

Return Values

No value is returned.

Related Information

Functions: **dce_cf_binding_entry_from_host(3dce)**, **dce_cf_get_cell_name(3dce)**, **dce_cf_get_host_name(3dce)**, **dce_cf_prin_name_from_host(3dce)**.

Books: *OSF DCE Administration Guide*.

dce_cf_get_cell_name

Purpose Returns the local cell name

Library **libdce.a**

Synopsis **#include <dce/dce_cf.h>**

```
public void dce_cf_get_cell_name(
        char **cellname,
        unsigned long *status);
```

Parameters

Input

None.

Input/Output

cellname The address of a string pointer. This pointer will be set by the function to point to a buffer containing the cellname.

Output

status Returns the status code from this operation. The status code is a value that indicates whether the routine completed successfully and if not, why not.

Possible status codes and their meanings are as follows:

dce_cf_st_ok	Operation successfully completed.
dce_cf_e_file_open	File open error.
dce_cf_e_no_mem	No memory available.
dce_cf_e_no_match	No cellname entry in the DCE configuration file.

Description

The **dce_cf_get_cell_name( )** routine searches the DCE configuration file for the local cell's name. If the name is found, **dce_cf_get_cell_name( )** allocates (by a call to **malloc( )**) a buffer for it, copies the name into the buffer, and returns the buffer's address in the *cellname* input parameter.

The configuration file is searched by a call to **dce_cf_get_name_by_key( )**. **dce_cf_get_cell_name( )** opens and closes the file automatically.

Note: Cell names are case insensitive. Cell names returned by DCE routines default to lowercase. If you are doing string comparisons on cell names returned by DCE routines, you must convert your strings to lowercase before performing the comparisons.

Cautions

The memory for a returned name string is allocated by **malloc( )**, and must be freed by the caller of **dce_cf_get_cell_name( )**.

The DCE 1.0 version of this routine is limited to processing lines of text whose length is less than 1024 characters.

Files

dcelocal/**dce_cf.db** The machine's local DCE configuration file (where *dcelocal* is usually something like **/opt/dcelocal**).

Return Values

No value is returned.

Related Information

Functions: **dce_cf_binding_entry_from_host(3dce)**, **dce_cf_find_name_by_key(3dce)**, **dce_cf_get_host_name(3dce)**, **dce_cf_prin_name_from_host(3dce)**.

Books: *OSF DCE Administration Guide*.

dce_cf_get_host_name

Purpose Returns the hostname relative to the local cell root

Library **libdce.a**

Synopsis **#include <dce/dce_cf.h>**

public void dce_cf_get_host_name(
char ***hostname*,
unsigned long **status*);

Parameters

Input

None.

Input/Output

hostname The address of a string pointer. This pointer will be set by the function to point to a buffer containing the hostname.

Output

status Returns the status code from this operation. The status code is a value that indicates whether the routine completed successfully and if not, why not.

Possible status codes and their meanings are as follows:

dce_cf_st_ok	Operation successfully completed.
dce_cf_e_file_open	File open error.
dce_cf_e_no_mem	No memory available.
dce_cf_e_no_match	No hostname entry in the DCE configuration file.

Description

The **dce_cf_get_host_name( )** routine searches the DCE configuration file for the local host's name relative to the local cell's root. If the name is found, **dce_cf_get_host_name( )** allocates (by a call to **malloc( )**) a buffer for it, copies the name into the buffer, and returns its address in the *hostname* input parameter.

The configuration file is searched by a call to **dce_cf_get_name_by_key( )**. **dce_cf_get_host_name( )** opens and closes the file automatically.

Note: Cell names are case insensitive. Cell names returned by DCE routines default to lowercase. If you are doing string comparisons on cell names returned by DCE routines, you must convert your strings to lowercase before performing the comparisons.

Cautions

The memory for a returned name string is allocated by **malloc( )**, and must be freed by the caller of **dce_cf_get_host_name( )**.

The DCE 1.0 version of this routine is limited to processing lines of text whose length is less than 1024 characters.

Files

dcelocal/**dce_cf.db** The machine's local DCE configuration file (where *dcelocal* is usually something like **/opt/dcelocal**).

Return Values

No value is returned.

Related Information

Functions: **dce_cf_binding_entry_from_host(3dce)**, **dce_cf_find_name_by_key(3dce)**, **dce_cf_get_cell_name(3dce)**, **dce_cf_prin_name_from_host(3dce)**.

Books: *OSF DCE Administration Guide*.

dce_cf_prin_name_from_host

Purpose Returns the host's principal name

Library **libdce.a**

Synopsis

```
#include <dce/dce_cf.h>
PUBLIC void dce_cf_prin_name_from_host(
          char *hostname,
          char **prin_name,
          unsigned long *status);
```

Parameters

Input

hostname The name of the host. If **NULL**, the configuration file is searched for the hostname, and that name, if found, is used.

Output

prin_name
The principal name associated with the specified host.

status Returns the status code from this operation. The status code is a value that indicates whether the routine completed successfully and if not, why not.

Possible status codes and their meanings are as follows:

dce_cf_st_ok Operation completed successfully.

dce_cf_e_file_open File open error.

dce_cf_e_no_mem No memory available.

dce_cf_e_no_match No hostname entry in the DCE configuration file.

Description

The **dce_cf_prin_name_from_host( )** routine returns the principal name associated with the *hostname* passed to it. If *hostname* is **NULL**, **dce_cf_prin_name_from_host( )** returns the principal name associated with the name returned by **dce_cf_get_host_name( )**.

Note: Cell names are case insensitive. Cell names returned by DCE routines default to lowercase. If you are doing string comparisons on cell names returned by DCE routines, you must convert your strings to lowercase before performing the comparisons.

Files

dcelocal/**dce_cf.db** The machine's local DCE configuration file (where *dcelocal* is usually something like **/opt/dcelocal**).

Return Values

No value is returned.

Related Information

Functions: **dce_cf_binding_entry_from_host(3dce)**, **dce_cf_find_name_by_key(3dce)**, **dce_cf_get_cell_name(3dce)**, **dce_cf_get_host_name(3dce)**.

Books: *OSF DCE Administration Guide*.

dce_cf_profile_entry_from_host

Purpose Returns the host profile entry

Library **libdce.a**

Synopsis **#include <dce/dce_cf.h>**

public void dce_cf_profile_entry_from_host(
 char **hostname*,
 char ***prof_name*,
 unsigned long **status)*;

Parameters

Input

hostname Specifies the name of the host. If **NULL**, the configuration file is searched for the hostname, and that name, if found, is used.

Output

prof_name
The profile entry associated with the specified host.

status Returns the status code from this operation. The status code is a value that indicates whether the routine completed successfully and if not, why not.

Possible status codes and their meanings are as follows:

dce_cf_st_ok	Operation completed successfully.
dce_cf_e_file_open	File open error.
dce_cf_e_no_mem	No memory available.
dce_cf_e_no_match	No hostname entry in the DCE configuration file.

Description

The **dce_cf_profile_entry_from_host( )** routine returns the profile entry string associated with the *hostname* passed to it. If *hostname* is **NULL**, the profile entry associated with the name returned by **dce_cf_get_host_name( )** is returned.

Note: Cell names are case insensitive. Cell names returned by DCE routines default to lowercase. If you are doing string comparisons on cell names returned by DCE routines, you must convert your strings to lowercase before performing the comparisons.

Files

dcelocal/**dce_cf.db** The machine's local DCE configuration file (where *dcelocal* is usually something like **/opt/dcelocal**).

Return Values

No value is returned.

Related Information

Functions: **dce_cf_find_name_by_key(3dce)**, **dce_cf_get_cell_name(3dce)**, **dce_cf_get_host_name(3dce)**, **dce_cf_prin_name_from_host(3dce)**, **dce_cf_binding_entry_from_host(3dce)**.

Books: *OSF DCE Administration Guide*.

Index

Symbols

A

B

C

D

E

F

G

H

M

N

O

P

R

S

T

U

V

W

Y

Notes

Notes

Notes

Notes

OPEN SOFTWARE FOUNDATION™

INFORMATION REQUEST FORM

Please send to me the following:

( ) OSF™ Membership Information

( ) OSF™ DCE License Materials

( ) OSF™ DCE Training Information

Contact Name ______________________________

Company Name ______________________________

Street Address ______________________________

Mail Stop ______________________________

City ______________ State _____ Zip __________

Phone ______________ FAX ______________

Electronic Mail ______________________________

MAIL TO:

Open Software Foundation
11 Cambridge Center
Cambridge, MA 02142

Attn: OSF™ DCE

For more information about OSF™ DCE call OSF Direct Channels at 617 621 7300.